A Special Issue of
Visual Cognition

Eye Guidance in Natural Scenes

Guest Editor

Benjamin W. Tatler
University of Dundee

T0347358

Routledge
Taylor & Francis Group

LONDON AND NEW YORK

First published 2009 by Psychology Press

Published 2018 by Routledge
2 Park Square, Milton Park, Abingdon, Oxon OX14 4RN
52 Vanderbilt Avenue, New York, NY 10017

First issued in paperback 2018

Routledge is an imprint of the Taylor & Francis Group, an informa business

Copyright © 2009 by Taylor & Francis

All rights reserved. No part of this book may be reprinted or reproduced or utilised in any form or by any electronic, mechanical, or other means, now known or hereafter invented, including photocopying and recording, or in any information storage or retrieval system, without permission in writing from the publishers.

Notice:
Product or corporate names may be trademarks or registered trademarks, and are used only for identification and explanation without intent to infringe.

British Library Cataloguing in Publication Data
A catalogue record for this book is available from the British Library

ISSN 1350-6285

Cover design by Design Deluxe
Typeset by Datapage (India) Private Limited, Chennai, India

ISBN 13: 978-1-138-99086-9 (pbk)
ISBN 13: 978-1-84872-715-1 (hbk)

Contents*

---

* This book is also a special issue of the journal *Visual Cognition* and forms issues 6 & 7 of
Volume 17 (2009). The page numbers are taken from the journal and so begin with p. 777.

VISUAL COGNITION, 2009, 17 (6/7), 777–789

Current understanding of eye guidance

Benjamin W. Tatler

University of Dundee, Dundee, UK

Visual sampling of the scene is at a premium in human vision. High acuity vision is restricted to the small foveal region at the centre of vision and the "saccade and fixate" strategy means that this window of high-resolution vision is only directed at an average of three to four locations in each second. It is therefore not surprising that understanding the factors that underlie decisions about where to allocate this valuable resource of foveal vision have been at the heart of eye movement research since the earliest objective recordings (Wade & Tatler, 2005). The earliest work on viewing complex scenes found that there were certain locations in scenes that were consistently looked at by most observers (Buswell, 1935). Buswell called these locations "centers of interest" and asked what it was about these locations that made them "interesting". He considered that there were two possibilities: That it was something external in the stimulus that attracted the viewers' eyes; or that it was something more internal to the viewer that reflected higher level cognitive "interest". Buswell favoured the latter explanation, and he famously showed that presenting the same image but with different instructions fundamentally changed the places that a viewer fixated; an observation that was confirmed by Yarbus (1967).

Given this demonstration and early favouring of top-down control of where we place our eyes in complex scenes, it is perhaps surprising that much of the subsequent consideration of how we view complex scenes has focused on the role of low-level factors in guiding attention. Why might this be? A wealth of literature on visual search demonstrated that basic visual features

Please address all correspondence to Benjamin W. Tatler, School of Psychology, University of Dundee, Dundee DD1 4HN, UK. E-mail: b.w.tatler@dundee.ac.uk

I would like to thank all authors and reviewers for their time and effort in ensuring that the set of papers included in this Special Issue are of the highest quality and reflect the current cutting edge in the field. I would particularly like to extend my gratitude to Jim Brockmole, who acted as action editor on the two submissions on which I was an author. Finally, I thank John Henderson, Mary Hayhoe, and Mike Land for valuable feedback on earlier versions of this editorial.

© 2009 Taylor & Francis
DOI: 10.1080/13506280902869213

can "capture" and guide our attention in simple displays (Wolfe, 1998). This work inspired its natural extension to more complex scene viewing: Koch and Ullman (1985) proposed that a set of basic features is extracted and combined to form an overall map of the visual conspicuity or "salience" in scenes and that this drives attention around the scene in a winner-takes-all manner. Itti and Koch (2000; Itti, Koch, & Niebur, 1998) translated this intuitive extension of the visual search literature into a computational model of salience.

The emergence of a quantitative model of complex scene viewing has had a profound impact on subsequent research. This impact has been highly divergent: On the one hand we have seen a large number of studies enthusiastically endorsing this model; on the other hand we now see emerging an equally large and enthusiastic number of studies criticizing it. Early evidence seemed to favour the model: If the low-level statistical content of fixated locations is compared to control locations there are robust differences, demonstrating nonrandom selection of basic visual features (e.g., Krieger, Rentschler, Hauske, Schill, & Zetzsche, 2000; Mannan, Ruddock, & Wooding, 1997; Parkhurst, Law & Niebur, 2002; Reinagel & Zador, 1999). However, more recently researchers have begun to question the implications of these observed correlations between features and fixations. First, correlations are typically small (Tatler, Baddeley, & Gilchrist, 2005) and restricted to small amplitude saccades (Tatler, Baddeley, & Vincent, 2006). Second, correlations do not necessarily imply causality (Einhäuser & König, 2003; Henderson, Brockmole, Castelhano, & Mack, 2007), and even correlations may disappear when the overall distribution of features across the scene is unusual (Tatler, 2007). Third, a growing number of studies have demonstrated that low-level models fail completely when the observer's behavioural task is varied (e.g., Einhäuser, Rutishauser, & Koch, 2008; Foulsham & Underwood, 2008; Rothkopf, Ballard, & Hayhoe, 2007). Despite mounting reports of failures of the original salience model, there has yet to emerge a strong alternative quantitative model. That is not to say that good alternatives have not been proposed (e.g., Sprague, Ballard, & Robinson, 2007), but they have yet to gather popular momentum. As a result, to a large extent we have reached somewhat of an impasse in our understanding of eye guidance when looking at complex scenes.

In this Special Issue we will see how to circumvent this impasse. The studies presented here offer a range of alternatives to purely low-level visual conspicuity that might better account for where we fixate, and also offer emerging alternative models of how we look at images of complex scenes. Importantly, the papers in this Special Issue also highlight the need to move the question on in a number of ways, including starting to think about when we move our eyes rather than simply where we look, considering the possibility of qualitatively different viewing modes, and remembering that a key challenge for this area is to consider eye guidance in real-world environments rather than simply when looking at static scenes in the lab.

WHEN IMAGE SALIENCE IS NOT ENOUGH

The first paper in this special issue is a timely reminder of Yarbus' (1967) classic demonstration that the instructions given to an observer radically change how he or she inspects the scene. DeAngelus and Pelz (2009 this issue) extend Yarbus' work by testing multiple observers (Yarbus only tested one) and employing modern analytical approaches. They replicate Yarbus' key observations and this is a timely reminder for us that task has such a fundamental influence on fixation placement. Indeed the early work of Buswell and Yarbus should really have precluded any purely bottom up accounts of eye guidance, and despite the fact that Itti and Koch (2000) conceded this, this message seems to have been somehow forgotten (or at least given less weight than it should have) in the field.

The second paper in this Special Issue complements the growing body of examples of situations in which a purely bottom-up model fails to adequately account for important aspects of natural behaviour. Underwood, Foulsham, and Humphrey (2009 this issue) show that the salience model cannot account for similarities that are observed between initially viewing a scene and later viewing it again as part of a recognition test. Furthermore, the model cannot account for how experts view scenes that are specific to their domain of expertise. This work extends recent demonstrations that the model fails for particular behavioural tasks, to show that it cannot account for repeated viewing effects or expertise.

Matsukura, Brockmole, and Henderson (2009 this issue) explore how introducing different types of changes to objects (either a new object appears or an existing object changes colour) in a scene during viewing alter the attentional priority given to the changed object. If the change is during a fixation then new objects receive greater priority than objects that change colour. However, if the change occurs during a saccade, appearances and colour changes receive equal priority. Importantly, low-level image salience does not account for any prioritization of changed objects: Objects of low or high salience are treated no differently by the oculomotor system. These data are used to suggest that attentional prioritization to changes in scenes is driven by online memory for objects rather than low-level visual factors.

ALTERNATIVE LEVELS OF SELECTION FOR EYE GUIDANCE

With a wealth of studies arguing against visual salience as a likely causal factor in eye guidance, the important challenge is to find alternative levels of selection that are better able to account for where humans fixate. The next four papers in this Special Issue rise to this challenge. We have previously seen that objects account for more fixations than salience does (Einhäuser, Spain, & Perona, 2008), but other levels of selection may also be important. Vincent, Baddeley, Correani, Troscianko, and Leonards (2009 this issue) use a novel mixture model technique to evaluate a range of hypotheses of eye guidance from simple features to high-level concepts of "foreground". They find that most of the fixations are explained by two factors: A tendency to look near the centre of the screen (Tatler, 2007) and looking at foreground objects. The mixture model technique is a promising new tool in the arsenal of scene perception researchers.

Cristino and Baddeley (2009 this issue) extend this idea into the realm of dynamic scenes, showing participants movies recorded while walking around city streets. Cristino and Baddeley find, like Vincent et al. (2009 this issue), that low-level factors are totally inadequate descriptors of where people fixate. Furthermore, even motion cues cannot explain fixation placement. They find that looking at the centre of the screen has some predictive power, but that the single best explanation of fixation placement is a world-centred bias to look slightly below the horizon (which of course changes position considerably throughout the video clips). Impressively, they demonstrate that this bias is not about anything physical in the video clips by inducing a perceived change in height relative to the horizon and showing that this perceived shift in the horizon shifts the world-centred bias.

In the ongoing debate about the relative importance of low- and high-level factors in eye guidance when viewing natural scenes, there is a surprising tendency to overlook what has been known for some time to have a profound impact of attentional guidance: The social cues provided by another person's gaze direction (Friesen & Kingstone, 1998). Birmingham, Bischof, and Kingstone (2009 this issue) add to this literature by attempting to resolve the ongoing debate about whether eyes are equivalent directional cues to nonsocial stimuli such as arrows (Gibson & Kingstone, 2006; Langton, Watt, & Bruse, 2000). Importantly Birmingham et al. use gaze and arrow cues in the context of photographs of real-world scenes, rather than using isolated gaze or arrow cues in Posner-like cueing paradigms. These authors find that arrows in natural scenes are not given any special attentional priority, but an individual's eyes receive a great deal of fixation by observers. In the context of these social scenes, in which people are often present, Birmingham et al. further demonstrate that a salience-based model of eye guidance accounts for little human viewing behaviour.

Magicians are masters of manipulating the tendency that humans have to follow another's gaze. Kuhn, Tatler, and Cole (2009 this issue) study observers' fixation behaviour and ability to detect the secret when viewing a video of a magician (Kuhn) performing a simple disappearance trick.

Kuhn et al. show that these social gaze cues are powerful factors in determining not only where people will fixate, but also the success of a magic trick. Misdirection often relies on multiple simultaneous cues to divert the viewer's attention but, crucially, Kuhn et al. tease apart the relative contribution of gaze cues and motion cues in misdirection.

EMERGING MODELS OF EYE GUIDANCE

The previous papers in this Special Issue show that concepts other than low-level image properties, such as behavioural tendencies to look at particular locations in the scene irrespective of content, concepts such as foreground objects and social factors, are better candidates for factors involved in deciding where to place the eyes. However, what is needed is a quantitative alternative to the salience map model that draws upon the kind of findings and observations in the first seven papers of this Special Issue. The next four papers all provide suggestions for components of such a model.

One of the most compelling recent development in modelling eye guidance came from Torralba, Oliva, Castelhano, and Henderson's (2006) model that incorporated the notion of contextual guidance to narrow down searching for objects in scenes to locations we have learnt are likely to contain the objects we are looking for. For example, we will look at walls to find paintings and surfaces to find mugs. Ehinger, Hidalgo-Sotelo, Torralba, and Oliva (2009 this issue) extend this model in the context of searching for people to include an object-detector. They find that a model that incorporates some notion of image salience, where observers expect to find people, and a person-detector does a rather good job of accounting for where observers fixate in images of natural scenes.

In a very complimentary approach, Kanan, Tong, Zhang, and Cottrell (2009 this issue) provide a model of fixation selection based upon a notion of early salience, spatial context, and a Bayesian description of object appearance. They train a probabilistic object detector such that a map of locations that share distinctive features of the target object in a visual search can be created. This object appearance map accounts for a large proportion of the places that human observes fixate in photographs of natural scenes. Like Ehinger et al. (2009 this issue), Kanan et al. find the best descriptive power is offered by a model that includes not only object appearance but also salience and spatial information about where targets are likely to occur. Both of these papers also show that when the three components are evaluated separately, salience alone accounts for little, whereas both of the other sources of information do quite a good job of predicting fixation placement in isolation.

Zelinsky and Schmidt (2009 this issue) take a slightly different approach to the sort of spatial relationships between target and scene that can be utilized. In some ways the notion of contextual guidance used by Ehinger et al. (2009 this issue) and Kanan et al. (2009 this issue) is rather rigid. We learn where an object is likely to occur for a particular class of scene—for example we learn that in outdoor urban scenes people tend to be on the ground plane. We then apply this prior learning to new scenes of the same class such that when we are faced with an outdoor urban scene and asked to look for people we will look preferentially at the ground plane. However, as Zelinsky and Schmidt point out, there are situations in which this strategy would not be helpful. If we are asked to "look at that person on the roof" our learnt expectation for finding people on the ground is not helpful. Yet as Zelinsky and Schmidt show, visual search can be rapidly constrained to a scene region defined in this way. This result shows that where we look can be constrained to scene regions referenced in the short term and does not rely solely on a history of learning where things are likely to be. Using scene regions to constrain search also highlights the need to consider how scenes are rapidly segmented early in viewing in order for such constraining to be possible.

A rather different approach to the previous three papers is taken by Tatler and Vincent (2009 this issue). These authors consider the possible role of systematic oculomotor biases to move the eyes in particular ways in fixation selection. Alarmingly for those still pinning their hopes on a salience model, Tatler and Vincent show that a blind model based only on systematic motor biases (with no visual input) far outperforms salience models in predicting fixation placement. This work complements recent advances in hand and arm motor research, which have demonstrated that much of natural hand behaviour can be explained by a very limited set of stereotypical combinations of joint movements (Ingram, Kording, Howard, & Wolpert, 2008). A simple model based on some description of low-level characteristics of the scene (actually a simple edge model does better than the full salience model) combined with oculomotor biases offers remarkably good predictive power.

These four papers offering alternative modelling components for explaining fixation selection have many things in common. Notably, they all still incorporate some notion of image salience. At least for the suggestions put forward by Ehinger et al. (2009 this issue), Kanan et al. (2009 this issue), and Tatler and Vincent (2009 this issue), all can be seen as modulators of a bottom-up featural description of the scene. While not explicitly stated in this way, Zelinsky and Schmidt's (2009 this issue) ideas could be implemented as a modifier of salience. As such, we could summarize the existing components in the emerging models of picture viewing as shown in Figure 1. Given the evidence from these four papers, such a model would be likely to have good predictive power. However, given the growing evidence against

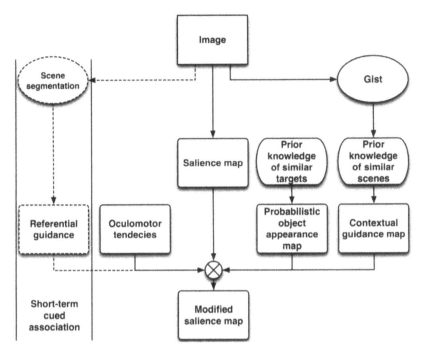

Figure 1. Summary of overall model of eye guidance based on papers by Ehinger et al. (2009 this issue), Kanan et al. (2009 this issue), Tatler and Vincent (2009 this issue), and Zelinsky and Schmidt (2009 this issue). The bottom-up salience map is modulated by contextual information (where targets are likely to be found), a probabilistic object appearance map and how the eyes tend to move. Short-term referential information can also modulate the map to constrain search to particular scene regions.

salience as a good basic model, is it really right to still place salience at the core of these models? This question will need to be considered carefully.

NEW CHALLENGES IN EYE GUIDANCE

All of the papers so far discussed have followed the "traditional" approach to studying eye guidance in natural scenes of focusing solely on where observers fixate and treating all fixations as equivalent in the analyses. The following four papers challenge this traditional approach in a number of important ways.

Henderson and Smith (2009 this issue) consider the important question of trying to understand when people move their eyes in natural scene viewing. Using a scene onset delay paradigm (Henderson & Pierce, 2008), Henderson and Smith suggest that fixations can be broadly grouped into those that wait for the scene to reappear before being terminated, and those that finish and move on to a new location even before the scene reappears. This distinction supports the idea that fixation duration is under mixed control: Involving both incoming visual information and a stochastic timer.

In the original conception of the salience model attention moved from peak to peak in the scene by imposing an inhibitory blob on each location as it was looked at to suppress this peak in the salience map and inhibit return to it. However, Smith and Henderson (2009 this issue) demonstrate that inhibition of return is not really a feature of scene viewing. Instead they show an increased frequency of returning to fixations that have just been looked at or were looked at two fixations ago. There is an increase in fixation duration before these returns but they are a common feature of natural scene viewing.

One thing we can take from the previous two papers is that it is not valid to treat all fixations as equal in modelling where people will saccade to next. We need to think about fixation durations and where the previous fixation was. Pannasch and Velichkovsky (2009 this issue) add to this argument by exploring their previous contention that there are two qualitatively different modes of viewing during scene inspection: An ambient mode for discerning overall spatial layout and a focal mode for more detailed, local processing (Velichkovsky, Joos, Helmert, & Pannasch, 2005). Velichkovsky and colleagues argue that these two modes are separable on the basis of eye movements: Ambient processing is characterized by short duration fixations associated with large amplitude saccades; focal processing is characterized by long duration fixations associated with small amplitude saccades (Unema, Pannasch, Joos, & Velichkovsky, 2005). In their current contribution, they extend this work to consider how the distractor effect might differ between these two modes of viewing.

DYNAMIC AND REAL SCENES

In the final three papers in this Special Issue we see a move away from the static scenes that have been used in the earlier papers (with the exception of Cristino and Baddeley, 2009 this issue, and also Kuhn et al., 2009 this issue, who both used video scenes) and indeed in much of the research that has attempted to quantify fixation placement. A notable (but not solitary) exception to this is Rothkopf et al. (2007), who used a virtual environment to consider the relative roles of task and salience on fixation selection. They found strong effects of task not only on what objects are looked at but also on the locations within objects that are fixated. However, Itti and Koch's (2000) salience model could not account for the data in any condition and predicted very different looking behaviour.

't Hart et al. (2009 this issue) make a much-needed comparison between viewing a real-world environment, a video of the same environment, and static snapshots from the environment. Using their innovative EyeSeeCam (Einhäuser et al., 2007), they find robust differences in eye guidance between real-world viewing, video viewing, and static scene viewing. Biases to look at the centre of photographic scenes produce artificially inflated measures of interobserver consistency, with far lower consistency when viewing video sequences of the same scenes. This work argues for the need to study eye guidance in the context of dynamic scenes rather than static scenes, where biases artificially distort viewing behaviour.

Droll and Eckstein (2009 this issue) consider how sensitive we are to detecting changes in a real-world setting. As people walk laps of a building, a number of target objects are changed. Droll and Eckstein find that the more people look at objects before they change, the more likely they are to detect the change, extending what we know about fixation time and change detection in static scenes (e.g., Hollingworth & Henderson, 2002) to a real environment. Droll and Eckstein also find that how much people looked at the objects, both before and after the change, varied depending on the instructions given: When asked to remember as much possible for a later test, target objects were fixated for longer than when asked simply to walk around. This result is reminiscent of the classic work of Buswell and Yarbus, which was reexamined by DeAngelus and Pelz in the first paper (2009 this issue).

The final paper, by Ballard and Hayhoe (2009 this issue), offers a critical review of eye guidance in the context of natural behaviour, both in real world and virtual environments. This paper argues strongly that if we are to understand eye guidance we must understand it within the context of behaviour. We have known for some time that task fundamentally changes fixation behaviour, yet many studies are based on viewing static images, often without an explicit task in mind. Importantly, Ballard and Hayhoe suggest a way that we can move approaches to modelling eye guidance forward: They suggest that modelling fixations on the basis of reward for uncertainty reduction about task relevant quantities in the environment can provide new insights into how fixations are targeted in natural behaviour.

EYE GUIDANCE IN NATURAL SCENES: WHERE NEXT?

In this Special Issue we have seen that the case against a low-level salience model now seems overwhelming. More than this we have been presented with a range of alternative factors that might better account for where people fixate. These better descriptions of the levels at which fixation selection may be decided should be used in the currently emerging new models of eye guidance. At present all emerging ideas covered in this Special Issue still include a role for salience, yet is this really necessary? Not only must we bear this in mind in our emerging alternative models, but efforts should be united to combine the different approaches being taken in order to see whether we can arrive at a more unified theoretical explanation of why we look where we do in complex scenes. However, perhaps the biggest challenge facing us in this area is to recognize the need to move away from static scene viewing into dynamic environments. It is peculiar that quantitative models of eye guidance have so far been derived exclusively from static scene viewing paradigms, yet perhaps the most profound insights about fixation placement are to be found in studies of eye movements during natural behaviour (for reviews see Hayhoe & Ballard, 2005; Land, 2006; Land & Tatler, 2009). For example, these studies show, with far more elegance even than Yarbus, how tightly coupled eye movements are to behavioural goals. This tight coupling is not only spatial but also temporal. Furthermore, Steinman (2003) reminds us that fundamental aspects of how we employ our oculomotor apparatus change between simply looking and imagining a task compared to actually engaging in a motor act (Epelboim et al., 1995, 1997). These cautionary notes raise serious concerns about how safely we can generalize our findings from static scene viewing to real behaviour.

Progress in this direction is certainly starting to be made. Ballard, Hayhoe, and colleagues have suggested task-based models of gaze allocation in virtual environments (Rothkopf et al., 2007) based upon reward maximization (Sprague et al., 2007) and have shown that familiarity (and deviation from it) has a strong influence on gaze allocation (Karacan & Hayhoe, 2008). It is vital that we rise to the challenge of moving studies of eye guidance firmly into natural settings in the next few years and evaluate whether our emerging models of eye guidance during scene viewing are anything more than descriptions of how we look at pictures.

REFERENCES

Ballard, D. H., & Hayhoe, M. M. (2009). Modelling the role of task in the control of gaze. *Visual Cognition*, *17*(6/7), 1185–1204.

Birmingham, E., Bischof, W., & Kingstone, A. (2009). Get real! Resolving the debate about equivalent social stimuli. *Visual Cognition*, *17*(6/7), 904–924.

Buswell, G. T. (1935). *How people look at pictures: A study of the psychology of perception in art*. Chicago: University of Chicago Press.

Cristino, F., & Baddeley, R. J. (2009). The nature of the visual representations involved in eye movements when walking down the street. *Visual Cognition*, *17*(6/7), 880–903.

DeAngelus, M., & Pelz, J. (2009). Top-down control of eye movements: Yarbus revisited. *Visual Cognition*, *17*(6/7), 790–811.

Droll, J., & Eckstein, M. (2009). Gaze control, change detection and the selective storage of object information while walking in a real world environment. *Visual Cognition, 17*(6/7), 1159–1184.

Ehinger, K., Hidalgo-Sotelo, B., Torralba, A., & Oliva, A. (2009). Modelling search for people in 900 scenes: A combined source model of eye guidance. *Visual Cognition, 17*(6/7), 945–978.

Einhauser, W., & Konig, P. (2003). Does luminance-contrast contribute to a saliency map for overt visual attention? *European Journal of Neuroscience, 17*(5), 1089–1097.

Einhauser, W., Rutishauser, U., & Koch, C. (2008). Task-demands can immediately reverse the effects of sensory-driven saliency in complex visual stimuli. *Journal of Vision, 8*(2), 1–19.

Einhäuser, W., Schumann, F., Bardins, S., Bartl, K., Böning, G., Schneider, E., & König, P. (2007). Human eye-head co-ordination in natural exploration. *Network: Computation in Neural Systems, 18*(3), 267–297.

Einhauser, W., Spain, M., & Perona, P. (2008). Objects predict fixations better than early saliency. *Journal of Vision, 8*(14), 11–26.

Epelboim, J., Steinman, R. M., Kowler, E., Pizlo, Z., Erkelens, C. J., & Collewijn, H. (1995). The function of visual search and memory in two kinds of sequential looking tasks. *Vision Research, 37*, 2597–2607.

Epelboim, J., Steinman, R. M., Kowler, E., Pizlo, Z., Erkelens, C. J., & Collewijn, H. (1997). Gaze-shift dynamics in two kinds of sequential looking tasks. *Vision Research, 37*(18), 2597–2607.

Foulsham, T., & Underwood, G. (2008). What can saliency models predict about eye movements? Spatial and sequential aspects of fixations during encoding and recognition. *Journal of Vision, 8*(2), 1–17.

Friesen, C. K., & Kingstone, A. (1998). The eyes have it! Reflexive orienting is triggered by nonpredictive gaze. *Psychonomic Bulletin and Review, 5*(3), 490–495.

Gibson, B. S., & Kingstone, A. (2006). Visual attention and the semantics of space: Beyond central and peripheral cues. *Psychological Science, 17*, 622–627.

Hayhoe, M., & Ballard, D. H. (2005). Eye movements in natural behavior. *Trends in Cognitive Sciences, 9*(4), 188–193.

Henderson, J. M., Brockmole, J. R., Castelhano, M. S., & Mack, M. L. (2007). Visual saliency does not account for eye movements during search in real-world scenes. In R. P. G. van Gompel, M. H. Fischer, W. S. Murray, & R. L. Hill (Eds.), *Eye movements: A window on mind and brain* (pp. 537–562). Oxford, UK: Elsevier.

Henderson, J. M., & Pierce, G. L. (2008). Eye movements during scene viewing: Evidence for mixed control of fixation durations. *Psychonomic Bulletin and Review, 15*, 566–573.

Henderson, J. M., & Smith, T. J. (2009). How are eye fixation durations controlled during scene viewing? Further evidence from a scene onset delay paradigm. *Visual Cognition, 17*(6/7), 1055–1082.

Hollingworth, A., & Henderson, J. M. (2002). Accurate visual memory for previously attended objects in natural scenes. *Journal of Experimental Psychology: Human Perception and Performance, 28*(1), 113–136.

Ingram, K. N., Kording, K. P., Howard, I. S., & Wolpert, D. M. (2008). The statistics of natural hand movements. *Experimental Brain Research, 188*(2), 223–236.

Itti, L., & Koch, C. (2000). A saliency-based search mechanism for overt and covert shifts of visual attention. *Vision Research, 40*(10–12), 1489–1506.

Itti, L., Koch, C., & Niebur, E. (1998). A model of saliency-based visual attention for rapid scene analysis. *IEEE Transactions on Pattern Analysis and Machine Intelligence, 20*(11), 1254–1259.

Kanan, C., Tong, M. H., Zhang, L., & Cottrell, G. W. (2009). SUN: Top-down saliency using natural statistics. *Visual Cognition, 17*(6/7), 979–1003.

Karacan, H., & Hayhoe, M. M. (2008). Is attention drawn to changes in familiar scenes? *Visual Cognition, 16*(2–3), 356–374.

Koch, C., & Ullman, S. (1985). Shifts in selective visual-attention—Towards the underlying neural circuitry. *Human Neurobiology, 4*(4), 219–227.

Krieger, G., Rentschler, I., Hauske, G., Schill, K., & Zetzsche, C. (2000). Object and scene analysis by saccadic eye-movements: An investigation with higher-order statistics. *Spatial Vision, 13*(2–3), 201–214.

Kuhn, G., Tatler, B. W., & Cole, G. C. (2009). You look where I look! Effect of gaze cues on overt and covert attention in misdirection. *Visual Cognition, 17*(6/7), 925–944.

Land, M. F. (2006). Eye movements and the control of actions in everyday life. *Progress in Retinal and Eye Research, 25*(3), 296–324.

Land, M. F., & Tatler, B. W. (2009). *Looking and acting: Vision and eye movements in natural behaviour.* Oxford, UK: Oxford University Press.

Langton, S. R. H., Watt, R. J., & Bruce, V. (2000). Do the eyes have it? Cues to the direction of social atention. *Trends in Cognitive Sciences, 4*(2), 50–58.

Mannan, S. K., Ruddock, K. H., & Wooding, D. S. (1997). Fixation sequences made during visual examination of briefly presented 2D images. *Spatial Vision, 11*(2), 157–178.

Matsukara, M., Brockmole, J. R., & Henderson, J. M. (2009). Overt attentional prioritization of new objects and feature changes during real-world scene viewing. *Visual Cognition, 17*(6/7), 835–855.

Pannasch, S., & Velichkovsky, B. M. (2009). Distractor effect and saccade amplitudes: Further evidence on different modes of processing in free exploration of visual images. *Visual Cognition, 17*(6/7), 1109–1131.

Parkhurst, D. J., Law, K., & Niebur, E. (2002). Modeling the role of salience in the allocation of overt visual attention. *Vision Research, 42*(1), 107–123.

Reinagel, P., & Zador, A. M. (1999). Natural scene statistics at the centre of gaze. *Network-Computation in Neural Systems, 10*(4), 341–350.

Rothkopf, C. A., Ballard, D. H., & Hayhoe, M. M. (2007). Task and context determine where you look. *Journal of Vision, 7*(14), 1–20.

Smith, T. J., & Henderson, J. M. (2009). Facilitation of return during scene viewing. *Visual Cognition, 17*(6/7), 1083–1108.

Sprague, N., Ballard, D. H., & Robinson, A. (2007). Modeling embodied visual behaviors. In *ACM transactions on applied perception, 4*(2). doi.acm.org/10.1145/1265957.1265960.

Steinman, R. M. (2003). Gaze control under natural conditions. In L. M. Chalupa & J. S. Werner (Eds.), *The visual neurosciences* (pp. 1339–1356). Cambridge, MA: MIT Press.

Tatler, B. W. (2007). The central fixation bias in scene viewing: Selecting an optimal viewing position independently of motor biases and image feature distributions. *Journal of Vision, 7*(14), 1–17.

Tatler, B. W., Baddeley, R. J., & Gilchrist, I. D. (2005). Visual correlates of fixation selection: Effects of scale and time. *Vision Research, 45*(5), 643–659.

Tatler, B. W., Baddeley, R. J., & Vincent, B. T. (2006). The long and the short of it: Spatial statistics at fixation vary with saccade amplitude and task. *Vision Research, 46*, 1857–1862.

Tatler, B. W., & Vincent, B. T. (2009). The prominence of behavioural biases in eye guidance. *Visual Cognition, 17*(6/7), 1029–1054.

't Hart, M., Vockeroth, J., Schumann, F., Bartl, K., Schneider, E., Konig, P., et al. (2009). Gaze allocation in natural stimuli: Comparing free exploration to head-fixed viewing conditions. *Visual Cognition, 17*(6/7), 1132–1158.

Torralba, A., Oliva, A., Castelhano, M. S., & Henderson, J. M. (2006). Contextual guidance of eye movements and attention in real-world scenes: The role of global features in object search. *Psychological Review, 113*(4), 766–786.

Underwood, G., Foulsham, T., & Humphrey, K. (2009). Saliency and scan patterns in the inspection of real-world scenes: Eye movements during encoding and recognition. *Visual Cognition, 17*(6/7), 812–834.

Unema, P. J. A., Pannasch, S., Joos, M., & Velichkovsky, B. M. (2005). Time course of information processing during scene perception: The relationship between saccade amplitude and fixation duration. *Visual Cognition, 12*(3), 473–494.

Velichkovsky, B. M., Joos, M., Helmert, J. R., & Pannasch, S. (2005). Two visual systems and their eye movements: Evidence from static and dynamic scene perception. In B. G. Bara, L. Barsalou, & M. Bucciarelli (Eds.), *Proceedings of the XXVII conference of the Cognitive Science Society* (pp. 2283–2288). Mahwah, NJ: Lawrence Erlbaum Associates, Inc.

Vincent, B. T., Baddeley, R. J., Correani, A., Troscianko, T., & Leonards, U. (2009). Do we look at lights? Using mixture modelling to distinguish between low- and high-level factors in natural image viewing. *Visual Cognition, 17*(6/7), 856–879.

Wade, N. J., & Tatler, B. W. (2005). *The moving tablet of the eye: The origins of modern eye movement research.* New York: Oxford University Press.

Wolfe, J. M. (1998). Visual search. In H. Pashler (Ed.), *Attention* (pp. 13–74). Hove, UK: Psychology Press.

Yarbus, A. L. (1967). *Eye movements and vision.* New York: Plenum Press.

Zelinsky, G. J., & Schmidt, J. (2009). An effect of referential scene constraint on search implies scene segmentation. *Visual Cognition, 17*(6/7), 1004–1028.

VISUAL COGNITION, 2009, 17 (6/7), 790–811

Top-down control of eye movements: Yarbus revisited

Marianne DeAngelus and Jeff B. Pelz

Chester F. Carlson Center for Imaging Science, Rochester Institute of Technology, Rochester, NY, USA

Alfred Yarbus (1967) reported that an observer's eye movement record varied based on high-level task. He found that an observer's eye movement patterns during freeview were dramatically different than when given tasks such as "Remember the clothes worn by the people." Although Yarbus' work is often cited to demonstrate the task-dependence of eye movements, it is often misrepresented; Yarbus reported results for only one observer, but authors commonly refer to Yarbus' "observers". Additionally, his observer viewed the painting for 21 minutes with optical stalks attached to the sclera and with his head severely restricted. Although eye movements are undoubtedly influenced by high-level tasks, it is not clear how Yarbus' results reflect his unique experimental conditions. Because of Yarbus' role in the literature, it is important to determine the extent to which his results represent a sample of naïve observers under more natural conditions. We replicated Yarbus' experiment using a head-free eyetracker with 17 naïve observers. The presentations were self-paced; viewing times were typically an order of magnitude shorter than the times Yarbus imposed. Eye movement patterns were clearly task dependent, but some of the differences were much less dramatic than those shown in Yarbus' now-classic observations.

Key words: Attention; Eye movements; Visual cognition.

The doctoral work of Alfred Lukianovich Yarbus (alternatively spelled Iarbus) was published in book form as *The Role of Eye Motion in Vision Processes* in 1965 in Moscow (Iarbus, 1965). In 1967, it was translated into English by Basil Haigh and Lorrin Riggs (editor) and published as *Eye Movements and Vision* (Yarbus, 1967). The book covered both the ingenious eyetracking devices he devised to perform his experiments and the research he performed with those devices. Yarbus examined and characterized the mechanics of the oculomotor system, including the velocities and durations

Please address all correspondence to Jeff B. Pelz, Chester F. Carlson Center for Imaging Science, Rochester Institute of Technology, 54 Lomb Memorial Drive, Rochester, NY 14623, USA. E-mail: pelz@cis.rit.edu

The authors wish to acknowledge Jason Babcock and Constantin Rothkopf for their valuable contributions.

© 2009 Taylor & Francis
DOI: 10.1080/13506280902793843

of different types of eye movements. His book includes photographic records of corrective saccades, curved saccades, and eye movements of patients with disorders such as nystagmus and glaucoma. Figure 1 shows a number of the miniature optical devices, or suction "caps", designed by Yarbus that were attached to the eye to record eye movements or project stabilized retinal images. An entire chapter is devoted to the perceptual effects of stabilized retinal images, including blank fields, fields of high luminance and colour contrast, and flickering objects.

Eye movement patterns were recorded for observers viewing both stationary and moving objects, including simple stimuli, text, and optical illusions. The last chapter of *Eye Movements and Vision* shows records of observers viewing complex objects such as paintings and photographs. Although he was not the first researcher to conduct this sort of analysis (see, e.g., Buswell, 1935), he was one of the first to investigate the relationship between eye movement patterns and high-level cognitive factors. In Figures 107–112 of his book, Yarbus shows photographic records of eye movement patterns while viewing I. E. Repin's painting, "They Did Not Expect Him" (1884). The politically significant painting, portraying a Russian revolutionary returning from exile, was well known at the time. In Figure 2 (Yarbus' Figure 109), Yarbus showed a set of seven eye movement patterns for one observer as he or she viewed the painting under different instructions. In the first viewing, the observer was not given a specific instruction, but only asked to look at the painting. Before each of the subsequent six viewings, the instructions were: "Estimate the material circumstances of the family in the picture", "Give the ages of the people", "Surmise what the family had been doing before the arrival of the 'unexpected visitor'", "Remember the clothes worn by the people", "Remember the position of people and objects in the room", and "Estimate how long the 'unexpected visitor' had been away from the family".

There are striking differences in the eye movement patterns among the different conditions. These differences are more pronounced than among records of seven different observers freely viewing the painting without instruction, shown in Figure 107 of Yarbus' book. From this experiment, Yarbus concluded that the eyes "fixate on those elements of an object which

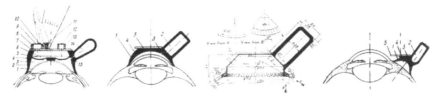

Figure 1.   Diagrams of suction "caps". The rightmost cap is designed to record eye movements. From Yarbus (1967, pp. 30–33).

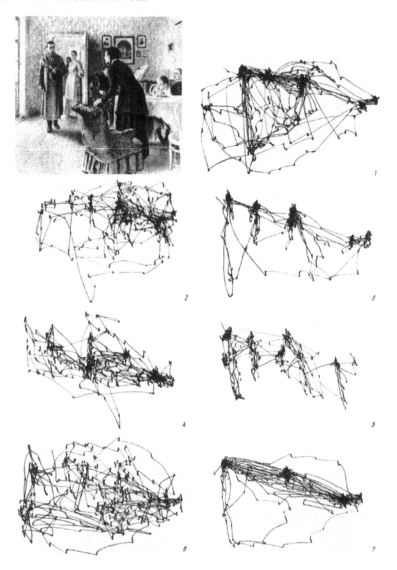

Figure 2. Figure 109 from Yarbus (1967, p. 174): Seven records of eye movements by the same subject. Each record lasted 3 minutes. The subject examined the reproduction with both eyes. 1) Free examination of the picture. Before the subsequent recording sessions, the subject was asked to: 2) estimate the material circumstances of the family in the picture; 3) give the ages of the people; 4) surmise what the family had been doing before the arrival of the "unexpected visitor"; 5) remember the clothes worn by the people; 6) remember the position of the people and objects in the room; 7) estimate how long the "unexpected visitor" had been away from the family.

carry or may carry essential or useful information" (Yarbus, 1967, p. 211). The eyes are not reactively drawn to salient, low-level properties of the image such as bright regions or edges. Instead, the elements fixated are those that provide the most information for the task at hand. As the task changes, so does the "informativeness" of certain regions, thereby changing the observer's viewing behaviour. Furthermore, the patterns and locations of eye movements give insight into what the observer was thinking.

Yarbus also noted a "cyclic" pattern of eye movements. Acknowledging that the 3-minute viewing time was more than long enough to fixate on the important regions of the picture, he noted the fact that once these regions were fixated, the observer did not move on to examine the secondary elements and details in the picture. To further investigate the temporal order of regions fixated, he repeated the 3-minute freeview task while changing the photographic plate every 25 s. From these records he noted similar scanpaths in which the observer looked at these primary regions again and again throughout the full viewing time. Yarbus concluded from other freeview experiments with additional complex images that this "cycle" can last from a few seconds to many tens of seconds (Yarbus, 1967, pp. 175, 193, 194).

IMPLICATIONS

The results from this experiment are significant in that they demonstrate a "top-down" component of visual selection, demonstrating the active nature of the human visual system. An observer's cognitive goal and past experiences interact with the visual stimulus in order to execute an appropriate behaviour. The system is not passive; it does not randomly or uniformly sample the visual environment, nor does it simply react to the stimulus. Guy T. Buswell had reported earlier that, "The directions given prior to looking at a picture have a marked influence upon the character of perception" (1935, p. 144). He based that statement on experiments comparing observers' eye movements when they viewed images without instruction to those made during (1) visual search, (2) after reading a page of descriptive material about the picture, or (3) when asked which of two images was preferred. Buswell's work was likely influenced by his thesis adviser, Charles H. Judd, who investigated the relationship between eye movements and the perception of visual illusions (Judd, 1905; Judd & Courten, 1905). Buswell's work predated Yarbus' by three decades; Yarbus took the investigation of the relationship between eye movement patterns and high-level cognitive factors beyond Buswell's pioneering work and has received far more attention in recent years.

YARBUS' METHODS

Yarbus' Figure 109 is very well known and often cited in literature concerning eye movements, behaviour, top-down control of oculomotor function, and high-level scene perception. The fact that is often overlooked is that the records published are for only one, unidentified observer. There is no reference in *Eye Movements and Vision* (1967) to other observers performing these tasks or producing similar results, and the original Russian journal article (Iarbus, 1961) contains the same set of records as shown in Figure 109 of the translated text.

It must also be noted that each of the photographic records was made as the observer viewed the picture for a full 3 minutes. During the recording, the observer's eye was anaesthetized and his eyelids were taped open with heated strips of adhesive plaster as seen in Figure 3. Figure 1 shows the small suction device ("cap") holding a small mirror that was firmly attached to the sclera. Light projected onto the mirror and reflected onto a piece of photographic film created the eye movement record. The observer's head was constrained using the chin and forehead rests seen in Figure 3.

The results of Yarbus' experiment are important and have been widely referenced as among the first to demonstrate the task-dependent nature of saccadic eye movements. The fact that his result was based on a single,

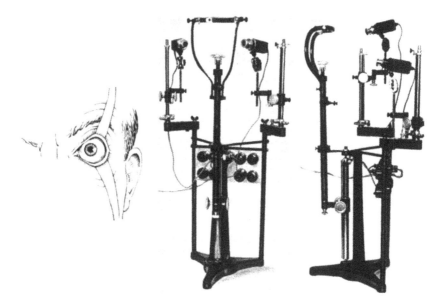

Figure 3. Left: Configuration of eyelids and strips of adhesive plaster during recording of eye movements. Right: Apparatus used in recording eye movements. The setup contains chin and forehead rests, light sources, and a control panel. From Yarbus (1967, pp. 41, 44).

unidentified observer was sufficient reason to replicate the experiment with a larger sample of naïve observers. The restrictive, intrusive, (and likely painful) nature of the instrumentation available to Yarbus was further motivation to repeat the experiment with contemporary eyetracking systems. We were also interested in examining the eye movement patterns of observers who were free to view the painting for only as much time as they thought necessary to answer the questions posed, rather than being forced to continue viewing for three minutes on each of the seven presentations. Finally, the relatively high-resolution, 2-D data output by modern eyetracking instrumentation allows the application of new analytical tools that were not available to Yarbus when he performed his pioneering research.

METHODS

Gaze tracking

Gaze position was determined by an integrated eye/head-tracking system consisting of an Applied Science Laboratories Series 501 video-based eyetracker ("ASL") and a Polhemus 3-Space Fastrak Magnetic Head Tracker ("MHT"). The MHT uses a fixed transmitter mounted just behind the observer and a small receiver attached to the ASL headgear. Position (x, y, z) and orientation (azimuth, elevation, roll) of the receiver are reported with respect to the transmitter. Combining the eye-in-head signal from the ASL with the head-in-space signal from the MHT provides a gaze-in-space vector that is used to determine the intersection of gaze on the display. The system allows image-centric gaze monitoring without constraining natural head movements. Position and orientation of the MHT transmitter is critical to the system calibration. To ensure repeatability, a three-axis laser level was affixed to the transmitter stand and three reference marks were placed on the ceiling, the base of the stimulus display, and an adjacent wall. Before each trial, the lasers were checked to ensure that the relative position and orientation of the transmitter and display were correct.

Calibration

The eye/head gaze tracking system was calibrated at the start of each session, and monitored every 10 images throughout a trial. Calibration was repeated if the reported gaze position fell outside circles of 1° radius surrounding the calibration check points.

Calibration consisted of optical alignment of the cameras and illumination source with the observer's eye and scene, defining nine calibration points on the image display, and capturing the vector difference between pupil centre and the first-surface corneal reflection at each of the nine points. The MHT system corrects for head movements, but initial calibration was performed with the head stable. Rather than use a mechanical constraint for calibration, observers held their head stable by maintaining a point projected from a semiconductor laser mounted to the ASL headgear within the circle about the central calibration point. Once the calibration was completed and verified, the laser was turned off and the observer was free to move his/her head naturally.

Gaze accuracy

The accuracy of the output fixation locations is dependent on several factors. First, because the video system tracks the retroreflection from the retina and the corneal reflection, differences between observers can affect performance. Using the MHT in conjunction with the eyetracker can introduce error if the headgear moves with respect to the head during the experiment. In a previous study in which this system was used (Babcock, 2002), angular deviation between fixation points and target calibration points (during calibration checks) was found to range between 0.4° and 1.1° across 26 observers, with an average deviation of 0.7° of visual angle. Additional uncertainty of fixation location may be introduced by the algorithm used to classify fixations and saccades, discussed later. An eye movement record was discarded if the final angular deviation was greater than 1.0°.

Fixation, saccade, and blink classification

Gaze position in the image plane was captured at 60 Hz, with no field averaging. Fixations, saccades, blinks, and any track losses were extracted from this data stream using an adaptive-velocity threshold; the threshold used to distinguish between fixations and saccades changes dynamically with the amount of noise in the signal, which varies between observers. See Rothkopf and Pelz (2004) for details on the detection algorithm.

Observers

Twenty-five observers (16 male, 9 female, ages 18–45 years, mean = 24 years, $SD = 5.9$) were compensated for participating in the experiment. All had normal or corrected-to-normal vision (only contact lenses were allowed) and were naïve to the purpose of the experiment. The Rochester Institute of

Technology Institutional Review Board approved the study, and informed consent was obtained from each observer after an explanation of the nature and possible consequences of the study.

Stimulus display

Images were displayed on a 50-inch Pioneer 503CMX Plasma display, driven by 1280×768 digital RGB input via a Pioneer PDA-5002 video card in linear display mode. While observers were free to move their heads, they were seated approximately 40-inches from the display, at which distance it subtended 50° of visual angle horizontally and 35° vertically. Images were presented in 24-bit colour at a resolution of 1280×768 pixels. Figure 4 shows the experimental setup. Repin's painting did not fill the available screen size and was presented at a resolution of 870×768 pixels, subtending a visual angle of $40° \times 35°$.

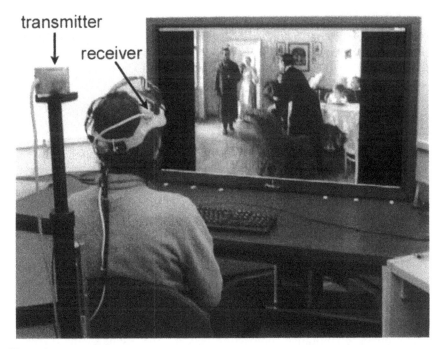

Figure 4. Experimental setup showing the plasma display, the eyetracking headgear, the magnetic head tracker transmitter, and receiver.

Replication of experiment

Yarbus' tasks were replicated within a larger experiment in which observers viewed a set of 57 digital images of paintings, photographs, and drawings. Observers were told to simply view the remaining artwork. The viewing was self-paced; the observer pressed the spacebar to move on to the next image. Between every 10 images, the observer was asked to look at a sequence of nine points to check the accuracy of the track. Observers were recalibrated if needed. Following the calibration check, a screen with a written instruction was presented. These instructions are the same as those reported by Yarbus (1967), and were also presented in the same order. (For the no-instruction "Freeview" task, Repin's painting was shown randomly within the first 10 images without any instruction; it was simply another painting within the set of random images.) The only exception was that "Estimate the material circumstances of the family in the picture" was reworded as "Estimate the financial circumstances of the family in the picture" because during a pilot experiment some observers did not readily understand the meaning of the original wording. When the observer had read the instruction, he or she pressed the spacebar to view Repin's "They Did Not Expect Him". The observer then performed the task, which in most cases involved answering questions out loud. When the observer completed the task, the spacebar was pressed to freely view the next random image. Including the calibration checks, instruction screens, and repetitions of Repin's painting, there were 78 images displayed during the experiment. The experiment lasted between 11 and 20 minutes. Of the 25 observers who performed the experiment, 17 met the one-degree calibration criterion throughout the full trial and were included in the subsequent analysis.

Although the focus of the study was to replicate Yarbus' tasks under more natural viewing conditions with a larger set of observers, we did replicate Yarbus viewing durations with one observer (male, age 28); eye movements were recorded as he viewed Repin's painting in 3-minute intervals for each of the seven tasks. For this experiment, no other images were shown between the tasks. This experiment lasted 21 minutes, plus the time the observer spent reading the instruction screens.

RESULTS

Given that the results published by Yarbus were very qualitative, and lacked any information about the temporal sequence of viewing, it is difficult to make a direct, quantitative comparison between the results of the present experiment and those reported by Yarbus. In the following sections, several qualitative and quantitative methods are used to compare the eye movement patterns of observers across the different tasks and viewing conditions.

Self-terminated viewing

Scanpaths. Figure 5 shows eye movement records of two observers as they performed each of the seven tasks during this experiment. For Observer A, shown on the left, the viewing times ranged from 6 to 92 s. Although the times are all well under 3 minutes, the eye movement patterns are remarkably similar to those published by Yarbus. Fixations in the "Freeview", "Ages", and "How long away" tasks fell primarily on faces and figures. The "Financial" and "Position" tasks elicited more spatially distributed patterns of fixations. Observer B represents an atypical observer, whose eye movement patterns are not drastically different among tasks. The view times were

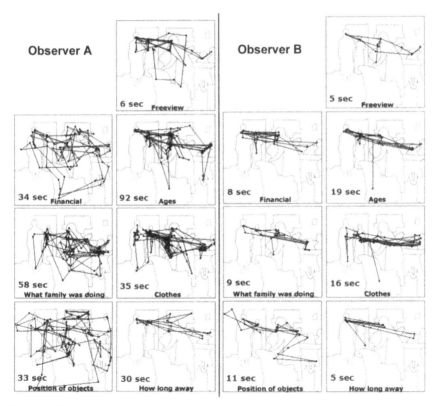

Figure 5. Eye movement records from two observers as they performed each of the seven tasks. Observer A represents an observer whose view patterns resembled those published by Yarbus. Observer B represents an atypical observer, whose view patterns did not differ significantly among tasks.

also shorter, ranging from 5 to 19 s. Both observers completed all tasks and answered questions out loud; Observer A gave more thoughtful and detailed answers compared with Observer B, which accounts for the differences in total task time.

Total viewing time. Whereas Yarbus had an enforced 3-minute viewing time, the self-terminated experiment allows us to examine how much time an observer spent performing each of the seven tasks. Figure 6 shows the total viewing time for each observer in each task. Viewing times were for the most part an order of magnitude less than in Yarbus' experiment. For the "Freeview" task, observers viewed the painting for only nine s on average. Nineteen seconds was the average time observers spent answering the question, "Estimate the financial circumstances." When asked to give the ages of the people, the painting was viewed for an average of 50 s, which is significantly longer than any other task. For the tasks "Surmise what the family had been doing", "Remember the clothes", and "Remember the

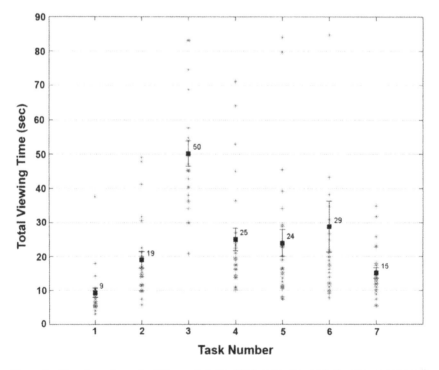

Figure 6. View times for each of the seven tasks. Black rectangles mark the average across all observers. Error bars represent one standard error of the mean. Tasks: 1: Freeview; 2: Financial circumstances; 3: Give the ages; 4: Surmise what family was doing; 5: Remember the clothes; 6: Remember the position of people and objects; 7: Estimate how long the visitor was away.

position of people and objects", the image was viewed for an average of 25, 24, and 29 s, respectively. The last task, "Estimate how long the visitor has been away", was completed in an average of 15 s.

Fixation duration.   Another measure that was not reported by Yarbus was the duration of fixations in each task. Figure 7 shows histograms of fixation durations pooled across observers for the seven tasks. Listed on

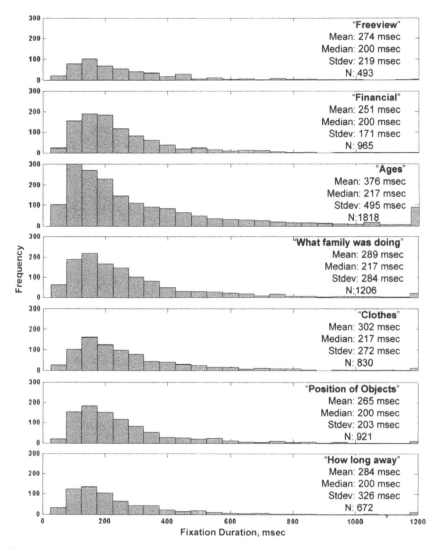

Figure 7.   Histograms of fixation durations for each task across all observers.

each graph are the mean, median, and standard deviation of the distribution, and number of fixations. All the tasks had median fixation durations of near 200 ms. Additionally, all but one task showed a peak in the histogram near 150 ms; the histogram for the task "Give the ages of the people" peaks at only 100 ms, with 22% of fixations lasting 100 ms or less. Interestingly, this task also elicited the longest fixations; about 7% (133) fixations were longer than 1 s in duration. Yarbus noted that his observer had few saccades between faces, suggesting long fixation times.

Regions of interest. Yarbus' results focused entirely on the spatial distribution of fixations, in the form of photographic records shown in Figure 2 and comments derived from those records. Specifically, Yarbus often commented on the attention given to primary (faces and figures), secondary (furniture and objects in the foreground), and background elements of the image. We sought to quantify the amount of time an observer viewed these regions and to compare our results with Yarbus' commentary.

The image of Repin's painting was segmented into 22 different regions (e.g., the man's face, the man's figure, chairs, floor, etc.). The regions and associated labels are shown in Figure 8. The total gaze duration in each of these regions was found for every observer. These durations were then normalized by the viewing time for each observer and task to produce the percentage of time spent viewing each region. The results for each task are also shown in Figure 8, averaged across all observers.

During the freeview task, 20% of the time was spent fixating on the man's face, followed by the faces of the mother, wife, maid, and children. This result agrees with Yarbus' observer's behaviour; the most fixations fell on the faces of the people followed by the figures.

The distribution of gaze for the task "Estimate how long the 'unexpected visitor' was away" is very similar to that of the freeview task. Again the faces received the most fixations. More of the viewers' time, around 35%, was spent looking at the man's face for this task. His figure and the faces of the mother and children were also important. For this task, Yarbus noted particularly intensive movements between the faces of the children and man.

The task "Give the ages of the people" resulted in a more uniform distribution across the faces, with very little attention given to background elements. Yarbus reported that for this task, all of the observer's attention was concentrated on the faces, with few saccades between faces.

For the task, "Estimate the financial circumstances of the family", the faces were again the most attended-to regions. However, the clothing and furniture received more fixations than in previous tasks. Yarbus' observer paid particular attention to the women's clothing, armchair, and tabletop.

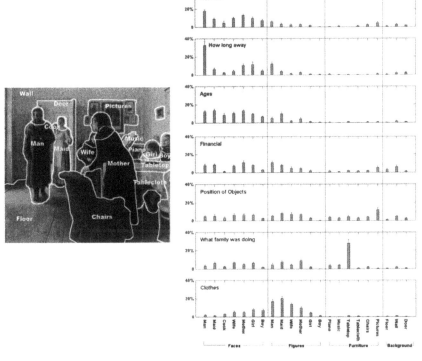

Figure 8. Left: Image segmented into 22 regions with associated labels. Right: Percentage of time spent viewing each region. Error bars represent standard error of the mean across 17 observers.

For the task, "Remember the position of people and objects in the room", every region received fixations in most cases, producing a more uniform distribution of gaze durations throughout the image. The pictures on the wall were examined for a larger fraction of time (12%) than in other tasks. The more uniform distribution across primary, secondary, and background elements agrees with Yarbus' report that his observer examined the whole room and all of the objects.

When asked to "surmise what the family had been doing before the arrival of the 'unexpected visitor'", the tabletop was evidently the most informative, as viewers spent 30% of their time looking at it. The piano and sheet music also received a larger percentage of viewing time than in other tasks. These are also the regions that Yarbus' observer attended to the most: "[T]he observer directed his attention particularly to the objects arranged on the table, the girl's and the woman's hands, and to the music" (Yarbus, 1967, p. 192).

Last, when asked to "remember the clothes worn by the people", viewers spent the majority of time examining the figures in the image, as did Yarbus' observer. The faces of the people in the image were invariably fixated, regardless of the task.

Between-observer variability. To measure the influence of task on viewing behaviour, the between-observer variability and between-task variability were compared. The fraction of time spent viewing each of the regions in the image can be thought of as a 22-element feature vector. As a measure of between-observer variability within each task, the Euclidean distance between each possible pair of vectors was found. The average distances within each task are shown in Figure 9. Also shown is the between-task (within-observer) distance, averaged across all observers; 0.39. For the first six tasks, the between-observer variability is below the between-task variability, indicating that the eye movement patterns across observers for that task were more similar than the patterns of one person performing different tasks. "Give the ages" task was the most similar between observers, with an average distance of 0.25, suggesting similar viewing strategies (e.g., most attention given to the faces). The average distance for the "How long

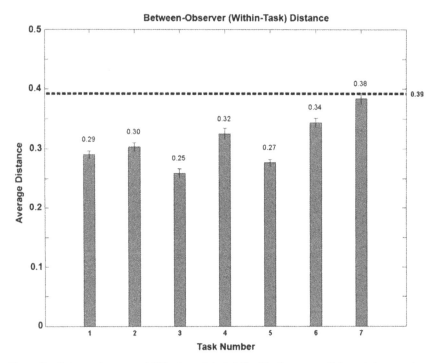

Figure 9. Between-observer variability for each task defined by the average distance between region histogram vectors. Error bars represent one standard error of the mean. The dotted line represents the within-observer (between-task) variability, averaged across 17 observers.

away" task, 0.38, was very close to the within-observer distance, suggesting that observers attended to different regions when performing that task. This was the last and shortest task; it is possible that some observers did not refixate on informative regions and instead used information gathered during previous viewings.

Enforced three-minute view, all tasks

Scanpaths.   Yarbus' enforced 3-minute view time was replicated for a single observer. By the end of the experiment, he had been looking at the painting for 21 minutes. Figure 10 shows the eye movement patterns as well as percentage of time spent per region of interest. When compared to the average behaviour during the self-terminated condition, shown in Figure 8, there are many similarities. This may support Yarbus' report of "cyclic" eye movement patterns in which the same informative regions are re-fixated

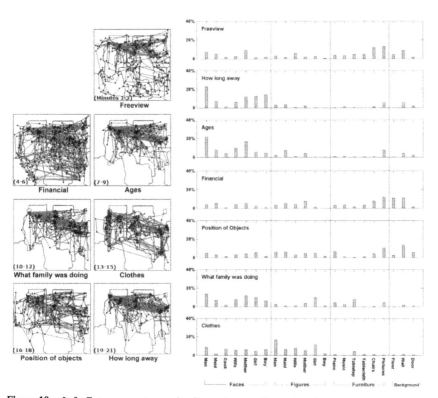

Figure 10.   Left: Eye movement records of one observer. For each task, the observer viewed the painting for 3 minutes. The minutes in which each task was performed are labelled in the corner of each record. Right: Percentage of time one observer spent viewing each region as he viewed the image for 3 minutes per task.

throughout the extended view time. For example, in the "How long away" task, the observer spent most of his time looking at the man's face, and the expressions on the faces of the mother, girl, and boy; these were also the most fixated regions in Figure 8. The observer reported that he was trying to guess whether both of the children recognized the man. For the "Financial" and "Position of Object" tasks, the histograms are more uniform, as they were for the self-terminated condition. For the "Ages" task, this observer's behaviour was also similar in that almost all fixations fell on the faces, although he did spend some time examining the pictures on the wall.

There were also some dissimilarities between this observer's viewing behaviour and the results of the self-terminated condition. For example, the histogram for "Clothes" shows that the observer spent almost an equal amount of time looking at the people's faces as he did at their clothing. When guessing "What the family was doing", the observer did examine the tabletop, but unlike the self-terminated task where observers spent almost 30% of their time studying it, this observer spent less than 10% of the time fixating the tabletop. Instead, more time was spent examining the faces of the people in the room; the observer reported that by the end of the task, he was developing a story about the characters in the scene, their personalities, and what they were doing.

For the "Freeview" task, although the observer did spend time looking at the faces in the scene, many of the other objects, or "secondary details" were attended to, particularly the furniture and pictures on the wall. This result differs from both the self-terminated results as well as the behaviour of Yarbus' observer. It is possible that this observer's behaviour was similar to Yarbus' at the beginning of the experiment, and changed as time went on. In the next section we will investigate the effect of the enforced 3-minute view time on this task.

Temporal order.   Yarbus noted that over several minutes, the eye movement "record obtained will clearly show that, when changing its points of fixation, the observer's eye repeatedly returns to the same elements of the picture. Additional time spent on perception is not used to examine the secondary elements, but to reexamine the most important elements" (Yarbus, 1967, p. 193). In an additional experiment, he found that an observer's eye movement patterns were similar during each of 25-s intervals during a 3-minute free examination of the painting.

To determine if the observer's viewing behaviour was indeed cyclic, or whether it changed over time, we examined the temporal order of regions fixated (i.e., shifts of gaze) for the "Freeview" task, shown in Figure 11. These regions are grouped into three areas of interest: Faces, figures, and background/furniture. This grouping corresponds to the elements Yarbus referred to as primary (faces and figures) and secondary (other foreground

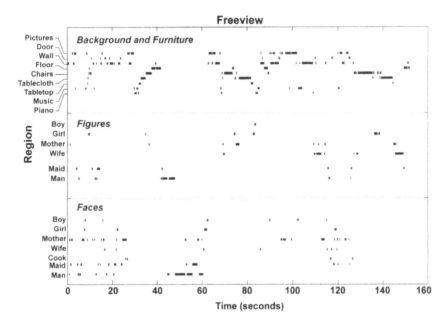

Figure 11. Temporal order for one observer during the "Freeview" task. The length of each line represents fixation duration. Each vertical level represents a different region. The bottom section is all of the Face regions. The regions in the middle section are the Figure regions. The top section is all other regions. (The time does not extend to the full 3 minutes, or 180 s, because the time during blinks and saccades has been removed.)

items and background). During the first 20–30 s of viewing, the observer made many short fixations on each of the faces, most of the figures, and almost all the background elements. For the next 30 s, the observer seemed to change behaviour. Gaze durations become longer, and were spent on the background elements for 10 s, then to the man's figure, and then to the man's face. During the next 30 s, the background elements were again examined. After that, there were again short fixations distributed among the faces, figures, and background, which is similar to the behaviour at the beginning of the task. For the rest of the viewing time, the background elements and figures were examined with long gaze durations.

In the "Clothes" task, again we see a change in viewing behaviour, illustrated in Figure 12. During the first half of the viewing time, the faces and clothes are each examined in turn with long gaze durations. During the second half, the background elements are examined, and gaze shifts frequently and more quickly among different regions.

The "Financial" task, shown in Figure 13, represents a task in which the behaviour is more consistent over time: Short fixations are distributed among all the areas throughout the viewing period.

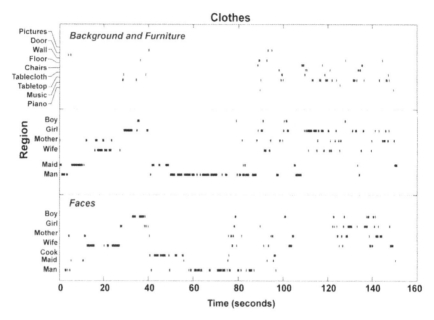

Figure 12. Temporal order of fixations during "Remember the clothes" task.

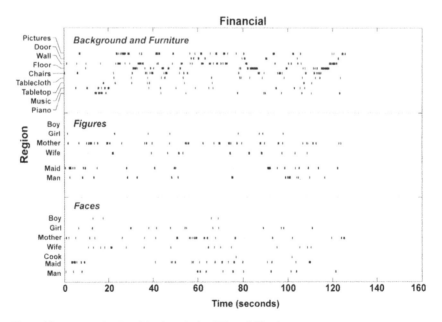

Figure 13. Temporal order of fixations during "Financial" task.

From these visualizations we see that our observer did indeed fixate on primary regions (faces) throughout the viewing time. However, Yarbus' notion that an observer would repeat the same scanpath over and over, without moving on to secondary objects is too severe a generalization.

CONCLUSIONS

Alfred Yarbus' classical experiment showed the influence of task on oculomotor behaviour. In his experiment, Yarbus had one observer repeatedly view a painting seven times for 3 minutes each time; before each viewing the observer was given a different instruction. From records of the spatial pattern of eye movements, Yarbus' concluded that the observer's fixations repeatedly fell on regions that were most important or "informative" for the particular task, forming a cyclic pattern throughout the 3-minute viewing time.

We replicated the experiment with 17 naïve observers using a free-head, video-based eyetracker. Viewing times were self-terminated. Observers performed each of the seven tasks that Yarbus used in his experiment while viewing a large-field reproduction of I. E. Repin's painting, "They Did Not Expect Him". The tasks were: (1) Freeview (no instruction); (2) "Estimate the financial circumstances of the family in the picture"; (3) "Give the ages of the people"; (4) "Surmise what the family had been doing before the arrival of the 'unexpected visitor'"; (5) "Remember the clothes worn by the people"; (6) "Remember the position of people and objects in the room"; and (7) "Estimate how long the 'unexpected visitor' had been away from the family".

The average view time for each task was 9, 19, 50, 25, 24, 29, and 15 s, respectively; these times are significantly less than the enforced 3-minute view time of Yarbus' observer. The task, "Give the ages of the people", elicited both the shortest and longest fixation durations; 22% of fixations were 100 ms or shorter, and 7% were longer than 1 s. All other tasks had similar distributions of gaze durations with median durations near 200 ms.

Most observers' eye movement patterns were subjectively similar to those reported by Yarbus, with faces invariably fixated, and the overall viewing pattern varying with instruction. A few observers, especially those with shorter viewing times, did not show dramatic shifts with instruction.

A Euclidean-distance metric between the feature vectors describing the distribution of gaze within regions of interest in the painting was used as a measure of both between-task and between-observer variability. All tasks except for "How long away" resulted in between-observer average distances that were less than the between-task distance. The "Give the ages" task resulted in the smallest distance of all tasks, indicating that for this task the eye movement patterns were most similar among the observers. The "How long away" task showed the most variability among observers, suggesting that observers used different viewing strategies to complete this task.

Yarbus' observation of a "cyclic" behaviour of eye movements was also investigated by examining the temporal sequences of fixations of one observer who performed each of the seven tasks with an enforced 3-minute view time. The viewing behaviour for the "Financial" task was consistent throughout the viewing time in that the observer frequently shifted his gaze among faces, figures, and background objects. Other tasks, including "Remember the clothes", show a distinct change in behaviour. For this task, the observer began the task by examining the clothes and faces of the people in the scene, with some fairly long gaze durations. Halfway through the viewing time, the observer began to examine furniture and background elements. Yarbus' observer did not show this behaviour of moving attention to secondary elements, but instead spent the entire 3 minutes refixating on the "informative" regions. This cyclic behaviour may in part be a result of the uncomfortable setup of his experiment, which may have made his observer conscious of where he was looking. In doing so, the observer may have changed his viewing behaviour to adhere strictly to the given instructions. It is also possible that an observer, even a naïve observer, having looked at the same painting for over 20 minutes, would begin to consciously narrow his or her gaze based on the instructions.

Yarbus' basic result, that eye movement patterns are tied to the immediate task, is fundamental to the so-called "bottom-up/top-down debate". It is in this context that many of the references to his work are made (e.g., Baars, 1988, Ballard, Hayhoe, Pook, & Rao, 1997; Gould, 1976; Hoffman & Subramanium, 1995), and recent research continues to show the importance of top-down influence on eye movement patterns (e.g., Einhäuser, Rutishauser, & Koch, 2008, Rothkopf, Ballard, & Hayhoe, 2007). Yet a significant literature exists supporting bottom-up models that predict fixation density or scanpath sequences based on low-level image features. In an early instantiation, Koch and Ullman (1985) proposed a network that calculated the relative conspicuity of each location in the visual scene based on the low-level features. Work on such "saliency-map" methods continues, with some researchers attempting to merge the bottom-up and top-down approaches (Canosa, 2005; Itti & Koch, 2001; Parkhurst, Law, & Niebur, 2002; Peters & Itti, 2008). The importance and visibility of Yarbus' work is likely to grow in the foreseeable future as the community continues to work toward models of that successfully merge the two approaches.

REFERENCES

Baars, B. J. (1988). *A cognitive theory of consciousness*. New York: Cambridge University Press.

Babcock, J. B. (2002). *Eye tracking observers during color image evaluation tasks*. Unpublished MS thesis. Rochester Institute of Technology, Rochester, NY.

Ballard, D. H., Hayhoe, M. M., Pook, P. K., & Rao, R. P. N. (1997). Deictic codes for the embodiment of cognition. *Behavioral and Brain Sciences, 20*, 723–742.

Buswell, G. T. (1935). *How people look at pictures: A study of the psychology of perception in art*. Chicago: University of Chicago Press.

Canosa, R. L. (2005). Modeling selective perception of complex, natural scenes. *International Journal on Artificial Intelligence, 14*(1–2), 233–260.

Einhäuser, W., Rutishauser, U., & Koch, C. (2008). Task-demands can immediately reverse the effects of sensory-driven saliency in complex visual stimuli. *Journal of Vision, 8*(2):2, 1–19.

Gould, J. D. (1976). Looking at pictures. In R. A. Monty & J. W. Senders (Eds.), *Eye movements and psychological processes* (pp. 323–346). Hillsdale, NJ: Lawrence Erlbaum Associates, Inc.

Hoffman, J. E., & Subramanium, B. (1995). The role of visual attention in saccadic eye movements. *Perception and Psychophysics, 57*, 787–795.

Iarbus, A. L. (1961). Eye movements during examination of complex objects (in Russian). *Biofizika, 6*, 207–212.

Iarbus, A. L. (1965). *Rol' dvizheniya glaz v protsesse zreniya* [The role of eye motion in vision processes] (in Russian). Moscow: Nauka Press.

Itti, L., & Koch, C. (2001). Computational modeling of visual attention. *Nature Reviews Neuroscience, 2*(3), 194–203.

Judd, C. H. (1905). The Müller-Lyer illusion. *Psychological Review Monographs, 7*(Suppl. 29), 55–82.

Judd, C. H., & Courten, H. C. (1905). The Zöllner illusion. *Psychological Monographs, 7*, 112–139.

Koch, C., & Ullman, S. (1985). Shifts in selective visual attention: Towards the underlying neural circuitry. *Human Neurobiology, 4*, 219–227.

Parkhurst, D., Law, K., & Niebur, E. (2002). Modeling the role of salience in the allocation of visual selective attention. *Vision Research, 42*(1), 107–123.

Peters, R. J., & Itti, L. (2008). Applying computational tools to predict gaze direction in interactive visual environments. *ACM Transactions in Applied Perception, 5*(2), 1–19.

Rothkopf, C. A., Ballard, D. H., & Hayhoe, M. M. (2007). Task and context determine where you look. *Journal of Vision, 7*(14):16, 1–20.

Rothkopf, C. A., & Pelz, J. B. (2004). Head movement estimation for wearable eye tracker. In *Proceedings of the Eye Tracking Research and Application symposium* (ETRA 2004) (pp. 123–130). San Antonio, TX: ACM.

Yarbus, A. L. (1967). *Eye movements and vision* (B. Haigh, Trans.). New York: Plenum Press.

VISUAL COGNITION, 2009, 17 (6/7), 812–834

Saliency and scan patterns in the inspection of real-world scenes: Eye movements during encoding and recognition

Geoffrey Underwood, Tom Foulsham, and
Katherine Humphrey

University of Nottingham, Nottingham, UK

How do sequences of eye fixations match each other when viewing a picture during encoding and again during a recognition test, and to what extent are fixation sequences (scan patterns) determined by the low-level visual features of the picture rather than the domain knowledge of the viewer? The saliency map model of visual attention was tested in two experiments to ask whether the rank ordering of regions by their saliency values can be used to predict the sequence of fixations made when first looking at an image. Experiment 1 established that the sequence of fixations on first inspection during encoding was similar to that made when looking at the picture the second time, in the recognition test. Experiment 2 confirmed this similarity of fixation sequences at encoding and recognition, and also found a similarity between scan patterns made during the initial recognition test and during a second recognition test 1 week later. The fixation scan patterns were not similar to those predicted by the saliency map model in either experiment, however. These conclusions are qualified by interactions involving the match between the content of the image and the domain of interest of the viewers.

Keywords: Scene perception; Saliency; Scanpaths; Eye movements; Domain knowledge.

Saliency map models of visual attention make strong predictions about the direction of our eyes when we first look at a picture of a natural scene. Conspicuous regions of an image are expected to gain early inspection by virtue of the early acquisition of low-level visual information about regions that are readily discriminated from their surroundings. Changes in colour and intensity, for example, identify a region as being visually salient, and the

---

Please address all correspondence to Geoffrey Underwood, School of Psychology, University of Nottingham, Nottingham NG7 2RD, UK.

E-mail: geoff.underwood@nottingham.ac.uk

This research was supported by project grant EP/E006329/1 from the EPSRC (UK) to GU.

© 2009 Taylor & Francis
DOI: 10.1080/13506280902771278

model identifies these regions as being most likely to attract our attention. This advantage of salient over nonsalient regions is considered to be short-lived, however, and once the meaning of the scene has been appreciated after the first few fixations, then top-down conceptual processes will dominate and the viewer's attention will no longer be captured by conspicuous regions. The two experiments described here assess the saliency map model as a predictor of sequences of fixations. If viewers move their eyes according to the peaks on the saliency map—looking first at the most salient region, and then the next most salient region, and so on—then a fixation sequence will be established that may persist over time and over repeated viewings of the same image. We recorded the locations of eye fixations of viewers when they first looked at a collection of images, and again when they looked at the same images in a recognition test some time later. Comparing the fixation sequences on separate viewings provides a test of extended saliency map model, and a test of the stability of fixation sequences over repeated viewings.

One of the more explicit and fully formalized models of the visual saliency map hypothesis was proposed by Itti and Koch (2000), who developed an algorithm that measures the saliency of an image objectively, by the identification of peaks in the distribution of colour, intensity, and orientation. The saliency distribution generates predictions as to where attention should be directed and forms the basis of a model of visual attention. For each of the visual characteristics a separate conspicuity map is first computed by searching for change relative to adjacent regions. The separate maps are then combined to find saliency peaks, with a change in any of the three characteristics resulting in an increase in the saliency value assigned to that region of the image.

What distinguishes the Itti and Koch (2000) saliency map model is that it has been implemented in software that can be used to identify the saliency peaks in an image, and these peaks then form the basis for predictions about the sequence of fixation of objects. The Itti and Koch algorithm operationalizes image saliency purely on the basis of an analysis of bottom-up featural information. The generation of a saliency map and an associated sequence of fixations can be seen in Figure 1A, in which the most visually salient region of the image is the area around the skyline on the centre left, where the dark outline of tree contrasts against a bright sky. The algorithm picks this region as having the greatest saliency value, and this is represented in Figure 1B by the brightness of that area. The rank ordering of the saliency peaks then provides a prediction about the ordering of fixations, and the peaks are identified in Figure 1C. The predicted fixations in Figure 1C can be contrasted against the actual fixations of one human viewer in Figure 1A. This contrast is presented for illustrative purposes only, and it is significant that the participant whose fixations are recorded in Figure 1A has a

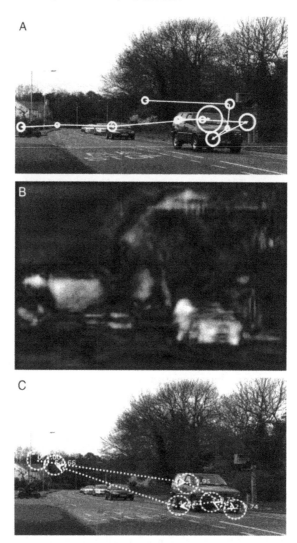

Figure 1. A recorded sequence of fixations made while inspecting a scene (A), a raw saliency map of the scene (B), and the predicted sequence according to a bottom-up saliency map (C). The original image, from which the saliency map in B is generated, was shown in colour. In Image A (actual fixations), the circles represent fixations, with the diameter indicating duration. The first fixation was near to the centre of the picture and after 11 saccades the final fixation was on the motorcycle on the left of the picture. The saliency peaks in Image B are represented here as the brightest areas, and are used to determine the predicted sequence of fixations in C, with the most salient region being on the left of the image at the edge between a tree and the sky, and the next four most salient regions are around the car in the foreground.

professional interest in motoring and in motorcycling in particular. One purpose of the second experiment reported here is to evaluate the saliency map hypothesis with viewers who have prior domain knowledge and special interest in the images being inspected.

Studies that have supported the saliency map model of visual attention have often used search tasks with simple geometric displays of targets and distractors (e.g., Lamy, Leber, & Egeth, 2004; Nothdurft, 2002), but the model also makes predictions about eye fixations with other images. Parkhurst, Law, and Niebur (2002) presented a range of images, including photographs of real-world scenes as well as computer-generated fractals. The saliency values of regions in each image provided a good prediction of the locations of eye fixations during the few seconds available for inspection. This experiment provided early empirical support for a purely bottom-up account of visual attention during scene perception, although the task used by Parkhurst et al. raises questions about the role of top-down conceptual processes. Their task was to look around the images, with no other purpose than to remain looking at the screen. When we look at a scene there is often a purpose, as when looking for one's coat on a crowded coat-stand in a restaurant, for example, or when looking for a specific food jar in a kitchen cupboard. At these times we can look for an object according to its individual characteristics, and brightly coloured but task-irrelevant objects do not usually capture our attention (but see Foulsham & Underwood, in press, for a case of a search task when distractor objects had a greater effect when they were visually salient than when they were inconspicuous). When we search scenes we do so purposely, and with cognitive override of visual saliency. When viewers look at real-world scenes in preparation for a sentence verification task they scan the whole photograph to encode as much content as possible (Underwood, Jebbett, & Roberts, 2004), but when the sentence is presented first and they know what aspect of the scene is most relevant, then fixations can be directed towards the objects targeted by the sentence. We have established the relationship between task purpose and image saliency in experiments that used the same pictures in different tasks (Foulsham & Underwood, 2007; Underwood & Foulsham, 2006; Underwood, Foulsham, van Loon, Humphreys, & Bloyce, 2006)—saliency can be potent during picture encoding but less so during the search for a specific target. When instructed to inspect scenes in preparation for a recognition test, then fixations followed the predictions of the saliency map model, with conspicuous objects attracting early fixations. When instructed to decide whether the scene contained a specific target object, however, a highly salient nontarget distractor object was not fixated in preference to a less salient target. Saliency determined the early capture of attention in these experiments, but only when there was no object-based purpose to the inspection.

A limitation of saliency as a predictor of fixation locations is also apparent in change detection experiments, where salient regions do not capture attention (Stirk & Underwood, 2007; Underwood, Templeman, Lamming, & Foulsham, 2008). A single object was changed between two images of the same scene in these experiments, and the object was either very conspicuous when changed (one of the three most salient items in the scene) or inconspicuous (not in the top 10). The saliency of the changed item did not affect detection in either a flicker paradigm with alternating images (Stirk & Underwood, 2007), or in a comparative visual search task in which both images were presented side-by-side (Underwood et al., 2008). High saliency does not always attract early fixations and more recent models of real-world scene perception take the purpose of inspection and the scene semantics into account and do not rely exclusively on bottom-up processes (Navalpakkam & Itti, 2005; Torralba, Oliva, Castelhano, & Henderson, 2006).

To provide the saliency map model with a good chance of predicting fixation behaviour a task should be used that has enabled effects to been found, and so the present experiments used a recognition memory task. In each experiment we first presented photographs of real-world scenes, and then presented them again, mixed with an equal number of previously unseen images. The task was to say which were the new images and which had been presented earlier. In this task there is an established influence of visual saliency, with conspicuous regions attracting early attention, and the two experiments here examined the possibility that saliency may have an influence on the second viewing of the image, and the possibility that saliency can influence the ordinal sequence of fixations during inspection.

SCANPATHS AND SCAN PATTERNS

What determines where the viewer's eyes will move next? We are interested here with the pattern or sequence of fixations that is generated during a particular viewing period or that is associated with a particular picture. These patterns can be referred to as *scanpaths* (Noton & Stark, 1971a,b,c) or *scan patterns* (Henderson, 2003). Early researchers investigating the locations of fixations made during picture perception recorded a large variation in the sequences of fixations made, but regular patterns did emerge (Buswell, 1935; Yarbus, 1967). When viewers are allowed prolonged inspection of an image their fixations are not randomly located, and neither are they regularly distributed across space, as we might suppose if the visual system were trying to sample the whole scene uniformly (see Figure 1). In the example here the viewer's fixations start in the centre of the image, and then focus on a series of interesting objects, especially the brightly coloured car in the foreground, the speed camera on the right, and finishing with the motorcycle on the left. Fixations have largely avoided areas of the scene that are uniform or devoid of interest, such as the sky, the trees, and the roadway. We tend to look at interesting or informative parts of a scene. If looking at a picture containing people, fixations tend to be focused on their faces (see for example, Buswell, 1935; Yarbus, 1967) and within faces fixations are concentrated on the eyes (see, for example, Birmingham, Bischof, & Kingstone, 2008; Langton, Watt, & Bruce, 2000). The pictures used in the two experiments described here did not contain images of people, to avoid problems associated with the social saliency of human faces.

In addition to being tied to the visual features present in a stimulus, the pattern of eye movements made by an observer is known to vary according to the task being undertaken. In his often-cited early work on eye movements, Yarbus (1967) highlighted the fact that scanpaths exhibited when viewing the same stimulus would be quite different if the viewer was given a different task. Two commonly studied experimental tasks are looking at a scene in order to remember it for later and searching a scene for a specific target (e.g., Henderson, Weeks, & Hollingworth, 1999; Underwood & Foulsham, 2006). The between-subjects variation in scanpaths has led some to label scanpaths as distinctively idiosyncratic, presumably reflecting personal knowledge, experience, or viewing strategy. To study these top-down aspects of overt attention it is useful to be able to compare scanpaths across viewings, stimuli, and individuals. Before looking at this technique in more detail, we need to distinguish between the observation of fixation sequences and the scanpath theory for which the comparison of sequences is particularly important.

Scanpath theory comprises an ambitious set of ideas that were originally proposed by Noton and Stark (1971a,b,c). The theory describes scanpaths as controlled by internal, cognitive models representing the viewer's expectations of the scene. These models might represent the saccades involved in viewing a picture or scene as a kind of structure or syntax that binds together the features processed at fixation. When viewing the same scene again, as in the test phase of a recognition experiment, a scanpath might be reinvoked or checked against the external stimulus. The theory argued that inspection of an image resulted in the formation of a "feature ring" of sensorimemory traces of image regions and motor memory traces of saccades, and that specific oculomotor activity becomes associated with regions of interest in the image. The main evidence for scanpath theory came from experiments showing that fixation sequences recurred when stimuli were reviewed in a recognition task. In the earliest papers, this conclusion was reached based on subjective observation of the patterns shown by each viewer, and there was no quantification of the similarity between the scanpaths. However, in a later study by Stark and Ellis (1981), the regularity of fixation sequences was determined by Markov matrices to establish the transition probabilities of sequences to determine whether they have occurred more frequently than would be expected by chance. The Markov matrix method for the identification of short sequences of fixations has been used in different applications, but is limited by the number of fixations that can be compared within any sequence (e.g., Underwood, Chapman, Brocklehurst, Underwood, & Crundall, 2003). Other researchers have reported the presence of repetitive scanpaths when inspecting and then imagining a picture using a more workable serial-order method that compares strings in terms of the number of editing operations necessary to convert one to the other. This string-editing comparison process is used here (Brandt & Stark, 1997; Laeng & Teodorescu, 2002).

Little empirical support has been found for scanpath theory and there are common observations that it would seem to have trouble explaining. For example, it is not necessary to move one's eyes to encode or recognize the gist of a picture (e.g., Biederman, Rabinowitz, Glass, & Stacy, 1974; Potter, 1976), even if eye movements are used at other times. There is no evidence to support the idea that the features of an image are remembered in combination with the motor signals associated with saccades resulting in their fixation, and the apparently large amount of variability within the patterns shown by a single person viewing the same stimulus also makes a strong version of scanpath theory untenable (Mannan, Ruddock, & Wooding, 1996). Fisher, Karsh, Breitenbach, and Barnette (1983) concluded that the appearance of scanpaths was the product of correlations between fixation locations and high information areas independently of sequence. The distinction between *local* and *global* scanpaths, to emphasize consistent patterns of successive fixations and the overall distribution of fixations over a longer time scale (Groner, Walder, & Groner, 1984), goes some way to answering this objection, but the absence of a weight of evidence has resulted in scanpath theory falling into disuse. Given the difficulty in supporting its assumptions, Henderson (2003) cautioned against use of the term scanpath due to its association with this theory. Accordingly, we will use the term *scan patterns*, in order to be clear that we are not accepting the assumptions of scanpath theory and we will not examine the specifics of scanpath theory or any other particular approach to the control of eye movements.

In the following two experiments we compared the sequence of fixations made during the first inspection of a photograph against the sequence made when judging whether the picture has been seen before (a recognition memory test), looking for a correspondence between the sequence predicted by the saliency map hypothesis and the sequence made by observers. In the second experiment we also investigated the role of domain knowledge in overriding the effects of visual saliency.

EXPERIMENT 1

The role of visual saliency in scan patterns during encoding and recognition

This experiment examines eye movements both at first viewing, and when looking at the same images later, during a recognition memory test. Does saliency influence the sequences of fixations in both tasks, or is recognition more similar to a search task where the viewer neglects visual saliency during the search for specific objects?

The experiment gives the opportunity to provide a more comprehensive analysis of the saliency map model by looking at fixation sequences. This experiment reevaluates the evidence for repetitive scan patterns and asks if the sequences of fixations at encoding of a picture of a real-world scene and recognition of that picture are similar. Such a finding might be explained by the bottom-up determinants of attention suggested by the saliency map model. If this is the case, then repeated scan patterns are expected not because they are encoded in any way by the observer, but because in both cases they are determined by the saliency values of different regions of the picture. The saliency analyses here allow this possibility to be investigated by the comparison of fixation sequences over different stages of the experiment and against the predictions of the model.

Method

Participants.   One group of 21 student volunteers took part. All had normal or corrected-to normal vision and were naive as to the purpose of the experiment. Inclusion in the study was contingent on reliable eye tracking calibration and in particular on maintaining a central fixation at the beginning of each presentation.

Materials and apparatus.   An SMI EyeLink I system was used to monitor eye movements. The system was head mounted and sampled pupil position from the right eye every 4 ms, with spatial accuracy to within $0.5°$. Acceleration of $35°/s$ or more defined the end of a fixation and the beginning of a saccade. A chinrest was used to minimize head movements and ensure a constant viewing position, and head position was recorded remotely.

A set of 90, high-resolution digital photographs of natural scenes was prepared as stimuli, sourced from a commercially available CD-ROM collection ("Art Explosion"). They were presented on a colour computer monitor at a resolution of 1024 × 768 pixels. A fixed viewing distance of 60 cm gave an image that subtended 31 × 25 degrees of visual angle. The images depicted showed exterior and interior scenes featuring houses, landscapes, furniture, and other natural objects. Of these pictures, half were designated "old" and were shown in both encoding and test phases; the other half were labelled "new" and were shown only during the recognition test.

Saliency maps were generated using Itti and Koch's (2000) algorithm, to identify the five most salient regions for each picture. The only further criterion for stimuli was that all five salient regions were noncontiguous; those pictures where the same or overlapping regions were reselected by the model were replaced.

Design. All participants viewed the same stimuli under the same task conditions. Test pictures were inspected under two successive viewing conditions: Encoding and recognition.

Procedure. Following the standard EyeLink calibration procedure, participants were shown written instructions telling them to inspect the pictures in preparation for a memory test. They then viewed a set of six photographs with similar characteristics as the test set, to gain task practice. Participants then viewed the same set, mixed with six new photographs, in a random order. In each case they made a keyboard response to indicate "old" pictures they had seen before or "new", unseen pictures. Following the practice phase, the experiment proper began. In the encoding phase all 45 encoding stimuli were presented in a randomized order. Each picture was preceded by a drift-correct marker and a fixation cross which ensured that fixation at picture onset was in the centre of the screen. Each picture was presented for 3 s and participants were free to scan the picture, after which the picture was offset and the beginning of the next trial was indicated by the appearance of a central drift correct marker.

The recognition test was a two-alternative forced-choice (2AFC) task that began immediately after all 45 encoding stimuli had been presented. During this phase 90 pictures (the 45 encoding pictures which were now "old", plus 45 new images not previously seen) were presented in a random order in exactly the same way as in the encoding phase and participants responded old or new using the keyboard. In order to facilitate an ideal comparison between encoding and test phases, each picture was again shown for 3 s. As we are principally interested in the sequences of fixations here, the speed of response will not be considered further.

Results

Overall, recognition performance was 77% accurate, and the incorrect trials were discarded from further analysis. Trials were also excluded where the fixation at picture onset was not within the central region, which was ensured by fixation of a drift correct marker. The two main questions addressed by this experiment are whether individuals' scan patterns during initial inspection are reliably similar to those for the same pictures when they are at test, and whether the saliency map model predicts scanning patterns in encoding and in recognition.

Are sequences of fixations similar at encoding and at later recognition? Inspection of the sequences of fixations made when viewing a picture on the first (encoding) and second occasion (recognition), indicates that some repetitions are evident. Similar regions were often inspected soon after picture onset in the two viewings and in some cases scan patterns were identical for the first few fixations. The first task is to quantify this similarity between fixation sequences. The technique used here is the string editing or edit-distance method (Brandt & Stark, 1997; Choi, Mosley, & Stark, 1995; Hacisalihzade, Allen, & Stark, 1992; Josephson & Holmes, 2002). This involves turning a sequence of fixations into a string of characters by dividing the stimulus into labelled regions. The similarity between two strings is then computed by calculating the minimum number of editing steps required to turn one string into the other. The algorithm for calculating the minimum editing cost is presented in detail in Brandt and Stark (1997).

To convert fixation sequences into character strings, a 5×5 grid was first overlaid onto the pictures, so that fixation locations can be identified by a single character. The resulting 25 regions were labelled with the characters A to Y, reading from left to right and from top to bottom. Fixations were then labelled, according to their spatial coordinates, resulting in a character string representing all the fixations made in this viewing. So, if a viewer looked first at the grid at the top left of a picture, and then at each of the other four grids at the top, moving from left to right, the string sequence would be labelled ABCDE. The first fixation on the picture, which was always in the centre, was removed before comparing strings, and any adjacent fixations on the same regions were condensed into one gaze. This was done as it is the global movements that are of interest here, rather than the small readjustments which combine to give one gaze on a region. Strings were limited to the first five letters, and similarity scores were computed for each participant viewing each picture. In those trials where fewer than five fixations remained after condensing gazes, the paired string was cropped to the same length.

The average similarity between fixation sequences during encoding and the same picture during the recognition test was 0.2734 ($SD = 0.042$) where a perfect match would have a value of 1. In order to assess whether these similarity values are higher than would expected by chance, comparison with a null condition is necessary. Estimation of the similarity value to be expected by chance is clearly a contentious matter, with Type I and Type II errors at risk. We could estimate chance on the basis of hypothetical fixations made randomly across the image, or on the basis of locations of actual fixations made by each participant looking at other images. We first consider both estimates here. The probability that two randomly placed fixations will be on the same region is 1/25, although this is a slightly liberal estimate for the similarity due to chance given the constraint that no two consecutive fixations will be on the same region. A computer simulation compared 1000 randomly generated pairs of five letter strings and gave an average similarity of 0.0417 between any two of these generated strings. However, viewers do not look at the regions of pictures randomly, with their fixations distributed evenly across all regions, and so this similarity value is likely to be unrepresentative of any actual fixation sequence. Our preferred alternative is to take each picture viewed by each participant and compare the scan pattern string for that picture against a different picture seen by the same participant. Fixation sequence strategies and location preferences are then taken into account, and regions that are generally avoided are less influential because they will be discounted in both strings. We paired each viewer's fixation sequence for each picture with another fixation sequence from a picture selected at random. The two sequences from each viewer therefore reflected any individual tendencies to fixate regions in a personal or habitual fashion. This procedure delivers an average string similarity of 0.122, and this is the value of chance used here. The comparison of scan pattern strings recorded during picture encoding and during picture recognition (0.2734) is reliably higher than would be expected using this value of chance, $t(20) = 4.49$, $p < .001$.

Are sequences of fixations predicted by the saliency model? The model analyses pictures to find the most salient region, then the next most salient region, and so on, and this sequence can be used to predict the sequence of fixations that an observer would make, if the observer's fixation locations were determined by region saliency alone. The similarities between strings of fixations predicted by the saliency model and fixations observed during encoding of each picture can be compared against the fixation sequences predicted by the saliency model. The similarity score between the order of fixations observed during encoding and the order predicted by the model was 0.0693 ($SD = 0.0179$). This similarity score was not different to the score expected by chance (string similarity of 0.122 using chance derived from actual fixations rather than hypothesized random fixations).

Whichever estimate of chance is used the model fails to predict the temporal order of those fixations.

EXPERIMENT 2

The role of domain knowledge in scan patterns during encoding and recognition

In Experiment 1 the scan patterns recorded during a recognition test were more similar to the patterns seen during the first inspection of the picture than would be expected by chance. Comparing performance during a recognition test against performance during encoding may have obscured the analysis, however, because encoding and recognition are different tasks, and viewers would have been inspecting the pictures for very different purposes. During recognition, for example, viewers may have been searching for a specific feature of an image to confirm that they had or had not seen it previously, whereas during encoding the important features of the scene would be inspected, related to each other, and used to form a new representation in preparation for the test. During encoding the distinguishing features of the image may be identified and during recognition the image may be checked for possession of those distinguishing features. The purpose of inspection leads to very different patterns of inspection, as Yarbus (1967) demonstrated with multiple purposes applied to the same image, and as Underwood et al. (2004) demonstrated when viewers were asked either to encode a picture or to search for the answer to a previously presented question. If recognizing a picture involves the search for an object that is familiar, then comparing the scan patterns at encoding and at recognition could not be expected to provide the best estimate of similarity. A better estimate would be provided by a comparison of scan patterns on two successive viewings of a picture where the purpose of inspection is held constant.

The current experiment offers the chance to further investigate the similarity of scan patterns on encoding and second viewing of a naturalistic picture and how this is influenced by saliency. It also offers the opportunity to explore how domain knowledge influences the affect of saliency on scan patterns, and whether a combination of top-down and bottom-up factors determine scan patterns during visual inspection.

Method

Participants. All participants were undergraduates at Nottingham University, and consisted of 15 American Studies and 15 Engineering students. A requirement of the American Studies group was that they had to have taken a core module on "The American Civil War". All participants had normal or corrected-to-normal vision. Inclusion in the study was contingent on reliable eyetracking calibration and three participants had to be replaced due to equipment/calibration failure.

Materials and apparatus. Eye position was recorded using an SMI iVIEW X Hi-Speed eyetracker, which uses an ergonomic chinrest and provides gaze position accuracy to within $0.2°$. The system parses samples into fixations and saccades based on velocity across samples, with a spatial resolution of $0.01°$, a processing latency of less than 0.5 ms and a sampling rate of 240 Hz. A set of 90 high-resolution digital photographs were prepared as stimuli, sourced from the same CD-ROM collection used for Experiment 1. Of this set of 90 pictures, 30 were engineering-specific, 30 were Civil War specific, and 30 were of natural scenes such as gardens, parks, and landscapes (control stimuli). The engineering pictures showed images of machinery, and the Civil War pictures showed collections of uniforms and other military artifacts. Half of each category were designated "old" and shown in both encoding and test phases; the other half were labelled "new" and were shown only as fillers at test. Another 45 pictures were selected for use as the "new" stimuli in the delayed recognition test. Pictures were presented on a colour computer monitor at a resolution of 1600×1200 pixels. The monitor measured 43.5 cm $\times$ 32.5 cm, and a fixed viewing distance of 98 cm gave an image that subtended approximately 25×19 degrees of visual angle.

Saliency maps were generated using Itti and Koch's (2000) model to identify the first four simulated shifts and thus indicate the first five most salient regions for each picture. A further criterion for stimuli was that all five salient regions were noncontiguous. As before, those pictures where the same or overlapping regions were reselected by the model were replaced.

Design. The experiment used a 2×3 mixed design, with two specialist groups of participants and three specific types of stimuli. All participants viewed the same stimuli under the same task conditions. Test pictures were inspected under each of three successive viewing conditions: Encoding, immediate recognition, and delayed recognition.

Procedure. Following a nine-point calibration procedure, participants were shown written instructions asking them to inspect the following pictures in preparation for a memory test.

In a practice phase designed to familiarize participants with the equipment, the displays, and the task, they were shown a set of five photographs that were similar to the ones in the experimental set, but did not fall into any of the three distinct experimental categories. Participants were not told to look for anything in particular in any of the pictures but were asked to look at them in preparation for a memory test. Following the practice phase, the first stage of the experiment began. There were 45 stimuli (15 engineering pictures, 15 Civil War pictures, and 15 natural scenes) presented in a randomized order. Each picture was preceded by a fixation cross, which ensured that fixation at picture onset was in the centre of the screen. Each picture was presented for 3 s, during which time participants moved their eyes freely around the screen. This presentation format and the 2AFC task are the same as was used in Experiment 1.

After all 45 pictures had been presented, participants were informed that they were going to see a second set of pictures and had to decide whether each picture was new (never seen before) or old (from the previous set of pictures) by making a keyboard response.

During this phase, 90 pictures were presented in a random order; 45 of these were old and 45 new. In order to facilitate an ideal comparison between encoding and test phases, each picture was again shown for 3 s. One week after the original recognition test, participants returned to the laboratory and were shown 90 test pictures again, with task again being to say whether they had seen each picture during the original encoding phase. Of the 90 pictures, 45 had been shown during the encoding phase and during the first recognition phase, and 45 were new to the experiment.

Results

The purpose of the recognition test with pictures from different domains of study was to establish a difference between the two groups of participants. Recognition accuracy in deciding whether pictures had been seen previously did indeed depend upon the viewer's knowledge of the picture's content. During the first recognition test Engineers were more accurate at recognizing the engineering pictures, $t(14) = 2.85$, $p < .05$, and American Studies students were more accurate with the American Civil War pictures, $t(14) = 2.54$, $p < .05$. There was no difference between groups in the recognition of the neutral pictures, $t(14) = 1.60$. The superior performance of domain specialists in remembering pictures from their field of interest is shown in Figure 2.

As in Experiment 1, the scan patterns of the first five fixations observed during the encoding phase and during the immediate recognition test were quantified by the string-edit method, to generate similarity scores that had a maximum value of 1. The resultant values are shown in Figure 3A. These scores were compared to a chance value estimated by the same procedure as in Experiment 1: Each viewer's scanpath from each picture was paired with another scanpath from another picture seen by that viewer and the similarity recorded. This gives a mean scanpath similarity of 0.1148 (cf. the value of

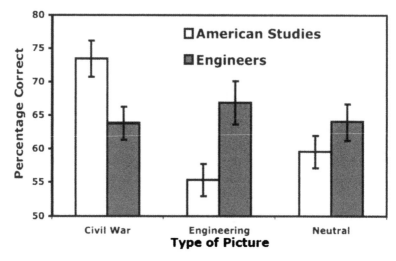

Figure 2.   Recognition accuracy in the test applied immediately after presentation of the pictures for encoding, for the two groups of viewers and the three types of pictures (Experiment 2).

0.122 in Experiment 1). All comparisons showed the string similarities between encoding and test to be reliably greater than chance. Strings of fixation locations were similar for American Studies undergraduates inspecting Civil War pictures, $t(14) = 9.54$, $p < .001$, engineering pictures, $t(14) = 10.89$, $p < .001$, and neutral scenes, $t(14) = 9.89$, $p < .001$. The two scan patterns were also similar for Engineers looking at Civil War pictures, $t(14) = 8.69$, $p < .001$, at engineering pictures, $t(14) = 13.23$, $p < .001$, and at neutral pictures, $t(14) = 8.11$, $p < .001$.

Scan patterns during picture encoding were also compared with those observed during the second recognition test. This test occurred 1 week after the pictures had been seen for the first time. A mixed-model ANOVA found reliable main effects of picture type, $F(2, 28) = 18.36$, $MSE = 0.058$, $p < .001$, and participant group, $F(1, 28) = 7.29$, $MSE = 0.029$, $p < .05$, and there was also an interaction between these two factors, $F(2, 56) = 43.615$, $MSE = 0.139$, $p < .001$. The interaction is illustrated in Figure 3B, where it can be seen that the similarity score between the two scan patterns was greater when participants inspected pictures within their field of interest. Pairwise comparisons confirmed this impression, with both American Studies undergraduates and Engineers showing scan patterns that were reliably more similar between encoding and the delayed test for those pictures that were domain-specific (both contrasts at $p < .05$), and these domain-specific similarity scores were the only scores that were reliably greater than chance (both $p < .05$).

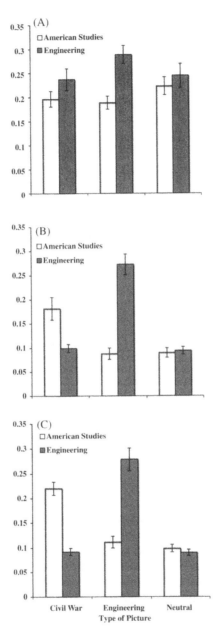

Figure 3. Scan pattern string similarity between encoding and the first (immediate) recognition test (A), between encoding and the second (delayed) recognition test (B), and between the first (immediate) and the second (delayed) recognition tests (C) in Experiment 2.

To match the task processes, this study presented the recognition test twice, and so a further comparison was made between scan patterns during the immediate and delayed picture recognition tests. The similarity scores are shown in Figure 3C. A mixed-model ANOVA found a reliable main effect of type of picture, $F(2, 28) = 31.84$, $MSE = 0.077$, $p < .001$, and no effect of participant group ($F < 1$), but there was an interaction between these two factors, $F(2, 56) = 68.25$, $MSE = 0.164$, $p < .001$. Pairwise comparisons found that for both American Studies undergraduates and Engineers, scan patterns were reliably more similar between the immediate and delayed test when they inspected pictures that were within their domain of interest. That is, American Studies students had higher string similarity scores for their two recognition viewings of Civil War pictures than they did for engineering pictures ($p < .001$) or for neutral scenes ($p < .001$). Engineering students showed the opposite pattern, with greater string similarities for engineering pictures than for Civil War pictures ($p < .001$) or for neutral pictures ($p < .001$). Only these two domain-specific similarity scores were reliably greater than the value estimated for chance (both $p < .001$).

The scan patterns generated from first viewing of a picture were again compared to the scan patterns predicted by the saliency model (Itti & Koch, 2000) on the basis of the five most salient regions being expected to be fixated in order of the magnitude of their estimated saliency. The comparison between model-predicted and observed fixation sequences in Experiment 1 delivered nonsupportive results—the model did not predict scan patterns during picture encoding. The results from Experiment 2 also failed to support the model. The similarity between observed and predicted scan patterns was no better than would be expected by chance when the images were domain-specific. When stimuli were not domain specific, the similarity score was less than the estimated chance level (see Figure 4). There was a reliable between-groups difference in viewing Civil War stimuli, $F(1, 28) = 52.50$, $MSE = 0.099$, $p < .001$, and a reliable between-groups difference in viewing engineering stimuli, $F(1, 28) = 48.75$, $MSE = 0.067$, $p < .001$. There was no difference between groups when viewing neutral stimuli, $F(1, 28) = 1.40$. For the Civil War pictures, pairwise comparisons found that scan patterns from American Studies undergraduates were reliably less similar to sequences predicted by the saliency model than were the Engineers' scan patterns ($p < .001$). Conversely, for the engineering pictures, scan patterns from Engineers were reliably less similar to scan patterns predicted by saliency than those from the American Studies undergraduates ($p < .001$). The natural scenes were similar to engineering pictures for American Studies undergraduates and had higher string similarity than Civil War pictures ($p < .001$), whereas for Engineering undergraduates the neutral pictures had string similarities more like the Civil War pictures and less like the engineering scenes ($p < .001$). Domain

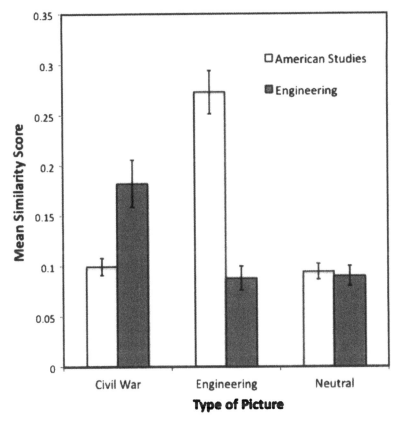

Figure 4. Comparing the string similarity scores in Experiment 2 against the predictions of the saliency model. The similarity between a scan pattern sequences made on during the encoding phase and the sequence predicted by the model was calculated using the edit-distance method.

specialists were less likely to perform according to the predictions of the saliency model when viewing pictures from their domain of interest.

DISCUSSION

In both experiments images of real-world scenes were shown for a few seconds, and then a recognition test performed, with viewers discriminating between old and new pictures. Eye fixations were recorded throughout, and fixation sequences were quantified for comparison between phases of the experiments. In the second experiment there were two notable additions to the procedure: The recognition test was repeated after a week, and the participants had special preexisting domain knowledge of one-third of the pictures shown. The experiments were designed to establish the value of visual saliency in guiding eye fixation sequences. Can saliency values be used to predict sequences of fixations, and can the top-down knowledge of the viewer override any bottom-up effects of saliency?

Sequences of fixations were compared, to determine the similarity of the scan patterns during encoding and recognition, and to evaluate the predictions of the saliency model in the sequence of initial fixations. In the second experiment, we also made comparisons with inspections during a delayed recognition test, when participants returned to the laboratory a week after the initial test.

In both experiments, viewers' scan patterns at encoding were more similar to those made when inspecting the same picture at test than would be expected by chance. Two scan patterns from the same viewer and same picture might be similar on different occasions for a number of reasons, including the role of picture memory and the role of the saliency map. Similarity might be due to the sequence being generated by the same person with a general scanning strategy, rather than being due to a coded sequence for that particular stimulus in response to the individual features and objects depicted in the image. A general scanning strategy might be to start looking at the centre of the picture and make a series of stereotyped saccades to the centre of each quadrant, or to make an invariant sequence of fixations moving from left to right and down the picture. General scanning strategies would show only minimal sensitivity to the content of the picture, in contrast with the content-dependent scanning illustrated by Yarbus (1967). This possibility was checked using the fixation sequences in the recognition phase by each old test picture being arbitrarily paired with a new picture and the fixation strings on each compared. The same person is then performing the same recognition task but with a different picture, and so any sequence similarity provides an estimate of a scanning strategy, and cannot result from an influence of picture memory or of bottom-up visual factors. This established that scan patterns were indeed similar when a viewer looks at two different pictures, confirming the role of stereotypical scanning strategies, but scan patterns were even more similar when the same picture was inspected, confirming the role of picture features in the guidance of fixation locations.

Sequences of fixations over repeated viewings tended to be more similar to each other if the viewer had special knowledge of the content of the image. When Engineers and American Civil War students looked at pictures taken from their own domain of interest, they were more likely to generate consistent scan patterns. This domain-dependent stability was also seen in the similarity between saliency-predicted sequences and those recorded during the first viewing (Figure 4).

The first new result of interest concerns predictions of the saliency map model about sequences of fixations. According to the model, a viewer's eyes and attention should be attracted first by the most salient region in an image, and then to the second most salient region, and so on. This is not only a model of which regions attract fixations, but also the order in which they are fixated. The similarity of fixation sequences between encoding and recognition supports the view that when we look at a picture a second time we are guided to the same regions as when we looked at it originally. The absence of similarity between observed and model-predicted scan patterns suggests that the sequence of fixations is determined by processes that are independent of the saliency values of the inspected regions. This is perhaps unsurprising given that the model does not take into account the distance between saliency peaks. Saccade amplitudes tend to be just a few degrees (e.g., Henderson et al., 1999; Tatler, Baddeley, & Vincent, 2006), but the saliency model selects its peaks regardless of the distance between them. If the first and second highest peaks happen to be 15° apart, the model predicts that these will be the first two regions to be fixated. This would constitute an unusually large saccade. It is more likely that the second peak would be fixated if 3° from the first peak, however, and so a model that is blind to interpeak distance allows only a conservative estimate of a match between observed and predicted scan patterns. A more sophisticated saliency map model will take the distance between peaks into account in making predictions about fixation sequences.

In Experiment 1 the comparison between fixation sequences was between those made during encoding and during recognition, and because these are different tasks engaging different cognitive processes, we introduced an additional phase in Experiment 2, a second recognition task. This resulted in a second new finding, in which a comparison between two recognition tasks, performed a week apart, eliminated the important differences between tasks. When comparing the two recognition tasks, in which the same viewers looked at the same pictures on separate occasions, there was a similarity between the scan patterns of the first few fixations. The stability of the scan patterns over time is of particular interest here.

The final extension to our earlier results qualifies the other conclusions: Fixation sequences depend upon whether a viewer is looking at a picture of specialist interest. In comparing scan patterns during the different phases of the experiment, specialists tended to produce more consistent sequences of fixations when looking at images from their own domain. This result is interesting because it is evidence of individual scan patterns that are picture based rather than being the product of general scanning strategies. If scan patterns were the product of a habitual and stereotypical saccade-generator routine, or indeed of the low-level visual characteristics of an image, then we would expect invariant similarity scores. Instead, when comparing fixation sequences for pictures from different domains of interest, the similarity between scan patterns varied. There was sensitivity to the content of the picture here, with individuals varying their scanning behaviour according to what they were looking at.

It is arguable that these experiments do not provide a fair test of the saliency map model. We have looked for stable scan patterns over extended periods of time and over repeated viewings of images, but the model only claims to predict the initial allocation of attention on first sight of an image, during the first few fixations. Thereafter, the scene semantics are said to determine the guidance of eye movements. We have, perhaps, sought a test of the predictions of the model that is inappropriate. However, we can now conclude that the model cannot be extended to predict the order of a repeated sequence of fixations when viewing an image a second or third time.

The influence of the knowledge and interest of the individual viewer on the locations of fixations, at the exclusion of an influence of visual saliency, requires that another qualification be placed on the generality of the saliency map hypothesis. We have previously concluded that this model makes good predications about fixations in free-viewing and general encoding tasks, and that it performs poorly in search tasks. We now know that the model does not make invariably good predictions about fixations in an encoding task, and that the knowledge of the viewer can override any low-level influences.

REFERENCES

Biederman, I., Rabinowitz, J. C., Glass, A. L., & Stacy, E. W. (1974). On the information extracted from a glance at a scene. *Journal of Experimental Psychology, 103*, 597–600.

Birmingham, E., Bischof, W. F., & Kingstone, A. (2008). Gaze selection in complex social scenes. *Visual Cognition, 16*, 341–355.

Brandt, S. A., & Stark, L. W. (1997). Spontaneous eye movements during visual imagery reflect the content of the visual scene. *Journal of Cognitive Neuroscience, 9*, 27–38.

Buswell, G. T. (1935). *How people look at pictures: A study of the psychology of perception in art.* Chicago: University of Chicago Press.

Choi, Y. S., Mosley, A. D., & Stark, L. (1995). Sting editing analysis of human visual search. *Optometry and Vision Science, 72*, 439–451.

Fisher, D. F., Karsh, R., Breitenbach, F., & Barnette, B. D. (1983). Eye movements and picture recognition: Contribution or embellishment? In R. Groner, C. Menz, D. F. Fisher, & R. A. Monty (Eds.), *Eye movements and psychological functions* (pp. 193–210). Hillsdale, NJ: Lawrence Erlbaum Associates, Inc.

Foulsham, T., & Underwood, G. (2007). How does the purpose of inspection influence the potency of visual saliency in scene perception? *Perception, 36*, 1123–1138.

Foulsham, T., & Underwood, G. (in press). Does conspicuity enhance distraction? Saliency and eye landing position when searching for objects. *Quarterly Journal of Experimental Psychology.*

Groner, R., Walder, F., & Groner, M. (1984). Looking at faces: Local and global aspects of scanpaths. In A. Gale & F. Johnson (Eds.), *Theoretical and applied aspects of eye movement research* (pp. 523–533). Amsterdam: Elsevier.

Hacisalihzade, S. S., Allen, J. S., & Stark, L. (1992). Visual perception and sequences of eye movement fixations: A stochastic modelling approach. *IEEE Transactions on Systems, Man, and Cybernetics, 22,* 474–481.

Henderson, J. M. (2003). Human gaze control during real-world scene perception. *Trends in Cognitive Sciences, 7,* 498–504.

Henderson, J. M., Weeks, P. A., & Hollingworth, A. (1999). The effects of semantic consistency on eye movements during complex scene viewing. *Journal of Experimental Psychology: Human Perception and Performance, 25,* 210–228.

Itti, L., & Koch, C. (2000). A saliency-based search mechanism for overt and covert shifts of visual attention. *Vision Research, 40,* 1489–1506.

Josephson, S., & Holmes, M. E. (2002). Attention to repeated images on the World-Wide Web: Another look at scanpath theory. *Behavior Research Methods, Instruments, and Computers, 34,* 539–548.

Laeng, B., & Teodorescu, D. S. (2002). Eye scanpaths during visual imagery reenact those of perception of the same visual scene. *Cognitive Science, 26,* 207–231.

Langton, S. R. H., Watt, R. J., & Bruce, V. (2000). Do the eyes have it? Cues to the direction of social attention. *Trends in Cognitive Sciences, 4,* 50–59.

Lamy, D., Leber, A., & Egeth, H. E. (2004). Effects of task relevance and stimulus-driven salience in feature-search mode. *Journal of Experimental Psychology: Human Perception and Performance, 30,* 1019–1031.

Mannan, S., Ruddock, K., & Wooding, D. (1996). The relationship between the locations of spatial features and those of fixations made during visual examination of briefly presented images. *Spatial Vision, 10,* 65–188.

Navalpakkam, V., & Itti, L. (2005). Modeling the influence of task on attention. *Vision Research, 45,* 205–231.

Nothdurft, H.-C. (2002). Attention shifts to salient targets. *Vision Research, 42,* 1287–1306.

Noton, D., & Stark, L. (1971a). Eye movements and visual perception. *The Scientific American, 224,* 34–43.

Noton, D., & Stark, L. (1971b). Scanpaths in eye movements during pattern perception. *Science, 171,* 308–311.

Noton, D., & Stark, L. (1971c). Scanpaths in saccadic eye movements while viewing and recognizing patterns. *Vision Research, 11,* 929–942.

Parkhurst, D., Law, K., & Niebur, E. (2002). Modelling the role of salience in the allocation of overt visual attention. *Vision Research, 42,* 107–123.

Potter, M. C. (1976). Short-term conceptual memory for pictures. *Journal of Experimental Psychology: Human Learning and Memory, 2,* 509–522.

Stark, L., & Ellis, S. R. (1981). Scanpaths revisited: Cognitive models direct active looking. In D. F. Fisher, R. A. Monty, & J. W. Senders (Eds.), *Eye movements: Cognition and visual perception* (pp. 193–227). Hillsdale, NJ: Lawrence Erlbaum Associates, Inc.

Stirk, J. A., & Underwood, G. (2007). Low-level visual saliency does not predict change detection in natural scenes. *Journal of Vision, 7*(10), Pt. 3, 1–10.

Tatler, B. W., Baddeley, R. J., & Vincent, B. T. (2006). The long and the short of it: Spatial statistics at fixation vary with saccadic amplitude and task. *Vision Research, 46,* 1857–1862.

Torralba, A., Oliva, A., Castelhano, M. S., & Henderson, J. M. (2006). Contextual guidance of eye movements and attention in real-world scenes: The role of global features in object search. *Psychological Review, 113*(4), 766–786.

Underwood, G., Chapman, P., Brocklehurst, N., Underwood, J., & Crundall, D. (2003). Visual attention while driving: Sequences of eye fixations made by experienced and novice drivers. *Ergonomics, 46,* 629–646.

Underwood, G., & Foulsham, T. (2006). Visual saliency and semantic incongruency influence eye movements when inspecting pictures. *Quarterly Journal of Experimental Psychology, 59,* 1931–1949.

Underwood, G., Foulsham, T., van Loon, E., Humphreys, L., & Bloyce, J. (2006). Eye movements during scene inspection: A test of the saliency map hypothesis. *European Journal of Cognitive Psychology, 18,* 321–342.

Underwood, G., Jebbett, L., & Roberts, K. (2004). Inspecting pictures for information to verify a sentence: Eye movements in general encoding and in focused search. *Quarterly Journal of Experimental Psychology, 57A,* 165–182.

Underwood, G., Templeman, E., Lamming, L., & Foulsham, T. (2008). Is attention necessary for object identification? Evidence from eye movements during the inspection of real-world scenes. *Consciousness and Cognition, 17,* 159–170.

Yarbus, A. L. (1967). *Eye movements and vision.* New York: Plenum.

VISUAL COGNITION, 2009, 17 (6/7), 835–855

Overt attentional prioritization of new objects and feature changes during real-world scene viewing

Michi Matsukura, James R. Brockmole, and John M. Henderson

Department of Psychology, University of Edinburgh, Edinburgh, UK

The authors investigated the extent to which a change to an object's colour is overtly prioritized for fixation relative to the appearance of a new object during real-world scene viewing. Both types of scene change captured gaze (and attention) when introduced during a fixation, although colour changes captured attention less often than new objects. Neither of these scene changes captured attention when they occurred during a saccade, but slower and less reliable memory-based mechanisms were nevertheless able to prioritize new objects and colour changes relative to the other stable objects in the scene. These results indicate that online memory for object identity and at least some object features are functional in detecting changes to real-world scenes. Additionally, visual factors such as the salience of onsets and colour changes did not affect prioritization of these events. We discuss these results in terms of current theories of attention allocation within, and online memory representations of, real-world scenes.

Keywords: Attention; Visual memory; Oculomotor capture; Real-world scenes; Gaze control.

The guidance of the eyes through a scene is an active process of interrogating scene regions relevant to one's goals (e.g., Antes, 1974; Buswell, 1935; Hayhoe, Shrivastava, Mruczek, & Pelz, 2003; Henderson, Brockmole, Castelhano, & Mack, 2007; Henderson & Hollingworth, 1998; Land, Mennie, & Rusted, 1999; Mackworth & Morandi, 1967; Torralba, Oliva, Castelhano, & Henderson, 2006;

Please address all correspondence to James Brockmole, now at Department of Psychology, University of Notre Dame, 118-C Hagger Hall, Notre Dame, IN 46556, USA. E-mail: James. Brockmole@nd.edu

This research was made possible by a grant from the Economic and Social Research Council (RES-000-22-2484) awarded to James Brockmole and John Henderson. We thank Krista Ehinger and Michael Mack for invaluable technical assistance. We also thank Carrick Williams, Geoff Cole, Robert Rauschenberger, Angus Gellatly, and an anonymous reviewer for their comments and suggestions during the course of this project.

M. Matsukura is now at the University of Iowa, IA, USA.

© 2009 Taylor & Francis
DOI: 10.1080/13506280902868660

Yarbus, 1967). However, in order to achieve some balance between the need to selectively focus on task-relevant stimuli and the need to be interrupted by other important events, the goal-directed control of gaze is not absolute and can be disrupted. For example, dynamic changes to visual displays such as the sudden emergence of a new object (Boot, Kramer, & Peterson, 2005b; Brockmole & Henderson, 2005b, 2008; Irwin, Colcombe, Kramer, & Hahn, 2000; Theeuwes, Kramer, Hahn, & Irwin, 1998; Theeuwes, Kramer, Hahn, Irwin, & Zelinsky, 1999), the disappearance of an object (Brockmole & Henderson, 2005a), or changes to an object's colour or luminance (Irwin et al., 2000) can exogenously draw gaze, a circumstance referred to as *oculomotor capture*.[1]

The vast majority of oculomotor capture research has considered the priority given to new objects that appear in simple visual arrays of geometric shapes (Boot et al., 2005a; Irwin et al., 2000; Theeuwes et al., 1998, 1999). To take the seminal paper on the topic as an illustrative example, Theeuwes et al. (1998) presented observers with six grey circles surrounding a central fixation point. Five circles then turned red and letters were revealed in each circle. Observers were to move their eyes to the remaining grey circle and identify the letter presented within it. Critically, along with the revelation of the search target, an additional red item appeared in the display. Although this new item was never the target of search, the eyes moved toward the onset on approximately 50% of trials. Fixations on the onset were atypically brief, suggesting that the saccade to the target was programmed, but before the eye movement could be executed to this target, the onset interrupted the goal-directed eye movement.

More recent experiments have begun to consider analogous effects during real-world scene viewing. In a series of studies, Brockmole and Henderson (2005a, 2005b, 2008) asked observers to study photographs of scenes for a later memory task. During the study period, an object was added to each display. As expected, observers had a strong tendency to fixate these new objects very soon after their appearance at rates much higher than expected by chance. The degree of prioritization, however, depended on whether the new object appeared during a fixation (so that it was accompanied by a motion transient) or during a saccadic eye movement (which, due to saccadic suppression, eliminated the transient signal). New objects that appeared during fixations were fixated twice as often as those that appeared during saccades, indicating that, although low-level transient motion signals enhance the prioritization of new objects for viewing, they are not required

---

[1] Covert measures of *attention capture* whereby involuntary shifts of attention to dynamic singletons are measured through reaction time or response accuracy have a rich history (see Rauschenberger, 2003, and Simons, 2000, for reviews). Because our focus is on the capture of gaze, we will not review the covert capture literature in depth.

for prioritization to occur. This is not merely a quantitative distinction, however; it is also one of kind. Prioritization of new objects during saccades did not occur as quickly as it did during fixations. Additionally, prioritization of new objects during saccades, but not during fixations, was affected by manipulations of memory for the scene. These two results indicate that the effects observed during saccades are qualitatively different from those observed during fixations. Fast, exogenous, and robust oculomotor capture requires a transient motion signal, but, without such a signal, new objects are nevertheless prioritized for viewing as slower and less reliable memory processes are engaged to guide gaze. Brockmole and Henderson (2005b) termed this second mechanism *memory-guided prioritization*. Hence, the overt prioritization of new objects in real-world scenes can be mediated by both exogenous and endogenous mechanisms.

Although the research described above demonstrates how gaze control is affected by the appearance of new objects in a visual display or scene, it is less clear how gaze might be affected by changes to the surface features of *existing* objects that are visible throughout the viewing period. In the present study, we investigated whether and under what conditions sudden changes to an existing object's colour can attract gaze, and if so, whether this attraction can be driven by oculomotor capture and/or memory-guided prioritization. By investigating the extent to which each of these mechanisms is sensitive to changes to surface features of objects in real-world scenes, we aimed to determine the extent to which the overt attention system is tuned to identify and prioritize scene changes that do not involve the appearance of a new object, and the nature of the object feature information retained in online memory representations that is functional in detecting dynamic scene changes.

OCULOMOTOR CAPTURE

The evidence reviewed above indicates that transient motion signals lead to oculomotor capture when they coincide with the appearance of a new object. One goal of this study was to determine whether these transient signals lead to oculomotor capture when they are correlated with feature changes to existing objects. If new objects play a special role in oculomotor capture (cf. Yantis, 1993, 1998, 2000; Yantis & Gibson, 1994; Yantis & Hillstrom, 1994; Yantis & Jonides, 1996), then changes to surface features of existing objects such as their colours may not attract gaze. Only one previous study has used an oculomotor capture paradigm to investigate this question. Irwin et al. (2000) presented observers with four red circles around a central fixation cross. After a short delay, letters were revealed in the centre of each circle while one circle simultaneously turned grey and an additional red circle was onset. In separate conditions, observers were to report the letter contained within either the grey circle or within the onset. When the target was defined by the colour singleton, the presence of the onset captured gaze. When the target was in the onset, the colour singleton also captured gaze, but only if colour singletons were previously used as targets in the experiment. These results suggest that, while onsets capture gaze regardless of an observer's task or prior experience, transient colour changes do not attract gaze automatically, but can be induced to do so if they were previously related to the observer's goals.

Irwin et al.'s (2000) study provided important insight into the prominence of new objects in attracting gaze, but it is limited in an important way: Colour changes always occurred concurrently with onsets. In other words, the authors examined how well transient changes to existing objects capture gaze when a suddenly appearing new object is simultaneously competing for attention. In this situation, it is impossible to ascertain the efficacy with which feature changes can independently attract gaze. Resolving this ambiguity in the context of real-world scene viewing is one goal of the present study.

MEMORY-GUIDED PRIORITIZATION

In addition to investigating the control of oculomotor capture by changes to an object's surface features, we also aimed to advance our understanding of memory-guided prioritization. According to Brockmole and Henderson's (2005a, 2005b, 2008) conceptualization of this mechanism, when scene changes are not marked by a transient motion signal, observers can compare the perceived scene with a stored memory representation derived from prior discrete views (for similar arguments for such a comparison mechanism, see Henderson & Castelhano, 2005; Hollingworth & Henderson, 2002; Hyun, Woodman, Vogel, Hollingworth, & Luck, in press; Zelinsky, 2001). According to this hypothesis, when a perceived object lacks a corresponding representation in memory, this object is prioritized for viewing. An important question to ask of this mechanism, therefore, concerns the specificity with which memory representations of objects and scenes are maintained in working memory and the degree of mismatch that is necessary for prioritization to take place. In the case of an onset, the sudden appearance of a new object generates a substantial mismatch between the perceived scene and the corresponding representation of the scene in memory. Changes to existing objects, however, are more subtle. For example, the degree to which colour changes to an object can be detected depends on how well these surface properties are maintained in the online memory representations constructed over the course of scene viewing as well as their functionality in guiding attention. Therefore, the second goal of this report was to determine the degree to which memory-based control of attention can be used to detect changes to scenes in which the featural properties of existing objects change.

VISUAL SALIENCE IN OCULOMOTOR CAPTURE AND MEMORY-GUIDED PRIORITIZATION

In addition to being visually surprising events (see Itti & Baldi, in press, for a computational modelling approach to visually based surprise), the addition of a new object or a change in an existing object's visual features is likely to alter low-level visual characteristics of a scene. However, previous work on oculomotor capture and memory-guided prioritization (at least as they operate within real-world scenes) has treated all scene changes as visual equals. Hence, although it is known that the semantic nature of sudden scene changes can influence the rates at which they are prioritized for viewing (Brockmole & Henderson, 2008), it is unknown to what degree low-level visual attributes of objects are also important. In an effort to provide insight into this question, a final goal of this report was to investigate the potential importance of *visual salience* in oculomotor capture and memory-guided prioritization.

A major theme throughout much of this Special Issue specifically, and the gaze control literature generally, is the extent to which gaze is correlated with visual salience, or the conspicuity of a scene region within the global visual context (Foulsham & Underwood, 2007; Henderson et al., 2007; Itti & Koch, 2000; Koch & Ullman, 1985; Parkhurst, Law, & Niebur, 2002; Tatler, Baddely, & Gilchrist, 2005; Torralba et al., 2006). As a means of extending this discussion to oculomotor capture, we asked whether the visual salience of the new or altered object modulates the extent to which that object is prioritized for viewing. We accomplished this goal by examining whether critical objects that either scored very low or very high in salience were differentially prioritized (details of salience calculation in methods section). If the visual prominence of an object makes it more likely to be prioritized, regardless of its identity, then gaze should be allocated to highly salient objects more than to nonsalient objects when they appear (or change) in a scene.

THE CURRENT STUDY

Observers viewed photographs of real-world scenes for 10 s each (Figure 1). As a cover task, observers were instructed to memorize each scene for a later memory test (in actuality, no such test was given). During viewing, a change to each scene was effected during a fixation (to explore oculomotor capture) or a saccade (to examine memory-guided prioritization) after 5 s had elapsed

Before Change   After Change

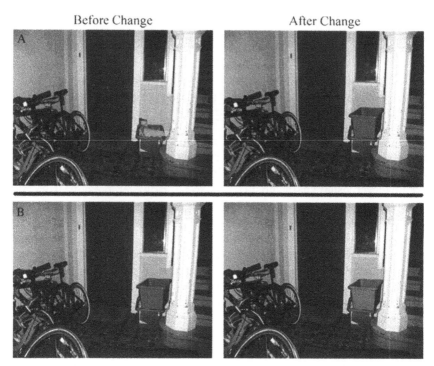

Figure 1. An example scene used in this study for both before (left panels) and after (right panels) the scene change: (A) Onset, (B) Colour change. To view this figure in colour, please see the online issue of the Journal.

since the beginning of a trial. Within each scene, a critical object was selected (e.g., the recycle bin in Figure 1). For one group of observers, the critical object was added to the scene either during a fixation or during a saccade (Figure 1A), replicating Brockmole and Henderson (2005b). The data from this group provided a baseline against which the behavioural consequences of colour changes on gaze could be contrasted. For a second group of observers, the same critical objects were present in the scene from the beginning of the trial, but changed colour mid-way through scene viewing (Figure 1B).[2] If transient changes to a scene are prioritized either via attention capture or memory-guided prioritization, then the critical objects should be viewed more often than expected by chance immediately after the change takes place. By comparing the strength of the prioritization effect

---

[2] This method resulted in postchange scenes that were not identical in the new object and colour change conditions. However, it allowed a direct comparison between the situations where a particular object appeared in a scene and when that same particular object changed its features.

separately for both new objects and feature changes, we can determine which types of scene change are the strongest attractors of gaze as well as the conditions under which these influences are evident. By comparing the strength of the prioritization effect separately for high and low salience objects, we can determine the extent to which prioritization of scene changes is dependent on their visual conspicuity.

METHOD

Participants

Thirty-six University of Edinburgh undergraduates with normal or corrected-to-normal vision were paid £4.00 for their participation in a single 30-minute experimental session (mean age = 21.9, range 18–26). Participants were randomly divided into three equal groups (details below).

Stimuli

Stimuli consisted of full-colour photographs of 30 real-world scenes. Initially, two photographs of each scene were taken, differing only in the presence or absence of a single *critical object* (Figure 1A). Photographs were digitally edited to eliminate minor differences in shadow and spatial displacement between each shot. Local luminance was closely approximated in each scene version (on average luminance for the critical objects was slightly, but not reliably, smaller than the backgrounds in the object-absent versions). We additionally created alternate versions of these photographs in which the colour of the critical object in each scene was altered (see Figure 1B). These colour changes were produced through a series of a pixel-wise manipulations in CIE L*a*b* colour space, which represents any colour independently of luminance. Thus, we were able to change the colour of the critical object without affecting its physical luminance level.

A saliency map was generated for each scene using the salience model popularized by Itti and Koch (2000). Based on this approach, a saliency map was generated for each scene using the Saliency Toolbox for Matlab (Walther & Koch, 2006; see also www.saliencytoolbox.net) using default parameter values. For each scene, a region of interest was defined by the smallest imaginary rectangle that could surround the critical object. For each of these regions, the average saliency value within the corresponding portion of the saliency map was calculated. Fourteen critical objects were classified as "salient items" with an average salience score of .51. Sixteen critical objects were classified as "nonsalient items" with an average salience score of .05 (see Figure 2).

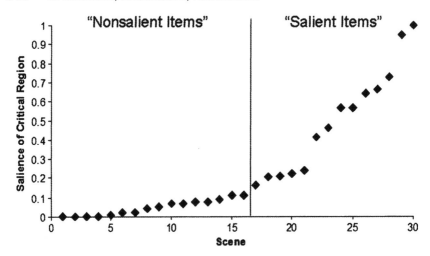

Figure 2. Mean salience value of pixels within the critical region within each of the 30 scenes. Sixteen scenes were considered to have nonsalient critical regions; fourteen scenes were considered to have salient critical regions.

Photographs were displayed at a resolution of 800 × 600 pixels in 24-bit colour and subtended 37° horizontally and 27.5° vertically at a viewing distance of 81 cm. Eight pictures of the scenes used in this experiment were also used by Brockmole and Henderson (2005a, 2005b) and 22 pictures of the scenes were created for this study. The new scenes replaced scenes from Brockmole and Henderson's original set in which the critical objects were black or white as these colours could not be altered without influencing their luminance. Stimuli were also replaced in which a colour change produced semantic inconsistency in a scene (e.g., a package of sausages in a freezer suddenly changing from a natural brown to an unnatural blue). In such cases, it would be difficult to separate prioritization patterns caused by colour change per se and the semantic inconsistency it would generate (see Brockmole & Henderson, 2008, for discussion of how semantic inconsistency affects attention capture and memory-guided prioritization).

Apparatus

Stimuli were presented on a 21-inch CRT monitor with a screen refresh rate of 120 Hz. Throughout each trial, the spatial position of each observer's right eye was sampled at a rate of 1000 Hz by a tower-mounted EyeLink 2K eyetracking system (SR Research, Inc.) running in pupil and corneal-reflection mode, resulting in an average spatial accuracy of 0.15°. An eye movement was classified as a saccade if its amplitude exceeded 0.2° and either (a) its velocity exceeded 30°/s or (b) its acceleration exceeded 9500°/s.

Chin and forehead rests stabilized head position and kept viewing distance constant.

Design and procedure

Observers were randomly assigned to one of three conditions: The *onset condition*, the *colour condition*, and the *control condition*. The task in all conditions was the same; observers were instructed to memorize each scene in preparation for a subsequent memory test (in actuality, the test was never given). In the onset condition, a single critical object was added to the scene, whereas in the colour condition the colour of the critical object (present from the start of the trial) was altered. These scene changes occurred after 5 s had elapsed from the beginning of a trial (details later). In the control condition, these same critical objects were visible throughout the trial. This control condition allowed us to determine the baseline rate at which the critical objects were fixated when they were not suddenly added or changed during viewing. No explicit instructions regarding scene changes were given to observers in any condition.

All observers began the experimental session by completing a calibration routine that mapped the output of the eyetracker onto the display position. Calibration was constantly monitored throughout the experiment and was adjusted when necessary (a drift correction was applied at the start of each trial). Observers began each trial by fixating a dot in the centre of the display. When they were ready to view the stimulus, a photograph was displayed for 10 s. For observers in the onset and colour conditions, new objects were added or altered while an observer was studying a scene by seamlessly switching the photograph presented on the display with its associated counterpart that contained either the additional object or the altered colour (depending on the observer's condition assignment). Furthermore, critical objects were added or altered during either a saccade or a fixation. These scene changes were yoked to the first saccadic eye movement that occurred after 5 s had elapsed from the beginning of the trial. When scene changes were to occur during a saccade, their occurrence coincided with the detection of this saccade (*saccade trials*). By contrast, when scene changes were to occur during a fixation, they were executed 100 ms after the start of the first saccade launched after 5 s of viewing time. This 100-ms delay was long enough to allow the critical saccade to terminate but short enough that a subsequent saccade could not be launched before the scene change (see Brockmole & Henderson, 2005a, 2005b, 2008, for successful use of this method). Thus, the eyes were stable when scene changes occurred (*fixation trials*). The successful trial-by-trial application of these principles was examined post hoc (see below).

RESULTS AND DISCUSSION

Linking onsets and colour changes to saccadic eye movements required a liberal threshold for saccade detection. As well as enabling us to execute these scene changes during saccades on the majority of saccade trials, this procedure also led to false alarms by the saccade detection algorithm. New objects were successfully onset during a fixation on 96% of fixation trials and during a saccade on 67% of saccade trials. Colour changes were successfully executed during a fixation on 92% of fixation trials and during a saccade on 69% of saccade trials. All remaining trials were excluded from the reported analyses. Two types of analysis were conducted (see Brockmole & Henderson, 2005a, 2005b). First, we determined the probability that the critical object was fixated after its appearance or colour change relative to the probability that it was fixated when it did not suddenly appear nor change colour. Evidence for prioritization requires that the critical objects be fixated more than expected by chance. Second, we examined the speed with which the critical object was fixated following its appearance or alteration in the scene. Prioritization based on oculomotor capture should be evident sooner than that based on memory-guided prioritization.

New objects

Probability of fixating the new object.   For each scene, a region of interest was defined by the smallest imaginary rectangle that could surround the critical object. Fixations were sorted based on whether they fell within or outside these regions of interest. We restricted our analysis to the first four fixations following the appearance of the new object (denoted as *ordinal fixation positions* 1, 2, 3, and 4, respectively). Fixation 1 denotes the termination of the first saccade launched after the critical change occurred to the scene. Therefore, it is the first fixation that could be influenced by the change. If the new object captures observers' gaze, then observers' eyes should be quickly directed to the location of the scene change with greater-than-chance probability. This chance level was obtained from the control condition where, on average, 7% of fixations were localized on the critical object. We refer to this probability as *the baseline rate of viewing.* After a new object appears, the probability of fixating the critical object should exceed this baseline rate if it draws attention.

Initial analyses considered the probability that the critical object was fixated as a function of trial type (fixation vs. saccade), ordinal fixation position (Fixations 1–4), and salience (salient items vs. nonsalient items). In the corresponding repeated-measures analysis of variance (ANOVA), the main effect of salience was not reliable ($p = .45$), nor did it interact with any other factor (all $ps > .13$). Our remaining analyses, therefore, collapsed across this factor and are illustrated in Figure 3 (refer to Table 1 for breakdown of performance as a function of salience).

Ninety-five per cent confidence intervals indicated that, for both fixation and saccade trials, the new object was fixated more frequently than the baseline rate of viewing at all four ordinal fixation positions. Fixation and saccade trials were contrasted with a 2 (trial type) × 4 (ordinal fixation position) repeated-measures ANOVA. On average, the new object was fixated more often when it appeared during a fixation (61% of fixations) than when it appeared during a saccade (27% of fixations), which led to a reliable main effect of trial type, $F(1, 11) = 40.9$, $p < .0001$. The new object

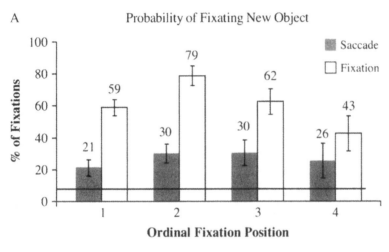

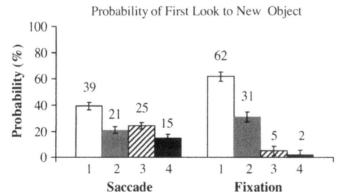

Figure 3.   Results: New objects. (A) The mean probability of fixating the new object as a function of trial type (saccade vs. fixation) and ordinal fixation position (Fixations 1–4). The solid line illustrates the baseline rate of viewing (chance). (B) The probability with which the first look to the new object occurred at each of the first four fixations after its appearance. Error bars represent 95% within-subjects confidence intervals (Loftus & Masson, 1994).

TABLE 1
Mean percentage of fixations (with standard deviation) falling on new objects and
colour changes broken down by ordinal fixation number, trial type, and visual salience

| Trial type | Ordinal fixation number | | | |
	1	*2*	*3*	*4*
New objects				
Fixation condition				
Nonsalient items	58 (5.2)	80 (3.7)	66 (5.3)	41 (6.5)
Salient items	55 (5.2)	77 (5.1)	58 (7.4)	40 (9.8)
Saccade condition				
Nonsalient items	18 (6.2)	23 (6.0)	25 (5.6)	22 (6.2)
Salient items	22 (5.8)	36 (6.9)	33 (6.2)	28 (6.6)
Colour changes				
Fixation condition				
Nonsalient items	27 (6.1)	45 (4.6)	48 (5.8)	40 (6.0)
Salient items	40 (5.2)	50 (6.1)	44 (6.4)	45 (7.6)
Saccade condition				
Nonsalient items	22 (6.0)	29 (7.4)	31 (9.3)	26 (7.2)
Salient items	15 (6.8)	40 (10)	45 (10)	37 (9.0)

was not fixated equally at all ordinal fixation positions, however, which also led to a reliable main effect of ordinal fixation position, $F(3, 33) = 7.2$, $p < .001$. For both fixation and saccade trials, the new item was fixated more often during Fixation 2 than any other fixation position. However, on fixation trials, the probability of fixating the new objects dropped dramatically from Fixation 2 to Fixation 4, whereas on saccade trials, the probability of fixating the new item remained relatively stable throughout. These distinctly different frequency patterns produced a reliable interaction of trial type and ordinal fixation position, $F(3, 33) = 5.9$, $p < .002$. These patterns qualitatively replicate those reported by Brockmole and Henderson (2005a, 2005b). Observers fixated newly appearing objects more often than expected by chance, regardless of whether they appeared during a saccade or a fixation. However, the transient signal that accompanies the onset of a new object in fixation trials drew observers' eyes more often than the appearance of a new object without such a signal (saccade trials).[3]

Number of eye movements to first fixation on new objects.   Despite reliable effects of ordinal fixation position in the analysis above, it is difficult to assess the temporal trend in prioritization from fixation frequency data

---

[3] A similar conclusion follows from analysis of trial-level effects. The new object was fixated within the first four fixations after its appearance in the scene on 85% of trials in the fixation condition and on 40% of trials in the saccade condition, $p < .001$.

because both initial fixations and refixations are combined. The number of fixations intervening between the onset of the new object and an observer's first fixation on that object, however, does reveal how quickly the object is prioritized. On average, when occurring during a fixation, the new object was first fixated 1.5 fixations after the onset. In contrast, when occurring during a saccade, the new object was fixated 4.0 fixations after onset, $t(11) = 4.7$, $p < .0007$. On fixation trials, 98% of all first looks to the new object occurred in the first four fixations after its appearance. On saccade trials, this rate fell to 68%, $t(11) = 10.2$, $p < .0001$. These disproportionate rates of viewing indicate that new objects with transient onsets draw attention more readily than those without a transient signal.

To obtain a more fine-grain picture of prioritization speed, we analysed the probability with which the first fixation on the critical object occurred at each of the ordinal fixation positions, given that it was fixated within this temporal range. Figure 3B illustrates these probabilities as a function of trial type. The probability of the first look to the new object occurring at each of the four ordinal fixation positions differed, $F(3, 33) = 32.8$, $p < .0001$, and these differences were not equal for saccade and fixation trials, $F(3, 33) = 34.5$, $p < .0001$.[4] On fixation trials, 62% of first looks to the new object occurred at Fixation 1. This was followed by a rapid decline at each of the next ordinal fixation positions. Only 7% of these first looks occurred at Fixations 3 and 4 combined. In contrast, on saccade trials, 39% of the first looks occurred at Fixation 1. The moderate decrease followed with 21% of first looks occurring at Fixation 2, and an additional 40% at Fixations 3 and 4 combined. Compared with onsets on fixation trials, prioritization of new objects appearing during saccades was temporarily protracted. These results also qualitatively replicate those reported by Brockmole and Henderson (2005b). In conjunction with the fixation frequency analysis depicted in Figure 3A, we conclude that, like Brockmole and Henderson (2005a, 2005b, 2008), a transient signal increases both the probability that the new object is prioritized and the speed with which the prioritization takes place.

Colour changes

Probability of fixating colour changes. As with new objects, initial analyses considered the probability that the critical object was fixated as a function of trial type (fixation vs. saccade), ordinal fixation position (Fixations 1–4), and salience (salient items vs. nonsalient items). In the

---

[4] To avoid issues of multicollinearity introduced by expressing the number of first looks to the onset at each of ordinal fixation position as a conditional probability, we performed the ANOVA on the raw number of times the first look occurred at each fixation position (see Brockmole & Henderson, 2005b).

corresponding repeated-measures ANOVA, the main effect of salience was not reliable ($p = .15$), nor did it interact with any other factor (all $ps > .15$). Therefore, our remaining analyses collapsed across this factor and are illustrated in Figure 4 (refer to Table 1 for breakdown of performance as a function of salience).

Ninety-five percent confident intervals indicated that, for both fixation and saccade trials, colour changes were fixated more frequently than the baseline rate of viewing at all four ordinal fixation positions. A 2 (trial

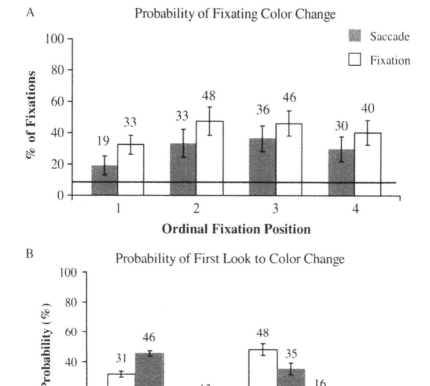

Figure 4.   Results: Colour changes. (A) The mean probability of fixating the colour change as a function of trial type (saccade vs. fixation) and ordinal fixation position (Fixations 1–4). The solid line illustrates the baseline rate of viewing (chance). (B) The probability with which the first look to the critical object occurred at each of the first four fixation position after its colour changed. Error bars represent 95% within-subjects confidence intervals (Loftus & Masson, 1994).

type) × 4 (ordinal fixation position) repeated-measures ANOVA revealed a marginal difference in the probability of fixating the critical regions between fixation (42%) and saccade (30%) trials, $F(1, 11) = 4.5$, $p = .057$.[5] Like a sudden appearance of an object in Experiment 1, colour changes to existing objects were not fixated equally at all ordinal fixation positions, $F(3, 33) = 5.7$, $p < .001$, with the probability of fixating the critical object greatest at Fixation 2. However, prioritization patterns across the four ordinal fixation positions were very similar for fixation and saccade trials and the interaction of trial type (fixation vs. saccade) and ordinal fixation position was not reliable, $F(3, 33) < 1$.

Number of eye movements to first fixation on colour changes.   On average, there was no reliable difference in the speed with which the critical object was first fixated when colour changes occurred during a fixation (4.0 fixations after colour change) and when they occurred during a saccade (4.7 fixations after colour change), $t(11) = 1.06$, $p = .31$. On fixation trials, 72% of all first looks to the target object occurred in the first four fixations after the colour changed, whereas on saccade trials, 67% of all first looks to the critical object occurred in the first four fixations, $t(11) = 3.2$, $p < .008$.

Figure 4B illustrates the probability that the critical object was first fixated at each of the four ordinal fixation positions given that it was viewed within this range of fixations. The probability that the first look to the critical object occurred at each of the first four ordinal fixation positions differed, $F(3, 33) = 15.7$, $p < .0001$, and these differences were not equal for saccade and fixation trials, $t(11) = 4.5$, $p < .001$. Specifically, on fixation trials, 48% of first looks to the critical object occurred at Fixation 1, which was followed by progressive decline with only 23% of first looks occurring at Fixations 3 and 4 combined. However, on saccade trials, the probability of first look peaked at Fixation 2 rather than Fixation 1, then declining to 17% at Fixations 3 and 4 combined. Although the differences in prioritization speed between fixation and saccade trials was less striking than that observed for new objects, these results nevertheless indicate that, relative to fixation trials, prioritization of the critical object was somewhat slower on saccade trails.

---

[5] The choice of using four ordinal fixation positions was arbitrary and was used here to parallel results presented in our prior studies (Brockmole & Henderson, 2005a, 2005b). An ANOVA considering only the first three ordinal fixation positions revealed a reliable effect of trial type, $F(1, 11) = 4.73$, $p = .05$, demonstrating a prioritization effect specific to the transient signal. The analysis of trial-level effects also supports this conclusion; observers looked to the colour change on 54% of trials in the fixation condition and on 34% of trials in the saccade condition ($p < .01$).

New objects versus colour changes

The preceding results indicate that sudden changes to an existing object's colour are prioritized. These results also suggest that memory for scenes includes not only what objects are present, but also some aspects of their surface features (i.e., colour). To more fully characterize the effects of colour change on attentional prioritization, we contrasted fixation and saccade trials across new object and colour change conditions with separate 2 (change type) × 4 (ordinal fixation position) mixed-model ANOVAs for each trial type. For fixation trials, main effects of change type, $F(1, 22) = 18.1$, $p < .001$, and ordinal fixation position, $F(3, 66) = 10.8$, $p < .001$, were observed. These factors also interacted, $F(3, 66) = 4.9$, $p < .01$. Within fixation trials, although colour changes were prioritized, new objects that suddenly appeared during scene viewing were fixated more often than colour changes. These results suggest that onsets capture attention more effectively than colour changes in real world scenes (see Boot, Brockmole, & Simons, 2005a; Gibson & Jiang, 1998; Irwin et al., 2000; Jonides & Yantis, 1988, for similar demonstrations with nonscene stimuli). For saccade trials, only a main effect of ordinal fixation position was observed, $F(3, 66) = 4.3$, $p < .01$ (all other $Fs < 1$). Thus, when a transient signal was not present, new objects and colour changes were prioritized with equal efficiency.

The speed of prioritization was also contrasted across the new object and colour change conditions). On fixation trials, qualitative patterns of first fixation probabilities were similar across change types, but quantitative differences were observed as a reliable interaction between change type (i.e., experiment) and ordinal fixation position, $F(3, 66) = 9.28$, $p < .01$. Although first looks to scene changes were most likely at Fixation 1 in both cases, colour changes were more likely to be fixated first later in the trial than onsets. For saccade trials, the interaction between change type and ordinal fixation position was not reliable, $F(3, 66) = 1.02$, $p = .39$. Thus, without a transient signal, new objects and colour changes were prioritized with equal speed.

DISCUSSION

The present study investigated the extent to which changes to an object's colour are prioritized for viewing relative to the appearance of a new object. New objects appeared, and object feature changes occurred, either during a fixation so that they were accompanied by transient motion signals or during a saccade so that these transient signals were eliminated. Replicating previous findings (Brockmole & Henderson, 2005a, 2005b, 2008), new objects were powerful attracters of gaze by two separable mechanisms. When new objects appeared during a fixation, over half of the next four fixations were directed to these new objects. Furthermore, over 60% of all first looks to the new object occurred with the fixation immediately following the onset. These results indicate that transient onsets capture attention quickly and reliably. Gaze was also directed to new objects that appeared without a transient signal (i.e., during a saccade) at rates far greater than chance. However, prioritization of these objects occurred less often and more slowly than objects accompanied by a transient motion signal.

The consequence of a colour change to an existing object on gaze was qualitatively very similar to that caused by new objects. Colour changes were prioritized for viewing regardless of their transient status, but those that occurred during a fixation received more frequent and faster prioritization than those that occurred during a saccade. However, important quantitative differences were apparent between the efficacy with which a colour change draws gaze and that observed when a new object appears in a scene. With respect to oculomotor capture, transient onsets captured gaze more often than transient colour changes. This is a result that refines and extends the conclusions reached by Irwin et al. (2000) regarding the capture of attention by colour singletons. First, as in simple displays, colour changes to an existing object can capture attention in real-world scenes. Second, capture by a colour change does not require the critical object to be a singleton in an otherwise homogenous display. Third, colour changes capture attention less often than new objects even when these two types of change occur independently from one another.

With respect to memory-guided prioritization, no differences were observed between the prioritization given to colour changes and to new objects. This result has two major implications for conceptualization of online scene memory. First, object surface feature information (i.e., colour) in a display is incidentally stored in the online representations that are generated during scene viewing, extending previous demonstrations that object identity, position, and orientation are maintained in memory (e.g., Aivar, Hayhoe, Chizk, & Mruczek, 2005; Henderson & Hollingworth, 1999, 2003; Hollingworth, 2004, 2006, 2007; Hollingworth & Henderson, 2000, 2002; Smilek, Eastwood, & Merikle, 2000; Tatler, Gilchrist, & Land, 2005; Tatler, Gilchrist, & Rusted, 2003). However, this conclusion contrasts somewhat with recent arguments that colour information is not useful in the guidance of visual search for known targets through real-world scenes (Ehinger & Brockmole, 2008), although a variety of task differences existed between these studies. Therefore, determining the conditions under which colour is used to guide attention constitutes an important avenue for continued research. Second, when current views are compared to those stored in memory, a change to the colour of an object is as conspicuous as a change produced by the onset of an entirely new object. The behavioural equivalence of these conditions suggests that a sudden change to an object's colour may require an observer to create a new object file in visual working memory (Treisman & Gelade, 1980), but further research on this possibility is required (see Mitroff & Alvarez, 2007, for evidence that surface features such as colour may not determine object files).

While the prioritization of new objects can be affected by their semantic identity (Brockmole & Henderson, 2008), the results of the present study suggest that both oculomotor capture and memory-guided prioritization operate independently of at least some visual factors. Newly appearing nonsalient objects were prioritized for viewing—regardless of the mechanisms involved—just as efficaciously as highly salient objects. Similar results were obtained for colour changes. This result reinforces the prominence of a transient motion signal in the generation of oculomotor capture and suggests that the features of salient objects are no more likely to be retained in memory than those of nonsalient objects.

In summary, we can draw five general conclusions regarding the prioritization of new objects and changes in the surface features of existing objects. First, both new objects and colour changes can capture overt attention during real-world scene viewing. This finding not only supports the ecological validity of prior oculomotor capture studies but also provides clear evidence that these effects can be observed even when scene changes do not constitute singletons in an otherwise homogeneous display. Second, a strong "new object" theory of attention capture seems to be false, at least in the context of oculomotor capture during real-world scene viewing. Colour changes did not result in physically new objects in the displays, but they nevertheless captured overt attention. Third, the robustness of oculomotor capture is not equal for all types of scene change. In this case colour changes did not capture attention as efficiently as new objects. This pattern suggests that while physically new objects are not required for oculomotor capture, they nevertheless are given higher priority than feature changes. Fourth, memory-guided prioritization is not limited to the onset (or offset) of an object. When transient signals were absent, colour changes were prioritized just as well as new objects, suggesting some level of psychological equivalence between these two types of scene change. Finally, although prioritization can be influenced by semantic factors (Brockmole & Henderson, 2008), both oculomotor capture and memory-guided prioritization of new objects and colour changes are independent of visual salience.

REFERENCES

Aivar, M. P., Hayhoe, M. M., Chizk, C. L., & Mruczek, R. E. B. (2005). Spatial memory and saccadic targeting in a natural task. *Journal of Vision, 5,* 177–193.

Antes, J. R. (1974). The time course of picture viewing. *Journal of Experimental Psychology, 103,* 62–70.

Boot, W. R., Brockmole, J. R., & Simons, D. J. (2005a). Attention capture is modulated in dual-task situations. *Psychonomic Bulletin and Review, 12,* 662–668.

Boot, W. R., Kramer, A. F., & Peterson, M. S. (2005b). Oculomotor consequences of abrupt object onsets and offsets: Onsets dominate oculomotor capture. *Perception and Psychophysics, 67,* 910–928.

Brockmole, J. R., & Henderson, J. M. (2005a). Object appearance, disappearance, and attention prioritization in real-world scenes. *Psychonomic Bulletin and Review, 12,* 1061–1067.

Brockmole, J. R., & Henderson, J. M. (2005b). Prioritization of new objects in real-world scenes: Evidence from eye movements. *Journal of Experimental Psychology: Human Perception and Performance, 31,* 857–868.

Brockmole, J. R., & Henderson, J. M. (2008). Prioritizing new objects for eye fixation in real-world scenes: Effects of object–scene consistency. *Visual Cognition, 16,* 375–390.

Buswell, G. T. (1935). *How people look at pictures.* Chicago: University of Chicago Press.

Ehinger, K. A., & Brockmole, J. R. (2008). The role of color in visual search in real-world scenes: Evidence from contextual cueing. *Perception and Psychophysics, 70,* 1366–1378.

Foulsham, T., & Underwood, G. (2007). Can the purpose of inspection influence the potency of visual saliency in scene perception? *Perception, 36,* 1123–1138.

Gibson, B. S., & Jiang, Y. (1998). Surprise! An unexpected color singleton does not capture attention in visual search. *Psychological Science, 9,* 176–182.

Hayhoe, M. M., Shrivastava, A., Mruczek, R., & Pelz, J. B. (2003). Visual memory and motor planning in a natural task. *Journal of Vision, 3,* 49–63.

Henderson, J. M., Brockmole, J. R., Castelhano, M. S., & Mack, M. (2007). Visual saliency does not account for eye movements during search in real-world scenes. In R. van Gompel, M. Fischer, W. Murray, & R. Hill (Eds.), *Eye movements: A window on mind and brain* (pp. 537–562). Oxford, UK: Elsevier.

Henderson, J. M., & Castelhano, M. S. (2005). Eye movements and visual memory for scenes. In G. Underwood (Ed.), *Cognitive processes in eye guidance* (pp. 213–235). New York: Oxford University Press.

Henderson, J. M., & Hollingworth, A. (1998). Eye movements during scene viewing: An overview. In G. Underwood (Ed.), *Eye guidance while reading and while watching dynamic scenes* (pp. 269–293). Oxford, UK: Elsevier.

Henderson, J. M., & Hollingworth, A. (1999). The role of fixation position in detecting scene changes across saccades. *Psychological Science, 5,* 438–443.

Henderson, J. M., & Hollingworth, A. (2003). Eye movements and visual memory: Detecting changes to saccade targets in scenes. *Perception and Psychophysics, 65,* 58–71.

Hollingworth, A. (2004). Constructing visual representations of natural scenes: The roles of short- and long-term visual memory. *Journal of Experimental Psychology: Human Perception and Performance, 30,* 519–537.

Hollingworth, A. (2006). Visual memory for natural scenes: Evidence from change detection and visual search. *Visual Cognition, 14,* 781–807.

Hollingworth, A. (2007). Object-position binding in visual memory for natural scenes and object arrays. *Journal of Experimental Psychology: Human Perception and Performance, 33,* 31–47.

Hollingworth, A., & Henderson, J. M. (2000). Semantic informativeness mediates the detection of changes in natural scenes. *Visual Cognition, 7,* 213–235.

Hollingworth, A., & Henderson, J. M. (2002). Accurate visual memory for previously attended objects in natural scenes. *Journal of Experimental Psychology: Human Perception and Performance, 28,* 113–136.

Hyun, J.-S., Woodman, G. F., Vogel, E. K., Hollingworth, A., & Luck, S. J. (in press). The comparison of visual working memory representations with perceptual inputs. *Journal of Experimental Psychology: Human Perception and Performance.*

Irwin, D. E., Colcombe, A. M., Kramer, A. F., & Hahn, S. (2000). Attentional and oculomotor capture by onset, luminance and color singletons. *Vision Research, 40*, 1443–1458.

Itti, L., & Baldi, P. F. (in press). Bayesian surprise attracts human attention. *Vision Research.*

Itti, L., & Koch, C. (2000). A saliency-based search mechanism for overt and covert shifts of visual attention. *Vision Research, 40*, 1489–1506.

Jonides, J., & Yantis, S. (1988). Uniqueness of abrupt visual onset in capturing attention. *Perception and Psychophysics, 43*, 346–354.

Koch, C., & Ullman, S. (1985). Shifts in selective visual attention: Towards the underlying neural capacity. *Human Neurobiology, 4*, 219–227.

Land, M., Mennie, N., & Rusted, J. (1999). The roles of vision and eye movements in the control of activities of daily living. *Perception, 28*, 1311–1328.

Loftus, G. R., & Masson, M. E. J. (1994). Using confidence intervals in within-subject designs. *Psychonomic Bulletin and Review, 1*, 476–490.

Mackworth, N. H., & Morandi, A. J. (1967). The gaze selects informative details within pictures. *Perception and Psychophysics, 2*, 547–552.

Mitroff, S. R., & Alvarez, G. A. (2007). Space and time, not surface features, guide object persistence. *Psychonomic Bulletin and Review, 14*, 1199–1204.

Parkhurst, D., Law, K., & Niebur, E. (2002). Modeling the role of salience in the allocation of overt visual selective attention. *Vision Research, 42*, 107–123.

Rauschenberger, R. (2003). Attentional capture by auto- and allo-cues. *Psychonomic Bulletin and Review, 10*, 814–842.

Simons, D. J. (2000). Attentional capture and inattentional blindness. *Trends in Cognitive Sciences, 4*, 147–155.

Smilek, D., Eastwood, J. D., & Merikle, P. M. (2000). Does unattended information facilitate change detection? *Journal of Experimental Psychology: Human Perception and Performance, 26*, 480–487.

Tatler, B. W., Baddeley, R. J., & Gilchrist, I. D. (2005). Visual correlates of eye movements: Effects of scale and time. *Vision Research, 45*, 643–659.

Tatler, B. W., Gilchrist, I. D., & Land, M. F. (2005). Visual memory for objects in natural scenes: From fixations to object files. *Quarterly Journal of Experimental Psychology: Human Experimental Psychology, 58A*, 931–960.

Tatler, B. W., Gilchrist, I. D., & Rusted, J. (2003). The time course of abstract visual representation. *Perception, 32*, 579–592.

Theeuwes, J., Kramer, A. F., Hahn, S., & Irwin, D. E. (1998). Our eyes do not always go where we want them to go: Capture of the eyes by new objects. *Psychological Science, 9*, 379–385.

Theeuwes, J., Kramer, A. F., Hahn, S., Irwin, D. E., & Zelinsky, G. J. (1999). Influence of attentional capture on oculomotor control. *Journal of Experimental Psychology: Human Perception and Performance, 25*, 1595–1608.

Torralba, A., Oliva, A., Castelhano, M., & Henderson, J. M. (2006). Contextual guidance of eye movements and attention in real-world scenes: The role of global features in object search. *Psychological Review, 113*, 766–786.

Treisman, A. M., & Gelade, G. (1980). A feature-integration theory of attention. *Cognitive Psychology, 12*, 97–136.

Walther, D., & Koch, C. (2006). Modeling attention to salient proto-objects. *Neural Networks, 19*, 1395–1407.

Yantis, S. (1993). Stimulus-driven capture and attentional control settings. *Journal of Experimental Psychology: Human Perception and Performance, 19*, 676–681.

Yantis, S. (1998). Objects, attention, and perceptual experience. In R. Wright (Ed.), *Visual attention* (pp. 187–214). New York: Oxford University Press.

Yantis, S. (2000). Goal-directed and stimulus-driven determinants of attentional control. In S. Monsell & J. Driver (Eds.), *Attention and performance XVIII* (pp. 73–103). Cambridge, MA: MIT Press.

Yantis, S., & Gibson, B. S. (1994). Object continuity in motion perception and attention. *Canadian Journal of Experimental Psychology, 48,* 182–204.

Yantis, S., & Hillstrom, A. P. (1994). Stimulus-driven attentional capture: Evidence from equiluminant visual objects. *Journal of Experimental Psychology: Human Perception and Performance, 20,* 95–107.

Yantis, S., & Jonides, J. (1996). Attentional capture by abrupt visual onsets: New perceptual objects or visual masking? *Journal of Experimental Psychology: Human Perception and Performance, 22,* 1505–1513.

Yarbus, A. (1967). *Eye movements and vision.* New York: Plenum Press.

Zelinsky, G. J. (2001). Eye movements during change detection: Implications for search constraints, memory limitations, and scanning strategies. *Perception and Psychophysics, 63,* 209–225.

VISUAL COGNITION, 2009, 17 (6/7), 856–879

Do we look at lights? Using mixture modelling to distinguish between low- and high-level factors in natural image viewing

Benjamin T. Vincent

School of Psychology, University of Dundee, Dundee, UK

Roland Baddeley, Alessia Correani, Tom Troscianko, and Ute Leonards

Department of Experimental Psychology, University of Bristol, Bristol, UK

The allocation of overt visual attention while viewing photographs of natural scenes is commonly thought to involve both bottom-up feature cues, such as luminance contrast, and top-down factors such as behavioural relevance and scene understanding. Profiting from the fact that light sources are highly visible but uninformative in visual scenes, we develop a mixture model approach that estimates the relative contribution of various low and high-level factors to patterns of eye movements whilst viewing natural scenes containing light sources. Low-level salience accounts predicted fixations at luminance contrast and at lights, whereas these factors played only a minor role in the observed human fixations. Conversely, human data were mostly explicable in terms of a central bias and a foreground preference. Moreover, observers were more likely to look near lights rather than directly at them, an effect that cannot be explained by low-level stimulus factors such as luminance or contrast. These and other results support the idea that the visual system neglects highly visible cues in favour of less visible object information. Mixture modelling might be a good way forward in understanding visual scene exploration, since it makes it possible to measure the extent that low-level or high-level cues act as drivers of eye movements.

Keywords: Eye movements; Bottom-up; Top-down; Salience; Lights.

Please address all correspondence to Benjamin T. Vincent, School of Psychology, University of Dundee, Dundee, DD1 4HN, UK. E-mail: b.t.vincent@dundee.ac.uk

This work was completed whilst BTV was at University of Bristol, supported by EPSRC grant GR/S47953/01; AC by the British Academy (SG-38465). RJB was funded by EPSRC Research Grant no. EP/C516303/1. We thank our reviewers for their helpful suggestions. AC are now at the School of Psychology, University of Birmingham, Birmingham B15 2TT, UK.

© 2009 Taylor & Francis
DOI: 10.1080/13506280902916691

In natural situations we are usually unaware of where we look and just rely on the effectiveness of our saccadic control system to provide sensible fixation locations for the performance of vision-based cognitive tasks. For a given static image, visual scan patterns are sometimes very similar across observers, particularly during the first few seconds of exposure (Antes, 1974; Buswell, 1935; Mackworth & Morandi, 1967; Noton & Stark, 1971; Tatler, Baddeley, & Gilchrist, 2005), and this is even more strongly the case when observers view videos of dynamic scenes (see Smith & Henderson, this issue 2009). This is consistent with the notion that there are particular visual characteristics of visual scenes that attract fixations. Fixations may potentially be elicited by areas of high contrast, such as edges, corners, symmetry (e.g., Locher & Nodine, 1987), and also by more complex forms such as irregular contours (e.g., Loftus & Mackworth, 1978; Richards & Kaufman, 1969). Models taking into account such bottom-up driven and exogenous factors in visual scene exploration propose that fixation of particular targets is achieved by calculating a set of feature maps (such as edges, contrast, and colour) and then combining them together in a linear weighted sum (e.g., Itti & Koch, 2000; Parkhurst & Niebur, 2003). Indeed, the argument that locations in the visual scene are selected on the basis of their feature composition is supported by observations of robust differences in feature properties between fixated and nonfixated locations (Baddeley & Tatler, 2006; Krieger, Rentschler, Hauske, Schill, & Zetzsche, 2000; Mannan, Ruddock, & Wooding, 1997; Parkhurst, Law, & Niebur, 2002; Parkhurst & Niebur, 2003; Reinagel & Zador, 1999; Tatler et al., 2005).

In addition to such low-level parameters (Liversedge & Findlay, 2000), visual scan patterns depend strongly on high-level parameters, such as an individual's intentional state, their experience, memory, and the task that has to be performed in relation to the exploration of the visual image (e.g., Yarbus, 1967). Eyetracking in humans completing tasks such as driving (Land & Horwood, 1995; Land & Lee, 1994), preparing cups of tea (Land & Hayhoe, 2001), making a sandwich (Hayhoe, 2000), or playing cricket (Land & McLeod, 2000) convincingly demonstrate that eye movements precede action, actively seeking out pertinent information about the world. In other words, task-relevant top-down driven information largely influences eye movement behaviour in natural viewing situations. This view (see review by Hayhoe & Ballard, 2005) would assert that the spatiotemporal demands of tasks are the causal factors in attentional allocation. Such a view is entirely consistent with the fact that visual features that are and are not selected for fixation do differ, but only by very small amounts (Tatler & Vincent, this issue 2009), which dissipates with eccentricity (Tatler, Baddeley, & Vincent, 2006). Moreover, a role for high-level (top-down or endogenous) effects could account for the fact that scan patterns often diverge both between and within observers (Mannan et al., 1997).

But how exactly do we identify the different low-level and high-level factors and the role they might play in determining the final fixation behaviour of participants exploring natural images? And how are we able to distinguish between these different factors without having to investigate low-level and high-level factors separately?

First, we would need images of natural scenes with highly visible information that is at the same time irrelevant to human behaviour, such as natural lights in everyday outdoor scenes. Indeed, under typical daytime luminance conditions, objects relevant to goal-directed behaviour usually reflect light while light-emitting objects, such as the sun, are less likely to be relevant for the task at hand. Yet the luminance (and by inference visibility) of light-emitting objects is likely to be several orders of magnitude higher than the luminance of a simultaneously present reflecting objects (e.g., the unobscured solar disk has a luminance of order 10^9 cd/m^2; Karandikar, 1955), while reflecting objects have a typical daytime luminance around 500 cd/m^2). Any fixation selection mechanism based on low-level optical visibility should therefore automatically prioritize light-emitting objects (see our calculation at the end of Experiment 2), taking away important processing time from potential task-relevant reflecting objects. To allow task-related priority for less visible reflecting objects, one would predict the selective neglect of optically highly visible information (such as light-emitting objects) in favour of less visible (here light-reflecting) objects. Even though the amount of light reaching the eyes can be varied by changes in the reflecting properties of object surfaces, or by changes in illumination levels, it is generally assumed that such a distinction cannot be made at the retinal level, at which only information about flux and spectral composition are available. However, we know that a distinction between illumination and reflectance must somehow be recovered at a later stage in the visual system, making it possible to perceptually distinguish between light-emitting and light-reflecting objects, but the neural mechanisms for this process are still unclear (for a discussion on this issue see Correani, Scott-Samuel, & Leonards, 2006; Gilchrist, 2007; Leonards, Troscianko, Lazeyras, & Ibanez, 2005). Estimating the relationship between eye movements and light sources when observers explore their visual environment permits new insights into the question how low-level and high-level processes influence eye movement patterns.

Second, we would need a method that can take into account well-definable low-level features such as luminance contrast on one hand, and less definable high-level factors on the other, in the same data set at the same time. One way of trying to solve this problem of high- versus low-level factor contribution to visual scene exploration has been to allow feature based salience models (Itti & Koch, 2000; Parkhurst & Niebur, 2003) the ability to alter the relative importance of different visual feature dimensions in a top-down manner (Navalpakkam & Itti, 2005). However, a study of such a system showed both theoretical problems with the notion as well as limited ability to achieve the aim of fixating target objects in natural scenes (Vincent, Troscianko, & Gilchrist, 2007).

We therefore propose another approach, namely the analysis of high- versus low-level factor contribution to scene exploration in terms of a mixture model (Everitt & Hand 1981), which we demonstrate in Figure 1 (see Experiment 1's Methods section for further information). We express the

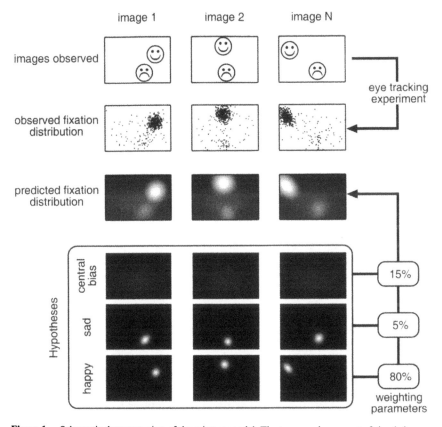

Figure 1. Schematic demonstration of the mixture model. The top row shows a set of simple images consisting of happy and sad faces. Using an eyetracker, one can obtain an observed set of fixations (second row). We can use the mixture model to evaluate the role of various hypotheses, or fixation generators, which gave rise to these fixations. Here we show three such hypotheses: Observers have a central bias; they fixate happy faces; or sad faces. The mixture model calculates the optimal weighting parameters, such that the probability that the observed distributions were generated from the predicted fixation distribution (third row) is maximized. We omit many possible hypotheses from the diagram for simplicity, but the flexibility of the approach is such that any type of hypothesis that can be represented as a 2-D mask can be considered.

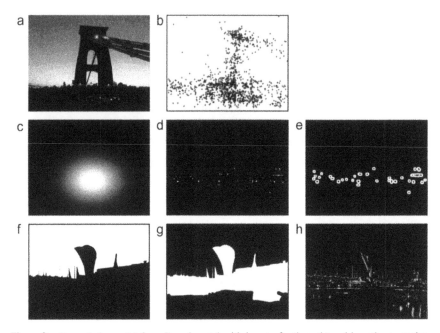

Figure 2. Example image (a) from Experiment 1 with human fixations (b) and hypotheses masks: Central bias (c), lights (d), around lights (e), sky (f), and foreground (g) luminance contrast (h). The uniform random hypothesis is not shown. To view this figure in colour, please see the online issue of the Journal.

combined set of fixations for all the images participants explored in terms of a mixture of separate factors/hypotheses or "fixation generators". These hypotheses are described as two-dimensional probability distributions, and can be thought of as spatial masks (see for example Figures 1, 2, and 3). Low-level image driven hypotheses are created rather simply with standard image processing techniques: Edge maps can be obtained by filtering with oriented Gabors, for example. High-level hypotheses such as "look at lights" or "foreground" can be created by defining a spatial mask corresponding to these regions using any software paint package. Thus, hypotheses are described by spatial masks that have higher values (probability densities) at image regions at which the hypothesis predicts fixations to be directed. We can then answer questions about any structure in the fixations in terms of how important the different hypotheses are in generating the observed fixation data. As a side effect, we can label each fixation with the probability with which it was generated by each hypothesis.

The goal of the present set of experiments was to investigate the hypothesis that human observers neglect highly visible objects (such as light sources) in favour of less visible, but more informative (reflecting) objects in natural environments, by introducing mixture modelling to account for both

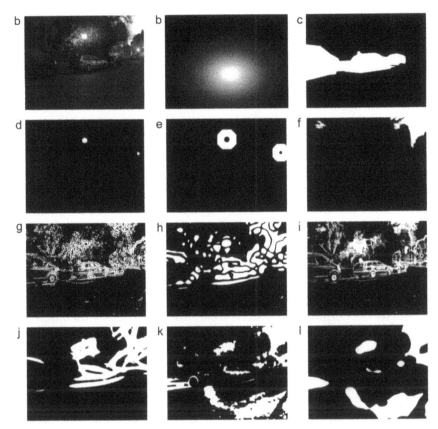

Figure 3. An example image from Experiment 2 (a) with its associated hypotheses: The central bias (b) which was the same for all images, foreground (c), lights (d), around lights (e), sky (f), luminance contrast at high (g) and low (h) spatial frequencies, edges at high (i) and low (j) spatial frequencies, and luminance extremes at high (k) and low (l) spatial frequencies. To view this figure in colour, please see the online issue of the Journal.

"low-level" stimulus parameters (e.g., luminance and contrast) as well as "high-level" parameters. In two experiments, we collected fixation data from human observers viewing natural scenes and evaluated the ability of a range of low- and high-level hypotheses of fixation generation. Modulations in the setups of the two experiments and the amounts of hypotheses introduced as possible fixation generators allowed us to test the reliability of our results, and to ensure they were not parochial to the particular images used, specific presentation times, or the particular implementation of low-level feature maps. To control whether low-level salience models would predict fixation instead of neglect of light sources, we used the mixture model to evaluate the set of hypotheses as introduced in Experiment 2, but based upon fixations generated by Walther and Koch's (2006) salience model instead of those found in our observers. Major discrepancies in the fixation behaviour of the salience model and our human observers for the same image sets would permit us to conclude that the visual system were indeed able to neglect highly visible image features. Such a result could be produced either by active avoidance mechanisms acting on top of low-level factors, or simply by low-level factors playing little or no role in eye guidance.

EXPERIMENT 1

Methods

Subjects

Twenty healthy volunteers (13 females, 7 males), aged between 18 and 39 years (mean age 22.85 ± 5.88 SD) participated in the eye movement data collection of Experiment 1. All participants had normal or corrected-to-normal vision, and all but two (the authors AC and UL) were naïve with respect to the purpose of the experiment. Volunteers gave their informed written consent in accordance with the Declarations of Helsinki, and experiments were approved by the Ethical Committee of the Department of Experimental Psychology, University of Bristol.

Stimuli and experimental procedure

Participants were asked to look at a series of nine images (e.g., Figure 2a) presented on an 18-inch flat screen monitor for 20 s per image, in any manner participants chose. Images subtended a visual angle of $35.2° \times 28°$ and were all photographs of city scenes taken in Bristol (England), containing a large variety of objects and people. Images were taken around dusk because that allows both lights and reflecting objects to lie within the dynamic range of the camera. All pictures included artificial lights (e.g., street lamps or car lights), reflections, and shadows. Before the experiment began, participants were informed that they would have to answer some questions about the images later to ensure that they viewed the images attentively. To ensure that all participants had the same scan starting point at image onset, subjects fixated a central point between image presentations.

Two-dimensional eye movements were recorded with the Eyelink II (SR Research Ltd.). The experimental session was preceded by a nine-point grid calibration and validation. Between trials, the fixation circle reappeared to correct for drifts due to head movements. The sampling rate was set to 500 Hz and the spatial resolution was typically less than $0.3°$ of visual angle.

Hypotheses

For every image we constructed two-dimensional (2-D) spatial hypotheses (masks) that embody a range of hypothesized fixation generators. All these 2-D masks were normalized to sum to unit area such that they represented probability distributions over space. With the exception of the central bias hypothesis, all masks were binary.

1. Lights: In a low-level salience driven system with input from luminance or contrast, one would expect that lights would be highly visible and account for a fair portion of the fixations. Masks around light sources were generated manually (see Figure 2d).
2. Around lights: Light sources are highly visible, but potentially damaging to the retina and rarely containing important information with respect to goal-directed action; instead, participants might fixate near lights (see Figure 2e) to explore objects lit by the lights.
3. Local luminance contrast: Similarly, if subjects show a strong bias to fixating regions surrounding lights, this could be a by-product of these regions having high luminance contrast. To test whether simple contrast is sufficient to account for fixations, we included a luminance contrast map. These were calculated by convolving the image with difference of Gaussian filters with centre and surround variances of $0.017°$ and $0.034°$, respectively, with zero DC, and then thresholding the image to form a binary spatial mask such that the hypothesis represents the regions of highest contrast (see Figure 2h).
4. Sky: A large effect of preference to fixate lights could simply be because people fixate to regions of highest luminance. As a control against such an interpretation of results for Hypothesis 1, we constructed hypotheses for each image that consisted of the sky, usually the area with the most extreme luminance (see Figure 2f). If there were a large preference for this hypothesis in addition to the lights hypothesis, then a low-level explanation for the "lights" hypothesis would seem more plausible.
5. Foreground: Most natural scenes can be split into potentially interesting foreground, and less interesting background. Independent of any other high-level hypotheses, one would expect subjects to fixate the foreground more than the background, and any differences due to more specific hypotheses have to be above and beyond a gross difference in the fixation of foreground and background, before they would be classed as interesting. Because there is no automated algorithm to define foreground regions, we resorted to the manual tracing of foreground areas by a third-party observer who was naïve to the aims of the experiment and did not have access to the fixation data of our observers (see Figure 2g). Note that the foreground region is a

high-level notion; therefore, it is possible that different people might differ on exactly what they define as foreground.

6. Central bias: A large number of studies have observed that subjects fixate more often towards the centre of the image than the edges (e.g., He & Kowler, 1989). This is not due to centrally located features, nor a centrally located initial fixation location (Tatler, 2007). Regardless of the unknown basis of the central bias, any effects need to be above and beyond a general preference for fixating the centre to be of interest. This bias was modelled by a Gaussian (see Figure 2c). The best fitting mean and covariance matrix of this Gaussian was estimated as part of the expectation maximization algorithm described later.

7. Random/uniform: A fixation from the "random/uniform" hypothesis occurs at all locations with equal probability. All models should have such a "catch-all" hypothesis to deal with any fixations that are not explicable by any more interpretable causes. If the other causes provide a good model for the data, the weighting of this hypothesis will be low. Any contribution of this hypothesis represents fixations over all the images that were not better accounted for by other tested or untested hypotheses.

Eye movement analysis.   Eye movement analysis for each participant was restricted to the eye with the better spatial eye movement measurement accuracy. The eye-position data were analysed offline by an automatic saccade detection procedure. Saccade onset was defined as a change in eye position with a minimum velocity of $30°/s$ or minimal acceleration threshold of $8000°/s^2$ and a fixation began after the velocity fell below this value for five successive samples.

Mixture model and statistical analysis.   If $X_{1...N} = \{x, y\}$ is a set of N fixation locations, the probability distribution of fixation locations across all images (I) is $P(X) = \prod_I P(I = k)P(X|I)$, where $P(X|I = k)$ is the distribution for image k, and $P(I = k) = 1/v$ is the probability of a given image which we take to be equal for all v images.

To decompose this probability distribution $P(X|I)$ into a set of fixation generators, the most natural way is to express it in terms of a mixture of different causes, each associated with a given probability $P(C_c)$: For example, $P(X|I) = \Sigma_c P(C_c)P(X|I = k, C_c)$, where $P(C_c)$ is the probability of fixations being due to the generator/cause c. Because we are assuming a mixture model $\Sigma_c P(C_c) = 1$, we are left with the problem of defining the causes $P(X|I = k, C_c)$, estimating the most likely (e.g., maximum likelihood) probabilities associated with these hypotheses $P(C_c)$, and estimating any parameters associated with each of the hypotheses. The hypotheses are defined as 2-D spatial probability distributions (note that essentially they are images). Any hypothesis, as long as it assigns a probability equal or greater than zero to any location and where the sum of probabilities equals one, can be treated as a simple fixation density model.

To find the most probable values of $P(C)$, the expectation maximization (EM) algorithm by Dempster, Laird, and Rubin (1977) can estimate $P(C)$ and the parameters of the central bias model. If these hypotheses have in addition any associated parameters, these can also be found with only a few passes through the data, as long as the parameters of the distributions have sufficient statistics so that they can be efficiently estimated.

It is worth giving a short description of the expectation maximization (EM) algorithm (for more detail see for instance Bishop, 1995). Though the EM algorithm is one of the most used in statistics, machine learning, and engineering, it is not widely known in psychology. The EM algorithm is used when a model is to be fit to the data to maximize the likelihood of the data, and the problem could easily be optimized, if the value of some unmeasured variable were known. In this case, the variable is the probability that each individual fixation came from each of the seven/twelve different hypotheses: $P(C_c)$. It is clear that if this were known, then finding the most probable parameters would be trivial. The EM algorithm works by iterating two steps, and is guaranteed to find a local maximum of the likelihood. The first step (the expectation step) goes through the data, and, assuming that the current model is correct, labels each data point (fixation location) with the probability it came from each of the seven/twelve hypotheses (these probabilities are known as the responsibilities). This is followed by the maximization step, where it is assumed that the responsibilities are correct, and the parameters of the various hypotheses are then set to their maximum likelihood values ($P(C)$ for each hypothesis and the mean and covariance matrices for the central bias model). Reasonable estimates are reached within 30 iterations of these two steps, but we used 300.

The EM algorithm calculates the maximum likelihood values of probabilities $P(C)$ of our 7 (Experiment 1) or 12 (Experiment 2) hypotheses and the best-fitting Gaussian model of the central bias, but to estimate the precision of these estimates, 95% confidence limits were constructed by creating 200 bootstrap data sets by sampling with replacement, and fitting the model to each of these data sets (Efron & Tibshirani, 1993).

Note that we chose to model fixation distributions as a weighted sum (mixture) of probability distributions associated with different hypotheses. This is almost certainly a simplification: Our model assumes that each fixation is due to one and only one cause, not some (necessarily nonlinear) interaction between causes. Despite this, we think that a mixture-of-causes model is often an appropriate model to apply when asking questions about the interaction between high-level and low-level causes for a number of reasons. The first reason is simplicity. Simplicity comes in two kinds. First, the model is easy to understand: All the causes are simply proposals as to where we fixate, and their combination rule (weighted average) is also easy to conceptualize. The results of an analysis (the relative probabilities of the various hypotheses) are more straightforward to interpret than, say, the weights of even a simple neural network. Second, not only is the analysis simple to understand, but so is the algorithm used to optimize the hypothesis probabilities. There are no learning rates, regulators, or priors; and the algorithm, a simplification of the common EM algorithm for the mixture of Gaussian's model, consists of only 10 or so lines of Matlab code. This means that different groups, with the same data and set of hypotheses, will readily reach the same conclusion. This is not true of many models, especially ones with many parameters, optimized by gradient descent. Moreover, the algorithms converge in seconds (rather than hours in the case of some regularized generalized linear models), which is not an insignificant advantage.

Another reason to use a mixture-of-causes model is directly related to its simplicity, namely its identifiability and statistical efficiency. Smallish data sets can uniquely specify the weights of the mixture. This is particularly important, since we perform statistical testing based on bootstrap estimates of the variability of weighting parameters. Again, a more flexible model of how various fixation causes could interact would need more parameters. Not only would these parameters be less interpretable, but there was a greater probability of having multiple solutions, in addition to requiring larger data sets to reliably specify these parameters. Although it is perfectly possible to collect large data sets, an analysis method that works well with small data sets does always seem preferable. Note that identifiability is only strictly true if the hypotheses have no tuneable parameters, and efficiency is only maintained if any tuneable hypotheses have sufficient statistics. We only have one tuneable hypothesis (the central bias—see Methods), but since this is a Gaussian, it has sufficient statistics. We also found, that as long as this is initialized to a broad centralized bias, this causes no problems: The same solution was found every time independently of initial conditions. A mixture model where all (or more than one) hypotheses had tuneable parameters would not have these advantages.

One could argue that a far simpler approach would be to count the frequency of fixations falling within each hypothesis over all the images, and normalize for the area of each hypothesis. Simpler methods are generally preferable, but this metric would be confounded with spatial location of the hypotheses (due to the central bias effect) and would also not be appropriate for hypotheses that spatially overlap. The mixture model approach avoids both of these problems. By using the mixture model and by making the approximation that each fixation is due to one and only one fixation generator, we get a highly interpretable model that can be estimated with small data sets and optimized quickly and easily. As a first pass to interpreting the interaction between high- and low-level factors in eye movements, this seems a sensible compromise.

Examining each hypothesis in isolation.   The mixture model allows us to calculate the best multivariate explanation of the observed pattern of fixations, but just as when applying multivariate analysis to the data, it is worth checking if individual factors/hypotheses are significant in isolation or simply as a component of the more complicated model. To do this, we calculated whether the number of fixations occurring within a given mask-defined area was greater than chance (note that this is not the same as testing if this hypothesis made a significant contribution to explaining the eye movements). The statistic we used was the log ratio of two measures, $\log(\alpha_i/\beta_i)$. The first measure α_i, is the proportion of fixations within the hypothesis defined mask for that image. This is a measure of how well the hypothesis described the fixations. However, this does not account for the possibility that some locations may be fixated more or less than average (e.g., central bias effect). Therefore we calculated β_i, which is a measure of how often fixations are made to the masked area, but for all fixations excluding those to the current image.

The log ratio measure will be zero if fixation probability is equal to chance; however, it will be significantly higher than zero if hypothesis-defined regions are fixated above chance. Again, this significance was assessed using bootstrap estimated 95% confidence limits (Efron & Tibshirani, 1993).

Results

The mixture model's evaluation of the hypotheses' ability to explain fixation behaviour is shown in Table 1. The "sky" hypothesis was unable to account for any fixations (0%, 95% confidence intervals 0%–0%). This does not mean that no fixations were made to the sky, but that they could *all* be better accounted for by other hypotheses. Our log ratio statistic confirms a significant tendency to not look at the sky and to look instead at all other regions, supportive of a similar suggestion by Tatler et al. (2005). Contrast, or some correlated quantity, does seem to have a significant yet marginal role in fixation behaviour. But above and beyond what can be accounted for due to contrast, participants were nearly 10 times more likely to look near, but not directly at, lights (2.6%) than to look directly at them (0.29%). Therefore the notion that we look near lights because they are areas of high luminance contrast is not supported by this analysis.

TABLE 1
Results from Experiment 1

Hypothesis	Probability, $P(C_c)$, and (95% confidence intervals)	Log ratio metric (95% confidence intervals)
Sky	0.0% (0.0%–0.0%)	−0.6492 (−1.255, −0.129)
At lights	0.29% (0.13%–0.44%)	0.8460 (0.625, 1.067)
Around lights	2.62% (2.17%–3.03%)	0.9636 (0.745, 1.149)
Contrast	0.83% (0.54%–1.17%)	0.4664 (0.218, 0.741)
Random/uniform	13.34% (11.9%–14.46%)	
Central bias	34.21% (32.63%–35.93%)	
Foreground	48.7% (47.07%–50.12%)	1.4312 (1.073, 1.740)

The most likely probabilities for the fixation generators together with their 95% confidence limits are shown (second column). The parameters for the best fitting Gaussian for the central bias hypothesis were: Mean x = 537, y = 485; *SD* x = 201.2, y = 139.94. The log ratio statistic (third column) evaluates hypotheses in isolation. For all, the log ratio is significantly different from zero, showing that all hypotheses elicit more fixations than would be expected by chance. The one exception is for the sky, for which it elicits fewer fixations than expected by chance.

In contrast to these hypotheses, we found 34.2% of fixations could be accounted for by simply looking towards the centre of an image. We found that this central bias is not actually central, but centred about two-thirds of the way down from the top of the image. This is not surprising, as the "horizon line" (Sedgwick, 1980) of our images varied between the bottom and the centre of the images, being on average around one-third of the way from the bottom. When viewing a landscape, the horizon line is an informative place to start one's viewing; moreover, it might also reflect a strong photographer's bias for image composition.

The mixture model also showed that a very high 48.7% of fixation can be accounted for by humans looking to foreground regions. 13.34% of fixations were attributed to the uniform (control) hypotheses and can be interpreted as either genuine uniformly random fixation behaviour or the more likely possibility of purposeful but as yet unaccounted for targeting behaviour.

EXPERIMENT 2

To test the reliability of the results of Experiment 1 and to ensure they were not parochial to the particular images used, the rather long presentation times, or the particular implementation of the low-level feature maps, a second experiment was conducted. Experiment 2 used different and larger dataset of natural images (66 as opposed to 9), with larger sized light sources and decreased participant viewing time (5 s rather than 20). In order to compare human fixation behaviour to that predicted by a low-level account, we used the mixture model to evaluate the same expanded set of hypotheses as in Experiment 2, but based upon fixations generated by the salience model (Walther & Koch, 2006). All other details are similar to Experiment 1 unless otherwise specified.

Methods

Subjects

A total of 20 volunteers (10 females, 10 males), aged between 18 and 36 years (mean age 22.00 ± 4.9 *SD*) participated in Experiment 2.

Stimuli and experimental procedure

Participants viewed 99 natural images, mostly taken in Bristol (33 daylight images without light sources and 66 images at dusk including light sources, reflections, and shadows as in Experiment 1). The 33 daylight images, included to divert people from our actual hypothesis, were excluded from later analysis. Furthermore, this time participants were asked to identify and count the number of non-Bristol images. All 66 dusk-images remained for inclusion in the analysis (e.g., Figure 3a and Figure 4, left column). The total viewing time per image was reduced to 5 s. There was an average of five light sources in each image, and they had an average size of 0.91 degrees ($SD \pm 1.1$ degrees).

Hypotheses

In order to investigate the role of low-level feature properties in more detail, the range of hypotheses was expanded to include a central bias, foreground, at lights, around lights, at sky, and high and low spatial frequency luminance contrast, edges, and luminance extremes (see Figure 3). Rather than using continuous valued maps as the hypotheses (which makes various assumptions about output linearity/nonlinearity assumptions of feature detectors), we opted for a simple threshold for all of the additional hypotheses. We set this at 20% such that one-fifth of the area of the image was occupied by the hypothesis. The exact value was arbitrary, but it embodies the notion that the one-fifth of the image with highest edge value, etc. could be fixated by this hypothesis.

- Edges: Baddeley and Tatler (2006) found that high frequency edge information is a better predictor of fixation behaviour and luminance contrast is a simple correlate of this or some other causal factor. Therefore, in the second experiment we included edge hypotheses at both high and low spatial frequencies (see Figure 3i and j). Multiple

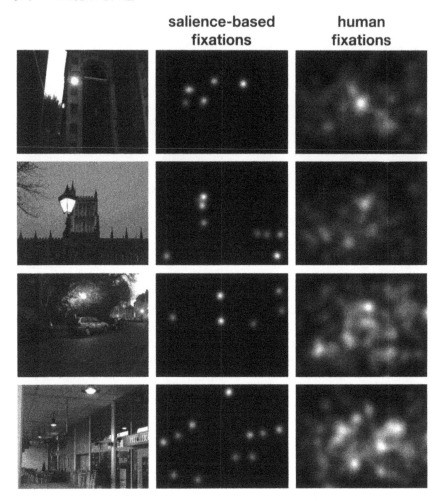

Figure 4. Example images from Experiment 2, salience-based fixation density (not salience maps) and recorded human fixation density. Salience-based fixations tended to cycle round a few salient locations, often fixating light sources, and failing to account for human variability. To view this figure in colour, please see the online issue of the Journal.

maps were calculated by convolving the natural image with Gabor filters at eight orientations. The final edge map consisted of the maximum value across each edge orientation, pixel-wise. Gabors had a spatial frequency of 2.9 cpd for the high spatial frequency edge maps and 0.29 cpd for the low.

- Contrast: This hypothesis was slightly modified as compared to the first experiment by using the simpler Laplacian filter, and was calculated at both high ($\sigma = 1.72°$) and low ($\sigma = 3.4°$) spatial scales (see Figure 3g and h).

- Luminance extremes: We included a luminance extreme hypothesis which consisted of both darkest and lightest areas of the scene for a number of reasons. First, when interpreting fixation behaviour to the sky, which is typically bright, this hypothesis allows us determine if we avoid fixating the sky because of some high-level knowledge that it is unimportant or simply on the basis that it is bright. Again, this hypothesis was evaluated at high and low spatial scales (see Figure 3k and l). Luminance extreme maps were calculated by blurring the luminance of the images, with Gaussians of standard deviation of $1.72°$ and $3.4°$ for high and low spatial frequency maps, respectively. The absolute difference between these blurred luminance values and the mean image luminance value was calculated. The threshold applied was such that the top 10% and bottom 10% of luminance values were included in the mask region.

Salience model-based fixation generation. Fixations based upon the natural images viewed by subjects in Experiment 2 were calculated using the latest salience software (available from http://www.saliencytoolbox.net). Default parameters were used; full details of the algorithm can be found in Walther and Koch (2006). Because the salience model produces the same set of fixations for a given image, it was not appropriate to run the algorithm multiple times to mirror multiple human observers as tested in Experiment 2. Instead, one set of 29 fixations was generated per image, which matched the maximum number of fixations that humans made within the 5 s stimulus presentations used in Experiment 2.

Results

The results from Experiment 2 (Table 2) are in agreement with those of Experiment 1. Again, there was no evidence for actively fixating sky regions (0%) or luminance extremes (0%). Also looking directly at lights was again very rare (0.39%). Moreover, we again found evidence for significantly increased scanning around lights (by a factor of 4.4 compared to "at lights") and this was above and beyond any fixations accounted for by luminance contrast, luminance extremes, or any other tested hypothesis. Moreover, the greatest proportion of eye movements could again be attributed to viewing foreground regions (24.6%) and central bias (56.8%), which increased from Experiment 1 (34.21%). It is possible that the overall spatial biases could be well described by a Gaussian central bias + uniform component, in which case the change in the sum of these combined hypotheses is only 47.55% to

TABLE 2
Results from Experiment 2

| Condition | Human | | Salience model |
	Percentage of eye movements (95% confidence interval)	Number of fixations	Percentage of eye movements (SD)
Random/uniform	3.26 (3.22–3.30)	1031	5.07 (0.04)
Foreground	24.60 (24.48–24.71)	7804	15.51 (0.17)
Central bias	56.80 (56.69–56.93)	18020	4.19 (0.13)
At lights	0.39 (0.38–0.41)	125	20.38 (0.14)
Around lights	1.73 (1.70–1.76)	549	0.49 (0.03)
Sky	0.00 (0.00–0.00)	0	0.00 (0.00)
Contrast			
High sf	4.01 (3.95–4.07)	1274	3.24 (0.05)
Low sf	3.61 (3.56–3.67)	1147	43.84 (0.16)
Edginess			
High sf	3.96 (3.88–4.05)	1255	2.71 (0.06)
Low sf	1.62 (1.59–1.65)	514	2.03 (0.04)
Luminance extreme			
High sf	0.00 (0.00–0.00)	2	2.55 (0.07)
Low sf	0.00 (0.00–0.00)	0	0.00 (0.00)

The table shows the most likely probabilities for the expanded, 12 possible fixation generators together with their 95% confidence limits assessed using a bootstrap technique (second column). To give a more intuitive feel for this result, also given is the approximate number of fixations that each hypothesis was responsible for (the mixing fraction times the total number of fixations; third column). The findings from the first dataset are repeated. The parameters for the best fitting Gaussian for the central bias hypothesis were: Mean x = 513, y = 426; SD x = 207, y = 120. Results of salience model driven fixations are shown in the fourth column with standard deviations. sf = spatial frequency.

60.06%. The hypotheses in Experiment 2 were able to account for a greater proportion of fixations than those in Experiment 1, as only 3.6% were attributed to the uniform hypothesis compared to the 13.3% in Experiment 1.

We evaluated the full set of hypotheses from Experiment 2 using the mixture model with fixations produced by the salience model (see Figure 4 and Methods section Experiment 2) and compared the results to the fixations produced by our human observers (see Figure 4, Figure 5, and Table 2). The only hypotheses for which the salience model approximated human fixation behaviour were for those with marginal contributions (sky, luminance extremes, edges, uniform/random, high frequency luminance contrast, and around lights; see Figure 5). In contrast, "looking at lights" and "low spatial frequency luminance contrast" were powerful explanations of the behaviour of the salience model, but hardly played a role in explaining human fixation behaviour. The central bias explained a minor degree of

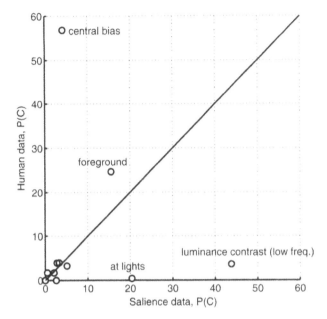

Figure 5.   Comparing human fixations with the outcome of the salience model. If the salience model accurately predicted how humans fixate images, all data points would lie on the diagonal line. This is only approximately true for a subset of hypotheses that are poor at explaining fixation in both humans and the salience model (sky, luminance extremes, edges, uniform/random, high frequency luminance contrast, and around lights). However, for highly predictive hypotheses, either the salience model fixates things that humans do not (lights and low frequency luminance contrast) or the salience model fails to capture the dominant fixation behaviour of humans (i.e., central bias and foreground).

fixation behaviour in the salience model, yet it was the most predictive factor in human fixation behaviour. The role of fixating foreground regions is similar in humans and the salience model; however, the salience model does not have any concept of foreground. From our data it is not possible to determine precisely why the foreground was fixated by the salience model. However, a putative explanation would be that the foreground might contain low-level feature cues present in the salience model, but absent from our list of hypotheses (such as colour), *and* that the presence/absence of these features correlated with foreground regions.

Discussion

Using a mixture model to calculate the relative importance of various low- and high-level factors in fixation behaviour simultaneously, we addressed the question whether people look at highly visible but action-uninformative light sources. The mixture model approach enabled the comparison of low-level hypotheses, such as looking at areas of high luminance, contrast, edges, or at light sources, with high-level hypotheses, such as fixating around lights, or to foreground regions for the same data set in the same analysis. After taking random behaviour and central bias into account, the majority of fixations were to a high-level defined area of foreground; a much smaller fraction of fixations were attributable to fixating low-level features such as luminance contrast, edges, or lights. Even though light sources were highly visible, subjects neglected them relative to the salience model. Instead, they fixated around the lights (see also Leonards et al., 2007). It thus seems that (a) light-emitting objects are ignored in visual scene exploration despite their high visibility, and (b) mixture modelling is indeed a powerful tool to assess the relative importance of different hypotheses in generating the eye movement patterns under different behavioural tasks.

Several caveats have to be considered. First, is the limited dynamic range of the computer screen insufficient to invoke salience-based orienting, specifically orienting towards lights? There is no specification in low-level salience models about what dynamic range is a prerequisite of feature-driven fixations nor what *would* drive fixation behaviour if the dynamic range of monitors was insufficient to invoke saliency. But it might therefore be of interest to repeat these experiments in the future under real world conditions.

Second, could the inaccuracy of the eyetracker affect our results? We first examined if inaccuracy might have affected the degree to which humans fixated lights relative to the salience model. Considering the "lights" and "around lights" hypotheses together (in Experiment 2), a total of 2.12% of human fixations could be accounted for; however, a total of 20.87% of salience model's fixations was accounted for. Therefore, we can be confident that even in the presence of some eyetracker error, the overall fixations in the local region of lights is approximately 10 times less common than predicted by the low level salience account. Did eyetracker error influence the ratio of "at" and "around lights" hypotheses? Out of the 66 images in Experiment 2 there were a total of 325 light sources (an average of five per image). These were large, on average subtending just under 0.91 degrees ($SD \pm 1.1$ degrees). Given that the accuracy (as measured by the standard deviation) of eye movements is approximately proportional to 7% of their magnitude (van Beers, 2007), and the majority of eye movements are short, the inaccuracy of the subjects' eye movements could not account for the observed pattern of "avoiding lights".

Third, most of our fixations were best explained by the hypothesis of a central bias. Could the high role for the central bias be due to its flexible parameters whilst the other hypotheses had fixed parameters? Even though we cannot entirely exclude the possibility of overfitting of the central bias, it seems unlikely given the low spatial complexity of a large Gaussian blob. Lack of flexible parameters in low-level hypotheses such as edges could have limited their ability to account for fixations; however, our results are consistent with a range of studies all using a variety of methods to calculate feature maps (Einhäuser, Spain, & Perona, 2008; Nyström & Holmqvist, 2008; Tatler et al., 2005; Tatler & Vincent, this issue 2009).

Fourth, in common with any multivariate analysis, the contribution of any single hypothesis has to be interpreted in relation to the other hypotheses. For example, the output of the mixture model in terms of percentage contribution of each hypothesis will subtly shift depending on what other hypotheses are and are not considered. The mixing coefficients would be different if we included additional hypotheses, based on colour for example. This quality means that the mixture model may not be the best approach if trying to elucidate fundamentally "fixed" contributions of various hypotheses, if such a concept is even meaningful. However, it does allow one to evaluate the relative importance of multiple hypotheses. Furthermore, it allows you to know how much you *cannot* explain: For example, in Experiment 1 we found the uniform random fixation hypothesis accounted for ~13% of fixations, but this decreased in Experiment 2 to 3.26%. This is in part due to the inclusion of more hypotheses, which could better explain the data.

Finally, our whole model was based on the assumption that each fixation is caused by a single hypothesis; thus, each fixation is due to one and only one cause. This may of course not be the case: Fixations may be the product of some potentially very complex and nonlinear combination of multiple different causes—in our example, fixations around lights might have been driven by luminance contrast, edges, and "around lights" factors at the same time. However, taking a modelling approach that accounts for fixations being the product of possible linear or nonlinear combinations of hypotheses would result in a significantly more complex model with increased parameters and greatly decreased confidence in the values of those parameters given the same eye movement data. We are aware that our approach is therefore highly simplified, which should be considered when it comes to discussing models on visual scene exploration in general. However, for the question we were interested in here, we feel this simplified assumption was a reasonable approximation to make.

Mixture modelling.   The real advantage of the mixture model compared to the log ratio metric was that it allowed us to consider multiple hypotheses concurrently: The "lights" hypothesis demonstrates this point. The log ratio metric (in Experiment 1) of $+0.846$ (95% confidence intervals: 0.625–1.067) showed that if we ask the question, "Do we look at lights at above chance levels?", the answer would be affirmative. However, this simple statistic fails to account for the fact that this result may have been produced by other hypotheses. When we consider multiple hypotheses in Experiment 1, then the role of lights is only 0.29% (95% confidence intervals: 0.13%–0.44%): The mixture model shows that the vast majority of, but not all, fixations to lights are better explained by other hypotheses. In this way, it is perhaps difficult to establish what the precise causal factors behind fixations are; however, the mixture model at least provides a framework whereby more and more hypotheses can be added into consideration. Higher weightings in the mixture model indicates that those hypotheses are better able to account for the data, and could be argued to be better causal explanations, relative to other explanations.

A key factor for our example is that mixture models deal with hypotheses of varying specificity. Because each hypothesis (spatial mask) sums to a total area of 1, the probability mass for points within spatially specific hypotheses (e.g., lights) will be very high relative to a spatially broad hypothesis, such as "sky". If we considered a single image, with a fixation in both the sky and on a light, the mixture model would assign a higher weighting to the lights hypothesis due to the different probability masses. This is perhaps not the result we would like. However, each hypothesis is considered over multiple scenes. Because of this, very specific hypotheses will only have high weightings, if a high proportion of fixations occur within its area *over many images*. So, highly specific hypotheses that happen by chance to be fixated in only a few scenes—but not the rest—will not receive high weightings as they can be accounted for by other hypotheses. This may provide some insight into why the central bias scored so highly in the mixture model: It is a good explanation of fixation behaviour over multiple images, and those fixations were not better explained by other hypotheses.

Eye guidance in natural scenes.   Within the limits of these concerns, it remains tempting to speculate about the implications of our results in a more general way for the understanding of eye guidance made to natural scenes. In Experiment 1, we found only 3.7% of eye movements could be attributed to "low-level" hypotheses. Whilst increasing the number of such hypotheses in Experiment 2 led to their increased importance of 13.2%, this still comparatively low role of low-level hypotheses is in line with other estimates; for example, by measuring differences in feature composition at fixated and nonfixated locations, only a relatively minor role could be attributed to low-level image features (area under receiver operating curves of 0.55–0.65; Tatler et al., 2005; Tatler & Vincent, this issue 2009). It is clear that almost all explorations of the role of low-level statistics in fixation selection will overestimate their role. Regions in images that are interesting for high-level reasons (such as faces, food, friends, . . .), tend to have also more low-level visual structure. Regions that are very rarely of interest for high-level reasons (sky, the floor, blank walls), tend to have very little low-level visual structure. Even if low-level features had *no* causal role in guiding eye movements, there would still be reliable differences in the statistics at fixated and nonfixated locations as observed. Although our results are not strong enough to ascertain this point, our method does allow high- and low-level factors to be quantitatively evaluated for the first time. We saw a vastly smaller role for these low-level effects than sometimes assumed. This therefore questions the ability of low-level, task-independent salience to offer causal explanations of eye guidance in natural scene viewing.

The large discrepancy between low-level feature driven hypotheses and higher level hypotheses or spatial factors raises an unavoidable question: Just how much can be understood about eye guidance in natural scenes by studying how image features are combined in more complex ways? Given the very high role for central biases and the importance of other forms of bias (Tatler & Vincent, this issue 2009) then, perhaps a more profitable direction would be to examine these further. Does a central bias, which is made to computer-displayed images, have any meaningful analogue in natural behaviour? If not, then it is not immediately clear how understanding viewing to computer-displayed images will map on to real behaviour, even if they are photos of natural scenes. Our results suggest that a greater understanding of eye guidance in natural scenes could be reached from investigating traditionally termed top-down processes.

CONCLUSIONS

Using mixture modelling to test the hypothesis that the visual system treats light-emitting and light-reflecting objects in different ways, neglecting fixation of light-emitting objects in natural images despite their high optical visibility, we found that fixation of light sources was indeed very unlikely. Instead, visual fixations occurred near light sources, an effect that could not be explained by low-level features such as luminance contrasts or luminance maxima, and was not predicted by a typical salience model. It thus seems as if the visual system neglects highly visible, but uninformative objects in favour for less visible but action-informative ones in foreground and central regions.

REFERENCES

Antes, J. R. (1974). The time course of picture viewing. *Journal of Experimental Psychology, 103,* 62–70.

Baddeley, R., & Tatler, B. (2006). High frequency edges (but not contrast) predict where we fixate: A Bayesian system identification analysis. *Vision Research, 46*(18), 2824–2833.

Bishop, C. M. (1995). *Neural networks for pattern recognition.* Oxford, UK: Oxford University Press.

Buswell, G. T. (1935). *How people look at pictures.* Chicago: University of Chicago Press.

Correani, A., Scott-Samuel, N. E., & Leonards, U. (2006). Luminosity—a perceptual "feature" of light-emitting objects? *Vision Research, 46*(22), 3915–3925.

Dempster, A., Laird, N., & Rubin, D. (1977). Maximum likelihood from incomplete data via the EM algorithm. *Journal of the Royal Statistical Society, 39B*(1), 1–38.

Efron, B., & Tibshirani, R. J. (1993). *An introduction to the bootstrap.* New York: Chapman & Hall.

Einhäuser, W., Spain, M., & Perona, P. (2008). Objects predict fixations better than early saliency. *Journal of Vision, 8*(14), 11–26.

Everitt, B. S., & Hand, D. J. (1981). *Finite mixture distributions.* London: Chapman & Hall.

Gilchrist, A. L. (2007). Lightness and brightness. *Current Biology, 17*, R267–R269.

Hayhoe, M. (2000). Visual routines: A functional account of vision. *Visual Cognition, 7*, 43–64.

Hayhoe, M., & Ballard, D. (2005). Eye movements in natural behavior. *Trends in Cognitive Sciences, 9*(4), 188–193.

He, P. Y., & Kowler, E. (1989). The role of location probability in the programming of saccades: Implications for "center-of-gravity" tendencies. *Vision Research, 29*, 1165–1181.

Itti, L., & Koch, C. (2000). A saliency-based search mechanism for overt and covert shifts of visual attention. *Vision Research, 40*, 1489–1506.

Karandikar, R. V. (1955). Luminance of the sun. *Journal of the Optical Society of America, 45*, 483–488.

Krieger, G., Rentschler, I., Hauske, G., Schill, K., & Zetzsche, C. (2000). Object and scene analysis by saccadic eye-movements: An investigation with higher-order statistics. *Spatial Vision, 13*(2–3), 201–214.

Land, M. F., & Hayhoe, M. M. (2001). In what ways do eye movements contribute to everyday activities? *Vision Research, 41*, 3559–3565.

Land, M. F., & Horwood, J. M. (1995). Which parts of the road guide steering. *Nature, 377*, 339–340.

Land, M. F., & Lee, D. N. (1994). Where we look when we steer. *Nature, 369*, 742–744.

Land, M. F., & McLeod, P. (2000). From eye movements to actions: How batsmen hit the ball. *Nature Neuroscience, 3*, 1340–1345.

Leonards, U., Baddeley, R., Gilchrist, I. D., Troscianko, T., Ledda, P., & Williamson, B. (2007). Mediaeval artists: Masters in directing the observers' gaze. *Current Biology, 17*, R8–R9.

Leonards, U., Troscianko, T., Lazeyras, F., & Ibanez, V. (2005). Cortical distinction between the neural encoding of objects that appear to glow, and those that do not. *Cognitive Brain Research, 24*, 173–176.

Liversedge, S. P., & Findlay, J. M. (2000). Saccadic eye movements and cognition. *Trends in Cognitive Science, 4*, 6–14.

Locher, P. J., & Nodine, C. G. (1987). Symmetry catches the eye. In J. K. O'Regan & A. Levy-Schoen (Eds.), *Eye movements: From physiology to cognition* (pp. 353–361). Amsterdam and New York: North-Holland/Elsevier Science Publishers.

Loftus, G. R., & Mackworth, N. H. (1978). Cognitive determinants of fixation location during picture viewing. *Journal of Experimental Psychology: Human Perception and Performance, 4*, 565–572.

Mackworth, N. H., & Morandi, A. J. (1967). The gaze selects informative details within pictures. *Perception and Psychophysics, 2*, 547–552.

Mannan, S. K., Ruddock, K. H., & Wooding, D. S. (1997). Fixation patterns made during brief examination of two-dimensional images. *Perception, 26*(8), 1059–1072.

Navalpakkam, V., & Itti, L. (2005). Modeling the influence of task on attention. *Vision Research, 45*(2), 205–231.

Noton, D., & Stark, L. (1971). Scanpaths in saccadic eye movements while viewing and recognizing patterns. *Vision Research, 11*, 929–942.

Nyström, M., & Holmqvist, K. (2008). Semantic override of low-level features in image viewing—both initially and overall. *Journal of Eye Movement Research, 2*(2), 1–11.

Parkhurst, D., Law, K., & Niebur, E. (2002). Modelling the role of salience in the allocation of overt visual attention. *Vision Research, 42,* 107–123.

Parkhurst, D., & Niebur, E. (2003). Scene content selected by active vision. *Spatial Vision, 16,* 125–154.

Reinagel, P., & Zador, A. M. (1999). Natural scene statistics at the centre of gaze. *Network Computation in Neural Systems, 10,* 341–350.

Richards, W., & Kaufman, L. (1969). Centre-of-gravity tendencies for fixations and flow patterns. *Perception and Psychophysics, 5,* 81–84.

Sedgwick, H. A. (1980). The geometry of spatial layout in pictorial representation. In M. A. Hagen (Ed.), *The perception of pictures: Vol. 1. Alberti's window: The projective model of pictorial information* (pp. 33–88). New York: Academic Press.

Smith, T., & Henderson, J. (2009). Attentional synchrony in static and dynamic scenes. *Visual Cognition, 17*(6/7), 1083–1108.

Tatler, B. W. (2007). The central fixation bias in scene viewing: Selecting an optimal viewing position independently of motor biases and image feature distributions. *Journal of Vision, 7*(14), 1–17.

Tatler, B. W., Baddeley, R. J., & Gilchrist, I. D. (2005). Visual correlates of fixation selection: Effects of scale and time. *Vision Research, 45,* 643–659.

Tatler, B. W., Baddeley, R. J., & Vincent, B. (2006). The long and the short of it: Spatial statistics at fixation vary with saccade amplitude and task. *Vision Research, 46,* 1857–1862.

Tatler, B. W., & Vincent, B. T. (2009) The prominence of behavioural biases in eye guidance. *Visual Cognition, 17*(6/7), 1029–1054.

Van Beers, R. (2007). The sources of variability in saccadic eye movements. *Journal of Neuroscience, 27*(33), 8757–8770.

Vincent, B., Troscianko, T., & Gilchrist, I. D. (2007). Investigating a space-variant weighted salience account of visual selection. *Vision Research, 47,* 1809–1820.

Walther, D., & Koch, C. (2006). Modelling attention to salient proto-objects. *Neural Networks, 19,* 1395–1407.

Yarbus, A. L. (1967). *Eye movements and vision.* New York: Plenum Press.

VISUAL COGNITION, 2009, 17 (6/7), 880–903

The nature of the visual representations involved in eye movements when walking down the street

Filipe Cristino and Roland Baddeley

Department of Experimental Psychology, University of Bristol, Bristol, UK

In this paper we set out to answer two questions. The first aims to discover whether saccades are driven by low level image features (as suggested by a number of recent and influential models), a position we call image salience, or whether they are driven by the meaning and reward associated with the world, a position we call world salience. The second question concerns the reference frame in which the eye movements are planned. To answer these questions, we recorded six videos, using a head mounted camera, with the viewer walking down a popular shopping street in Bristol. As well as showing these videos to our participants, we also showed spatially and temporally filtered versions of them. We found that, at a coarse spatial scale, subjects viewed similar locations in the image, irrespective of the filtering, and that fixation distributions found when viewing videos with similar filtering were no more alike than if the filtering varied widely. Using a novel mixture modelling technique, we also showed that the most important reference frame was world-centred rather than head or body-based. This was confirmed by a second experiment where the fixation distributions to identical videos was systematically changed by using a swivelling tent that only altered subjects' perception of the gravitational vertical. We conclude that eye movements should not be understood in terms of image salience, or even information maximization, but in terms of the more flexible concept of reward maximization.

Keywords: Eye movements; Natural scenes; Video stimuli; Mixture modelling; World-centred reference frame.

In every second of the waking day we make an average of three eye movements. With each of these saccades we have to decide where to point the eyes, making this one of the most frequent decisions we make. As highly visual animals, many tasks simply cannot be done if we do not fixate the relevant locations making this decision not only frequent, but highly important for our survival.

Please address all correspondence to Filipe Cristino, Department of Experimental Psychology, University of Bristol, 12a Priory Road, Bristol BS8 1TU, UK. E-mail: F.cristino@ bristol.ac.uk

This work was supported by an EPSRC grant (REVERB).

© 2009 Taylor & Francis
DOI: 10.1080/13506280902834696

This decision of where to look is based, broadly speaking, on both high level (task-related) and low level (image-related) considerations but, despite much recent work, two fundamental questions relating to these processes remain. The first concerns the role of low level image features. Over recent years, a large amount of evidence has been accumulated, suggesting that the image characteristics at fixated locations differ from those at nonfixated locations. Fixated locations tend to have higher contrast, more edges, less extreme low spatial frequency luminance, and more motion than nonfixated locations (Baddeley & Tatler, 2006; Parkhurst & Niebur, 2003; Rajashekar, Cormack, & Bovik, 2003). This is not true for all fixated locations, but, based on these statistical differences, it is possible to discriminate between fixated and nonfixated locations up to about 70% of the time with chance being 50% (Baddeley & Tatler, 2006; Kienzle, Wichmann, Scholkopf, & Franz, 2007). A common (and natural) interpretation of this is that the eye movements are "driven" by these image differences; in other words, locations in images that are extreme in terms of their low level features are in some sense visually "salient". This position has been proposed by a number of recent high profile papers (Itti & Koch, 2001; Parkhurst, Law, & Niebur, 2002; Rajashekar, van der Linde, Bovik, & Cormack, 2007). Similar work has been done using dynamic stimuli. Itti (2005) found that low level saliency of video clips could account for 50% of the eye movements, with the most important predictors being motion and temporal change. Unfortunately these models even if performing above chance don't explain most of the eye movements. Recently, Tatler and Vincent (2009) showed that a fixation model just based on the biases of the oculomotor system (therefore blind to the visual input) can outperform most of the saliency maps based models.

An alternative interpretation of this observed correlation between image features and fixation is that it is not causal (Einhauser & Konig, 2003). Instead of eye movements being driven by low level visual features, it is suggested that subjects fixate behaviourally important objects or locations in the world (Oliva, Torralba, Castelhano, & Henderson, 2003). If, on average, the image features at behaviourally important locations are different from those at other locations, we would observe differences in the statistics of fixated and nonfixated locations, but it would be the behavioural importance of the locations that would be driving eye movements and not the low level features per se.

An example of such potential correlation is that people rarely look at the sky. Unless judging the weather or searching for aeroplanes, the sky rarely contains behaviourally important information so this is generally sensible behaviour. The sky is also brighter, has less contrast and fewer edges than most image locations. Therefore, simply not fixating the sky would result in robust statistical differences between image statistics at locations we fixate, as opposed to those we do not. This would be true despite these image differences themselves having no causal role. In the present paper, we will therefore contrast two positions. In the image salience position, a given image location is "salient" because of the presence of a particular set of image features. In contrast, in the world salience position, a location is salient not because of the particular features, but because of the reward or behavioural relevance of the object in the world that generated these features. This world has obviously to be inferred from these features, but any set of features that allow this world to be inferred will be deemed salient: There is a one to one mapping not between image salience and fixation probability, but the world that generated these features and fixation probability: In this "world salience" proposal, in contrast to the "image salience" interpretation, it is not the image characteristics driving the system, but the inferred world that generates the image.

Given images where a third of their area is both featureless and behaviourally unimportant (e.g., sky, blank walls, ceiling, ...), any fixation prediction model, based on any feature that discriminates between feature-less and feature rich locations, will perform with 66% accuracy. This is roughly the performance of most systems that attempt to predict fixations based on image statistics. In short, evidence for robust differences between the statistics at fixated location versus nonfixated locations is not evidence that these features are driving the system.

In normal experiments, with natural images used as stimuli, it is often not possible to distinguish between image and world salience proposals since they are likely to make the same predictions. Here we show that by using spatiotemporal filtered movies (where the filtering changes low level features but not the world signalled), it is possible to tell these positions apart. In particular, since the videos were taken with a head-mounted camera walking down the street, most of the high temporal frequencies will be around the edge of the movies (i.e., buildings, sky, and the road), and most of the low temporal frequencies will be near the centre (as most of the motion is generated by moving vehicles or pedestrians, which often are at the edges of the videos). If, when the movies are high pass temporally filtered, subjects preferentially view locations on the edge of the screen, whilst when the images are low pass temporally filtered, they preferentially view central locations; this is strong evidence for an "image salience" interpretation. If, in contrast, the movies (independent of filtering) generate similar patterns of fixations (because the inferred world that generated them is the same), this then argues for a world salience interpretation.

This brings us to the second issue. Following the recent literature (Foulsham & Underwood, 2008; Itti, 2005), even the most enthusiastic proponent of the low level salience models would not propose that eye movements are simply made to the next location of high visual salience;

some kind of high level-top down planning is required (Buswell, 1935; Land & Hayhoe, 2001; Yarbus, 1967). The spatial planning (reference frame) of multiple fixations has to be performed in a representation independent of the current eye position. The simplest representation in terms of the execution of eye movements would be if they were planned in a head or body-centred (egocentric) representation. Despite being easier to convert this representation into motor commands, it may instead be that eye movements are planned in a world centred representation, for instance a representation relative to the ground plane. Many behaviourally important locations (such as where my feet will be in three steps time; Patla & Vickers, 2003) will more naturally be described in such a reference frame.

There are a number of phenomena consistent with such high level, world-centred planning. Perhaps the simplest is that when viewing almost any image, far more eye movements are made to the centre of the image, independent of the head or eye position on onset (Vitu, Kapoula, Lancelin, & Lavigne, 2004), this effect is particularly significant for early fixations (Tatler, 2007). In these experiments, the head is fixed (as is the body), and although such biases are consistent with a head-centred, egocentric representation, they are also consistent with a world-centred representation. Foulsham, Kingstone, and Underwood (2008) showed recently that the horizontal bias in saccades (making saccades parallel to the horizon line) is "world centred". By displaying square images of landscapes, they demonstrated that people make more saccade along the horizon line even if they rotate the image within the square frame. By recording eye movements of subjects viewing movies, and observing if any centre-of-the-screen biases follow the screen coordinates or the world coordinates (or a combination of both), we can place constraints on the nature of the representations involved in eye movement planning: Do biases follow the screen, or the world described by the screen?

To answer these two questions about low and high level processes in fixation selection, we need a naturalistic stimulus for the subject to view. For this purpose we used a head-mounted camera (Sony DV camera mounted on a skateboard helmet) and walked down Park Street, a popular shopping street in Bristol, where we recorded six videos of two and half minutes each. We attempted to minimize any head movements, since these are very visually unsettling when the videos are watched later on (as the camcorder was mounted on the top of a helmet any brusque movement would have been amplified by the fact that the helmet could not be firmly fixed to the head).

As stimuli, these videos have three important characteristics. First, they are both natural (particularly to the Bristolians tested) and constantly changing. This is important because, from research on static images, the first four or five fixation locations are similar across different subjects, whereas later fixations show much greater variability between subjects (Tatler,

Baddeley, & Gilchrist, 2005). By using constantly changing stimuli, we hope to maximize the between subject consistency whilst maintaining the data rate of continuous viewing. Second, the pavement (sidewalk) was narrow and the videos were recorded with the cameraman looking straight forward. This meant that there were larger motion signals to the left and right side of the video (passing buildings, people, and cars) than at the centre, which was often the point of expansion (as can be seen in Figure 1). When we applied a spatiotemporal filter to the videos (see later), this resulted in higher temporal frequency information in the periphery than in the centre. This is potentially useful for distinguishing between motion and static feature generated saccades, the hypothesis being that these two different kinds of eye movements will go to different spatial locations. The final characteristic to take into account was that the street used for the experiment was not level, showing a rather large incline at several points, up to a gradient of 15%. This meant that, even though the head was approximately level, the "horizon line" of the image moved systematically as a function of time (Figure 1). As such, the relationship between the video and the world it represents changes systematically during presentation, allowing us to explore whether fixation behaviour follows the world or the screen coordinates.

Previous studies investigating salience effects have chosen to express subjects' fixation probability distributions as a function of the image properties (for instance calculating P(fixation | image) (Baddeley & Tatler, 2006; Henderson, 2003; Itti & Koch, 2001). The problem here is the mapping is potentially nonlinear and complicated (multidimensional), and if a relationship is not found (or found to be weak), a reasonable objection is that an incorrect form of mapping has been chosen. In this paper, in contrast, we choose to interpret subjects' spatial temporal fixation distributions in terms of other fixation distributions. In particular, we express the observed distributions of eye movements to the unfiltered videos in terms of a mixture of the subjects' fixation distributions observed when they view related but filtered scenes. In a normal experiment, if a participant fixates a road sign, two explanations of why the road sign was fixated occur: An image saliency interpretation may propose it is because of the features present (the locations luminance, orientation, contrast, or colour, etc.); in contrast, in terms of the world salience interpretation, this location is fixated because it is potentially behaviourally important (and therefore rewarding). With our approach, these two possibilities can be pulled apart as the sign will have varying low level features in each of the differently filtered videos. If low level image saliency is the cause of fixation, observers may only fixate the sign in the subset of the filtered videos where these features are still present. On the other hand, if the behaviourally important information available at that location in the world was the most important factor, then the sign will be fixated in all of the videos, as long as the filtering left enough information

Figure 1. Examples of frame shots filmed in Park Street, Bristol with our homemade helmet camera. On the right, picture of the video helmet worn by one of the authors (RB).

to identify this location as the location where the sign is present. Later we also include other mixture components attributable to egocentric and allocentric spatial biases to measure the relative importance of these two representations.

This paper shows that there is little evidence for "image salience" driven fixation and, instead, favours the theory that eye movements are driven by "world salience". It also shows that world-centred representation is very important, with an egocentric representation making an insignificant contribution to the observed eye movement distributions. It is also shows that manipulations altering the participants' perceived vertical change fixation behaviour, even when the stimuli and instructions remain identical.

EXPERIMENT 1

Method

Procedure.   In this first experiment, the task given to participants was to watch the movies and answer six basic questions after the viewing of each film (e.g., "Where was the post office?", "How many phone-boxes did you see?"). Participants did not know the questions before the start of the trial. The answers to these questions were recorded, but not for any purpose other than to ensure participants were paying attention to the stimuli and could interpret the filtered images. In this experiment, each participant saw seven different films. Presentation was counterbalanced so that no subject saw either the same video or the same filtering condition twice. Order of presentation was randomized between subjects.

Subjects.   Forty participants (of whom 37 were female) from our student pool took part in the study. One of the authors (RB) served as a subject as well as another member of our vision research group. All other participants were naive about the experiment. All had either normal vision or corrected to normal vision. The experiments were conducted in accordance with our Research Ethics committee.

Equipment.   The eyetracker used to conduct this experiment was the EyeLink II, produced by SR Research. The EyeLink II is a head mounted binocular eyetracking device with a sampling rate of 500 Hz. The stimuli were displayed on a Eizo Flexcan T965 CRT screen. In this experiment the screen resolution was set to 800×600 pixels giving a horizontal visual angle of 36 degrees and 30 degrees vertically. A nine-point calibration was performed before each film followed by a drift correction of the eyetracker. Saccade extraction was done using SR research normal saccadic filter with values of

30 deg/s^{-1} velocity threshold and 8000 deg/s^{-2} acceleration threshold. Participants were asked to lean against a chinrest situated 66 cm from the display screen.

Stimuli. The stimuli shown during the experiments were filmed in Bristol, walking down a busy shopping street (Park Street) using a consumer basic DV camera (Sony Handicam 400) at 25 frames per second (fps) with a resolution of 720×576 pixels (Standard Definition). The camera was attached to a homemade video helmet. The aim of such apparatus was to create video stimuli as natural as possible (Felsen & Dan, 2005). The camcorder saved the video recordings on miniDV tapes set to the minimum compression setting possible (DV codec). The film was then extracted to a raw format (RGB) and up-sampled to 50 fps using the properties of the interlaced framing used on most consumer cameras (conversion from 25 fps interlaced to 50 fps progressive using the Smart Bob Filter in VirtualDub; http://www.virtualdub.org/). This higher frame rate allowed us to perform higher temporal frequency filtering on the stimuli later on.

We used greyscale stimuli to minimize calibration issues, minimize the complexity of the experiment, and simplify later interpretation. The films were transformed into greyscale by retaining only the green channel of the RGB colour space (the green channel being a reasonable approximation to the human luminance channel; Webster, de Valois, & Switkes, 1990). After the greyscale conversion, each of the seven videos (165 s long) was spatiotemporally band-passed filtered to produce six different video conditions. Specifically, each video was filtered spatially between 0.25 cycles per degree and 5 cycles per degree, and temporally filtered from 0.58 to 12.5 Hz to produce six filtered versions of each video as shown in Figure 2. This resulted in a total of 49 different videos (seven original videos together with six different filtered versions of each). All the films were normalized by condition to have the same amount of average luminance per frame as well as gamma corrected for our screen. Gamma correction made the movies perceptually overexposed, hence slightly unnatural, but we decided to perform it for further statistical analysis and replication purposes. The films were then recompressed at the end of all the video processing (using the Xvid codec using a high bit-rate to avoid any compression artefacts). All the films were displayed during the experiments at 50 fps using the Experiment Builder software provided by SR research, which allowed a smooth and accurate display of the videos at a high frame rate.

Statistical analysis. Analysis of more than 24 million samples from the eye movement recording setup resulted in over 150,000 saccades being identified in the first experiment. For further analysis, the data was first spatially binned using bins of 4.5×4.5 degrees (each image was split into an

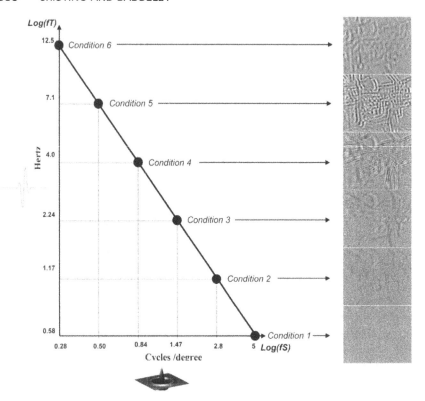

Figure 2. Characteristics of the six filtered versions of the video sequences. To investigate the possibility that separate low level spatial and temporal filter banks are used to determine where we move our eyes, as well as recording eye movements when the subjects were viewing the normal videos, we also created and presented six spatial temporal filtered versions of the videos. Each filter had a spatial and temporal bandwidth of one octave. The filters that allowed high frequency spatial information through (fine spatial detail), did not allow fine temporal frequency information through, and vice versa. This meant that filtered videos that contain only motion information (high temporal filtered: Condition 1, 2, and 3) would be expected to stimulate motion sensitive brain areas (often associated with MT), whilst filtered video conditions 4, 5, and 6 should preferentially stimulate high spatial resolution brain areas because of the fine detail of the videos (V4). Even if these anatomical speculations are not true, since the videos were made of a subject walking down a road, the locations with high temporal frequency energy (the edges of the video) will be different from those with low temporal frequencies. Therefore, if subjects are fixating low level features, they will look at different locations when viewing the different video conditions.

8×6 grid). The number of fixations within each bin was counted as a function of time and subject. Temporally, the data was binned with bins of 300 ms (this figure was not critical: Different temporal size bins of 200 ms or 250 ms were also tested but were not giving significantly different results). Because we used the binned frames as probability distributions, they were normalized to have a sum of one (the sum of all the bins within a frame equalled one).

The main statistical analysis used to model the data was based on a mixture modelling technique. Instead of characterizing eye movements as a function of low level features (edges, contrast, colour, luminance, etc.) or high level objects (cars, road, sky, etc.), we defined the probability distributions to unfiltered video in terms of the distribution of eye movements to filtered ones (Figure 3). This was achieved using a mixture modelling technique; the distribution to the unfiltered videos being expressed as a weighted sum of the probability distributions to the other conditions, where the weightings are all positive and must add up to one (they are probabilities). Mixture modelling is very popular in many areas of science and technology; for instance, it forms the basis of most models of speech recognition (Reynolds & Rose, 1995). Despite this, we believe it has not yet been widely used with psychology.

The mixture model is defined by the sum of the distributions of the six filter variants as well as a uniform distribution. Practically, this spatially uniform distribution accounts for any eye movements observed not accounted by the distributions of any of the filtered videos. Given this, the mixture model can be formalized as follows:

$$P(y_i|\vec{\pi}) = \sum_{k=1}^{K} \pi_k P(y_i|C_k) + \pi_{K+1} P(y_i|u) \tag{1}$$

Where the sum of the weights (π) of each mixture add up to one ($\Sigma\pi = 1$), and all mixture weights are positives ($\pi_k > 0$ for each filter condition k). The first term Equation 1 gives the probability P that a fixation in the unfiltered video (y_i) where i is a binned sample is produced by the filtered video (C_k); the second term defines the uniform distribution with u (the uniform value) being one over the numbers of bins (~ 0.02). In addition to expressing the unfiltered video fixation distributions in terms of both the filtered distributions and a uniform distribution, we also explored adding extra mixture components to account for other potential effects.

More specifically, two mixture components were added. The first consisted of a spatial Gaussian distribution in world-centred coordinates (see later), that can be used to account for fixations that reliably occur at a given location in world coordinates. The second was a Gaussian distribution in screen coordinates that can be used to investigate the strength of a widely observed bias for fixations towards the centre of the screen. This mixture model could then be described as:

$$P(y_i|\vec{\pi},\Theta) = \sum_{k=1}^{K} \pi_k P(y_i|C_k) + \sum_{j=K+1}^{J} \pi_j P(y_i|\mu_j, \sigma_j) + \pi_{J+1} P(y_i|u) \tag{2}$$

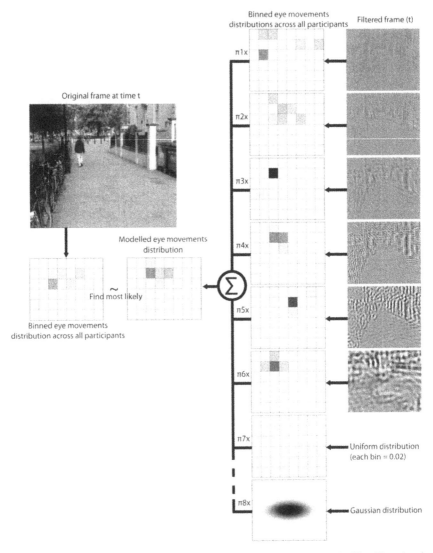

Figure 3.   Mixture model for a single frame. Eye movements collected for each video (filtered and unfiltered) were coarsely binned spatially and temporally. The mixture model represented the fixations to the unfiltered videos as a function of the filtered ones (as well as Gaussian distributions for the more complex models). The EM algorithm then found the weights (π) and the parameters associated with the Gaussians. Parameters were found using all the frames of all the videos.

where the second term of Equation 2 defines the Gaussians mixtures with its two parameters μ, σ (the mean and standard deviation, respectively). The mixture model is now defined not only with the weight vector $\vec{\pi}$, but as well with the parameters Θ, which includes all the Gaussian parameters.

The "world bias" was intended to represent a coordinate system based on the subject's perception of the horizon. We used subjects' estimate of the location of the horizon line as the basis of the world coordinate system. To estimate this, three observers were asked to view all six videos and, using a mouse, to mark at all times their best estimate of the horizon line. This was done using a purpose-built programme. A horizontal line was overlaid on top of the video while the film was being played to show were the mouse was pointing and, for better accuracy, the videos were shown at half their real speed (25 fps). All three observers had a very similar view on the location of the horizon line for all six videos (as it was quite often easy to judge). The mean estimate of the three observers of the horizon line was used for later analysis. The horizon line position was used as an anchor for the Gaussian mixture representing the world coordinate system in the mixture model.

To identify the optimal mixing fractions (π) and the parameters associated with the Gaussians distributions representing the world and screen biases (Θ), the values that maximized the log likelihood were found. This was done using the Expectation Maximization (EM) algorithm (Dempster, Laird, & Rubin, 1977), which is a well-established general algorithm to estimate maximum likelihood solution when the likelihood functions include latent variables.

The EM algorithm alternates between two steps: The Expectation step (E-step), where it computes the expected likelihood for the complete data set for a certain value of the latent variables (the Q function), and a Maximization step (M-step), where it reestimates all the parameters by maximizing the Q function. Once a new set of parameters is found, a new E-step is computed. This process continues until the maximum likelihood converges. The EM algorithm is only guaranteed to find a local maxima of the likelihood, so we ran the algorithm with multiple initial conditions. All were found to converge to the same solution and we believe that there are no significant local minima for this problem.

In Equation 1, the EM algorithm only computed the mixture weights (π), whereas in Equation 2 the means and standards deviation parameters (Θ) of the Gaussian distributions associated with the screen and world coordinates were also estimated.

To compute the similarity between the fixation distributions across the different conditions, we calculated the Pearson's product moment correlation between the distributions, averaged over time. If the fixation distributions for two similarly filtered videos are more alike than those obtained from videos where the filtering varied widely, this will be revealed by this statistic.

Results

We first calculated the spatial-temporal probability distribution of subjects' fixations to both the unfiltered and filtered videos, and found the optimal combination of the filtered image generated fixations to recreate the fixations observed when watching the unfiltered video. The "image salience" and "world salience" hypotheses should generate very different predictions about these distributions.

More importantly, because of the pattern of motions induced by people walking down the street, there will be much more high temporal/low spatial frequency energy in the periphery, and more low temporal/high spatial frequency information at the centre of the screen. This, together with the low level image statistics being more alike, would lead us to predict that fixation distributions from similar filtered images will be more similar than those from images filtered with very dissimilar filters (the distributions of fixations generated when observing videos filtered in Conditions 1 and 2 (Figure 2), will be more similar than those generated when observing videos filtered in Conditions 1 and 6 for instance).

This contrasts with a very different set of predictions from the "world salience" hypothesis. In this case, despite drastically different visual stimuli, all video sequences will signal the same behavioural significance and hence have the same level of salience: The fixation distributions for the high passed filtered images would be to similar locations in the low passed videos. Second, the information that allows us to infer what is going on in the world will generate similar fixations. Besides some roll off at high and low temporal and spatial frequencies due to the effects of the contrast modulation function, all filtered video distributions will contribute to describing the unfiltered video distributions.

As shown in Table 1, the saccade distributions were as similar for images viewed with very different filtering and very similar filtering. The relatively low correlation coefficients ($r=.425$) found are probably due to the fact that the estimates of the probability distributions for each time period were based only on a small number of samples (sampling noise will systematically lower the observed correlations).

We computed the correlation coefficients between the probability distributions resulting from subjects viewing each filter bank,to compare the similarity of fixations in filtered clips that are close to each others' (e.g., filter condition 1 and 2) than far from each other (e.g., filter condition 1 and 6). As can be seen in Figure 4, the pattern observed strongly favours a world saliency interpretation, where similarity in the world is more important than similarity in features in determining where we look, $r = -.101$, $p = .6$.

This interpretation is also supported by the mixture weights shown in Figure 5 where each filtered condition contribute significantly towards

TABLE 1
Pearson's correlation coefficients between all the coarsely binned probability
distributions observed when the subjects viewed the six filtered videos

	Condition 2	Condition 3	Condition 4	Condition 5	Condition 6
Condition 1	.465029	.432254	.395177	.384403	.400332
Condition 2	—	.468498	.441618	.424787	.387747
Condition 3	—	—	.472262	.458009	.413949
Condition 4	—	—	—	.444826	.440933
Condition 5	—	—	—	—	.4526

Widely differing filtering results in similar levels of correlation to neighbouring ones. This is what
we would expect if world salience rather than low level feature salience was driving the system.

describing the fixations to the unfiltered film. The eye movements when
viewing the Condition 5 video are more similar to those to the unfiltered
video, simply because we believe this condition (because of the contrast
modulation function) lets more information in.

We then explored the role of adding two high level reference frames; one
consisting of a Gaussian distribution in a screen-based coordinate system,
and one of a Gaussian distribution in a world-based coordinate system

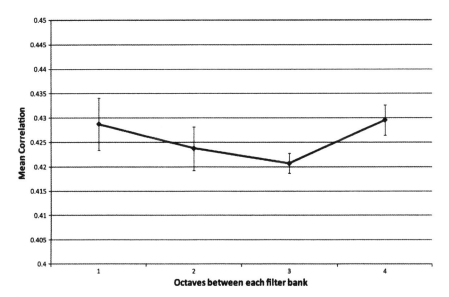

Figure 4. Mean correlations coefficients between each filter conditions for different bank distances
(e.g., one octave as described in Figure 3 is the difference between filter condition 1 and 2, or 4 and 5;
two octaves is the difference between filter condition 2 and 4; and so on). A regression analysis showed
a nonsignificant effect of the number of octaves between filters and the mean correlations, $r = -.101$,
$p = .6$, meaning that eye movements were made to similar location despite videos having different low
level features. Error bar represent $+/-$ SE (across filtered clips).

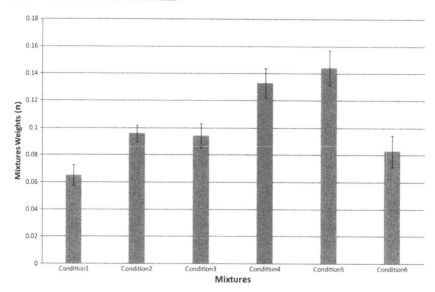

Figure 5. Mixtures weights (π) found by the EM algorithm. The probabilities of eye movements to unfiltered videos are represented in terms of the distribution of eye movement to filtered ones. The uniform distribution mixture is not shown in the graph for clarity but has a weight of 0.38. Error bars are the +/− SE found using a bootstrap procedure.

(expressed relative to the "horizon line"). The results were unambiguous (Figure 7). By far the most important single predictor of fixation density (with a mixing fraction of 36%) is where in the world the fixation is directed (Figure 6). This distribution (7.2 degrees under the perceived horizon line) is slightly shifted to the right as in most of our movies (4.5 out of 6) behaviourally important "content" (people, cars, etc.) was on the right-hand side of the picture (on the left often being buildings). The screen bias, which

Figure 6. Two typical scenes of the stimuli used in Experiments 1 and 2. The horizontal black line represents the horizon as found by the three observers. Linked to it is the Gaussian distribution (as found by the mixture model) representing the "world bias".

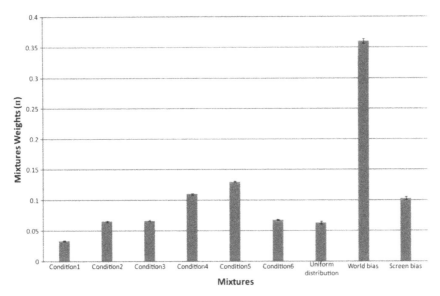

Figure 7.   Mixtures weights (π) found by the EM algorithm when two spatial biases are added. The probabilities of eye movements to unfiltered videos are represented in terms of the distribution of eye movement to filtered ones, and in terms of two Gaussian distributions (one in a screen-based coordinate system and one in a horizon line-based coordinate system). Error bars are the +/- SE calculated using a 10,000 bootstrap procedure.

is often reported in other studies as having a strong impact on fixation patterns (people having a tendency to fixate in the middle of the screen) only accounts for 10.5% of fixation in the unfiltered video. The relative contribution of the six filtered videos does not change when extra mixtures are added: The extra mixtures added assume the role previously taken by the uniform distribution.

Obviously, by adding more and more mixtures to our model, a higher likelihood will be found, even if the additional models do not account for important structure in the data. To take into account this model complexity issue, we used the Bayesian Information Criterion (BIC) to compare the models (this technique attempts to control for the number of free parameters; Schwarz, 1978). Table 2 reports the BIC weights (Wagenmakers & Farrell, 2004), which are broadly speaking a normalization of the BICs across several models, allowing an easy comparison and under some conditions can be interpreted as posterior probabilities. The BIC can be used to choose which of a number of models best accounts for the data and, for the situation tested here, it is clear that the best model only uses the output of the world bias (BIC weight = 0.23) system in combination with the distributions associated with viewing filtered videos. In short, the better

TABLE 2
BIC weights for several mixture models

Mixture used (6 filtered ones +)	BIC weight
Uniform distribution	0.1704
Screen bias	0.1218
World bias	0.2313
Uniform distribution + Screen bias	0.1462
Uniform distribution + World bias	0.1123
Uniform distribution + World bias + Screen bias	0.2180

The preferred model: The best compromise between the fit to the data and the number of degrees of freedom is the one with the highest BIC weight. As it can be seen, the best model ignores the contribution due to screen bias and uses the distributions associated with the world-centred reference frame and those associated with viewing the filtered videos.

fit found by the next best model (including both a uniform distribution and a screen bias) is not justified by the additional parameters needed to achieve it.

These experimental results provide indirect evidence that the most important reference frame used for planning eye movements is one in world, rather than screen, coordinates. This was tested more directly in the second experiment.

EXPERIMENT 2

Method

Procedure.   For this second experiment only the six unfiltered movies were used. Participants watched three films with the tent in the *low* position, and the other three in the *high* position. No participant watched the same movie twice and the displaying order of the movies, as well as the initial position of the box (high or low) was randomized across subjects. After watching the first three movies, participants were asked to leave the room for a few minutes to "get a cup of coffee or some water". This allowed the experimenter to change the tent tilting position without having the participant asking or wondering what was the tent purpose. After the experiment, the experimenter asked informally if they realized that the tent had moved, and all but one did not realize the change in the apparatus setup.

Subjects.   Twelve paid subjects took part in the experiment (of which eight were female). No participant did both experiments and all were naive to the purpose of the research.

Equipment. As for Experiment 1, the same eyetracker with the same settings were used to record the eye movements of the participants. In this experiment a homemade tent was built using aluminium profiles covered with a blue chessboard pattern material (Figure 8). The full size of the box was 220 cm long × 120 cm high × 80 cm wide. Participants were seated 100 cm from the screen, giving a screen size of 21 × 16 degrees. The participant–monitor distance was increased for this experiment to allow the tent to have a greater effect on peripheral vision. The tent was hinged around the screen with two possible settings positions: A *low* setting, where the tent was tilted backwards (20 degrees) to give participants the impression of falling forwards, and a *high* setting, tilted 20 degrees forwards to leave the participant feeling as if they were tilted backwards (Figure 8).

Statistical analysis. In this experiment, we were interested in the effect of the tent on the vertical fixation landings. We compared average vertical fixation positions for all fixations when the videos were viewed in the high tent position, and when the tent was viewed in the low position.

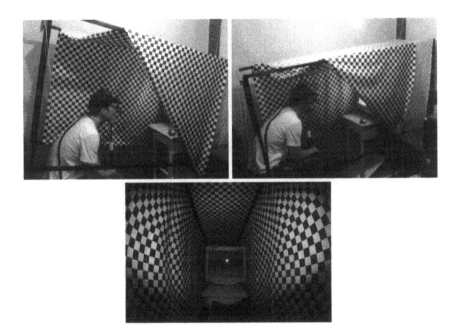

Figure 8. The tent. The pictures show the tent, with its side open, in both positions (high on the left and low on the right). The bottom picture shows the view observed by participants when viewing the monitor. By changing the angle of the tent, the subjects' estimate of vertical was changed. To view this figure in colour, please see the online issue of the Journal.

Results

To provide more direct evidence that the most important reference frame used for planning eye movements is one in world, rather than screen, coordinates, the second experiment recorded eye movements of 12 participants observing the unfiltered video, the only difference between the two different conditions being the presence of a different peripheral cue to vertical (induced by a swivelling tent). Other than this, all aspects of the presentation were identical for the two conditions. None of the participants reported side effects on being inside the tent, other than an unsettling sense of things "not being straight". The screen where the videos were displayed did not move independently of the tent position.

Across movies, a highly statistically significant effect was observed on the average vertical fixation position of fixations across the two conditions (paired t-test between participants), with a difference of means of 0.52 degrees, $SD = 0.16$, $t(11) = 3.213$, $p < .001$. Fixation distributions can be seen in Figure 9. These distributions show clearly the effect of the estimated horizon (as induced by the presence of the tent) on the landing positions. This provides direct evidence that a world-based coordinate system is used in planning fixations since there was no difference in the

Figure 9. Vertical saccade distributions and means of all the participants for a single film (4) overlaid on a single frame. A vertical shift can be observed between the distribution in white (tent in the "high" position) and the distribution in black (tent in the "low" position).

videos viewed, only a peripherally induced difference in the perceived gravitational vertical.

GENERAL DISCUSSION

Our analysis shows two main results. The first is that it is not image salience but world salience (inferred from the visual properties of the world) that drives the gross spatial distribution of fixations. We determined this from the finding that fixation distributions were similar when viewing the same video in different filtered conditions, even when the filtered videos had uncorrelated features. The highest weight of the filtered video (Condition 5) appeared simply to be determined by the spatiotemporal contrast sensitivity function.

The second result is that, for the task studied here, the predominant spatial reference frame used to plan eye movements is world-centred rather than head or body centred. This was demonstrated by the fact that the Bayesian information criterion selected a model that included a world-centred bias (not a screen-based bias), and that a simple manipulation of the subjects' perception of gravitational vertical, whilst leaving all aspects of the experiment identical, was enough to make a sizeable shift in the average vertical eye position.

Insight from why this is happening be can be gained by considering three types of objects present in the studied videos. First, let's consider two objects that are at two extremes of visibility: A flock of seagulls taking off from a green, and the kerb between pavement and road. Although the extreme counter shading of the black-backed gull may be an effective camouflage pattern in a marine environment (Cott, 1940), the high contrast between its white belly and black back is highly visible when flying in a city street. This, together with the large motion signal issued by a bird in flight, means that in terms of any image salience model, particularly one that uses motion, these animals are of extreme salience. Despite this, and although our videos do feature a flock of seagulls taking off, to our surprise, none of our subjects fixated them.

On the other hand, the kerb, marking the boundary between pavement and road, has a low contrast; the materials and colours on both sides of the boundary are similar and there is no movement. Despite this, and unlike a moving seagull, it is vital for us to locate the kerb to avoid falling over. As such, we found that fixations to the kerb were highly frequent.

While watching the videos recreating the visual input people would experience whilst walking down a shopping street, one of the most common "objects" encountered are people. The face is (usually) the most informative region of a person, but subjects fixated people's feet far more often than their faces, and when they did fixate the face, it was almost always within virtual "touching distance". Fixation behaviour here appears to be driven by a compromise between avoiding collisions and, importantly, a social "cost" in making direct eye contact. As anyone who has visited a large British city knows, making direct eye contact at a distance is a strong social signal and, even though our subjects were simply watching videos in a darkened room, the simplest interpretation is that this was sufficient to engage their unconscious visual routines that were, in this case, more appropriate to walking down a street. In such situations, the informational utility of fixating passing people has to be balanced against the social cost of engaging direct eye contact. Though fixating people's feet provides less information about them, it is sufficient for avoiding collision and does not start fights, unwanted sexual advances or social awkwardness. Though less informative, fixating the feet is often more rewarding in the long term.

Before completely dismissing the image salience type frameworks, one consideration should be taken into account. All the analyses presented here were made at a very coarse spatial scale. The screen was split into a 6×8 grid for estimating fixation distributions, so what we were measuring was only the gross distribution of saccades; i.e., do you fixate the person on the right or fixate the ground below, not do you fixate the corner at the edge of the eye or its centre. It may well be that, although the macroscopic structure of fixation distributions is determined by the meaning of the world, the fine, detailed, microscopic structure of fixation distributions may be determined by more simple low level (and fast) image saliency considerations. Despite this, the most important aspect of fixation distributions in natural environments is their gross scale properties, and it is clear that these are, perhaps unsurprisingly, determined by the behavioural relevance of the objects out there rather than the low level features that happen to be associated with them.

The second result we obtained was that high level planning appeared predominantly to be performed in a world-centred representation (which we approximated as one expressed relative to the horizon line). Again, viewing the videos makes clear why any other strategy would be problematic. When walking down the road, due to self motion, almost all retinotopic locations move. The up and down motion caused by walking, the forward movement of the body, and objects that move relative to oneself simply because one is moving, are of less interest than any objects that are actually moving relative to the world. In an egocentric representation, self-generated movement cannot simply be discriminated from the actually moving objects. In contrast, in a world-centred representation, it is potentially easy to discriminate between actually moving objects (that are potentially interesting and should be fixated), from motion signals generated simply from the act of walking (and are hence highly predictable and not worth fixating). Making fixations in such a high level, world-centred representation is computationally demanding, but necessary if one is not to be swamped be the vast number of self-generated motion signals, and still be able to detect and fixate behaviourally relevant objects approaching at high speed.

In the first experiment we established that saccades are a function of the world and that we have a strong bias directly linked to where the horizon was perceived. We pursued this idea in the second experiment by trying to alter the perception of where the horizon is in the videos; not by changing the videos themselves (low level features), but by changing how participants would perceive them. Using a homemade tent, covered with checked material, we created an illusion for participants immersed inside that they were either slightly tilted forwards or backwards depending on the tent position. This significantly changed where participants looked in the video, resulting in saccades half a degree (0.52) vertically higher when the tent was tilted forwards than when it was tilted backwards. This effect once again demonstrates that low level features (same within the videos independently of the tent position) have less effect than the world saliency (which we can alter by changing the way participants watch the video).

This is relevant given the huge amounts of money currently being spent to purchase large, flat-screen television monitors. One of the chief attractions of these monitors is that they can be wall-mounted so as not clutter our living rooms, which often results in screens being positioned much higher than the traditional viewing location of their cathode-ray predecessors. Given the effect of reference frame we have observed, we strongly predict a significant change in where subjects will look on the screen when viewing wall-mounted televisions. This may well affect what we notice and attend to when watching TV, e.g., old re-runs may seem different the second time we view them.

In summary, given our highly foveated visual system, it is very important to point our eyes to informative locations. Object motion is potentially a very important cue to behavioural relevance: A moving object indicates a changing world, and that change represents potential opportunities and risks. Unfortunately, when moving around the world, motion on the retina (or any motion signal in head-based coordinates) is a very unreliable cue to object motion. When we move about, everything in our visual field moves, and the fastest moving locations do not in general correspond to fast moving objects. If we simply fixated fast moving locations we would be continually fixating walls we pass and our hands as we stride though the world. Motion is important, but for it to be worth fixating, we need to distinguish between motion signals generated by our own movement and motion signals generated by moving objects within the world. A retinal representation of movement will not allow this. Perhaps then, it is not surprising that we find evidence that eye movements are planned in a world-centred representation.

Again where we fixate is so important that it cannot be simply directed to locations that are extreme in terms of low level features (in effect what is calculated by most low level salience representations). How informative a location is for the current task is probably a better model (although more difficult to specify for realistic situations), but even this underplays the importance of eye movements. In England, when someone in a pub asks "Are you looking at me?", this is not a question about whether you find the low level features of his face the most visually distinctive, or even if his face provides the most task-related information; he is asking for a fight. A more general conception, based on reward, is required to understand why we look at people sometimes and not at others: Fixations can have very real costs as well as benefits.

REFERENCES

Baddeley, R. J., & Tatler, B. W. (2006). High frequency edges (but not contrast) predict where we fixate: A Bayesian system identification analysis. *Vision Research, 46*(18), 2824–2833.

Buswell, G. (1935). *How people look at pictures: A study of the psychology of perception in art.* Chicago: University of Chicago Press.

Cott, H. B. (1940). *Adaptive coloration in animals.* London: Methuen.

Dempster, A. P., Laird, N. M., & Rubin, D. B. (1977). Maximum likelihood from incomplete data via the EM algorithm. *Journal of the Royal Statistical Society, 39*(1), 1–38.

Einhauser, W., & Konig, P. (2003). Does luminance-contrast contribute to a saliency map for overt visual attention? *European Journal of Neuroscience, 17*(5), 1089–1097. DOI: 10.1046/j.1460-9568.2003.02508.x.

Felsen, G., & Dan, Y. (2005). A natural approach to studying vision. *Nature Neuroscience, 8*(12), 1643–1646. DOI: 10.1038/nn1608.

Foulsham, T., Kingstone, A., & Underwood, G. (2008). Turning the world around: Patterns in saccade direction vary with picture orientation. *Vision Research, 48*(17), 1777–1790. DOI: S0042-6989(08)00281-2.

Foulsham, T., & Underwood, G. (2008). What can saliency models predict about eye movements? Spatial and sequential aspects of fixations during encoding and recognition. *Journal of Vision, 8*(2), 1–17. DOI: 10.1167/8.2.6.

Henderson, J. M. (2003). Human gaze control during real-world scene perception. *Trends in Cognitive Sciences, 7*(11), 498–504.

Itti, L. (2005). Quantifying the contribution of low-level saliency to human eye movements in dynamic scenes. *Visual Cognition, 12*(6), 1093–1123.

Itti, L., & Koch, C. (2001). Computational modelling of visual attention. *Nature Reviews Neuroscience, 2*(3), 194–203.

Kienzle, W., Wichmann, F. A, Scholkopf, B., & Franz, M. O (2007). A nonparametric approach to bottom-up visual saliency. In: B. Schölkopf, J. Platt, & T. Hofmann (Eds.), *Advances in neural information processing systems: Vol. 19. Proceedings of the 2006 conference* (pp. 689–696). Cambridge, MA: MIT Press.

Land, M. F., & Hayhoe, M. (2001). In what ways do eye movements contribute to everyday activities? *Vision Research, 41*(25–26), 3559–3565.

Oliva, A., Torralba, A., Castelhano, M. S., & Henderson, J. M. (2003). Top-down control of visual attention in object detection. In *International conference on Image Processing* (Vol. 1, pp. 253–256). Los Alamitos, CA: IEEE Computer Society Press.

Parkhurst, D., Law, K., & Niebur, E. (2002). Modeling the role of salience in the allocation of overt visual attention. *Vision Research, 42*(1), 107–123.

Parkhurst, D. J., Niebur, E. (2003). Scene content selected by active vision. *Spatial Vision, 16*(2), 125–154. DOI: 12696858.

Patla, A., & Vickers, J. (2003). How far ahead do we look when required to step on specific locations in the travel path during locomotion? *Experimental Brain Research, 148*(1), 133–138. DOI: 10.1007/s00221-002-1246-y.

Rajashekar, U., Cormack, L., & Bovik, A. (2003). Image features that draw fixations. *In International conference on Image Processing* (Vol. 3, pp. 313–316). DOI:1109/ICIP.2003.1247244.

Rajashekar, U., van der Linde, I., Bovik, A., & Cormack, L. (2007). Foveated analysis of image features at fixations. *Vision Research, 47*(25), 3160–3172.

Reynolds, D. & Rose, R. (1995). Robust text-independent speaker identification using Gaussian mixture speaker models. *IEEE Transactions on Speech and Audio Processing, 3*(1), 72–83. DOI: 10.1109/89.365379.

Schwarz, G. (1978). Estimating the dimension of a model. *Annals of Statistics, 6*(2), 461–464.

Tatler, B. W. (2007). The central fixation bias in scene viewing: Selecting an optimal viewing position independently of motor biases and image feature distributions. *Journal of Vision, 7*(14), 4.

Tatler, B. W., Baddeley, R. J., & Gilchrist, I. D. (2005). Visual correlates of fixation selection: Effects of scale and time. *Vision Research, 45*(5), 643–659.

Tatler, B. W., & Vincent, B. T. (2008). Systematic tendencies in scene viewing. *Journal of Eye Movement Research, 2*(2), 5, 1–18.

Vitu, F., Kapoula, Z., Lancelin, D., & Lavigne, F. (2004). Eye movements in reading isolated words: Evidence for strong biases towards the center of the screen. *Vision Research, 44*(3), 321–338.

Wagenmakers, E. J., & Farrell, S. (2004). AIC model selection using Akaike weights. *Psychonomic Bulletin and Review, 11*(1), 192–196.

Webster, M., de Valois, K., & Switkes, E. (1990). Orientation and spatial-frequency discrimination for luminance and chromatic gratings. *Journal of the Optical Society of America, 7A*(6), 1034–1049.

Yarbus, A. L. (1967). *Eye movements and vision.* New York: Plenum Press.

VISUAL COGNITION, 2009, 17 (6/7), 904–924

Get real! Resolving the debate about equivalent social stimuli

Elina Birmingham

California Institute of Technology, Pasadena, CA, USA

Walter F. Bischof

University of Alberta, Edmonton, Canada

Alan Kingstone

University of British Columbia, Vancouver, Canada

Gaze and arrow studies of spatial orienting have shown that eyes and arrows produce nearly identical effects on shifts of spatial attention. This has led some researchers to suggest that the human attention system considers eyes and arrows as equivalent social stimuli. However, this view does not fit with the general intuition that eyes are unique social stimuli nor does it agree with a large body of work indicating that humans possess a neural system that is preferentially biased to process information regarding human gaze. To shed light on this discrepancy we entertained the idea that the model cueing task may fail to measure some of the ways that eyes are special. Thus rather than measuring the orienting of attention to a location cued by eyes and arrows, we measured the selection of eyes and arrows embedded in complex real-world scenes. The results were unequivocal: People prefer to look at other people and their eyes; they rarely attend to arrows. This outcome was not predicted by visual saliency but it was predicted by the idea that eyes are social stimuli that are prioritized by the attention system. These data, and the paradigm from which they were derived, shed new light on past cueing studies of social attention, and they suggest a new direction for future investigations of social attention.

Keywords: Social attention; Gaze perception; Attentional selection; Cuing paradigm; Scene perception.

Our everyday knowledge suggests that we are very interested in the attention of other people. Indeed, experience suggests that as social beings we are

Please address all correspondence to Elina Birmingham, 1200 E. California Blvd., California Institute of Technology, Pasadena, CA 91125, USA. E-mail: elinab@hss.caltech.edu

© 2009 Taylor & Francis
DOI: 10.1080/13506280902758044

quick to notice when people are looking at us; and when they are not looking at us we are quick to determine what they are looking at. This intuition, that we care about where other people are attending, has led to the birth of research in *social attention.*

Although there are several cues to the direction of another person's attention (e.g., gaze direction, head position, body position, pointing gestures), the above description suggests that gaze direction has a special status as an attentional cue (Emery, 2000; Langton, Watt, & Bruce, 2000). Morphologically, the human eye is equipped to promote fast discrimination of gaze direction, having the highest dark iris-to-white sclera contrast of all the primate eyes (Kobayashi & Koshima, 1997). Humans are not only very accurate at discriminating gaze direction (Cline, 1967; Gibson & Pick, 1963; Lord & Haith, 1974), but we also appear to have neural structures that are preferentially biased for processing gaze information. For instance, single cell recordings in monkeys show that the superior temporal sulcus (STS) has cells that are selective for different gaze directions, independent of head orientation (Perrett et al., 1985); and neuroimaging studies (e.g., Hoffman & Haxby, 2000; Pelphrey, Viola, & McCarthy, 2004) have similarly shown that the human STS seems to be especially activated by changes in gaze direction. Indeed, eye gaze is thought to be so important that it has been placed as the primary social attention cue in prominent models of social attention (Baron-Cohen, 1995; Perrett, Hietanen, Oram, & Benson, 1992).

Perhaps what makes eyes so unique is that in addition to implying where someone's attention is directed, they can be used to infer a wealth of other social information that we use on an everyday basis. For instance, eyes can help us determine what someone is feeling, thinking, or wanting (Baron-Cohen, Baldwin, & Crowson, 1997). Eyes are also used to modulate social interactions, by facilitating conversation turn-taking, exerting social dominance, and signalling social defeat or appeasement (Argyle & Cook, 1976; Dovidio & Ellyson, 1982; Ellsworth, 1975; Exline, 1971; Exline, Ellyson, & Long, 1975; Kendon, 1967; Kleinke, 1986; Lochman & Allen, 1981). Thus, both intuition and empirical evidence suggest that eyes are extremely important and unique social-communicative stimuli.

To measure the unique social importance of eyes, an abundance of research has examined the extent to which gaze direction can trigger an attention shift in others (what is sometimes called "joint attention"). Using the model gaze cueing task it is well-established that infants (Farroni, Johnson, Brockbank, & Simion, 2000; Hood, Willen, & Driver, 1998), preschool children (Ristic, Friesen, & Kingstone, 2002), and adults alike (Driver et al., 1999; Friesen & Kingstone, 1998; Langton & Bruce, 1999) will shift attention automatically to where others are looking. In the typical gaze cueing paradigm a participant is first shown a picture of a real or schematic face with the eyes looking either to the left or to the right. A target is then presented either at the gazed-at location or at the opposite location. The usual finding is that response time (RT) to detect a target is fastest when the target appears at the gazed-at (cued) location, consistent with the notion that attention was shifted there in response to where the gaze cue was looking. Because this effect emerges rapidly and occurs even when gaze direction does not predict where a target is going to appear, it is considered to measure *reflexive* orienting of attention to gaze direction.

This automatic gaze cueing effect was initially thought to be an effect that was unique to gaze, with other, well-learned directional stimuli, like arrows, failing to produce a reflexive attention effect (Jonides, 1981). It was therefore somewhat surprising when Ristic, Friesen and Kingstone (2002) and Tipples (2002) reported in separate investigations that central, spatially nonpredictive arrow cues produce a robust reflexive orienting effect; and Ristic et al. mapped out the time course of this attention effect for eyes and arrows and showed that they were very similar.

A number of subsequent studies have confirmed that the arrow cueing effect is very similar to the gaze cueing effect (e.g., Gibson & Bryant, 2005; Gibson & Kingstone, 2006; Hommel, Pratt, Colzato, & Godijn, 2001; Ristic, Wright, & Kingstone, 2007; see also Eimer, 1997). Indeed, even some of the more subtle attention effects that were initially thought to be unique to gaze cues have now been shown to occur for arrow cues as well. For instance, it was initially thought that only gaze cues produce reflexive orienting to a location despite observers' intention to shift attention volitionally somewhere else (Driver et al., 1999; Friesen, Ristic, & Kingstone, 2004). However, Tipples (2008) has shown convincingly that arrows, too, can produce this reflexive attention effect.

Similarly, brain lesion and neuroimaging studies are equivocal as to whether gaze and arrow cues engage different underlying neural systems. Specifically, although some neuropsychological studies suggest that there are different neural systems for gaze and arrow cueing (Kingstone, Friesen, & Gazzaniga, 2000; Ristic et al., 2002; Vuilleumier, 2002), the neuroimaging findings comparing gaze and arrow cueing are less clear. For instance, there is recent evidence that brain activation differences produced for gaze and arrow cueing may be partly due to the recruitment of different brain areas for visually analyzing gaze and arrow cues, and not necessarily for the subsequent shifts of attention (Hietanen, Nummenmaa, Nyman, Parkkola, & Hämäläinen, 2006; Tipper, Handy, Giesbrecht, & Kingstone, 2008). That is, when physical differences between the cues are controlled, gaze and arrow cues appear to engage the same brain systems (Tipper et al., 2008).

This convergence between gaze and arrow cues extends to overt shifts of attention. Ricciardelli, Bricolo, Aglioti, and Chelazzi (2002) found that when participants were asked to make a speeded eye movement to the left or right of fixation, as indicated by a central square stimulus, correct saccade latencies were fastest when an irrelevant central face gazed in the signalled saccade direction (congruent gaze). A similar effect occurred when an arrow replaced the gaze stimulus. In contrast, although *incongruent gaze* produced unwanted saccades in the incorrect direction, *incongruent arrows* did not. In a follow-up study, Kuhn and Benson (2007) implemented the same saccade paradigm as Ricciardelli et al., but used more traditional, "arrow-like" cues than did Ricciardelli et al. (who used simple arrowheads, e.g., < >). Kuhn and Benson now found that both incongruent gaze and arrow stimuli triggered incorrect saccades; although the response latency for incorrect saccades appeared to be somewhat shorter for gaze than arrow stimuli. Recently, however, this error latency difference between eyes and arrows was found to be unreliable (Kuhn & Kingstone, 2009).

Collectively, the extant data are equivocal with regard to the unique effects of gaze cueing. On the one hand, there are some studies that find subtle differences between gaze cueing and arrow cueing, but on the other hand often these differences are not observed. Overall, the evidence that gaze cueing is unique from arrow cueing is weak. Thus, even though we have an intuition that eye gaze is a special attentional stimulus, behavioural and neural evidence indicates that humans shift their attention in response to eyes and arrows in similar ways, and that this applies to both covert and overt orienting.

The broader implications of this conclusion are not altogether clear. Certainly, the finding that arrow cues produce near identical effects to gaze cues runs counter to our intuition that eyes are unique, special social attention stimuli. However, it could be simply that arrows are also important social stimuli, which explains why they, too, have the same effect on attention as eyes. This potential status of arrows has not been overlooked. For example, Kingstone, Smilek, Ristic, Friesen, and Eastwood (2003) wrote "arrows are obviously very directional in nature, and, like eyes, they have a great deal of social significance. Indeed, it is a challenge to move through one's day without encountering any number of arrows on signs and postings" (p. 178).

An alternative explanation of the data is that the cueing paradigm may be failing to capture key aspects about eyes that distinguish them as special social stimuli from other stimuli, like arrows. In other words, the general intuition that eyes are special is correct but the cueing paradigm may not be measuring what makes eyes distinct from arrows. The cueing paradigm may be merely measuring eyes and arrows on a dimension that they share strongly—their ability to communicate directional information such as left and right (Gibson & Kingstone, 2006). It is like taking a 150-pound person and a 150-pound rock, weighing them, and concluding that they are the same. They are the same, in terms of weight, but there is the intuition that they are not the same in many other ways. To demonstrate that, however, one would need a different way to measure the person and the rock, i.e., a different research approach would be called for. In much the same way, what may be needed in the area of social attention is a different research approach—one that better reflects our intuition that the human attention system cares about eyes in a way that is distinct from other stimuli in the environment. One possible avenue has recently been suggested by Kuhn and Kingstone (2009): "[A]lthough arrows and eye gaze may be of equal relevance when they are presented to the participant in isolation, key differences between social and nonsocial cues may only become apparent when they are embedded within a richer environment."

AN ALTERNATIVE RESEARCH APPROACH

An alternative approach for studying social attention is provided by considering the different components of attention that can be measured in experiments involving social stimuli. Rather than examining the orienting of attention in response to a cue (i.e., orienting *from* the cue to where the cue is pointing), we propose to study the selection of the cue itself (i.e., orienting *to* the cue). Consider a real-world example of social attention: You are riding a bicycle on campus and notice that your colleague is standing on the sidewalk and looking at something on the ground. Using her gaze direction, you orient your attention to see what she is looking at. It is clear from this example that there are at least two distinct stages of social attention: First, you select (orient to) your colleague's eyes as a key social stimulus, and, second, you orient your attention from her eyes to select the location/object that she is looking at. Importantly, cueing studies with central symbolic cues are specifically designed to test only one of these attentional components: Orienting in response to the cue. The *selection* of the cue is relatively trivial within the context of the cueing paradigm because the cue, that is, a gaze, arrow, word, or number stimulus, is presented at central fixation and typically in advance of the target object (Gibson & Kingstone, 2006). That is, the experimenter essentially *preselects* the cue and places it at fixation (the current focus of attention). As we found in the preceding section, when this selection process is omitted, the prevailing literature indicates that eyes and arrows are given equal priority by the attention system. Does this equivalence hold, however, when the *selection* of social cues is measured? In other words, will eyes and arrows be given equal priority when participants are provided with the opportunity to select them from a complex visual scene?

The aim of the present study was to examine whether this equivalence between eyes and arrows will hold when the *selection* component of social attention is measured. Specifically, will eyes and arrows be given equal priority when participants are provided with the opportunity to freely select stimuli from a complex real-world visual scene?

The fact that no studies have compared the selection of eyes versus arrows in complex settings is noteworthy given the strong tradition of research on selective attention (e.g., Broadbent, 1958, 1972; Deutsch & Deutsch, 1963; James, 1890; Moray, 1959; Neisser, 1967; Treisman, 1960). The basic assumption behind all these conceptualizations of selective attention is that humans possess a capacity limitation when it comes to handling information in the world. The implication of this capacity limitation is that we must select some items for processing at the expense of others (hence the term selective attention). Research on scene perception has consistently shown that when presented with a complex scene, observers tend to select (fixate) items that are informative (Buswell, 1935; Henderson, Weeks, & Hollingworth, 1999; Loftus & Mackworth, 1978; Yarbus, 1965/ 1967). When people are absent from visual scenes, this means that observers will look primarily at objects that add semantic meaning to the scene and scene regions with high amounts of visual information (Antes, 1974; Buswell, 1935; Henderson et al., 1999; Loftus & Mackworth, 1978). When people are present in a scene, observers look primarily at the eyes and faces of the people and devote less attention to the rest of the scene (Birmingham, Bischof, & Kingstone, 2007, 2008a, 2008b; Yarbus, 1965/1967). This suggests that when a person is presented in a scene, their eyes become important to understanding the scene. We have interpreted these findings as indicating that people fixate the eyes of others because they perceive the eyes to contain important social information. In support of this, observers' preference for eyes is enhanced by social tasks (e.g., describe where people in the scene are directing their attention) and by increasing the social content and activity of a scene (e.g., increasing the number of people actively doing something (Birmingham et al., 2008b). Thus, there is evidence suggesting that observers preferentially select gaze information from a complex scene, and that this reflects the fact that eyes are perceived to be informative social stimuli.

However, no studies have tested whether gaze would be preferentially selected if an arrow were also placed in the scene. Research using the cueing paradigm indicates that eyes and arrows are equivalent attentional cues, and that this reflects the fact that arrows, like eyes, are socially significant. One possible outcome then is that eyes and arrows will be selected to the same extent. An alternative possibility is that eyes will be preferentially selected over arrows. This finding would suggest that eyes and arrows do not have equal social relevance, and would dovetail with the general intuition that while eyes and arrows are both directional, eyes are unique in that they can communicate other social information, such as the emotion, intention, state of mind, and ages of other people. As such, eyes may be prioritized by the attention system. This outcome is not predicted by past gaze and arrow cueing studies.

METHOD

The present study examined the extent to which eyes and arrows are selected from complex scenes. We presented a variety of photographs of real-world scenes containing both people and arrows, and monitored observers' eye movements while they freely viewed the scenes. This allowed us to determine how often, and how quickly, observers select eyes and arrows.

Participants

Fifteen undergraduate students from the University of British Columbia participated in this experiment. All had normal or corrected to normal vision, and were naïve to the purpose of the experiment. Each participant received course credit for participation in a 1-hour session.

Apparatus

Eye movements were monitored using an Eyelink II tracking system. The online saccade detector of the eyetracker was set to detect saccades with an amplitude of at least $0.5°$, using an acceleration threshold of $9500°/s^2$ and a velocity threshold of $30°/s$.

Stimuli

Full colour photographs were collected from various sites on the World Wide Web.

Each picture was presented on a white 800×600 pixel canvas. Thus, in some cases, a picture that was slightly smaller than 800×600 pixels was surrounded by the white borders of the canvas. Image (canvas) size was 36.5×27.5 cm, corresponding to $40.1° \times 30.8°$ at the viewing distance of

---

Figure 1 (opposite).   Left: The scenes used in the experiment. A–C: Scenes with eyes and arrows; D–F: Scenes with large arrows; G: Scene without people. Middle: Overlays from all observers' fixations. There was a clear preference for the people in the scene, particularly their faces and eyes. Fewer fixations went to the arrows. Right: Saliency maps for each scene, with first fixations from all observers. First fixations tended to land on the nonsalient areas of the scene (black in the saliency map). To view this figure in colour, please see the online issue of the Journal.

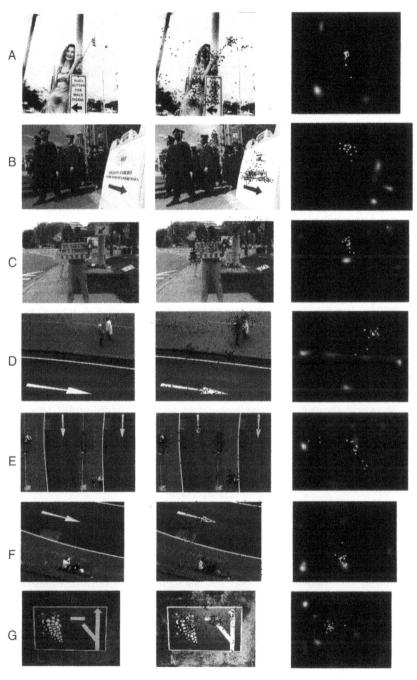

Figure 1 (*see caption opposite*)

50 cm. Twenty-three images were used in the present experiment: Six images contained both people and arrows, one image contained arrows but no people, and 16 remaining "filler" images were displayed (containing photographs of people, faces, and paintings). The critical seven arrow images analysed in the present experiment are shown in Figure 1 (left column).

Procedure

Participants were seated in a brightly lit room, and were placed in a chinrest so that they sat approximately 50 cm from the display computer screen. Participants were told that they would be shown several images, each one appearing for 15 s, and that they were to simply look at these images.

Before beginning the experiment, a calibration procedure was conducted. Participants were instructed to fixate a central black dot, and to follow this dot as it appeared at nine fixed locations on the screen in a random order. This calibration was then validated, a procedure that calculates the difference between the calibrated gaze position and target position and corrects for this error in future gaze position computations. After successful calibration and validation, the scene trials began.

At the beginning of each trial, a fixation point was displayed in the centre of the computer screen in order to correct for drift in gaze position. Participants were instructed to fixate this point and then press the spacebar to start a trial. The 23 pictures were shown in random order. Each picture was shown in the centre of the screen and remained visible until 15 s had passed, after which the picture was replaced with the drift correction screen.

RESULTS

Data handling

In keeping with previous reports (e.g., Birmingham et al., 2008a, 2008b; Smilek, Birmingham, Cameron, Bischof, & Kingstone, 2006) the data were handled in the following manner. For each image, an outline was drawn around each region of interest (e.g., "eyes", "arrow") and each region's pixel coordinates and area were recorded. We defined the following regions in this manner: Eyes, heads, bodies (including arms, torso, and legs), arrows,[1] and "other".

---

[1] We also conducted an analysis using just the heads of the arrows, which some might argue contain the most information. The pattern of results remained the same as what is reported here.

To determine what regions were of most interest to observers we computed *fixation proportions* by dividing the number of fixations for a region by the total number of fixations over the whole display. We corrected for area differences between regions and across scenes to control for the fact that large regions would, by chance alone, receive more fixations than small regions. This was accomplished by dividing the proportion score for each region by its area. These area-normalized data are shown in Table 1. Table 1 also shows the raw fixation proportions (not area-corrected). Note that although we analyse the area-normalized data, all the key significant effects are replicated when the uncorrected data are analysed, i.e., the significant preference to select eyes over arrows in people scenes, and to select other objects rather than arrows in the nonpeople scene.

To determine where observers' initial saccades landed in the visual scene, we computed the number of first fixations that landed in a region (*initial fixations*). The initial fixation was the first fixation made after the experimenter-controlled fixation at screen centre. These data were not area-corrected and are shown in Table 1.

To determine whether low-level properties of the scene—that is, *visual saliency*—could account for where observers committed their first fixation to the scene, we computed saliency maps according to Itti and Koch's (2000) model. Itti and Koch measure visual saliency of an image by identifying strong changes in intensity, colour, and local orientation. We used the Saliency Toolbox (Walther & Koch, 2005, 2006). As visual saliency has been hypothesized to have its greatest impact on the first saccade (Henderson et al., 1999; Parkhurst, Law, & Niebur, 2002; although see Tatler, Baddeley, & Gilchrist, 2005, for evidence that this is not the case), we focused our analysis on initial fixations.

We computed the average saliency of fixated scene locations and compared this to the average saliency of random locations sampled from the smoothed probability distribution of all first-fixation locations from participants' eye movement data across all scenes. This control value was chosen to account for the known bias to fixate the lower central regions of scenes (see Tatler, 2007, for more on the central fixation bias). This comparison allowed us to determine whether the saliency model accounted for first fixation position above what would be expected by chance.

Fixation proportions

Scenes with eyes and arrows.   Our main question of interest was whether eyes and arrows would be fixated to the same extent. Thus, we analysed the images containing both eyes and arrows, i.e., images with people who were large enough for the observer to see the eye region (Figure 1, A–C). The middle column of Figure 1(A–C) shows fixation plots for all subjects for

TABLE 1
Proportion of all fixations landing in each region (fixation proportions:
area-normalized and nonnormalized), and proportion of all first
fixations landing in each region (initial fixations)

Scene type	Region	Fixation proportion (area-normalized)	Fixation proportion (nonnormalized)	Initial fixations (nonnormalized)
Eyes and arrows	Eyes	0.45	0.09	0.20
	Heads	0.23	0.14	0.20
	Bodies	0.05	0.19	0.13
	Text	0.21	0.32	0.22
	Arrow	0.05	0.01	0.00
	Other	0.01	0.25	0.24
Large arrows	Heads	0.51	0.09	0.07
	Bodies	0.33	0.20	0.40
	Bench	0.09	0.09	0.13
	Arrow	0.05	0.08	0.00
	Other	0.02	0.54	0.40
No people	No-entry	0.53	0.26	0.07
	Grapes	0.27	0.37	0.93
	Arrow	0.17	0.11	0.00
	Other	0.03	0.26	0.00

these three images. Immediately noticeable from these plots is that observers concentrated their fixations primarily on the people, particularly their eyes. Observers rarely fixated the arrows.

To confirm these impressions, we conducted a repeated measures ANOVA on the area-normalized fixation proportions (see Table 1) with region (eyes, heads, bodies, text, arrows, and "other"—the remainder of the scene) as a factor. This analysis revealed a highly significant effect of region, $F(5, 70) = 50.98$, $p < .0001$. Pairwise comparisons (Tukey-Kramer multiple comparisons test) revealed that observers fixated the eyes more than any other region ($p < .05$). The next most frequently fixated regions were heads and text, which were fixated more than bodies and arrows, and the rest of the scene, $ps < .05$. Confirming our impression from Figure 1, arrows were not fixated often in these scenes. Thus, to answer the main question of our study, eyes were fixated more frequently than arrows, which were hardly fixated at all.

Scenes with larger arrows.   One might wonder if observers failed to show a preference for arrows in the previous analysis because they were relatively inconspicuous given that they were smaller than the people in the scene (Figure 1, scenes A–C). To address this issue we analysed three other scenes in which the arrows were large and the people were small (indeed, their eyes were not clearly visible, Figure 1, D–F). Fixation plots for these images are shown in Figure 1 (D–F, middle column). Again, it is immediately noticeable that observers focused mostly on the people, particularly the heads of the people, and that few fixations were committed to the arrows. Even the empty bench in Scene E, where people would be expected, seemed to receive more fixations than the arrows in the scene. For these scenes, we analysed fixation proportions as a function of region (heads, bodies, bench, arrows, other). Note that the eyes were not visible because the people were small (also because of the viewing angle) and thus eyes were not analysed. The ANOVA revealed an effect of region, $F(4, 56) = 83.62$, $p < .00001$, with heads being fixated more than any other region (Tukey Kramer, $p < .05$). Bodies were the next most fixated, and more so than benches, arrows, and other items, all $ps < .05$ (see Table 1). Thus, despite their very large size, arrows were again fixated infrequently relative to the people. Note that as the data are *proportions* of fixations as a function of region, one cannot directly compare the data for Scenes D–F to Scenes A–C, as the content of the scenes (and thus the regions of interest) are not constant; however, it is unequivocal that in all cases fixations were committed preferentially to eyes when they were available, and frequently to heads when eyes were not available; and in all cases fixations were rarely committed to arrows.

Scenes with no people. The results thus far have demonstrated that observers care very little about arrows placed in scenes containing people. It appears that as social beings, observers allocate their attention primarily to other people, particularly their eyes and heads. What happens when no people are in the scene? Given that arrows have been thought of as socially relevant objects (Kingstone et al., 2003; Tipples, 2002), would they receive preferential attention when placed among other objects when there are no people present? We analysed the data for the scene in Figure 1(G). For the analysis the scene was parsed into four regions: The "no-entry" sign, the drawing of grapes, the arrow, and other (remaining items of the scene). The fixation plot in Figure 1(G) shows that relative to the no-entry sign and the grapes, the arrow was fixated infrequently. The data are summarized in Table 1. An ANOVA on the fixation proportions revealed an effect of region, $F(3, 42) = 135.78$, $p < .00001$, with pairwise comparisons revealing that observers looked more at the no-entry sign than any other region (Tukey-Kramer, $p < .05$). The next most fixated region was "grapes", which was fixated more than the arrow, $p < .05$. All three of these regions were fixated more often than the remainder of the image (other), $p < .05$ when area-normalized. These data suggest that observers show little interest in the arrow relative to other main scene items.

Initial fixations

Scenes with eyes and arrows.   Although the fixation proportions showed that eyes were fixated more frequently than arrows, these were computed over the entire viewing period. Thus, the analyses of fixation proportions might reflect more voluntary or strategic viewing patterns that developed over time. The very first fixation, on the other hand, reveals which regions attract attention immediately upon the appearance of the scene. We reasoned that if arrows capture attention as strongly as eyes, then this would be reflected in the first fixation being just as likely to land on an arrow as an eye region. Thus, we analysed the proportion of first fixations (the first fixation after the experimenter-controlled fixation at centre) that landed on eyes, heads, bodies, arrows, or other (see Table 1). These data were not area normalized. There was a significant effect of region, $F(5, 70) = 3.61, p < .01$, with eyes, heads, text, and the remainder of the scene all equally likely to receive the first fixation, and all more likely than the arrow, which never received the first fixation (Tukey-Kramer, $p < .05$).

Scenes with larger arrows.   Larger arrows were also never fixated first (Table 1). An ANOVA revealed an effect of region, $F(4, 56) = 9.33, p < .0001$. Bodies and other were both most likely to get the first fixation, more so than any other region, (Tukey-Kramer, $p < .05$). As with scenes containing smaller arrows, larger arrows never received the first fixation.

Scenes with no people.   An ANOVA revealed an effect of region (no-entry, grapes, arrow, other), $F(3, 42) = 70.38, p < .0001$. The grapes were highly likely to be fixated first, and more so than the no-entry sign (Tukey-Kramer, $p < .05$). The arrow and the rest of the scene were never fixated first.

Visual saliency

Saliency of the location of subjects' first fixations was compared to a chance-based estimate (called *biased-random*) that takes into account the bias to fixate the lower central regions of the scene. Figure 1 (right column) shows all observers' first fixations overlaid on the saliency maps of each image. To determine whether the saliency model accounted for first fixation position above what would be expected by chance, nonparametric statistics (Mann-Whitney U tests) were performed to compare the medians of *fixated* saliency and *biased-random* saliency.

The fixated saliency was very low (0.0022), and was no different from biased-random saliency (0.0027, $p > .50$). Thus, saliency at fixated locations was no higher than would be expected by chance. In fact, observers generally fixated nonsalient regions in the scenes. Figure 1 demonstrates this nicely, showing that fixations tended to land on the black parts of the saliency map.

DISCUSSION

The aim of present study was to determine whether eyes and arrows are selected to the same extent within complex scenes. Although cueing studies have found that observers orient in response to central directional gaze and arrow cues in similar ways, these studies do not inform us whether the attentional system *selects* eyes and arrows to the same extent.

One possibility was that observers might select arrows as often as eyes. This would be consistent with research using the cueing paradigm showing that gaze and arrows are equivalent attentional cues, suggesting that they may be of equal social relevance. An alternative possibility was that eyes would be preferentially selected over arrows. This finding would suggest that eyes and arrows do not have equal social relevance, and would be in line with the general intuition that while eyes and arrows are equivalent at conveying directional information, eyes are special social stimuli because, for example, unlike arrows, they can communicate other important social information about people such as their age, identity, emotions, and inner attentional states. As such, one would expect humans to prioritize information from eyes over arrows.

The results of the present study were clear. When both eyes and arrows were visible in a scene, the majority of fixations went to the eyes, and very few went to the arrows (Table 1). Furthermore, an analysis of the first fixations made in the scenes revealed that observers never fixated an arrow first. Instead, participants were equally likely to fixate the eyes, heads, and text on the first fixation. This finding suggests that when people are presented with scenes containing eyes and arrows, eyes (and heads and text) capture attention but arrows do not. Moreover, we found that when observers are provided with extended periods of time to view natural scenes, they continue to show interest in the people, particularly their eyes, and continue to essentially ignore the arrows.

A general preference for people persisted in scenes in which the arrow was large and the people were small. We were interested in whether making the arrow large in comparison to the people, and reducing the eye information in the scene, would enable arrows to be prioritized. However, in those images, the arrows were again rarely fixated. Instead, the heads were fixated the most frequently overall. Again, the arrows were never fixated first. Thus, even when arrows were large, and eyes were unavailable, arrows did not receive many fixations overall relative to the people in the scene.

We were also interested in exploring whether an arrow would be preferentially selected when placed in a scene without people. Given that arrows have been thought of as social tools (Kingstone et al., 2003), one might expect them to receive more attention than other, presumably less social objects (as intuited, for instance, from the gaze/arrow cueing literature). Thus, we showed an image of a road sign with other graphic components (a "no-entry" symbol and a bunch of grapes). However, the data revealed that observers again fixated the arrow less often than the other elements of the scene. In addition, the arrow was never fixated first, but the grapes often were. Thus, although this is a single scene, the initial data suggest that even when arrows are placed within a scene without people, they do not receive much attention,

Finally, we analysed the contribution of visual saliency to observers' fixation placement. The saliency at fixated locations was remarkably low, and no higher than what would be expected by chance. This agrees with other recent studies suggesting that visual saliency provides a poor account of eye fixation patterns in complex visual scenes (Cerf, Harel, Einhäuser, & Koch, 2008; Henderson, Brockmole, Castelhano, & Mack, 2007; Nystrom & Holmqvist, 2008; Tatler, 2007; Torralba, Oliva, Castelhano, & Henderson, 2006), particularly when the task is active. In fact, it appears that task demands can completely override the effects of visual saliency in complex visual displays (Einhauser, Rutishauser, & Koch, 2008; Foulsham & Underwood, 2008; Nystrom & Holmqvist, 2008; Rothkopf, Ballard, & Hayhoe, 2007).

Before we move onto the implications of these findings, we must note some of the limitations of our study that warrant future investigation. For instance, the small number of test images along with our choice of filler images, which all contained at least one person but no arrows, could have biased observers' viewing behaviour to look at the people. However, we do not believe that this was driving observers' fixations, as we have shown in previous work that observers show a strong bias to look at the eyes when people and nonpeople images are interleaved (Birmingham, Bischof, & Kingstone, 2007). It is also noteworthy that in the real world one is repeatedly exposed to images of people and real people alike. Indeed, if anything one might reasonably make the argument that by repeatedly presenting images containing arrows to our participants we risked over-estimating how often observers normally select arrows. While that concern does not seem to have manifested itself in the present study, the traditional model cueing paradigm, which normally preselects and presents an arrow stimulus to observers for hundreds of trials, does seem vulnerable to concerns of this nature.

There are several important implications of the present findings. First, to answer the main question of the study, when eyes and arrows are presented within complex scenes and observers are allowed to select items for further processing, observers show a profound preference to select eyes rather than arrows. This is consistent with the neural evidence that humans possess brain mechanisms that are preferentially biased to processing eyes (e.g., Hoffman & Haxby, 2000; Pelphrey et al., 2004; Perrett et al., 1985). Thus, although eyes and arrows are equally good at conveying directional information, and hence produce equivalent effects on shifts of spatial attention within the cueing paradigm, they are not given equal priority by the attention system via selection within complex scenes. On the contrary, observers show a bias to select information from people's eyes.

Second, arrows were not only selected less often than eyes, they were typically selected less often than most other scene regions. This was true even when the arrows were large, and when people were absent from the scene. What makes this finding interesting is that even though it is clear that an arrow will produce reflexive shifts of attention within the context of the cueing paradigm, observers show very little interest in arrows within the context of complex scenes. One interpretation of these findings is that the importance of arrows as social communicative tools may be restricted to situations in which direction or location information is task-relevant (e.g., following an exit sign on the highway; determining which lane is the turning lane, etc.). Indeed, the cueing paradigm is just that—a situation in which the task is to detect a target at a location on the screen. There, even though arrow direction is not spatially informative about where the target will appear, spatial location is a task-relevant dimension, i.e., the only factor over which the target may vary is its spatial position, and the only factor over which the cue may vary is whether it is spatially congruent or incongruent with the target. That said, it may be worthwhile for future studies to map out fixation performance to eyes and arrows within complex scenes under task instructions that emphasize either gaze or arrows in order to determine if, when, and for how long, observers demonstrate a selection bias for arrows. Based on previous work that has shown that people have a profound bias to look at eyes and heads regardless of task instruction (Birmingham et al., 2008b; Cerf et al., 2008), it is possible that any selection bias for arrows may be fleeting.

A third implication of the present study is that despite a general preference to select people from complex scenes, there appears to be a hierarchy to the selection of "people parts". If the people are large enough so that the eyes are visible, observers will concentrate their fixations on the eyes, followed by the heads, and then the bodies. If the people are too small for the eyes to be discriminated, then observers will concentrate their fixations on the heads, followed by the bodies. Thus, although there is a general preference for people, observers preferentially fixate the eyes if they are available, then heads, then bodies. This is consistent with Perrett et al.'s (1992) model of social attention, in which gaze is at the top of a hierarchy of social attention cues, followed by head position, and then body position.

Fourth, in light of the data indicating an enormous preference to select eyes over arrows, we can return to our initial consideration of the cueing literature, which indicates that eyes and arrows are equivalent social cues. This position must be rejected. We favour the alternative view that the similarity between gaze and arrow cues within the cueing paradigm occurs because the cueing paradigm is not measuring much of what makes eyes and arrows different. Indeed, because similar cueing effects are found for gaze, arrows, words (Hommel et al., 2001), wagging tongues (Downing, Dodds, & Bray, 2004), and even eyes and arrows drawn within a gloved hand (Quadflieg, Mason, & Macrae, 2004), it appears that the cueing paradigm may measure how well different cues convey directional information. In other words, working from the basic intuition that eyes are very different social stimuli from arrows, one may conclude that the similarity found between eyes and arrows in the cueing paradigm tells us about the limitations of the cueing paradigm rather than the social equivalence of eyes and arrows.

We do not mean to suggest that using the cueing paradigm to study the orienting of attention in response to gaze direction is necessarily unimportant. However, it may be the case that the cueing paradigm is not measuring how this process occurs in the real world, where different stimuli are embedded in rich social contexts and compete for selection. We propose that a more favourable research approach is one that tries to measure social attention in more real-world settings. For instance, Kuhn and Land (2006) showed that the vanishing ball illusion, in which a ball is perceived to have vanished in mid-air, relies strongly on social attention cues from the magician performing the trick. That is, when the magician pretends to toss a ball upwards but secretly conceals the ball in the palm of his hand, observers are much more likely to perceive the ball travelling upward and vanishing when the magician looks upwards with the fake toss than when he looks down at his hand. Furthermore, on real throws on which the ball is physically present, instead of simply tracking the ball with their eyes, observers often make fixations to the magician's face before looking at the ball. This suggests that observers select information about the magician's attention in order to predict the position of the ball. Kuhn and Land's study thus provides an excellent example of how social attention, both with regard to *orienting to (selecting) social cues* and *orienting in response to social cues*, can be studied successfully using rich, complex stimuli.

Furthermore, it would certainly be advantageous to move from eye monitoring people while they view *images* of people to eye monitoring people while they view *real* people. By definition, images of people cannot attend to the observer while the observer is attending to them. This stands in sharp contrast to many situations in real life. There is some intriguing initial research that has begun to examine the effects of social attention in real-world settings (e.g., Gullberg, 2002; Kuhn & Tatler, 2005; Tatler & Kuhn, 2007). For example, recent work has shown that the effect of misdirection in a cigarette magic trick (occurring when the magician looks at one hand while secretly dropping a cigarette with the other, giving the impression that the cigarette has "vanished") is stronger in live demonstrations than in videotaped demonstrations (Kuhn, Tatler, Findlay, & Cole, 2008). Such findings suggest that eye gaze is a more powerful social attention stimulus in the real world than in images of the real world. This possibility opens up an enormous range of questions that investigations of social attention will most certainly begin to explore.

REFERENCES

Antes, J. R. (1974). The time course of picture viewing. *Journal of Experimental Psychology, 103*(1), 62–70.

Argyle, M., & Cook, M. (1976). *Gaze and mutual gaze.* Cambridge, UK: Cambridge University Press.

Baron-Cohen, S. (1995). *Mindblindness: An essay on autism and theory of mind.* Cambridge, MA: MIT Press.

Baron-Cohen, S., Baldwin, D. A., & Crowson, M. (1997). Do children with autism use the speaker's direction of gaze strategy to crack the code of language? *Child Development, 68,* 48–57.

Birmingham, E., Bischof, W. F., & Kingstone, A. (2007). Why do we look at eyes? *Journal of Eye Movement Research, 1*(1), 1–6.

Birmingham, E., Bischof, W. F., & Kingstone, A. (2008a). Gaze selection in complex social scenes. *Visual Cognition, 16*(2/3), 341–355.

Birmingham, E., Bischof, W. F., & Kingstone, A. (2008b). Social attention and real world scenes: The roles of action, competition, and social content. *Quarterly Journal of Experimental Psychology, 61*(7), 986–998.

Broadbent, D. E. (1958). *Perception and communication.* London: Pergamon Press.

Broadbent, D. E. (1972). *Decision and stress.* New York: Academic Press.

Buswell, G. T. (1935). *How people look at pictures.* Chicago: University of Chicago Press.

Cerf, M., Harel, J., Einhäuser, W., & Koch, C. (2008). Predicting human gaze using low-level saliency combined with face detection. *Advances in neural information processing systems, 20,* 241–248.

Cline, M. G. (1967). The perception of where a person is looking. *American Journal of Psychology, 80,* 41–50.

Deutsch, J. A., & Deutsch, D. (1963). Attention: Some theoretical considerations. *Psychological Review, 70,* 80–90.

Dovidio, J. F., & Ellyson, S. L. (1982). Decoding visual dominance: Attributions of power based on relative percentages of looking while speaking and looking while listening. *Social Psychology Quarterly, 43,* 106–113.

Downing, P. E., Dodds, C. M., & Bray, D. (2004). Why does the gaze of others direct visual attention? *Visual Cognition, 11,* 71–79.

Driver, J., Davis, G., Ricciardelli, P., Kidd, P., Maxwell, E., & Baron-Cohen, S. (1999). Gaze perception triggers visuospatial orienting by adults in a reflexive manner. *Visual Cognition, 6,* 509–540.

Eimer, M. (1997). Uninformative symbolic cues may bias visual-spatial attention: Behavioral and electrophysiological evidence. *Biological Psychology, 46,* 67–71.

Einhauser, W., Rutishauser, U., & Koch, C. (2008). Task-demands can immediately reverse the effects of sensory-driven saliency in complex visual stimuli. *Journal of Vision, 8*(2), 1–19.

Ellsworth, P. C. (1975). Direct gaze as a social stimulus: The example of aggression. In P. Pliner, L. Krames, & T. Alloway (Eds.), *Nonverbal communication of aggression* (pp. 71–89). New York: Plenum.

Emery, N. J. (2000). The eyes have it: The neuroethology, function and evolution of social gaze. *Neuroscience and Biobehavioral Reviews, 24,* 581–604.

Exline, R. (1971). Visual interaction: The glances of power and preferences. *Nebraska Symposium on Motivation, 19,* 163–206.

Exline, R. V., Ellyson, S. L., & Long, B. (1975). Visual behavior as an aspect of power role relationships. In P. Pliner, L. Krames, & T. Alloway (Eds.), *Nonverbal communication of aggression* (pp. 21–52). New York: Plenum Press.

Farroni, T., Johnson, M. H., Brockbank, M., & Simion, F. (2000). Infants' use of gaze direction to cue attention: The importance of perceived motion. *Visual Cognition, 7,* 705–718.

Foulsham, T., & Underwood, G. (2008). What can saliency models predict about eye movements? Spatial and sequential aspects of fixations during encoding and recognition. *Journal of Vision, 8*(2), 1–17.

Friesen, C. K., & Kingstone, A. (1998). The eyes have it! Reflexive orienting is triggered by nonpredictive gaze. *Psychonomic Bulletin and Review, 5,* 490–495.

Friesen, C. K., Ristic, J., & Kingstone, A. (2004). Attentional effects of counterpredictive gaze and arrow cues. *Journal of Experimental Psychology: Human Perception and Performance, 30,* 319–329.

Gibson, B. S., & Bryant, T. A. (2005). Variation in cue duration reveals top-down modulation of involuntary orienting to uninformative symbolic cues. *Perception and Psychophysics, 67,* 749–758.

Gibson, B. S., & Kingstone, A. (2006). Visual attention and the semantics of space: Beyond central and peripheral cues. *Psychological Science, 17,* 622–627.

Gibson, J. J., & Pick, A. (1963). Perception of another person's looking. *American Journal of Psychology, 76,* 86–94.

Gullberg, M. (2002). Eye movements and gestures in human interaction. In J. Hyönä, R. Radach, & H. Deubel (Eds.), *The mind's eyes: Cognitive and applied aspects of eye movements* (pp. 685–703). Oxford, UK: Elsevier.

Henderson, J. M., Brockmole, J. R., Castelhano, M. S., & Mack, M. (2007). Visual saliency does not account for eye movements during visual search in real-world scenes. In R. van Gompel, M. Fisher, W. Murray, & R. Hill (Eds.), *Eye movement research: Insights into mind and brain.* Oxford, UK: Elsevier.

Henderson, J. M., Weeks, P. A., Jr., & Hollingworth, A. (1999). The effects of semantic consistency on eye movements during scene viewing. *Journal of Experimental Psychology: Human Perception and Performance, 25*(1), 210–228.

Hietanen, J. K., Nummenmaa, L., Nyman, M. J., Parkkola, R., & Hämäläinen, H. (2006). Automatic attention orienting by social and symbolic cues activates different neural networks: An fMRI study. *Neuroimage, 33,* 406–413.

Hoffman, E. A., & Haxby, J. V. (2000). Distinct representations of eye gaze and identity in the distributed human neural system for face perception. *Nature Neuroscience, 3,* 80–84.

Hommel, B., Pratt, J., Colzato, L., & Godijn, R. (2001). Symbolic control of visual attention. *Psychological Science, 12,* 360–365.

Hood, B. M., Willen, J. D., & Driver, J. (1998). Adult's eye trigger shifts of visual attention in human infants. *Psychological Science, 9,* 131–134.

Itti, L., & Koch, C. (2000). A saliency-based search mechanism for overt and covert shifts of visual attention. *Vision Research, 40*, 1489–1506.

James, W. (1890). *Principles of psychology.* New York: Holt.

Jonides, J. (1981). Voluntary versus automatic control over the mind's eye's movement. In T. Field & N. Fox (Eds.), *Attention and performance IX* (pp. 187–203). Hillsdale, NJ: Lawrence Erlbaum Associates, Inc.

Kendon, A. (1967). Some functions of gaze-direction in social interaction. *Acta Psychologica, 26*, 22–63.

Kingstone, A., Friesen, C. K., & Gazzaniga, M.S. (2000). Reflexive joint attention depends on lateralized cortical connections. *Psychological Science, 11*, 159–166.

Kingstone, A., Smilek, D., Ristic, J., Friesen, C. K., & Eastwood, J. D. (2003). Attention, researchers! It's time to pay attention to the real world. *Current Directions in Psychological Science, 12*, 176–180.

Kleinke, C. L. (1986). Gaze and eye contact: A research review. *Psychological Bulletin, 100*, 78–100.

Kobayashi, H., & Kohshima, S. (1997). Unique morphology of the human eye. *Nature, 387*, 767–768.

Kuhn, G., & Benson, V. (2007). The influence of eye-gaze and arrow pointing distractor cues on voluntary eye movements. *Perception and Psychophysics, 69*(6), 966–971.

Kuhn, G., & Kingstone, A. (2009). Look away! Eyes and arrows engage oculomotor responses automatically. *Perception and Psychophysics.*

Kuhn, G., & Land, M. F. (2006). There's more to magic than meets the eye! *Current Biology, 16*(22), R950–R951.

Kuhn, G., & Tatler, B. W. (2005). Magic and fixation: Now you don't see it, now you do. *Perception, 34*(9), 1155–1161.

Kuhn, G., Tatler, B. W., Findlay, J. M., & Cole, G. G. (2008). Misdirection in magic: Implications for the relationship between eye gaze and attention. *Visual Cognition, 16*(2–3), 391–405.

Langton, S. R. H., & Bruce, V. (1999). Reflexive visual orienting in response to the social attention of others. *Visual Cognition, 6*, 541–568.

Langton, S. R. H., Watt, R. J., & Bruce, V. (2000). Do the eyes have it? Cues to the direction of social attention. *Trends in Cognitive Sciences, 4*, 50–58.

Lochman, J. E., & Allen, G. (1981). Nonverbal communication of couples in conflict. *Journal of Research in Personality, 15*, 253–269.

Loftus, G. R., & Mackworth, N. H. (1978). Cognitive determinants of fixation location during picture viewing. *Journal of Experimental Psychology: Human Perception and Performance, 4*(4), 565–572.

Lord, C., & Haith, M. M. (1974). The perception of eye contact. *Perception and Psychophysics, 16*, 413–416.

Moray, N. (1959). Attention in dichotic listening: Affective cues and the influence of instructions. *Quarterly Journal of Experimental Psychology, 11*, 56–60.

Neisser, U. (1967). *Cognitive psychology.* New York: Appleton-Century-Crofts.

Nyström, M., & Homlqvist, K. (2008). Semantic override of low-level features in image viewing—both initially and overall. *Journal of Eye Movement Research, 2*(2), 1–11.

Parkhurst, D., Law, K., & Niebur, E. (2002). Modeling the role of salience in the allocation of overt visual attention. *Vision Research, 42*, 107–123.

Pelphrey, K. A., Viola, R. J., & McCarthy, G. (2004). When strangers pass: Processing of mutual and averted social gaze in the superior temporal sulcus. *Psychological Science, 15*, 598–603.

Perrett, D. I., Hietanen, J. K., Oram, M. W., & Benson, P. J. (1992). Organisation and functions of cells responsive to faces in the temporal cortex. *Philosophical Transactions of the Royal Society of London, Series B, 335*, 23–30.

Perrett, D. I., Smith, P. A. J., Potter, D. D., Mistlin, A. J., Head, A. S., Milner, A. D., & Jeeves, M. A. (1985). Visual cells in the temporal cortex sensitive to face view and gaze direction. *Proceedings of the Royal Society of London: Series B, 223*, 293–317.

Quadflieg, S., Mason, M. F., & Macrae, C. N. (2004). The owl and the pussycat: Gaze cues and visuospatial orienting. *Psychonomic Bulletin and Review, 11*(5), 826–831.

Ricciardelli, P., Bricolo, E., Aglioti, S. M., & Chelazzi, L. (2002). My eyes want to look where your eyes are looking: Exploring the tendency to imitate another individual's gaze. *Neuroreport, 13*(17), 2259–2264.

Ristic, J., Friesen, C. K., & Kingstone, A. (2002). Are eyes special? It depends on how you look at it. *Psychonomic Bulletin and Review, 9*, 507–513.

Ristic, J., Wright, A., & Kingstone, A. (2007). Attentional control and reflexive orienting to gaze and arrow cues. *Psychonomic Bulletin and Review, 14*, 964–969.

Rothkopf, C. A., Ballard, D. H., & Hayhoe, M. M. (2007). Task and context determine where you look. *Journal of Vision, 7*(14), 1–20.

Smilek, D., Birmingham, E., Cameron, D., Bischof, W. F., & Kingstone, A. (2006). Cognitive ethology and exploring attention in real world scenes. *Brain Research, 1080*, 101–119.

Tatler, B. W. (2007). The central fixation bias in scene viewing: Selecting an optimal viewing position independently of motor biases and image feature distributions. *Journal of Vision, 7*(14), 1–17.

Tatler, B. W., Baddeley, R. J., & Gilchrist, I. D. (2005). Visual correlates of fixation selection: Effects of scale and time. *Vision Research, 45*, 643–659.

Tatler, B. W., & Kuhn, G. (2007). Don't look now: The magic of misdirection. In R. P. G. van Gompel, M. H. Fischer, W. S. Murray, & R. L. Hill (Eds.), *Eye movements: A window on mind and brain* (pp. 697–714). Oxford, UK: Elsevier.

Tipper, C., Handy, T., Giesbrecht, B., & Kingstone, A. (2008). Brain responses to biological relevance. *Journal of Cognitive Neuroscience, 20*(5), 879–891.

Tipples, J. (2002). Eye gaze is not unique: Automatic orienting in response to noninformative arrows. *Psychonomic Bulletin and Review, 9*, 314–318.

Tipples, J. (2008). Orienting to counterpredictive gaze and arrow cues. *Perception and Psychophysics, 70*, 77–87.

Torralba, A., Oliva, A., Castelhano, M. S., & Henderson, J. M. (2006). Contextual guidance of eye movements and attention in real-world scenes: The role of global features in object search. *Psychological Review, 113*, 766–786.

Treisman, A. M. (1960). Contexual cues in selective listening. *Quarterly Journal of Experimental Psychology, 12*, 242–248.

Vuilleumier, P. (2002). Perceived gaze direction in faces and spatial attention: A study in patients with parietal damage and unilateral neglect. *Neuropsychologia, 40*(7), 1013–1026.

Walther, D., & Koch, C. (2005). Saliency Toolbox (Ver. 2.0) [Computer software]. Retrieved November 2, 2005, from, http://www.saliencytoolbox.net

Walther, D., & Koch, C. (2006). Modeling attention to salient proto-objects. *Neural Networks, 19*, 1395–1407.

Yarbus, A. L. (1967). *Eye movements and vision* (B. Haigh, Trans.). New York: Plenum Press. (Original work published 1965)

VISUAL COGNITION, 2009, 17 (6/7), 925–944

You look where I look! Effect of gaze cues on overt and covert attention in misdirection

Gustav Kuhn

Durham University, Durham, UK

Benjamin W. Tatler

Dundee University, Dundee, UK

Geoff G. Cole

Durham University, Durham, UK

We designed a magic trick in which misdirection was used to orchestrate observers' attention in order to prevent them from detecting the to-be-concealed event. By experimentally manipulating the magician's gaze direction we investigated the role that gaze cues have in attentional orienting, independently of any low level features. Participants were significantly less likely to detect the to-be-concealed event if the misdirection was supported by the magician's gaze, thus demonstrating that the gaze plays an important role in orienting people's attention. Moreover, participants spent less time looking at the critical hand when the magician's gaze was used to misdirect their attention away from the hand. Overall, the magician's face, and in particular the eyes, accounted for a large proportion of the fixations. The eyes were popular when the magician was looking towards the observer; once he looked towards the actions and objects being manipulated, participants typically fixated the gazed-at areas. Using a highly naturalistic paradigm using a dynamic display we demonstrate gaze following that is independent of the low level features of the scene.

Keywords: Covert attention; Eye movements; Gaze cueing; Gaze following; Overt attention; Social attention.

Our subjective perception of the world is one of full coherence, yet our conscious representation is rather limited (Rensink, 2002). Rather than

Please address all correspondence to Gustav Kuhn, Department of Psychology, University of Durham, South Road, Durham DH1 3LE, UK. E-mail: Gustav.Kuhn@Durham.ac.uk

This research was funded by the Wolfson Research Institute, University of Durham. We also thank Daniel Smilek, Greg Zelinsky, and James Brockmole for their helpful comments.

© 2009 Taylor & Francis
DOI: 10.1080/13506280902826775

processing all of the sensory information, the visual system selects the information that is of importance through the systematic orientation of both covert and overt attention. The latter process is achieved by directing the fovea, capable of encoding high acuity visual information, to spatial locations that are of importance. Enhanced processing can also occur in the absence of eye movements, namely through the deployment of covert attention (Posner, 1980).

Over the past years much research has been conducted identifying the mechanism behind attentional orienting. In the covert attention literature it has become apparent that people automatically orient their attention towards certain stimulus features (e.g., Wolfe & Horowitz, 2004). For example, events such as the onset of an object (e.g., Cole, Kuhn, & Liversedge, 2007; Yantis & Jonides, 1990), onset of motion (Abrams & Christ, 2003), or objects looming towards the observer capture our attention (Cole & Liversedge, 2006; Franconeri & Simons, 2003). Although certain events, such as the onset of new objects are capable of capturing attention in the absence of a unique visual transient (Cole & Kuhn, 2009) attentional orienting in response to these stimulus properties is largely driven by luminance transients (Franconeri, Hollingworth, & Simons, 2005).

A key component of attentional orientation is the overt orientation of the eyes. A large volume of research has been aimed at exploring the factors that underlie and influence what locations we select as the targets of fixation in complex scenes (since Buswell, 1935). Traditionally, the debate about the factors responsible for fixation selection has centred on the bottom-up/top-down dichotomy (see Henderson, 2003), mirroring the issues that have been explored in visual search literature (see Wolfe & Horowitz, 2004). While people no longer argue for selection being *either* bottom-up *or* top-down, the debate continues about the relative influence of these two orienting processes (as reflected throughout this Special Issue).

Current models, derived mainly from static scene viewing, favour a view in which higher level factors such as behavioural task (Einhauser, Rutishauser, & Koch, 2008), expertise with similar scenes (Underwood, Foulsham, & Humphrey, 2009, this issue), spatial expectation for object location (Ehinger, Hidalgo-Sotelo, Torralba, & Oliva, 2009, this issue), and object appearance (Kanan, Kanan, Zhang, & Cottrell, 2009, this issue) modulate or even override a basic low-level form of attentional capture based on image conspicuity or salience (Itti & Koch, 2000). Other behavioural biases such as the general tendency to look near the centre of monitor displays (Tatler, 2007) and the tendency to make particular eye movements more frequently than others (Tatler & Vincent, 2009, this issue) have also been shown to influence where observers fixate.

A surprising omission from the high-level cues so far investigated in the context of emerging models of eye guidance when viewing complex scenes is gaze cueing. Where an individual attends can be strongly influenced (perhaps event automatically) by where another individual is attending (Driver et al., 1999; Friesen & Kingstone, 1998). Using a Posner (1980) type precueing task it has been shown that participants detect targets occurring in the gazed-at location more rapidly than when they occur at a non-gazed-at location, even when the gaze is nonpredictive of the target location, thus suggesting that gaze direction results in automatic orienting of covert attention. Similarly, gaze cues also affect people's overt attentional deployment (Kuhn & Benson, 2007; Kuhn & Kingstone, 2009; Mansfield, Farroni, & Johnson, 2003; Ricciardelli, Bricolo, Aglioti, & Chelazzi, 2002). For example, if participants are required to look at targets presented either to the left or the right of a centrally presented face whose gaze is either congruent or incongruent to the intended saccade direction, participants often followed the distractor gaze even though the gaze direction was nonpredictive (Kuhn & Benson, 2007; Ricciardelli et al., 2002) or counterpredictive of the intended saccade direction (Kuhn & Kingstone, 2009), thus arguing that this type of gaze following may even be automatic.

Presenting faces in isolation and at the centre of the observer's gaze means not only is the face's gaze the only directional cue available, but also that it is preselected as the fixation target for the observer (they do not need to initially orient to the face to infer gaze direction). Numerous studies have shown that nonsocially relevant directional cues such as arrows trigger automatic shifts in both overt (Friesen, Ristic, & Kingstone, 2004; Hommel, Pratt, Colzato, & Godijn, 2001; Tipples, 2002) and covert attention (Kuhn & Benson, 2007; Kuhn & Kingstone, 2009). It is therefore likely that any directional cue presented in isolation will result in attentional orienting. The true influence of social attention may therefore only be understood if we examine the role of gaze cueing in a richer context, i.e., in natural scenes.

To date, few studies have investigated attentional orienting in response to gaze cues when the face is presented in a more natural environment (Birmingham, Bischof, & Kingstone, 2009, this issue). Results from the social attention literature predict attention should be directed towards areas that are being looked at by the central figure in the display. Indeed, Fletcher-Watson, Findlay, Leekam, and Benson (2008) showed that that participants spent more time looking at the object being fixated by the scene character than would be predicted by chance. Similarly, Castelhano, Wieth, and Henderson (2007) measured participants' eye movements whilst they were looking at sequences of scene photographs that told a story. Their results showed that the actor's face was highly likely to be fixated and participants' next saccade was often directed towards the object that was the focus of the actor's gaze direction.

One problem in interpreting studies using naturalistic displays, as the results cited earlier, is that we cannot be sure that the location cued by the gaze of the central figure in the display is not also cued by other factors. For example, the cued location may have different or conspicuous low-level feature properties and thus be favoured by a salience-type selection mechanism. Alternatively (or additionally) the gaze-cued location may be of central importance to the higher level interpretation of the scene, this being the target of any high-level selection mechanism. This is particularly problematic in natural scenes: Indeed the question could be raised about why the central figure is looking at that location in the first place. Is it to do with the visual or semantic prominence of the location? In the extreme we could suggest that the cooccurrence of attention at the mutually gazed location is not a reflection of a tendency to follow another's gaze, but a common mechanism underlying fixation selection (such as the latest modifications to Itti's salience framework; Itti & Koch, 2001).

There are two ways in which the above concern about whether gaze cueing really influences fixation selection in social scenes can be addressed. First, we can artificially manipulate where the depicted characters in the scene are looking. Dukewich and Klein (2008) did exactly this: They measured participants' eye movements whilst looking at art and digitally manipulated the gaze direction of the central figure. By manipulating the gaze direction, this approach allowed for the independent assessment of the degree to which attentional orienting is influenced by the gaze direction of the central figure. Rather surprisingly, their results demonstrated that participants viewing behaviour was only weekly influenced by the central character's gaze direction. The images used by Dukewich and Klein consisted of rather abstract artistic paintings, which may have been too artificial to engage full social processing, and thus reduced the effectiveness of the gaze manipulation. Furthermore, by digitally changing gaze direction all other directional cues in the paintings, such as the character's head and body direction and the location of other objects in the scenes, were no longer consistent with the character's manipulated gaze direction.

Alternatively, we can find a situation in which a component of the natural behaviour is to decouple gaze direction and conspicuous events. Magic offers an ideal opportunity for this (see Kuhn, Amlani, & Rensink, 2008; Macknik et al., 2008) because some tricks explicitly use the magician's gaze direction to misorient the observer attention at the crucial moments (Lamont & Wiseman, 1999). We have developed magic tricks that allow us to consider the extent to which an observer's gaze is misdirected by the magician's gaze (Kuhn & Tatler, 2005; Kuhn, Tatler, Findlay, & Cole, 2008). In these magic tricks misdirection is used to prevent participants from detecting a visually salient event. By measuring participants' eye movements whilst watching this misdirection trick we can evaluate the extent to which overt attention has been manipulated. Moreover, analogous to approaches that use change detection and inattentional blindness as measures of covert attention

(Tse, 2004), the detection of the to-be-concealed event provides us with an index of covert attention (see Kuhn & Findlay, in press, for a full discussion on how detection provides an index of covert attention rather than inference). Previous studies using misdirection tricks have demonstrated that detection of the event was independent of where people were looking, thus demonstrating that misdirection may involve misdirecting covert rather than overt attention. Similarly, in the vanishing ball illusion, Kuhn and Land (2006) demonstrated that although social cues could be used to deceive participants' expectations and as such what they saw, participants' eye movements were not fooled the magician's gaze. Based on these previous results it therefore remains to be seen whether social cues effectively misdirect overt attention, when used in isolation.

Using a combination of both live performances and video presentations of performances, we have shown that participants' eye movements were strongly driven by the magician's social cues, i.e., where he was looking (Kuhn & Land, 2006; Tatler & Kuhn, 2007). However, the magician's gaze cues are rarely used in isolation. Instead magicians typically employ a combination of additional attentional cues such as movement or changes in contrast so as to maximize the misdirection's propensity. The extent to which gaze cues are responsible for this attentional misdirection above all of the other cues, remains unclear. For example, in Tatler and Kuhn (2007) the cigarette "disappearance" (i.e., dropping the cigarette into his lap) is concealed by the magician gazing at his other (empty) hand, whilst at the same time waving this empty hand so providing strong motion cues at this location. It is therefore unclear whether the observer's fixation of the empty hand is driven primarily by motion or gaze cues.

Within the context of the magic trick it is possible to disentangle gaze-cueing effects from the effects of other cues. That is, there can be situations in which the magician's gaze cues are effectively in conflict with both the low-level cues in the scene (e.g., both the waving empty hand and the white cigarette dropping against a black background provide what must be visually salient events) and the behavioural goals of the observer (when instructed to work out how the magician made the cigarette disappear the hand in which the cigarette is held is central to the high level goals of the observer). Thus, in the case of the dropping object, gaze can be used to cue either the waving, empty hand (the normal situation for misdirecting the viewer; here referred to as the misdirection condition) or the hand dropping the object (here referred to as the nonmisdirection condition). By comparing the gaze allocation and detection probabilities in these two situations, we can effectively disentangle the influence of gaze and low-level motion cues in misdirection. Not only does this approach offer new insights into how a magician achieves successful misdirection of his audience, but also it allows insights into the relationship between gaze cues and other cues in the allocation of attention in natural, social settings.

METHOD

Participants

Thirty-two students from Durham University took part in the study (mean age = 25.3; 19 female, 13 male). Participants were either paid or received course credits.

Material

Two versions of the misdirection trick were recorded. The effect[1] in this magic trick was the disappearance of a lighter (see Figure 1 for a description of the trick; video can be downloaded from http://www.dur.ac.uk/gustav. kuhn/papers/KuhnetalVisCog2009/Material.htm). In this trick the magician picks up a lighter with his left hand and lights it. He then pretends to take the flame with his right hand, and gradually moves it away from the hand that is holding the lighter. In the misdirection condition the magician looks at the right hand throughout the manoeuvre. Once the right hand has reached the other side, whilst still looking at it, he snaps his fingers, waves his hand and reveals that it is empty. The misdirection employed involves a combination of cues in particular the waving hand and the magician's gaze direction, which is directed towards the right hand. At the same time the lighter is dropped into the lap. The drop is fully visible. The magician now directs his gaze to his left hand, raises it, and snaps his fingers to reveal that his left hand is now also empty and the lighter has disappeared. The sequence in the nonmisdirection condition was identical to the original misdirection trick with the exception that at the time when the right hand goes to pick up the flame, the magician's gaze is directed towards the left hand holding the lighter, rather than following the right hand. The magician's social cues were therefore contrary to the misdirection (see Figure 1). As can be seen from the timeline, the timing of most of the movements in both conditions took place at virtually the same time.

The magic trick was filmed using a digital video camera (PAL, JVC, GR-D240EK) at 25 fps, and then sampled using Adobe Premier (720 × 576). All of the video editing was carried out using Adobe Premier and Adobe

---

[1] In the magic literature the term "effect" refers to what the spectator sees, whilst method describes how the trick is done (Lamont & Wiseman, 1999).

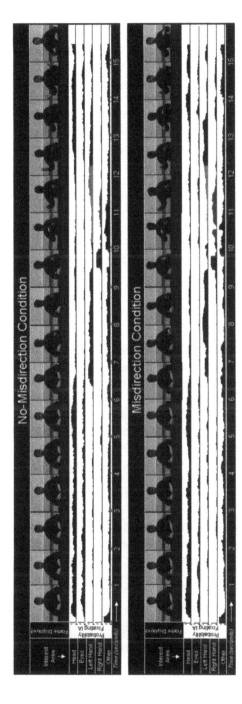

Figure 1. Time lines of the magic tricks performed for the nonmisdirection and the misdirection conditions. Time (in s) is represented along the x-axis. To illustrate what was happening at any particular time the frames corresponding to the particular time on the x-axis are included. The frame located at the 0–1 interval is the frame presented at time 0, the frame located at the 1–2 interval is frame presented at time 1 s etc. ... the number in the parenthesis are the times at which the events take place (in s). In the misdirection condition (bottom plane) the video clip starts with a 5 s still image of the magician looking ahead (1–5). He then looks at the lighter located on the table which he picks up with his left hand (5–7) and lights it (7–9). He then pretends to take the flame and gradually moves it away from the hand holding the lighter (9–10). In the misdirection condition the magician looks at the right hand throughout the manoeuvre. Once the right hand has reached the other side, whilst still looking at the right hand, he snaps his fingers, waves his hand and reveals that it is empty (10–11). The misdirection employed involves a combination of cues in particular the waving hand and the magician's gaze direction, which is directed towards the right hand. At the same time the lighter is dropped into the lap. The drop takes place in full view. The magician now directs his gaze to his left hand (11–12), raises it, and snaps his fingers to reveal that his left hand is now also empty and the lighter has disappeared (12–14). The sequence in the nonmisdirection condition was identical to the original misdirection trick with the exception that at the time when the right hand goes to pick up the flame, the magician's gaze is directed towards the left hand holding he lighter, rather than following the right hand. The difference between the two conditions take place between 10.2 and 12.1 s. As can be seen from the timeline, the timing of most of the movements in both conditions took place at virtually the same time. Below each of the time lines are five bar charts which plot the probability of participants looking at any of the five interest areas against time. To view this figure in colour, please see the online issue of the Journal.

Photoshop. The duration of the trick from beginning to end was 10.48 s (262 frames).

The entire clip was exported as a film strip and edited using Adobe Photoshop. For both conditions the dropping lighters, which were visible for three frames, were removed using the stamp tool. Footage from a different trial using the same lighter was then digitally inserted to these frames. This meant that the dropping lighters in both conditions were identical and thus were equally perceptible. One hundred and twenty-five still frames were added to the beginning of the clip and 50 frames were added to the end of the clip resulting in the entire clip lasting 517 frames. The film strips were then converted back into avi files. The video clips were presented using SR Research Experiment Builder software which guaranteed accurate frame display timing. The movies were displayed on a 21 inch CRT monitor (75 Hz). Screen resolution was set to 600×800 pixels so that the video clip filled most of the screen. Eye movements were recorded monocularly (left eye) using an SR-Research Eyelink II eyetracker (500 Hz). Viewing distance was 63 cm and the head was fixed using a chinrest.

Procedure

Participants were informed that they were about to see a video clip of a magic trick and that their task was to discover how this trick was done. The eye tracker was then calibrated using a 9 point calibration procedure, which was immediately followed by a validation procedure. Calibrations were accepted if the mean error was less than $0.5°$. Immediately after the magic trick participants were asked whether they saw how the lighter disappeared. If they answered yes, they were asked to describe what they saw. If they answered no, they were asked to speculate about the method they thought might have been used to make the lighter disappear. All participants were urged to differentiate between what they saw and how they thought it was done. Kuhn and Findlay (in press) showed that if the dropping lighter is digitally removed, thus making it invisible, participants did not falsely claim to see it drop, thus demonstrating that reports of detecting the lighter provide reliable indexes of what people have seen rather than inferences.

Dynamic scene analysis: Data preparation

In static scene viewing an interest area can be defined for each image and we can calculate eye movement statistics such as total number of fixations or dwell time per interest area. Analysing eye movements in dynamic scenes generates numerous additional challenges which need to be addressed. First, objects are likely to move over time and as such the interest area can change in location from frame to frame. Second, if the object changes in depth or orientation the perceived size and shape of the object may change over time. Third, if there are several objects in different depth planes, some objects are likely to become occluded by others, thus providing us with potentially overlapping interest areas. The first two issues can be solved by tracking objects as they move in time and adjusting the location and the size of the interest area as the object of interest changes. The second issue is more problematic, which is why in the present study, we tried to design a magic trick that avoided occlusion of objects as much as possible.

Five different interest areas were defined for each frame: Head, eyes, left hand right hand, and other (including everything else). Each area of interest was defined manually on every frame of the videos. Rather than defining each interest area by the exact outline of the object, they were defined by spheres, which were centred on the object of interest (see Figure 2). The size of these spheres was held constant throughout the trial and the size was selected to ensure that the entire object of interest was covered throughout the trial. As most of the actions took place in the same plane, and the camera angle was constant, the size of the objects did not vary much and thus the spheres were relatively accurate approximations of the true area covered by the object of interest. There was relatively little occlusion. When the right hand takes the flame from the left hand the two hands touch each other thus resulting in an overlap interest areas (nonmisdirection condition, 10 frames; misdirection condition, 11 frames), the interest area had to be

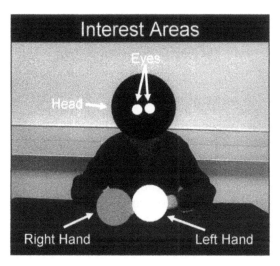

Figure 2. The interest areas (IA) as defined on the first frame. The relative sizes of the interest areas sizes in both the misdirection and the nonmisdirection conditions were as follows: Head = 4.98%, eyes = 0.28%, left hand = 1.61%, right hand = 1.61%.

adjusted manually. For the remainder of the frames there was no occlusion, thus resulting in mutually exclusive interest areas.

Data analysis was conducted using custom written software, which analysed the data on a frame by frame basis. Data acquisition was at 500 Hz, thus resulting in 20 samples per frame of the stimulus video. In static scene viewing eye movements are typically analysed in terms of fixation durations, or overall dwell times. In dynamic scenes, the interest area is likely to change on each frame, and participants often track slowly moving objects thus making this type of analysis rather problematic. We therefore propose a somewhat different approach. Rather than using a fixation-based analysis, we analysed eye movements for each gaze location sample, by classifying each sample according to which interest area was being looked at. By doing this we can calculate the proportion of participants looking at each interest area at any point in time (i.e., number of participants fixating interest area divided by total number of participants).[2]

RESULTS

Detection rates

In the nonmisdirection condition, nine participants (56%) detected the lighter drop compared to two participants (12.5%) in the misdirection condition. Although the dropping lighters in both conditions were identical, participants in the misdirection condition were significantly less likely to detect it than participants in the nonmisdirection condition, $\chi^2 = 7.46$, $p = .021$. The magician's gaze direction therefore played a significant role in the effectiveness of misdirecting participants' attention.

Overt versus covert misdirection

Our results clearly demonstrate that the magician's gaze direction was influential in misdirecting participants' attention. However, which type of attention was being manipulated? Did the magician's gaze direction help misdirect where participants were looking, and thus act upon participants' overt attention, or was the misdirection more covert in nature? In order to investigate this question we analysed participants' gaze positions at the time of the drop. The dropping lighter was visible on three frames. Fixations at the time of the drop were defined as fixation positions on the second frame of the drop (10th eye movement sample). Figure 3 shows participants' fixation

---

[2] In the context of this analysis, the term fixation will be used rather loosely, whereby fixations refer to gaze coordinates at each sample.

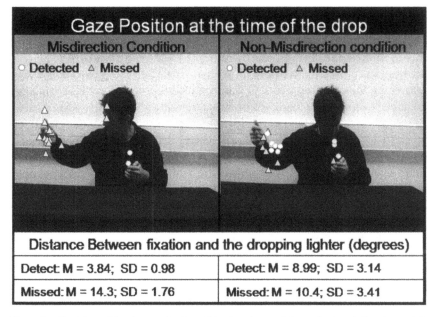

Gaze Position at the time of the drop	
Misdirection Condition	Non-Misdirection condition
○ Detected △ Missed	○ Detected △ Missed
Distance Between fixation and the dropping lighter (degrees)	
Detect: M = 3.84; SD = 0.98	Detect: M = 8.99; SD = 3.14
Missed: M = 14.3; SD = 1.76	Missed: M = 10.4; SD = 3.41

Figure 3. Participants' fixations at the time of the drop for participants in the misdirection and the nonmisdirection condition. Table 1 denotes the distances between the fixation and the dropping lighter for participants who missed the drop and those who detected it for both conditions (in degrees). To view this figure in colour, please see the online issue of the Journal.

points at the time of the drop. The aim of the misdirection was to direct attention away from the dropping lighter. We can therefore use the distance between the participants' fixation and the dropping lighter as an index of the strength of the overt misdirection. This figure also includes the distances between participants' fixations and the dropping lighter (in degrees). Overall, participants in the nonmisdirection condition fixated significantly closer to the dropping lighter than participants in the misdirection condition, $t(30) =$ 2.65, $p = .013$, thus demonstrating that the magician's gaze direction affected overt attention. From the mean distances shown in Figure 3, there would appear to be an interaction between misdirection conditions and detection of the drop. However, with only two detected trials in the misdirection condition, it is hard to assess this possibility.

Thus far, we have only focused on participant's eye movements at a particular point in time, namely in the middle of the drop. However, as we are dealing with events that develop over time, it is more informative to analyse the data over time. The line graphs below each of the time lines in Figure 1 plot the proportion of participants looking at each of the areas of interest. These types of graphs allow us to depict and analyse participants' gaze behaviour over time (see also Kuhn & Land, 2006).

Overall analysis

The first striking feature is that most of the data are captured by the defined areas of interest (head, eyes, left hand, right hand). Although the areas of interest only covered 8.5% of the total area, 70% of all eye movements were captured by these interest areas. Given that the background in these displays is relatively uniform it might seem less surprising that participants spend relatively little time looking at it. However, these results clearly demonstrate that participants look at the key areas where the trick is being performed. Similar to previous studies (Birmingham, Bischof, & Kingstone, 2008a, 2008b; Birmingham et al., 2009, this issue; Smilek, Birmingham, Cameron, Bischof, & Kingstone, 2006) once the interest areas were weighted for size (see Figure 2 for relative size of the interest areas), the eyes accounted for an exceptionally high proportion of fixations (60.2%), followed by the left hand (21.3%), the head (9.8%), and the right hand (8.1%).

By looking at the time line it becomes apparent that the popularity of different interest areas varies systematically with time. Whilst viewing the still image in which the magician looks towards the viewer, most of the data are captured by the eyes and the head (up to 5 s). However, once the scene becomes animated (5 s and onwards), the left and the right hand rapidly gain in popularity. The dynamic aspect of the scene strongly influences participants' eye movement behaviour. On an informal level it is apparent that for most of the time, the hand that is being looked at by the magician becomes the most popular interest area, but when the magician is looking towards the observer, the eyes and the head gain popularity.

Gaze following over time

Throughout most of the trick, the magician's gaze is directed towards the object that is being manipulated, thus making it difficult to assess the unique contributions that the magician's gaze makes. However, as we experimentally manipulated the magician's gaze direction in orchestrating his misdirection we can evaluate the independent effect that the gaze direction has on overt attention. In the misdirection condition, the magician uses his right hand and the gaze direction to draw attention away from the left hand, which takes place between frames 256 and 303. In the nonmisdirection condition, attention is only drawn away from the lighter hand using (movements of) the left hand, whilst his gaze is directed towards the left hand. If the gaze direction affects overt attention we would expect participants in the misdirection condition to spend less time looking at the left-hand interest area than participants in the nonmisdirection condition. Table 1 shows the proportion of time spent looking at each of the interest areas for the two

TABLE 1
Percentage of time spent looking at each of the interest areas during the time in which
the two conditions differed from each other (frames 256–303)

Interest area	Nonmisdirection		Misdirection	
	Mean	SE	Mean	SE
Head	5.46	2.81	9.24	2.81
Eyes	0.63	2.85	7.88	2.85
LH	32.0	5.87	14.1	5.87
RH	14.7	3.80	34.9	3.80
Other	47.0	5.49	33.5	5.49

conditions. Indeed, participants in the nonmisdirection condition spent significantly more time looking at the left hand than participants in the misdirection conditions, thus demonstrating that the magician's gaze cues were effective at orienting overt attention away from the left hand, $t(30) = 2.16$, $p = .039$. Moreover, participants in the misdirection condition spent significantly more time looking at the right hand than participants in the nonmisdirection condition, $t(30) = 3.75$, $p = .001$. These results demonstrate that the magician's social cues significantly reoriented participants' overt attention away from the left hand and towards the right hand and that this reorienting of attention was independent of any low level features.

Covert attention

Six of the participants who detected the drop in the nonmisdirection condition looked towards the waving hand, and one of the participants fixated the left hand yet missed the lighter drop, thus suggesting that detection of the drop was not solely related to where participants were looking. Indeed, similar to previous findings (Kuhn & Tatler, 2005; Kuhn, Tatler, et al., 2008), participants who detected the drop fixated no closer to the lighter than those who missed it, $t(14) < 1$. These results demonstrate that the misdirection did not merely involve manipulating participants' overt attention. Thus, participants did not miss the drop because of limited retinal resolution, which suggest that the misdirection was more covert in nature.

In the misdirection condition, there was a clear relationship between where participants were looking and whether they detected it. The two participants who detected the drop fixated the left hand, whereas all of the participants who missed it fixated elsewhere. Indeed there was a significant difference in visual eccentricity and detection, $t(14) = 8.1$, $p < .0005$. However, as there were only two participants who detected the drop, the generalizability of these results must be treated with caution.

DISCUSSION

Misdirection involves systematically manipulating people's attention so as to prevent the observer from detecting certain events. Typically magicians use a wide range of techniques, of which the strategic use of eye gaze has been particularly highlighted (Lamont & Wiseman, 1999; Sharpe, 1988). By experimentally manipulating a misdirection trick, we isolated the role that gaze cues have in orchestrating attention. Our results showed that participants were significantly less likely to detect the to-be-concealed event if the misdirection was supported by the magician's social cues, thus demonstrating that the magician's gaze direction plays an important role in directing peoples' attention. By analysing participants' eye movements at the time of the drop, we could gain an insight into the type of attention that was being manipulated, and the extent to which gaze cues influence participants' overt attentional allocation. Participants in the nonmisdirection condition fixated significantly closer to the dropping lighter than participants in the misdirection condition, thus demonstrating that the magician's gaze direction influenced participants' overt attention. However, for participants in the nonmisdirection condition there was no difference in visual eccentricity between participants who detected the drop and those who missed it, thus suggesting that the misdirection involved both the manipulation of overt and covert attention. Moreover, by disentangling the influence of gaze cues from other cues (such as the motion of the waving, empty hand), we have for the first time demonstrated that the social gaze cues were not the sole cues that are able to misdirect observers' attention.

One interpretation of the difference between the two conditions is that in the misdirection condition both the overt and covert attention of the participants was misdirected away from the dropping lighter. In the nonmisdirection condition the participants' overt attention is still misdirected away from the drop (75% were looking at the empty right hand at the time of the drop), presumably because of the motion cues in the waving hand. However, participants' attention was less strongly misdirected in the nonmisdirection condition in two distinct ways: First, gaze direction at the time of the drop was on average closer to the dropping lighter and so overt attention was less strongly misdirected. This implies a role for gaze cueing on overt attentional allocation. Second, participants were far more likely to detect the drop whether they were fixating near the drop or near the empty right hand. This suggests that irrespective of overt misdirection, participants' covert attention was less strongly misdirected in the nonmisdirection condition; we can speculate that the magician's gaze direction might cue covert attentional allocation to the gazed-at location.

Previous studies using static scenes have shown that faces, and in particular the eye region, are particularly salient features of a scene (Birmingham et al.,

2008a, 2008b; Smilek et al., 2006). Our results dovetail this proposition by demonstrating that participants spent a large proportion of their time looking at the eyes. Once the interest areas were controlled for size, the eye region accounted for most of the data. However, the popularity of this interest area systematically varied with time. In particular the eyes were popular when the magician was looking towards the observer; once he started to move his hand and look towards the actions and objects being manipulated, the areas that were being looked at became more popular. This finding coincides with a simple rule in magic which states that: "If you want the audience to look at you, look at them; If you want the audience to look at something else, look at it" (Kuhn, Amlani, & Rensink, 2008), and with our previous studies (Kuhn & Land, 2006; Tatler & Kuhn, 2007).

Where another person is looking is likely to be of potential interest. Similar to other low level cues, such as luminance changes or the onset of motion, gaze cues are correlated with events that are of potential interest and as such warrant attentional allocation. Indeed numerous papers using gaze cueing tasks (see Frischen, Bayliss, & Tipper, 2007, for a review) have argued that people's attention is automatically oriented towards areas that are being looked at. For example, it has been shown that even when instructed to saccade in the opposite direction to where a distractor gaze is looking participants often followed the gaze in the cued but unintended direction even when the gaze was non- or counterpredictive of the intended saccade direction, thus highlighting the prepotency of gaze following (Kuhn & Benson, 2007; Kuhn & Kingstone, 2009; Ricciardelli et al., 2002). However, in most of the previous studies, the gaze cues are preselected, and the stimulus displays are rather artificial. Though consistent, and statistically reliable, the magnitude of these cueing effects is rather small. Our study found reliable gaze cueing effects using one trial, compared to the hundreds of trials typically required in conventional task. This suggests that increasing the ecological validity of the stimulus may also amplify the gaze cueing effect. By investigating social attention using rather impoverished displays we may thus be underestimating the true power of these types of attentional cues (Kingstone, Smilek, & Eastwood, 2008). However, the present study differs from the above cited ones in that participants were not explicitly instructed to ignore the gaze cue. Whilst our study demonstrates that under normal conditions people show a strong tendency to follow another person's gaze, it is agnostic as to the automaticity of this gaze following.

In misdirection, a combination of cues are used to orchestrate the spectator's attention. For example, the magician looks at the lighter whilst lighting it, thus creating both a general interest as well as salient low level features such as luminance contrast and movement. Merely focusing on the correlation between the magician's gaze direction and participants eye movements therefore cannot necessarily inform us about the actual contribution that gaze cues make in orienting attention. However, as the social cues were manipulated experimentally, we can identify the contributions that the gaze cue made independently of all other features. By measuring the distance between the lighter and the fixation at the time of the drop we obtain an index of how influential the misdirection was upon overt attention. Indeed, participants in the nonmisdirection condition fixated more closely to the lighter than those in the misdirection condition thus demonstrating that participants' eye movements were influenced by where the magician was looking. Over the course of the performance of the trick (i.e., during the time of the drop), we found that participants in the nonmisdirection condition spent more time looking at the left hand than participants in the misdirection condition. However, participants in the misdirection condition spent significantly more time looking at the right hand than participants in the nonmisdirection condition. This supports the notion that the magician's gaze cueing during the trick influenced the participants' gaze allocation above and beyond any influence of nongaze cues, such as low-level visual conspicuity, motion, or higher level task goals. To our knowledge this is the first experimental dissection of gaze cues from these other attentional cues.

In the nonmisdirection condition, 44% of the participants failed to see the lighter drop even though the magician's gaze was directed towards the dropping lighter. Although the magician's social cues played an important role in manipulating participants' attention, they clearly do not account for all of the misdirection. Misdirection involves a combination of attentional techniques. In this trick the misdirection works by initially drawing attention to the lighter which is being lit (high luminance contrast of the flame is used to capture attention), and then drawn away by the right hand which pretends to grab the flame, and then in a slow continuous motion moves to the right. At the time of the drop, the magician snaps his right fingers thus creating a motion transient which is though to attract additional attention and thus misdirect from the dropping lighter. In the nonmisdirection condition, the effectiveness of the misdirection is largely driven by these motion signals. The fact that most (75%) of the participants looked towards the moving hand highlights the importance that these motion transients play in capturing overt attention. Furthermore, this result highlights that it is not due to gaze cues alone that participants look at the empty right hand in the normal performance of this type of trick (the misdirection condition).

Our finding that people still look at the waving hand in the nonmisdirection condition suggests that motion cues might be important in gaze allocation. Traditionally the scene viewing literature has focused on static scenes. Although it is possible to find anecdotal situations in which the world we are viewing approximates to a static scene—such as viewing a table to find a set of keys—it is rarely the case that we operate in a truly static visual domain. Even when searching the table for our keys we are likely to move objects during the search and change our viewpoint by moving around ourselves. Thus, it is crucial to study attentional allocation under more dynamic viewing conditions. In the attentional capture literature it has become apparent that although perceptual features such as the onset of new objects may capture our attention in the absence of a transient overtly (Brockmole & Henderson, 2005) and covertly (Cole & Kuhn, 2009), most attentional capture results from luminance transients. Moreover, studies that have investigated eye movement behaviour in dynamic scenes have demonstrated that motion contrasts are more predictive of people's saccade targets than static features such as intensity variance or orientation contrast (Carmi & Itti, 2006). Our results further highlight the importance that motion transients can play in guiding peoples' eye movements. Although the onset of motion has been shown to capture attention, continuous motion is not thought to do so (Abrams & Christ, 2003). Here however, the continuous motion of moving the hand from one side to the other appears to be particularly attractive. In the nonmisdirection condition, half of the participants' gaze followed the right hand as it moved across the screen. The use of continuous motion in terms of gestures is often used in misdirection to orchestrate attention (Macknik et al., 2008). Our data demonstrate just how powerful these types of cues are, and future research could benefit from exploring the role of these types of gestures in attention research.

With regard to this Special Issue of *Visual Cognition*, we feel that our data speak to a much-neglected component of the decision about where to fixate in complex natural environments: Where others in the environment themselves are looking. To date the vast majority of research has considered static scenes, often without people, or at least the influence of the people in the scenes has not been thoroughly explored. Instead debate has centred on the relative contributions of low-level stimulus cues and high-level task goals in influencing where people fixate. Of course, social gaze cues could be thought of as just another example of a high-level task goal effect—for example we could assume that the task of the observer is to monitor where others are attending because these locations may be important to us as well. However, given the prepotent capturing effect of social gaze cues on observers' attention (Kuhn & Kingstone, 2009), it may be that these cues are effectively a type of cue in their own right—that is, something more than just bottom-up or top-down. Whatever type of cue we want to class gaze cues as, it is clearly time to acknowledge that these have a prominent influence on where humans fixate in dynamic social settings.

REFERENCES

Abrams, R. A., & Christ, S. E. (2003). Motion onset captures attention. *Psychological Science*, *14*(5), 427–432.

Birmingham, E., Bischof, W. F., & Kingstone, A. (2008a). Gaze selection in complex social scenes. *Visual Cognition*, *16*(2/3), 341–356.

Birmingham, E., Bischof, W. F., & Kingstone, A. (2008b). Social attention and real world scenes: The roles of action, competition, and social content. *Quarterly Journal of Experimental Psychology*, *61*(7), 986–999.

Birmingham, E., Bischof, W. F., & Kingstone, A. (2009). Get real! Resolving the debate about equivalent social stimuli. *Visual Cognition*, *17*(6/7), 904–924.

Brockmole, J. R., & Henderson, J. M. (2005). Object appearance, disappearance, and attention prioritization in real-world scenes. *Psychonomic Bulletin and Review*, *12*(6), 1061–1067.

Buswell, G. T. (1935). *How people look at pictures*. Chicago: University of Chicago Press.

Carmi, R., & Itti, L. (2006). Visual causes versus correlates of attentional selection in dynamic scenes. *Vision Research*, *46*(26), 4333–4345.

Castelhano, M. S., Wieth, M. S., & Henderson, J. M. (2007). I see what you see: Eye movements in real-world scenes are affected by perceived direction of gaze. In L. Paletta & E. Rome (Eds.), *Attention in cognitive systems* (pp. 252–262). Berlin: Springer.

Cole, G. G., & Kuhn, G. (2009). Appearance matters: Attentional orienting by new objects in the precuing paradigm. *Visual Cognition*, *17*(5), 755–776.

Cole, C. G., Kuhn, G., & Liversedge, S. P. (2007). Onset of illusory figures attenuates change blindness. *Psychonomic Bulletin & Review*, *14*(5), 939–943.

Cole, G. G., & Liversedge, S. L. (2006). Change blindness and the primacy of object appearance. *Psychonomic Bulletin & Review*, *13*, 588–593.

Driver, J., Davies, M., Ricciardelli, P., Kidd, P., Maxwell, E., & Baron-Cohen, S. (1999). Gaze perception triggers reflective visuospatial orienting. *Visual Cognition*, *6*(5), 509–540.

Dukewich, K. R., & Klein, R. M. (2008). The effect of gaze on gaze direction while looking at art. *Psychonomic Bulletin and Review*, *15*(6), 1141–1147.

Ehinger, K., Hidalgo-Sotelo, B., Torralba, A., & Oliva, A. (2009). Modeling search for people in 900 scenes: A combined source model of eye guidance. *Visual Cognition*, *17*(6/7), 945–978.

Einhauser, W., Rutishauser, U., & Koch, C. (2008). Task-demands can immediately reverse the effects of sensory-driven saliency in complex visual stimuli. *Journal of Vision*, *8*(2), 1–19.

Fletcher-Watson, S., Findlay, J. M., Leekam, S. R., & Benson, V. (2008). Rapid detection of person information in a naturalistic scene. *Perception*, *37*(4), 571–583.

Franconeri, S. L., Hollingworth, A., & Simons, D. J. (2005). Do new objects capture attention? *Psychological Science*, *16*(4), 275–281.

Franconeri, S. L., & Simons, D. J. (2003). Moving and looming stimuli capture attention. *Perception and Psychophysics*, *65*, 999–1010.

Friesen, C. K., & Kingstone, A. (1998). The eyes have it! Reflexive orienting is triggered by nonpredictive gaze. *Psychonomic Bulletin and Review*, *5*(3), 490–495.

Friesen, C. K., Ristic, J., & Kingstone, A. (2004). Attentional effects of counterpredictive gaze and arrow cues. *Journal of Experimental Psychology: Human Perception and Performance*, *30*(2), 319–329.

Frischen, A., Bayliss, A. P., & Tipper, S. P. (2007). Gaze cueing of attention: Visual attention, social cognition, and individual differences. *Psychological Bulletin*, *133*(4), 694–724.

Henderson, J. M. (2003). Human gaze control during real-world scene perception. *Trends in Cognitive Science*, *7*(11), 498–504.

Hommel, B., Pratt, J., Colzato, L., & Godijn, R. (2001). Symbolic control of visual attention. *Psychological Science*, *12*(5), 360–365.

Itti, L., & Koch, C. (2001). Computational modelling of visual attention. *Nature Reviews Neuroscience, 2*(3), 194–203.

Kanan, C., Tong, M. H., Zhang, L., & Cottrell, G. W. (2009). SUN: Top-down saliency using natural statistics. *Visual Cognition, 17*(6/7), 979–1003.

Kingstone, A., Smilek, D., & Eastwood, J. D. (2008). Cognitive ethology: A new approach for studying human cognition. *British Journal of Psychology, 99*, 317–340.

Kuhn, G., Amlani, A. A., & Rensink, R. A. (2008). Towards a science of magic. *Trends in Cognitive Sciences, 12*(9), 349–354.

Kuhn, G., & Benson, V. (2007). The influence of eye-gaze and arrow pointing distractor cues on voluntary eye movements. *Perception and Psychophysics, 69*(6), 966–971.

Kuhn, G., & Findlay, J. M. (in press). Misdirection, attention and awareness: Inattentional blindness reveals temporal relationship between eye movements and visual awareness. *Quarterly Journal of Experimental Psychology.* Advance online publication. Retrieved May 19, 2009. doi:10.1080/17470210902846757

Kuhn, G., & Kingstone, A. (2009). Look away! Eyes and arrows engage oculomotor responses automatically. *Perception and Psychophysics, 71*(2), 314–327.

Kuhn, G., & Land, M. F. (2006). There's more to magic than meets the eye. *Current Biology, 16*(22), R950–R951.

Kuhn, G., & Tatler, B. W. (2005). Magic and fixation: Now you don't see it, now you do. *Perception, 34*(9), 1155–1161.

Kuhn, G., Tatler, B. W., Findlay, J. M., & Cole, G. G. (2008). Misdirection in magic: Implications for the relationship between eye gaze and attention. *Visual Cognition, 16*(2–3), 391–405.

Lamont, P., & Wiseman, R. (1999). *Magic in theory.* Hartfield, UK: Hermetic Press.

Macknik, S. L., King, M., Randi, J., Robbins, A., Teller, Thompson, J., et al. (2008). Attention and awareness in stage magic: Turning tricks into research. *Nature Reviews Neuroscience, 9*(11), 871–879.

Mansfield, E. M., Farroni, T., & Johnson, M. H. (2003). Does gaze perception facilitate overt orienting? *Visual Cognition, 10*(1), 7–14.

Posner, M. I. (1980). Orienting of attention. *Quarterly Journal of Experimental Psychology, 32*, 3–25.

Rensink, R. A. (2002). Change detection. *Annual Review of Psychology, 53*, 245–277.

Ricciardelli, P., Bricolo, E., Aglioti, S. M., & Chelazzi, L. (2002). My eyes want to look where your eyes are looking: Exploring the tendency to imitate another individual's gaze. *Neuroreport, 13*(17), 2259–2264.

Sharpe, S. (1988). *Conjurers psychological secrets.* Calgary, AB: Hades Publications.

Smilek, D., Birmingham, E., Cameron, D., Bischof, W., & Kingstone, A. (2006). Cognitive ethology and exploring attention in real-world scenes. *Brain Research, 1080*, 101–119.

Tatler, B. W. (2007). The central fixation bias in scene viewing: Selecting an optimal viewing position independently of motor biases and image feature distributions. *Journal of Vision, 7*(14), 1–17.

Tatler, B. W., & Kuhn, G. (2007). Don't look now: The magic of misdirection. In R. P. G. van Gompel, M. H. Fischer, W. S. Murray, & R. L. Hill (Eds.), *Eye movements: A window on mind and brain* (pp. 697–714). Oxford, UK: Elsevier.

Tatler, B. W., & Vincent, B. T. (2009). The prominence of behavioural biases in eye guidance. *Visual Cognition, 17*(6/7), 1029–1054.

Tipples, J. (2002). Eye gaze is not unique: Automatic orienting in response to uninformative arrows. *Psychonomic Bulletin and Review, 9*(2), 314–318.

Tse, P. U. (2004). Mapping visual attention with change blindness: New directions for a new method. *Cognitive Science, 28*(2), 241–258.

Underwood, G., Foulsham, T., & Humphrey, K. (2009). Saliency and scan patterns in the inspection of real-world scenes: Eye movements during encoding and recognition. *Visual Cognition*, *17*(6/7), 812–834.

Wolfe, J. M., & Horowitz, T. S. (2004). What attributes guide the deployment of visual attention and how do they do it? *Nature Reviews Neuroscience*, *5*(6), 495–501.

Yantis, S., & Jonides, J. (1990). Abrupt visual onsets and selective attention—Voluntary versus automatic allocation. *Journal of Experimental Psychology: Human Perception and Performance*, *16*(1), 121–134.

VISUAL COGNITION, 2009, 17 (6/7), 945–978

Modelling search for people in 900 scenes: A combined source model of eye guidance

Krista A. Ehinger and Barbara Hidalgo-Sotelo

Department of Brain and Cognitive Sciences, Massachusetts Institute of Technology, Cambridge, MA, USA

Antonio Torralba

Computer Science and Artificial Intelligence Laboratory, and Department of Electrical Engineering and Computer Science, Massachusetts Institute of Technology, Cambridge, MA, USA

Aude Oliva

Department of Brain and Cognitive Sciences, Massachusetts Institute of Technology, Cambridge, MA, USA

How predictable are human eye movements during search in real world scenes? We recorded 14 observers' eye movements as they performed a search task (person detection) in 912 outdoor scenes. Observers were highly consistent in the regions fixated during search, even when the target was absent from the scene. These eye movements were used to evaluate computational models of search guidance from three sources: saliency, target features, and scene context. Each of these models independently outperformed a cross-image control in predicting human fixations. Models that combined sources of guidance ultimately predicted 94% of human agreement, with the scene context component providing the most explanatory power. None of the models, however, could reach the precision and fidelity of an attentional map defined by human fixations. This work puts forth a benchmark for computational models of search in real world scenes. Further improvements in

Please address all correspondence to Aude Oliva, Department of Brain and Cognitive Sciences, Massachusetts Institute of Technology, Cambridge, MA, USA. E-mail: oliva@mit.edu

KAE and BH-S contributed equally to the work. The authors would like to thank two anonymous reviewers and Benjamin Tatler for their helpful and insightful comments on an earlier version of this manuscript. KAE was partly funded by a Singleton graduate research fellowship and by a graduate fellowship from an Integrative Training Program in Vision grant (T32 EY013935). BH-S was funded by a National Science Foundation Graduate Research Fellowship. This work was also funded by an NSF CAREER award (0546262) and a NSF contract (0705677) to AO, as well as an NSF CAREER award to AT (0747120). Supplementary information available on the following website: http://cvcl.mit.edu/SearchModels

© 2009 Taylor & Francis
DOI: 10.1080/13506280902834720

modelling should capture mechanisms underlying the selectivity of observers' fixations during search.

Key words: Computational model; Contextual guidance; Eye movement; Real world scene; Saliency; Target feature; Visual search

Daily human activities involve a preponderance of visually guided actions, requiring observers to determine the presence and location of particular objects. How predictable are human search fixations? Can we model the mechanisms that guide visual search? Here, we present a dataset of 45,144 fixations recorded while observers searched 912 real world scenes and evaluate the extent to which search behaviour is (1) consistent across individuals and (2) predicted by computational models of visual search guidance.

Studies of free viewing have found that the regions selected for fixation vary greatly across observers (Andrews & Coppola, 1999; Einhauser, Rutishauser, & Koch, 2008; Parkhurst & Neibur, 2003; Tatler, Baddeley, & Vincent, 2006). However, the effect of behavioural goals on eye movement control has been known since the classic demonstrations by Buswell (1935) and Yarbus (1967) showing that observers' patterns of gaze depended critically on the task. Likewise, a central result emerging from studies of oculomotor behaviour during ecological tasks (driving, e.g., Land & Lee, 1994; food preparation, e.g., Hayhoe, Shrivastava, Mruczek, & Pelz, 2003; sports, e.g., Land & McLeod, 2000) is the functional relation of gaze to one's momentary information processing needs (Hayhoe & Ballard, 2005).

In general, specifying a goal can serve as a referent for interpreting internal computations that occur during task execution. Visual search— locating a given target in the environment—is an example of a behavioural goal which produces consistent patterns of eye movements across observers. Figure 1 (later) shows typical fixation patterns of observers searching for pedestrians in natural images. Different observers often fixate remarkably consistent scene regions, suggesting that it is possible to identify reliable, strategic mechanisms underlying visual search and to create computational models that predict human eye fixations.

Various mechanisms have been proposed which may contribute to attention guidance during visual search. Guidance by statistically unexpected, or salient, regions of a natural image has been explored in depth in both modelling and behavioural work (e.g., Bruce & Tsotsos, 2006; Itti, Koch, & Niebur, 1998; Koch & Ullman, 1985; Li, 2002; Rosenholtz, 1999; Torralba, 2003a). Numerous studies have shown that regions where the local statistics differ from the background statistics are more likely to attract an observer's gaze. Distinctive colour, motion, orientation, or size constitute the

(a) High inter-observer agreement

(b) Low inter-observer agreement

Figure 1. Examples of target-absent scenes with (a) high and (b) low inter-observer agreement. Dots represent the first three fixations from each observer. To view this figure in colour, please see the online issue of the Journal.

most common *salient* attributes, at least in simple displays (for a review, Wolfe & Horowitz, 2004). Guidance by saliency may also contribute to early fixations on complex images (Bruce & Tsotsos, 2006; Harel, Koch, & Perona, 2006; Itti & Koch, 2000; Parkhurst, Law, & Niebur, 2002; van Zoest, Donk, & Theeuwes, 2004), particularly when the scene context is not informative (Parkhurst et al., 2002; Peters, Iyer, Itti, & Koch, 2005) or during free viewing. In natural images, it is interesting to note that objects are typically more salient than their background (Elazary & Itti, 2008; Torralba, Oliva, Castelhano, & Henderson, 2006), so oculomotor guidance processes may use saliency as a heuristic to fixate objects in the scene rather than the background.

In addition to bottom-up guidance by saliency, there is a top-down component to visual attention that is modulated by task. During search, observers can selectively attend to the scene regions most likely to contain the target. In classical search tasks, target features are an ubiquitous source of guidance (Treisman & Gelade, 1980; Wolfe, 1994, 2007; Wolfe, Cave, & Franzel, 1998; Zelinsky, 2008). For example, when observers search for a red target, attention is rapidly deployed towards red objects in the scene. Although a natural object, such as a pedestrian, has no single defining feature, it still has statistically reliable properties (upright form, round head, straight body) that could be selected by visual attention. In fact, there is considerable evidence for target-driven attentional guidance in real world search tasks (Einhauser et al., 2008; Pomplun, 2006; Rao, Zelinsky, Hayhoe, & Ballard, 2002; Rodriguez-Sanchez, Simine, & Tsotsos, 2007; Tsotsos et al., 1995; Zelinsky, 2008).

Another top-down component which applies in ecological search tasks is scene context. Statistical regularities of natural scenes provide rich cues to target location and appearance (Eckstein, Drescher & Shimozaki, 2006; Hoiem, Efros, & Hebert, 2006; Oliva & Torralba, 2007; Torralba & Oliva, 2002, 2003). Within a glance, global information can provide useful information about spatial layout and scene category (Greene & Oliva, 2009; Joubert, Rousselet, Fize, & Fabre-Thorpe, 2007; McCotter, Gosselin, Sowden, & Schyns, 2005; Renninger & Malik, 2004; Rousselet, Joubert, & Fabre-Thorpe, 2005; Schyns & Oliva, 1994). Categorical scene information informs a viewer of which objects are likely to be in the scene and where (Bar, 2004; Biederman, Mezzanotte, & Rabinowitz, 1982; de Graef, Christiaens, & d'Ydewalle, 1990; Friedman, 1979; Henderson, Weeks, & Hollingworth, 1999; Loftus & Mackworth, 1978). Furthermore, global features can be extracted quickly enough to influence early search mechanisms and fixations (Castelhano & Henderson, 2007; Chaumon, Drouet, & Tallon-Baudry, 2008; Neider & Zelinky, 2006; Torralba et al., 2006; Zelinsky & Schmidt, this issue 2009).

In the present work, we recorded eye movements as observers searched for a target object (a person) in over 900 natural scenes and evaluated the predictive value of several computational models of search. The purpose of this modelling effort was to study *search guidance*, that is, where observers look while deciding whether a scene contains a target. We modelled three sources of guidance: bottom-up visual saliency, learned visual features of the target's appearance, and a learned relationship between target location and scene context. The informativeness of these models, individually and combined, was assessed by comparing the regions selected by each model to human search fixations, particularly in target-absent scenes (which provide the most straightforward and rigorous comparison).

The diversity and size of our dataset (14 observers' fixations on 912 urban scenes)[1] provides a challenge for computational models of attentional guidance in real world scenes. Intelligent search behaviour requires an understanding of scenes, objects and the relationships between them. Although humans perform this task intuitively and efficiently, modelling visual search is challenging from a computational viewpoint. The combined model presented here achieves 94% of human agreement on our database; however, a comprehensive understanding of human search guidance will benefit from mutual interest by cognitive and computer vision scientists alike.

EXPERIMENTAL METHOD

Participants

Fourteen observers (18–40 years old, with normal acuity) were paid for their participation ($15/hour). They gave informed consent and passed the eyetracking calibration test.

Apparatus

Eye movements were recorded at 240 Hz using an ISCAN RK-464 video-based eyetracker. Observers sat at 75 cm from the display monitor, 65 cm from the eyetracking camera, with their head centred and stabilized in a headrest. The position of the right eye was tracked and viewing conditions were binocular. Stimuli were presented on a 21-inch CRT monitor with a resolution of 1024 × 768 pixels and a refresh rate of 100 Hz. Presentation of the stimuli was controlled with Matlab and Psychophysics Toolbox (Brainard, 1997; Pelli, 1997). The following calibration procedure was

---

[1] The complete dataset and analysis tools will be made available at the authors' website.

performed at the beginning of the experiment and repeated following breaks. Participants sequentially fixated five static targets positioned at 0° (centre) and at 10° of eccentricity. Subsequently, the accuracy of the calibration was tested at each of nine locations evenly distributed across the screen, including the five calibrated locations plus four targets at $+/-5.25°$ horizontally and vertically from centre. Estimated fixation position had to be within 0.75° of visual angle for all nine points, otherwise the experiment halted and the observer was recalibrated.

Stimuli

The scenes consisted of 912 colour pictures of urban environments, half containing a pedestrian (target present) and half without (target absent). Images were of resolution 800 × 600 pixels, subtending 23.5 × 17.7 ° of visual angle. When present, pedestrians subtended on average 0.9 × 1.8° (corresponding to roughly 31 × 64 pixels). For the target-present images, targets were spatially distributed across the image periphery (target locations ranged from 2.7 ° to 13 ° from the screen centre; median eccentricity was 8.6°), and were located in each quadrant of the screen with approximately equal frequency.[2]

Procedure

Participants were instructed to decide as quickly as possible whether a person was present in the scene. Responses were registered via the keyboard, which terminated the image presentation. Reaction time and eye movements were recorded. The first block consisted of the same 48 images for all participants, and was used as a practice block to verify that the eye could be tracked accurately. The experiment was composed of 19 blocks of 48 trials each and 50% target prevalence within each block. Eyetracking calibration was checked after each block to ensure tracking accuracy within 0.75° of each calibration target. Each participant performed 912 experimental trials, resulting in an experiment duration of 1 hour.

Eye movement analysis

Fixations were identified on smoothed eye position data, averaging the raw data over a moving window of eight data points (33 ms). Beginning and end

---

[2] See additional figures on authors' website for distribution of targets and fixations across all images in the database.

positions of saccades were detected using an algorithm implementing an acceleration criterion (Araujo, Kowler, & Pavel, 2001). Specifically, the velocity was calculated for two overlapping 17 ms intervals; the onset of the second interval was 4.17 ms after the first. The acceleration threshold was a velocity change of 6°/s between the two intervals. Saccade onset was defined as the time when acceleration exceeded threshold and the saccade terminated when acceleration dropped below threshold. Fixations were defined as the periods between successive saccades. Saccades occurring within 50 ms of each other were considered to be continuous.

HUMAN EYE MOVEMENTS RESULT

Accuracy and eye movement statistics

On average, participants' correct responses when the target was present (hits) was 87%. The false alarm rate (fa) in target-absent scenes was 3%. On correct trials, observers' mean reaction time was 1050 ms (1 standard error of the mean or SEM = 18) for target-present and 1517 ms (1 SEM = 14) for target-absent. Observers made an average of 3.5 fixations (excluding the initial central fixation but including fixations on the target) in target-present scenes and 5.1 fixations in target-absent scenes. The duration of "search fixations" exclusively (i.e., exploratory fixations excluding initial central fixation and those landing on the target) averaged 147 ms on target-present trials and 225 ms on target-absent trials. Observers spent an average of 428 ms fixating the target-person in the image before indicating a response.

We focused our modelling efforts on predicting locations of the first *three* fixations in each scene (but very similar results were obtained when we included all fixations). We introduce next the measures used to compare search model's predictions and humans' fixations.

Agreement among observers

How much eye movement variability exists when different observers look at the same image and perform the same task? First, we computed the regularity, or agreement among locations fixated by separate observers (Mannan, Ruddock, & Wooding, 1995; Tatler, Baddeley, & Gilchrist, 2005). As in Torralba et al. (2006), a measure of inter-observer agreement was obtained for each image by using the fixations generated by all-except-one observers. The "observer-defined" image region was created by assigning a value of 1 to each fixated pixel and 0 to all other pixels, then applying a Gaussian blur (cutoff frequency = 8 cycles per image, about 1° visual angle). The observer-defined region was then used to predict fixations of the excluded observer. For each image, this process was iterated for all observers. Thus, this measure reflected how consistently different observers selected similar regions to fixate. Figure 1 shows examples of target-absent scenes with high and low values of inter-observer agreement.

Not all of the agreement between observers is driven by the image, however—human fixations exhibit regularities that distinguish them from randomly selected image locations. Tatler and Vincent (this issue 2009) present compelling evidence that robust oculomotor biases constrain fixation selection independently of visual information or task (see also Tatler, 2007). Qualitatively, we observe in our dataset that the corners of the image and the top and bottom edges were less frequently fixated than regions near the image centre. We therefore derived a measure to quantify the proportion of inter-observer agreement that was independent of the particular scene's content (see also Foulsham & Underwood, 2008; Henderson, Brockmole, Castelhano, & Mack, 2007). Our "cross-image control" was obtained using the procedure described previously, with the variation that the observer-defined region for one image was used to predict the excluded observer's fixations from a *different* image selected at random.

The Receiver Operating Characteristic (ROC) curves for inter-observer agreement and the cross-image control are shown in Figure 2. These curves show the proportion of fixations that fall within the fixation-defined map (detection rate) in relation to the proportion of the image area selected by the map (false alarm rate). In the following, we report the area under the curve (AUC), which corresponds to the probability that the model will rank an actual fixation location more highly than a nonfixated location, with a value ranging from .5 (chance performance) to 1 (perfect performance) (Harel et al., 2006; Renninger, Verghese, & Coughlan 2007; Tatler et al., 2005).

The results in Figure 2 show a high degree of inter-observer agreement, indicating high consistency in the regions fixated by different observers for both target-absent scenes (AUC = .93) and target-present scenes (AUC = .95). Overall, inter-observer agreement was higher in target-present than in target-absent scenes, $t(805) = 11.6$, $p < .0001$, most likely because fixating the target was the primary goal of the search. These agreement curves represent an upper bound for comparing performance of the computational models with human fixations. Furthermore, the cross-image control produced an AUC of .68 and .62 for target-absent and target-present scenes respectively (random chance: AUC = .5). The cross-image control line represents the proportion of human agreement due to oculomotor biases and other biases in the stimuli set, and serves as the lower bound on the performance of the models.

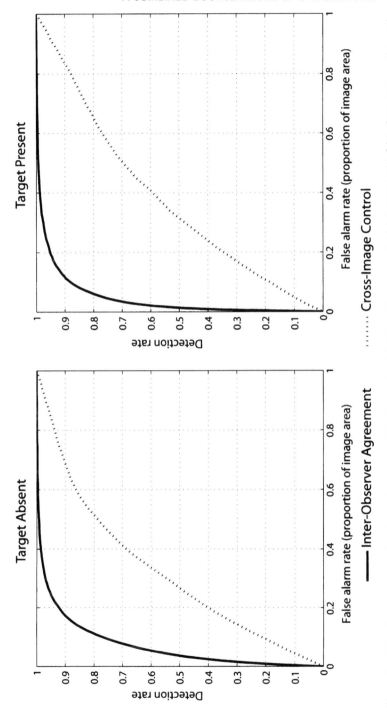

Figure 2. Inter-observer agreement and cross-image control for target-absent (left) and target-present (right) scenes. The false alarm rate, on the x-axis, corresponds to the proportion of the image selected by the model.

MODELLING METHODS

Here we used the framework of visual search guidance from Torralba (2003b) and Torralba et al. (2006). In this framework, the attentional map (M), which will be used to predict the locations fixated by human observers, is computed by combining three sources of information: Image saliency at each location (M_S), a model of guidance by target features (M_T), and a model of guidance by the scene context (M_C).

$$M(x, y) = M_S(x, y)^{\gamma 1} \, M_T(x, y)^{\gamma 2} \, M_C(x, y)^{\gamma 3} \qquad (1)$$

The exponents ($\gamma 1$, $\gamma 2$, $\gamma 3$), which will act like weights if we take the logarithm of Equation 1, are constants that are required when combining distributions with high-dimensional inputs that were independently trained, to ensure that the combined distribution is not dominated by one source (the procedure for selecting the exponents is described later). Together, these three components (M_S, M_T, and M_C) make up the combined attentional map (M).

Figure 3 illustrates a scene with its corresponding saliency, target features, and scene context maps, as well as a combined map integrating the three sources of guidance. Each model makes predictions, represented as a surface map, of the regions that are likely to be fixated. The best model should capture as many fixations as possible within as finely constrained a region as possible. In the following sections, we evaluate the performance of each of the three models individually, followed by a model combining sources of attentional guidance.

Guidance by saliency

Computational models of saliency are generally based on one principle: They use a mixture of local image features (e.g., colour and orientation at various spatial scales) to determine regions that are local outliers given the statistical distribution of features across a larger region of the image. The hypothesis underlying these models is that locations whose properties differ from neighbouring regions or the image as a whole are the most informative. Indeed, rare image features in an image are more likely to be diagnostic of objects (Elazary & Itti, 2008; Torralba et al., 2006), whereas repetitive image features or large homogenous regions are unlikely to be object-like (Bravo & Farid, 2006; Rosenholtz, Li, & Nakano, 2007).

Computing saliency involves estimating the distribution of local features in the image. Here we used the statistical saliency model described in Torralba et al. (2006), including the use of an independent validation set to determine an appropriate value for the exponent.[3] The independent

---

[3] In our validation set, the best exponent for the saliency map was .025, which is within the optimal range of .01–.3 found by Torralba et al. (2006).

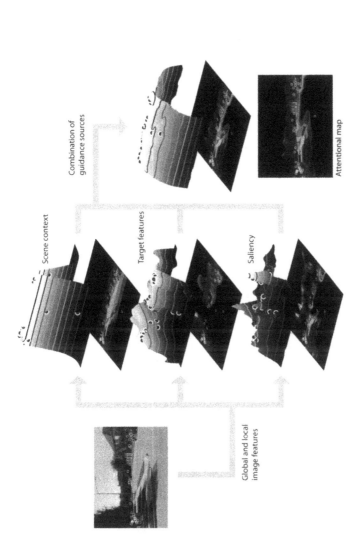

Figure 3. Illustration of a target-present image from the dataset, with the computational maps for three sources of guidance, and the combined attentional map. The flattened maps show the image regions selected when the model is thresholded at 30% of the image. To view this figure in colour, please see the online issue of the Journal.

validation set was composed of 50 target-present and 50 target-absent scenes selected randomly from the 912 experimental images and excluded from all other analyses. Figure 4 shows maps of the best and worst predictions of the saliency model on our stimuli set.

Guidance by target features

To date, the most well-studied sources of search guidance are target features (for reviews, see Wolfe, 2007; Zelinsky, 2008). Identifying the relevant features of an object's appearance remains a difficult issue, although recent computer vision approaches have reached excellent performance for some object classes (i.e., faces, Ullman, Vidal-Naquet, & Sali, 2002; cars, Papageorgiou & Poggio, 2000; pedestrians, Dalal & Triggs, 2005; cars, bicycles, and pedestrians, Serre, Wolf, Bileschi, Riesenhuber, & Poggio, 2007; Torralba, Fergus, & Freeman, 2008). Here, we used the person detector developed by Dalal and Triggs (2005) and Dalal, Triggs, and Schmid (2006) to model target features, as their code is available online[4] and gives state of the art detection performance at a reasonable speed.

Implementation of the DT person detector. The Dalal andTriggs (DT) detector is a classifier-based detector that uses a scanning window approach to explore the image at all locations and scales. The classifier extracts a set of features from each window and applies a linear Support Vector Machine (SVM) to classify the window as belonging to the target or background classes. The features are a grid of Histograms of Oriented Gradients (HOG) descriptors. The detector is sensitive to the gross structure of an upright human figure but relatively tolerant to variation in the pose of the arms and legs. We trained various implementations of the DT detector with different training set sizes and scanning window sizes, but here we report the only the results from implementation which ultimately gave the best performance on our validation set.[5] This implementation used a scanning window of 32×64 pixels and was trained on 2000 upright, unoccluded pedestrians, along with their left–right reflections. Pedestrians were cropped from images in the LabelMe database (Russell, Torralba, Murphy, & Freeman, 2008) and reduced in size to fill three-quarters of the height of the detection window. Negative training examples consisted of 30 randomly selected 32×64 pixel patches from 2000 images of outdoor scenes which did not contain people. None of the experimental stimuli were used as training images. The training process was as described in Dalal and Triggs (2005).

---

[4] See people detector code at http://pascal.inrialpes.fr/soft/olt/
[5] See the authors' website for details and results from the other implementations.

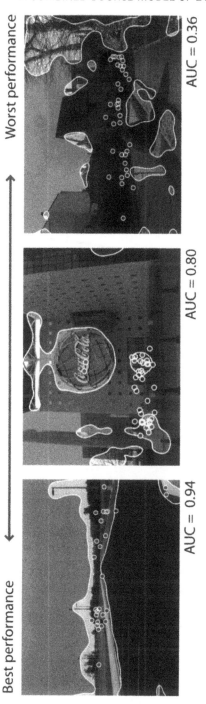

Figure 4. Saliency maps of the best and worst predictions on the dataset, and one mid-range image, with their AUC values. The highlighted region corresponds to 20% of the image area. Dots represent human fixations. To view this figure in colour, please see the online issue of the Journal.

The detector was tested on our stimuli set with cropped, resized pedestrians from our target-present scenes serving as positive test examples and 32×64 pixel windows from our target-absent scenes serving as negative test examples. Figure 5 shows the detection performance of our selected DT model implementation.[6] This implementation gave over 90% correct detections at a false positive rate of 10%, confirming the reliability of the DT detector on our database. Although this performance might be considered low given the exceptional performance of the DT detector on other image sets, the scenes used for our search task were particularly challenging: Targets were small, often occluded, and embedded in high

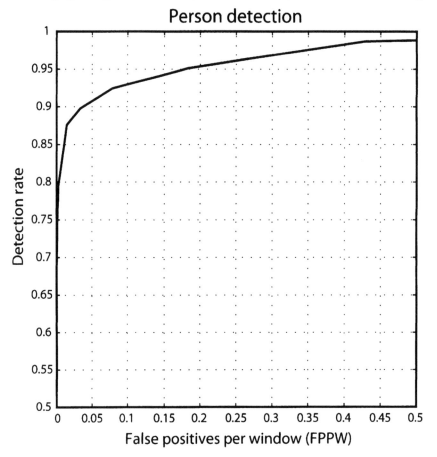

Figure 5. The ROC curve of the best implementation of the DT pedestrian detector, tested on our stimuli set. To view this figure in colour, please see the online issue of the Journal.

---

[6] See the authors' website for the detection curves of the other model implementations.

clutter. It is worth nothing that our goal was not to detect target-people in the dataset, but to use a reliable object detector as a *predictor* of human search fixations.

Target features map.   To generate target features maps for each image, the detector was run using a sliding window that moved across the image in steps of eight pixels. Multiscale detection was achieved by iteratively reducing the image by 20% and rerunning the sliding window detector; this process was repeated until the image height was less than the height of the detector window (see Dalal & Triggs, 2005, for details). This meant that each pixel was involved in many detection windows, and therefore the detector returned many values for each pixel. We created the object detector map (M_T) by assigning to each pixel the highest detection score returned for that pixel (from any detection window at any scale). As with the saliency map, the resulting object detector map was raised to an exponent (.025, determined by iteratively varying the exponent to obtain the best performance on the validation set) and then blurred by applying a Gaussian filter with 50% cutoff frequency at 8 cycles/image. Figure 6 shows maps of the best and worst predictions of the target features model on our stimuli set.

Guidance by scene context features

A mandatory role of scene context in object detection and search has been acknowledged for decades (for reviews, Bar, 2004; Chun, 2003; Oliva & Torralba, 2007). However, formal models of scene context guidance face the same problem as models of object appearance: They require knowledge about how humans represent visual scenes. Several models of scene recognition have been proposed in recent years (Bosch, Zisserman, & Muñoz, 2008; Fei Fei & Perona, 2005; Grossberg, & Huang, 2009; Lazebnik, Schmidt, & Ponce, 2006; Oliva & Torralba, 2001; Renninger & Malik, 2004; Vogel & Schiele, 2007), with most of the approaches summarizing an image's "global" features by pooling responses from low-level filters at multiple scales and orientations sampled over regions in the image.

Our model of scene context implements a top-down constraint that selects "relevant" image regions for a search task. Top-down constraints in a people-search task, for example, would select regions corresponding to sidewalks but not sky or trees. As in Oliva and Torralba (2001), we adopted a representation of the image using a set of "global features" that provide a holistic description of the spatial organization of spatial frequencies and orientations in the image. The implementation was identical to the description in Torralba et al. (2006), with the exception that the scene context model incorporated a finer spatial analysis (i.e., an 8×8 grid of

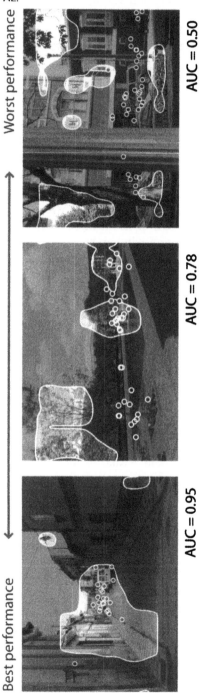

Figure 6. Target features maps (thresholded at 20% of the image area). Dots represent human fixations. To view this figure in colour, please see the online issue of the Journal.

nonoverlapping windows) and was trained on more images (1880 images). From each training image, we produced 10 random crops of 320×240 pixels to generate a training set with a uniform distribution of target locations. As in Torralba et al., the model learned the associations between the global features of an image and the location of the target. The trained computational context model compared the global scene features of a *novel* image with learned global scene features to predict the image region most highly associated with the presence of a pedestrian. This region is represented by a horizontal line at the height predicted by the model. Figure 7 shows maps of the best and worst predictions of the scene context model on our stimuli set.

There are cases of the scene context model failing to predict human fixations simply because it selected the wrong region (see Figures 7 and 8). In these cases, it would be interesting to see whether performance could be improved by a "context oracle", in which the true context region is known. It is possible to approximate contextual "ground truth" for an image by asking observers to indicate the best possible context region in each scene (Droll & Eckstein, 2008). With this information, we can establish an upper bound on the performance of a model based solely on scene context.

Evaluating the ground truth of scene context: A "context oracle".   Seven new participants marked the context region for pedestrians in each scene in the database. The instructions were to imagine pedestrians in the most plausible places in the scene and to position a horizontal bar at the height where the heads would be. Participants were encouraged to use cues such as the horizon, the heights of doorways, and the heights of cars and signs in order to make the most accurate estimate of human head height. Image presentation was randomized and self-paced. Each participant's results served as an individual "context model", which identified the contextually relevant location for a pedestrian for each scene. The "context oracle" was created by pooling responses from all observers. Context oracle maps (Figure 8), were created by applying a Gaussian blur to the horizontal line selected by each observer, and then summing the maps produced by all participants.

Guidance by a combined model of attention

The three models were combined by multiplying the weighted maps as shown in Equation 1. The weights ($\gamma 1 = 0.1$, $\gamma 2 = 0.85$, $\gamma 3 = 0.05$) were selected by testing various weights in the range [0,1] to find the combination which gave the best performance on the validation set. Examples of combined source model maps are shown in Figure 9.

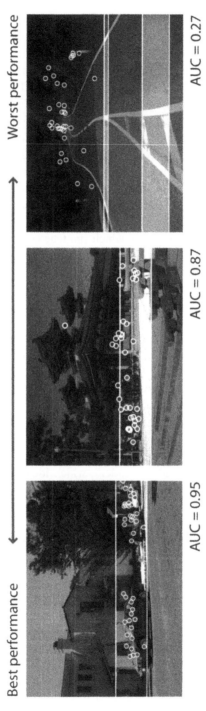

Figure 7. Scene context maps (thresholded at 20% of the image area). Dots represent human fixations. To view this figure in colour, please see the online issue of the Journal.

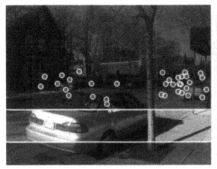 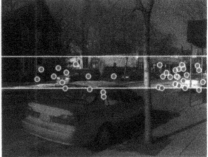

(a) Scene context model   (b) Context oracle

Figure 8. Comparison between (a) the computationally defined scene context map and (b) the empirically defined context oracle map for a single image (maps are thresholded at 20% of the image area; dots represent fixations). To view this figure in colour, please see the online issue of the Journal.

MODELLING RESULTS

The ROC curves for all models are shown in Figure 10 and the performances are given in Table 1. Averaging across target-absent and target-present scenes, the scene context model predicted fixated regions with greater accuracy (AUC = .845) than models of saliency (.795) or target features (.811) alone. A combination of the three sources of guidance, however, resulted in greater overall accuracy (.895) than any single source model, with the overall highest performance given by a model that integrated saliency and target features with the "context oracle" model of scene context (.899). Relative to human agreement, the purely computational combined model achieved 94% of the AUC for human agreement in both target-present and target-absent scenes. When the context oracle was substituted for the scene context model, the combined model achieved on average 96% of the AUC of human agreement.

Saliency and target features models

The saliency model had the lowest overall performance, with an AUC of .77 and .82 in target-absent and target-present scenes. This performance is within the range of values given by other saliency models predicting fixations in free viewing tasks (AUC of .727 for Itti et al., 1998; .767 for Bruce & Tsotsos, 2006; see also Harel et al., 2006).

The best example shown in Figure 4 is typical of the type of scene in which the saliency model performs very well. The saliency model does best in scenes with large homogenous regions (sky, road), and in which most of the

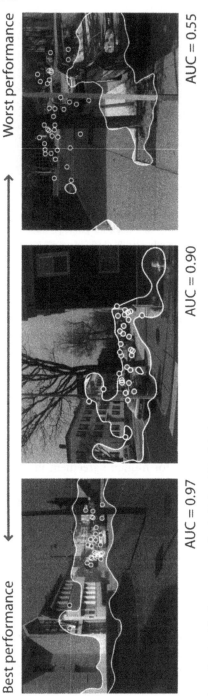

Figure 9. Combined source maps (thresholded at 20% of the image area). Dots represent human fixations. To view this figure in colour, please see the online issue of the Journal.

TABLE 1
Summary of performance of human observers, single source models, and combined
source of guidance models

	Area under curve	Performance at 20% threshold	Performance at 10% threshold
Target-absent scenes			
Human agreement	.930	.923	.775
Cross-image control	.683	.404	.217
Saliency model	.773	.558	.342
Target features model	.778	.539	.313
Scene context model	.845	.738	.448
Context oracle	.881	.842	.547
Saliency × Target features	.814	.633	.399
Context × Saliency	.876	.801	.570
Context × Target features	.861	.784	.493
Combined source model	.877	.804	.574
Combined model, using context oracle	.893	.852	.605
Target-present scenes			
Human agreement	.955	.952	.880
Cross-image control	.622	.346	.186
Saliency model	.818	.658	.454
Target features model	.845	.697	.515
Scene context model	.844	.727	.451
Context oracle	.889	.867	.562
Saliency × Target features	.872	.773	.586
Context × Saliency	.894	.840	.621
Context × Target features	.890	.824	.606
Combined source model	.896	.845	.629
Combined model, using context oracle	.906	.886	.646

salient features coincide with the region where observers might reasonably expect to find the target. This illustrates the difficulty in determining how saliency influences eye movement guidance: In many cases, the salient regions of a real world scene are also the most contextually relevant regions. In fact, recent studies suggest that the correlation between saliency and observer's fixation selection may be an artefact of correlations between salience and higher level information (Einhauser et al., 2008; Foulsham & Underwood, 2008; Henderson et al., 2007; Stirk & Underwood, 2007; Tatler,

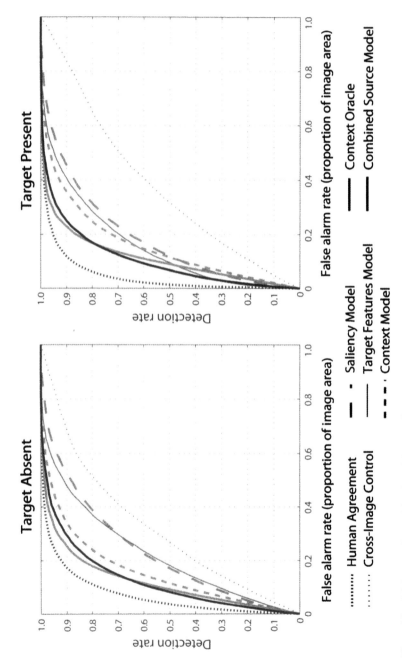

Figure 10. ROC curves for models. The ROC curves for human agreement and cross-image control correspond respectively to the upper and lower bounds of performance against which models were compared. To view this figure in colour, please see the online issue of the Journal.

2007). The saliency model can also give very poor predictions of human fixations in some scenes, as shown by the example in Figure 4. In a search task, saliency alone is a rather unreliable source of guidance because saliency is often created by an accidental feature (such as a reflection or a differently coloured gap between two objects) that does not necessarily correspond to an informative region.

In target-present scenes, not surprisingly, the target features model (AUC = .85) performed significantly better than the saliency model, $t(404) = 4.753$, $p < .001$. In target-absent scenes, however, the target features model (AUC = .78) did not perform significantly above the saliency model, $t(405) < 1$. Interestingly, both models were significantly correlated with each other, $r = .37$, $p < .001$, suggesting that scenes for which the saliency model was able to predict fixations well tended to be scenes in which the target features model also predicted fixations well.

Figure 5 shows target-absent images for which the target features model gave the best and worst predictions. Similar to the saliency model, the target features model tended to perform best when most of the objects were concentrated within the contextually relevant region for a pedestrian. Also like the saliency model, the target features model performed poorly when it selected accidental, nonobject features of the image (such as tree branches that happened to overlap in a vaguely human-like shape). It is important to note that the performance of the target features model is not due solely to fixations on the target. In the target-absent scenes, there was no target to find, yet the target features model was still able to predict human fixations significantly above the level of the cross-image control. Even in target-present scenes, replacing predictions of the target features model with the *true* location of the target (a "target oracle") did not explain the target model's performance on this dataset.[7]

Context models

Overall, scene context was the most accurate single source of guidance in this search task. The computational model of scene context predicted fixation locations with an AUC of .85 and .84 in target-absent and target-present scenes, respectively. The scene context model performed significantly better than the target features model in target-absent scenes, $t(405) = 11.122$, $p < .001$, although the two models did not significantly differ in target-present scenes, $t(404) < 1$.

---

[7] See the authors' website for a comparison of the ROC curves of the target features model and the target oracle.

In the majority of our scenes, the computational scene context model gave a very good approximation of the location of search fixations. The first and second images in Figure 7 show the model's best and median performance, respectively, for target-absent scenes. In fact, the context model failed to predict fixated regions (i.e., had an AUC below the mean AUC of the cross-image control) in only 26 target-absent scenes and 24 target-present scenes. Typical failures are shown in Figures 7 and 8: In a few scenes, the model incorrectly identifies the relationship between scene layout and probable target location. In order to get around this problem and get a sense of the true predictive power of a context-only model of search guidance, we used the "context oracle". The empirically determined context oracle should be able to distinguish between cases in which the context model fails because it fails to identify the appropriate context region, and cases in which it fails because human fixations were largely outside the context region.

Overall performance of the context oracle was .88 and .89 for target-absent and target-present images, respectively. The context oracle performed significantly better than the computational model of scene context in target-absent, $t(405) = 8.265$, $p < .001$, and target-present, $t(404) = 8.861$, $p < .001$, scenes. Unlike any of the computational models, the context oracle performed above chance on all images of the dataset; at worst, it performed at about the level of the average AUC for the cross-image control (.68 for target-absent scenes). Examples of these failures are shown in Figure 11.

Combined source models

A combined source model that integrated saliency, target features, and scene context outperformed all of the single source models, with an overall AUC of .88 in target-absent scenes and .90 in target-present scenes (see Table 1). The combined guidance model performed better than the best single source model (scene context) in both target-absent, $t(405) = 10.450$, $p < .001$, and target-present, $t(404) = 13.501$, $p < .001$, scenes.

Across the image set, performance of the combined model was strongly correlated with that of the scene context model, $r = .80$, $p < .001$ in target-absent scenes. The combined model was also moderately correlated with the saliency model, $r = .51$, $p < .001$ in target-absent scenes, and the target features model correlated weakly, $r = .25$, $p < .001$ in target-absent scenes. Taken together, this suggests that the success or failure of the combined model depended largely on the success or failure of its scene context component, and less on the other two components.

In order to analyse the combined model in greater detail, we also tested partial models that were missing one of the three sources of guidance (see Table 1). Removing the saliency component of the combined model

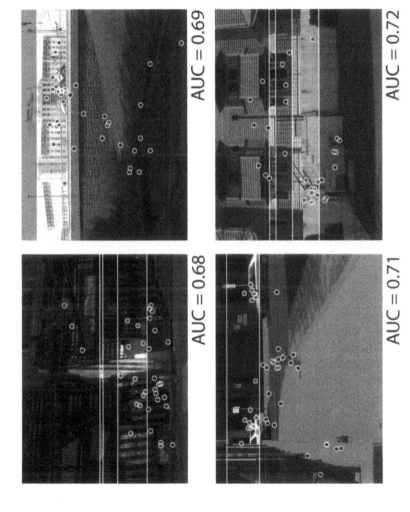

Figure 11. Target-absent scenes on which the context oracle performed the worst, with their corresponding AUC values. Maps are thresholded at 20% of the image area; dots represent fixations. To view this figure in colour, please see the online issue of the Journal.

produced a small but significant drop in performance in target-absent, $t(405) = 6.922$, $p < .001$, and target-present, $t(404) = 2.668$, $p < .01$, scenes. Likewise, removing the target features component of the model also produced a small but significant drop in performance in target-absent, $t(405) = 5.440$, $p < .001$, and target-present, $t(404) = 10.980$, $p < .001$, scenes. The high significance value of these extremely small drops in performance is somewhat deceptive; the reasons for this are addressed in the Discussion. Notably, the largest drop in performance resulted when the scene context component was removed from the combined model: target-absent, $t(405) = 17.381$, $p < .001$; target-present, $t(404) = 6.759$, $p < .001$.

Interestingly, the combined source model performed very similarly to the empirically defined context oracle. The difference between these two models was not significant in target-absent, $t(405) = -1.233$, $p = .218$, or target-present, $t(404) = 2.346$, $p = .019$, scenes.

Finally, the high performance of the context oracle motivated us to substitute it for the scene context component of the combined model, to see whether performance could be boosted even further. Indeed, substituting the context oracle for computational scene context improved performance in both target-absent, $t(405) = 5.565$, $p < .001$, and target-present, $t(404) = 3.461$, $p = .001$, scenes. The resulting hybrid model was almost entirely driven by the context oracle, as suggested by its very high correlation with the context oracle, $r = .97$, $p < .001$ in target-absent scenes.

DISCUSSION

We assembled a large dataset of 912 real world scenes and recorded eye movements from observers performing a visual search task. The scene regions fixated were very consistent across different observers, regardless of whether the target was present or absent in the scene. Motivated by the regularity of search behaviour, we implemented computational models for several proposed methods of search guidance and evaluated how well these models predicted observers' fixation locations. On the target-absent scenes of the dataset, the scene context model generated better predictions (it was the best single map in 276 out of the 406 scenes) than saliency (71 scenes) or target features (59 scenes) models. Even in target-present scenes, scene context provided better predictions (191 of 405 scenes) than saliency (72 scenes) but only slightly more than target features (142 scenes). Ultimately, combining models of attentional guidance predicted 94% of human agreement, with the scene context component providing the most explanatory power.

Although the combined model is reasonably accurate at predicting human fixations, there is still room for improvement. Moving forward, even small improvements in model specificity will represent a significant achievement. Our data shows that human observers are reasonable predictors of fixations even as map selectivity increases: 94% and 83% accuracy for selected region sizes of 20% and 10%, respectively. In contrast, the accuracy of all models fell off drastically as map selectivity increased and a region size of roughly 40% is needed for the combined model to achieve the same detection rate as human observers. Figure 12 illustrates this gap between the best computational model and human performance: Observers' fixations are tightly clustered in very specific regions, but the model selects a much more general region containing many nonfixated objects. In the following, we offer several approaches that may contribute to an improved representation of search guidance in real world scenes.

In our work, a "context region" is operationally defined as an association between certain scene regions and the presence of a target. Under this definition, a context region can be specified for any class of target and modelled using many representations. In this study, our model of scene context generated predictions based on a learned association between a representation of global image statistics and the location of a person in the scene. Compared to a model of image saliency or a model of target-like features, we found that a scene context model was better able to predict the region where people would look, regardless of whether the target was present in the scene. Moreover, the high overall accuracy of a *computational* combined source model was matched by an *empirically* derived context oracle, created by an independent set of participants marking the region which they deemed most likely to contain the target. In target-absent scenes, there was a substantial correlation between the context oracle and human agreement, $r = .54$, $p < .001$, and also between the context oracle and the combined model, $r = .50$, $p < .001$. This suggests that examining failures of the context oracle may hint at ways in which the combined model's representation fails to match human search patterns.

Figure 11 shows the worst performance of the context oracle for target-absent scenes. Why was contextual guidance insufficient for predicting the fixated regions of these scenes? One reason may be that our model of the context region did not adequately represent the real context region in certain complex scenes. We modelled the context region as a single height in the image plane, which is appropriate for most images (typically pedestrians appear on the ground plane and nowhere else). However, when the scenes contain multiple surfaces (such as balconies, ramps, and stairs) at different heights, the simplified model tends to fail. Improving the implementation of scene context to reflect that observers have expectations associated with multiple scene regions may reduce the discrepancy between model predictions and where observers look.

In addition, observers may be guided by contextual information beyond what is represented here. It is important to note that scene context can be

(a) Combined computational model

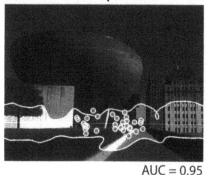 

AUC = 0.95   AUC = 0.95

(b) Region defined by human fixations

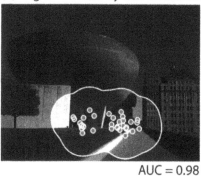 

AUC = 0.98   AUC = 0.98

Figure 12. Illustration of the discrepancy between regions selected by (a) the combined computational model and (b) human fixations. To view this figure in colour, please see the online issue of the Journal.

represented with a number of approaches. Associations between the target and other *objects* in the scene, for example, may also contribute to search guidance (Kumar & Hebert, 2005; Rabinovich, Vedaldi, Galleguillos, Wiewiora, & Belongie, 2007; Torralba, Murphy, & Freeman, 2005, 2007). In our search task, for example, the presence of a person may be more strongly associated with a doorway than a garbage can. The role of semantic influences in search guidance remains an interesting and open question. Zelinsky and Schmidt (this issue 2009) explore an intermediate between search of semantically meaningful scenes and search in which observers lack expectations of target location. They find evidence that scene segmentation and flexible semantic cues can be used very rapidly to bias search to regions associated with the target (see also Eckstein et al., 2006; Neider & Zelinsky, 2006).

Scene context seems to provide the most accurate predictions in this task, which provokes the question: Is scene context *typically* the dominant source of guidance in real world search tasks? Similarly, how well do the findings of this study generalize to search for other object classes? Our search task may be biased towards context-guided search in the following ways. First, observers may have been biased to adopt a context-based strategy rather than relying on target features simply because the target pedestrians were generally very small (less than 1% of image area) and often occluded, so a search strategy based mainly on target features might have produced more false alarms than detections. Second, the large database tested here represented both semantically-consistent associations (pedestrians were supported by surfaces; Biederman et al., 1982) and location-consistent associations (pedestrians were located on *ground* surfaces). As a result, even when the target was absent from the scene, viewers expected to find their target within the context region, and therefore the scene context model predicted fixations more effectively than the target features or saliency models. Searching scenes in which the target location violated these prior expectations (e.g., person on a cloud or rooftop) might bias the pattern of fixations such that the emphasis on each source of guidance would be different from the current model.

A fully generalizable model of search behaviour may need to incorporate flexible weights on the individual sources of search guidance. Consider the example of searching for a pen in an office. Looking for a pen from the doorway may induce strategies based on convenient object relations, such as looking first to a desk, which is both strongly associated with the target and easy to discriminate from background objects. On the other hand, looking for a pen while standing in front of the desk may encourage the use of other strategies, such as searching for pen-like features. It follows that the features of the target may vary in informativeness as an observer navigates through their environment. A counting task, for example, may enhance the importance of a target features model (see Kanan, Tong, Zhang, & Cottrell, this issue 2009). The implications for the combined source model of guidance are that, not only would the model benefit from an improved representation of target features (e.g., Zelinsky, 2008), saliency (see Kanan et al., this issue 2009), or context, but the weights themselves may need to be flexible, depending on constraints not currently modelled.

In short, there is much room for further exploration: We need to investigate a variety of natural scene search tasks in order to fully understand the sources of guidance that drive attention and how they interact. It is important to acknowledge that we have chosen to implement only one of several possible representations of image saliency, target features, or scene context. Therefore, performance of the individual guidance models discussed in this paper may vary with different computational approaches. Our aim, nevertheless, is to set a performance benchmark for how accurately a model representing combined sources of guidance can predict where human observers will fixate during natural search tasks.

CONCLUDING REMARKS

We present a model of search guidance that combines saliency, target features, and scene context, and accounts for 94% of the agreement between human observers searching for targets in over 900 scenes. In this people-search task, the scene context model proves to be the single most important component driving the high performance of the combined source model. None of the models, however, fully capture the selectivity of the observer-defined attentional map. A comprehensive understanding of search behaviour may require that future models capture mechanisms that underlie the tight clustering of search fixations.

REFERENCES

Andrews, T. J., & Coppola, D. M. (1999). Idiosyncratic characteristics of saccadic eye movements when viewing different visual environments. *Vision Research, 39*, 2947–2953.

Araujo, C., Kowler, E., & Pavel, M. (2001). Eye movements during visual search: The cost of choosing the optimal path. *Vision Research, 41*, 3613–3625.

Bar, M. (2004). Visual objects in context. *Nature Reviews Neuroscience, 5*, 617–629.

Biederman, I., Mezzanotte, R. J., & Rabinowitz, J. C. (1982). Scene perception: Detecting and judging objects undergoing relational violations. *Cognitive Psychology, 14*, 143–177.

Bosch, A., Zisserman, A., & Muñoz, X. (2008). Scene classification using a hybrid generative/discriminative approach. *IEEE Transactions on Pattern Analysis and Machine Intelligence, 30*, 712–727.

Brainard, D. H. (1997). The Psychophysics Toolbox. *Spatial Vision, 10*, 433–436.

Bravo, M. J., & Farid, H. (2006). Object recognition in dense clutter. *Perception & Psychophysics, 68*(6), 911–918.

Bruce, N., & Tsotsos, J. K. (2006). Saliency based on information maximization. *Advances in Neural Information Processing Systems, 18*, 155–162.

Buswell, G. T. (1935). *How people look at pictures.* Oxford, UK: Oxford University Press.

Castelhano, M. S., & Henderson, J. M. (2007). Initial scene representations facilitate eye movement guidance in visual search. *Journal of Experimental Psychology: Human Perception and Performance, 33*, 753–763.

Chaumon, M., Drouet, V., & Tallon-Baudry, C. (2008). Unconscious associative memory affects visual processing before 100 ms. *Journal of Vision, 8*(3), 1–10.

Chun, M. M. (2003). Scene perception and memory. In D. E. Irwin & B. H. Ross (Eds.), *The psychology of learning and motivation: Advances in research and theory* (Vol. 42, pp. 79–108). San Diego, CA: Academic Press.

Dalal, N., & Triggs, B. (2005). Histograms of oriented gradients for human detection. *IEEE Conference on Computer Vision and Pattern Recognition, 2*, 886–893.

Dalal, N., Triggs, B., & Schmid, C. (2006). Human detection using oriented histograms of flow and appearance. *European Conference on Computer Vision, 2*, 428–441.

De Graef, P., Christiaens, D., & d'Ydewalle, G. (1990). Perceptual effects of scene context on object identification. *Psychological Research*, *52*, 317–329.

Droll, J., & Eckstein, M. (2008). Expected object position of two hundred fifty observers predicts first fixations of seventy seven separate observers during search. *Journal of Vision*, *8*(6), 320.

Eckstein, M. P., Drescher, B. A., & Shimozaki, S. S. (2006). Attentional cues in real scenes, saccadic targeting and Bayesian priors. *Psychological Science*, *17*, 973–980.

Einhäuser, W., Rutishauser, U., & Koch, C. (2008). Task-demands can immediately reverse the effects of sensory-driven saliency in complex visual stimuli. *Journal of Vision*, *8*(2), 1–19.

Elazary, L., & Itti, L. (2008). Interesting objects are visually salient. *Journal of Vision*, *8*(3), 1–15.

Fei Fei, L., & Perona, P. (2005). A Bayesian hierarchical model for learning natural scene categories. *IEEE Proceedings in Computer Vision and Pattern Recognition*, *2*, 524–531.

Foulsham, T., & Underwood, G. (2008). What can saliency models predict about eye movements? Spatial and sequential aspects of fixations during encoding and recognition. *Journal of Vision*, *8*(2), 1–17.

Friedman, A. (1979). Framing pictures: The role of knowledge in automatized encoding and memory of gist. *Journal of Experimental Psychology: General*, *108*, 316–355.

Greene, M. R., & Oliva, A. (2009). Recognition of natural scenes from global properties: Seeing the forest without representing the trees. *Cognitive Psychology*, *58*(2), 137–179.

Grossberg, S., & Huang, T.-R. (2009). ARTSCENE: A neural system for natural scene classification. *Journal of Vision*, *9*, 1–19.

Harel, J., Koch, C., & Perona, P. (2006). Graph-based visual saliency. *Advances in Neural Information Processing Systems*, *19*, 545–552.

Hayhoe, M., & Ballard, D. (2005). Eye movements in natural behavior. *Trends in Cognitive Sciences*, *9*, 188–194.

Hayhoe, M., Shrivastava, A., Mruczek, R., & Pelz, J. B. (2003). Visual memory and motor planning in a natural task. *Journal of Vision*, *3*, 49–63.

Henderson, J. M., Brockmole, J. R., Castelhano, M. S., & Mack, M. (2007). Visual saliency does not account for eye movement during visual search in real-world scenes. In R. van Gompel, M. Fischer, W. Murray, & R. Hill (Eds.), *Eye movement research: Insights into mind and brain* (pp. 537–562). Oxford, UK: Elsevier.

Henderson, J. M., Weeks, P. A., Jr., & Hollingworth, A. (1999). Effects of semantic consistency on eye movements during scene viewing. *Journal of Experimental Psychology: Human Perception and Performance*, *25*, 210–228.

Hoiem, D., Efros, A. A., & Hebert, M. (2006). Putting objects in perspective. *IEEE Conference on Computer Vision and Pattern Recognition*, *2*, 2137–2144.

Itti, L., & Koch, C. (2000). A saliency-based search mechanism for overt and covert shifts of visual attention. *Vision Research*, *40*, 1489–1506.

Itti, L., Koch, C., & Niebur, E. (1998). A model of saliency-based visual attention for rapid scene analysis. *IEEE Transactions in Pattern Analysis and Machine Vision*, *20*(11), 12–54.

Joubert, O., Rousselet, G., Fize, D., & Fabre-Thorpe, M. (2007). Processing scene context: Fast categorization and object interference. *Vision Research*, *47*, 3286–3297.

Kanan, C., Tong, M. H., Zhang, L., & Cottrell, G. W. (2009). SUN: Top-down saliency using natural statistics. *Visual Cognition*, *17*(6/7), 979–1003.

Koch, C., & Ullman, S. (1985). Shifts in visual attention: Towards the underlying circuitry. *Human Neurobiology*, *4*, 219–227.

Kumar, S., & Hebert, M. (2005). A hierarchical field framework for unified context-based classification. *IEEE International Conference on Computer Vision*, *2*, 1284–1291.

Land, M. F., & Lee, D. N. (1994). Where we look when we steer. *Nature*, *369*, 742–744.

Land, M. F., & McLeod, P. (2000). From eye movements to actions: How batsmen hit the ball. *Nature Neuroscience*, *3*, 1340–1345.

Lazebnik, S., Schmidt, C., & Ponce, J. (2006). Beyond bags of features: Spatial pyramid matching for recognizing natural scene categories. *IEEE Conference on Computer Vision and Pattern Recognition, 2*, 2169–2178.

Li, Z. (2002). A saliency map in primary visual cortex. *Trends in Cognitive Sciences, 6*(1), 9–16.

Loftus, G. R., & Mackworth, N. H. (1978). Cognitive determinants of fixation location during picture viewing. *Journal of Experimental Psychology: Human Perception and Performance, 4*, 565–572.

Mannan, S., Ruddock, K. H., & Wooding, D. S. (1995). Automatic control of saccadic eye movements made in visual inspection of briefly presented 2-D images. *Spatial Vision, 9*, 363–386.

McCotter, M., Gosselin, F., Sowden, P., & Schyns, P. G. (2005). The use of visual information in natural scenes. *Visual Cognition, 12*, 938–953.

Neider, M. B., & Zelinsky, G. J. (2006). Scene context guides eye movements during visual search. *Vision Research, 46*, 614–621.

Oliva, A., & Torralba, A. (2001). Modeling the shape of the scene: A holistic representation of the spatial envelope. *International Journal of Computer Vision, 42*, 145–175.

Oliva, A., & Torralba, A. (2006). Building the gist of a scene: The role of global image features in recognition. *Progress in Brain Research: Visual Perception, 155*, 23–36.

Oliva, A., & Torralba, A. (2007). The role of context in object recognition. *Trends in Cognitive Sciences, 11*(12), 520–527.

Papageorgiou, C., & Poggio, T. (2000). A trainable system for object detection. *International Journal of Computer Vision, 38*(1), 15–33.

Parkhurst, D. J., Law, K., & Niebur, E. (2002). Modeling the role of salience in the allocation of overt visual attention. *Vision Research, 42*, 107–123.

Parkhurst, D. J., & Niebur, E. (2003). Scene content selected by active vision. *Spatial Vision, 16*(2), 125–154.

Pelli, D. G. (1997). The VideoToolbox software for visual psychophysics: Transforming numbers into movies. *Spatial Vision, 10*, 437–442.

Peters, R. J., Iyer, A., Itti, L., & Koch, C. (2005). Components of bottom-up gaze allocation in natural images. *Vision Research, 45*, 2397–2416.

Pomplun, M. (2006). Saccadic selectivity in complex visual search displays. *Vision Research, 46*, 1886–1900.

Rabinovich, A., Vedaldi, A., Galleguillos, C., Wiewiora, E., & Belongie, S. (2007). Objects in context. *IEEE International Conference on Computer Vision*, 1–8.

Rao, R. P. N., Zelinsky, G., Hayhoe, M. M., & Ballard, D. H. (2002). Eye movements in iconic visual search. *Vision Research, 42*, 1447–1463.

Renninger, L. W., & Malik, J. (2004). When is scene identification just texture recognition? *Vision Research, 44*, 2301–2311.

Renninger, L. W., Verghese, P., & Coughlan, J. (2007). Where to look next? Eye movements reduce local uncertainty. *Journal of Vision, 7*(3), 1–17.

Rodriguez-Sanchez, A. J., Simine, E., & Tsotsos, J. K. (2007). Attention and visual search. *International Journal of Neural Systems, 17*(4), 275–288.

Rosenholtz, R. (1999). A simple saliency model predicts a number of motion popout phenomena. *Vision Research, 39*, 3157–3163.

Rosenholtz, R., Li, Y., & Nakano, L. (2007). Measuring visual clutter. *Journal of Vision, 7*(2), 1–22.

Rousselet, G. A., Joubert, O. R., & Fabre-Thorpe, M. (2005). How long to get to the "gist" of real-world natural scenes? *Visual Cognition, 12*, 852–877.

Russell, B., Torralba, A., Murphy, K., & Freeman, W. T. (2008). LabelMe: A database and web-based tool for image annotation. *International Journal of Computer Vision, 77*, 157–173.

Schyns, P. G., & Oliva, A. (1994). From blobs to boundary edges: Evidence for time- and spatial-scale-dependent scene recognition. *Psychological Science, 5,* 195–200.

Serre, T., Wolf, L., Bileschi, S., Riesenhuber, M., & Poggio, T. (2007). Object recognition with cortex-like mechanisms. *IEEE Transactions on Pattern Analysis and Machine Intelligence, 29*(3), 411–426.

Stirk, J. A., & Underwood, G. (2007). Low-level visual saliency does not predict change detection in natural scenes. *Journal of Vision, 7*(10), 1–10.

Tatler, B. W. (2007). The central fixation bias in scene viewing: Selecting an optimal viewing position independently of motor biases and image feature distributions. *Journal of Vision, 7*(14), 1–17.

Tatler, B. W., Baddeley, R. J., & Gilchrist, I. D. (2005). Visual correlates of fixation selection: Effects of scale and time. *Vision Research, 45*(5), 643–659.

Tatler, B. W., Baddeley, R. J., & Vincent, B. T. (2006). The long and the short of it: Spatial statistics at fixation vary with saccade amplitude and task. *Vision Research, 46*(12), 1857–1862.

Tatler, B. W., & Vincent, B. T. (2009). The prominence of behavioural biases in eye guidance. *Visual Cognition, 17*(6/7), 1029–1054.

Torralba, A. (2003a). Contextual priming for object detection. *International Journal of Computer Vision, 53*(2), 169–191.

Torralba, A. (2003b). Modeling global scene factors in attention. *Journal of Optical Society of America, 20A*(7), 1407–1418.

Torralba, A., Fergus, R., & Freeman, W. T. (2008). 80 million tiny images: A large dataset for non-parametric object and scene recognition. *IEEE Transactions on Pattern Analysis and Machine Intelligence, 30,* 1958–1970.

Torralba, A., Murphy, K. P., & Freeman, W. T. (2005). Contextual models for object detection using boosted random fields. *Advances in Neural Information Processing Systems, 17,* 1401–1408.

Torralba, A., Murphy, K. P., & Freeman, W. T. (2007). Sharing visual features for multiclass and multiview object detection. *IEEE Transactions on Pattern Analysis and Machine Intelligence, 29*(5), 854–869.

Torralba, A., & Oliva, A. (2002). Depth estimation from image structure. *IEEE Pattern Analysis and Machine Intelligence, 24,* 1226–1238.

Torralba, A., & Oliva, A. (2003). Statistics of Natural Images Categories. *Network: Computation in Neural Systems, 14,* 391–412.

Torralba, A., Oliva, A., Castelhano, M., & Henderson, J. M. (2006). Contextual guidance of eye movements and attention in real-world scenes: The role of global features in object search. *Psychological Review, 113,* 766–786.

Treisman, A., & Gelade, G. (1980). A feature integration theory of attention. *Cognitive Psychology, 12,* 97–136.

Tsotsos, J. K., Culhane, S. M., Wai, W. Y. K., Lai, Y. H., Davis, N., & Nuflo, F. (1995). Modeling visual-attention via selective tuning. *Artificial Intelligence, 78,* 507–545.

Ullman, S., Vidal-Naquet, M., & Sali, E. (2002). Visual features of intermediate complexity and their use in classification. *Nature Neuroscience, 5,* 682–687.

Van Zoest, W., Donk, M., & Theeuwes, J. (2004). The role of stimulus-driven and goal-driven control in saccadic visual selection. *Journal of Experimental Psychology: Human Perception and Performance, 30,* 746–759.

Vogel, J., & Schiele, B. (2007). Semantic scene modeling and retrieval for content-based image retrieval. *International Journal of Computer Vision, 72*(2), 133–157.

Wolfe, J. M. (1994). Guided Search 2.0: A revised model of visual search. *Psychonomic Bulletin and Review, 1,* 202–228.

Wolfe, J. M. (2007). Guided Search 4.0: Current progress with a model of visual search. In W. Gray (Ed.), *Integrated models of cognitive systems* (pp. 99–119). New York: Oxford Press.

Wolfe, J. M., Cave, K. R., & Franzel, S. L. (1989). Guided Search: An alternative to the feature integration model for visual search. *Journal of Experimental Psychology: Human Perception and Performance, 15*, 419–433.

Wolfe, J. M., & Horowitz, T. S. (2004). What attributes guide the deployment of visual attention and how do they do it? *Nature Reviews Neuroscience, 5*(6), 495–501.

Yarbus, A. (1967). *Eye movements and vision.* New York: Plenum Press.

Zelinsky, G. J. (2008). A theory of eye movements during target acquisition. *Psychological Review, 115*, 787–835.

Zelinsky G. J., & Schmidt, J. (2009). An effect of referential scene constraint on search implies scene segmentation. *Visual Cognition, 17*(6/7), 1004–1028.

VISUAL COGNITION, 2009, 17 (6/7), 979–1003

SUN: Top-down saliency using natural statistics

Christopher Kanan, Mathew H. Tong, Lingyun Zhang, and Garrison W. Cottrell

Department of Computer Science and Engineering, University of California San Diego, La Jolla, CA, USA

When people try to find particular objects in natural scenes they make extensive use of knowledge about how and where objects tend to appear in a scene. Although many forms of such "top-down" knowledge have been incorporated into saliency map models of visual search, surprisingly, the role of object appearance has been infrequently investigated. Here we present an appearance-based saliency model derived in a Bayesian framework. We compare our approach with both bottom-up saliency algorithms as well as the state-of-the-art Contextual Guidance model of Torralba et al. (2006) at predicting human fixations. Although both top-down approaches use very different types of information, they achieve similar performance; each substantially better than the purely bottom-up models. Our experiments reveal that a simple model of object appearance can predict human fixations quite well, even making the same mistakes as people.

Keywords: Attention; Saliency; Eye movements; Visual search; Natural statistics.

The arboreal environments that early primates evolved within demanded keen eyesight to support their ability to find targets of interest (Ravosa & Savakova, 2004; Regan et al., 2001). The ability to visually search for fruits and other foods while avoiding camouflaged predators such as snakes is essential for survival. However, the amount of information in the visual world presents a task too overwhelming for the visual system to fully process

Please address all correspondence to Christopher Kanan, Department of Computer Science and Engineering, University of California San Diego, 9500 Gilman Drive, Mail Code 0404, La Jolla, CA, 92093-0404, USA. E-mail: ckanan@cs.ucsd.edu

The authors would like to thank Antonio Torralba and his colleagues for sharing their dataset of human fixations, the LabelMe image database and toolbox, and a version of their bottom-up saliency algorithm. We would also like to thank Paul Ruvolo, Matus Telgarsky, and everyone in GURU (Gary's Unbelievable Research Unit) for their feedback and advice. This work was supported by the NIH (Grant No. MH57075 to GWC), the James S. McDonnell Foundation (Perceptual Expertise Network, I. Gauthier, PI), and the NSF (Grant No. SBE-0542013 to the Temporal Dynamics of Learning Center, GWC, PI and IGERT Grant No. DGE-0333451 to GWC and V. R. de Sa). CK is also funded by a Eugene Cota-Robles fellowship.

© 2009 Taylor & Francis
DOI: 10.1080/13506280902771138

concurrently (Tsotsos, 1990). Saccadic eye movements are an overt manifestation of the visual system's attempt to focus the fovea on important parts of the visual world in a serial manner (Henderson, 1992). In order to accomplish this feat, numerous brain structures, including visual cortex, the frontal eye fields, superior colliculus, the posterior parietal cortex, and the lateral geniculate nucleus (O'Connor, Fukui, Pinsk, & Kastner, 2002) are involved in determining where the next fixation should be directed (Schall, 2002). These brain regions are thought to compute, or influence the computation of, saliency maps, which guide eye movements to regions of interest (Koch & Ullman, 1985; see Itti & Koch, 2001, for a review).

Although the saliency map was originally intended to model covert attention, it has achieved great prominence in models of overt visual attention. In this context, saliency maps attach a value to each location in the visual field given the visual input and the current task, with regions of higher salience being more likely to be fixated. This framework has been extensively used to model eye movements, an overt form of attentional shift. What makes something salient depends on many factors. Generally in the modelling literature it has been assumed a region is salient if it differs greatly from its surroundings (Bruce & Tsotsos, 2006; Gao & Vasconcelos, 2007; Itti, Koch, & Niebur, 1998; Rosenholtz, 1999). Our model, SUN (Saliency Using Natural statistics; Zhang, Tong, & Cottrell, 2007; Zhang, Tong, Marks, Shan, & Cottrell, 2008), defines bottom-up saliency as deviations from the natural statistics learned from experience, and is a form of the kind of "novelty" detector useful in explaining many search asymmetries (see Wolfe, 2001, for a review of the asymmetries).

Recently, the ability of purely bottom-up models to predict human fixations during free viewing has been questioned. It is not clear if bottom-up saliency plays a causal role in human fixation, even if the correlations between predictions and fixations were stronger (Einhäuser & König, 2003; Tatler, 2007; Underwood, Foulsham, van Loon, Humphreys, & Bloyce, 2006). However, it has long been clear that bottom-up models are inadequate for modelling eye movements when top-down task requirements are involved, both intuitively and via some of the earliest studies of eye movements (Buswell, 1935; Einhäuser, Rutishauser, & Koch, 2008; Hayhoe & Ballard, 2005; Yarbus, 1967). For example, when searching for a person in an image, looking for something relatively tall, skinny, and on the ground will provide a more efficient search than hunting for the scene's intrinsically interesting features.

Several approaches have attempted to guide attention based on knowledge of the task, the visual appearance, or features, of the target. Perhaps the best known is Wolfe's Guided Search model (1994), which modulates the response of feature primitives based on a number of heuristics. Others have incorporated top-down knowledge into the computation of a saliency map.

Gao and Vasconcelos (2005) focus on features that minimize classification error of the class or classes of interest with their Discriminative Saliency model. The Iconic Search model (Rao & Ballard, 1995; Rao, Zelinsky, Hayhoe, & Ballard, 1996; Rao, Zelinsky, Hayhoe, & Ballard, 2002) uses the distance between an image region and a stored template-like representation of feature responses to the known target. Navalpakkam and Itti's work (2005) finds the appropriate weight of relevant features by maximizing the signal to noise ratio between the target and distractors. Turano, Garuschat, and Baker (2003) combine basic contextual location and appearance information necessary to complete a task, showing vast improvements in the ability to predict eye movements. The Contextual Guidance model (Ehinger, Hidalgo-Sotelo, Torralba, & Oliva, this issue 2009; Oliva, Torralba, Castelhano, & Henderson, 2003; Torralba, Oliva, Castelhano, & Henderson, 2006) uses a holistic representation of the scene (the *gist*) to guide attention to locations likely to contain the target, combining top-down knowledge of where an object is likely to appear in a particular context with basic bottom-up saliency.

One of the virtues of probabilistic models is that experimenters have absolute control over the types of information the model can use in making its predictions (Geisler & Kersten, 2002; Kersten & Yuille, 2003). As long as the models have sufficient power and training to represent the relevant probability distributions, the models make optimal use of the information they can access. This allows researchers to investigate what information is being used in a biological system, such as the control of human eye fixations.

In this paper we examine two probabilistic models, each using different types of information, that predict fixations made while counting objects in natural scenes. Torralba et al.'s (2006) Contextual Guidance model makes use of global features to guide attention to locations in a scene likely to contain the target. Our model, SUN, contains a top-down component that guides attention to areas of the scene likely to be a target based on appearance alone. By comparing the two approaches, we can gain insight into the efficacy of these two types of knowledge, both clearly used by the visual system, in predicting early eye movements.

THE SUN FRAMEWORK

It is vital for animals to rapidly detect targets of interest, be they predators, food, or targets related to the task at hand. We claim this is one of the goals of visual attention, which allocates computational resources to potential targets for further processing, with the preattentive mechanism actively and rapidly calculating the probability of a target's presence at each location using the information it has available. We have proposed elsewhere (Zhang et al., 2007, 2008) that this probability *is* visual saliency.

Let z denote a point in the visual field. In the context of this paper, a point corresponds to a single image pixel, but in other contexts, a point could refer to other things, such as an object (Zhang et al., 2007). We let the binary random variable C denote whether or not a point belongs to a target class,[1] let the random variable L denote the location (i.e., the pixel coordinates) of a point, and let the random variable F denote the visual features of a point. Saliency of a point z is then defined as $p(C=1 \mid F=f_z, L=l_z)$ where f_z represents the feature values observed at z, and l_z represents the location (pixel coordinates) of z. This probability can be calculated using Bayes' rule:

$$s_z = p(C = 1|F = f_z, L = l_z)$$

$$= \frac{p(F = f_z, L = l_z|C = 1)p(C = 1)}{p(F = f_z, L = l_z)}$$

After making the simplifying assumptions that features and location are independent and conditionally independent given $C = 1$, this can be rewritten as:

$$s_z = \frac{p(F = f_z|C = 1)p(L = l_z|C = 1)p(C = 1)}{p(F = f_z)p(L = l_z)}$$

$$= \underbrace{\frac{1}{p(F = f_z)}}_{\substack{\text{Independent} \\ \text{of target} \\ \text{(bottom-up saliency)}}} \underbrace{p(F = f_z|C = 1)}_{\text{Likelihood}} \underbrace{p(C = 1|L = l_z)}_{\text{Location Prior}}$$

$$\underbrace{}_{\substack{\text{Dependent on target} \\ \text{(top-down saliency)}}}$$

These assumptions can be summarized as entailing that a feature's distribution across scenes does not change with location, regardless of whether or not it appears on a target.

SUN can be interpreted in an information theoretic way by looking at the log salience, log s_z. Since the logarithm is a monotonically increasing function, this does not affect the ranking of salience across locations in an image. For this reason, we take the liberty of using the term saliency to refer both to s_z and to log s_z, which is given by:

---

[1] In other contexts, we let C denote the particular class of interest, e.g., people, mugs, or paintings.

$$\log s_z = \underbrace{-\log p(F = f_z)}_{\substack{\text{Self-information:} \\ \text{Bottom-up saliency}}} + \underbrace{\log p(F = f_z | C = 1)}_{\substack{\text{Log likelihood:} \\ \text{Top-down knowledge} \\ \text{of appearance}}} + \underbrace{\log p(C = 1 | L = l_z)}_{\substack{\text{Location prior:} \\ \text{Top-down knowledge} \\ \text{of target's location}}}$$

Our first term, $-\log p(F=f_z)$, depends only on the visual features observed at the point, and is independent of any knowledge we have about the target class. In information theory, $-\log p(F=f_z)$ is known as the *self-information* of the random variable F when it takes the value f_z. Self-information increases when the probability of a feature decreases—in other words, rarer features are more informative. When not actively searching for a particular target (the *free-viewing* condition), a person or animal's attention should be directed to any *potential* targets in the visual field, despite the features associated with the target class being unknown. Therefore, the log-likelihood and location terms are omitted in the calculation of saliency. Thus, the overall saliency reduces to the self-information term: $\log s_z = -\log p(F=f_z)$. This is our definition of bottom-up saliency, which we modelled in earlier work (Zhang et al., 2007, 2008). Using this term alone, we were able to account for many psychological findings and outperform many other saliency models at predicting human fixations while free-viewing.

Our second term, $\log p(F=f_z | C = 1)$, is a log-likelihood term that favours feature values consistent with our knowledge of the target's appearance. The fact that target appearance helps guide attention has been reported and used in other models (Rao et al., 1996; Wolfe, 1994). For example, if we know the target is green, then the log-likelihood term will be much larger for a green point than for a blue point. This corresponds to the top-down effect when searching for a known target, consistent with the finding that human eye movement patterns during iconic visual search can be accounted for by a maximum likelihood procedure which computes the most likely location of a target (Rao et al., 2002).

The third term, $\log p(C = 1 | L = l_z)$, is independent of the visual features and reflects any prior knowledge of where the target is likely to appear. It has been shown that if the observer is given a cue of where the target is likely to appear, the observer attends to that location (Posner & Cohen, 1984). Even basic knowledge of the target's location can be immensely useful in predicting where fixations will occur (Turano et al., 2003).

Now, consider what happens if the location prior is uniform, in which case it can be dropped as a constant term. The combination of the first two terms leads to the pointwise mutual information between features and the presence of a target:

$$-\underbrace{\log p(F = f_z)}_{\substack{\text{Self-information:} \\ \text{Bottom-up saliency}}} + \underbrace{\log p(F = f_z | C = 1)}_{\substack{\text{Log likelihood:} \\ \text{Top-down knowledge} \\ \text{of appearance}}} = \underbrace{\log \frac{p(F = f_z, C = 1)}{p(F = f_z)p(C = 1)}}_{\text{Pointwise mutual information}}.$$

This implies that for known targets the visual system should focus on locations with features having the most mutual information with the target class. This is very useful for detecting objects such as faces and cars (Ullman, Vidal-Naquet, & Sali, 2002). This combination reflects SUN's predictions about how appearance information should be incorporated into overall saliency, and is the focus of the present paper. SUN states that appearance-driven attention should be directed to combinations of features closely resembling the target but that are rare in the environment. Assuming targets are relatively rare, a common feature is likely caused by any number of nontargets, decreasing the feature's utility. SUN looks for regions of the image most likely to contain the target, and this is best achieved by maximizing the pointwise mutual information between features and the target class.

In the special case of searching for a single target class, as will be the case in the experiments we are trying to model, $p(C = 1)$ is simply a constant. We can then extract it from the mutual information, thus:

$$
\begin{aligned}
\underbrace{\log \frac{p(F = f_z, C = 1)}{p(F = f_z)p(C = 1)}}_{\text{Pointwise mutual information}} &= \log \frac{p(F = f_z, C = 1)}{p(F = f_z)} - \log p(C = 1) \\
&= \log p(C = 1 | F = f_z) - \log p(C = 1) \\
&= \log p(C = 1 | F = f_z) + \text{const.}
\end{aligned}
$$

Hence, what we have left can be implemented using any classifier that returns probabilities.

In summary, SUN's framework is based on calculating the probability of a target at each point in the visual field and leads naturally to a model of saliency with components that correspond to bottom-up saliency, target appearance, and target location. In the free-viewing condition, when there is no specific target, saliency reduces to the self-information of a feature. This implies when one's attention is directed only by bottom-up saliency, moving one's eyes to the most salient points in an image can be regarded as maximizing information sampling, which is consistent with the basic assumption of Bruce and Tsotsos (2006). When a particular target is being searched for, as in the current experiments, our model implies the best features to attend to are those having the most pointwise mutual information, which can be modelled by a classifier. Each component of SUN functionally corresponds to probabilities we think the brain is computing. We do not know precisely how the brain implements these calculations, but as a functional model, SUN invites investigators to use the probabilistic algorithm of their choice to test their hypotheses.

EXPERIMENT

When searching for a target in a scene, eye movements are influenced by both the target's visual appearance and the context, or gist, of the scene (Chun & Jiang, 1998). In either case the pattern of fixations differs significantly compared to when a person is engaged in free-viewing. Although the development of robust models of object appearance is complicated by the number of scales, orientations, nonrigid transformations, and partial occlusions that come into play when viewing objects in the real world, even simple models of object appearance have been more successful than bottom-up approaches in predicting human fixations during a search task (Zelinsky, Zhang, Yu, Chen, & Samaras, 2006). These issues can be evaded to some extent through the use of contextual guidance. Many forms of context can be used to guide gaze ranging from a quick holistic representation of scene content, to correlations of the objects present in an image, to a deeper understanding of a scene.

Here we examine SUN's appearance-driven model $p(C = 1|F = f_z)$, denoted $p(C = 1|F)$ hereafter with other terms abbreviated similarly, and the Contextual Guidance model described by Torralba et al. (2006). Our appearance model leaves out many of the considerations listed previously, but nevertheless it can predict human eye movements in task-driven visual search with a high level of accuracy. The Contextual Guidance model forms a holistic representation of the scene and uses this information to guide attention instead of relying on object appearance.

METHODS

Human data

We used the human data described in Torralba et al. (2006), which is available for public download on Torralba's website (http://people.csail.mit.edu/torralba/GlobalFeaturesAndAttention/). For completeness, we give a brief description of their experiment. Twenty-four Michigan State University undergraduates were assigned to one of three tasks: Counting people, counting paintings, or counting cups and mugs. In the cup- and painting-counting groups, subjects were shown 36 indoor images (the same for both tasks), and in the people-counting groups, subjects were shown 36 outdoor images. In each of them, targets were either present or absent, with up to six instances of the target appearing in the present condition. Images were shown until the subject responded with an object count or for 10 s, whichever came first. Images were displayed on an NEC Multisync P750 monitor with a refresh rate of 143 Hz and subtended $15.8° \times 11.9°$. Eyetracking was performed using a Generation 5.5 SRI Dual Purkinje Image Eyetracker with a refresh rate of 1000 Hz, tracking the right eye.

Stimuli used in simulations

The training of top-down components was performed on a subset of the LabelMe dataset (Russell, Torralba, Murphy, & Freeman, 2008), excluding the set used in the human experiments and the data from video sequences. We trained on a set of 329 images with cups/mugs, and 284 with paintings, and 669 with people in street scenes. Testing was performed using the set of stimuli shown to human subjects.

Contextual Guidance model and implementation

Torralba et al. (2006) present their Contextual Guidance model, which is a Bayesian formulation of visual saliency incorporating the top-down influences of global scene context. Their model is

$$p(C = 1, \ L|F, G) = p(F|G)^{-1}p(F|C = 1, \ L, \ G)p(L|C = 1, G)p(C = 1|G)$$

where G represents a scene's global features, a set of features that captures a holistic representation or gist of an image. F, C, and L are defined as before. Global features are calculated by forming a low dimensional representation of a scene by pooling the low-level features (the same composing F) over large portions of the image and using principal component analysis (PCA) to reduce the dimensionality further. The $p(F|G)^{-1}$ term is their bottom-up saliency model and the authors approximate this conditional distribution with $p(F)^{-1}$, using the statistics of the current image (a comparison of this form of bottom-up saliency with SUN's was performed in (Zhang et al., 2008)). The remaining terms are concerned with top-down influences on attention. The second term, $p(F|C = 1, L, G)$, enhances features of the attended location L that are likely to belong to class in the current global context. The contextual prior term $p(L|C = 1, G)$ provides information about where salient regions are in an image when the task is to find targets from class C. The fourth and final term $p(C = 1 | G)$ indicates the probability of class being present within the scene given its gist. In their implementation both $p(F\,|\,C=1, L, G)$ and $p(C=1\,|\,G)$ are omitted from the final model. The model that remains is $p(C=1, L\,|\,F, G) \approx p(F)^{-1}p(L\,|\,C=1, G)$, which combines the bottom-up saliency term with the contextual priors in order to determine the most salient regions in the image for finding objects of class . To avoid having saliency consistently dominated by one of the two terms, Torralba et al. apply an exponent to the local saliency term: $p(C=1, L\,|\,F, G) \approx p(F)^{-\gamma}p(L\,|\,C=1, G)$, where γ is tuned using a validation set.

Our use of Bayes' rule to derive saliency is reminiscent of the Contextual Guidance model's approach, which contains components roughly analogous to SUN's bottom-up, target appearance, and location terms. However, aside from some semantic differences in how overall salience is defined, the conditioning of each component on a coarse description of the scene, the global gist, separates the two models considerably. SUN focuses on the use of natural statistics learned from experience to guide human fixations to areas of the scene having an appearance similar to previously observed instances of the target, whereas the Contextual Guidance model guides attention to locations where the object has been previously observed using the scene's gist. Although both probabilistic models rely on learning the statistics of the natural world from previous experience, the differences between the formulations affect the meaning of each term, from the source of statistics used in calculating bottom-up saliency to how location information is calculated.

As was done in Torralba et al. (2006), we train the gist model $p(L\,|\,C=1, G)$ on a set formed by randomly cropping each annotated training image 20 times, creating a larger training set with a more uniform distribution of object locations. One difference from Torralba et al. is that we use a nonparametric bottom-up salience model provided to us by Torralba that performs comparably to the original, but is faster to compute. Otherwise, we attempted to be faithful to the model described in Torralba et al. For our data, the optimal γ was 0.20, which is different than what was used in Torralba et al., but is within the range that they found had good performance. Our reimplementation of the Contextual Guidance model performs on par with their reported results; we found no significant differences in the performance measures.

SUN implementation

Recall when looking for a specific target, guidance by target appearance is performed using the sum of the self-information of the features and the log-likelihood of the features given a class. Although we developed efficient ways of estimating the self-information of features in earlier work (Zhang et al.,

2008), accurately modelling log $p(F|C=1)$ or $p(F, C=1)$ for high dimensional feature spaces and many object classes is difficult. Instead, as described earlier, we extract the log $p(C=1)$ term (equations repeated here for convenience), which results in a formulation easily implementable as a probabilistic classifier:

$$\log \underbrace{\frac{p(F, C = 1)}{p(F)p(C = 1)}}_{\text{Pointwise mutual information}} = \log \frac{p(F, C = 1)}{p(F)} - \log p(C = 1)$$

$$= \log p(C = 1|F) - \log p(C = 1)$$
$$= \log p(C = 1|F) + \text{const.}$$

The probabilistic classifier we use is a support vector machine (SVM) modified to give probability estimates (Chih-Chung & Chih-Jen, 2001). SVMs were chosen for their generally good performance with relatively low computational requirements. An SVM is simply a neural network with predefined hidden unit features that feed into a particularly well-trained perceptron. The bottom-up saliency term, $-\log p(F)$, is still implicitly contained in this model. For the remainder of the paper, we omit the logs for brevity since as a monotonic transform it does not influence saliency.

The first step in our algorithm for $p(C=1|F)$ is to learn a series of biologically inspired filters that serve as the algorithm's features. In SUN's bottom-up implementation (Zhang et al., 2008), we used two different types of features to model $p(F)^{-1}$: Difference of Gaussians at multiple scales and filters learned from natural images using independent component analysis (ICA; Bell & Sejnowski, 1995; Hyvärinen & Oja, 1997). Quantitatively, the ICA features were superior, and we use them again here. When ICA is applied to natural images, it yields filters qualitatively resembling those found in visual cortex (Bell & Sejnowski, 1997; Olshausen & Field, 1996). The FastICA algorithm[2] (Hyvärinen & Oja, 1997) was applied to 11-pixel× 11-pixel colour natural image patches drawn from the Kyoto image dataset (Wachtler, Doi, Lee, & Sejnowski, 2007). This window size is a compromise between the total number of features and the amount of detail captured. We used the standard implementation of FastICA with its default parameters. These patches are treated as 363 ($11 \times 11 \times 3$) dimensional feature vectors normalized to have zero mean. After all of the patches are extracted, they are whitened using PCA, where each principal component is normalized to unit length. This removes one dimension due to mean subtraction, resulting in 362 ICA filters of size $11 \times 11 \times 3$. When used this way, ICA permits us to learn the statistical structure of the visual world. This approach has been used in biologically inspired models of both face and object recognition

---

[2] Software available at http://www.cis.hut.fi/projects/ica/fastica/

(Shan & Cottrell, 2008) and visual attention (Bruce & Tsotsos, 2006; Zhang et al., 2008).

To learn $p(C = 1 | F)$, we find images from the LabelMe dataset (Russell et al., 2008) containing the current class of interest, either people, cups, or paintings. Each image is normalized to have zero mean and unit standard deviation. Using the target masks in the annotation data, $d \times d \times 3$ square training patches centred on the object are cropped from the images, with each patch's size d chosen to ensure the patch contains the entire object. Random square patches of the same size are also collected from the same images, which serve as negative, background examples for $C = 0$. These came from the same images used to train the Contextual Guidance model. In selecting positive training example patches from the image set, our algorithm ignored objects that consumed over 50% of the training image (permitting negative examples to be taken from the same image) or less than 0.2% of the image (which are too small to extract reliable appearance features). Given the large number of images containing people in street scenes, we chose 800 patches of people randomly from those available. This resulted in 800 patches of people (533 negative examples[3]), 385 patches of mugs (385 negative examples), and 226 patches of paintings (226 negative examples).

We apply our filters to the set of patches, resizing the filters to each patch's size to produce one response from each filter per patch. We multiply each response by $11^2/d^2$ to make the responses invariant to d's value and then take the absolute value to obtain its magnitude. The dimensionality of these responses was reduced using PCA to 94 dimensions, a number chosen by cross-validation as explained next.

Three probabilistic SVMs (Chih-Chung & Chih-Jen, 2001) were trained, using the v-SVC algorithm (Scholkopf, Smola, Williamson, & Bartlett, 2000) with a Gaussian kernel, to discriminate between people/background, paintings/background, and mugs/background. The number of principal components, the same for each SVM, and the kernel and v parameters for each of the SVMs were chosen using five-fold cross-validation using the training data. The number of principal components was chosen to maximize the combined accuracy of the three classifiers. The kernel and v parameters of the three SVMs were independently selected for a given number of principal components. We did not tune the classifiers' parameters to match the human data. Even though our appearance-based features are quite simple, the average cross-validation accuracy across the three classifiers on the training patches was 89%.

Since the scale at which objects appear varies greatly, there is no single optimal scale to use when applying our classifier to novel images. However,

---

[3] Due to the limited memory capacity of the development machine, the number of background examples for each class was chosen to be at most $\lfloor 800(2/3) \rfloor = 533$ per object class.

objects do tend to appear at certain sizes in the images. Recall that we resized the filters based on the patch size, which was in turn based on the masks people placed on the objects. Hence, we have a scale factor for each training example. Histogramming these showed that there were clusters of scales that differed between the three classes of objects. To take advantage of this information and speed up classification, we clustered the resizing factors by training a one-dimensional Gaussian mixture model (GMM) with three Gaussians using the Expectation-Maximization algorithm (Dempster, Laird, & Rubin, 1977). The cluster centres were initialized using the k-Means + + algorithm (Arthur & Vassilvitskii, 2007). The three cluster centres found for each class are used to resize the filters when computing $p(C = 1 | F)$. By learning which scales are useful for object recognition, we introduce an adaptive approach to scale invariance, rather than the standard approach of using an image pyramid at multiple octaves. This lets us avoid excessive false positives that could arise in the multiple octave approach. For example, at a very coarse scale, a large filter applied to an image of a person visiting an ancient Greek temple would probably not find the person salient, but might instead find a column that looks person-like.

To calculate $p(C = 1 | F)$, for a test image I, we preprocess the image in the same way as the training images. First, we normalize I to have zero mean and unit variance, then we apply the three scale factors indicated by the cluster centres in the GMM for the object class. For each of our three scales, we enlarge the ICA filter according to the cluster's mean and normalize appropriately. We convolve each of these filters with the image and take the absolute value of the ICA feature response. These responses are projected onto the previously learned principal components to produce a 94 dimensional feature vector. The SVM for class C provides an estimate of $p(C = 1 | F, S = s)$ for each scale s. This procedure is repeated across the image for all three scales. Each of the maps at scale s is then smoothed using a Gaussian kernel with a half-amplitude spatial width of $1°$ of visual angle, the same procedure that Torralba et al. (2006) used to smooth their maps in order to approximate the perceptual capabilities of their human subjects. Combining the probability estimates from the three scales at each location is done by averaging the three estimates and smoothing the combined map again using the same Gaussian kernel. This helps ensure the three maps are blended smoothly. Smoothing also provides a local centre of mass, which accounts for the finding that when two targets are in close proximity saccades are made to a point between the two salient targets, putting both in view (Deubel, Wolf, & Hauske, 1984; Findlay, 1983). The same SVM classifier is used for each of the three scales.

RESULTS

In order to compare the ability of SUN's appearance-based saliency model and the Contextual Guidance model of Torralba et al. (2006) to predict human fixations, we have adopted two different performance measures. Our first measure is the same as used in Torralba et al.: It evaluates the percentage of human fixations being made to the top 20% most salient regions of the saliency map for each subject's first five fixations. Our second measure of performance is the area under the ROC curve (AUC). It eliminates the arbitrary nature of the 20% threshold evaluation, assessing the entire range of saliency values and revealing the robustness of a particular approach. With this metric, pixels are predicted to be attended or unattended based on whether they are above or below the current saliency threshold; plotting the hit and false alarm rates through all thresholds creates an ROC curve, with the area under the ROC curve being a measure of a model's ability to predict human fixations (Bruce & Tsotsos, 2006; Tatler, Baddeley, & Gilchrist, 2005). However, the patterns of performance with this second metric remained the same as with the first, so we focus on the first in our discussion (see Figure 3b for AUC data).

Due to the tendency of people to fixate near the centre of the screen in free-viewing experiments, it is frequently the case that a Gaussian (or other function decreasing with eccentricity) tuned to the distribution of human

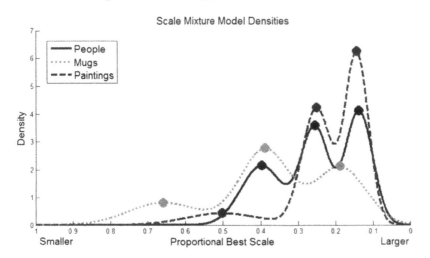

Figure 1.   The three Gaussian mixture model densities learned from the size of the objects in the training data. When searching for a particular object, the cluster centres, indicated by filled circles, are used to select the scales of the ICA filters used to extract features from the image. Note that since the inverse values are clustered a value of 0.1 corresponds to enlarging the original ICA filters to 110 × 110 × 3 while a value of 0.8 only enlarges the filter slightly to 14 × 14 × 3. To view this figure in colour, please see the online issue of the Journal.

Person Search   Mug Search   Painting Search

Figure 2. Gaussians fit to the eye movements of subjects viewing these scenes while performing these tasks. Data for eye movements came directly from the test set. By treating these as saliency masks, we can assess the performance of a model that solely makes use of the kinds of eye movements people make performing these tasks.

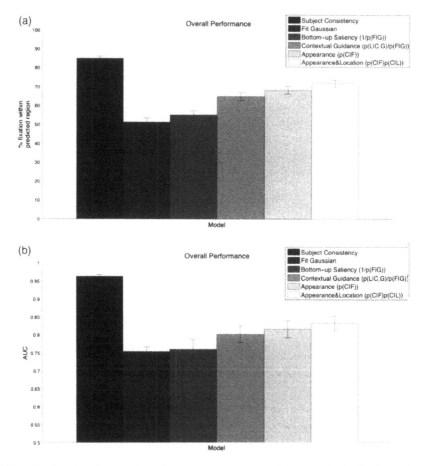

Figure 3. Overall performance in predicting human gaze, across all images and tasks. See the text for a description of the models. (a) Performance assessed by looking at the percentage of fixations falling within the top 20% most salient regions of each image. (b) Performance assessed by looking at the area under the ROC curve. To view this figure in colour, please see the online issue of the Journal.

fixations will outperform state-of-the-art bottom-up saliency algorithms (Le Meur, Le Callet, & Barba, 2007; Tatler, 2007; Tatler et al., 2005; Zhang et al., 2008). Instead of compensating for these biases as was done in Tatler et al. (2005) and Zhang et al. (2008), we instead assessed whether performance was greater than what could be achieved by merely exploiting them. We examined the performance of a Gaussian fit to all of the human fixations in the *test data* for each task. Each Gaussian was treated as a saliency map and used to predict the fixations of each subject. Since this includes the current image, this may be a slight overestimate of the actual performance of such a Gaussian. As shown in Figure 3a, there is no significant difference between our implementation of Torralba et al.'s bottom-up saliency and the Gaussian blob, $t(107) = 1.391$, $p = .0835$. Furthermore, all methods incorporating top-down knowledge outperformed the static Gaussian, $t(107) = 5.149276$, $p < .00001$ for contextual guidance, $t(107) = 6.356567$, $p < .0001$ for appearance.

To evaluate how consistent the fixations are among subjects, we determined how well the fixations of seven of the subjects can predict the fixations of the eighth using the procedure of Torralba et al. (2006). This was done by creating a mixture of Gaussians, with a Gaussian of 1° of visual angle placed at each point of fixation for first five fixations from seven of the subjects, to create a map used to predict where the eighth will fixate. We use the same performance measure described earlier. Figures 3 and 4 include these results and Figures 5–8 include subject consistency maps made using this approach.

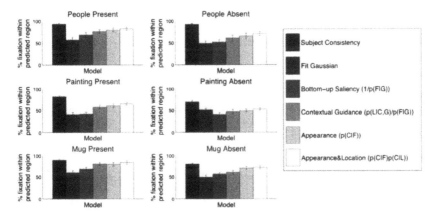

Figure 4. Performance of each model by task and condition. The condition refers to whether or not at least one instance of the target was present. The three tasks were counting people, paintings, and cups. The text provides a description for the six models presented. The performance scores indicate what percentage of fixations fell within the top 20 most salient regions for each image. To view this figure in colour, please see the online issue of the Journal.

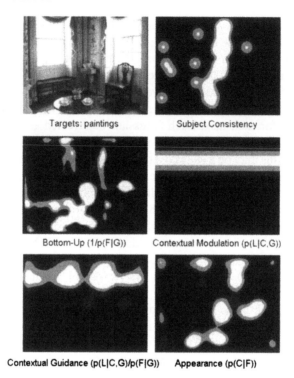

Figure 5. The human fixations and saliency maps produced during a search for paintings. Light grey (yellow), grey (green), and dark grey (blue) correspond to the top 10, 20, and 30% most salient regions respectively. Note that the horizontal guidance provided by contextual guidance is particularly ill-suited to this image, as the attention of both the human subjects and the appearance model is focused on the vertical strip of painting-like wallpaper between the two windows. This figure was selected by identifying images where the Contextual Guidance model and SUN most differed. To view this figure in colour, please see the online issue of the Journal.

We find appearance provides a better match to the human data, with the overall performance of SUN's appearance model outperforming the contextual-guidance model when their performance on each task-image pair is compared, $t(107) = 2.07$, $p < .05$. Surprisingly, even though the two models of task-based saliency differ considerably in the kind of information they use they both perform similarly overall, with most differences losing statistical significance when a smaller number of images are used in finer levels of analysis (e.g., over tasks or individual fixations).

However, great insight can be gained on the strengths and weaknesses of the two approaches by examining the kinds of saliency maps they produce in greater detail. In order to examine this question, we computed the Euclidean distance between the salience map for each image and task between the Contextual Guidance model, $p(L \mid C, G) \, p(F \mid G)^{-1}$, and SUN, $p(C \mid F)$. In

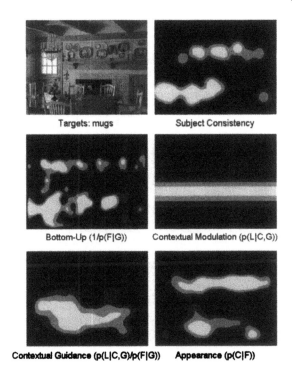

Figure 6.   The human fixations and saliency maps produced during a search for cups. Contextual guidance outperformed appearance modelling on this image, although it does not capture the two distinct regions where cups seem most likely two appear. Note than both human subjects and the attention-guidance system are drawn to the cup-like objects above the fireplace. As in Figure 5, light grey (yellow), grey (green), and dark grey (blue) correspond to the top 10, 20, and 30% most salient regions respectively, and this figure was also selected by identifying images where the Contextual Guidance model and SUN most differed. To view this figure in colour, please see the online issue of the Journal.

Figures 5 and 6, we show two of the maps where the disagreement is large. As can be seen from these images, in these cases, the gist model tends to select single horizontal bands (it is restricted to modelling L along the vertical dimension only) making it difficult to model human fixations that stretch along the vertical dimension, or are bimodal in the vertical dimension. Our appearance model has no such restriction and performs well in these situations. However, these are both limitations of the Contextual Guidance model as implemented, and not necessarily with the concept of contextual guidance itself.

In Figure 7, we show a case of maximal agreement. Here, the images tend to be "canonical" in that the objects of interest are well-described by a horizontal band, and hence both models can capture the salient regions.

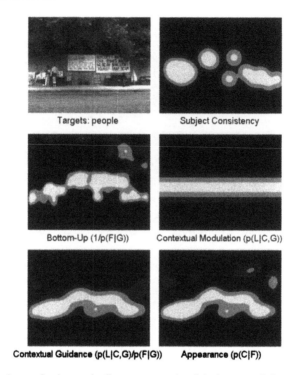

Figure 7. The human fixations and saliency maps produced during a search for people. Here the various models largely agree upon the most salient region of the image. This figure was selected by identifying the image where the Contextual Guidance model and SUN are most similar. As in Figures 5 and 6, light grey (yellow), grey (green), and dark grey (blue) correspond to the top 10, 20, and 30% most salient regions respectively. To view this figure in colour, please see the online issue of the Journal.

Furthermore, most of the interesting textures are confined to a small region of the scene, so even purely bottom-up methods perform comparably.

The predictions of the Contextual Guidance and our appearance model generally coincide quite well with the human data, but some differences are

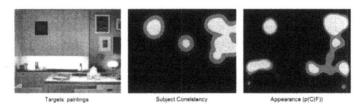

Figure 8. When instructed to find paintings and shown this image, the subjects fixate the television embedded in the cabinet, since it qualitatively looks very much like a painting. SUN makes a similar mistake. To view this figure in colour, please see the online issue of the Journal.

visually apparent when comparing the maps. This is partially due to thresholding them for display purposes—black regions are not expected to be devoid of fixations, but the models do predict that other regions are more likely to be attended. Additionally, the images in Figures 5 and 6 were chosen as examples where appearance and context differed most, suggesting that these images may be particularly interesting or challenging. However, the subject consistency results in Figures 3 and 4 demonstrate that both models are far from sufficient and must be improved considerably before a complete understanding of fixational eye movements is achieved.

The images in Figures 6 and 8 show the appearance model's "hallucinations" of potential targets. In Figure 6, there are several objects that might be interpreted as cups and attract gaze during a cup search. In Figure 8, the model confuses the television embedded in the cabinet with a painting, which is the same mistake the subjects make. Torralba et al. (2006) predicted appearance will play a secondary role when the target is small, as is the case here where targets averaged $1°$ visual angle for people and cups. In support of this prediction, they evaluated the target masks as a salience model, and found the target's location was not a good indicator of eye fixations. What was missing from this analysis is that an appearance model can capture fixations that would be considered false alarms under the "fixate the target" goal assumed by using the target's locations. Both our model and the subjects' visual attention are attracted by objects that appear similar to the target. In this experiment, appearance seemed to play a large role in guiding humans fixations, even during early saccades (we report averages over the first five) and the target absent condition.

We also evaluated how well the task-based models compare to purely bottom-up models. The appearance model of SUN and the Contextual Guidance model both perform significantly better than the Torralba et al. (2006) bottom-up saliency model, $t(107) = -6.440620$, $p < .0001$ for contextual guidance, $t(107) = -7.336285$, $p < .0001$ for appearance. The top-down models also perform significantly better than SUN's bottom-up saliency model, which was outlined in the Framework section. Since the two bottom-up models perform comparably on this task, $t(107) = -1.240$, $p = .109$, and SUN's bottom-up component is not of particular interest in the current work, we use the bottom-up component of the Contextual Guidance model in our comparison. See Zhang et al. (2008) for a discussion of how these two models of saliency relate.

Finally, we evaluated how the full SUN model would perform when the location term was included. The LabelMe set provides an object mask indicating the location of each object. We fit a Gaussian with a diagonal covariance matrix to each relevant mask and then averaged the Gaussian responses at each location, after adjusting appropriately to the scale of a given image. The resulting masks provide an estimation of $p(L|C)$. The term

$p(C|L)$ is simply $p(L|C) \times p(C)/p(L)$, which is constant over an image and does not affect overall salience. We see that its inclusion improves our overall performance significantly, $t(107) = 5.105662$, $p < .0001$. We intend to explore these findings further in future work.

DISCUSSION

The experiments we conducted were designed to elucidate the similarities and differences between two models of visual saliency that are both capable of modelling human gaze in a visual search task involving finding and counting targets. Our results support previous findings showing models of bottom-up attention are not sufficient for visual search (Einhäuser et al., 2008; Henderson et al., 2007), and that when top-down knowledge is used, gaze can be better predicted (Torralba et al., 2006; Zelinsky et al., 2006). Although SUN performs significantly better than our reimplementation of the Contextual Guidance model, the differences are small, and both models can assuredly be improved. This coincides well with the results reported by Ehinger et al. (this issue 2009). It is still unclear which plays a larger role when performing visual search in images of real world scenes, appearance or contextual information; presumably, a combination of both could be better than either alone.

We provide computational evidence rejecting the assertion of Torralba et al. (2006) that appearance plays little role in the first few fixations when the target is very small. Their claim was based partly on the limitations of the human visual system to detect small objects, particularly in the periphery. In support of this hypothesis, they found using the labelled regions (e.g., the area labelled "painting") as the salience model does not completely predict where people look. What their analysis overlooks is that the regions of the image containing targets cannot predict fixations in regions of the image that *look like* targets. Our coarse features capture the kind of similarity that could be computed by peripheral vision, resulting in the assignment of high salience to regions having an appearance similar to the target object class, allowing an appearance model to predict eye movements accurately even in the target-absent condition. The most recent version of the Contextual Guidance model (Ehinger et al., this issue 2009) incorporates object appearance (their target-feature model), and they find its performance is about the same as bottom-up saliency in the target absent condition using a dataset consisting of pedestrians in outdoor scenes. This may be because they used a sophisticated pedestrian detection algorithm in contrast to our coarse features, but a deeper investigation is needed.

In this work, we did not use the standard image pyramid with scales being separated by octaves, which has been the standard approach for over

20 years (Adelson, Anderson, Bergen, Burt, & Ogden, 1984). However, an image pyramid does not seem appropriate in our model since an object's representation is encoded as a vector of filter responses. Besides wasting computational resources, using arbitrary scales can also lead to almost meaningless features during classification since the test-input is so different from the input the classifier was trained with. Instead, we learned which scales objects appear at from the training data. Torralba and Sinha (2001) use a similar approach to learn which scales should be used, except their model performs a regression using scene context to select a single scale for a target class. SUN's scale selection may have been impaired since the distribution of object sizes in the training set is not the same as in the test set, which generally contains smaller objects. However, remedying this by screening the training data would be contrary to the importance we place on learning natural statistics.

Both SUN's appearance model and the Contextual Guidance model suffer from several noticeable flaws. In both models a separate module is learned for each object class. This is especially a problem for SUN. Humans have the ability to rule out objects after fixating them because they can be identified. Our classifiers are only aware of how the object class they are trained on differs from the background. Hence, when searching for mugs, the mug model has not learned to discriminate paintings from mugs, and so it may produce false alarms on paintings. The use of a single classifier for all classes would remedy this problem; however, current state-of-the-art approaches in machine learning (e.g., SVMs) are not necessarily well suited for learning a large number of object classes. A one-layer neural network with softmax outputs trained on all the classes may be a feasible alternative, as its parameters scale linearly with the number of classes.

In future work, we intend to investigate how different types of top-down (and bottom-up) knowledge can be combined in a principled way. In Torralba et al. (2006), a fixed weighting parameter is used between bottom-up and top-down knowledge, but it seems unlikely that different types of top-down knowledge should be always weighted the same way. If searching for a target with an unreliable appearance but a consistent location, it seems reasonable to weight the location information higher. A method of dynamically selecting the weight depending on the task, visual conditions, and other constraints is likely to significantly improve visual saliency models.

Another important enhancement needed by many saliency models is the explicit incorporation of a retina to model scanpaths in scenes. This has been investigated a few times in models using artificial stimuli (Najemnik & Geisler, 2005; Renninger, Coughlan, Verghese, & Malik, 2005; Renninger, Verghese, & Coughlan, 2007) with each fixation selected to maximize the amount of information gained. Currently SUN produces a static saliency map, with equal knowledge of all parts of the image. Incorporating foveated vision would better model the conditions under which we make eye movements. Likewise, using experiments freed of the monitor would increase the realism of the experimental environment (e.g., Einhäuser et al., 2007); currently our findings are restricted to images displayed on a screen, and it is unclear how well they will generalize.

In conclusion, we have described and evaluated two distinct top-down visual attention models which both excel at modelling task-driven human eye movements, especially compared to solely bottom-up approaches, even though the type of top-down information each uses is considerably different. However, comparing the modelling results with human data it is clear that there is much room for improvement. Integrating appearance, location, and other pieces of top-down information is likely to further improve our ability to predict and understand human eye movements. The probabilistic frameworks we examined are powerful tools in these investigations, allowing investigators to develop models with tightly controlled information access and clearly stated assumptions permitting hypotheses about the information contributing to eye movement control and visual attention to be readily evaluated.

REFERENCES

Adelson, E. H., Anderson, C. H., Bergen, J. R., Burt, P. J., & Ogden, J. M. (1984). Pyramid methods in image processing. *RCA Engineer, 29*(6), 33–41.

Arthur, D., & Vassilvitskii, S. (2007). K-means+ +: The advantages of careful seeding. *SODA '07: Proceedings of the eighteenth annual ACM-SIAM symposium on Discrete algorithms* (pp. 1027–1035). Society for Industrial and Applied Mathematics, Philadelphia, PA.

Bell, A., & Sejnowski, T. (1995). An information-maximisation approach to blind separation and blind deconvolution. *Neural Computation, 7*(6), 1129–1159.

Bell, A., & Sejnowski, T. (1997). The independent components of natural scenes are edge filters. *Vision Research, 37*(23), 3327–3338.

Bruce, N., & Tsotsos, J. (2006). Saliency based on information maximization. *Advances in neural information processing systems, 18*, 155–162.

Buswell, G. (1935). *How people look at pictures: A study of the psychology of perception in art.* Chicago: University of Chicago Press.

Chih-Chung, C., & Chih-Jen, L. (2001). *LIBSVM: A library for support vector machines* [Computer software]. Retrieved from http://www.csie.ntu.edu.tw/~cjlin/libsvm

Chun, M. M., & Jiang, Y. (1998). Contextual cueing: Implicit learning and memory of visual context guides spatial attention. *Cognitive Psychology, 36*, 28–71.

Dempster, A., Laird, N., & Rubin, D. (1977). Maximum likelihood from incomplete data via the EM algorithm. *Journal of the Royal Statistical Society, 39*, 1–38.

Deubel, H., Wolf, W., & Hauske, G. (1984). The evaluation of the oculomotor error signal. In *Theoretical and applied aspects of eye movement research* (pp. 55–62). Amsterdam: North-Holland.

Ehinger, K., Hidalgo-Sotelo, B., Torralba, A., & Oliva, A. (2009). Modeling search for people in 900 scenes: Close but not there yet. *Visual Cognition, 17*(6/7), 945–978.

Einhäuser, W., & König, P. (2003). Does luminance-contrast contribute to a saliency map of overt visual attention? *European Journal of Neuroscience, 17*, 1089–1097.

Einhäuser, W., Rutishauser, U., & Koch, C. (2008). Task-demands can immediately reverse the effects of sensory-driven saliency in complex visual stimuli. *Journal of Vision, 8*(2), 1–19.

Einhäuser, W., Schumann, F., Bardins, S., Bartl, K., Böning, G., Schneider, E., & König, P. (2007). Human eye-head co-ordination in natural exploration. *Network: Computation in Neural Systems, 18*(3), 267–297.

Findlay, J. M. (1983). Visual information for saccadic eye movements. In A. Hein & M. Jeannerod (Eds.), *Spatially orientated behavior* (pp. 281–303). New York: Springer-Verlag.

Gao, D., & Vasconcelos, N. (2005). Discriminant saliency for visual recognition from cluttered scenes. *Advances in Neural Information Processing Systems, 17*, 481–488.

Gao, D., & Vasconcelos, N. (2007). *Bottom-up saliency is a discriminant process.* Paper presented at the IEEE conference on Computer Vision and Pattern Recognition (CVPR), Rio de Janeiro, Brazil.

Geisler, W. S., & Kersten, D. (2002). Illusions, perception and Bayes. *Nature Neuroscience, 5*(6), 508–510.

Hayhoe, M., & Ballard, D. H. (2005). Eye movements in natural behavior. *Trends in Cognitive Sciences, 9*(4), 188–194.

Henderson, J. M. (1992). Object identification in context: The visual processing of natural scenes. *Canadian Journal of Psychology, 46*, 319–342.

Henderson, J. M., Brockmole, J. R., Castelhano, M. S., & Mack, M. L. (2007). Visual saliency does not account for eye movements during visual search in real-world scenes. In R. van Gompel, M. Fischer, W. Murray, & R. Hill (Eds.), *Eye movements: A window on mind and brain.* Oxford, UK: Elsevier.

Hyvärinen, A., & Oja, E. (1997). A fast fixed-point algorithm for independent component analysis. *Neural Computation, 9*(7), 1483–1492.

Itti, L., & Koch, C. (2001). Computational modeling of visual attention. *Nature Reviews Neuroscience, 3*(3), 194–203.

Itti, L., Koch, C., & Niebur, E. (1998). A model of saliency-based visual attention for rapid scene analysis. *IEEE Transactions on Pattern Analysis and Machine Intelligence, 20*(11), 1254–1259.

Kersten, D., & Yuille, A. (2003). Bayesian models of object perception. *Current Opinion in Neurobiology, 13*, 1–9.

Koch, C., & Ullman, S. (1985). Shifts in selective visual attention. *Human Neurobiology, 4*, 219–227.

Le Meur, O., Le Callet, P., & Barba, D. (2007). Predicting visual fixations on video based on low-level visual features. *Vision Research, 14*(19), 2483–2498.

Najemnik, J., & Geisler, W. (2005). Optimal eye movement strategies in visual search. *Nature, 434*, 387–391.

Navalpakkam, V., & Itti, L. (2005). Modeling the influence of task on attention. *Vision Research, 45*, 205–231.

O'Connor, D. H., Fukui, M. M., Pinsk, M. A., & Kastner, S. (2002). Attention modulates responses in the human lateral geniculate nucleus. *Nature Neuroscience, 5*(11), 1203–1209.

Oliva, A., Torralba, A., Castelhano, M., & Henderson, J. (2003). Top-down control of visual attention in object detection. In *Proceedings of international conference on Image Processing* (pp. 253–256). Barcelona, Catalonia: IEEE Press.

Olshausen, B. A., & Field, D. J. (1996). Emergence of simple-cell receptive field properties by learning a sparse code for natural images. *Nature, 381*(6583), 607–609.

Posner, M. I., & Cohen, Y. (1984). Components of attention. In H. Bouma & D. G. Bouwhuis (Eds.), *Attention and performance X* (pp. 55–66). Hove, UK: Lawrence Erlbaum Associates Ltd.

Rao, R., & Ballard, D. (1995). An active vision architecture based on iconic representations. *Artificial Intelligence, 78*, 461–505.

Rao, R., Zelinsky, G., Hayhoe, M., & Ballard, D. (1996). Modeling saccadic targeting in visual search. *Advances in Neural Information Processing Systems, 8*, 830–836.

Rao, R., Zelinsky, G., Hayhoe, M., & Ballard, D. (2002). Eye movements in iconic visual search. *Vision Research, 42*(11), 1447–1463.

Ravosa, M. J., & Savakova, D. G. (2004). Euprimate origins: The eyes have it. *Journal of Human Evolution, 46*(3), 355–362.

Regan, B. C., Julliot, C., Simmen, B., Vienot, F., Charlse-Dominique, P., & Mollon, J. D. (2001). Fruits, foliage and the evolution of primate colour vision. *Philosophical Transactions of the Royal Society, 356*, 229–283.

Renninger, L. W., Coughlan, J., Verghese, P., & Malik, J. (2005). An information maximization model of eye movements. *Advances in Neural Information Processing Systems, 17*, 1121–1128.

Renninger, L. W., Verghese, P., & Coughlan, J. (2007). Where to look next? Eye movements reduce local uncertainty. *Journal of Vision, 7*(3), 1–17.

Rosenholtz, R. (1999). A simple saliency model predicts a number of motion popout phenomena. *Vision Research, 39*, 3157–3163.

Russell, B. C., Torralba, A., Murphy, K. P., & Freeman, W. T. (2008). LabelMe: A database and web-based tool for image annotation. *International Journal of Computer Vision, 77*(1–3), 157–173.

Schall, J. D. (2002). The neural selection and control of saccades by the frontal eye field. *Philosophical Transactions of the Royal Society, 357*, 1073–1082.

Scholkopf, B., Smola, A., Williamson, R. C., & Bartlett, P. L. (2000). New support vector algorithms. *Neural Computation, 12*, 1207–1245.

Shan, H., & Cottrell, G. (2008). *Looking around the backyard helps to recognize faces and digits.* Paper presented at the IEEE conference on Computer Vision and Pattern Recognition (CVPR).

Tatler, B. W. (2007). The central fixation bias in scene viewing: Selecting an optimal viewing position independently of motor biases and image feature distributions. *Journal of Vision, 7*(14), Pt. 4, 1–17.

Tatler, B. W., Baddeley, R. J., & Gilchrist, I. D. (2005). Visual correlates of fixation selection: Effects of scale and time. *Vision Research, 45*(5), 643–659.

Torralba, A., Oliva, A., Castelhano, M. S., & Henderson, J. M. (2006). Contextual guidance of eye movements and attention in real-world scenes: The role of global features in object search. *Psychological Review, 113*(4), 766–786.

Torralba, A., & Sinha, P. (2001). Statistical context priming for object detection. *Proceedings of the International Conference on Computer Vision* (pp. 763–770). Vancouver, Canada: IEEE Computer Society.

Tsotsos, J. (1990). Analyzing vision at the complexity level. *Behavioral and Brain Sciences, 13*(3), 423–445.

Turano, K., Garuschat, D., & Baker, F. (2003). Oculomotor strategies for the direction of gaze tested with a real-world activity. *Vision Research, 43*, 333–346.

Ullman, S., Vidal-Naquet, M., & Sali, E. (2002). Visual features of intermediate complexity and their use in classification. *Nature Neuroscience, 5*(7), 682–687.

Underwood, G., Foulsham, T., van Loon, E., Humphreys, L., & Bloyce, J. (2006). Eye movements during scene inspection: A test of the saliency map hypothesis. *European Journal of Cognitive Psychology, 18*, 321–343.

Wachtler, T., Doi, E., Lee, T.-W., & Sejnowski, T. J. (2007). Cone selectivity derived from the responses of the retinal cone mosaic to natural scenes. *Journal of Vision, 7*(8), Pt. 6, 1–14.

Wolfe, J. M. (1994). Guided Search 2.0: A revised model of visual search. *Psychonomic Bulletin and Review, 1*, 202–228.

Wolfe, J. M. (2001). Asymmetries in visual search: An introduction. *Perception and Psychophysics, 63*(3), 381–389.

Yarbus, A. L. (1967). *Eye movements and vision.* New York: Plenum Press.

Zelinsky, G., Zhang, W., Yu, B., Chen, X., & Samaras, D. (2006). The role of top-down and bottom-up processes in guiding eye movements during visual search. *Advances in Neural Information Processing Systems, 18,* 1569–1576.

Zhang, L., Tong, M. H., & Cottrell, G. W. (2007). Information attracts attention: A probabilistic account of the cross-race advantage in visual search. In D. S. McNamara & J. G. Trafton (Eds.), *Proceedings of the 29th annual conference of the Cognitive Science Society* (pp. 749–754). Austin, TX: Cognitive Science Society.

Zhang, L., Tong, M. H., Marks, T. K., Shan, H., & Cottrell, G. W. (2008). SUN: A Bayesian framework for saliency using natural statistics. *Journal of Vision, 8*(7), Pt. 32, 1–20. Retrieved from http://journalofvision.org/8/7/32/, DOI:10.1167/8.7.32.

VISUAL COGNITION, 2009, 17 (6/7), 1004–1028

An effect of referential scene constraint on search implies scene segmentation

Gregory J. Zelinsky and Joseph Schmidt

Department of Psychology, Stony Brook University, Stony Brook, NY, USA

Subjects searched aerial images for a UFO target, which appeared hovering over one of five scene regions: Water, fields, foliage, roads, or buildings. Prior to search scene onset, subjects were either told the scene region where the target could be found (specified condition) or not (unspecified condition). Search times were faster and fewer eye movements were needed to acquire targets when the target region was specified. Subjects also distributed their fixations disproportionately in this region and tended to fixate the cued region sooner. We interpret these patterns as evidence for the use of referential scene constraints to partially confine search to a specified scene region. Importantly, this constraint cannot be due to learned associations between the scene and its regions, as these spatial relationships were unpredictable. These findings require the modification of existing theories of scene constraint to include segmentation processes that can rapidly bias search to cued regions.

Keywords: Visual search; Scene context; Aerial images; Region segmentation; Eye movements.

Most visual search studies are designed so as to prevent searchers from having foreknowledge of a target's location.[1] This is typically accomplished by using arrays of randomly positioned targets and distractors. However, whereas these randomization procedures are necessary and important for studying certain aspects of search (e.g., the efficiency of feature-based guidance), they do not accurately reflect search as it exists in the real world. This is because search

---

[1] Of course many studies have also used spatial precues to manipulate the expected location of a target (e.g., Palmer, Ames, & Lindsey, 1993; Zelinsky, 1999), but these explicit spatial cueing situations are not the focus of this paper.

Please address all correspondence to Gregory J. Zelinsky, Department of Psychology, Stony Brook University, Stony Brook, NY 11794-2500, USA. Email: Gregory. Zelinsky@stonybrook.edu

This work was supported by the National Science Foundation under Grant IIS-0527585 and by the National Institute of Mental Health under Grant 2-R01-MH63748 to GJZ. We thank Zainab Karimjee, Alyssa Fasano, Rosa Vespia, and Mariya Norenberg for help with stimulus creation and data collection.

© 2009 Taylor & Francis
DOI: 10.1080/13506280902764315

happens in the context of scenes, and scenes provide many clues to the likely location of a target. Some of these clues stem from the rapid and automatic segmentation of a scene into surfaces and objects (e.g., Biederman, 1981; Boyce, Pollatsek, & Rayner, 1989; Hummel & Biederman, 1992; Marr, 1982; Palmer, 1975; Sanocki, 2003; see also Intraub, 1989). By excluding broad regions of a scene's background, this early contextual information can bias search to the important parts of a scene, a bias that persists even when these parts are unlikely to correspond to a target (e.g., Neider & Zelinsky, 2006b; see also Neider & Zelinsky, 2008). Other scene context effects arise from prior knowledge of a target's likely location. If a target was viewed previously at a given location in the scene (e.g., Brockmole, Castelhano, & Henderson, 2006; Brockmole & Henderson, 2006; Chun & Jiang, 1998; Chun, 2000), or if it tends to appear at predictable locations in a particular category of scene (e.g., Eckstein, Drescher, & Shimozaki, 2006; Oliva, Torralba, Castelhano, & Henderson, 2003), these locations can be inspected first, thereby increasing search efficiency. Still other scene constraints are best described as semantic (e.g., Henderson, Weeks, & Hollingworth, 1999). When searching for your car there is no reason to scrutinize every cloud in the sky (Neider & Zelinsky, 2006a). This study explored a middle ground between a totally unconstrained search with no prior information about a target's location, and a highly constrained search with multiple sources of scene context providing clues as to the possible location of the target. Specifically, subjects were told the region of the scene that contained a target, but these regions appeared at unpredictable scene locations. We did this so as to begin teasing apart the various ways that scene context might facilitate search.

Early work addressing the contextual factors affecting search defined context in terms of the spatial configurations of items. For example, Chun and Jiang (1998) had subjects search for items appearing in either new configurations or configurations that repeated over trials. They found that search was more efficient when configurations repeated, and interpreted this benefit as evidence for the learning and use of item configurations to guide search (but see Kunar, Flusberg, Horowitz, & Wolfe, 2007). In subsequent work, Chun and Jiang (1999) demonstrated that this contextual cueing is not limited to learned spatial configurations. Subjects searched for a target among randomly positioned distractors under consistent-mapping (particular targets were paired with particular distractors) and variable-mapping (no association between targets and distractors) conditions. They found that search was more efficient with consistent mapping, which they again interpreted as a contextual cueing effect; subjects learned to associate a particular set of distractors with a particular target, thereby creating a more specific template for search guidance. Extending these findings to scenes, if one is looking for a difficult to find target (e.g., a bee), it might be helpful to search for larger and more discriminable objects (e.g., flowers) that often cooccur with these targets (see also Bar, 2004; Bar & Aminoff, 2003; Brockmole et al., 2006; Eckstein et al., 2006).

Although it is important to understand the contextual constraints imposed by non-targets on search, scenes are much more than simple collections of objects. The elements of a scene are coherently organized into a sort of story, the scene's gist, and this coherence can be the source of much semantic information. Henderson et al. (1999) were among the first to study this semantic source of scene constraint in the context of a search task. Motivated by a previous claim that scene-inconsistent objects are detected sooner (Loftus & Mackworth, 1978), they had subjects search for a target that was either consistent with a scene (e.g., a microscope in a laboratory) or inconsistent with a scene (e.g., a microscope in a bar). Contrary to the earlier claim, they found that scene-consistent targets were fixated by gaze *before* scene-inconsistent targets. They attributed this difference to an expectation of where a target might be located in a given scene; because microscopes *should* appear on work tables, subjects tended to inspect these surfaces first. Although not the focus of their study, this finding provided the first clear evidence for search being guided by scene context (see also Castelhano & Henderson, 2007; and Henderson, 2003, 2005, 2007, for reviews).

As exemplified by the Henderson et al. (1999) study, the early work on scene context centred on the effects of inconsistent objects (see also Antes & Penland, 1981; de Graf, de Troy, & d'Ydewalle, 1992; Friedman, 1979). This work also relied almost exclusively on line drawings of scenes as stimuli. Line drawings are useful in that they preserve a great deal of the scene's semantic information. However, a great deal of potentially search-relevant information about a scene is also lost, including colour (e.g., Goffaux et al., 2005) and direction of lighting (e.g., Enns & Rensink, 1990). More recently, Neider and Zelinsky (2006a) revisited the relationship between scene context and search, asking whether general semantic knowledge of targets and scenes is used to guide search irrespective of consistency. Their stimuli were computer-generated rendered scenes depicting a mountainous desert land-scape; objects in the scene were therefore not only coherently organized, they were also embedded in a relatively rich context of surface, colour, and lighting information. Although all of the search targets were scene consistent (a jeep, blimp, and helicopter), these targets were either scene constrained, meaning that the scene suggested a target-consistent region (ground for jeeps and the sky for blimps), or scene unconstrained, meaning that the target could appear anywhere in the scene (a helicopter can appear in the sky or on the ground). Subjects detected the scene-constrained targets faster and with fewer eye movements compared to the scene-unconstrained target. They also directed more initial saccades to the ground when searching for the jeep and to the sky when searching for the blimp, even when the target did not appear in the scene. These findings were interpreted as evidence for a rapid top-down biasing of search behaviour by scene context to target-consistent scene regions.

The Neider and Zelinsky (2006a) study provided clear experimental evidence for the biasing of search to likely target regions in a scene, but the mechanism underlying this direction of search was left unspecified. One straightforward explanation for such scene context effects might appeal to target expectancy. If a target is likely to appear at a given location in a scene, due either to its having appeared there before or because of learned spatial associations with other scene objects, these expectancies could act as a sort of spatial cue (e.g., Chun & Jiang, 1998), allowing the information at this cued location to be weighted in the search decision. The optimal weighting of this information can be formalized using Bayesian decision theory (Eckstein, Shimozaki, & Abbey, 2002; Green & Swets, 1966; Kersten, Mamassian, & Yuille, 2004; Palmer et al., 1993; Shaw, 1982), with the probability of the target appearing at a given scene location referred to as a Bayesian prior. Previous work has shown that Bayesian ideal observer models can do an excellent job of describing overt search behaviour in the context of nonscene stimuli (Eckstein, Beutter, & Stone, 2001; Najemnik & Geisler, 2005; see also Geisler, Perry, & Najemnik, 2006). Eckstein et al. (2006) extended this approach to more realistic search contexts. They had subjects search for either a predictably located target (a lamp on a table) or an unpredictably located target (a lamp on a bed), and found that initial saccades landed closer to the targets at predictable scene locations. This expectancy effect was quantified in terms of a Bayesian model, one adapted for use with realistic scenes. The model combined visual evidence for the target with differential weightings reflecting contextual cues to produce a posterior probability map indicating the target's likely location in a scene. Good agreement was found between this model and the observed behavioural data, suggesting that a Bayesian framework offers a viable explanation for effects of scene context on search.

To date, a model developed by Torralba, Oliva, Castelhano, and Henderson (2006; see also Oliva et al., 2003; Torralba, 2003) offers the most specific and comprehensive description of how search can be constrained by scene context. The principle theoretical advance of this model is its use of a scene classification method to delineate scene-specific regions that are likely to contain a given target. Global features, derived from the outputs of local filters at multiple scales, colours, and orientations, are first used to classify a scene as a particular type (e.g., a street scene or an indoor room scene; see also Oliva & Torralba, 2001, 2006). Top-down knowledge of where targets appeared in other scenes of this type, obtained from a prior training phase, is then used to bias search to corresponding locations (coarsely defined) in the target scene. If a scene was classified as a city street and the target was a pedestrian, search might therefore be contextually constrained to a region spanning the bottom of the scene, corresponding to where pedestrians are typically located. In parallel with this global contextual constraint, local saliency values are computed using a method similar to the one described in Itti and Koch (2000). These global and local constraints are combined within a Bayesian framework, with search being guided to scene locations that tend to have both a high saliency value and a strong contextual constraint. The model was tested using mug, painting, and pedestrian targets, and in each case was able to predict, better than a saliency model alone, where subjects chose to direct their first couple of fixations when searching for the same targets in the same scenes. These findings are significant in at least two respects. First, they provide a very specific theoretical framework for understanding scene constraints on search; constraints stem from a rapid classification of a scene, combined with biases introduced through learned associations between a scene type and a target. Second, the model demonstrates how scene constraints can be implemented without appeal to image segmentation processes; constraints arise directly from the global scene context, individual objects or regions in a scene do not need to be segmented or identified.

This discussion makes clear that scene constraints can originate from many sources: Implicitly learned spatial relationships between targets and distractor positions (Chun & Jiang, 1998) or explicitly learned relationships between targets and scenes (Neider & Zelinsky, 2006a), relationships between highly salient scene objects and less salient targets (Eckstein et al., 2006), or global contextual relationships between specific targets and scene types (Torralba et al., 2006). In this paper we investigate another type of scene constraint, and evaluate its potential to guide search in the absence of guidance from the other forms. Specifically, we are interested in one's ability to rapidly constrain their search for a target to an arbitrary region of a scene, one that is designated immediately prior to the search task. Such a situation describes many real world uses of scene constraint, particularly with respect to linguistically defined targets. Imagine you are at a park with a friend, who suddenly exclaims: "Look at that duck on the grass!" The phrase "on the grass" creates an immediate and temporary relationship between a target (duck) and a scene region (grass), which can be used to exclude as potential targets the ducks that may be swimming in the water or flying overhead. This form of constraint, which we consider to be one expression of a larger class of *referential* scene constraints (see also Logan, 1995), cannot be explained as a contextual cueing effect (Chun & Jiang, 1998), as the constraint provides no information about where the cued region is located in the scene. For the same reason this constraint cannot be easily explained by Bayesian learning. The significance of the relationship between "duck" and "grass" is a result of the target-defining expression and is not the product of learned associations (indeed, ducks may be more associated with water than grass). To distinguish this type of constraint from global context (Torralba et al., 2006), we use scenes having unpredictable spatial relationships to regions. Knowledge of the scene type and target region can therefore not be used to contextually constrain search, as the region might be located anywhere in the scene. To the extent that region cueing affects search, we should find that fewer eye movements are needed to acquire region-specified targets (relative to an unspecified condition), and an overall larger proportion of search fixations in the cued region. Finding evidence for task specific scene constraints under these conditions would require models of search to reconsider the inclusion of a scene segmentation process, as constraints could not be imposed until after the scene appears.

METHOD

Participants

Twenty undergraduate students from Stony Brook University participated for course credit. All had normal or corrected to normal vision, by self-report, and were naïve with regard to the purpose of the experiment.

Stimuli and apparatus

Search scenes were aerial images of Long Island, New York, as viewed from an altitude of 800–1200 feet above sea level (Google Earth). We obtained images from a relatively narrow geographical area so as to minimize dramatic differences between scenes, and to maximize the likelihood of including the same types of regions in each scene. Specifically, scenes were selected so as to depict five identifiable categories of regions: *Foliage*—trees, shrubs, or heavy brush, *roads*—highways, streets, or paved areas, *buildings*—houses or commercial structures, *water*—ocean, ponds, streams, and *fields*—open areas of grass or dirt (see Figure 1). All regions were delineated by three independent raters, and scenes were discarded when any rater failed to agree on the regions. The final 30 scenes, although visually very diverse, were also therefore similar in that each region type appeared in every scene. Importantly, we used aerial images as stimuli so as to sever learned spatial relationships between a scene and its regions. Whereas scenes typically place strong spatial constraints on their regions (e.g., a sky region is typically found at the top of a landscape scene), such associations do not exist for aerial images. The locations of regions in our scenes were completely unpredictable; roads and houses could appear at any position and orientation, and water could be found at the top, sides, or middle of a scene in addition to its more standard bottom location.

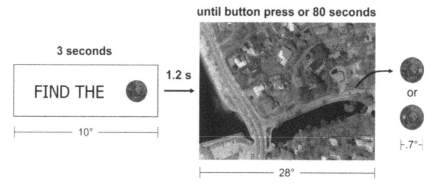

Figure 1. The experimental procedure. Each trial began with a 3 s presentation of a target cue (left). The cue either specified the target region (e.g., "Find the <target> over the road") or left the target region unspecified (as shown). The search scene appeared after a 1.2 s delay (with central fixation) and remained until the judgement (or 80 s). A semitransparent white dot was drawn on the left or right side of the target in the search scene (right), and the subject's task was to indicate the placement of this dot under time pressure. To view this figure in colour, please see the online issue of the Journal.

The search target was a flying saucer (Figure 1). As in the case of aerial views, which break the typical spatial relationships between a scene and its regions, a saucer target is desirable in the context of this study as it is essentially a nonsense object for which there exists no strong association to any region of a scene. Unlike a car, for which there exists a strong association to a road, a flying saucer is equally at home hovering over a field or a building. The saucer image was obtained from the Web and altered in appearance (Photoshop CS2) so as to be moderately difficult to detect in the search scenes. The size and appearance of the target was held constant throughout the experiment. Targets subtended 0.7° of visual angle (32 pixels in diameter) as viewed in the 28° × 21° search scenes (1280 × 960 pixels). Saucer targets were digitally inserted into images such that, over trials, each of the five scene regions was equally likely to contain a target. Placement of a target within a given region was pseudorandom, reflecting an attempt to have target locations be distributed as evenly as possible in scenes so as to discourage position biases.

Stimuli were presented in colour on a ViewSonic 19-inch flat-screen CRT monitor at a refresh rate of 100 Hz. The experiment was controlled by Experiment Builder (SR Research, Ver. 1.4.624), running under Microsoft Windows XP. Eye movement and manual RT data were collected using the EyeLink II eyetracking system (SR Research). Eye position was sampled at 500 Hz, and saccades were detected using default settings. Head position and viewing distance (72 cm) were fixed with a chinrest, and all responses were made with a gamepad controller attached to the computer's USB port.

Judgements were made with the left and right index-finger triggers; trials were initiated with a button operated by the right thumb.

Design and procedure

Foreknowledge of the scene region containing the target was manipulated in specified and unspecified cueing conditions. In the unspecified condition, subjects would see a cue consisting of the words "Find the", followed by a picture of the saucer target (Figure 1, left). The specified condition was identical, except for the addition of the phrase "over the X", where X would be either "foliage", "road", "building", "water", or "field". A region-specified cue might therefore read: "Find the <picture of target> over the field." Subjects engaged in an unspecified search would therefore be looking for the saucer target alone, whereas subjects conducting a specified search would be looking for the same target in a specific scene region. Target region specification was a within-subjects variable, with specified and unspecified trials randomly interleaved.

The 30 different scenes were each repeated five times, yielding a total of 150 experimental trials per subject. Each of the five scene repetitions corresponded to the placement of a target in one of the five region types, meaning that a target appeared only once in a given region for a given scene. The 150 trials were evenly divided into specified and unspecified conditions, and within each specification condition targets appeared equally often (15 times) in each of the five scene regions. Target assignment to a region in a given scene was counterbalanced over subjects such that a target appeared in each region of every scene an equal number of times under both specified and unspecified conditions. Trial order was also randomized over subjects so as to minimize the accidental clumping of trials from a given condition, and any effects that this might have on the data.

The experiment began with a nine-point calibration routine needed to map eye position to screen coordinates. A calibration was not accepted until the average error was less than $0.4°$ and the maximum error was less than $0.9°$, and six calibrations were conducted throughout the experiment. Subjects started each trial by fixating a central point and pressing a button on the gamepad. This buttonpress also "drift corrected" the eyetracker, a compensation that corrects for any small head movements that might have occurred since the last calibration. The cue was then displayed for 3 s followed by another central dot for 1.2 s, which served to return gaze to the centre of the screen. The search display then appeared, and remained on the screen until the target judgement or until 80 s had elapsed.

The testing context was: "UFOs have invaded Long Island!" Subjects were asked to find the extraterrestrial target and to indicate its type. Two types of search targets were created by inserting a white dot into either the left or right side of the saucer image presented at preview (Figure 1, right). Subjects indicated a left or right dot on the saucer by pressing the left or right triggers of the game pad, respectively. The task was therefore search, followed by a left/right discrimination judgement. A target was present on every trial, and subjects were instructed to make their judgements as quickly as possible while maintaining accuracy. There were 20 practice trials, and the entire experiment lasted approximately 90 min.

RESULTS AND DISCUSSION

Errors in this task indicated either a failure to find the target within 80 s or an incorrect left/right discrimination judgement. Both of these events were rare. Average error rates in the specified and unspecified conditions were 2% or less, and the maximum average error for any individual region condition was only 5%. Error trials were excluded from all subsequent analyses.

How efficiently were subjects able to find the saucer targets under region specified and unspecified conditions? If a cue can be used to restrict search to the target region we would expect subjects to find the target faster, and to do so with fewer eye movements, on region specified trials. To test these hypotheses we analysed for each trial the time needed to fixate within $1.5°$ of the target's centre, and the corresponding number of fixations (see Table 1). Both predictions were confirmed using repeated measures ANOVA. When the target region was specified subjects needed less time to fixate the target, $F(1, 19) = 28.66$, $p < .001$, and acquired the target with fewer fixations, $F(1, 19) = 35.59$, $p < .001$. These patterns are consistent with an effect of referential scene constraint on search; information from the cue was used to

TABLE 1

Mean time to fixate the target and mean number of fixations until reaching the target ($1.5°$) for correct trials, grouped by region and cue condition

Region	Time to fixate the target (ms)		Number of fixations to the target	
	Specified	Unspecified	Specified	Unspecified
Water	830 (77)	1132 (94)	4.5 (0.25)	5.5 (0.36)
Building	3269 (241)	4728 (357)	12.9 (0.86)	17.8 (1.22)
Foliage	2465 (175)	3176 (312)	10.0 (0.68)	12.5 (1.02)
Road	1908 (160)	4050 (454)	8.3 (0.59)	15.4 (1.34)
Field	2495 (296)	2911 (435)	9.9 (0.96)	11.5 (1.39)
Mean	2194 (109)	3199 (209)	9.1 (0.41)	12.5 (0.67)

Values in parentheses indicate one standard error of the mean (SEM).

flexibly constrain search to the target region, thereby increasing search efficiency.

As indicated in Table 1, there were also large and significant differences between regions in both time-to-target, $F(4, 76) = 35.09$, $p < .001$, and fixations-to-target, $F(4, 76) = 39.74$, $p < .001$. Targets over water were detected the fastest and with the fewest fixations when compared to all other regions (all $ps < .001$), and targets over buildings were by far the most difficult to detect (all $ps < .03$). These region differences also interacted with cue specificity, as indicated by significant Region × Cue interactions: Time-to-target, $F(4, 76) = 4.21$, $p < .01$, fixations-to-target, $F(4, 76) = 4.17$, $p < .01$. To better understand these interactions we conducted post hoc comparisons between specified and unspecified conditions for each region type. Except for the field region, $t(19) \leq .91$, $p \geq .37$, subjects acquired targets faster and with fewer fixations when the target region was specified, $t(19) \geq 2.28$, $p \leq .02$. This suggests that the benefit derived from target region cueing is fairly robust and not highly dependent on region type. The absence of a cueing benefit for fields may be due to the unusually high degree of variability specific to this region, which ranged from manicured green backyards to irregular tan patches of wild grass and dirt.

We know from the previous analysis that cueing the target region produced a clear search benefit, but was this benefit derived from a restriction of search to the cued region? To begin addressing this question we analysed the distribution and proportional density of fixations in each scene, which we visualize in the form of heat maps (Figure 2). Heat maps are useful in that they provide an intuitive sense of how gaze was allocated during the search of a given scene. For example, from the two scenes illustrated in Figure 2 it is clear that subjects were able to use a region cue to restrict their search to the cued region, as indicated by the localized patches of high fixation density. When the road region was specified search was confined to the road (Figure 2A), and when the building region was specified search was concentrated on the buildings (Figure 2C). Subjects viewing the same scenes in the unspecified region condition showed dramatically different behaviour (Figure 2B and D). Their search was distributed far more broadly over the scenes (more green), and they showed much less agreement in their fixation locations, resulting in uniformly low fixation densities (fewer patches of red). We therefore have a preliminary explanation for the cueing benefits reported in Table 1; subjects were able to restrict their search to the cued region, resulting in a faster search with fewer fixations.

Heat maps are largely a data visualization tool; to better quantify referential scene constraint in this study we computed the proportion of fixations that each subject devoted to the target region, normalized by region

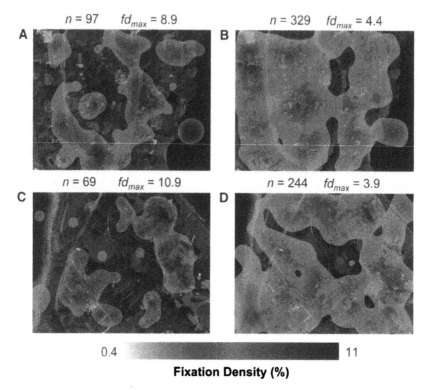

$n = 97$ $fd_{max} = 8.9$ $n = 329$ $fd_{max} = 4.4$

$n = 69$ $fd_{max} = 10.9$ $n = 244$ $fd_{max} = 3.9$

0.4   11

Fixation Density (%)

Figure 2. Fixation density heat maps indicating the distribution and relative proportion of fixations for two representative scenes, averaged over subjects and grouped by cue condition. Maps were normalized by dividing local measures of fixation frequency by the total number of fixations made to a given scene. Greater fixation density (i.e., a larger proportion of fixations) is represented by movement from green to red. (For readers of the print version of this paper, red is indicated by the dark areas within light patches.) Only those fixations occurring after the initial saccade of a trial and until the first fixation on the target were included in this analysis, and fixation densities less than 10% of the peak density on a given map were excluded for clarity. The total number of fixations (n) and the maximum fixation density (fd_{max}) are noted above each example. (A) Region specified trial: "Find the <target> over the road". (B) The corresponding region unspecified trial: "Find the <target>". (C) Region specified trial: "Find the <target> over the building". (D) The corresponding region unspecified trial: "Find the <target>". To view this figure in colour, please see the online issue of the Journal.

area.[2] To derive this normalized proportion measure, one experimentally naïve rater first demarcated every instance of each of the five regions in every scene, thereby creating interest areas that could be used in conjunction with

---

[2] We use the term "target region" to refer to the collective instances in a given scene of the region type containing the target, not the specific region in which the target is actually located. For example, if the saucer is located over a building, all fixations on any building are considered fixations in the target region.

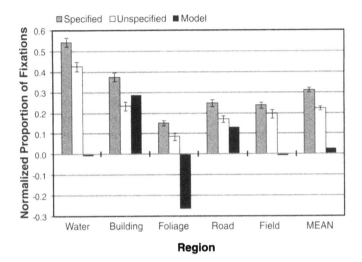

Figure 3.   Proportion of fixations in the target region, grouped by region type and normalized for region area. Grey bars, region specified condition; white bars, region unspecified condition; black bars, data from a saliency-based model. Data are only from fixations leading up to the first fixation within 1.5° of the target on each trial; excluded are the initial central fixations, fixations accompanying the discrimination judgement, and data from trials in which the target was never fixated. Errors bars indicate one standard error of the mean.

the eyetracker's data analysis software (Dataviewer; SR Research). With the specification of these regions we then computed the proportion of fixations per target region, but these proportions varied with the area of the target region in a given scene; if the target area is very large in a given scene, a greater proportion of fixations might fall in this region simply due to chance.[3] To correct for this area confound we obtained the proportion of the target area in each scene, then subtracted this value from the proportion of target region fixations on a trial-by-trial basis (see also Neider & Zelinsky, 2006a). If subjects randomly fixated locations in a scene, this normalized proportion of target region fixations would therefore be zero. Conversely, to the extent that subjects were successful in constraining their search to the cued region, their normalized proportion of fixations in the target region would not only be greater than chance, but significantly higher than the corresponding proportions under region unspecified conditions.

Figure 3 plots these normalized proportions as a function of target region type and cue condition. Analyses of these data revealed a significantly higher proportion of target region fixations in the specified condition compared to

---

[3] So as to minimize biases arising from initial central fixation and target inspection during discrimination, this analysis starts with the fixation following the initial saccade and ends with the first fixation within 1.5° of the target.

the unspecified condition, $F(1, 19) = 83.94$, $p < .001$. This difference is consistent with our interpretation of cueing benefits in terms of a constriction of the search space to the specified region. As in the case of time-to-target and fixations-to-target, there was also a main effect of region type, $F(4, 76) = 111.99$, $p < .001$, and an interaction between region and specificity, $F(4, 76) = 3.31$, $p < .02$; using a referential cue to restrict search is easier for some regions than others. This interaction, however, was carried by the field region, which showed only a marginally significant effect of specificity, $t(19) = 1.87$, $p = .078$. For all other regions the cue effect was large and highly reliable, $t(19) \geq 3.79$, $p \leq .001$. Again, we attribute this lacklustre benefit of field cues to this region's high variability, making foreknowledge of a field target relatively uninformative.

Although not the focus of this study, it is also interesting that fixations in the unspecified conditions were concentrated in the target regions clearly more than what would be expected by chance (all $ps < .001$). We interpret these above-chance fixation rates as evidence for target guidance. Even in the absence of a region cue subjects might still use the saucer's features to guide their search, and as search is steadily guided to the target (Zelinsky, Rao, Hayhoe, & Ballard, 1997) the proportion of target region fixations should increase. Search was guided most efficiently to targets over water (all $ps < .001$), followed by targets over buildings (all $ps \leq .02$). The road and field conditions showed comparable levels of guidance, with both differing from the other three region types (all $ps \leq .02$). The least amount of guidance was found for the foliage region (all $ps < .001$), due perhaps to the fact that foliage was the region with the largest average scene area and was therefore most susceptible to a floor effect introduced by the normalization procedure.

The previous analyses demonstrated a clear search benefit from target region specification, but how soon is this scene constraint available to the search process? To better understand how search is restricted to the target region over time, we calculated the cumulative probability of fixating the target region as a function of saccade number. If this scene constraint unfolds slowly, it may take several saccades before differences between specified and unspecified conditions are expressed. However, if search can be rapidly narrowed to the target region, then evidence for scene constraint might be observed within the first couple of eye movements.

The results of this analysis are shown in Figure 4. Data averaged across region are shown in the upper left, with the other panels showing data grouped by region. Cumulative probability of target region fixation is plotted as a function of six saccade bins, with each bin spanning two eye movements. If the target region was fixated following the first or second saccade, this would be registered in the ≤ 2 saccade bin; if the first fixation in the target region did not occur until after the ninth saccade, this event

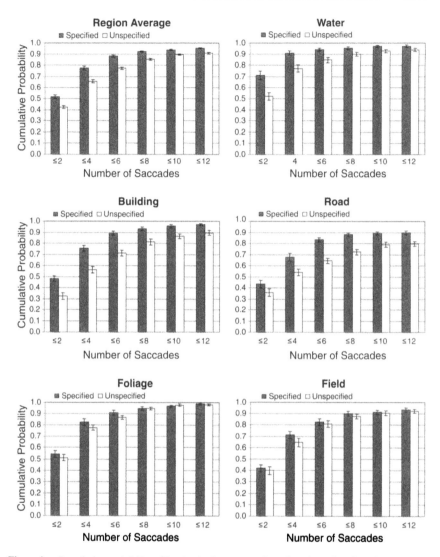

Figure 4. Cumulative probability of fixating in the target region, plotted as a function of saccade and grouped by specificity condition and region. Initial central fixations were excluded from this analysis, and error bars indicate one standard error of the mean.

would be counted in the ≤ 10 saccade bin. As expected from the previous analysis, we found significant main effects of specificity, $F(1, 19) = 64.34$, $p < .001$, and region type, $F(4, 76) = 29.74$, $p < 001$, as well as an interaction between the two, $F(4, 76) = 4.34$, $p < .01$. Separate repeated-measures ANOVAs performed on individual regions revealed that the water, $F(1, 19) = 13.83$, $p = .001$, building, $F(1, 19) = 32.84$, $p < .001$, and road,

$F(1, 19) = 22.70$, $p < .001$, regions all showed significant differences between specified and unspecified conditions, but that this cueing benefit did not extend to the foliage, $F(1, 19) = 1.10$, $p > .30$, and field, $F(1, 19) = .60$, $p > .44$, regions. This selective expression of a cueing benefit is not surprising; the field region consistently showed little or no effect of region specificity, and the typically large area of a scene devoted to foliage made it more likely that a saccade would land in this region even in the absence of a region cue.

More importantly, the relationship between cue specificity and region type was qualified by a significant three-way interaction with the number of saccades, $F(20, 380) = 2.25$, $p < .01$; not only did the probability of subjects fixating in the target region vary with cue specificity, these cueing benefits appeared sooner for some region types than others. To more closely examine the time course of these benefits for the water, building and road regions, we performed post hoc tests on the probability of target region fixation after the first two saccades. These analyses revealed highly significant effects of specificity for the water and building regions, $t(19) \geq 4.28$, $p < .001$. The fact that these target regions were preferentially fixated so early during search (see also Torralba et al., 2006) suggests a specific mechanism of scene constraint, one in which search is actually guided by the visual features of the target regions. Interestingly, the cueing benefit for roads reached significance only after four saccades, $t(19) = 3.01$, $p < .01$, suggesting that search guidance to this region was delayed relative to water and buildings. Referential scene constraints can therefore be very fast acting, but are not equally fast for all regions.

Can a purely bottom-up search model account for aspects of our data? It is clear from the outset that a model based entirely on feature contrast would not be able to capture the effects of referential scene constraint reported in this paper. Referential scene constraints are an obvious expression of top-down control, and as such are outside the scope of these models (for additional discussion of how saliency-based models are limited in this respect, see: Einhäuser & König, 2003; Foulsham & Underwood, 2007; Tatler, Baddeley, & Gilchrist, 2005; Turano, Geruschat, & Baker, 2003; Underwood & Foulsham, 2006; Vincent, Troscianko, & Gilchrist, 2007; Zelinsky, 2008). However, subjects in our task also differentially fixated scene regions even in the absence of region cueing (e.g., Figure 3, white bars). We attributed this fixation variability in the unspecified condition to differential target guidance between regions, but it is possible that strictly bottom-up factors might also explain these differences. Might subjects have preferred to fixate targets in the water because the target is more salient in this local context?

To address this possibility we used the saliency-based model developed by Zelinsky and colleagues (Zelinsky, Zhang, Yu, Chen, & Samaras, 2006; see also Chen & Zelinsky, 2006) to evaluate the independent contributions of bottom-up and top-down factors in guiding search. This bottom-up model first separates the search image into an intensity channel and two opponent-process colour channels, red minus green and blue minus yellow. Visual features are then extracted via application of steerable two-dimensional Gaussian-derivative filters, the identical filters used in Zelinsky (2008). The current implementation used first-order and second-order Gaussians, four orientations (0°, 45°, 90°, and 180°), and three scales (7, 15, and 31 pixels), resulting in 24 feature maps per intensity-colour channel. The 24 feature maps for each channel were combined into a single map using the nonlinear normalization procedure described in Itti, Koch, and Niebur (1998), and these three combined maps were then averaged to create the final saliency map. Note that this method of computing salience differs from the method described by Itti and colleagues (Itti & Koch, 2000; Itti et al., 1998) in the specific filters that were used and in the method of obtaining feature contrast; our approach obtained contrast directly from the Gaussian-derivative filter responses rather than through the application of Difference-of-Gaussian (DoG) filters. However, despite these differences in pilot testing these methods yielded very similar estimates of bottom-up salience. We gave the model the same stimuli presented to subjects, and had it generate eye movements until simulated gaze landed within 1.5° of the target (as in the behavioural experiment) or until 100 fixations were produced, whichever came first.

This saliency-based model did a poor job of characterizing our subjects' behaviour. These deficiencies fall into three categories. First, whereas subjects looked within 1.5° of the target on the vast majority of trials (~95%), quite often the model failed to acquire the saucer target even after 100 fixations. These miss rates varied with target region, with the model failing to acquire the target on 90%, 83%, 43%, 37%, and 13%, of the foliage, water, field, road, and building trials, respectively. With the possible exception of cases in which a target appeared over a building, the model was therefore largely unable to complete these search tasks (see also Zelinsky, 2008). Second, on those trials in which the model ultimately acquired the target, it did so after an unrealistically large number of fixations: 71, 48, 44, 31, and 30 fixations in the water, road, field, building, and foliage regions, respectively. Third, the model's normalized distribution of fixations differed from human behaviour for several of the scene regions, as illustrated for correct trials by the black bars in Figure 3. This was particularly true for the water, field, and foliage regions. Water and field target regions were fixated by the model at chance, meaning that a random placement of fixations in the scene would have produced the same proportion of fixations in these regions. In contrast, subjects showed strong guidance to targets in these regions, especially the water. Similarly, the foliage target region was fixated well below chance by the model, whereas subjects clearly devoted an above-chance proportion of their fixations to this region. Only in the case of the building and road regions did the model's behaviour approximate that of subjects. These partial successes were often due to the high contrast created between the light grey of a roadway and the surrounding green grass, or a building and its cast shadow.

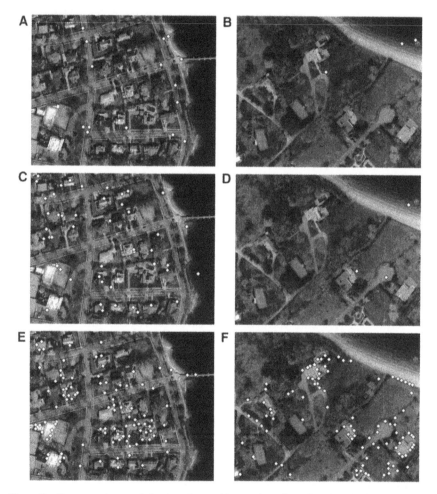

Figure 5. Representative search fixations from subjects and a saliency-based model for two scenes. (A) Behavioural data from one subject when the road region was specified. (C) Behavioural data for the corresponding scene without region specification. (E) Corresponding data from the model. (B) Behavioural data from one subject when the water region was specified. (D) Behavioural data for the corresponding scene without region specification. (F) Corresponding data from the model. Note that the model generally failed to inspect the water and foliage regions regardless of target placement. To view this figure in colour, please see the online issue of the Journal.

The examples in Figure 5 illustrate the previously described deficiencies of the saliency-based model, and contrast the behavioural differences between specified and unspecified conditions. The top two panels make clear that subjects were able to confine their search to cued regions. Figure 5A shows a restriction of search to the road region, and Figure 5B shows a near immediate direction of gaze to the water. In the absence of referential constraints, subjects made more fixations to more regions (Figure 5C), or needed more eye movements to fixate the target region (Figure 5D), but eventually managed to find the saucer target. This is not true of the model, which in both cases failed to find the target in its first 100 fixations (Figure 5E and 5F). This was even the case when the target "popped out" for human observers (Figure 5B and 5D). Apparently, the target region that proved easiest for subjects (i.e., water; see Table 1) was one of the most challenging for the saliency-based model. In summary, saliency differences either cannot explain the observed region variability in fixation behaviour, or the tested model was too insensitive to the subtle feature contrast signals (e.g., between the water and the saucer target) used by our subjects to direct gaze.

GENERAL DISCUSSION

This paper documents the existence and use of a previously unstudied form of scene constraint, one arising from categorical foreknowledge of the scene region containing a target. Our evidence for this constraint takes the form of multiple and converging data from manual and eye movement measures. Search times were faster when the target region was known compared to when it was unknown, suggesting that subjects were able to partially restrict their search to the cued region. This narrowing of the search space was explicitly demonstrated by the fewer fixations needed to reach the search target, and by the disproportionate distribution of these fixations in the target region, far more so than what would be expected by chance. Cued target regions also tended to be fixated sooner, with significant effects of region specification appearing as early as the first two saccades. This evidence for early scene constraint suggests that search was guided to the cued region; not only was search largely confined to these cued regions, these regions were actively sought out.

All of these patterns are consistent with the use of a referential variety of scene constraint, one in which a target can be specified in relation to another scene component, in this case a region. These referential constraints differ from other forms of scene constraint in that they can be introduced moments before a search and can be flexibly changed from task to task using the same scenes (i.e., they are not dependent on learned associations between specific scenes and scene elements). This combination of qualities makes this variety of scene constraint potentially important in social or interactive search situations, such as when one person communicates to another the whereabouts of a search target (e.g., Brennan, 2005; Brennan, Chen, Dickinson, Neider, & Zelinsky, 2008; Neider, Chen, Dickinson, Brennan, & Zelinsky, 2005; see also Logan, 1995, for discussion of a related linguistic constraint on search using nonscene stimuli). There is also a conceptual relationship between referential scene constraints and the work by Tanenhaus and colleagues (e.g., Tanenhaus, Spivey-Knowlton, Eberhard, & Sedivy, 1995), particularly with regard to the role of scalar adjectives in referential communication (Brown-Schmidt & Tanenhaus, 2006), and also recent work showing that such constraints can be used almost immediately (e.g., Dahan & Tanenhaus, 2005; Huettig & Altmann, 2005).

Existing theories of search are not well suited to explain this evidence for referential scene constraint. Most theories of search fall into one of two categories: Those that assume the existence of a target template and the top-down guidance of search to patterns matching this template (e.g., Wolfe, 1994; Zelinsky, 2008), and those that assume that search is guided predominantly by bottom-up properties of the search scene, such as feature contrast (e.g., Itti & Koch, 2000; Theeuwes, 2004). Top-down search theories cannot account for the observed differences between specified and unspecified conditions, as the same target appeared in the same regions in each condition. Bottom-up theories are similarly inadequate in explaining these data, as we demonstrated by having a bottom-up model search for the saucer target in the same scenes viewed by our subjects. As expected, not only did this model fail to capture the human ability to confine search to the cued region, it also made too many fixations and often failed to acquire the target entirely, even under conditions that were easy for human observers (e.g., water).

Our findings are even problematic for theories of search tailored to the explanation of scene context effects. Indeed, our intent was to explore the limitations of these previous approaches by focusing on a very specific form of referential constraint, one that describes a middle ground between more common scene constraints (with all semantic associations intact) and situations in which subjects have no information as to a target's location in a scene. For example, we can rule out explanations relying on learned spatial relationships between targets and regions (e.g., Chun & Jiang, 1998; Eckstein et al., 2006) because these relationships were unpredictable in our study; subjects knew the target region but did not know where this region would be located in the scene. Similarly, the mechanism for constraint used in the Torralba et al. (2006) model would not apply to this study, for two reasons. First, this model used scene classification to impose spatial constraints; our scenes were all relatively similar aerial views of Long Island, placing them in the same scene category and removing the information needed for a differential biasing of scene locations. Second, even if one were to assume that our scenes were categorized at a more subordinate level (e.g., scenes with big fields, or lots of roads), this more specific categorization could not be used to impose spatial scene constraints, as the locations of these regions would remain unpredictable. The model would therefore behave similarly if asked to find the target "over the field" versus "over the building", because it would have no idea where either region would be located in the scene. In the absence of this top-down information, the Torralba et al. approach would degenerate into a purely bottom-up search model, which we have already demonstrated to be inadequate to describe our data. In summary, the constraints described by contextual cueing theory and Bayesian approaches, as well as the Torralba et al. scene context model, are all undoubtedly important in a wide variety of search tasks, but the current task is not one of these. We have isolated a form of referential scene constraint that is potentially widely used to describe targets as part of our normal social discourse, yet cannot be easily explained by any of these popular approaches.

If existing theories of scene context and search cannot explain our data, what other processes might underlie our observed effect of region specificity? We believe that our data cannot be explained without appeal to some form of scene segmentation, as this would be the only means by which subjects could determine the location of the cued region in a given scene.

The suggestion that segmentation might underlie scene constraint is theoretically important. The Torralba et al. (2006) model assumed the existence of dedicated global features for the categorization of various scene types (Oliva & Torralba, 2001, 2006), thereby making it possible to impose scene constraints without segmenting a scene into objects or regions. This is desirable, as scene segmentation is an open problem; if one can describe scene constraints while side-stepping segmentation, so much the better. However, as evidenced by our data it may not be possible to avoid segmentation entirely. Indeed, Torralba et al. provided only an implementation proof showing the feasibility of using global context to describe scene constraints in their search tasks; they did not demonstrate that their subjects were similarly relying exclusively on global information. Perhaps their subjects were instead using rapid scene segmentation, in conjunction with semantic cueing, to confine their search, as this would have produced the same pattern of search guidance. By demonstrating scene constraints under conditions unfavourable to global contextual cueing, we partially tease apart these competing explanations and provide indirect support for the involvement of scene segmentation. This does not mean that global context is unimportant in the production of scene constraints; it is quite likely that no single approach, segmentation, global context, or Bayesian, tells the whole story. However, our findings do suggest that additional work is needed to exclude alternative hypotheses so as to better understand the relative contributions of each constraint on search guidance.

Implicating scene segmentation in search is one thing, specifying the role of this segmentation process in guiding search is quite another. There are at least two possibilities. The first presumes the rapid segmentation and recognition of the regions in a scene (*full segmentation* hypothesis), combined with guidance from semantic cues. If a search scene is segmented into recognized regions, and the subject knows that the target appears over a road, they might semantically constrain their search to this region. To meaningfully affect search this region recognition would have to occur very rapidly. Rapid recognition has already been demonstrated for scenes (e.g., Biederman, 1981; Intraub, 1989; Li, VanRullen, Koch, & Perona, 2002; Oliva & Schyns, 1997; Potter, 1976; Potter, Staub, & O'Connor, 2004; Schyns & Oliva, 1994), and even objects embedded in scenes (e.g., Thorpe, Fize, & Marlot, 1996); it is therefore plausible that individual scene regions might also be recognized in time to guide the first couple of eye movements during search. Alternatively, segmentation might be tied more closely to the specific search task. Upon presentation of the region cue subjects might consult their long-term memory to obtain region-specific visual features based on previous viewings of this region type in similar scenes. Following presentation of the search scene these features could be compared to those obtained from the automatic and parallel analysis of the scene by early visual processes. This comparison would serve to coarsely delineate the cued region in the search scene, thereby making unnecessary the need to fully segment and recognize each of the scene's regions. One practical consequence of this *search-specific segmentation* process would be the frequent performance of two sequential search tasks, one for the cued target region and the other for the actual target within this region.

Future work might distinguish between these hypotheses by using briefly presented catch trials in conjunction with spatial probes appearing in either cued or noncued scene regions. According to the full-segmentation hypothesis, subjects should be able to report the identity of the probed region regardless of whether it was cued, as all regions would have been segmented and recognized. However, the search-specific segmentation hypothesis predicts that good region identification should be limited to the cued region.

REFERENCES

Antes, J., & Penland, J. (1981). Picture context effects on eye movement patterns. In D. Fisher, R. Monty, & J. Senders (Eds.), *Eye movements: Cognition and visual perception* (pp. 157–170). Hillsdale, NJ: Lawrence Erlbaum Associates, Inc.

Bar, M. (2004). Visual objects in context. *Nature Neuroscience Reviews, 5*, 617–629.

Bar, M., & Aminoff, E. (2003). Cortical analysis of visual context. *Neuron, 38*, 347–358.

Biederman, I. (1981). On the semantics of a glance at a scene. In M. Kubovy & J. R. Pomerantz (Eds.), *Perceptual organization* (pp. 213–253). Hillsdale, NJ: Lawrence Erlbaum Associates, Inc.

Boyce, S. J., Pollatsek, A., & Rayner, K. (1989). Effect of background information on object identification. *Journal of Experimental Psychology: Human Perception and Performance, 15,* 556–566.

Brennan, S. E. (2005). How conversation is shaped by visual and spoken evidence. In J. Trueswell & M. Tanenhaus (Eds.), *Approaches to studying world-situated language use: Bridging the language-as-product and language-action traditions* (pp. 95–129). Cambridge, MA: MIT Press.

Brennan, S. E., Chen, X., Dickinson, C., Neider, M. B., & Zelinsky, G. J. (2008). Coordinating cognition: The costs and benefits of shared gaze during collaborative search. *Cognition, 106,* 1465–1477.

Brockmole, J. R., Castelhano, M. S., & Henderson, J. M. (2006). Contextual cueing in naturalistic scenes: Global and local contexts. *Journal of Experimental Psychology: Learning, Memory, and Cognition, 32,* 699–706.

Brockmole, J. R., & Henderson, J. M. (2006). Using real-world scenes as contextual cues for search. *Visual Cognition, 13,* 99–108.

Brown-Schmidt, S., & Tanenhaus, M. K. (2006). Watching the eye when talking about size: An investigation of message formulation and utterance planning. *Journal of Memory and Language, 54,* 592–609.

Castelhano, M. S., & Henderson, J. M. (2007). Initial scene representations facilitate eye movement guidance in visual search. *Journal of Experimental Psychology: Human Perception and Performance, 33,* 753–763.

Chen, X., & Zelinsky, G. J. (2006). Real-world visual search is dominated by top-down guidance. *Vision Research, 46,* 4118–4133.

Chun, M. M. (2000). Contextual cueing of visual attention. *Trends in Cognitive Sciences, 4,* 170–178.

Chun, M. M., & Jiang, Y. (1998). Contextual cueing: Implicit learning and memory of visual context guides spatial attention. *Cognitive Psychology, 36,* 27–71.

Chun, M. M., & Jiang, Y. (1999). Top-down attentional guidance based on implicit learning of visual covariation. *Psychological Science, 10,* 360–365.

Dahan, D., & Tanenhaus, M. K. (2005). Looking at the rope when looking for the snake: Conceptually mediated eye movements during spoken-word recognition. *Psychonomic Bulletin and Review, 12*(3), 453–459.

De Graf, P., de Troy, A., & d'Ydewalle, G. (1992). Local and global contextual constraints on the identification of objects in scenes. *Canadian Journal of Psychology, 46,* 489–508.

Eckstein, M. P., Beutter, B. R., & Stone, L. S. (2001). Quantifying the performance limits of human saccadic targeting during visual search. *Perception, 30,* 1389–1401.

Eckstein, M. P., Drescher, B., & Shimozaki, S. S. (2006). Attentional cues in real scenes, saccadic targeting and Bayesian priors. *Psychological Science, 17,* 973–980.

Eckstein, M. P., Shimozaki, S. S., & Abbey, C. K. (2002). The footprints of visual attention in the Posner cueing paradigm revealed by classification images. *Journal of Vision, 2,* 25–45.

Einhäuser, W., & König, P. (2003). Does luminance-contrast contribute to a saliency map for overt visual attention? *European Journal of Neuroscience, 17,* 1089–1097.

Enns, J. T., & Rensink, R. A. (1990). Influence of scene-based properties on visual search. *Science, 247,* 721–723.

Foulsham, T., & Underwood, G. (2007). How does the purpose of inspection influence the potency of visual salience in scene perception? *Perception, 36,* 1123–1138.

Friedman, A. (1979). Framing pictures: The role of knowledge in automatized encoding and memory for gist. *Journal of Experimental Psychology: General, 108,* 316–355.

Geisler, W. S., Perry, J. S., & Najemnik, J. (2006). Visual search: The role of peripheral information measured using gaze-contingent displays. *Journal of Vision, 6,* 858–873.

Goffaux, V., Jacques, C., Mouraux, A., Oliva, A., Rossion, B., & Schyns, P. G. (2005). Diagnostic colours contribute to early stages of scene categorization: Behavioural and neurophysiological evidences. *Visual Cognition, 12,* 878–892.

Green, D., & Swets, J. (1966). *Signal detection theory and psychophysics.* New York: Krieger.

Henderson, J. M. (2003). Human gaze control in real-world scene perception. *Trends in Cognitive Sciences, 7,* 498–504.

Henderson, J. M. (2005). Introduction to real-world scene perception. *Visual Cognition, 12,* 849–851.

Henderson, J. M. (2007). Regarding scenes. *Current Directions in Psychological Science, 16,* 219–222.

Henderson, J. M., Weeks, P., & Hollingworth, A. (1999). The effects of semantic consistency on eye movements during scene viewing. *Journal of Experimental Psychology: Human Perception and Performance, 25,* 210–228.

Huettig, F., & Altmann, G. T. M. (2005). Word meaning and the control of eye fixation: Semantic competitor effects and the visual world paradigm. *Cognition, 96,* B23–B32.

Hummel, J. E., & Biederman, I. (1992). Dynamic binding in a neural network for shape recognition. *Psychological Review, 99,* 480–517.

Intraub, H. (1989). Illusory conjunctions of forms, objects, and scenes during rapid serial visual search. *Journal of Experimental Psychology: Learning, Memory, and Cognition, 15,* 98–109.

Itti, L., & Koch, C. (2000). A saliency-based search mechanism for overt and covert shifts of visual attention. *Vision Research, 40,* 1489–1506.

Itti, L., Koch, C., & Niebur, E. (1998). A model of saliency-based visual attention for rapid scene analysis. *IEEE Transactions on Pattern Analysis and Machine Intelligence, 20,* 1254–1259.

Kersten, D., Mamassian, P., & Yuille, A. (2004). Object perception as Bayesian inference. *Annual Review of Psychology, 55,* 271–304.

Kunar, M. A., Flusberg, S. J., Horowitz, T. S., & Wolfe, J. M. (2007). Does contextual cueing guide the deployment of attention? *Journal of Experimental Psychology: Human Perception and Performance, 33,* 816–828.

Li, F. F., VanRullen, R., Koch, C., & Perona, P. (2002). Rapid natural scene categorization in the near absence of attention. *Proceedings of the National Academy of Sciences, USA, 99,* 9596–9601.

Loftus, G., & Mackworth, N. (1978). Cognitive determinants of fixation location during picture viewing. *Journal of Experimental Psychology: Human Perception and Performance, 4,* 565–572.

Logan, G. D. (1995). Linguistic and conceptual control of visual spatial attention. *Cognitive Psychology, 28,* 103–174.

Marr, D. (1982). *Vision.* San Francisco: Freeman.

Najemnik, J., & Geisler, W. S. (2005). Optimal eye movement strategies in visual search. *Nature, 434,* 387–391.

Neider, M. B., Chen, X., Dickinson, C., Brennan, S. E., & Zelinsky, G. J. (2005). Sharing eyegaze is better than speaking in a time-critical consensus task. In *Abstracts of the 46th annual meeting of the Psychonomic Society* (Vol. 10, No. 72). Toronto, Canada: Psychonomic Society.

Neider, M. B., & Zelinsky, G. J. (2006a). Scene context guides eye movements during visual search. *Vision Research, 46,* 614–621.

Neider, M. B., & Zelinsky, G. J. (2006b). Searching for camouflaged targets: Effects of target-background similarity on visual search. *Vision Research, 46,* 2217–2235.

Neider, M. B., & Zelinsky, G. J. (2008). Exploring set size effects in scenes: Identifying the objects of search. *Visual Cognition, 16,* 1–10.

Oliva, A., & Schyns, P. G. (1997). Coarse blobs or fine edges? Evidence that information diagnosticity changes the perception of complex visual stimuli. *Cognitive Psychology*, *34*, 107–772.

Oliva, A., & Torralba, A. (2001). Modeling the shape of the scene: A holistic representation of the spatial envelope. *International Journal of Computer Vision*, *42*, 145–175.

Oliva, A., & Torralba, A. (2006). Building the gist of a scene: The role of global image features in recognition. *Progress in Brain Research: Visual Perception*, *155*, 23–36.

Oliva, A., Torralba, A., Castelhano, M., & Henderson, J. M. (2003). Top-down control of visual attention in object detection. *IEEE International Conference on Image Processing*, *1*, 253–256.

Palmer, J., Ames, C., & Lindsey, D. (1993). Measuring the effect of attention on simple visual search. *Journal of Experimental Psychology: Human Perception and Performance*, *19*, 108–130.

Palmer, S. E. (1975). Visual perception and world knowledge: Notes on a model of sensory-cognitive interaction. In D. A. Norman & D. E. Rumelhart (Eds.), *Explorations in cognition* (pp. 279–307). San Francisco: Freeman.

Potter, M. C. (1976). Short term conceptual memory for pictures. *Journal of Experimental Psychology: Human Perception and Performance*, *2*, 509–522.

Potter, M. C., Staub, A., & O'Connor, D. H. (2004). Pictorial and conceptual representation of glimpsed pictures. *Journal of Experimental Psychology: Human Perception and Performance*, *30*, 478–489.

Sanocki, T. (2003). Representation and perception of scenic layout. *Cognitive Psychology*, *47*, 43–86.

Schyns, P. G., & Oliva, A. (1994). From blobs to boundary edges: Evidence for time- and spatial-scale-dependent scene recognition. *Psychological Science*, *5*, 195–200.

Shaw, M. (1982). Attending to multiple sources of information. *Cognitive Psychology*, *14*, 353–409.

Tanenhaus, M. K., Spivey-Knowlton, M. J., Eberhard, K. M., & Sedivy, J. C. (1995). Integration of visual and linguistic information in spoken language comprehension. *Science*, *268*, 1632–1634.

Tatler, B. W., Baddeley, R. J., & Gilchrist, I. D. (2005). Visual correlates of fixation selection: Effects of scale and time. *Vision Research*, *45*, 643–659.

Theeuwes, J. (2004). Top down search strategies cannot override attentional capture. *Psychonomic Bulletin and Review*, *11*, 65–70.

Thorpe, S., Fize, D., & Marlot, C. (1996). Speed of processing in the human visual system. *Nature*, *381*, 520–522.

Torralba, A. (2003). Modeling global scene factors in attention. *Journal of the Optical Society of America*, *20*, 1407–1418.

Torralba, A., Oliva, A., Castelhano, M., & Henderson, J. M. (2006). Contextual guidance of attention in natural scenes: The role of global features on object search. *Psychological Review*, *113*, 766–786.

Turano, K. A., Geruschat, D. R., & Baker, F. H. (2003). Oculomotor strategies for direction of gaze tested with a real-world activity. *Vision Research*, *43*(3), 333–346.

Underwood, G., & Foulsham, T. (2006). Visual saliency and semantic incongruency influence eye movements when inspecting pictures. *Quarterly Journal of Experimental Psychology*, *59*, 1931–1945.

Vincent, B. T., Troscianko, T., & Gilchrist, I. D. (2007). Investigating a space-variant weighted salience account of visual selection. *Vision Research*, *47*, 1809–1820.

Wolfe, J. M. (1994). Guided Search 2.0: A revised model of visual search. *Psychonomic Bulletin and Review*, *1*, 202–238.

Zelinsky, G. J. (1999). Precueing target location in a variable set size "nonsearch" task: Dissociating search-based and interference-based explanations for set size effects. *Journal of Experimental Psychology: Human Perception and Performance, 25*, 875–903.

Zelinsky, G. J. (2008). A theory of eye movements during target acquisition. *Psychological Review, 115*(4), 787–835.

Zelinsky, G. J., Rao, R., Hayhoe, M., & Ballard, D. (1997). Eye movements reveal the spatio-temporal dynamics of visual search. *Psychological Science, 8*, 448–453.

Zelinsky, G. J., Zhang, W., Yu, B., Chen, X., & Samaras, D. (2006). The role of top-down and bottom-up processes in guiding eye movements during visual search. In Y. Weiss, B. Scholkopf, & J. Platt (Eds.), *Advances in neural information processing systems* (Vol. 18, pp. 1609–1616). Cambridge, MA: MIT Press.

VISUAL COGNITION, 2009, 17 (6/7), 1029–1054

The prominence of behavioural biases in eye guidance

Benjamin W. Tatler and Benjamin T. Vincent

University of Dundee, Dundee, UK

When attempting to understand where people look during scene perception, researchers typically focus on the relative contributions of low- and high-level cues. Computational models of the contribution of low-level features to fixation selection, with modifications to incorporate top-down sources of information have been abundant in recent research. However, we are still some way from a model that can explain many of the complexities of eye movement behaviour. Here we show that understanding biases in *how* we move the eyes can provide powerful new insights into the decision about where to look in complex scenes. A model based solely on these biases and therefore blind to current visual information outperformed popular salience-based approaches. Our data show that incorporating an understanding of oculomotor behavioural biases into models of eye guidance is likely to significantly improve our understanding of where we choose to fixate in natural scenes.

Keywords: Behavioural bias; Fixation; Saccade amplitude; Saccade direction; Salience; Systematic tendency

Successfully completing many forms of behaviour requires that humans look in the right place at the right time. Ballard and colleagues described this as a "do-it-where-I'm-looking" visual strategy for completing complex tasks (Ballard et al., 1992); a finding that has been replicated across a range of studies of natural behaviour (e.g., Hayhoe, Shrivastava, Mruczek, & Pelz, 2003; Land & Hayhoe, 2001; Land, Mennie, & Rusted, 1999; Pelz & Canosa, 2001).

One reason why we look at the location we are interested in gathering information from is that the human retina evolved such that high quality

---

Please address all correspondence to Benjamin W. Tatler, School of Psychology, University of Dundee, Dundee DD1 4HN, UK. E-mail: b.w.tatler@activevisionlab.com or b.w.tatler@dundee.ac.uk

Both authors contributed equally to this manuscript. We thank Jim Brockmole, Aude Oliva, and Simon Liversedge for their comments on the submitted version of this manuscript. We also thank Roland Baddeley, Mark Bennett, Tim Dixon, Martin Fischer, Gesche Huebner, Casimir Ludwig, Wayne Murray, and Nick Wade for their comments and guidance during the preparation of this work.

© 2009 Taylor & Francis
DOI: 10.1080/13506280902764539

vision is restricted to the small ($\sim 2°$) fovea at the centre of vision. For many visually guided behaviours, the coarse information from peripheral vision is insufficient, thus requiring mechanisms to direct the foveae to appropriate locations. This has generated a large volume of research aimed at understanding how the eyes are guided (since Buswell, 1935).

FEATURE-BASED ACCOUNTS OF EYE GUIDANCE

One promising approach to understanding eye guidance has been to suppose that "basic" visual features, such as contrast, edges, colour, and motion, are extracted from the visual scene and used to direct the eyes (e.g., Wolfe & Horowitz, 2004). Support for this notion can be found from visual search paradigms in psychophysics, where manipulating visual features has clear consequences on the deployment of visual attention (Duncan & Humphreys, 1989; Treisman & Gelade, 1980; Wolfe, 1998). This notion of basic features guiding attention has been extended to natural scene viewing and formalized in models of eye guidance. One prominent such model is the visual salience model of Itti, Koch, and colleagues (Itti & Koch, 2000; Itti, Koch, & Niebur, 1998; Koch & Ullman, 1985). Here salience is operationalized as the output of a competitive process between a set of basic features (colour-, orientation-, and luminance-contrast) in order to produce an overall salience map of the scene. Eye guidance then unfolds from this using a winner-takes-all selection of the most salient location in the scene, with transient inhibition of fixated locations to avoid the model becoming stuck.

Despite the prominence of feature-based accounts of eye guidance in recent years, empirical evaluations of such models have shown that these are disappointingly poor at accounting for human fixation selection (e.g., Henderson, Brockmole, Castelhano, & Mack, 2007; Tatler, 2007; Tatler, Baddeley, & Gilchrist, 2005; Tatler, Baddeley, & Vincent, 2006). In particular, when the behavioural task is manipulated, feature-based models can fail almost completely (e.g., Einhäuser, Rutishauser, & Koch, 2008; Foulsham & Underwood, 2008; Underwood & Foulsham, 2006; Underwood, Foulsham, van Loon, Humphreys, & Boyce, 2006).

Selectively weighting the different feature channels in Itti's salience model (Navalpakkam & Itti, 2005) is one way to potentially improve feature-based accounts and incorporate some degree of high-level modulation (by effectively supplying top-down knowledge of the target of a visual search). However, even this modification of the salience model is very limited for finding real objects in images of natural scenes (Vincent, Troscianko, & Gilchrist, 2007).

More success has been found by incorporating top-down knowledge of where targets are likely to be found in natural scenes (Ehinger, Hidalgo-Sotelo,

Torralba, & Oliva, 2009 this issue; Torralba, 2003; Torralba, Oliva, Castelhano, & Henderson, 2006). Scene gist is used to categorize the scene and look up a spatial probability distribution of where the target is likely to be found. The spatial probability distribution is used to constrain the feature-level computations to these likely locations.

Despite continued research effort, we remain some way from a coherent understanding of the factors that underlie saccade target selection when viewing natural scenes and during natural behaviour.

REPHRASING EYE GUIDANCE PROBABILISTICALLY

The fundamental question at the heart of any account of eye guidance must be to understand the moment-to-moment relocation of gaze: That is, where will the eyes select as the target of the next fixation? A convenient way to phrase this question is in the language of probabilities. In general we can say that we are interested in knowing the probability of making a saccade to a location based upon all the information that the oculomotor system has available to it: P(saccade|data). Calculating this spatial probability distribution (or map) directly is not necessarily impossible, but by using Bayes's Theorem we can break this down into simpler components:

$$P(saccade \mid data) = \frac{P(data|saccade)}{P(data)} P(saccade) \tag{1}$$

The beauty of this approach is that the data could come from a variety of sources such as simple feature cues, derivations such as Itti's definition of salience, object-, or other high-level sources. Although this approach is extremely general and flexible in that manner, for the present study and for comparability with the studies discussed earlier, we will consider saccade target selection on the basis of the lower level cues of visual salience or simple visual features (in this case, edges).

The first right-hand term in Equation 1, P(data|saccade)/P(data), describes how the visual data might be involved in saccade target selection. Specifically, P(data|saccade) is the likelihood of particular visual data (say, particular image features) occurring at a saccade target location, and P(data) is the probability distribution of these visual data occurring in the environment. As such, dividing P(data|saccade) by P(data) effectively controls for the natural abundance of particular features within scenes. For example, if yellow items are commonly fixated then one may *initially* infer that yellow items predict fixations, but if yellow items are very common in the scene then yellow is a less effective predictor of eliciting fixations.

What is described in this first term bears a close resemblance to approaches previously employed to evaluate the possible involvement of visual features in eye guidance: Visual feature content at fixation—a measure of P(data|saccade)—is compared to features at control locations—an approximation of P(data)—and any differences are taken to imply nonrandom selection with respect to the visual feature under investigation (e.g., Baddeley & Tatler 2006; Krieger, Rentschler, Hauske, Schill, & Zetzsche, 2000; Mannan, Ruddock, & Wooding, 1997; Parkhurst, Law, & Niebur, 2002; Parkhurst & Neibur 2003; Reinagel & Zador, 1999; Tatler et al., 2005, 2006).

The second right-hand term in Equation 1 is the Bayesian prior, P(saccade). This term describes the probability of saccading to a location irrespective of the visual information at that location, or indeed anywhere in the scene. As such this term will encapsulate any "systematic tendencies" or "biases" in the manner in which we explore scenes with our eyes. Systematic tendencies in oculomotor behaviour can be thought of as regularities that are common across all instances of, and manipulations to, behavioural tasks. Whether or not such systematic biases in how we move our eyes can provide useful insight into predicting fixation selection has not been explored in previous studies of eye guidance. In the present paper we will explore whether understanding these biases can improve our understanding of the moment-to-moment decision about where to target with each saccade.

SYSTEMATIC TENDENCIES IN EYE GUIDANCE

In contrast to our underdeveloped ability to account for oculomotor selection, in other aspects of motor behaviour, there have been significant recent advances in our ability to model action selection (Körding & Wolpert, 2004). This progress can in part be attributed to recognizing that action selection is heavily influenced by the fact that motor behaviours are not all equally likely to be selected. For example, by recording hand movements during daily natural behaviour, it was found that certain combinations of finger movements are far more frequently selected than others (Ingram, Körding, Howard, & Wolpert, 2008). In fact, 60% of the variance of finger movements during natural behaviour could be described by only the first two principal components. The scale of this result clearly demonstrates that knowledge of this behavioural bias to select certain actions over others is highly informative in our ability to understand and model action selection.

Equivalent approaches have not been used to model visual selection, and our understanding of oculomotor behaviour remains underdeveloped. In the present paper we ask whether a similar approach to that being used to understand other aspects of motor control can be employed to improve current understanding of eye guidance when viewing natural scenes. Two clear questions emerge if we are to ask this: (1) Do oculomotor behavioural biases exist? (2) What is the relative informativeness of any such bias?

The first of these questions is addressed easily: Any survey of the eye movement literature reveals a wealth of support for the notion that there are systematic tendencies to select certain eye movements over others. For example, our oculomotor range is considerable, yet we are not equally likely to make saccades of all possible magnitudes. Instead, across a range of experimental paradigms and environments, saccade magnitudes show a positively skewed distribution, with a tendency to make small amplitude saccades (e.g., Bahill, Adler, & Stark, 1975; Gajewski, Pearson, Mack, Bartlett, & Henderson, 2005; Pelz & Canosa, 2001; Tatler et al., 2006). Similarly, we are far from uniform in selecting which direction to execute saccades in (e.g., Bair & O'Keefe, 1998; Lappe, Pekel, & Hoffmann, 1998; Lee, Badler, & Badler, 2002; Moeller, Kayser, Knecht, & König, 2004), with a higher frequency of horizontal saccades than vertical or oblique saccades (but for an exception to this pattern, Bahill et al., 1975, suggested that the majority of saccades made while walking around a real environment were oblique). In recent work, we explored the possibility that systematic tendencies may not be limited to the current saccade, but may exhibit sequential dependencies between successive saccades and fixations (Tatler & Vincent, 2008). We found that in many cases the properties of one saccade are influenced by the properties of the fixation and saccade that immediately preceded it (see also Hooge, Over, van Wezel, & Frens, 2005; Motter & Belky, 1998; Unema, Panasch, Joos, & Velichkovsky, 2005). These studies clearly illustrate that there exist systematic tendencies in the manner in which we move our eyes around a natural scene, and thus such tendencies may offer a previously untapped source of information about saccade target selection.

The second question will be the focus of the present report. Given that there is evidence for the existence of systematic tendencies in oculomotor control, we ask how informative these are as a component of models of eye guidance. Observing the existence of biases does not mean that they necessarily feature in the moment-to-moment selection of where to fixate. Instead, the observed overall biases may be a consequence of other decision factors, such as where visual information is in the world. As such, any identified biases need not be significant predictors of where each saccade is targeted. If this is the case, we might find that on a saccade-by-saccade basis, visual information predicts fixation selection, but oculomotor biases do not. However, if we find that oculomotor biases are themselves predictive of fixation selection beyond what can be predicted from visual information alone, then the tendency to move our eyes in particular ways can offer an informative component of our understanding of eye guidance.

If oculomotor biases are informative, it will be important to address the question of what these biases reflect: It is not the case that these necessarily reflect purely motoric factors; they may arise from a number of sources. For example, there may be high-level factors that influence these biases—when driving many saccades will be launched horizontally, whereas when batting in cricket vertical saccades will dominate as the ball is bowled (Land, 2006). Whatever the source of these biases, the finding that they are an informative component of fixation selection will be an important contribution to current approaches to modelling eye guidance. We will return to the issue of the possible sources of systematic oculomotor tendencies in the General Discussion.

An established technique for assessing how informative or predictive visual features are in eye guidance is to compare the visual feature content at fixated and control locations (e.g., Parkhurst et al., 2002; Parkhusrt & Niebur, 2003; Reinagel & Zador, 1999; Tatler et al., 2005). The logic is that if we can discriminate the feature content at fixated and control locations, then this feature is predictive of where will be fixated. Using techniques such as signal detection, we can further estimate the magnitude of the discrimination between fixated and control locations and use this as an indicator of the extent to which a feature can be informative about fixation selection. In the present report, we use the same principle of determining whether fixated and control locations can be discriminated. However, we extend this technique to allow us to consider not only the predictive power of visual features, but also that of oculomotor biases. To do this we extract not only the image features at each fixated and control location, but also the amplitude and direction of the saccade immediately preceding each of these real and control fixations (note that this is entirely possible for the control locations because we construct our control locations by sampling from fixations made on other images by the same participant). We evaluated how well we could predict saccade target selection by using a combination of signal detection theory and log-likelihood classifiers to discriminate fixated locations from control locations.

In order to assess the relative informativeness of visual features and oculomotor biases in eye guidance we first assessed how well visual features or oculomotor biases alone could be used to predict fixation selection. We then considered how these factors may combine to predict fixation, either as independent or interactive factors. When testing the ability to predict fixation selection on the basis of visual features, we decided to characterize these features in two different manners. First we used the popular current model of visual salience (Itti & Koch, 2000), which uses a competitive combination of visual feature channels to compute an overall conspicuity map. Second, based on previous work by one of the authors, we characterized visual features simply in terms of the edge intensity derived from the output of oriented Gabor filters, because when interactions between image features are accounted for edge intensity was found to be the maximally informative feature for predicting eye guidance (Baddeley & Tatler, 2006). Thus, the present study offers an opportunity not only to assess the relative predictive power of visual features and oculomotor biases, but also to compare the complex salience map model to a simple description of oriented edge information in scenes.

METHOD

Participants

All 22 participants were naïve to the purpose of the experiment and had normal or corrected-to-normal vision. Each received monetary reward (£5) or course credit towards their undergraduate psychology degree for taking part.

Stimuli and procedure

Each participant viewed 120 colour photographs of natural scenes: 40 indoor, and 80 outdoor scenes (Figure 3). Images were taken using a Nikon D2 digital SLR at a resolution of 4 megapixels and later resized to be 1600 × 1200 pixels and represented with 24-bit colour depth.

Images were displayed on a Viewsonic P225f 22-inch pure flat CRT monitor running at a refresh rate of 100 Hz. At the viewing distance of 57 cm, the images subtended approximately 40° horizontally and 30° vertically in the observer's field of view.

Participants were given no specific task instructions, merely being asked to freely view the images.[1] Each trial was preceded by a fixation marker positioned randomly within 10° of the centre of the screen. Images were presented for 5 s and were followed by a white noise mask.

Eye movement recording

Eye movements were recorded using an SR Research Ltd EyeLink II eyetracker, sampling pupil position at 500 Hz. Two nine-point grids were used to calibrate and then validate gaze position tracking. If the validation procedure returned a mean spatial accuracy of worse than ± 0.5°, the eye tracker was recalibrated. Eye position data were collected for the eye that

---

[1] Free viewing is often taken as a task that is free from higher level "baggage". However, this is not the case and free viewing comes with its own set of issues (Tatler et al., 2005). We chose this "task" for comparability with other recent studies that have evaluated low-level factors in eye guidance.

produced the better spatial accuracy as determined using the calibration. Saccades and fixations were defined using the saccade detection algorithm supplied by SR Research: Saccades were identified by deflections in eye position in excess of $0.1°$, with a minimum velocity of $30°s^{-1}$ and a minimum acceleration of $8000°s^{-2}$, maintained for at least 4 ms. We employed a minimum fixation duration of 50 ms. The first fixation in each trial was defined as the first fixation that began after the onset of the scene image. Thus, the fixation on the pretrial fixation marker was not included in the analyses.

Defining visual features and saccade characteristics for fixated locations

Visual features

Edges. Given our previous finding that edge information was more predictive of fixation behaviour than luminance or contrast information (Baddeley & Tatler, 2006), in the present paper we chose only to extract edge information at fixated and control locations. Edge information was quantified by convolving images with four oriented odd-phase Gabor patches (oriented at $0°$, $45°$, $90°$, and $135°$). The absolute values of each orientation map were used in order to capture unsigned difference from the mean. These orientation maps were combined and normalized by subtracting the mean of the combined map and dividing by its standard deviation, as in our previous work (Tatler et al., 2005). Edge maps were constructed over a range of spatial scales, using Gabors with envelope standard deviations from 0.625 to 20 cpd.

In order to extract edge information at fixation, $2° \times 2°$ patches were defined, centred around the point of the fixation as derived from the eyetracker record. The maximum edge feature value within this patch was then calculated and used as the value of edge information at fixation (see Figure 2).

Salience. We calculated the overall salience map for each image using the latest version of Itti's salience algorithm (available at http://www.saliency-toolbox.net). We used the default parameter settings for computing our salience maps. (For details of this algorithm, see Walther & Koch, 2006.) Just as for edge information, we extracted salience at fixation by taking the maximum value in a $2° \times 2°$ centred with respect to gaze.

Saccade characteristics

Saccade characteristics were also measured for each fixation, extracting the amplitude and direction of the saccade that brought the eye to bear on each fixated location (see Figure 2).

Defining visual features and saccade characteristics of control locations

Although we have direct access to fixated image regions from our empirical eye movement recordings, we must also define a set of control locations. There are several ways in which these control locations and their feature and saccade characteristics could be defined. One way to do this would be to uniformly sample values (of edge intensities, for example) within the range of edge intensities present in the image (see Figure 1); however, this has the drawback of not accounting for potential correlations in image features over the image. Such correlations may arise from the combination of: any compositional bias in capturing the display images (e.g., a tendency to take photographs with objects of interest in the centre); and any tendency to fixate some parts of images more than others (e.g., the central fixation bias, see Tatler, 2007).

Alternatively, these distributions could be created by uniformly and randomly sampling locations in the image (see Figure 1). This approach also has a drawback of not being a suitable control for the well-known nonrandom distribution of saccades over an image; there is a strong tendency to fixate the approximate centre of an image (Tatler, 2007).

We therefore employed a method used in our previous studies, which avoids the limitations of the two methods just described (Tatler et al., 2005). The method for creating control distributions of edge intensities, visual salience, saccade magnitudes, and saccade directions is shown schematically for one participant viewing one image in Figure 2.

First we compiled a list of x-y locations for fixations, together with the magnitudes and directions of the saccades that immediately preceded each of these fixations. These details were extracted for all fixations on all images excluding the one currently being analysed for this participant. We sampled from this list randomly a number of times equal to the number of actual fixations made on the current image. In doing this, we therefore sampled from actual saccades and fixation locations made by that participant but not on the current image. The control saccade magnitude and direction distributions were built up cumulatively with this procedure over all images and participants. The control feature distributions were constructed by using the sampled x-y locations to extract edge intensity from the current image. This procedure is a suitable way of constructing control image feature distributions because it accounts for the distribution of edge intensities on individual images, while also accounting for any spatial biases of the observer.

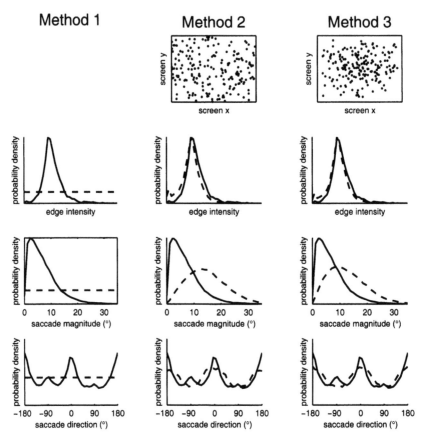

Figure 1. Methods for sampling nonfixated image locations. Distributions are shown for edge intensities, saccade amplitudes, and saccade directions for fixated (solid lines) and control (dashed lines) locations. In Method 1, a uniform distribution over each factor for the nonfixated locations is defined. In Method 2, we sample uniformly in space and construct the probability distributions of control locations from these locations. In Method 3, control distributions of locations were constructed by randomly sampling from the set of all fixations made by each individual observer on all images, excluding the current image. These coordinates were used to extract image feature information from the current image.

Assessing feature and saccade differences with a log likelihood ratio classifier

In order to assess how much we can predict about eye movements we constructed a simple classifier to distinguish fixated image patches (F) from control image patches (C). We calculated the performance at distinguishing F from C using a log likelihood threshold criterion with: Feature information (either edges or salience); saccade bias information; both feature and saccade bias information (assuming independence); feature

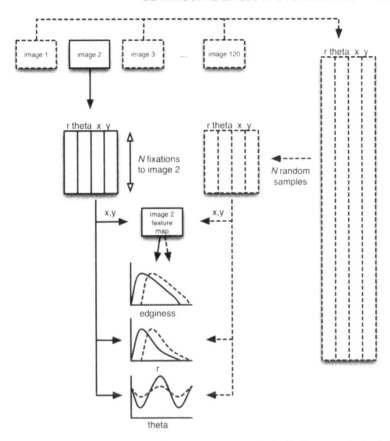

Figure 2. Schematic of how fixated (solid) and control (dashed) distributions are calculated. This example demonstrates the procedure for one particular participant viewing one particular image (Image 2) and is repeated over all images and participants. Fixated edge-intensities are simply drawn from the edge intensity map (of that image) at locations that subjects fixated. Distributions of saccade magnitudes and directions to actually fixated locations are simply calculated from the eyetracker data. Similar distributions for control locations are calculated by randomly sampling from a set of all actual fixations made by a participant to all images excluding Image 2. Saccade magnitude and directions come straight from this sample; edge intensities (and salience) are drawn from these locations but from the edge-intensity (or salience) map from Image 2.

and saccade bias (accounting for dependencies between these factors). The corresponding log likelihood ratios are, respectively:

$$\log\left[\frac{P(\text{feature}|F)}{P(\text{feature}|C)}\right] \tag{2}$$

$$\log\left[\frac{P(\text{magnitude}, \text{direction}|F)}{P(\text{magnitude}, \text{direction}|C)}\right] \tag{3}$$

$$\log \left[\frac{P(\text{feature, (magnitude, direction)}|F)}{P(\text{feature, (magnitude, direction)}|C)} \right] \tag{4}$$

$$\log \left[\frac{p(\text{feature, magnitude, direction}|F)}{p(\text{feature, magnitude, direction}|C)} \right] \tag{5}$$

In these equations, feature corresponds to edge intensity (see earlier) of a fixated location, magnitude is the amplitude of the saccade that brought the eye to the fixated location in degrees of visual angle, and direction is the direction in space of the saccade where $0°$ is rightwards, $-90°$ is upwards.

In order to compute the log likelihood ratios for particular patches, we need to define the likelihoods, which are simply probability distributions. We represented these probability distributions using histograms because they are nonparametric (thus containing no assumptions about the shape of the distributions). This approach does have a free parameter (number of histogram bins) per dimension of the probability distribution under consideration.

When producing these histograms, it was important to optimise the number of bins such that the best description of the underlying distributions was provided. We used tenfold cross validation to evaluate the generalization performance on the test set of data for histograms constructed using the training set. Increasing the number of bins will always fit the training data better, but as this effectively fits the noise in the data set as well as the signal, the performance on the test set will decrease beyond a certain number of bins. For the final results, we chose 20 bins for each dimension because this corresponded to a clear performance peak when accounting for dependencies between feature and saccade information, and had no impact on other conditions.

Of course building probability distributions from all of the fixated image patches and then testing the performance of this classifier on that very same data could lead to overfitting, with high performance for these data, but potentially poor generalization to unseen data. We avoided this issue by using tenfold cross validation. This splits the dataset up into 10 parts, so we build 10 sets of probability distributions and then report the performance measures on the corresponding 10 test portions of the data. Furthermore, the actual quantity reported is the mean and its 95% confidence intervals across the 10 cross-validation test sets as estimated by bootstrap (Efron & Tibshirani, 1993).

For any candidate image location, the log likelihood is calculated by using the appropriate equation from above (2, 3, 4, or 5). If the log likelihood ratio is greater than zero then that patch is more likely to have been fixated (F) than control (C). In this way, over many patches we can calculate percentage correct. To clarify, for a particular data point in the cross validation test set, the corresponding log likelihood is determined by linear interpolation from the log likelihood ratios calculated from the training set.

RESULTS AND DISCUSSION

Eye movement behaviour

Table 1 shows standard eye movement measures for our dataset. Figure 3 shows example plots of three images from this study overlaid with locations fixated by all participants (left column). We also show the human fixation locations superimposed onto salience maps (middle column) and edge maps (right column) for these scenes.

The Bayesian formulation of how we select the target of our next fixation can effectively be broken down into two constituent parts: that which involves the visual information in the scene: P(data|saccade)/P(data); and that which involves the systematic oculomotor tendencies: P(saccade). From this two-part expression of the problem we can postulate at least four simple hypotheses about how these factors may contribute to eye guidance: (1) Selection is based on visual features/salience alone; (2) selection is based on oculomotor tendencies alone, (3) selection involves independent contributions from visual features and oculomotor biases, and (4) visual features and oculomotor biases interact to select saccade targets. It is important to note that in all analyses that follow we were testing the ability of a classifier built on a portion of the dataset to generalise to *new, unseen* data. See the Method for further details.

Visual features

Salience. Using signal detection theory, we found that fixated and control locations could be discriminated. The area under the receiver operator curve (AUC) was 0.565 (with a 95% confidence interval of 0.562–0.568). This result is significantly different from chance discrimination (0.5), but the magnitude of the difference is quite small. A log-likelihood classifier

TABLE 1
Summary of eye movement measures between participants

	Mean	Median	Standard deviation
Number of fixations per image (5 s viewing period)	15.0	14.9	1.33
Fixation duration (ms)	258	250	26.3
Saccade amplitude (degrees)	7.03	7.22	0.982

All measures are reported to 3sf.

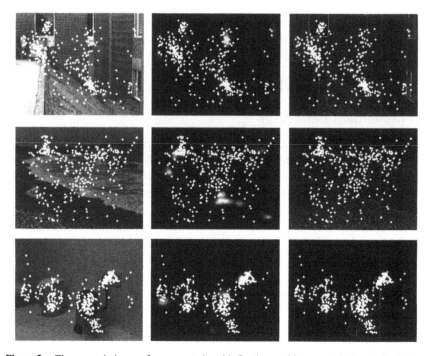

Figure 3.   Three sample images from our study, with fixation positions overlaid (small dots). For comparison, salience maps (middle column) and edge maps (right column) are shown for each image, onto which the fixation locations are also overlaid. Fixations are from all participants in the study. To view this figure in colour, please see the online issue of the Journal.

based on visual salience information alone was able to discriminate fixated from control locations with a performance (proportion correct) of 0.554 (95% confidence interval: 0.552–0.557).

Edges. For edge information, the AUC was 0.593 (95% confidence interval: 0.590–0.597). For the log-likelihood classifier, edge information provided a discrimination performance (proportion correct) of 0.562 (95% confidence interval: 0.559–0.564).

Our results for edge information alone and for Itti's full salience model result in very similar abilities to discriminate fixated and control locations. These findings are in line with previous studies, which have shown significant effects, but with low magnitude differences (e.g., Einhäuser, Spain, & Perona, 2008; Nyström & Holmqvist, 2008; Tatler et al., 2005).[2] These results

---

[2] It should be noted that some studies using different methods have reported higher ROC AUC values for Itti's salience map (e.g., Gao, Mahadevan, & Vasconcelos, 2008). However, our values fall in the range of previous studies and where in this range we fall does not undermine any comparisons of the *relative* predictive power of salience and motor biases in our dataset.

demonstrate that low-level visual information offers some predictive power, but is of limited informativeness in understanding eye guidance. It should also be noted that the simple edge model performed similarly to the full salience model (in fact it was significantly better for discriminating between fixated and control locations, $p < .001$). This result raises questions about the need for the more complex salience framework. A more parsimonious, yet equally effective description of eye guidance might therefore be that the portion of eye movement behaviour when looking at complex scenes that can be predicted from low-level information can be accounted for in terms of the edge information available in scenes. Previous work from our group has also suggested that when correlations between contrast, luminance, and edge information are accounted for, it is edges that provide the best ability to predict fixation selection, and that the apparent predictive power of other features can be attributed to their correlation with the occurrence of edges (Baddeley & Tatler, 2006).

Oculomotor tendencies

Next, we assessed how well oculomotor biases alone can be used to predict where human observers fixate. Figure 4 plots the interaction between saccade amplitude and direction in our dataset. Saccades in horizontal directions were more frequent than in vertical directions (see also Tatler & Vincent, 2008). Moreover, horizontal saccades tended to be of larger amplitude than vertical saccades. The plot in Figure 4 can also be seen as effectively a prior probability of saccade targeting in retinocentric space, with the centre of the plot representing the current location of the eye.

It should be noted that by assessing the predictive power of oculomotor biases alone, we are effectively testing an extreme and implausible hypothesis: We are effectively evaluating a model of fixation selection that is *blind* to visual information in the scene. If low-level visual salience is a prominent factor in selecting where to fixate we would expect that this extreme behavioural bias hypothesis should not perform as well as the salience or edge models. However, a log-likelihood classifier was able to discriminate fixated and control locations on the basis of oculomotor biases alone with a performance of 0.648 (95% confidence interval: 0.645–0.650). Therefore, feature-based accounts of eye guidance are outperformed when we know only about oculomotor biases and know *nothing* about image features. This striking result indicates that biases in how we move our eyes can be highly informative about the locations in the world that we select to look at. This result alone poses serious challenges to the existing feature- and salience-based frameworks for explaining eye movement behaviour. That we can do at least as well, if not considerably better, at predicting fixation selection

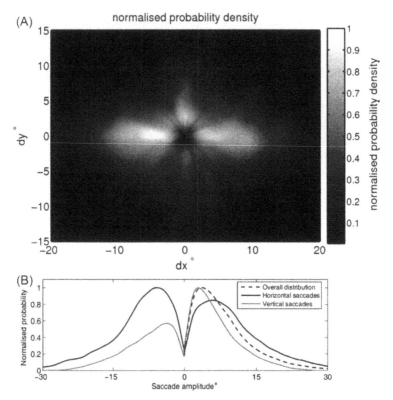

Figure 4. Saccadic biases. (A) The probability density of making saccades of particular magnitudes and directions. There is a clear bias to make saccades in horizontal directions more frequently than vertical directions, and to make vertical saccades more frequently than saccades in oblique directions. It is interesting to note that saccades were more frequently made in an upwards direction than in a downwards direction. (B) Cross-sections through the distribution plotted in (A). The dashed line shows the distribution of saccade amplitudes for saccades made in all directions. There were more longer saccades and fewer small amplitude saccades for horizontal saccades (solid black line) than for the overall distribution (dashed line). In contrast, vertical saccades (solid grey line) were more frequently of small amplitude than either the overall distribution, or horizontal saccades.

using only knowledge of how we tend to move the eyes, underlines the limited explanatory power of existing low-level frameworks.

Independent combination of visual features and oculomotor biases

Of course, both of the hypotheses tested here are straw men: No-one really suggests that eye guidance operates solely on the basis of low-level image properties. Similarly, oculomotor biases alone (with no contribution from visual input!) could not be the sole factor. Hence, in this and the following section we ask whether we can use oculomotor biases alongside visual feature information in order to increase our ability to account for where people fixate.

Performances (in terms of proportion correct) for classifiers based upon independent contributions of oculomotor biases and either salience (0.687, 95% confidence interval: 0.685–0.690) or edges (0.691, 95% confidence interval: 0.685–0.691) were better than for either oculomotor biases or visual features alone. Thus, we can see that accounting for both visual information and oculomotor characteristics improves our ability to discriminate locations that were fixated from control locations. We can use this result to suggest that using a combination of knowledge of what visual information is present in the scene and how humans tend to move their eyes is a useful and informative way of framing eye guidance.

Interactive combination of visual features and oculomotor biases

Finally, we considered the performance of a classifier based upon the interaction between oculomotor tendencies and visual features. For both the salience- and edge-based versions, we see very high levels of classification performance: For the interaction between salience and oculomotor characteristics, discrimination performance was 0.800 (95% confidence interval: 0.710–0.894). For the interaction between edge and oculomotor characteristics, discrimination performance was 0.822 (95% confidence interval: 0.785–0.862). Thus, there is clear evidence of a strong interaction, i.e., if any feature selection is occurring, then its nature varies over the visual field.

For ease of comparison we depict the performances of our various log-likelihood classifiers graphically in Figure 5. AUC values are also included for the salience- and edge-only classifiers in order to allow comparison to previous studies.

GENERAL DISCUSSION

Like a large number of researchers before us, we set out to ask how well we can explain where people fixate in images of natural scenes. However, unlike many previous studies, we chose to ask this question from a Bayesian point of view. Simply by posing the question of how we select the target of each saccade in this way, we immediately identified a previously neglected component of the moment-to-moment decision process: The prior probability of saccading to a location irrespective of the visual information present. This prior probability is interesting in two respects: First, it can be seen as capturing any systematic biases that exist in how we move our eyes around the visual environment. Second, we found it to be a highly informative component of eye guidance.

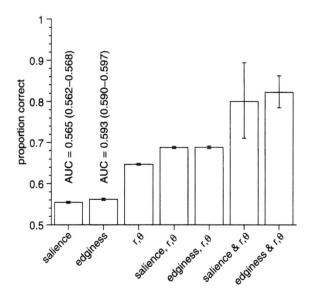

Figure 5. Performance of the classifiers. Performances, as proportion of correct classifications for each of the seven classifiers tested in the present study. From left to right, the classifiers tested the ability to correctly classify control and fixated locations on the basis of (1) Itti's salience model alone, (2) edge information alone, (3) saccade bias information (saccade amplitude, *r*, and saccade direction, θ) alone, (4) the independent combination of salience and oculomotor biases, (5) the independent combination of edges and oculomotor biases, (6) the interaction between salience and motor biases, and (7) the interaction between edges and oculomotor biases. Error bars indicate 95% confidence intervals across the 10 cross-validation test sets, estimated by bootstrap. For comparison to other studies we plot the area under the receiver operator curve (AUC) for salience and edge information-based fixation selection.

The ability to predict fixation selection from salience or visual features alone in our dataset was in line with a variety of recent studies that have shown significant but small predictive ability of low-level factors (e.g., Einhäuser, Spain, & Perona, 2008; Nyström & Holmqvist, 2008). Our finding that oculomotor biases alone were able to predict fixation selection better than salience or edge information clearly demonstrates that this is a useful source of information about where people will select as the target of each saccade. A visual priority map such as Itti's salience model is thus a much-oversimplified description of fixation selection. We have shown that by adding to this knowledge of where the eye currently is and how it tends to move, we can arrive at a surprisingly good description of what will be selected as the target of each new fixation.

Our Bayesian framing of the moment-to-moment relocation of gaze has thus provided a very simple account whereby fixation selection involves the combination of both the (low-level) visual information in the scene and the tendency to move the eyes in particular ways. Of course, expanding the account to include specific higher level cues will be crucial in further understanding fixation selection. Importantly, extrapolation to any number or any form of cues is achievable within the same simple Bayesian explanatory approach.

The origins and implications of oculomotor biases in eye guidance

Given the predictive power of oculomotor biases in our dataset it is important to consider these biases in more detail. As we stated in the introduction, the observation of oculomotor biases does not reveal their origin. Certainly, we do not suggest that these biases are purely motoric in origin. They may arise from a number of factors, from "low-level" biomechanics, to our learnt knowledge of the structure of the world and the distribution of objects of interest. We shall now consider some possible sources that may contribute to the observed biases.

Biomechanical factors

Oblique movements are executed by coordinating horizontal and vertical muscular activity (Becker & Jurgens, 1990) and may have lower efficiency (Pitzalis & Di Russo, 2001) than saccades that only involve horizontal or vertical components. It is plausible that there are costs associated with coordinating horizontal and vertical components of an eye movement such that movements accomplished primarily by only one set of oculomotor muscles are favoured (Smit, Van Gisbergen, & Cools, 1987; Viviani, Berthoz, & Tracey, 1977). A tendency to make smaller amplitude saccades in favour of larger amplitude saccades could again be argued on the basis of metabolic costs: The energy required to create greater tension in the muscles over a longer period of time for large saccades than for small saccades would mean that larger saccades were more costly. However, metabolic costs are unlikely to be a major factor in eye movement control because the inertia of the eyeball is very low (Carpenter, 1988; Robinson, 1964).

Saccade flight time and landing accuracy

Saccade targeting precision is likely to be influenced by peripheral acuity limits and "crowding" effects (e.g., Bouma, 1970; Stuart & Burian, 1962) and indeed smaller amplitude saccades tend to be more accurate (e.g., Becker, 1991). Thus, targeting accuracy could favour small saccades. Small amplitude saccades also minimise flight time (e.g., Carpenter, 1988; Collewijn, Erkelens, & Steinman, 1988; Robinson, 1964). As such, small amplitude saccades will minimize the time that vision is disrupted (e.g., Burr, Morrone, & Ross, 1994; Matin, 1974; Volkmann, 1976).

Uncertainty

An emerging theme in eye guidance is that saccades may reduce local uncertainty (Najemnik & Geisler, 2005;Renninger, Vergheese & Coughlan, 2007; Sprague, Ballard, & Robinson, 2007). The decline in sampling density with eccentricity in the retina is radially asymmetric, declining more rapidly with vertical eccentricity than with horizontal eccentricity (Curcio, Sloan, Kalina, & Hendrickson, 1990). This means that uncertainty increases more rapidly with eccentricity in vertical directions. At first this may appear to favour the opposite of our findings: that more vertical saccades should be observed. However, Najemnik and Geilser (2008) showed that an ideal observer that incorporated this asymmetry in visual sampling produced distributions of saccade direction and amplitude in a search task that closely match our observed distributions (their Figure 5). Thus, it would appear that the principle of using saccades to reduce uncertainty is consistent with our findings.

Distribution of objects of interest in the environment

Properties of the visual environment itself may result in a spatially variant utility function for saccade behaviour. Studies of natural scene statistics show that there is often most power in the horizontal directions, followed by vertical and finally oblique directions (Torralba & Oliva, 2003). It is interesting to compare this to the relative frequency of saccade directions we observed (Figure 4): Perhaps the abundance of horizontal and vertical form in natural scenes influences saccade targeting.

Not only are image statistics nonuniform, but they are also nonuniformly distributed in space. Baddeley (1997) showed that, from the autocorrelation function of natural scenes, any two features are *on average* more similar the closer they are in space. Correspondingly, regardless of where we fixate, features further from the fovea will become on average more different to the location currently fixated. Not only do correlations decrease with eccentricity, but the decrease is more rapid in the vertical direction than in the horizontal direction from fixation (Baddeley, 1997). Although the correlations in image statistics follow the same pattern over retinotopic space as does the distribution of oculomotor biases that we have described, it is hard to argue that these correlations might underlie our proposed saccade utility function. Indeed most saccade targeting models assume the opposite: Salience-based models (e.g., Itti & Koch, 2000; Parkhurst et al., 2002) identify locations with maximal difference from their surroundings as likely candidates for saccade targeting.

It may be that the biases are shaped at a much higher level. In natural tasks, objects of interest to us in completing the task will not be uniformly distributed around us. For example, when making tea in a kitchen (e.g., Land et al., 1999), the objects of interest will tend to lie in a horizontal envelope around us; on or near work surfaces, rather than on the floor or ceiling. Similar distributions of objects will occur in many real tasks, although of course there are exceptions. Could it be that the shape of the saccadic biases that we have measured reflects this asymmetric distribution of objects in the world around fixation? The idea that the distribution of photoreceptors may be optimized to object distributions has been suggested before (Lewis, Garcia, & Zhaoping, 2003). Lewis and colleagues used sampling theory to suggest that the distribution of objects in the visual environment was very similar to the distribution of cones in the human retina.

Task parameters

Finally, it is possible that different behavioural tasks favour different strategies for looking. That is, biases in oculomotor behaviour may arise from overall behavioural strategies. Anecdotally, this seems plausible given that it is easy to generate thought experiments that would favour particular sets of eye movements over others. There is also empirical evidence that saccade metrics vary between tasks (Rayner, Li, Williams, Cave, & Well, 2007; Steinman, 2003; Tatler et al., 2006) and strategies (Gilchrist & Harvey, 2006). However, there has yet to be a systematic exploration of this possibility.

Ecological validity of the described oculomotor biases

In the present study, data were collected with participants seated in a chair, viewing images presented on a computer screen and using a head-mounted eye tracker. As such, the experimental setting differs in a number of ways from natural behaviour and therefore caution must be exercised when extrapolating conclusions drawn about the nature of the prior knowledge and about its role in saccade behaviour to real-world settings. Two factors are particularly important when attempting to evaluate the ecological validity of our findings.

First, photographic scenes are in many ways removed from natural environments, in terms of the variation in luminance, depth cues and lack of dynamics. Furthermore, they are often compositionally biased by implicit or explicit tendencies of the photographer to place objects of interest near the centre of the scenes. Placing the scene within the bounds of a computer monitor is also likely to influence inspection behaviour. The $40° \times 30°$ monitor is much smaller than the approximately $180°$ horizontally $\times$ about $80°$ vertically human binocular field of view. Under natural conditions gaze shifts (incorporating eye, head, and body rotation) can be up to 180° (Land, 2004; Land et al., 1999). Certainly, saccade magnitude distributions are influenced by the extent of the image viewed: Although the long-tailed distribution remains, it scales to the size of the image observed (von Wartburg et al., 2007). Under natural viewing conditions, saccade amplitudes are much greater than when viewing a computer screen, with mean saccade amplitudes of up to 20° (Land et al., 1999). The screen not only influences the amplitudes of saccades but also introduces a strong bias to look near the centre of the screen, irrespective of the distribution of visual features in the scene (Tatler, 2007). Thus, the nature of the biases described in our study (Figure 4) may reflect aspects of the artificial nature of viewing images on a computer screen. However, we feel that this does not weaken our findings because our aim, like that of many other contemporary groups, was to consider the factors that allow us to explain eye movement behaviour in our experimental setting. Furthermore, even if the saccade biases look different during natural behaviour, they may still provide a highly informative component of the decision about where to target the next saccade.

Second, data were only collected for a single behavioural task in the present study. Theoretically, if we are to describe oculomotor biases fully we should marginalize fixation data over *all* possible behaviours. By limiting ourselves to only considering free viewing of scenes, the form of the saccadic biases may be of limited generalizability to other behavioural tasks.

Improving our description of oculomotor biases

It should be noted that our description of systematic tendencies in saccade generation is very simple: We describe this only in terms of the amplitude and direction of each saccade. Describing oculomotor biases in this way effectively treats each saccade as an independent event, yet we know that this is not the case: Previous studies have shown that the amplitude and direction of each saccade can be heavily influenced by the amplitude and direction of the preceding saccade and the duration of the fixation from which the saccade is launched (e.g., Tatler & Vincent, 2008; Unema et al., 2005). As such, a more comprehensive description of systematic oculomotor biases should incorporate these sequential effects into any model of eye guidance. Not only do we know that there are sequential dependencies between successive eye movements, but we also know that saccade behaviour changes over viewing time (Tatler et al., 2005). Understanding when an eye movement is launched is likely to offer further insights into behavioural biases and the moment-to-moment decision about where to fixate.

What is the future for salience models?

We feel that the research field has largely reached somewhat of an impasse in salience-based approaches to eye guidance. There abound reports of specific failures of the basic model to account for certain behavioural tasks. Certainly, consensus in the community is now that any low-level salience-type scheme will be quite limited in its ability to account for the complexities of eye movement behaviour. Our result that a visually blind model based only on biases in how we initiate saccades could dramatically outperform salience and edge models should in itself perhaps collectively motivate us to consider other lines of enquiry. As such, the challenge in this field must be to find the right way to move on from this impasse. We feel that an understanding of incorporating knowledge of *how* we tend to move our eyes will benefit emerging probabilistic models of eye guidance that attempt to incorporate higher level factors (Ehinger et al., 2009 this issue; Kanan et al., 2009 this issue).

REFERENCES

Baddeley, R. (1997). The correlational structure of natural images and the calibration of spatial representations. *Cognitive Science, 21*(3), 351–371.

Baddeley, R. J., & Tatler, B. W. (2006). High frequency edges (but not contrast) predict where we fixate: A Bayesian system identification analysis. *Vision Research, 46*, 2824–2833.

Bahill, A. T., Adler, D., & Stark, L. (1975). Most naturally occurring human saccades have magnitudes of 15 degrees or less. *Investigative Ophthalmology, 14*(6), 468–469.

Bair, W., & O'Keefe, L. P. (1998). The influence of fixational eye movements on the response of neurons in area MT of the macaque. *Visual Neuroscience, 15*(4), 779–786.

Ballard, D. H., Hayhoe, M. M., Li, F., Whitehead, S. D., Frisby, J. P., Taylor, J. G., et al. (1992). Hand eye coordination during sequential tasks. *Philosophical Transactions of the Royal Society of London Series B: Biological Sciences, 337*(1281), 331–339.

Becker, W. (1991). Saccades. In R. H. S. Carpenter (Ed.), *Vision and visual dysfuntion: Vol. 8. Eye movements* (pp. 95–137). Basingstoke: Macmillan.

Becker, W., & Jurgens, R. (1990). Human oblique saccades: Quantitative-analysis of the relation between horizontal and vertical components. *Vision Research, 30*(6), 893–920.

Bouma, H. (1970). Interaction effects in parafoveal letter recognition. *Nature, 226*(5241), 177–178.

Burr, D. C., Morrone, M. C., & Ross, J. (1994). Selective suppression of the magnocellular visual pathway during saccadic eye-movements. *Nature, 371*(6497), 511–513.

Buswell, G. T. (1935). *How people look at pictures: A study of the psychology of perception in art.* Chicago: University of Chicago Press.

Carpenter, R. H. S. (1988). *Movements of the eyes* (2nd ed.). London: Pion.

Collewijn, H., Erkelens, C. J., & Steinman, R. M. (1988). Binocular coordination of human vertical saccadic eye-movements. *Journal of Physiology London, 404,* 183–197.

Curcio, C. A., Sloan, K. R., Kalina, R. E., & Hendrickson, A. E. (1990). Human photoreceptor topography. *Journal of Comparative Neurology, 292*(4), 497–523.

Duncan, J., & Humphreys, G. W. (1989). Visual search and visual similarity. *Psychological Review, 96,* 433–458.

Efron, B., & Tibshirani, R. J. (1993). *An introduction to the bootstrap.* New York: Chapman & Hall.

Ehinger, K., Hidalgo-Sotelo, B., Torralba, A., & Oliva, A. (2009). Modeling search for people in 900 scenes: A combined source model of eye guidance. *Visual Cognition, 17*(6/7), 945–978.

Einhäuser, W., Rutishauser, U., & Koch, C. (2008). Task-demands can immediately reverse the effects of sensory-driven saliency in complex visual stimuli. *Journal of Vision, 8*(2), Pt. 2, 1–19.

Einhäuser, W., Rutishauser, U., & Koch, C. (2008). Task-demands can immediately reverse the effects of sensory-driven saliency in complex visual stimuli. *Journal of Vision, 8*(14), Pt. 2, 1–19.

Foulsham, T., & Underwood, G. (2008). What can saliency models predict about eye movements? Spatial and sequential aspects of fixations during encoding and recognition. *Journal of Vision, 8*(2):6, 1–17.

Gajewski, D. A., Pearson, A. M., Mack, M. L., Bartlett, F. N., & Henderson, J. M. (2005). Human gaze control in real world search. In L. Paletta, J. K. Tsotsos, E. Rome, & G. W. Humphreys (Eds.), *Attention and performance in computational vision* (pp. 83–99). Heidelberg, Germany: Springer-Verlag.

Gao, D., Mahadevan, V., & Vasconcelos, N. (2008). On the plausibility of the discriminant center-surround hypothesis for visual saliency. *Journal of Vision, 8*(7), Pt, 13, 11–18.

Gilchrist, I. D., & Harvey, M. (2006). Evidence for a systematic component within scan paths in visual search. *Visual Cognition, 14*(4–8), 704–715.

Hayhoe, M. M., Shrivastava, A., Mruczek, R., & Pelz, J. B. (2003). Visual memory and motor planning in a natural task. *Journal of Vision, 3*(1), 49–63.

Henderson, J. M., Brockmole, J. R., Castelhano, M. S., & Mack, M. L. (2007). Visual saliency does not account for eye movements during search in real-world scenes. In R. P. G. van Gompel, M. H. Fischer, W. S. Murray, & R. L. Hill (Eds.), *Eye movements: A window on mind and brain* (pp. 537–562). Oxford, UK: Elsevier.

Hooge, I. T. C., Over, E. A. B., van Wezel, R. J. A., & Frens, M. A. (2005). Inhibition of return is not a foraging facilitator in saccadic search and free viewing. *Vision Research, 45,* 1901–1908.

Ingram, K. N., Körding, K. P., Howard, I. S., & Wolpert, D. M. (2008). The statistics of natural hand movements. *Experimental Brain Research, 188*(2), 223–236.

Itti, L., & Koch, C. (2000). A saliency-based search mechanism for overt and covert shifts of visual attention. *Vision Research, 40*(10–12), 1489–1506.

Itti, L., Koch, C., & Niebur, E. (1998). A model of saliency-based visual attention for rapid scene analysis. *IEEE Transactions on Pattern Analysis and Machine Intelligence, 20*(11), 1254–1259.

Kanan, C., Tong, M., Zhang, L., & Cottrell, G. (2009). SUN: Top-down saliency. *Visual Cognition, 17*(6/7), 979–1003.

Koch, C., & Ullman, S. (1985). Shifts in selective visual-attention: Towards the underlying neural circuitry. *Human Neurobiology, 4*(4), 219–227.

Körding, K. P., & Wolpert, D. M. (2004). Bayesian integration in sensorimotor learning. *Nature, 427*(6971), 244–247.

Krieger, G., Rentschler, I., Hauske, G., Schill, K., & Zetzsche, C. (2000). Object and scene analysis by saccadic eye-movements: An investigation with higher-order statistics. *Spatial Vision, 13*(2–3), 201–214.

Land, M. F. (2004). The coordination of rotations of the eyes, head and trunk in saccadic turns produced in natural situations. *Experimental Brain Research, 159*(2), 151–160.

Land, M. F. (2006). Eye movements and the control of actions in everyday life. *Progress in Retinal and Eye Research, 25*(3), 296–324.

Land, M. F., & Hayhoe, M. M. (2001). In what ways do eye movements contribute to everyday activities? *Vision Research, 41*(25–26), 3559–3565.

Land, M. F., Mennie, N., & Rusted, J. (1999). The roles of vision and eye movements in the control of activities of daily living. *Perception, 28*(11), 1311–1328.

Lappe, M., Pekel, M., & Hoffmann, K. P. (1998). Optokinetic eye movements elicited by radial optic flow in the macaque monkey. *Journal of Neurophysiology, 79*(3), 1461–1480.

Lee, S. P., Badler, J. B., & Badler, N. I. (2002). Eyes alive. *ACM Transactions on Graphics, 21*(3), 637–644.

Lewis, A., Garcia, R., & Zhaoping, L. (2003). The distribution of visual objects on the retina: Connecting eye movements and cone distributions. *Journal of Vision, 3*(11), 893–905.

Mannan, S. K., Ruddock, K. H., & Wooding, D. S. (1997). Fixation sequences made during visual examination of briefly presented 2D images. *Spatial Vision, 11*(2), 157–178.

Matin, E. (1974). Saccadic suppression: A review and an analysis. *Psychological Bulletin, 81*, 899–917.

Moeller, G. U., Kayser, C., Knecht, F., & Konig, P. (2004). Interactions between eye movement systems in cats and humans. *Experimental Brain Research, 157*(2), 215–224.

Motter, B. C., & Belky, E. J. (1998). The guidance of eye movements during active visual search. *Vision Research, 38*(12), 1805–1815.

Najemnik, J., & Geisler, W. S. (2005). Optimal eye movement strategies in visual search. *Nature, 434*(7031), 387–391.

Najemnik, J., & Geisler, W. S. (2008). Eye movement statistics in humans are consistent with an optimal search strategy. *Journal of Vision, 8*(3), Pt. 4, 1–14.

Navalpakkam, V., & Itti, L. (2005). Modeling the influence of task on attention. *Vision Research, 45*(2), 205–231.

Nyström, M., & Holmqvist, K. (2008). Semantic override of low-level features in image viewing—both initially and overall. *Journal of Eye Movement Research, 2*(2), Pt. 2, 1–11

Parkhurst, D. J., Law, K., & Niebur, E. (2002). Modeling the role of salience in the allocation of overt visual attention. *Vision Research, 42*(1), 107–123.

Parkhurst, D. J., & Niebur, E. (2003). Scene content selected by active vision. *Spatial Vision, 16*(2), 125–154.

Pelz, J. B., & Canosa, R. (2001). Oculomotor behavior and perceptual strategies in complex tasks. *Vision Research, 41*(25–26), 3587–3596.

Pitzalis, S., & Di Russo, F. (2001). Spatial anisotropy of saccadic latency in normal subjects and brain-damaged patients. *Cortex, 37*(4), 475–492.

Rayner, K., Li, X., Williams, C. C., Cave, K. R., & Well, A. D. (2007). Eye movements during information processing tasks: Individual differences and cultural effects. *Vision Research, 47*(21), 2714–2726.

Reinagel, P., & Zador, A. M. (1999). Natural scene statistics at the centre of gaze. *Network—Computation in Neural Systems, 10*(4), 341–350.

Renninger, L. W., Vergheese, P., & Coughlan, J. (2007). Where to look next? Eye movements reduce local uncertainty. *Journal of Vision, 7*(3), 1–17.

Robinson, D. A. (1964). The mechanisms of human smooth pursuit eye movement. *Journal of Physiology, 180*(3), 569–591.

Smit, A. C., Van Gisbergen, J. A. M., & Cools, A. R. (1987). A parametric analysis of human saccades in different experimental paradigms. *Vision Research, 27*(10), 1745–1762.

Sprague, N., Ballard, D., & Robinson, A. (2007). Modeling embodied visual behaviors. *ACM Transactions on Applied Perception, 4*(2). doi.acm.org/10.1145/1265957.1265960.

Steinman, R. M. (2003). Gaze control under natural conditions. In L. M. Chalupa & J. S. Werner (Eds.), *The visual neurosciences*. Cambridge, MA: MIT Press.

Stuart, J. A., & Burian, H. M. (1962). A study of separation difficulty: Its relationship to visual acuity in normal and amblyopic eyes. *American Journal of Ophthalmology, 53*, 471–477.

Tatler, B. W. (2007). The central fixation bias in scene viewing: Selecting an optimal viewing position independently of motor biases and image feature distributions. *Journal of Vision, 7*(14), Pt. 4, 1–17.

Tatler, B. W., Baddeley, R. J., & Gilchrist, I. D. (2005). Visual correlates of fixation selection: Effects of scale and time. *Vision Research, 45*(5), 643–659.

Tatler, B. W., Baddeley, R. J., & Vincent, B. T. (2006). The long and the short of it: Spatial statistics at fixation vary with saccade amplitude and task. *Vision Research, 46*, 1857–1862.

Tatler, B. W., & Vincent, B. T. (2008). Systematic tendencies in scene viewing. *Journal of Eye Movement Research, 2*(2), Pt. 5, 1–18.

Torralba, A. (2003). Contextual priming for object detection. *International Journal of Computer Vision, 53*(2), 169–191.

Torralba, A., & Oliva, A. (2003). Statistics of natural image categories. *Network—Computation in Neural Systems, 14*(3), 391–412.

Torralba, A., Oliva, A., Castelhano, M. S., & Henderson, J. M. (2006). Contextual guidance of eye movements and attention in real-world scenes: The role of global features in object search. *Psychological Review, 113*(4), 766–786.

Treisman, A. M., & Gelade, G. (1980). A feature-integration theory of attention. *Cognitive Psychology, 12*, 97–136.

Underwood, G., & Foulsham, T. (2006). Visual saliency and semantic incongruency influence eye movements when inspecting pictures. *Quarterly Journal of Experimental Psychology, 59*(11), 1931–1949.

Underwood, G., Foulsham, T., van Loon, E., Humphreys, L., & Bloyce, J. (2006). Eye movements during scene inspection: A test of the saliency map hypothesis. *European Journal of Cognitive Psychology, 18*(3), 321–342.

Unema, P. J. A., Pannasch, S., Joos, M., & Velichkovsky, B. M. (2005). Time course of information processing during scene perception: The relationship between saccade amplitude and fixation duration. *Visual Cognition, 12*(3), 473–494.

Vincent, B. T., Troscianko, T., & Gilchrist, I. D. (2007). Investigating a space-variant weighted salience account of visual selection. *Vision Research, 47*(13), 1809–1820.

Viviani, P., Berthoz, A., & Tracey, D. (1977). Curvature of oblique saccades. *Vision Research, 17*(5), 661–664.

Volkmann, F. C. (1976). Saccadic suppression: A brief review. In R. A. Monty & J. W. Senders (Eds.), *Eye movements and psychological processes* (pp. 73–83). Hillsdale, NJ: Lawrence Erlbaum Associates, Inc.

Von Wartburg, R., Wurtz, P., Pflugshaupt, T., Nyffeler, T., Lüthi, M., & Müri, R. M. (2007). Size matters: Saccades during scene perception. *Perception, 36*(3), 355–365.

Walther, D., & Koch, C. (2006). Modeling attention to salient proto-objects. *Neural Networks, 19*, 1395–1407.

Wolfe, J. M. (1998). What can 1 million trials tell us about visual search? *Psychological Science, 9*(1), 33–39.

Wolfe, J. M., & Horowitz, T. S. (2004). What attributes guide the deployment of visual attention and how do they do it? *Nature Reviews Neuroscience, 5*(6), 495–501.

VISUAL COGNITION, 2009, 17 (6/7), 1055–1082

How are eye fixation durations controlled during scene viewing? Further evidence from a scene onset delay paradigm

John M. Henderson and Tim J. Smith

University of Edinburgh, Edinburgh, UK

Recent research on eye movements during scene viewing has focused on where the eyes fixate. But eye fixations also differ in their durations. Here we investigated whether fixation durations in scene viewing are under the direct and immediate control of the current visual input. In two scene memorization and one visual search experiments, the scene was removed from view during critical fixations for a predetermined delay, and then restored following the delay. Experiment 1 compared filled (pattern mask) and unfilled (grey field) delays. Experiment 2 compared random to blocked delays. Experiment 3 extended the results to a visual search task. The results demonstrate that fixation durations in scene viewing comprise two fixation populations. One population remains relatively constant across delay, and the second population increases with scene onset delay. The results are consistent with a mixed eye movement control model that incorporates an autonomous control mechanism with process monitoring. The results suggest that a complete gaze control model will have to account for both fixation location and fixation duration.

Keywords: Eye movement; Fixation duration; Gaze control; Naturalistic scene; Onset delay; Real-world scene.

During real-world scene exploration, viewers move their eyes from one scene region to another to process local visual information. Where viewers look in a scene is a strong indication of their focus of attention, and so recent studies of attention allocation during scene viewing have concentrated on explaining

Please address all correspondence to John M. Henderson, Psychology Department, 7 George Square, University of Edinburgh, Edinburgh EH8 9JZ, UK. E-mail: John.M.Henderson@ed.ac.uk

We thank Fernanda Ferreira, Robin Hill, George Malcolm, Antje Nuthmann, the members of the Visual Cognition Lab, and the Edinburgh Eye Movement Users Group for their feedback on this research. We also thank Ben Tatler, Geoff Underwood, and Boris Velichkovsky for their comments on an initial draft of this paper. The research reported here was supported by the Economic and Social Research Council of the UK (RES-062-23-1092).

© 2009 Taylor & Francis
DOI: 10.1080/13506280802685552

the processes that determine fixation locations (e.g., Baddeley & Tatler, 2006; Itti & Koch, 2000; Parkhurst & Neibur, 2003; Reinagel & Zador, 1999; Tatler, Baddeley, & Gilchrist, 2005; Torralba, Oliva, Castelhano, & Henderson, 2006; Underwood & Foulsham, 2006). However, the length of time the eyes remain in a given location (fixation duration) also varies considerably during scene viewing as a function of a variety of factors (Buswell, 1935; Findlay & Gilchrist, 2003; Henderson, 2003; Henderson & Hollingworth, 1998; Land & Hayhoe, 2001; Rayner, 1998). An open empirical question is whether this variability in fixation duration reflects underlying differences in online, moment-to-moment visual and cognitive processing (Henderson & Ferreira, 2004).

We can consider three general ways in which underlying processing might be related to fixation durations. *Process monitoring* proposes that the decision about when to terminate the current fixation and move the eyes is made on the basis of ongoing, moment-to-moment visual and cognitive analysis of the viewed scene. The strongest version of process monitoring involves *immediate control*, in which the duration of the current fixation is based on visual and cognitive processes taking place during that fixation (Henderson & Ferreira, 1990; Morrison, 1984; Rayner, 1998; Rayner & Pollatsek, 1981; Reichle, Pollatsek, Fisher, & Rayner, 1998). *Delayed control* instead assumes that the results of higher level visual and cognitive processes develop more slowly, exerting a delayed effect on subsequent fixation durations.

A second way in which underlying processing might be related to fixation duration involves *autonomous control*, wherein ongoing moment-to-moment scene analysis plays little role in determining fixation durations. The notion here is that the durations of many if not most fixations will be independent of moment-to-moment changes in visual and cognitive processing related to scene input. We can identify two subtypes of autonomous control. First, *timing control* proposes that individual fixation durations are primarily determined by an internal stochastic timer that is designed to keep the eyes moving at a constant rate. In this view, fixation durations are essentially a constant plus noise, a proposal that is compatible with theories of gaze control that focus solely on where the eyes move but do not consider when they move. Second, *parameter control* is a weaker version of autonomous control and assumes that fixation durations are based on a general oculomotor timing parameter that is set early in viewing to determine fixation durations, with the chosen parameter reflecting global viewing conditions such as the general nature of the image and viewing task. For example, the parameter might be set to a long value at the beginning of a difficult visual search task (Hooge, Vlaskamp, & Over, 2007), or to a longer value for scene memorization versus visual search (Henderson, Weeks, & Hollingworth, 1999). In both timing and parameter control versions of autonomous control, fixation durations are posited to be independent of immediate perceptual and cognitive processing.

Finally, *mixed control* suggests that fixation durations are based on some combination of the above processes. For example, fixation durations may be primarily the result of process monitoring, but might sometimes be influenced by preprogramming from a previous fixation (Morrison, 1984; Reichle et al., 1998). Or, fixation durations might be primarily controlled by process monitoring, but with an independent timing deadline when ongoing higher level processes take too long to complete (Henderson & Ferreira, 1990). As a third example, fixations might be terminated by an autonomous timer that is sometimes inhibited by higher level visual and cognitive processes, allowing for control based on timing plus late-acting (delayed) process monitoring (Yang & McConkie, 2001).

Understanding how fixation durations relate to underlying attentional and cognitive processes during scene viewing is a fundamental issue in visual cognition, but there is currently very little research investigating how individual fixation durations are controlled in scenes (Henderson, 2003, 2007). Scenes that are globally degraded by visual quality manipulations involving image luminance, contrast, and blur have been shown to influence fixation durations (Loftus, 1985; Loftus, Kaufman, Nishimoto, & Ruthruff, 1992; van Diepen, Wampers, & d'Ydewalle, 1998), and local image statistics also affect fixation durations. Similarly, viewing task can influence fixation durations (see Henderson & Hollingworth, 1998). But these effects could be due to a variety of types of control processes including process monitoring (immediate and delayed) and autonomous parameter control (Henderson, 2003; Henderson & Hollingworth, 1998). For instance, upon entering a poorly lit room, the oculomotor system might simply set a global parameter to increase the durations of all fixations. De Graef, Christiaens, and d'Ydewalle (1990) reported an effect of semantic consistency on the durations of the first fixations on objects. This result can be taken as support for immediate control by process monitoring, because it suggests that object recognition taking place during a fixation can produce an immediate effect on the duration of that fixation. However, in the De Graef et al. study, this effect only appeared late in scene viewing when a good deal of parafoveal processing of the objects may already have taken place, and so is also consistent with delayed control. Loschky, McConkie, Yang, and Miller (2005) reported that fixation durations increased at the time of particular display changes associated with eye movements, also consistent with immediate process monitoring control, but participants executed manual responses along with their eye movements, and the manual responses may themselves have been responsible for the increased fixation durations.

In the present study, to investigate the control of individual fixation durations in scene viewing, we used a *scene onset delay* paradigm (Henderson & Pierce, 2008; see also Morrison, 1984; Rayner & Pollatsek 1981; Shiori, 1993; van Diepen et al., 1998; Vaughan, 1982; Vaughan & Graefe, 1977). In this paradigm, participants examine photographs of real-world scenes while engaged in a viewing task. During the saccade just prior to a prespecified critical fixation, the scene is removed from the display. In this way, the scene is not visible when the eyes land in the critical fixation. Then, following a manipulated delay period, the scene reappears. The question we can ask with this paradigm is whether and how the duration of the critical fixation is influenced by the duration of the delay. We can also examine the influence of the delay on subsequent fixations. The different classes of theories make different predictions about the relationship between delay duration and observed fixation duration.

Process monitoring predicts that the duration of the delay should be reflected by the durations of subsequent fixations. Immediate control predicts that this influence should appear in the critical fixation itself, with critical fixation duration increasing with delay duration because the critical fixation should be held until adequate scene analysis has been achieved. Furthermore, immediate control predicts a shift in the underlying distribution of critical fixation durations, with the mode of the distribution increasing with increased delay. Models based on delayed control predict no effect of scene onset delay on the critical fixation, but instead an influence of the delay on the duration of a later fixation (Morrison, 1984; Rayner & Pollatsek, 1981; see also Vaughan, 1982).

Autonomous control predicts no specific effects of scene onset delay on critical or subsequent fixation durations. For example, parameter control predicts that a specific delay in a fixation will not be reflected by the duration of that fixation because durations are determined by global viewing conditions (e.g., the need to memorize the scene) rather than moment-to-moment changes in viewing conditions (e.g., the scene onset delay). The value of a general fixation duration parameter might be increased to reflect the fact that scene onset is sometimes delayed, but parameter control would not provide a way for the parameter to reflect the specific delay in any given fixation. That is, the parameter will not be influenced by moment-to-moment changes in visual or cognitive processes. Similarly, timing control predicts that the onset delay should affect neither the current fixation nor any subsequent fixation, because the underlying stochastic timer will determine fixation durations.

Finally, mixed control makes differing predictions depending on the nature of the mixture. For example, process monitoring supplemented with a deadline predicts that mean fixation duration will increase with delay, but some fixations (those that reach the deadline) will not wait out the delay when the deadline is reached first (Henderson & Ferreira, 1990). Timing control supplemented with delayed process monitoring predicts that mean fixation durations will increase with delay, with shorter duration fixations unaffected by delay and longer duration fixations open to inhibition from process monitoring. In this latter case the mode of the fixation duration distribution would remain constant (due to the timer) and the tail of the distribution would increase (due to those later saccades that are inhibited by process monitoring).

In an initial study using this method, we found evidence for mixed control (Henderson & Pierce, 2008). The present study extends this work in several important ways. First, we examined whether our evidence for mixed control might have been due to presenting a noise mask during the delay period (Experiment 1). Second, we investigated the predictability of the delay duration by contrasting random and blocked delay conditions (Experiment 2). Third, to ensure that the results were not peculiar to scene memorization, we extended the results to visual search (Experiment 3). Finally, we added several new analyses to probe more deeply the relationship between scene onset delay and fixation durations; these analyses provide additional insights into the nature of eye movement control during scene viewing.

EXPERIMENT 1

In an initial study using the scene onset delay paradigm, we found evidence for a form of mixed control involving both autonomous control and immediate process monitoring (Henderson & Pierce, 2008). However, in that study the onset delay was filled with a pattern mask. A pattern mask controls for phosphor persistence, but visual elements in the mask could potentially influence decisions about fixation termination. For example, pseudopatterns in the mask could potentially capture fixation and therefore extend fixation durations. An alternative to the pattern mask is a plain grey field. A grey field is conceptually more in keeping with an unfilled delay but has the potential problem of leaving a visual trace of the scene on the cathode ray tube (CRT) due to phosphor persistence. To make sure that the results of Henderson and Pierce were not an artefact of the mask, in Experiment 1 we contrasted the effects of a scene onset delay filled with a pattern mask (Experiment 1a) or a grey field (Experiment 1b). Delays in Experiment 1a were 0 (control), 100, 200, 400, 600, and 1200 ms, and in Experiment 1b were 0, 150, 300, 500, 800, and 1000 ms. The 0 ms delay control condition included the same computer code as the real delay conditions but immediately replaced the scene image with itself. Delay values were chosen pseudorandomly for each critical fixation within each scene.

Methods

Participants. Twenty-four members of the Edinburgh University community naïve with respect to the purposes of the study participated for payment, twelve each in Experiments 1a and 1b.

Apparatus. Eye movements were monitored with an SR Research Eyelink 1000. Eye position was sampled at 2000 Hz and saccades prior to critical fixations were detected with a 17-sample saccade detection model using a velocity trigger of 50°/s. For Experiment 1b, the tracker recorded at 1000 Hz and used a nine-sample saccade detection model with the same 50°/s velocity trigger. Viewing was binocular, but only the right eye was tracked. The images were presented on a 21-inch CRT monitor at a viewing distance of 90 cm with a refresh rate of 140 Hz. The experiment was controlled with SR Research Experiment Builder software.

Stimuli. Participants viewed 40 unique full-colour 800×600 pixel photographs of real-world scenes (20 outdoor, 20 indoor) from a variety of scene categories subtending a visual angle of $25.7° \times 19.4°$. The same 40 photographs were used in Experiments 1a and 1b.

Procedure. Each participant viewed all scenes for 65 fixations. Participants were told to view the scenes in preparation for a memory test that would be administered later and to ignore any occasional flicker they might notice. After the experiment the participants were informed that there would be no memory test and told the true intention of the study.

Scene onset delay was implemented using a saccade-contingent display change technique: The scene was removed from the CRT during the saccade just prior to the critical fixation (Figure 1). With this method the display change took place during the saccade when visual transients were suppressed, and the scene was already erased from the CRT when the critical fixation began. Scene onset delays took place every 10th fixation. Following the predetermined delay, the scene reappeared.

An experimental trial took place as follows. First, calibration was checked. Then, a randomly placed fixation point was presented on the CRT. Once the participant had fixated the point, the experimenter initiated the trial. The scene was then presented for 65 saccades, with a delay on every 10th saccade. Following the 65 saccades, the scene was terminated and calibration was checked for the next trial.

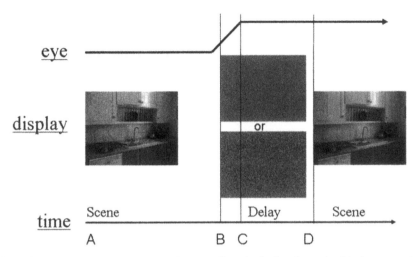

Figure 1.   Illustration of the scene onset delay paradigm. At the first time-point (A), the eyes are in the ninth fixation following the last delay. When the next saccade is detected (B) the display is changed so that when the eyes begin the following fixation (C) the scene has been removed from view. Following the specified delay (D) the scene reappears. The duration of the remaining saccade following the display change (C minus B) is subtracted from the specified delay (D minus B) to generate the actual delay that is plotted in subsequent figures.

Results

Critical fixations that began before the scene was completely erased from the CRT and in which the participant blinked were removed from analysis (Experiment 1a = 20.2%, Experiment 1b = 21.4%). Figure 2 shows the durations of all remaining fixations as a function of scene onset delay. Each nominal delay generated a small range of actual delays because the delay timer began during the saccade prior to the critical fixation (see Figure 1). The time of the remaining saccade prior to the critical fixation was therefore subtracted from the nominal delay to generate the actual delay plotted in Figure 2.

As can be seen in Table 1, mean fixation durations increased with onset delay in both Experiment 1a and 1b, (Greenhouse Geisser corrected due to violation of sphericity), $F(1.94, 21.39) = 24.747$, $p < .000$, and $F(2.38, 26.17) = 6.101$, $p < .01$. These results replicate those reported in reading (Morrison, 1984; Rayner & Pollatsek, 1981). As can be seen in Figure 2, the fixation duration distributions appeared to be bimodal (Henderson & Pierce, 2008; see also Morrison, 1984; Rayner & Pollatsek, 1981), with one mode increasing monotonically with delay and the second mode remaining constant across delay, making interpretation of the means problematic. To examine the nature of these distributions more carefully, we plotted histograms of fixation duration as a function of nominal delay duration.

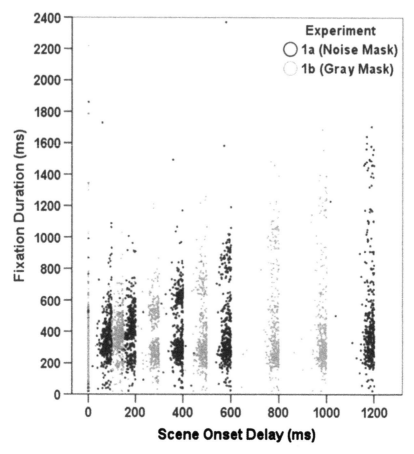

Figure 2. Fixation duration (ms) as a function of scene onset delay in Experiment 1. Each point represents one fixation, and all data are presented.

These distributions are shown in Figure 3. (Note again that actual delay duration varied depending on when during the saccade the display change took place; Figure 3 plots nominal rather than actual delay.) The bimodality implicit in Figure 2 is also apparent in Figure 3.

Following Henderson and Pierce (2008), we fit regression lines to the two distribution modes individually for each participant for all delays over 200 ms (see Figure 4). Table 2 shows the proportion of fixations in the lower population of fixations (upper mode proportion equals 1.00 minus lower mode proportion) for these delays. Table 2 indicates that the proportion of saccades initiated during the delay (lower population) increased with increasing delay, as found in previous studies of scene viewing (Henderson & Pierce, 2008) and reading (Morrison, 1984; Pollatsek & Rayner, 1981).

TABLE 1
Mean fixation durations (and standard errors) in ms for each scene onset delay condition across experiments

Exp							Scene onset delay				
	0	100	150	200	300	400	500	600	800	1000	1200
1a	270.5 (14.3)	369.4 (16.0)		417.1 (19.4)		418.9 (30.1)		459.9 (36.1)			518.6 (36.4)
1b	303.0 (21.0)		397.6 (34.5)		378.2 (22.6)		398.0 (25.8)		449.6 (40.2)	430.7 (41.9)	
2a	273.6 (16.3)				369.1 (16.5)	395.3 (15.6)		393.3 (28.5)	424.9 (26.9)		
2b	278.8 (15.9)				515.7 (46.6)	437.7 (65.6)		432.5 (37.5)	649.4 (157.5)		
3	261.7 (11.4)			401.0 (17.9)		433.9 (29.1)		456.6 (37.9)			499.0 (41.2)

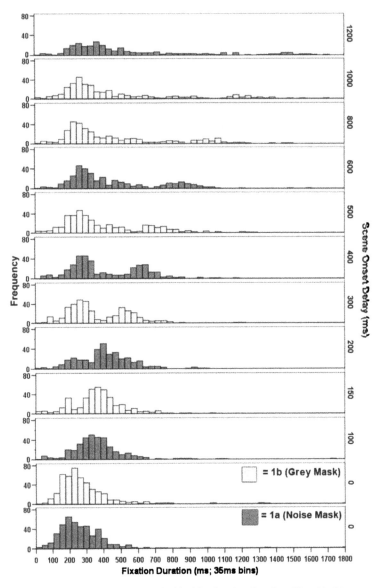

Figure 3. Histograms of the distribution of critical fixation durations (ms; 35 ms bins) in response to each scene onset delay condition (ms) for Experiments 1a (dark grey bars) and 1b (light grey bars).

The regression analysis for the upper modes showed that these fixation durations increased linearly and in a one-to-one relationship with delay: Pattern mask condition in Experiment 1a, slope = 1.056, y-intercept = 213 ms, $R^2 = .998$, $p < .013$; uniform grey mask condition in Experiment 1b,

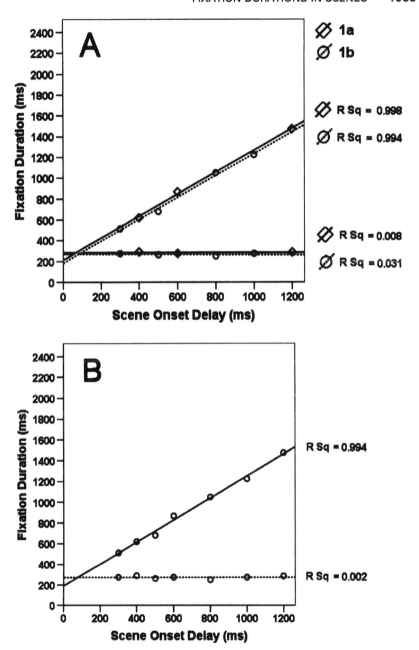

Figure 4. (A) Regression lines fit to the upper and lower fixation duration modes for Experiment 1a (diamonds and solid line) and 1b (circles and dotted line). (B) Data from the two experiments combined.

TABLE 2

Mean percentage (and standard errors) of critical fixations terminating during the delay (i.e., before the scene returned) across participants for each scene onset delay condition in each experiment. The saccadic inhibition gap was used to separate the lower from upper fixation duration populations

				Scene onset delay			
Exp.	300	400	500	600	800	1000	1200
1a		62.83 (2.5)		77.93 (2.17)			92.70 (1.38)
1b	57.55 (2.64)		76.08 (2.29)		85.51 (1.90)	90.63 (1.56)	
2a	60.44 (2.73)	73.52 (2.47)		85.63 (1.94)	87.96 (1.89)		
2b	37.64 (2.07)	67.95 (1.87)		85.51 (1.48)	68.86 (2.01)		
3		62.21 (1.98)		77.27 (1.70)			94.26 (0.97)

slope $= 1.051$, y-intercept $= 184$ ms, $R^2 = .994$, $p < .001$. The analysis for the lower modes demonstrates that these fixation durations remained constant across delay: Pattern mask condition in Experiment 1a, slope $= 0.002$, y-intercept $= 283$ ms, $R^2 = .008$, ns; uniform grey mask condition in Experiment 1b, slope $= -0.007$, y-intercept $= 270$ ms, $R^2 = .031$, ns.

The overall pattern of data was very similar for the uniform grey and pattern mask fillers, suggesting that the delay effect was not due either to phosphor persistence in a uniform field or to fixation capture by a patterned mask. Given this similarity, we collapsed across filler conditions and performed a new regression analysis for the combined data set. The regression analysis for the upper modes produced slope $= 1.061$, intercept $= 191$ ms, $R^2 = .994$, $p < .001$, and for the lower set of modes slope $= 0.002$, intercept $= 272$ ms, $R^2 = .002$, ns.

In summary, it appears that one population of fixations was extended in time as a function of scene onset delay (the upper population of fixations), consistent with immediate control by process monitoring, whereas a second substantial population of fixations (the lower population) remained relatively constant over delay, consistent with parameter, timing, and delayed control models.

Spillover. Do the effects of the scene onset delay carry over into subsequent fixations? To investigate this question, we analysed the duration of fixation $n + 1$, defined as the fixation immediately following the critical fixation (fixation n), as a function of the scene onset delay during the critical fixation. First, we examined fixation $n + 1$ following critical fixations that waited out the delay (Figure 5a). Unlike the critical fixation (n), the resulting duration distributions for fixation $n + 1$ were similar to the control (0 ms delay) condition. This finding differs slightly from those reported by Henderson and Pierce (2008), where a small main effect of delay on fixation

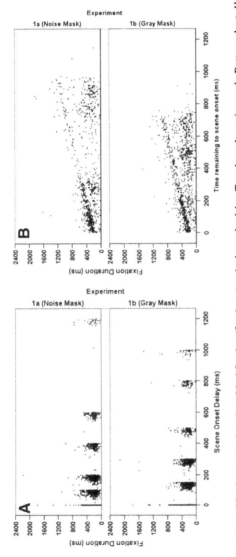

Figure 5. (A) Duration of fixation $n+1$ when the critical fixation (fixation n) waited out the delay. Top chart: 1a, noise mask; Bottom chart: 1b, grey mask. (B) Duration of fixation $n+1$ when fixation n did not wait out the delay. The time remaining plotted in the figure until the scene returns is contingent on the duration of the previous fixation.

$n + 1$ was observed, though that effect was not related to the duration of the delay. In contrast, these data showed no such effect, and so provide no evidence for "spillover" into fixation $n + 1$ of the scene onset delay from the critical fixation. The results suggest that when scene onset delay influenced the critical fixation, the influence was entirely restricted to that fixation. These results are not consistent with a delayed control model in which the influence of processing in a fixation extends to the next fixation.

We also examined the durations of fixations following the critical fixation in cases where the critical fixation terminated before the end of the delay. First, consider fixation $n + 1$ (Figure 5b): In this case, the eyes again landed on a blank display since the scene onset delay had not yet completed. Then, as in the critical fixation, the eyes could either wait out the remainder of the delay in this new fixation, or could again anticipate the reappearance of the scene and move before the end of the delay. As shown in Figure 5b, the pattern of data observed for the critical fixation was repeated for these $n + 1$ fixations: One population of fixations waited for the scene to return (the upper population), whereas other fixations (the lower population) again terminated before the scene returned. This same pattern was observed for the $n + 2$ and $n + 3$ fixations each time the eyes anticipated scene reappearance in the previous fixation.

Participant consistency.   As in Henderson and Pierce (2008), participant-by-participant analyses showed that the composite distributions reflected individual participant distributions. The two populations of fixation durations therefore cannot be attributed to different viewing strategies exhibited by different participant groups.

Saccadic inhibition.   Apparent in Figure 2 is a gap in the fixation duration distribution at each scene onset delay. This gap likely reflects saccadic inhibition induced by the reappearance of the scene after the delay (Reingold & Stampe, 2002). Could fixation durations be elevated in the delay conditions solely because of saccadic inhibition? Although the upper modes in each distribution could be partly due to fixations displaced upward (lengthened) by saccadic inhibition, this explanation cannot entirely account for the onset delay effect: Lengthened fixation durations are apparent earlier than the gap in the longer onset delay conditions. In fact, as can be seen in Figures 2 and 3 by comparing the 0 ms delay condition to any of the longer delay conditions, the gap in the latter conditions was present only because fixation durations had already increased. In other words, if fixations were not increased in duration over baseline due to the delay, there would be no fixations from which to create a gap. Saccadic inhibition cannot alone account for the longer fixation durations.

EXPERIMENT 2

Experiment 2 was designed to address whether the influence of the delay might be under the strategic control of the viewer, or whether instead it is a relatively automatic process. Following Morrison (1984), we investigated this question by comparing a condition in which the delays were randomly determined from fixation to fixation (Experiment 2a) with a condition in which the delays were constant for a given participant throughout the entire experiment (Experiment 2b). Henderson and Pierce (2008) also examined the influence of random versus blocked delays, but in that study the blocked delays changed from scene to scene, a manipulation that may not have been strong enough to induce a differential strategy from the random condition. In the present study, participants in the blocked condition received the same delay duration for the entire experiment. This manipulation therefore provides a strong test of the strategy hypothesis. In addition, the random versus blocked contrast provides a supplementary test of the autonomous parameter hypothesis: If a general parameter for fixation duration can be set based on global stimulus properties such as a predictable delay, then the delay should affect overall fixation duration values in the blocked but not the random delay condition.

Finally, the blocking manipulation provides an opportunity to investigate whether the tendency to delay saccades might be the result of learning. That is, perhaps participants begin by making fast saccades regardless of delay (autonomous control) but over the course of the experiment learn to wait out some or all of the delays (direct control). If this learning hypothesis is correct, then it could be that the lower population of fixations arises from early trials, and the upper population arises from later trials. A learning effect should be particularly pronounced in the blocked condition where the delay was predictable.

Methods

Participants.   Thirty-two participants naïve with respect to the purposes of the study took part in Experiment 2, 12 in Experiment 2a and 20 in Experiment 2b. None had participated in Experiment 1.

Apparatus.   Eye movements were tracked as in Experiment 1b.

Procedure.   Delays of 300, 400, 600, and 800 ms were used. The procedure was the same as in Experiment 1 with the following exceptions. In Experiment 2b the delay duration for a given participant did not vary within or across trials: Each trial involved five repetitions of the same delay plus one 0 ms (control) delay that was indistinguishable to the participant from nondelayed fixations. This created four participant groups, one for each delay condition, with four participants in each group. As in Experiment 1, the delay took place every 10th saccade. The delay filler was the noise field only.

Results

Onset delay.   Fixations that began prior to the display change completion and those on which the participant blinked were removed from analysis (Experiment 2a = 28.72%, Experiment 2b = 25.94%). Panel A of Figure 6 shows the durations of all remaining fixations as a function of scene onset delay across Experiments 2a (random, top panel) and 2b (blocked, bottom panel). The data from both experiments show the same pattern as observed in Experiment 1.

Regression lines were fit to the two modes of the fixation duration distributions for all delays over 200 ms. Table 2 shows the proportion of fixations in the lower population of fixations (upper mode proportion equals 1.00 minus lower mode proportion) for these delays. Fixation durations for the upper modes increased linearly and in a one-to-one relationship with delay: Random delay condition in Experiment 2a, slope = 1.021, y-intercept = 217 ms, R^2 = .989, $p < .01$; blocked delay condition in Experiment 2b, slope = 0.987, y-intercept = 244 ms, R^2 = .999, $p < .001$. These data again provide strong evidence for the existence of a set of fixations whose durations are under the immediate control of the current scene input. In contrast, the durations of the lower set of fixations remained constant across delay: Random delay condition in Experiment 2a, slope = 0.054, y-intercept = 271 ms, R^2 = .948, $p < .05$; blocked delay condition in Experiment 2b, slope = 0.139, y-intercept = 236 ms, R^2 = .800, *ns*.

Given that the data for the random and blocked delays produced nearly identical modes, we collapsed across the two conditions and performed a combined regression analysis. The regression analysis for the upper modes produced slope = 1.004, intercept = 230 ms, R^2 = .993, $p < .001$, and for the lower set of modes slope = 0.096, intercept = 252 ms, R^2 = .652, $p < .01$. Overall, the similarity of the data pattern across the random and blocked delay conditions provides strong evidence that the influence of onset delay on fixation duration is not a strategic effect.

Spillover.   As in Experiment 1, a spillover analysis was performed to test the delayed control hypothesis. First, we examined the durations of $n + 1$ fixations for those cases in which the critical fixations had waited out the delay. If scene absence in fixation n produced a delayed effect, we would expect fixation $n + 1$ to have a longer duration. Comparing the distribution of fixation durations for each delay condition to the control (0 ms delay) in

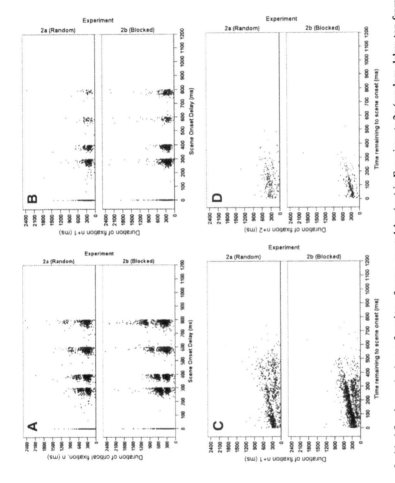

Figure 6. (A) Duration of critical fixation, *n* (ms) as a function of scene onset delay (ms) in Experiments 2a (random delay; top frame) and 2b (blocked delay; bottom frame). Each point represents one fixation, and all data are presented. (B) Duration of fixation *n*+1 when the critical fixation (fixation *n*) waited out the delay. (C) Duration of fixation *n*+1 when fixation *n* did not wait out the delay. The time remaining until the scene returns is contingent on the duration of the previous fixation. (D) Duration of fixation *n*+2 when fixation *n* and *n*+1 did not wait out the delay.

Figure 6B, it is clear that the durations were not abnormally lengthened in either the random delay condition of Experiment 2a (top panel of Figure 6B) or the blocked condition of Experiment 2b (bottom panel of Figure 6B). As in Experiment 1, the effect of the delay appeared to be restricted to the critical fixation.

We also examined the case in which fixation $n+1$ followed an anticipatory fixation n (Figure 6C). As in Experiment 1, in these cases, fixation $n+1$ produced a pattern similar to that observed for the critical fixations, with one population of fixations again terminating before the scene returned, and a second population waiting out the remainder of the delay. This pattern continued for up to four fixations during the delay (fixation $n+2$ is shown in Figure 6D) whether the delay was randomized or blocked.

Learning effects over trials.   To investigate whether learning influenced the results, we analysed the data as a function of ordinal trial number. Trials were divided into quartiles (trials 1–10, 11–20, 21–30, and 31–40) and the data plotted separately as a function of quartile and blocking condition. As can be seen in Figure 7 (top row), there was no evidence that the upper population of fixations appeared in later fixations only. Indeed, the plots were very similar for both early and late trials and in both the random and blocked delay conditions (Experiments 2a and 2b). It appears that the two populations of fixations manifest early and persist over trials.

Multiple delays were presented over the course of each trial. In addition to learning over trials, it is possible that oculomotor parameters changed over the short term due to learning within a trial. To test this possibility, we examined fixation durations as a function of delay duration and the ordinal delay number within a trial. These data are plotted in Figure 7 (bottom row). Once again, there was no evidence that the upper population of fixations appeared in later fixations only. And again, the plots were very similar for both early and late fixations and in both the random and blocked delay conditions (Experiments 2a and 2b).

In summary, the two-population pattern appears to be robust both across and within trials, consistent with the idea that it reflects a relatively stable set of oculomotor processes.

EXPERIMENT 3

In Experiments 1 and 2 and in Henderson and Pierce (2008), participants visually interrogated the scenes in preparation for an anticipated memory test. It is possible that given the need to memorize as much of each scene as possible within a fixed amount of time, participants were motivated to keep

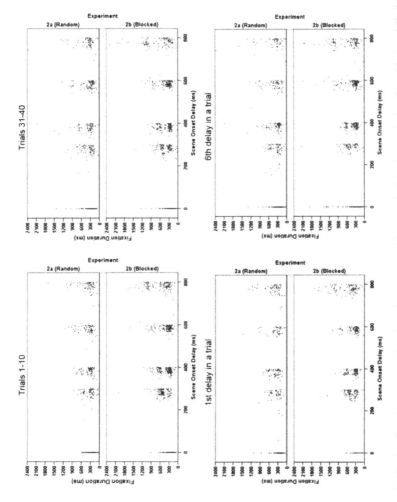

Figure 7. Experiment 2, Fixation duration (ms) as a function of scene onset delay (ms) in Experiments 2a (random delay) and 2b (blocked delay). Top row represents durations for early trials (1–10; top left) and late trials (31–40; top right). Bottom row represents durations for delays presented first (bottom left) or last (bottom right) in each trial.

the eyes moving at a constant rate. Such a strategy could lead to fixation durations that would be uninfluenced by moment-to-moment processing demands. If so, then changing the task to one in which viewing time is viewer-determined might encourage process monitoring. To test this hypothesis, we extended the scene onset delay paradigm to visual search. The search task involved locating and identifying a grey "T" or "L" embedded within each scene (e.g., Brockmole & Henderson, 2006). In this case, a decision was required in each fixation (is the target present here?) and the scene typically remained visible until the target was found. If the prior results were due to an eye movement control strategy peculiar to the memorization task, then we should see more emphasis on process monitoring in the search task where online decisions are necessary within fixations and display termination is viewer-determined. On the other hand, if the results of Experiments 1 and 2 were strategy- and task-independent, a similar pattern of results should be observed in Experiment 3 to those seen in Experiments 1 and 2.

To ensure an adequate number of critical fixations given the shorter scene presentation times in the search task, we increased the frequency of the onset delays to every sixth saccade. As in Experiments 1b and 2, a noise field was used as the delay filler.

Methods

Participants.   Twelve participants naïve with respect to the purposes of the study took part in Experiment 3. None had taken part in Experiments 1 or 2.

Apparatus.   Eye movements were measured as in Experiment 2b. The apparatus was the same as in Experiments 1 and 2.

Stimuli.   Participants viewed 60 unique 800×600 pixel colour photographs of real-world scenes from a variety of categories. A grey "T" or "L" target was embedded in each scene, with an equal number of each target type across scenes. More details about these stimuli can be found in Brockmole and Henderson (2006).

Procedure.   The procedure was the same as Experiment 1 with the following exceptions. Participants were told to search the scenes for an embedded "T" or "L" and to press one of two response buttons to indicate which target was present. They were shown examples of the targets embedded within scenes and were given practice with the task before the experiment. Participants were told to ignore any occasional flicker they might notice and concentrate on finding the targets. Scene onset delays of 0, 200, 400, 600, and 1200 ms were implemented as in Experiment 1a, but with scene onset delays taking place every sixth saccade. Unlike Experiments 1 and 2, the location of the initial fixation point was always at the centre of the display rather than randomly determined.

An experimental trial proceeded as follows. First, calibration was checked. Then, the fixation point was presented at the centre of the CRT screen. Once the participant had fixated this point, the experimenter initiated the scene. The scene was presented until the participant found the target or for 65 saccades, whichever came first.

Results

Onset delay.   Fixations that began prior to the display change completion and those on which the participant blinked were removed from analysis (25.94%). Figure 8a shows the duration of all remaining fixations as a function of scene onset delay. The data replicated the pattern observed in Experiments 1 and 2.

Regression lines were fit to the two modes of the fixation duration distributions for all delays. Table 2 shows the proportion of fixations in the lower population of fixations (upper mode proportion equals 1.00 minus lower mode proportion) for these delays. For the upper modes, fixation durations increased linearly and in a one-to-one relationship with delay: Slope = .961, y-intercept = 224 ms, $R^2 = 0.999$, $p < .01$. These values are similar to those of the random condition in Experiment 2a, and suggest that the results generalize across tasks. Once again, the durations of a second set of fixations remained constant across delay: Slope = -0.024, y-intercept = 276 ms, $R^2 = .481$, *ns.* Overall, the critical fixations were both qualitatively and quantitatively very similar in this search task and in the previous memorization task, suggesting that the influence of scene onset delay on fixation duration is a general phenomenon and not due to a strategy adopted for memorization.

Spillover.   The durations of fixation $n+1$ following critical fixation n were analysed to investigate whether the absence of a "spillover" effect of the scene onset delay in Experiments 1 and 2 was unique to the memorization task. As can be seen in Figure 8B, $n+1$ fixation durations following critical fixations that waited out the delay did not deviate from the 0 ms (control) condition. When fixation $n+1$ followed an anticipatory fixation n (Figure 8C), fixation $n+1$ again produced a pattern similar to that observed for the critical fixation. This pattern continued into the next $(n+2)$ fixation (Figure 8D).

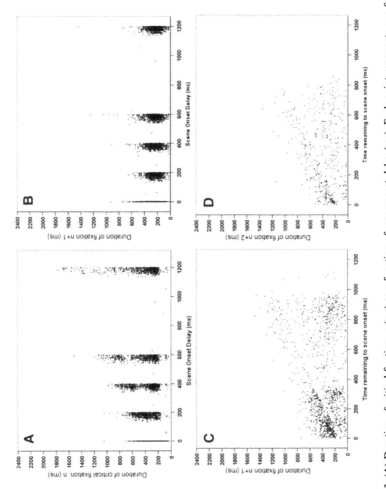

Figure 8. Experiment 3. (A) Duration of critical fixation, n (ms) as a function of scene onset delay (ms). Each point represents one fixation, and all data are presented. (B) Duration of fixation $n+1$ when the critical fixation (fixation n) waited out the delay. (C) Duration of fixation $n+1$ when fixation n did not wait out the delay. The time remaining until the scene returns is contingent on the duration of the previous fixation. (D) Duration of fixation $n+2$ when fixation n and $n+1$ did not wait out the delay.

GENERAL DISCUSSION

Fixation durations vary during real-world scene viewing. The present study investigated the degree to which this variability is controlled by the currently available visual input within a given fixation. To investigate this question, we used a scene onset delay paradigm in which the presence of the scene was delayed at the beginning of specific critical fixations. To implement the scene onset delay, a saccade-contingent display change technique was used to blank the scene during the saccade just prior to the critical fixation. Following a prespecified delay period, the scene returned to view. The main question was how the duration of the critical fixation would be affected by the onset delay. The results showed that the distribution of fixation durations changed as a function of delay. A set of early fixation durations was little influenced by the duration of the current delay. These fixations appeared to be insensitive to the current visual input. A second set of fixations increased in duration as a function of delay duration. These fixations appeared to be under the immediate influence of the current visual input. The present study extends the Henderson and Pierce (2008) results in three important ways by showing that this overall pattern is not a consequence of the use of a noise mask during the delay (Experiment 1), was not due to the predictability of the delay period or to learning the nature of the delay (Experiment 2), and generalizes across tasks (Experiment 3). Thus, the effects appear robust and general.

The results appear to be most consistent with a mixed control model of fixation duration in which an autonomous control component works to keep the eyes moving at a relatively constant rate independently of the current visual input, along with a process monitoring component that exerts an immediate influence extending the current fixation duration. The autonomous component leads to a set of fixation durations that are unaffected by the currently available scene input. The process monitoring component leads to another set of fixation durations that are lengthened with increasing delay of the current input.

What is the nature of the autonomous controller? Based on the lack of an effect of scene onset delay on fixations following the autonomously controlled critical fixations, the unaffected fixations do not seem to be the result of a delayed effect of process monitoring. There would appear to be two other possibilities. First, it could be that these fixations are controlled by a general fixation duration parameter that is set according to the nature of the stimulus and task, consistent with general parameter control (Hooge & Erkelens, 1998). However, we would expect that the mode of this population of fixations would change as a function of delay in the blocked condition when delay was predictably long versus predictably short. Contrary to this prediction, these fixation durations remained stable across the blocked delays, and indeed the modes were also very similar in the random and blocked conditions.

An alternative hypothesis is that these unaffected fixations were controlled by an autonomous timing mechanism that is independent of both general factors and the immediate stimulus. One way to think about the interaction of an autonomous timer and process monitoring is in terms of an inhibitory signal generated by process monitoring that can override saccades that would otherwise be generated from the timer (Findlay & Walker, 1999; Yang & McConkie, 2001). We have recently implemented a computational model based on this basic scheme as well as other known properties of the oculomotor system, and this model fits the data from this paradigm very well (Nuthmann, Smith, & Henderson, 2008).

The finding that stimulus–onset delay can influence the durations of at least some fixations provides an existence proof that fixations can be under direct control. This fact in turn opens the door to using fixation durations as a subtle measure of attention and ongoing perceptual and cognitive processes during scene viewing, as has been done to great benefit in the reading and psycholinguistics literatures. For example, in reading, fixation durations reflect stimulus properties as subtle as lexical frequency, more abstract representational systems like syntax, and high-level cognitive operations like semantic interpretation (Rayner, 1998). The fact that fixation durations are modulated in real time by the image available in a fixation during scene viewing suggests that it would be worth determining whether more subtle scene properties might also exert an immediate influence on fixation durations.

Implications for current accounts of scene viewing

The present results have important implications for current accounts of attention and eye movements in scene viewing. The dominant theories and the computational models that implement them focus solely on accounting for fixation locations (where people look) rather than fixation durations (how long they look there). For example, models based on visual saliency (e.g., Itti & Koch, 2000; Koch & Ullman, 1985; Neibur & Koch, 1996) or a combination of visual saliency and context (e.g., Torralba et al., 2006) have attempted to explain where participants look in complex images. If individual fixation durations can be treated as a constant (with noise), then there is no need to extend these models to explicitly account for duration. Furthermore, effects of visual or cognitive processes on aggregate measures of fixation time such as gaze duration (the sum of all fixations in a region of interest from initial entry to initial exit) could be accounted for within these current models, because if individual fixation durations are a constant, then increased gaze durations must entirely be the result of an increased probability of refixation (e.g., Henderson & Hollingworth, 2003; Henderson et al., 1999; Hollingworth, Williams, & Henderson, 2001). The same logic holds for other aggregate measures of fixation time such as total fixation duration (the sum of all fixations in a region including region reentries).

For example, consider a scan pattern over a kitchen scene in which a single fixation lands on a kettle and lasts for 330 ms. Now consider a second scan pattern in which two fixations lasting 330 ms each land on the kettle, so that the gaze duration (sum of fixations) is 660 ms. If fixation durations are constant as depicted here, the durations contain no additional information over the fixation count. Models designed to explain fixation placement would have to account for the fact that either one or two fixations had been placed on the kettle, but having done so, they would have no further obligation to offer an account of the difference in time spent on the kettle across the two cases. Now consider a third case in which the individual fixation duration reflects some aspect of ongoing visual or cognitive processing, with a longer fixation (say 540 ms) on the kettle when it is more difficult to identify (perhaps because it is an atypical artistic design) than when it is easier to identify. Here, a model designed to explain fixation placement would not be able to account for the systematic difference in the duration of the fixation across conditions, since the placement of the fixation (e.g., on the kettle) would be constant. More generally, such models would not be able to account for cases in which the number of fixations remains constant but the durations of those fixations changes systematically across conditions.

In sum, because current models of eye movements in scenes can potentially provide an account of the locations of fixations, they can also in principle account for the locations of refixations, giving them an architectural ability to explain differences in gaze durations or total fixation time by accounting for differences in refixations within a given scene region. However, models that focus on the where decision can not explain differences in individual fixation durations, or in summed fixation times that are a consequence of differences in individual fixation durations.

It is interesting to note that because individual fixation duration effects have been firmly established for eye movements in reading, the dominant current theoretical and computational models of eye movement control in that domain are driven by mechanisms that predict *when* the eyes will move (e.g., Carpenter, 2000; Engbert, Nuthmann, Richter, & Kliegl, 2005; Reichle et al., 1998; Reilly & Radach, 2003; Yang & McConkie, 2001). This situation is clearly different from that in the scene viewing literature. Given that individual fixation durations are also partially under direct control during scene viewing, as shown here, current computational models of scene perception need to be extended to explicitly account for fixation durations (Henderson, 2003, 2007). Such an extension would potentially lead to a constructive convergence of such models across scene viewing and reading.

REFERENCES

Baddeley, R. J., & Tatler, B. W. (2006). High frequency edges (but not contrast) predict where we fixate: A Bayesian system identification analysis. *Vision Research, 46*, 2824–2833.

Brockmole, J. R., & Henderson, J. M. (2006). Using real-world scenes as contexual cues for search. *Visual Cognition, 13*, 99–108.

Buswell, G. T. (1935). *How people look at pictures.* Chicago: University of Chicago Press.

Carpenter, R. H. S. (2000). The neural control of looking. *Current Biology, 10*, 291–293.

De Graef, P., Christiaens, D., & d'Ydewalle, G. (1990). Perceptual effects of scene context on object identification. *Psychological Research, 52*, 317–329.

Engbert, R., Nuthmann, A., Richter, E., & Kliegl, R. (2005). SWIFT: A dynamical model of saccade generation during reading. *Psychological Review, 112*, 777–813.

Findlay, J. M., & Gilchrist, I. D. (2003). *Active vision: The psychology of looking and seeing.* Oxford, UK: Oxford University Press.

Findlay, J. M., & Walker, R. (1999). A model of saccade generation based on parallel processing and competitive inhibition. *Behavioral and Brain Sciences, 22*, 661–721.

Henderson, J. M. (2003). Human gaze control during real-world scene perception. *Trends in Cognitive Sciences, 7*, 498–504.

Henderson, J. M. (2007). Regarding scenes. *Current Directions in Psychological Science, 16*, 219–222.

Henderson, J. M., & Ferreira, F. (1990). The effects of foveal difficulty on the perceptual span in reading: Implications for attention and eye movement control. *Journal of Experimental Psychology: Learning, Memory, and Cognition, 16*, 417–429.

Henderson, J. M., & Ferreira, F. (2004). Scene perception for psycholinguists. In J. M. Henderson and F. Ferreira (Eds.), *The interface of language, vision, and action: Eye movements and the visual world* (pp. 1–58). New York: Psychology Press.

Henderson, J. M., & Hollingworth, A. (1998). Eye movements during scene viewing: An overview. In G. Underwood (Ed.), *Eye guidance in reading and scene perception* (pp. 269–293). Oxford, UK: Elsevier.

Henderson, J. M., & Hollingworth, A. (2003). Eye movements and visual memory: Detecting changes to saccade targets in scenes. *Perception and Psychophysics, 65*, 58–71.

Henderson, J. M., & Pierce, G. L. (2008). Eye movements during scene viewing: Evidence for mixed control of fixation durations. *Psychonomic Bulletin and Review, 15*, 566–573.

Henderson, J. M., Weeks, P. A., Jr., & Hollingworth, A. (1999). Effects of semantic consistency on eye movements during scene viewing. *Journal of Experimental Psychology: Human Perception and Performance, 25*, 210–228.

Hollingworth, A., Williams, C. C., & Henderson, J. M. (2001). To see and remember: Visually specific information is retained in memory from previously attended objects in natural scenes. *Psychonomic Bulletin and Review, 8*, 761–768.

Hooge, I. T. C., & Erkelens, C. J. (1998). Adjustment of fixation duration in visual search. *Vision Research, 38*, 1295–1302.

Hooge, I. T. C., Vlaskamp, B. N. S., & Over, E. A. B. (2007). Saccadic search: On the duration of a fixation. In R. van Gompel, M. Fischer, W. Murray, & R. Hill (Eds.), *Eye movement research: Insights into mind and brain* (pp. 581–595). Oxford, UK: Elsevier.

Itti, L., & Koch, C. (2000). A saliency-based search mechanism for overt and covert shifts of visual attention. *Vision Research, 40,* 1489–1506.

Koch, C., & Ullman, S. (1985). Shifts in selective visual attention: Towards the underlying neural circuitry. *Human Neurobiology, 4,* 219–227.

Land, M. F., & Hayhoe, M. (2001). In what ways do eye movements contribute to everyday activities? *Vision Research, 41,* 3559–3565.

Loftus, G. R. (1985). Picture perception: Effects of luminance on available information and information-extraction rate. *Journal of Experimental Psychology: General, 114,* 342–356.

Loftus, G. R., Kaufman, L., Nishimoto, T., & Ruthruff, E. (1992). Effects of visual degradation on eye-fixation durations, perceptual processing, and long-term visual memory. In K. Rayner (Ed.), *Eye movements and visual cognition: Scene perception and reading* (pp. 203–226). New York: Springer.

Loschky, L. C., McConkie, G. W., Yang, J., & Miller, M. E. (2005). The limits of visual resolution in natural scene viewing. *Visual Cognition, 12,* 1057–1092.

Morrison, R. E. (1984). Manipulation of stimulus onset delay in reading: Evidence for parallel programming of saccades. *Journal of Experimental Psychology: Human Perception and Performance, 10,* 667–682.

Niebur, E., & Koch, C. (1996). Control of selective visual attention: Modeling the "where" pathway. *Neural Information Processing Systems, 8,* 802–808.

Nuthmann, A., Smith, T. J., & Henderson, J. M. (2008). Fixation durations in scene viewing: Experimental data and computational modeling [Abstract]. *Journal of Vision, 8*(6), 1107a. Retrieved from http://journalofvision.org/8/6/1107/.

Parkhurst, D. J., & Niebur, E. (2003). Scene content selected by active vision. *Spatial Vision, 16,* 125–154.

Rayner, K. (1998). Eye movements in reading and information processing: 20 years of research. *Psychological Bulletin, 124,* 372–422.

Rayner, K., & Pollatsek, A. (1981). Eye movement control during reading: Evidence for direct control. *Quarterly Journal of Experimental Psychology, 33.A,* 351–373.

Reichle, E. D., Pollatsek, A., Fisher, D. L., & Rayner, K. (1998). Toward a model of eye movement control in reading. *Psychological Review, 105,* 125–157.

Reingold, E. M., & Stampe, D. M. (2002). Saccadic inhibition in voluntary and reflexive saccades. *Journal of Cognitive Neuroscience, 14,* 371–388.

Reilly, R., & Radach, R. (2003). Glenmore: An interactive activation model of eye movement control in reading. In J. Hyönä, R. Radach, & H. Deubel (Eds.), *The mind's eye: Cognitive and applied aspects of eye movement research* (pp. 429–455). Amsterdam: Elsevier.

Reinagel, P., & Zador, A. M. (1999). Natural scene statistics at the centre of gaze. *Network: Computation in Neural Systems, 10,* 341–350.

Shiori, S. (1993). Postsaccadic processing of the retinal image during picture scanning. *Perception and Psychophysics, 53,* 305–314.

Tatler, B. W., Baddeley, R. J., & Gilchrist, I. D. (2005). Visual correlates of fixation selection: Effects of scale and time. *Vision Research, 45,* 643–659.

Torralba, A., Oliva, A., Castelhano, M. S., & Henderson, J. M. (2006). Contextual guidance of eye movements and attention in real-world scenes: The role of global features in object search. *Psychological Review, 113,* 766–786.

Underwood, G., & Foulsham, T. (2006). Visual saliency and semantic incongruency influence eye movements when inspecting pictures. *Quarterly Journal of Experimental Psychology, 59,* 1931–1949.

Van Diepen, P. M. J., Wampers, M., & d'Ydewalle, G. (1998). Functional division of the visual field: Moving masks and moving windows. In G. Underwood (Ed.), *Eye guidance in reading and scene perception* (pp. 337–355). Oxford, UK: Elsevier.

Vaughan, J. (1982). Control of fixation duration in visual search and memory search: Another look. *Journal of Experimental Psychology: Human Perception and Performance, 8*, 709–723.

Vaughan, J., & Graefe, T. (1977). Delay of stimulus presentation after the saccade in visual search. *Perception and Psychophysics, 22*, 201–205.

Yang, S. N., & McConkie, G. W. (2001). Eye movements during reading: A theory of saccade initiation times. *Vision Research, 41*, 3567–3585.

VISUAL COGNITION, 2009, 17 (6/7), 1083–1108

Facilitation of return during scene viewing

Tim J. Smith and John M. Henderson

University of Edinburgh, Edinburgh, UK

Inhibition of Return (IOR) is a delay in initiating attentional shifts to previously attended locations. It is believed to facilitate attentional exploration of a scene. Computational models of attention have implemented IOR as a simple mechanism for driving attention through a scene. However, evidence for IOR during scene viewing is inconclusive. In this study IOR during scene memorization and in response to sudden onsets at the last (1-back) and penultimate (2-back) fixation location was measured. The results indicate that there is a tendency for saccades to continue the trajectory of the last saccade (Saccadic Momentum), but contrary to the "foraging facilitator" hypothesis of IOR, there is also a distinct population of saccades directed back to the last fixation location, especially in response to onsets. Voluntary return saccades to the 1-back location experience temporal delay but this does not affect their likelihood of occurrence. No localized temporal delay is exhibited at 2-back. These results suggest that IOR exists at the last fixation location during scene memorization but that this temporal delay is overridden by Facilitation of Return. Computational models of attention will fail to capture the pattern of saccadic eye movements during scene viewing unless they model the dynamics of visual encoding and can account for the interaction between Facilitation of Return, Saccadic Momentum, and Inhibition of Return.

Keywords: Eye movement; Facilitation; Fixation duration; Gaze control; Inhibition of return; Naturalistic scene; Oculomotor capture; Real-world scene.

In order to accurately process a visual scene we must serially shift our attention. These overt attentional shifts create a sequence of fixations during which the eyes are relatively still and visual information is processed, interspersed with rapid eye movements (saccades) during which visual encoding is suppressed. Various models have been proposed that attempt to

---

Please address all correspondence to Tim J. Smith, Psychology, 7 George Square, University of Edinburgh, Edinburgh EH8 9JZ, UK. E-mail: tim.smith@ed.ac.uk

Thanks to the Edinburgh University Visual Cognition lab, Eye Movement User group, and Human Cognitive Neuroscience group for their feedback during early presentations of this data. These data were presented at the Rank Symposium on Representations of Visual World in the Brain (Grasmere, UK; 3–6 December 2007). This research was funded by ESRC grant RES-062-23-1092.

© 2009 Taylor & Francis
DOI: 10.1080/13506280802678557

reproduce the processes influencing fixation location. These models differ according to whether they prioritize bottom-up stimulus-based factors such as luminance contrast (Itti & Koch, 2001; Parkhurst, Law, & Niebur, 2002; Rosenholtz, 1999) or supplement bottom-up information with top-down memory-based factors such as scene semantics or viewing task (Navalpakkam & Itti, 2005; Rao, Zelinsky, Hayhoe, & Ballard, 2002; Sun, Fisher, Wang, & Gomes, 2008; Torralba, 2003; Torralba, Oliva, Castelhano, & Henderson, 2006; Vincent, Troscianko, & Gilchrist, 2007). However, all computational models operate in a similar fashion: Regions of a visual scene are ranked in terms of their conspicuity, i.e., their salience or task relevance, and attention shifts between these regions in decreasing rank order. In order to ensure that attention does not oscillate between the two regions of highest conspicuity an extra mechanism is required that decreases the likelihood of returning to a previously fixated region. The mechanism chosen for this purpose in all models that produce scan paths is Inhibition of Return (Itti & Koch, 2001; Navalpakkam & Itti, 2005; Parkhurst et al., 2002; Sun et al., 2008).

Inhibition of Return (IOR) is a behaviourally observed difficulty in orienting to a previously attended location. IOR results in longer manual and saccadic reaction times to targets presented at the last fixation location. The phenomenon was first reported by Posner and Cohen (1984) in the context of cueing paradigms but has subsequently been observed in visual search (Klein, 1988; Klein & MacInnes, 1999), reading (Rayner, Juhasz, Ashby, & Clifton, 2003; Weger & Inhoff, 2006), auditory and manual reaction tasks (Spence & Driver, 1998; Tassinari & Berlucchi, 1995) and search in three-dimensional environments (Thomas et al., 2006). It has been proposed that this *temporal* inhibition may have a *spatial* consequence: By inhibiting previously examined locations the probability of orienting to new locations will increase (Klein, 1988; Klein & MacInnes, 1999; Posner & Cohen, 1984). This "foraging facilitator" hypothesis is supported by evidence that during visual search, saccadic eye movements tend to be directed away from the last fixation location (Gilchrist & Harvey, 2000; Klein & MacInnes, 1999; Peterson, Kramer, Wang, Irwin, & McCarley, 2001), and saccades back to the last fixation location are preceded by longer fixations than saccades away from the last fixation location (Boot, McCarley, Kramer, & Peterson, 2004; Hooge, Over, van Wezel, & Frens, 2005; Klein & MacInnes, 1999; Snyder & Kingstone, 2000).

The prevalence of empirical support for IOR would appear to promote it as a suitable mechanism for inclusion in a model of natural attentional behaviour (e.g., Itti & Koch, 2001). However, although IOR is well established during the search of abstract object arrays, it is currently unclear whether IOR exists when viewing naturalistic visual scenes. During physical search of real-world scenes, participants rarely revisit searched locations (Gilchrist, North, & Hood, 2001; Thomas et al., 2006), but this may be the result of participants remembering where they have previously searched rather than a *spatial* consequence of IOR. When viewing natural visual scenes, viewer's fixations cluster around a small number of regions that are deemed significant by the viewer (Buswell, 1935; Yarbus, 1967). Viewers may revisit regions several times in order to encode information necessary for their viewing task (Yarbus, 1967), to detect changes (Henderson & Hollingworth, 1999), or to prepare for future actions (Mennie, Hayhoe, & Sullivan, 2006). Inhibition of these return fixations may be detrimental to the successful processing of the visual scene.

Hooge et al. (2005) examined eye movement behaviour during scene viewing and found that saccades landing precisely on the last fixation location (return saccades) occurred significantly more often than would be predicted by chance. Similar evidence of frequent and highly accurate return saccades has been demonstrated in monkeys during classic conjunction and feature search tasks (Motter & Belky, 1998). The accuracy of these saccades suggests that a mechanism may exist that facilitates, rather than inhibits immediate return when processing of the last fixation location is inadequate. We refer to this alternative mechanism as Facilitation of Return (FOR). Such a mechanism would be analogous to the regressive return saccades observed when reading difficult or ambiguous text (Rayner et al., 2003; Rayner & Pollatsek, 1989; Vitu, 2005). FOR may be needed for viewing realistic visual scenes because the complexity of the scene, number of objects, and difficulty in discriminating individual details may mean that a single fixation on an object is insufficient to extract all necessary information (Henderson & Pierce, 2008; Rayner, Smith, Malcolm, & Henderson, 2009). Further evidence for the relationship between processing during fixations and saccade programming can be found in Henderson and Smith (this issue 2009).

In order for IOR to provide a suitable mechanism for driving attention through a scene, fixations at previously viewed locations would have to occur significantly less often than fixations at novel locations. If, as suggested by Hooge et al. (2005), IOR does not function as a foraging facilitator, then it could not provide the mechanism required by current saliency-based computational models to keep the eyes moving through a scene.

Importantly, evidence against the *spatial* impact of IOR on the distribution of attention across a scene does not rule out the possibility that IOR has a *temporal* impact on attentional shifts during scene viewing. The classic measure of IOR is the time taken to initiate an attentional shift to the last location of attention (e.g., Posner & Cohen, 1984). Return saccades during scene viewing take longer to initiate than saccades elsewhere, confirming the *temporal* impact of IOR even in the absence of the *spatial* impact, i.e., decreased probability of return saccades (Hooge et al., 2005; Klein & MacInnes, 1999). However, the temporal effect usually associated with IOR also requires further subdivision to identify its true origin. Recent psychophysical evidence indicates that two saccades in the same direction (forward saccades) will be separated by a shorter fixation than two saccades in opposite directions (regressive saccades), even if the saccades do not land on a previous fixation location, i.e., are not regressive *return* saccades (Anderson, Yadav, & Carpenter, 2008). We refer to this phenomenon as Saccadic Momentum. This simple increase in fixation duration caused by reversing the direction of the eyes could account for the temporal effects previously attributed to IOR (Hooge et al., 2005; Klein & MacInnes, 1999). However, evidence from psychophysical studies has indicated that IOR only acts upon a small region (radius $\sim 4°$ of visual angle) around the last fixation location (Hooge & Frens, 2000) with inhibition decreasing with eccentricity (Dorris, Taylor, Klein, & Munoz, 1999). If saccades directed back to the last fixation during scene viewing are affected by this highly localized temporal IOR, they should exhibit latency greater than that caused by the simple reversal of the direction of the eyes (i.e., Saccadic Momentum).

The main goal of this study was to clear up the conflicting evidence for IOR and FOR during scene viewing. A thorough analysis of fixation location and fixation duration during scene memorization allowed the *spatial* (frequency of return saccades) and *temporal* (fixation duration) predictions of IOR and FOR to be tested. If IOR has a spatial impact on eye movement behaviour, return saccades will occur significantly less often than saccades to novel locations. By comparison, FOR would predict that return saccades are significantly more likely than saccades to randomly chosen novel locations. If IOR has a temporal impact on eye movement behaviour, saccades landing within a small region around previous fixation locations (regressive *return* saccades) will be preceded by significantly longer fixations than saccades in the opposite direction (forward saccades) or in the same direction but landing outside of this region (regressive *nonreturn* saccades), dissociating IOR from Saccadic Momentum. If return saccades are facilitated they may be quicker to initiate than fixations to novel locations. To test these hypotheses, the probability that a saccade is a return saccade and fixation durations preceding return saccades were analysed both during normal viewing and in response to peripheral onsets at the last (Experiment 1) and penultimate (Experiment 2) fixation locations.

EXPERIMENT 1

Method

Participants.   Sixteen members of the Edinburgh University community participated for payment (four male; mean age = 21 years, range 18–29). All participants had normal or corrected to normal vision and were naïve with respect to the purposes of the study.

Apparatus.   Eye movements were monitored by an SR Research Eyelink 1000 eyetracker. Fixation position was sampled at 1000 Hz and saccades prior to critical fixations were detected using a 17-sample saccade detection model with a velocity threshold of 30°/sec, an acceleration threshold of 8000°/s^2, and a minimum amplitude of 0.5°. Viewing was binocular, but only the right eye was tracked. The images were presented on a 21-inch CRT monitor at a viewing distance of 90 cm with a refresh rate of 140 Hz. The experiment was controlled with SR Research Experiment Builder software.

Stimuli.   Participants were presented 100 unique full-colour 800×600 pixel $\times$ 24 bit photographs of real-world scenes from a variety of scene categories (subtending a visual angle of 25.7° × 19.4°).

Procedure.   Participants were told to view the scenes in preparation for a memory test that would be administered after all trials. They were told that they may experience a brief flash while viewing the scenes. This was irrelevant to their task and they were told to ignore it. After the experiment, participants were informed that there would be no memory test and were told the true intention of the study.

An experimental trial took place as follows. First, calibration was checked using a central fixation point presented on the CRT. If gaze position was more than 0.5 degrees away from the fixation point a nine-point recalibration was performed. The scene was presented for an initial 1000 ms during which time the participant was free to explore. After 1000 ms, a critical fixation was identified and a pink square, 1° of visual angle in width, was presented for 250 ms in one of four positions on the circumference of a circle with the centre at the current fixation location and a radius equivalent to the amplitude of the last saccade. The angular deviation of the onsets from the last fixation was 0° (onset at the last fixation), 90°, 180° (onset in the same direction as the last saccade), or 270° (see Figure 1). If any of these points lay off the screen or the last saccade had an amplitude less than 1° (to exclude correction saccades), the program waited until the next suitable fixation to show the onset. Each participant was presented an equal number of onsets at each of the four locations randomly ordered and the location of onset within each scene was counterbalanced across participants.

After the onset had been presented for 250 ms, it was removed from the display and the participant was given a further 5000 ms to view the scene before the next trial began.

Figure 1.   Sequence of events in each trial. Participants initially viewed a scene for 1000 ms (circles indicate fixations). An onset (grey square; bright pink in the actual experiment) was then presented at one of four locations around the current fixation at relative angular deviation from the last fixation location: 0° (last fixation), 90°, 180°, 270°. Onset was presented for 250 ms during a fixation then removed. Participants were given a further 5000 ms to view each scene.

Results

To aid evaluation of the predictions of IOR and FOR, the results were analysed according to *spatial* (fixation probabilities) and *temporal* (preceding fixation duration) predictions.

Spatial: Fixation probability during normal viewing and following an onset

If IOR functions as a foraging facilitator during scene viewing we should observe a general tendency for saccades to be directed away from the last fixation location. This tendency can be examined by calculating the angular deviation of every saccade relative to the last fixation location. The angular deviation was calculated for all saccades except saccades following an onset and saccades in which the onset could not have been presented, i.e., the last saccade amplitude was less than 1° or any of the potential onset locations, 0°, 90°, 180°, and 270° fell off the display edge. After these exclusions 19,541 regular fixations remained. In our coding scheme, a regressive saccade has an angular deviation of 0° or 360°, whereas a forward saccade (continuing the vector of the last saccade) has an angular deviation of 180° (see Figure 1 for a map of angular deviation values).

Figure 2A illustrates the distribution of angular deviations relative to the last fixation. There is a very clear tendency to saccade away from the last fixation location (the peak of fixations with angular deviation 130–230°). We refer to this tendency as Saccadic Momentum. Previously this tendency has been interpreted as evidence for the foraging facilitator function of IOR (Klein & MacInnes, 1999). However, there is also a narrower but pronounced tendency to saccade back in the direction of the last fixation (angular deviations > 330° and < 30°). The prevalence of regressive saccades during normal viewing is not consistent with the interpretation of IOR as a foraging facilitator.

Inhibition is believed to be at the maximum for saccades that land at the last fixation location and decrease as the distance between the landing position and the last fixation location increases (Bennett & Pratt, 2001; Dorris et al., 1999; Hooge & Frens, 2000). The angular deviations in Figure 2A do not allow the dissociation of regressive saccades landing at the last fixation location from saccades that over- or undershoot. To test whether there was a specific bias against saccading to the last fixation location, the probability that the next fixation landed within 1 degree of visual angle of the last fixation location (0°) and three distance matched locations (90°,

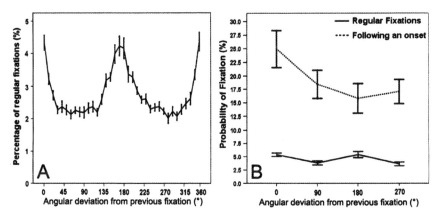

Figure 2.   (A) Angular deviation of all saccades during normal viewing relative to the last fixation (10° bins). See Figure 1 for map of angular deviations. (B) Mean probability (percentage of all fixations) of fixating four peripheral locations (0°, 90°, 180°, or 270° relative to the last fixation) during normal viewing (solid line) and in the fixation following an onset at the peripheral location (dotted line). Error bars represent +/−1 standard error.

180°, and 270°; see Figure 1) was calculated for all regular fixations in which the onset could have been presented and following an onset at the four locations. After all exclusions 19,541 regular fixations and 1220 fixations following onsets remained. A repeated-measures ANOVA of fixation probability (Figure 2B), with factors onset (free view vs. following an onset) and location (0°, 90°, 180°, and 270°), showed significant main effects of onset, $F(1, 15) = 48.372$, $MSE = 0.675$, $p < .001$, and location, $F(3, 45) = 4.478$, $MSE = 0.016$, $p < .01$, and a significant interaction, $F(3, 45) = 3.446$, $MSE = 0.012$, $p < .05$. This result indicates a clear increase in fixation probability in response to an onset across all four onset locations (the difference between the solid and dashed lines in Figure 2B). The interaction can be attributed to the difference in the effect of location between the onset conditions. A simple repeated-measures ANOVA (Greenhouse Geisser corrected due to violation of sphericity) within the normal viewing condition reveals a main effect of location, $F(1.67, 25.10) = 19.379$, $MSE = 0.003$, $p < .001$. As can be seen from Figure 2B (solid lines), this effect can be attributed to the probability of fixating the last fixation location (0°, $M = 5.4\%$, $SD = 1.3$) being higher than the probability at 90° ($M = 3.8\%$, $SD = 1.5$) or 270° ($M = 3.6\%$, $SD = 1.4$). There is no difference between the probability of fixating the last fixation location and the distance-matched location 180° away ($M = 5.4\%$, $SD = 1.4$). Planned post hoc comparisons reveal that the difference between the fixation probabilities at 0° and 180° are significantly different to those at 90° and 270° (all $ps < .001$).

A simple repeated-measures ANOVA of fixation probabilities following onsets (dashed lines in Figure 2B) reveals a main effect of location, $F(3, 45) = 3.815$, $MSE = 0.026$, $p < .05$. The expected low probability of fixation for onsets at the last fixation location was not observed. In fact, onsets at the last fixation location were fixated significantly more often (0°, $M = 25.0\%$, $SD = 13.6$) than onsets at 90° ($M = 18.4\%$, $SD = 10.5$; $p < .05$), 180° ($M = 15.8\%$, $SD = 11.0$; $p < .05$), and 270° ($M = 17.1\%$, $SD = 9.0$; $p < .05$). There were no other significant differences. This absence of inhibition for involuntary saccades back to the last fixation location further indicates an absence of any spatial impact of IOR during scene viewing, and instead suggests that viewers are more susceptible to oculomotor capture at the last attended location, consistent with Facilitation of Return.

Temporal: Fixation durations preceding normal saccades and following onsets

The classic measure of IOR used in attentional cueing paradigms is response time to a peripheral target (e.g., Posner & Cohen, 1984). In IOR studies investigating overt attentional shifts, this measure has been reinterpreted as the duration of a fixation preceding a critical saccade (Hooge et al.,

2005). Mean fixation durations preceding saccades landing within 1° of the last fixation location (0° angular deviation) and the three distance matched locations (90°, 180°, and 270°; see Figure 1) were calculated for all regular fixations in which the onset could have been presented and following an onset at the four locations. A repeated-measures ANOVA of preceding fixation duration (Figure 3), with factors onset (free view vs. following an onset) and location (0°, 90°, 180°, and 270°), showed significant main effects of onset, $F(1, 13) = 5.052$, $MSE = 3234$, $p < .05$, and location, $F(3, 39) = 10.028$, $MSE = 1520$, $p < .001$, but no interaction.[1] Planned post hoc comparisons revealed that the effect of onset is due to overall mean fixation durations being significantly longer during normal viewing ($M = 286.6$ ms, $SD = 10.34$) compared to following an onset ($M = 262.4$ ms, $SD = 7.23$; $p < .05$).

A simple repeated-measures ANOVA within the normal viewing condition (Figure 3, solid line) revealed a main effect of location, $F(3, 45) = 14.638$, $MSE = 1125$, $p < .001$. Planned post hoc comparisons revealed that return saccades were preceded by significantly longer fixations (0°, $M = 328.8$ ms, $SD = 67.01$) than saccades 90° ($M = 282.2$ ms, $SD = 42.5$; $p < .01$), 180° ($M = 250.9$ ms, $SD = 23.54$; $p < .001$), and 270° ($M = 284.1$ ms, $SD = 52.8$; $p < .01$) away from the last location. Saccades perpendicular to the current fixation (90° and 270°) were also preceded by significantly longer fixations than those directed straight ahead, 180° ($p < .01$). These results support previous evidence of a temporal delay when initiating voluntary saccades back towards the last fixation location (Hooge et al., 2005; Klein & MacInnes, 1999). However, the effect of location disappears when saccades

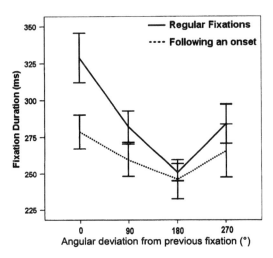

Figure 3.   Mean duration (ms) of the fixation preceding a fixation at the four locations (0°, 90°, 180°, or 270° relative to the last fixation) during normal viewing (solid line) and in the fixation following an onset at the peripheral location (dotted line).

are initiated in response to onsets (Figure 3, dashed line). A simple repeated-measures ANOVA of preceding fixation duration within the onset condition shows no main effect of location, $F(3, 39) = 1.001$, $MSE = 2590$, $p = .403$, ns (see Footnote 1). There is a trend for return saccades to be preceded by longer fixations ($0°$: $M = 278.7$ ms, $SD = 43$) than saccades directly away ($180°$: $M = 246$ ms, $SD = 50$), but this difference does not reach significance ($p = .116$, ns). These results indicate that there is no temporal evidence of IOR when return saccades are initiated in response to onsets at the last fixation location.

Temporal: Localized temporal effects on normal saccades relative to last fixation location

So far the results indicate that during normal scene viewing, return saccades are as common, if not more common, than saccades directed to any other location. Also, oculomotor capture by an onset at the last fixation location is more likely than by an onset elsewhere, and this capture shortens saccade initiation time. These results support the view that return to the last fixation location is spatially facilitated not inhibited. However, the finding that such return saccades are preceded by significantly longer fixation durations during normal viewing supports the idea of temporal IOR. Another interpretation of this temporal effect is that it is caused by Saccadic Momentum: The oculomotor bias to continue moving the eyes in the same direction. Our spatial data support the existence of such a bias (Figure 2A). If the longer preceding fixation duration is simply a function of the oculomotor cost introduced when the saccade trajectory is reversed, then the effect should increase linearly as the angular deviation from the last fixation location decreases. If, on the other hand, this difficulty with programming a voluntary refixation is due to localized inhibition of the last fixation location, then the difficulty should be a function of both the angular deviation and the spatial distance from the last fixation location.

To test the predictions of the Saccadic Momentum hypothesis versus localized temporal IOR, the location of all saccade targets were identified relative to the last fixation for the entire viewing period except for the fixations following an onset (Figure 4A). First, the angular deviation of all saccades from the last fixation was calculated and grouped into $45°$ bins (collapsed across bins with the same angular deviation clockwise and counterclockwise). Second, the difference between the amplitude of the next saccade and the last saccade was calculated. All saccades with

---

[1] Two participants had to be omitted from this analysis due to missing data in some conditions.

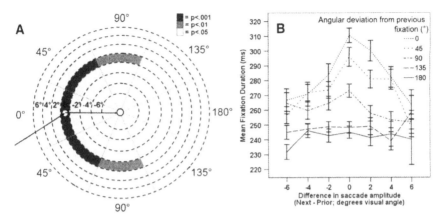

Figure 4. (A) Next saccade target location relative to current (centre spot) and last (left spot) fixations. Locations are binned in 45° regions beginning at the last fixation and encircling the current fixation. These regions are further divided according to the difference in amplitude between the next and last saccade (concentric rings; degrees of visual angle). Zone of IOR according to the significant peaks in preceding fixation durations is superimposed onto this chart: Black = $p < .001$, dark grey = $p < .01$, light grey = $p < .05$. (B) Mean fixation durations (ms) preceding fixations at the locations illustrated in A.

amplitudes less than 1° were removed to exclude corrective and microsaccades and only saccades with differences in saccade amplitudes greater than − 8° and less than 8° were included to exclude outliers. After exclusions, 22,024 fixations remained in the analysis. By combining these two measures the location of each saccade target relative to the last fixation could be identified. The mean duration of fixations preceding saccades to each region of this saccade target map were then calculated (Figure 4B).

A repeated-measures ANOVA with the factors angular deviation (0°, 45°, 90°, 135°, and 180°) and difference in saccade amplitude (− 6°, − 4°, − 2°, 0°, 2°, 4°, and 6°) revealed a main effect of angular deviation, $F(4, 60) = 21.660$, $MSE = 1761$, $p < .001$, difference in saccade amplitude, $F(6, 90) = 4.460$, $MSE = 1116$, $p < .01$, and a significant interaction, $F(24, 360) = 1.852$, $MSE = 1768$, $p < .01$. The main effect of angular deviation is due to a linear increase in mean preceding fixation duration as angular deviation decreases. This cost associated with reversing saccade direction, i.e., Saccadic Momentum, could completely account for the longer fixations preceding return saccades demonstrated in Figure 4B and previously attributed to IOR (Hooge et al., 2005; Klein & MacInnes, 1999). However, there is also evidence of localized temporal IOR. When saccades are directed back towards the last fixation location (0° angular deviation) there is a main effect of difference in saccade amplitude (repeated-measures ANOVA within the 0° angular deviation condition),

$F(6, 90) = 4.091$, $MSE = 1392$, $p < .001$, due to saccades landing within $+/-2°$ of the last fixation location being preceded by significantly longer fixations (0°: $M = 316.8$ ms, $SD = 53.43$) than saccades that over- ($-6°$: $M = 264.9$ ms, $SD = 37.95$, $p < .001$) or undershoot the last fixation (6°: $M = 266.8$ ms, $SD = 12.5$, $p < .05$). The effect of difference in saccade amplitude is also observed for saccades directed 45° away from the last fixation, $F(6, 90) = 5.837$, $MSE = 786$, $p < .001$. Angular deviations of 90° show a peak in fixation durations preceding saccades of the same amplitude as the last saccade but this does not result in a main effect of difference in saccade amplitude. Angular deviations of 180° and 135° showed no effect of difference in saccade amplitude on preceding fixation duration.

The peak in preceding fixations visible in Figure 4B can be extracted by performing pairwise t-tests within each angular deviation condition and projecting the significant differences relative to a baseline ($+/-6°$ difference in saccade amplitude) on to the saccade target map (Figure 4A). The resulting region represents the saccades affected by localized temporal IOR independent of the latency attributed to Saccadic Momentum.

In combination, the results of Experiment 1 confirm the existence of temporal IOR during scene viewing but not its spatial function as a foraging facilitator. The majority of saccades are directed away from the last fixation but there is also a distinct population returning to the last fixation location. These voluntary return saccades will take longer to initiate due to the lag associated with reversing the direction of the saccade (Saccadic Momentum) and localized temporal IOR acting on saccades with the same amplitude as the last saccade. However, if refixation of the last location is required this temporal IOR does not appear to stop it from happening.

EXPERIMENT 2

The temporal IOR affecting return saccades during normal viewing in experiment 1 disappeared when the return saccade was triggered by an onset. Similar weak inhibition of return saccades has been observed during search of complex scenes (Klein & MacInnes, 1999) and coloured object arrays (Paul & Tipper, 2003). Facilitation of Return to the last fixation location has been attributed to either greater conspicuity of the 1-back location due to the recency of its processing and representation in memory, or to delayed shifting of covert attention to the current fixation location (Klein, 2000; Klein & MacInnes, 1999; Lupianez, Milliken, Solano, Weaver, & Tipper, 2001; Paul & Tipper, 2003). Up to 300 ms following the appearance of an attentional cue, attentional shifts to the cue are facilitated (Posner & Cohen, 1984). After 300 ms such shifts are inhibited (Posner & Cohen, 1984). This crossover time is roughly equivalent to the average duration of fixations during scene viewing (Henderson, 2003), suggesting that attentional shifts back to the last fixation location may be facilitated early on in a fixation. In previous studies (Klein & MacInnes, 1999; Paul & Tipper, 2003), IOR reappeared when saccades were directed to the penultimate fixation location (2-back). By the time the fixation is 2-back, facilitation for this location is believed to have ended and inhibition taken its place. Whether saccades to the 2-back location are inhibited or facilitated during scene viewing was investigated in Experiment 2.

Method

The stimuli, apparatus and procedure for Experiment 2 were identical to Experiment 1. The only difference between Experiments 1 and 2 was the location of the onset (see Figure 5). After 1000 ms of scene exploration, a

Figure 5. Sequence of events in each trial. Participants initially viewed a scene for 1000 ms (circles indicate fixations). An onset (grey square; bright pink in the actual experiment) was then presented at one of four locations around the current fixation at relative angular deviation from the penultimate fixation location: 0° (penultimate fixation), 90°, 180°, 270°. Onset was presented for 250 ms during a fixation then removed. Participants were given a further 5000 ms to view each scene.

critical fixation was identified and a bright pink square (1° of visual angle) was abruptly presented for 250 ms in one of four locations on the circumference of a circle with its origin at the current fixation point and radius equal to the distance between the current fixation and the penultimate fixation (2-back). The angular deviation of the abrupt onset from the penultimate fixation location was 0° (back in the direction of the penultimate fixation), 90°, 180° (away from the penultimate fixation), or 270°. If any of these points lay off the screen or the distance to the penultimate fixation location was less than 1° (to exclude correction saccades) the computer waited until the next suitable fixation. Each participant saw an equal number of onset cues at each of the four locations randomly ordered, with onset location within each scene counterbalanced across participants. After the onset was removed the scene remained in view for 5000 ms.

Participants. Sixteen Edinburgh University first year Psychology students took part for course credit (seven male; mean age = 19.75 years, range 18–27).

Results

Spatial: Fixation probability during normal viewing and following an onset

To first check whether saccades were biased away from the penultimate fixation location, we calculated the angular deviation of every saccade (except those from fixations immediately following the onset) relative to the penultimate fixation location. Only saccades in which the onset could have been presented were used: The distance to the penultimate fixation location had to be greater than 1° and all potential onset locations (0°, 90°, 180°, and 270°) had to lie on the screen (see Figure 5 for map of angular deviations relative to 2-back). After all exclusions, 16,881 fixations remained. Figure 6A illustrates the distribution of angular deviations relative to the last fixation. The tendency for saccades to be directed away from the 2-back location was less pronounced than observed in Experiment 1 relative to the 1-back location, but it was still present. The intervening saccade could have been in any direction relative to the 2-back location, but given that the majority probably continued the vector of the last saccade (as shown in Figure 2A), when the next saccade was directed away from the 1-back location it was also away from the 2-back. Similarly, the cumulative pattern of angular deviations may also account for the distinct population of saccades directed back towards the 2-back location (Figure 6A, angular deviations > 330° and < 30°): A saccade in the direction of the 2-back fixation may also be in the same direction as

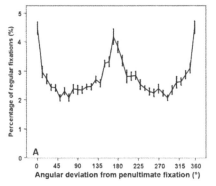
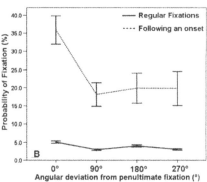

Figure 6. (A) Angular deviation of all saccades during normal viewing relative to penultimate fixation (10° bins). See Figure 5 for map of angular deviations. (B) Mean probability (percentage of all fixations) of fixating four peripheral locations (0°, 90°, 180°, or 270° relative to the penultimate fixation) during normal viewing (solid line) and in the fixation following an onset at the peripheral location (dotted line). Error bars represent $+/-1$ standard error.

1-back. However, irrespective of where the intervening fixation was located, if the 2-back location had been spatially inhibited there would be no peak in the frequency of angular deviations around 0°.

To examine whether these return saccades hit the penultimate fixation location, the probability that the next fixation landed within 1 degree of visual angle of the penultimate fixation location and three distance matched locations (see Figure 5) was calculated for all regular fixations in which the onset could have been presented (16,881 fixations) and following an onset at the four locations (1302 fixations). A repeated-measures ANOVA of fixation probability (Figure 6B), with factors onset (free view vs. following an onset) and location (0°, 90°, 180°, and 270°), showed significant main effects of onset, $F(1, 15) = 29.427$, $MSE = 0.042$, $p < .001$, and location, $F(3, 45) = 17.382$, $MSE = 0.004$, $p < .001$, and a significant interaction, $F(3, 45) = 11.353$, $MSE = 0.004$, $p < .001$. The interaction can be attributed to the 0° location having significantly greater fixation probability following an onset than any other location ($ps < .001$, planned post hoc comparison). A simple repeated-measures ANOVA within the normal viewing condition (Figure 6B, solid line) revealed a significant main effect of location, $F(3, 45) = 44.338$, $MSE = 0.00004$, $p < .001$, with saccades directed back to the 2-back location (0°, $M = 5.10\%$, $SD = 1.23$) significantly more likely than saccades directed 90° ($M = 2.99\%$, $SD = 0.83$; $p < .001$), 180° ($M = 4.03\%$, $SD = 1.30$; $p < .05$) and 270° ($M = 3.06\%$, $SD = 0.84$; $p < .001$) away. Also, saccades directed away from the 2-back location (180°) were significantly more likely than perpendicular saccades (90° and 270°, $ps < .001$). A similar repeated-measures ANOVA within the onset condition also revealed a main effect of location, $F(3, 45) = 14.236$, $MSE = 0.008$, $p < .001$, but this effect was only due to return saccades (0°, $M = 35.9\%$, $SD = 15.7$) being significantly more likely than saccades directed 90° ($M = 19.2\%$, $SD = 13.2$; $p < .001$), 180° ($M = 19.9\%$, $SD = 16.7$; $p < .001$), and 270° ($M = 19.8\%$, $SD = 18.9$; $p < .001$) away. There were no other significant differences.

The fixation probability results indicate that there was no evidence of more pronounced IOR for the 2-back fixation location. In fact, the return probability was greater than the probability of a fixation at the other three distance-matched locations both during normal viewing and following an onset, consistent with FOR at the penultimate fixated location.

Temporal: Fixation durations preceding normal saccades and following onsets

Are the saccades back to the penultimate fixation location delayed due to IOR? A repeated-measures ANOVA of preceding fixation duration for 2-back (Figure 7A) with factors onset (free view vs. following an onset) and location (0°, 90°, 180°, and 270°) showed a significant main effect of onset, $F(1, 11^2) = 6.497$, $MSE = 5435.647$, $p < .05$, no significant main effect of location, $F(3, 33) = 0.281$, $MSE = 1728.551$, $p = .782$, ns, and a significant interaction of the two factors, $F(3, 33) = 3.236$, $MSE = 2346.535$, $p < .05$. The absence of a main effect of location can be attributed to the interaction with onset. A simple

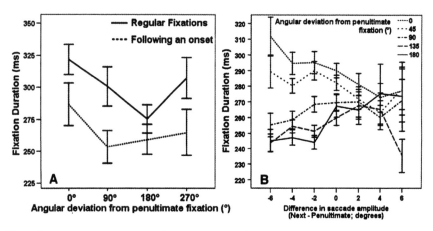

Figure 7. (A) Mean duration (ms) of the fixation preceding a fixation at the four locations (0°, 90°, 180°, or 270° relative to the penultimate fixation) during normal viewing (solid line) and in the fixation following an onset at the peripheral location (dotted line). Error bars represent $+/-1$ standard error. (B) Mean fixation durations (ms) preceding all saccades during normal viewing classified according to angular deviation from the penultimate fixation (lines) and difference in saccade amplitude (next—distance to penultimate location; x-axis).

---

[2] Four subjects had to be omitted from this analysis due to missing data in some conditions.

repeated-measures ANOVA within the free-view condition (Figure 7A, solid line), showed a main effect of location, $F(3, 45) = 5.789$, $MSE = 1033.8$, $p < .01$, with saccades directed to the 2-back location ($0°$, $M = 321.8$ ms, $SD = 47.11$) preceded by significantly longer fixations than saccades directed to the $180°$ location ($M = 275.6$ ms, $SD = 43.68$; $p < .001$). No other differences were significant. The main effect of location disappeared following onsets (Figure 7A, dotted line), $F(3, 33) = 1.478$, $MSE = 2814.758$, $p < .239$, *ns*, as did the pairwise differences between onset locations, although there is a nonsignificant trend for saccades directed to the 2-back location ($0°$, $M = 289.0$ ms, $SD = 67.97$) to be preceded by longer fixations than saccades to the $180°$ location ($M = 259.36$ ms, $SD = 46.05$), $t(14) = 1.916$, $p = .076$, *ns*.

Temporal: Localized temporal effects on normal saccades relative to penultimate fixation location

As in Experiment 1, the results for Experiment 2 indicate that during normal viewing, saccades back to a previously fixated location take significantly longer to initiate than saccades directed away from the previously visited location and that this delay is overridden by facilitation following an onset. This delay may be due to the oculomotor lag associated with reversing the eyes, i.e., Saccadic Momentum, or localized temporal IOR. To look for any evidence of localized temporal IOR all saccades during normal viewing were categorized according to their angle relative to the 2-back location (angular deviation) and the difference between the distance covered by the saccade and the distance between the current fixation and the 2-back location (difference in saccade amplitude). All saccades with amplitudes less than $1°$ were removed to exclude corrective and micro-saccades and only saccades with differences in saccade amplitudes between $-8°$ and $+8°$ were included to exclude outliers. After exclusions, 25,406 fixations remained in the analysis. A repeated-measures ANOVA of preceding fixation durations with the factors angular deviation ($0°$, $45°$, $90°$, $135°$, and $180°$) and difference in saccade amplitude ($-6°$, $-4°$, $-2°$, $0°$, $2°$, $4°$, $6°$) revealed a main effect of angular deviation, $F(4, 60) = 8.687$, $MSE = 2098.8$, $p < .001$, but no main effect of difference in saccade amplitude, $F(6, 90) = 1.138$, $MSE = 1445.9$, $p = .35$, *ns*, and a trend towards an interaction, $F(24, 360) = 1.458$, $MSE = 1204.6$, $p = .078$, *ns*. The results are shown in Figure 7B. Mean preceding fixation duration generally increased linearly as angular deviation decreased, although the effect was not as clear as in Experiment 1 due to an interaction with difference in saccade amplitude, i.e., change in gradient. This interaction is probably due to the indeterminate nature of the intervening saccade. Unlike in Experiment 1, the angular deviation relative to the penultimate fixation location does not accurately express the change in saccade vector as the last saccade may have already reversed direction relative to 2-back saccade.

Even given the variable impact of angular deviation on preceding fixation duration, localized temporal IOR should still be visible as a selective peak in preceding fixation durations when saccades are directed back to the 2-back location, i.e., 0° angular deviation and 0° difference in saccade amplitude. A repeated-measures ANOVA within the 0° angular deviation condition revealed no effect of difference in saccade amplitude, $F(6, 90) = 1.324$, $MSE = 1324.8$, $p = .255$, ns. There was also no effect of difference in saccade amplitude within any of the other angular deviation conditions except 135°, $F(6, 90) = 3.204$, $MSE = 713.6$, $p < .01$. Therefore, there was no evidence that saccades directed back to the 2-back fixation location were preceded by significantly longer fixations than those in the same direction but with shorter or longer amplitudes. These results are consistent with Saccadic Momentum but not with localized temporal IOR.

GENERAL DISCUSSION

The experiments presented here investigated whether IOR influences eye movements during naturalistic scene viewing. There were three main findings. First and foremost, the probability of returning the eyes to previous fixation locations is higher than predicted if IOR were functioning as a "foraging facilitator" (Klein, 1988; Klein & MacInnes, 1999; Posner & Cohen, 1984). The probability that a saccade returns to the last (1-back) and penultimate (2-back) fixation locations was greater than or equal to other distance-matched locations with and without an onset at those locations. This finding provides evidence against the view that IOR drives attention through a scene by decreasing the probability of return (Klein, 1988; Klein & MacInnes, 1999; Posner & Cohen, 1984) but complements evidence of above-chance levels of return saccades reported during psychophysical studies (Motter & Belky, 1998), array search (Peterson et al., 2001), and scene viewing (Hooge et al., 2005).

Second, evidence of IOR was found in the time taken to initiate a saccade to the last (1-back) fixation location during normal viewing. Saccades directed within $+/-2°$ of the last fixation location or with similar amplitudes but an angular deviation from the last fixation of up to 90° were preceded by significantly longer fixations than saccades in the same direction but with longer or shorter amplitudes. This zone of IOR is not observed for involuntary saccades (i.e., those initiated in response to onsets) or relative to the penultimate (2-back) fixation location. Although our analysis does not allow us to investigate the precise spatial extent of the zone of IOR, the $+/-2°$ is similar to the region previously reported in psychophysical studies (Bennett & Pratt, 2001; Berlucchi, Tassinari, Marzi, & Di Stefano, 1989; Dorris et al., 1999; Hooge & Frens, 2000; Maylor & Hockey, 1985; Tassinari, Aglioti, Chelazzi, Marzi, & Berlucchi, 1987).

Third, we found that the saccadic latency effects for return saccades previously attributed to IOR (Horton, 2005; Klein & MacInnes, 1999) can be accounted for by Saccadic Momentum, i.e., the tendency for saccades to continue the trajectory of the last saccade, and the oculomotor lag associated with reversing direction. We found that the time taken to initiate a saccade was inversely proportional to the angular deviation from the last fixation. For saccades in the direction of the last fixation, this delay was supplemented by localized inhibition for saccades with the same amplitude as the last saccade. However, for saccades relative to the penultimate saccade, no such localized inhibition was present and the delay in initiating these saccades can be entirely attributed to Saccadic Momentum. Similar evidence that attention is biased towards continuing in the same direction as the last attentional shift can be found in reaction times during covert attentional shifts (Bennett & Pratt, 2001; Pratt, Adam, & McAuliffe, 1998; Pratt, Spalek, & Bradshaw, 1999), and saccade initiation times in cueing tasks (Anderson et al., 2008; Ro, Pratt, & Rafal, 2000), double-step tasks (Hou & Fender, 1979; Komoda, Festinger, Phillips, Duckman, & Young, 1973) and during free-viewing of scenes (Tatler & Vincent, this issue 2009). Other systematic tendencies in eye movement behaviour during scene viewing such as a bias of fixations towards the screen centre and a prevalence of horizontal and vertical saccades have recently been reported by Tatler and colleagues (Tatler, 2007; Tatler & Vincent, 2008). It is an open question how saccadic momentum interacts with these screen biases. An examination of the distribution of critical fixation locations in the present study revealed no obvious bias towards the centre for any of the potential onset locations. We are confident that facilitation of return and saccadic momentum cannot be attributed to screen biases in the present study although more intelligent baselines such as cumulative fixation locations across all participants and the distribution of visual features may be used in the future to control for such biases.

Our study is the first to dissociate the impact of Saccadic Momentum from IOR during scene viewing. Future investigations of IOR must perform a similar dissociation if they are to ensure differences in saccade initiation time can be attributed to IOR and not Saccadic Momentum.

Can the complex pattern of localized temporal IOR, spatial FOR, and Saccadic Momentum be accommodated by current theories of IOR and attentional control? The zone of IOR observed relative to the last fixation location in Experiment 1 (Figure 4A) is compatible with the view that the neural structure subserving IOR is the superior colliculus (SC; Danziger, Fendrich, & Rafal, 1997; Dorris et al., 1999; Posner, Rafal, Choate, & Vaughn, 1985; Rafal, Calabresi, Brennan, & Sciolto, 1989; Sapir, Soroker,

Berger, & Henik, 1999; Taylor & Klein, 1998). The neurons of the intermediate layer of the superior colliculus are organized into an oculo-centric map (Robinson, 1972) with each neuron discharging action potentials for saccades of particular amplitudes and directions (Wurtz & Goldberg, 1972). Activation of saccade neurons in one region of the saccade target map creates complementary inhibition of saccade neurons on the opposite side of the map (Munoz & Istvan, 1998). The spatial extent of inhibition observed in our study is similar to the region of reduced activation observed in the monkey superior colliculus when preparing a saccadic eye movement to a previously attended location (Dorris, Everling, Klein, & Munoz, 2002; Dorris et al., 1999). This inhibition is believed to spread to adjacent regions (Munoz & Istvan, 1998) affecting neurons coding saccades in the same direction and saccades in a different direction but with the same amplitude. This separation between direction and distance may explain why the region of IOR observed in our study also affected saccades with the same amplitude as the last saccade but with angular deviations up to 90°.

However, patterns of activation and inhibition in the superior colliculus cannot account for the Facilitation of Return observed in Experiments 1 and 2. It has been proposed that the superior colliculus is not alone in creating IOR but that it is acted upon by other cortical regions (Dorris et al., 2002; Klein, 2000; Mayer, Seidenberg, Dorflinger, & Rao, 2004). One candidate region is the frontal eye fields (Dorris et al., 2002; Lepsien & Pollmann, 2002; Ro, Farnè, & Chang, 2003), which is involved in the programming of voluntary saccades (Henik, Rafal, & Rhodes, 1994; Ro, Henik, Machado, & Rafal, 1997; Ro et al., 2000) and the inhibition of reflexive saccades (Rafal, Machado, Ro, & Ingle, 2000). During normal viewing, the command to initiate a voluntary saccade back to the last fixation comes through the FEF but is delayed due to the neural inhibition in the superior colliculus. When an onset occurs at the last fixation location, it is believed to be the FEF that implements the voluntary command to suppress the reflexive saccade generated by the superior colliculus (Ro et al., 2003). Such a pattern of increased saccadic latency to sudden onsets is typically observed using sparse cueing displays (e.g., Posner & Cohen, 1984). However, in our experiments the complexity of the stimuli seems to necessitate a higher frequency of voluntary return fixations. These voluntary return commands could be mediated by the FEF but experience temporal delay due to the neural inhibition present in the target region of the superior colliculus.

This division between cortical commands and neural inhibition of the oculocentric map in the superior colliculus may also explain why we find no localized temporal IOR for the 2-back location. When a return saccade is programmed back to the 2-back fixation location, the saccade amplitude and direction required to reach the 2-back location no longer matches the saccade originally used to leave that location because of the intervening fixation. Therefore, a cortical command to saccade to the 2-back location will receive no neural inhibition in the superior colliculus because the new oculocentric coordinates of the 2-back location do not match the old oculocentric coordinates. Any inhibition of a 2-back return saccade would have to be generated cortically (Danziger et al., 1997) and, if such tagging occurs, it does not result in temporal IOR.

Why, when previous studies have reported return probabilities lower than chance (Boot et al., 2004; Gilchrist & Harvey, 2000; McCarley, Wang, Kramer, & Irwin, 2003; Peterson et al., 2001), do we observe return probabilities significantly above chance level? One possible factor is the complexity of stimuli and processing required during each fixation in scene viewing. All studies previously demonstrating return probabilities lower than chance used very sparse search arrays or saccade targets requiring simple discrimination (Boot et al., 2004; Gilchrist & Harvey, 2000; McCarley et al., 2003; Peterson et al., 2001). When the discrimination task (Motter & Belky, 1998; Peterson et al., 2001) or object complexity increased (Hooge et al., 2005; Paul & Tipper, 2003), return probability increased to above chance level (~ 3–4%). With more complexity, processing of foveal information may not have been completed during a single fixation, necessitating a return saccade. As the complexity of the visual scene reaches that of the real world, FOR, rather than IOR, may be more suitable for accurate processing of the complex visual details. Supporting evidence for a switch from IOR to FOR during scene viewing has been recently reported during scene memorization, preference judgement, and free viewing (Dodd, van der Stigchel, & Hollingworth, in press). With more complex, real-world encoding tasks, adequate processing of foveal information may not be completed before a saccade is initiated (Henderson & Pierce, 2008; Rayner et al., 2009). If the saccade programming system cannot be relied upon to hold fixation until adequate visual encoding has finished, a compensatory system which represents previously fixated locations and facilitates return saccades would be required. Such a system drives regressive saccades during reading (Rayner et al., 2003; Rayner & Pollatsek, 1989; Vitu, 2005) and appears to be in operation in the task presented here. Further experiments are required to understand whether FOR, IOR, and Saccadic Momentum are fundamental properties of the oculomotor system or under strategic control depending on viewing task or moment-by-moment processing requirements.

Implications for computational models of attentional control

All current computational models of attentional control during scene viewing require a mechanism for driving attention through conspicuous regions in a scene (Itti & Koch, 2001; Navalpakkam & Itti, 2005; Parkhurst et al., 2002; Sun et al., 2008). Without such a system, the model would either be trapped on the highest region of conspicuity or oscillate between the two regions of highest conspicuity. Selective inhibition of a limited number of previously visited locations via IOR is usually chosen as a way to ensure that this does not happen (Itti & Koch, 2001; Navalpakkam & Itti, 2005; Parkhurst et al., 2002; Sun et al., 2008). IOR may be adequate within a model of attentional behaviour during the exploration of sparse displays, but as we have demonstrated here, during scene viewing return saccades occur more often than would be permitted by an ideal IOR system.

A first step towards capturing the natural frequency of return saccades would be to replace IOR with Saccadic Momentum: Weighing the probability for saccades that continue the trajectory of the last saccade higher than return saccades. Tatler and Vincent (this issue 2009) present a model incorporating biases in saccade amplitudes and directions that predicts human fixations during scene viewing more accurately than a system based only on image features. By incorporating the systematic tendencies of the human attentional system, a computational model may manifest behaviour similar to that exhibited in the studies presented here without the need for an explicit IOR system.

However, such probabilistic models would fail to capture the functional role of return saccades. Systematic tendencies and localized inhibition may modify the probabilities of a location being fixated given the saccade history, but higher order control mechanisms can still override these tendencies and choose to return to a previous location. Return saccades may occur for a variety of reasons such as inadequacy of processing, significance of the region, a change at the location, or to acquire more details and consolidate its representation in memory (Henderson, Weeks, & Hollingworth, 1999). Modelling these factors would require a representation of the cognitive relevance of fixated objects, the degree of processing occurring during each fixation, and the adequacy of this processing. Where the eyes go next is not just based on what is in the visual scene (e.g., its visual saliency), or where the eyes have been previously (e.g., memory), but what processing has happened along the way. By representing the processing that happens during every fixation, attentional models will be able to account for the real-time factors, both top-down and bottom-up, affecting saccade programming during scene viewing (for a first attempt at modelling these factors during scene viewing see Nuthmann, Smith, & Henderson, 2008).

CONCLUSION

This study investigated whether the inclusion of IOR in models of attentional control during scene viewing is justified. No evidence that IOR functions as a foraging facilitator was found. Return saccades to both the last (1-back) and penultimate (2-back) fixation locations occur as often as saccades in other directions and are facilitated when an unexpected event occurs at the last fixation location. Evidence for IOR was only found in the time taken to initiate a voluntary saccade back to the last fixation location. These results highlight an important dissociation between the spatial and temporal aspects of saccade programming, with FOR characterizing the former process and IOR the latter. The absence of a spatial impact of IOR on saccade programming during scene viewing indicates that IOR does not provide the mechanism required by computational models to drive attention through a scene. Instead such models should look to modelling the dynamics of processing during each fixation.

REFERENCES

Anderson, A. J., Yadav, H., & Carpenter, R. H. S. (2008). Directional prediction by the saccadic system. *Current Biology, 18*(8), 614–618.

Bennett, P. J., & Pratt, J. (2001). The spatial distribution of inhibition of return. *Psychological Science, 12,* 76–80.

Berlucchi, G., Tassinari, G., Marzi, C. A., & Di Stefano, M. (1989). Spatial distribution of the inhibitory effect of peripheral non-informative cues on simple reaction time to non-fixated visual targets. *Neuropsychologia, 27*(2), 201–221.

Boot, W. R., McCarley, J. S., Kramer, A. R., & Peterson, M. S. (2004). Automatic and intentional memory processes in visual search. *Psychonomic Bulletin and Review, 11,* 854–861.

Buswell, G. T. (1935). *How people look at pictures: A study of the psychology of perception in art.* Chicago: University of Chicago Press.

Danziger, S., Fendrich, R., & Rafal, R. D. (1997). Inhibitory tagging of locations in the blind field of hemianopic patients. *Consciousness and Cognition, 6,* 291–307.

Dodd, M. D., van der Stigchel, S., & Hollingworth, A. (in press). Novelty is not always the best policy: Inhibition of return and facilitation of return as a function of visual task. *Psychological Science.*

Dorris, M. C., Everling, S., Klein, R., & Munoz, D. P. (2002). Contribution of the primate superior colliculus to inhibition of return. *Journal of Cognitive Neuroscience, 14,* 1256–1263.

Dorris, M. C., Taylor, T. L., Klein, R. M., & Munoz, D. P. (1999). Influence of previous visual stimulus or saccade on saccadic reaction times in monkey. *Journal of Neurophysiology, 81,* 2429–2436.

Gilchrist, I. D., & Harvey, M. (2000). Refixation frequency and memory mechanisms in visual search. *Current Biology, 10,* 1209–1212.

Gilchrist, I. D., North, A., & Hood, B. (2001). Is visual search really like foraging? *Perception and Psychophysics, 30*(12), 1459–1464.

Henderson, J. M. (2003). Human gaze control during real-world scene perception. *Trends in Cognitive Sciences, 7*(11), 498–504.

Henderson, J. M., & Hollingworth, A. (1999). The role of fixation position in detecting scene changes across saccades. *Psychological Science, 10*(5), 438–443.

Henderson, J. M., & Pierce, G. L. (2008). Eye movements during scene viewing: Evidence for mixed control of fixation durations. *Psychonomic Bulletin and Review, 15,* 566–573.

Henderson, J. M., & Smith, T. J. (2009). How are eye fixation durations controlled during scene viewing? Evidence from a scene onset delay paradigm. *Visual Cognition, 17*(6/7), 1055–1082.

Henderson, J. M., Weeks, P. A., & Hollingworth, A. (1999). The effects of semantic consistency on eye movements during complex scene viewing. *Journal of Experimental Psychology: Human Perception and Performance, 25*(1), 210–228.

Henik, A., Rafal, R. D., & Rhodes, D. (1994). Endogenously generated and visually guided saccades after lesions of the human frontal eye fields. *Journal of Cognitive Neuroscience, 6*, 400–411.

Hooge, I. T., & Frens, M. A. (2000). Inhibition of saccade return (ISR): Spatial-temporal properties of saccade programming. *Vision Research, 40*, 3415–3426.

Hooge, I. T., Over, E. A., van Wezel, R. J., & Frens, M. A. (2005). Inhibition of return is not a foraging facilitator in saccadic search and free viewing. *Vision Research, 45*, 1901–1908.

Horton, J. C. (2005). Vision restoration therapy: Confounded by eye movements. *British Journal of Ophthalmology, 89*(7), 792–794.

Hou, R. L., & Fender, D. H. (1979). Processing of direction and magnitude by the saccadic eye-movement system. *Vision Research, 19*, 1421–1426.

Itti, L., & Koch, C. (2001). Computational modelling of visual attention. *Nature Reviews Neuroscience, 2*(3), 194–203.

Klein, R. M. (1988). Inhibitory tagging system facilitates visual search. *Nature, 334*(6181), 430–431.

Klein, R. M. (2000). Inhibition of return. *Trends in Cognitive Sciences, 4*(4), 138–147.

Klein, R. M., & MacInnes, W. J. (1999). Inhibition of return is a foraging facilitator in visual search. *Psychological Science, 10*, 346–352.

Komoda, M. K., Festinger, L., Phillips, L. J., Duckman, R. H., & Young, R. A. (1973). Some observations concerning saccadic eye movements. *Vision Research, 13*, 1009–1020.

Lepsien, J., & Pollmann, S. (2002). Covert reorienting and inhibition of return: An event-related fMRI study. *Journal of Cognitive Neuroscience, 14*, 127–144.

Lupianez, J., Milliken, B., Solano, M., Weaver, B., & Tipper, S. P. (2001). On the strategic modulation of the time course of facilitation and inhibition of return. *Quarterly Journal of Experimental Psychology, 54*, 753–773.

Mayer, A. R., Seidenberg, M., Dorflinger, J. M., & Rao, S. M. (2004). An event-related fMRI study of exogenous orienting: Supporting evidence for the cortical basis of inhibition of return? *Journal of Cognitive Neuroscience, 16*(7), 1262–1271.

Maylor, E., & Hockey, R. (1985). Inhibitory component of externally controlled covert orienting in visual space. *Journal of Experimental Psychology: Human Perception and Performance, 11*, 777–787.

McCarley, J. S., Wang, R. F., Kramer, A. F., & Irwin, D. E. (2003). How much memory does oculomotor search have? *Psychological Science, 14*, 422–426.

Mennie, N., Hayhoe, M., & Sullivan, B. (2006). Look-ahead fixations: Anticipatory eye movements in natural tasks. *Experimental Brain Research, 179*(3), 427–442.

Motter, B. C., & Belky, E. J. (1998). The guidance of eye movements during active visual search. *Vision Research, 38*, 1805–1815.

Munoz, D. P., & Istvan, P. J. (1998). Lateral inhibitory interactions in the intermediate layers of the monkey superior colliculus. *Journal of Neurophysiology, 79*, 1193–1209.

Navalpakkam, V., & Itti, L. (2005). Modeling the influence of task on attention. *Vision Research, 45*(2), 205–231.

Nuthmann, A., Smith, T. J., & Henderson, J. M. (2008). Fixation durations in scene viewing: Experimental data and computational modeling. *Journal of Vision, 8*(6), 1107–1107.

Parkhurst, D., Law, K., & Niebur, E. (2002). Modeling the role of salience in the allocation of overt visual attention. *Vision Research, 42*(1), 107–123.

Paul, M. A., & Tipper, S. P. (2003). Object-based representations facilitate memory for inhibitory processes. *Experimental Brain Research, 148*, 283–289.

Peterson, M. S., Kramer, A. F., Wang, R. F., Irwin, D. E., & McCarley, J. S. (2001). Visual search has memory. *Psychological Science, 12*, 287–292.

Posner, M. I., & Cohen, Y. (1984). Components of visual orienting. In H. Bouma & D. G. Bouwhuis (Eds.), *Attention and performance X: Control of language processes* (pp. 531–556). Hove, UK: Lawrence Erlbaum Associates Ltd.

Posner, M. I., Rafal, R. D., Choate, L., & Vaughn, J. (1985). Inhibition of return: neural basis and function. *Cognitive Neuropsychologia, 2*, 211–228.

Pratt, J., Adam, J., & McAuliffe, J. (1998). The spatial relationship between cues and targets mediates inhibition of return. *Canadian Journal of Experimental Psychology, 52*, 213–216.

Pratt, J., Spalek, T., & Bradshaw, E. (1999). The time to detect targets at inhibited and non-inhibited location: Preliminary evidence for attentional momentum. *Journal of Experimental Psychology: Human Perception and Performance, 25*, 730–746.

Rafal, R. D., Calabresi, P., Brennan, C., & Sciolto, T. (1989). Saccade preparation inhibits reorienting to recently attended locations. *Journal of Experimental Psychology: Human Perception and Performance, 15*, 673–685.

Rafal, R. D., Machado, L., Ro, T., & Ingle, H. (2000). Looking forward to looking: Saccade preparation and the control of midbrain visuomotor reflexes. In S. Monsell & J. Driver (Eds.), *Attention and performance XVIII: Control of cognitive performance* (pp. 155–174). Cambridge, MA: MIT Press.

Rao, R. P. N., Zelinsky, G. J., Hayhoe, M. M., & Ballard, D. H. (2002). Eye movements in iconic visual search. *Vision Research, 42*(11), 1447–1463.

Rayner, K., Juhasz, B., Ashby, J., & Clifton, C. (2003). Inhibition of saccade return in reading. *Vision Research, 43*, 1027–1034.

Rayner, K., & Pollatsek, S. (1989). *The psychology of reading.* London: Prentice Hall.

Rayner, K., Smith, T. J., Malcolm, G., & Henderson, J. M. (2009). Eye movements and visual encoding during scene perception. *Psychological Science, 20*, 6–10.

Ro, T., Farnè, A., & Chang, E. (2003). Inhibition of return and the human frontal eye fields. *Experimental Brain Research, 150*, 290–296.

Ro, T., Henik, A., Machado, L., & Rafal, R. D. (1997). Transcranial magnetic stimulation of the prefrontal cortex delays contralateral endogenous saccades. *Journal of Cognitive Neuroscience, 9*, 433–440.

Ro, T., Pratt, J., & Rafal, R. D. (2000). Inhibition of return in saccadic eye movements. *Experimental Brain Research, 130*, 264–268.

Robinson, D. A. (1972). Eye movements evoked by collicular stimulation in the alert monkey. *Vision Research, 12*, 1795–1808.

Rosenholtz, R. (1999). A simple saliency model predicts a number of motion popout phenomena. *Vision Research, 39*(19), 3157–3163.

Sapir, A., Soroker, N., Berger, A., & Henik, A. (1999). Inhibition of return in spatial attention: Direct evidence for collicular generation. *Nature Neuroscience, 2*, 1053–1054.

Snyder, J. J., & Kingstone, A. (2000). Inhibition of return and visual search: How many separate loci are inhibited? *Perception and Psychophysics, 62*, 452–458.

Spence, C., & Driver, J. (1998). Inhibition of return following an auditory cue: The role of central reorienting events. *Experimental Brain Research, 118*, 352–360.

Sun, Y., Fisher, B., Wang, H., & Gomes, M. (2008). A computer vision model for visual-object-based attention and eye movements. *Computer Vision and Image Understanding, 112*, 126–142.

Tassinari, G., Aglioti, S., Chelazzi, L., Marzi, C. A., & Berlucchi, G. (1987). Distribution in the visual field of the costs of voluntarily allocated attention and of the inhibitory after-effects of covert orienting. *Neuropsychologia, 25*, 55–71.

Tassinari, G., & Berlucchi, G. (1995). Covert orienting to non-informative cues: Reaction time studies. *Behavioural Brain Research, 71*, 101–112.

Tatler, B. W. (2007). The central fixation bias in scene viewing: Selecting an optimal viewing position independently of motor biases and image feature distributions. *Journal of Vision, 7*(14), 1–17.

Tatler, B. W., & Vincent, B. T. (2008). Systematic tendencies in scene viewing. *Journal of Eye Movement Research, 2*(5), 1–18.

Tatler, B. W., & Vincent, B. T. (2009). The prominence of behavioural biases in eye guidance. *Visual Cognition, 17*(6/7), 1029–1054.

Taylor, T. L., & Klein, R. M. (1998). On the causes and effects of inhibition of return. *Psychonomic Bulletin and Review, 5*, 625–643.

Thomas, L. E., Ambinder, M. S., Hsieh, B., Levinthal, B., Crowell, J. A., Irwin, D. E., et al. (2006). Fruitful visual search: Inhibition of return in a virtual foraging task. *Psychonomic Bulletin and Review, 13*, 891–895.

Torralba, A. (2003). Modeling global scene factors in attention. *Journal of the Optical Society of America A: Optics Image Science and Vision, 20*(7), 1407–1418.

Torralba, A., Oliva, A., Castelhano, M. S., & Henderson, J. M. (2006). Contextual guidance of eye movements and attention in real-world scenes: The role of global features in object search. *Psychological Review, 113*(4), 766–786.

Vincent, B., Troscianko, T., & Gilchrist, I. (2007). Evaluating the weighted salience account of eye movements. *Journal of Vision, 7*(9), 959–959.

Vitu, F. (2005). Visual extraction processes and regressive saccades in reading. In G. Underwood (Ed.), *Cognitive processes in eye guidance* (pp. 1–32). Oxford, UK: Oxford University Press.

Weger, U. W., & Inhoff, A. W. (2006). Attention and eye movements in reading: Inhibition of return predicts the size of regressive saccades. *Psychological Science, 17*, 187–191.

Wurtz, R. H., & Goldberg, M. E. (1972). Activity of superior colliculus in behaving monkey: III. Cells discharging before eye movements. *Journal of Neurophysiology, 35*, 575–586.

Yarbus, A. L. (1967). *Eye movements and vision.* New York: Plenum Press.

VISUAL COGNITION, 2009, 17 (6/7), 1109–1131

Distractor effect and saccade amplitudes: Further evidence on different modes of processing in free exploration of visual images

Sebastian Pannasch and Boris M. Velichkovsky

Applied Cognitive Research/Psychology III, Technische Universitaet Dresden, Germany

In view of a variety of everyday tasks, it is highly implausible that all visual fixations fulfil the same role. Earlier we demonstrated that a combination of fixation duration and amplitude of related saccades strongly correlates with the probability of correct recognition of objects and events both in static and in dynamic scenes (Velichkovsky, Joos, Helmert, & Pannasch, 2005; Velichkovsky, Rothert, Kopf, Dornhoefer, & Joos, 2002). In the present study, this observation is extended by measuring the amount of the distractor effect (characterized as a prolongation of visual fixation after a sudden change in stimulation; see Pannasch, Dornhoefer, Unema, & Velichkovsky, 2001) in relation to amplitudes of the preceding saccade. In Experiment 1, it is shown that retinotopically identical visual events occurring 100 ms after the onset of a fixation have significantly less influence on fixation duration if the amplitude of the previous saccade exceeds the parafoveal range (set on 5° of arc). Experiment 2 demonstrates that this difference diminishes for distractors of obvious biological value such as looming motion patterns. In Experiment 3, we show that saccade amplitudes influence visual but not acoustic or haptic distractor effects. These results suggest an explanation in terms of a shifting balance of at least two modes of visual processing in free viewing of complex visual images.

Keywords: Ambient processing; Distractor effect; Fixation duration; Focal processing; Intermodal processing; Saccade amplitude; Scene perception; Two visual systems.

Please address all correspondence to Sebastian Pannasch, Applied Cognitive Research/ Psychology III, Technische Universitaet Dresden, Helmholtzstrasse 10, 01069 Dresden, Germany. E-mail: pannasch@applied-cognition.org

We thank Marina Danilova, Sven-Thomas Graupner, Sonja Gruen, Jens Helmert, Junji Ito, Andrei Nikolaev, Ben Tatler, Tim Smith, and one anonymous reviewer for their helpful suggestions and comments on the manuscript. This research was supported by grants from the European Commission to BMV (Network of Excellence COGAIN 511598 and NEST-Pathfinder projects MINET 043297 and PERCEPT 043261).

© 2009 Taylor & Francis
DOI: 10.1080/13506280902764422

The importance of eye movements for visual perception and cognition is undisputable (Buswell, 1935; Stratton, 1906; Yarbus, 1967). During the inspection of complex scenes, we perform on average three to four saccadic eye movements per second, which implies that neural processing operations aimed at scene segmentation, feature binding, and identification of image components are accomplished in about 200 ms. However, individual fixations greatly vary in their duration as do conditions and requirements of everyday tasks. This makes it highly improbable that the same neural computations are taking place during different fixations. This aspect of active vision has for a long time been neglected by the students of perception. Despite the fact that pioneering work on the understanding of the role of eye movements was often focused on the investigation of scenes and pictures, most of the influential research contributions in the last decades dealt with simple stimuli and artificial viewing tasks of the "fixate-and-jump" type (e.g., Deubel & Schneider, 1996; Findlay & Walker, 1999).

Although research on tasks such as reading (Rayner, 1978, 1998) and visual search (Vaughan, 1982) has resulted in a number of models explaining the control of fixation duration, recent efforts were focused on under-standing of the spatial target selection (Foulsham & Underwood, 2008; Hayhoe & Ballard, 2005; Itti & Koch, 2001; Tatler, Baddeley, & Vincent, 2006; Torralba, Oliva, Castelhano, & Henderson, 2006). One exception is a study by Henderson and Pierce (2008), who tested whether fixation duration is under direct or indirect control of the visual scene. In their experiments a scene onset delay paradigm was used, in order to investigate the degree to which fixation durations are under control of the availability of the current scene. The authors described two populations of fixations. Whereas a certain proportion of fixations was prolonged with respect to the scene onset delay, other fixations remained unaffected by the display change. The findings for the first group are interpreted as evidence for mechanisms of direct control of fixations. This investigation however leaves a number of questions open. One is the baseline probability for the survival of fixations, e.g., 100 or 800 ms after their beginning. When this baseline information is taken into account, the delay of scene onset results in a less dramatic prolongation of fixations than one reported in the study. Second, the authors do not provide an independent description of features that would enable to differentiate fixations under direct and indirect control. Finally, it remains unclear what neurophysiological mechanisms are or could be responsible for the existence of different groups of fixations.

In search of factors that may clarify the control mechanisms of fixations, we attempted to differentiate classes of fixations based on the existence of two basic modes of visual processing. Though earlier statements can be found (Bernstein, 1947), this distinction came to prominence with a special issue of *Psychologische Forschung* in 1967 (Ingle, Schneider, Trevarthen, & Held,

1967). Succeeding approaches emphasized two distinct cortical mechanisms of primates' vision, dorsal and ventral pathways (Milner & Goodale, 1995, 2008; Ungerleider & Mishkin, 1982). Accordingly, dorsal stream activity can be related to spatial localization and sensorimotor coordination, whereas the ventral visual pathway is involved in identification (e.g., Norman, 2002). One of the recent developments in the field is an emphasis on the role of the frontoparietal feedback system in the active programming of the spatial exploration of the scene contrasted with more stimuli-driven analysis of features of visual input by the structures of occipital and temporal cortex (Corbetta, Patel, & Shulman, 2008).

In line with this neurophysiological concept, we demonstrated in several studies that a combination of fixation durations and saccade amplitudes strongly correlates with the probability of recognition of scene fragments in both static and dynamic settings. This was shown for the correct reaction to hazardous events in a virtual driving simulation (Velichkovsky, Rothert, Kopf, Dornhoefer, & Joos, 2002), and for the recognition of cut-outs of natural images (Velichkovsky, Joos, Helmert, & Pannasch, 2005). In the latter study, the recognition of cut-outs of a previously seen visual scene was distinguished according to the fixation duration and the saccadic amplitude during the inspection. Correct answers were given with a higher probability if the part of the scene was inspected by relatively long fixations (>180 ms) accompanied with saccades of less than 5 deg. It was concluded that combining fixation duration and saccadic amplitude can provide indications of the processing mode: "Ambient processing mode" characterized by short fixations and long saccades is related to the overall spatial orientation in a scene, whereas long fixations—often accompanied by short saccades—are expressions of "focal processing" serving the identification of objects.

The goal of the present investigation is to contribute to this discussion using a simpler paradigm based on the presentation of distractors in relation to the fixation onset. Since the first report by Lévy-Schoen (1969) a large body of data demonstrated an increase in saccadic reaction time when a target stimulus appears together with a visual distractor (Walker, Kentridge, & Findlay, 1995). In most of the experiments, saccadic latencies were analysed within a "fixate-and-jump" paradigm: Subjects had to fixate a designated point on the screen and execute a single saccade once the target (and distractors) appeared. The gaze-contingent paradigm (McConkie & Rayner, 1975) allows distractor experiments in continuous tasks such as reading and free picture viewing (Pannasch, Dornhoefer, Unema, & Velichkovsky, 2001; Reingold & Stampe, 2000). Furthermore, it has been shown that the resulting effects are modulated by the neurophysiological level of processing (Reingold & Stampe, 2002) and can be partially explained within a framework of novelty-based reactions such as the orienting response (Graupner, Velichkovsky, Pannasch, & Marx, 2007).

For the present purpose it is important to note that the magnitude of the distractor effect can be related to differences in the experimental manipulation (e.g., eccentricity of distractor). This effect can also be interpreted—in free viewing—as a prolongation of the actual fixation. Finding differences in the amount of the distractor effect can be understood as a nearly online indicator of information processing in contrast to previous studies where a differentiation was only possible with a post hoc analysis of recognition (Velichkovsky et al., 2002, 2005). More specifically, we aimed to investigate the modulation of the distractor effect in relation to the amplitude of the preceding saccade, which has never been reported before. In our previous work, the distinction between processing modes was based on the combination of fixations and subsequent saccades. This differentiation cannot be applied in the current study since presenting a distractor affects the ongoing fixation and might also influence the following saccade. Therefore the classification of processing modes is based on the last eye movement parameter unaffected by a distractor—the amplitude of the preceding saccade.

It could be expected that ambient (directed at the spatial layout) and focal (directed at the objects and their features) processing differentially modulates the detection of visual sensory events. Both, our previous results (Velichkovsky et al., 2002, 2005) and newly revisited neurophysiological models (Corbetta et al., 2008) suggest that under dominance of the dorsal pathway, i.e., during ambient exploration, the processing of visual input, including distractors, would generally be diminished. One special case could be distractors of obvious biological significance, e.g., stimuli imitating a rapidly approaching object. In other words, one can expect that some resources of attentive processing are preserved even during ambient mode for dealing with biologically important information (Kahneman, 1973). Another hypothesis that had to be verified in the experiments concerns the question about the locus of the visual distractor effect: Is it more "visual" or more "distractor" effect, i.e., related to amodal mechanisms of the novelty-based responses? The answer to this particular question could be given by using distractors of different modalities.

In a more technical vein, experiments like this demand definition of several parametric values; first of all, the range of saccade amplitudes that can be considered as dividing the domains of ambient and focal processing. A simple rule of thumb that was validated in previous studies with static images is to take saccadic amplitudes at around 5° as the criterion to differentiate between the relative dominance of ambient or focal processing modes (Velichkovsky et al., 2002, 2005). This is a measure that also corresponds to the anatomical data on the parafoveal area of the adult human eye (Polyak, 1941; Wyszecki & Stiles, 1982) and to electrophysiological indicators (Billings, 1989; Thickbroom, Knezevic, Carroll,

& Mastaglia, 1991). The second parameter that was kept constant across the experiments was the delay of distractor presentation after the beginning of fixation. The selected delay was 100 ms. It is therefore larger than the temporal zone of saccadic suppression (Vallines & Greenlee, 2006). At the same time, the delay is short enough to test the majority of initially selected fixations, even if nearly 100 ms are additionally required for the full evolving of the distractor effect (Graupner et al., 2007; Reingold & Stampe, 2000).

EXPERIMENT 1

By distinguishing fixations in relation to the preceding saccadic amplitude, we expect stronger distractor effects for fixations in the focal mode rather than those related to ambient processing. To study this hypothesis it is necessary to control for the distractor's eccentricity as increasing the spatial distance between a distractor and the current fixation location reduces the influence of the distracting event (Honda, 2005; Walker, Deubel, Schneider, & Findlay, 1997). Since this observation was made in simple fixate-and-jump experiments, it is important to study if a similar relationship can be identified during free visual exploration.

Method

Subjects.   Sixteen healthy volunteers (11 females and 5 males) with a mean age of 25.3 years ($SD = 4.9$) took part in this experiment. All subjects had normal or corrected to normal vision and received either course credit or €7 for participation in the study conducted in conformity with the declaration of Helsinki.

Apparatus.   Participants were seated in a dimly illuminated, sound-attenuated room. Eye movements were sampled monocularly at 250 Hz using the EyeLink I eyetracking system (SR Research, Ontario, Canada) with online detection of saccades and fixations and a spatial accuracy of $< 0.5°$. Fixation onset was detected and transmitted to the presentation system with a delay of approximately 12 ms. A 9-point calibration and validation was performed according to the guidelines outlined by Stampe (1993) before the start of the first trial and after the break. Saccades were identified by deflections in eye position in excess of $0.1°$, with a minimum velocity of $30°/s^{-1}$ and a minimum acceleration of $8000°/s^{-2}$, maintained for at least 4 ms. The minimum fixation duration threshold was set to 100 ms. The first fixation in each trial was defined as the first fixation that began after the onset of the image. Pictures were displayed using a GeForce2 MX card and a CRT display (19-inch Iiyama Vision Master 451) at 1152×864 pixels at a refresh rate of 100 Hz. Viewed from a distance of

90 cm, the screen subtended a visual angle of 25.7° horizontally and 19.3° vertically.

Stimuli and design.   Forty digitized paintings by European seventeenth- to nineteenth-century artists were used as stimuli with a size of 1152 × 864 pixels and 24 bit colour depth. During each trial, visual distractors were presented 100 ms after the fixation onset with a duration of 75 ms. Distractors were of circular shape with a size of 50 pixels (~1.38°). They were implemented as a colour inversion for chromatic and luminance values of the designated image region (RGB values for each pixel were transformed into the equivalent value on the colour scale, e.g., a value of 5 was converted to 250). Distractors were shown at 11 different horizontal positions in relation to the current fixation location (0, 2, 4, 6, 8, or 10° to the left or to the right of it). Within one trial 22 distractors were presented in randomized order, resulting in two presentations at each position per trial.

Procedure.   Each subject was informed of the purpose of the study as an investigation of eye movement patterns in perception of art. Participants were asked to study the images in order to answer five questions regarding scene content after the picture offset (e.g., "Was there a painting on the wall?"). They were aware of the distractor presentations, but instructed to ignore them. The experimental session was run in four consecutive blocks, each containing 10 pictures with 5 min break after the second block. In total, the session took 90 min to complete. Before each trial, a drift correction was performed. Picture presentation began with an initial 5 s period without distractors, followed by the relevant experimental presentation. After an intervening delay of 2 s, questions regarding the picture content were shown. Within the experiment, distractors were presented at every fifth fixation. They were triggered by the fixation onset with a stimulus–onset asynchrony (SOA) of 100 ms. If a fixation was terminated before reaching the SOA, the program waited for the next suitable fixation resulting in more then five fixations between the distractors in such a particular case. The presentation algorithm also considered the relative position of the fixation on the image, i.e., if the fixation-distractor distance would result in a distractor outside the image, the direction was switched and the distractor appeared at the opposite position. The image presentation lasted until the respective number of distractors of each category was presented (on average, about 55 s).

Data analysis.   Data analyses were carried out using SPSS 14.0 and MATLAB 7.1. Raw eye movement data were preprocessed before statistical analysis. All fixations shorter than 100 ms or outside the presentation screen were excluded from analyses. According to earlier findings (Harris, Hainline, Abramov, Lemerise, & Camenzuli, 1988; Velichkovsky, Dornhoefer,

Pannasch, & Unema, 2000), fixations were expected to reveal a right skewed distribution where the median represents a more reliable value than the mean. Therefore, for statistical testing the respective median values were subjected to repeated measures analyses of variance (ANOVA). Partial eta-squared values were additionally reported in order to provide indicators of the potential practical significance of differences. For data analyses only the fixations and saccades at the time of distractor presentation and the two adjacent to this event were considered. Accordingly, 50.5% ($N = 76547$) of the overall dataset were used for subsequent statistical analyses.

Results

To investigate the effects of the distractors at the different positions, fixation durations of the baseline and the distractor condition were compared. As baseline we used the median duration of the two fixations preceding and following the distractor. A $2 \times 6 \times 2$ repeated measures ANOVA was conducted on the medians of fixation duration with direction (left vs. right), eccentricity (0, 2, 4, 6, 8, and 10° distance from the fixation location) and distractor (distractor vs. baseline), all serving as within-subjects factors. No effect was found for direction, $F < 1$, but for eccentricity, $F(5, 75) = 16.45$, $p < .001$, $\eta^2 = .523$, and for distractor, $F(1, 15) = 245.66$, $p < .001$, $\eta^2 = .942$. Furthermore, a significant interaction was obtained for Position × Distractor, $F(5, 75) = 30.53$, $p < .001$, $\eta^2 = .671$, demonstrating a larger influence of distractors within the foveal and parafoveal range (up to 5° away from the fixation location, within a range of 317–357 ms). For distractors appearing in the periphery (further away than 5° from the fixation location) the effect remains relatively stable (within a range of 300–308 ms; see Figure 1). No further interaction was found.

Since a prolongation of fixations was obtained, we were interested if this distractor effect is also modulated by processing mode. A distinction was made between fixations preceded by saccades with amplitudes of less or equal than 5° and fixations with preceding amplitudes of larger than 5°. As described earlier, the first category was assumed as belonging to focal processing (henceforth focal), whereas the second was referred to ambient processing (henceforth ambient). According to this definition, distractor and baseline fixations were classified. Subsequently, the difference values (distractor minus baseline fixations) for each category were computed. Because no differences were obtained concerning the location of distractors to the left or to the right from fixation position, this factor was not further considered. The resulting differences are shown in Figure 2.

Difference values were applied to a 6×2 repeated measures ANOVA with eccentricity (0, 2, 4, 6, 8, and 10° distance from the fixation location) and

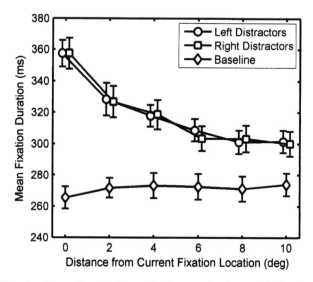

Figure 1. Mean durations and standard errors for distractor fixations and the baseline in respect of the distractor distance from the fixation position.

processing (ambient vs. focal) serving as within-subjects factors. A significant main effect was found for eccentricity, $F(5, 75) = 17.62$, $p < .001$, $\eta^2 = .540$. Post hoc testing revealed reliable differences between distractors at $0°$ and those that appeared at $4°$ and further away, $p < .05$. Also a

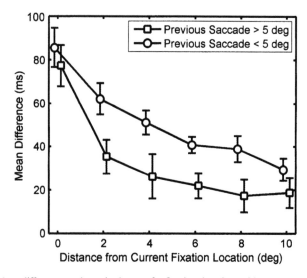

Figure 2. Mean differences and standard errors for fixation durations with respect to the amplitudes of the previous saccade.

significant difference was obtained for the factor processing, $F(1, 15) =$ 14.160, $p = .002$, $\eta^2 = .486$, with no further interaction, $F < 1$. The main effect was largest for distractors at the current fixation location (82 ms at 0° eccentricity) and became smaller with increasing eccentricity (24 ms at 10° eccentricity). Single paired t-tests on the difference values of distractor effects with respect to the previous saccadic amplitude revealed significant differences for distractors shown in the range of 2–8°, $t(15) \geq 2.43$, all ps $< .028$ (Bonferroni corrected).

Discussion

Our results are in line with earlier reports on differences in the influence of visual distractors in relation to their eccentricity. For four out of six eccentricities, in the range from 2° to 8°, we also found the expected differences of the distractor effect depending on the amplitude of the preceding saccade. This latter effect was absent at the foveal location of distractors leading to a steeper decline of distractor effect with increasing eccentricity of presentation when the tested fixations followed long-range saccades.

The notable exception of the distractor effect at the foveal location is similar to the picture of saccadic recalibration of presaccadic positions for shortly presented stimuli (Bischof & Kramer, 1968; McConkie & Currie, 1996; Müsseler, van der Heijden, Mahmud, Deubel, & Ertsey, 1999). However these effects were observed at earlier temporal intervals than 100 ms after the beginning of a new fixation as it was in our experiment. The same can be said about saccadic suppression. One possible explanation is related with the double nature of our stimuli used as distractors. They consisted of changes of both colour and luminance within the picture. It is known that the locus of interference of large saccades is the magnocellular pathway which is responsible to luminance variation in space and time (Burr, Morrone, & Ross, 1994; Vallines & Greenlee, 2006). Accordingly, saccades have a relatively weak influence on chromatically modulated components of distractors that can be efficiently processed in the foveal region.

EXPERIMENT 2

A nearly neglected aspect of the distractor effect is its dependency on dynamic parameters of the distractors. Because all existing studies are limited to the presentation of single simple stimuli, almost nothing is known about possible effects of the presentation of biologically important stimuli. This question is of particular interest from the perspective of the distinction of two modes of visual processing. While ambient processing can be generally connected with a shallower processing, according to the classical theory of attention as mental effort (see Kahneman, 1973), some residual resources may always be preserved for an in-depth processing of a limited set of stimuli with an a priori biological value. A looming optical pattern that normally signifies an approaching visual object is an example of such a stimulus. In the following experiment we compared the prolongation of visual fixations in dependence on the presentation of three types of distractors. We used single static stimuli as well as shrinking and expanding optical patterns.

Method

Subjects. Sixteen healthy volunteers (6 females and 10 males) with a mean age of 22.5 years ($SD = 2.9$) took part in this experiment. All subjects had normal or corrected to normal vision and received either course credit or €7 for participation in the study conducted in conformity with the declaration of Helsinki.

Apparatus and stimuli. Experiment 2 used the same apparatus and stimuli as described in Experiment 1.

Design. During each trial, visual distractors were presented in relation to the fixation position; 100 ms after the fixation onset and with duration of 75 ms. In contrast to Experiment 1, three subsequent distractors were shown during one fixation, resulting in a total distractor presentation time of 225 ms.

The distractors consisted of circular rings of three different sizes. The inner radius of the ring was always 0.375° but the outer radius could be either of 0.45°, 0.525°, or 0.60°. They were centred to the actual coordinates of the fixation and implemented by inverting the colour of the region between the inner and the outer radius. If a fixation was selected for the distractor presentation (see Experiment 1 for details) two different distractor sequences were possible. Distractors were presented in either an expanding or a shrinking manner. In the first case, it started with the smallest outer radius and expanded to the largest outer radius (i.e., from 0.45° to 0.60°), whereas in case of shrinking distractors the sequential procedure was the other way round. In addition, single distractors (circular ring with an inner radius of 0.375° and an outer radius of 0.45°) were presented (instead of three subsequent distractors) in order to test for the general distractor effect compared to Experiment 1. Within one trial 25 distractors (20 of the respective distractor type and 5 single distractors) were presented.

Procedure.   Each subject was informed of the purpose of the study as an investigation of eye movement patterns in perception of art paintings before signing their consent. The viewing task and procedure was the same as in Experiment 1. The experimental session was run in two consecutive blocks, each containing 20 pictures. Within a block only one distractor type (expanding or shrinking) was shown together with the single distractors, but each subject received all distractor types within one session. The order of the distractor type presentation was balanced across the subjects. On average, the presentation of an image lasted for about 55 s. In total, the experimental session took 90 min to complete with a 5 min break between the blocks.

Data analysis.   Eye movement data were preprocessed and filtered by the same routines as described in Experiment 1. Accordingly, 63.9% ($N = 59291$) of fixations and saccades of the overall dataset were used for subsequent statistical analyses.

Results

To investigate the effects of different distractor types, fixation durations of the distractor condition were compared with the baseline (median of the two fixations before and after the distractor presentation). A 3×2 repeated measures ANOVA was conducted on the median fixation duration with distractor type (single, expanding, and shrinking distractors) and distractor (distractor vs. baseline), both serving as within-subjects factors. We obtained significant differences for distractor type, $F(2, 30) = 5.72$, $p = .008$, $\eta^2 = .276$, and for distractor, $F(1, 15) = 58.88$, $p < .001$, $\eta^2 = .797$ (see Figure 3). Post hoc testing yielded significance only between the single distractors and the expanding distractors, $p < .001$. Moreover there was a significant interaction for Distractor type $\times$ Distractor, $F(2, 30) = 5.85$, $p = .007$, $\eta^2 = .281$, resulting from a smaller influence of single distractors ($M = 314$ ms) compared to shrinking and expanding distractors ($Ms = 335$ and 350 ms). The presentation of dynamic distractors within a fixation resulted in a stronger prolongation of the affected fixation (21–36 ms).

In order to investigate this effect on a finer grained level, we again distinguished distractor and baseline fixations on the basis of the amplitude of the preceding saccade (ambient vs. focal; see Experiment 1 for further description). Subsequent to this classification, differences between distractor and baseline fixations were calculated (see Figure 4). A 3×2 repeated measures ANOVA was conducted on the resulting values with distractor type (single, shrinking, and expanding) and processing (ambient vs. focal), both serving as within-subjects factors. A significant effect was found for

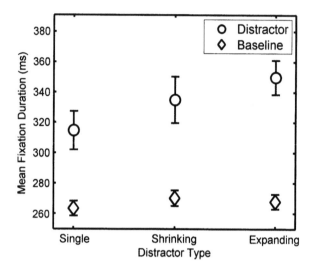

Figure 3. Mean fixation durations and standard errors for the different distractor types and the respective baseline.

distractor type, $F(2, 30) = 6.04$, $p = .006$, $\eta^2 = .287$. Moreover, a significant effect of processing was found, $F(1, 15) = 4.62$, $p = .048$, $\eta^2 = .235$, with no further interaction, $F(2, 30) = 2.62$, $p = .089$. Bonferroni corrected post hoc testing yielded stronger influences on fixations for expanding distractors than for single and shrinking distractors, $p < .05$ ($Ms = 79$ vs. 52 and 53 ms).

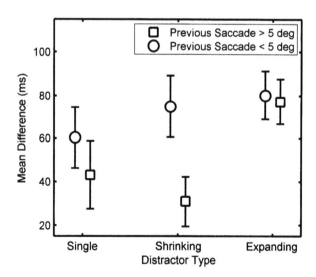

Figure 4. Mean difference values and standard errors for distractor types in relation to the amplitude of the previous saccade.

The results of this analysis demonstrate a distinct relationship between the effect of distractors and the mode of processing. For the focal processing, the outcome is similar to the results of the previous analysis for the general effect versus the baseline. Moreover, the effects for single distractors are similar to distractors that were shown at the eccentricity of 0° in Experiment 1. With dynamic distractors, a strong difference is found for shrinking (focal vs. ambient: $Ms = 75$ vs. 31 ms) but not for expanding distractors (focal vs. ambient: $Ms = 80$ vs. 77 ms).

Discussion

As expected, we found a stronger distractor effect for the dynamic visual stimulation as compared with single stimuli. Of particular interest for the purpose of our study was the analysis of the amount of this effect depending on the amplitude of the preceding saccade. Such analysis revealed a picture of results, which dissociates influences of two changing optical patterns of stimulation on the duration of fixations. When in presumably focal mode of processing, immediately after short-range saccades, both types of dynamic distractors showed approximately the same effect on tested fixations, the results were quite different in what we consider to support the ambient processing mode, i.e., after long-range saccades. Here a much stronger distractor effect of expanding patterns was discovered.

The special quality of optically and acoustically looming stimuli has been shown in a number of psychophysical and neurophysiological studies (Bruce, Green, & Georgeson, 1996; Lappe, 2004; Maier, Neuhoff, Logothetis, & Ghazanfar, 2004). For the first time, this was demonstrated with respect to the oculomotor distractor effect. However a significant difference between shrinking and expanding distractors was found only in context of large-range saccades. As in the case of distributed attention (Treisman, 2006), ambient mode of visual processing implies a generally shallower processing of input by simultaneously preserving the alerting function of vision for a limited set of objects of potential biological significance.

EXPERIMENT 3

Considering the mechanisms of the distractor effect, one has to be aware of a number of components influencing the final picture of oculomotor behaviour. Besides initial stages of sensory information processing, there are several other important mechanisms; for example, the inhibitory networks at the levels of superior colliculus, amygdala, and perhaps the premotor cortex (Reingold & Stampe, 2002, 2004). Previous results suggest that the distractor effect should also be considered within a broader category of novelty-based reactions of organisms such as startle and orienting reaction (Graupner et al., 2007). In the following experiment, we attempted to clarify whether the relationship of saccadic amplitude and the distractor effect is specifically related to processes within visual systems or perhaps reflects some more general states and intermodal processing. The simplest way to differentiate visual and nonvisual components of processing is to use presentation of intermodal distractors. The bulk of evidence supports the possible effect of acoustic and somatosensory distractors on the latency of saccades and fixation duration (Amlot, Walker, Driver, & Spence, 2003; Pannasch et al., 2001). Based on these results, visual, auditory, and haptic distractors were investigated in the same setting of free exploration of complex visual images.

Method

Subjects.   Sixteen healthy volunteers (7 females and 9 males) with a mean age of 23.6 years ($SD = 3.4$) took part in this experiment. All subjects had normal or corrected to normal vision and received either course credit or €7 for participation in the study conducted in conformity with the declaration of Helsinki.

Apparatus.   Experiment 3 used the same apparatus for eye movement recording and stimulus presentation as described in Experiment 1.

Stimuli and design.   Twenty of the pictures used in Experiment 1 were used as stimuli. During each trial, visual, auditory, or haptic distractors were presented 100 ms after a fixation onset with duration of 75 ms. Visual distractors had the same features as single distractors in Experiment 2. Auditory distractors consisted of pure sinusoidal 1000 Hz tones and were produced by a standard PC soundcard. The tones had a duration of 75 ms including 5 ms rise and fall time. They were presented at a sound pressure level of 70 dB binaurally via insert earphones (EartoneTM 3A). To generate haptic distractors, a custom-made stimulation device was produced that was controlled by a parallel input–output board (PIO-24 II, BMC Messsysteme, Maisach, Germany) which was connected to the PC running the experiment. Haptic distractors were implemented via a blunt metal pin which pushed against the left index finger for 75 ms. The stimulation was clearly perceivable but not painful. Visual distractors appeared on screen at the spatial location of the selected fixation; auditory and haptic distractors were presented without any spatial relation to the selected fixation.

Procedure.   Each subject was informed of the purpose of the study as an investigation of eye movement patterns in perception of art. The viewing task and procedure was the same as in Experiment 1. The experimental session was run in four consecutive blocks, with a presentation of five pictures within each. Within three of the four blocks distractors of only one modality appeared; in the fourth block distractors of all modalities were mixed. The order of blocks was balanced across the subjects. During each trial 21 distractors of the same modality or in the mixed block 7 of each were shown (see Experiment 1 for a description of the distractor presentation). On average, each trial lasted for about 55 s. In total, the experimental session took 60 min to complete, with a 5 min break following the second block.

Data analysis. To ensure the comparability eye movement data of the current study was preprocessed and filtered by the same routines as described for Experiment 1. Accordingly, 57.4% ($N = 41738$) of fixations and saccades of the overall dataset were used for subsequent statistical analyses.

Results

To investigate the effects of distractors of different modalities, fixation durations affected by distractors of the different modalities (visual, auditory, and haptic) were compared with the respective baseline fixations (median of the two fixations before and after the distractor presentation). We were also interested if there is a difference for the continuous presentation of distractors of one modality within one block against the mixed presentation of distractors of different modalities within one block. A $2 \times 3 \times 2$ repeated measures ANOVA was conducted on the medians fixation duration with block (continuous vs. mixed), modality (visual, auditory, and haptic), and distractor (distractor vs. baseline) all serving as within-subjects factors. No effect was found for block, $F(1, 15) = 2.68$, $p = .122$, but for modality, $F(2, 30) = 39.05$, $p < .001$, $\eta^2 = .722$ and for distractor, $F(1, 15) = 83.81$, $p < .001$, $\eta^2 = .848$. Significant interactions were obtained for modality and distractor, $F(2, 30) = 31.15$, $p < .001$, $\eta^2 = .675$ (see Figure 5), as well as for block and distractor, $F(1, 15) = 8.61$, $p = .010$, $\eta^2 = .365$. This latter interaction is due to the difference in distractor fixations (continuous vs. mixed block; $Ms = 324$ vs. 343 ms) since the baseline is the same ($Ms = 280$ vs. 278). A closer look at the finding reveals that it is mainly based on the visual distractors (continuous vs. mixed block; $Ms = 387$ vs. 428 ms). For other modalities the continuous vs. mixed presentation makes only marginal differences (auditory: $Ms = 301$ vs. 312 ms; haptic: 284 vs. 289 ms, correspondingly). Moreover, Bonferroni corrected paired t-tests for modality and distractor effect revealed significant influences on the fixation

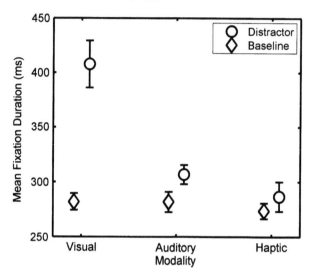

Figure 5.   Mean fixation durations and standard errors for distractor and baseline fixation in relation to the modality of the presented distractor.

duration for visual and acoustic, $ps < .001$, but not for haptic distractors, $p = .065$.

Again, the distractor effect was investigated in relation to the amplitude of the previous saccade. Due to the nonsignificant main effect for block in the previous analysis, this factor was not further considered. We distinguished fixations in the baseline and those probed by distractors on the basis of the amplitude of the preceding saccade (ambient vs. focal; see Experiment 1 for further description). Subsequent to this classification, differences between distractor and baseline were calculated (see Figure 6).

Difference values were entered into a 3×2 repeated measures ANOVA with modality (visual, auditory, and haptic) and processing (ambient vs. focal), both serving as within-subjects factors. Significant main effects were found for modality, $F(2, 30) = 66.40$, $p < .001$, $\eta^2 = .816$, and for processing, $F(1, 15) = 7.68$, $p = .014$, $\eta^2 = .339$. Post hoc testing revealed stronger effects for visual distractors ($M = 108$ ms) compared to auditory and haptic distractors ($Ms = 21$ and 11 ms, respectively). In addition, an interaction was obtained, $F(2, 30) = 9.00$, $p = .001$, $\eta^2 = .375$, resulting from the fact that the ambient-focal classification differentiated between fixations affected by visual distractors (about 47 ms). In the case of auditory and haptic modalities, any influence of saccadic amplitude is absent.

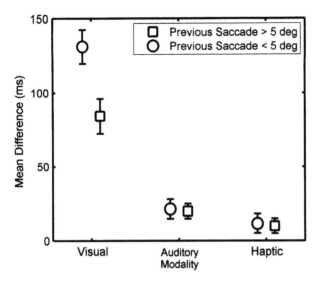

Figure 6. Difference values and standard errors for each distractor modality in relation to the amplitude of the preceding saccade.

Discussion

The results of this experiment demonstrate that the dependency of the distractor effect on the amplitude of preceding saccades is associated with the visual modality of presentation. Both auditory and haptic distractors had only a weak influence on the prolongation of fixations; moreover, this influence was independent of the saccadic context. Thus, the data from Experiment 3 testify that the visual distractor effect can be used for investigating differences in the mode of visual information processing, for example, in relation to the involvement of dorsal and ventral streams of visual processing in the regulation of eye movements (Burr et al., 1994; Velichkovsky et al., 2005).

Additional evidence for the locus of this effect could be collected with the repeated presentation of distractors and the analysis of habituation in the fixation duration (Graupner et al., 2007). In a preliminary way, one can predict no interaction of saccadic amplitudes and the rate of habituation, at least for fast habituation processes that seem to avoid cortical processing. At the same time, slow habituation, which usually develops over periods of minutes and hours, shows a correlation with the changes in visually evoked cortical ERPs and in that slow habituation might be related to one of the two modes of visual processing. A stronger overall effect for visual distractors was obtained in this experiment in comparison to Experiments 1 and 2. This might be due to the combined presentation of distractors of different modalities counteracting any form of habituation.

As demonstrated previously, habituation is more expressed in the case of homogeneous (unimodal) distractors (Graupner et al., 2007).

GENERAL DISCUSSION

Our goal in the study was a further analysis of information processing during separate visual fixations in a free viewing of complex images. In accordance with earlier findings on recognition performance (Velichkovsky et al., 2002, 2005) and recent neurophysiological models (Corbetta et al., 2008), we assumed a stronger influence of visual distractors during the focal as compared with ambient processing mode. This latter distinction was operationalized by taking into account the amplitude of saccades preceding the fixations in question: Fixations that resulted from saccades outside of the parafoveal range were considered as related to the ambient processing with its reliance on the global spatial layout of the environment. In this particular mode of processing, stimuli-driven influences such as additionally presented visual distractors could be of less importance.

We measured the influence of distractors on visual fixations effect depending on the retinotopic position of distractors (Experiment 1), their spatial-temporal patterning (Experiment 2) and the possible multimodality of the described effect (Experiment 3). In all three experiments, the differences in the size of the distractor effect in relation to the saccadic amplitude were confirmed. In terms of Henderson and Pierce (2008), fixation duration is under less direct control of the visual scene following saccade amplitudes outside the parafoveal range.

As every saccade is a complex biomechanical event changing conditions for visual information processing in a number of ways, alternative explanations for this basic result have to be considered. First of all, large saccades sometimes miss their targets, so that a short corrective saccade may follow after a preliminary stopping of eyes in the "undershot" position. However, precorrective fixations usually are of very short duration, substantially less than 100 ms (Otero-Millan, Troncoso, Macknik, Serrano-Pedraza, & Martinez-Conde, 2008; Velichkovsky et al., 2000; Yarbus, 1967). By presenting distractors 100 ms after the beginning of the selected fixations, we automatically excluded this possibility of explaining the results. Another explanation is the saccadic suppression (Dodge, 1900, Latour, 1962; Lee et al., 2007) that can be particularly pronounced in the case of large-scale saccadic eye movements. But an analysis of temporal relationships again makes this alternative a relatively unlikely explanation. Accordingly, suppression anticipates saccades by 50 ms, is maximal at the moment of saccadic onset, and outlasts saccades by nearly 50 ms at most (Vallines & Greenlee, 2006; Zuber & Stark, 1966). No saccadic suppression was discovered beyond this interval. This rules out an influence of saccadic suppression on the processing of distractors presented 100 ms after the saccade offset. Furthermore, one could argue that repetitive fixations (refixations) explain our findings. Regions of higher visual complexity are usually fixated with higher frequencies, longer durations, and the preceding saccades often are relatively short (Rajashekar, van der Linde, Bovik, & Cormack, 2007). Even if refixations are similar to focal fixations, this hypothesis alone does not explain the current findings, for instance, the differences of effects for expanding and shrinking distractors (Experiment 2). In addition, refixations were thoroughly controlled and excluded as a possible explanation in one of our previous studies (Velichkovsky et al., 2005).

Thus, the preferable hypothesis is that of a relation between eye movements and modes of visual processing. The conclusion is in general agreement with previous studies, which used such measures of visual performance as recognition (Velichkovsky et al., 2002, 2005) and, indirectly, with recent descriptive analysis of relationships between saccadic amplitudes and duration of fixations in visual processing of complex images (Tatler & Vincent, 2008; Unema, Pannasch, Joos, & Velichkovsky, 2005). Additionally it is supported by data from Experiment 3. Though the distractor effect (as a novelty-based reaction of the organism; see Graupner et al., 2007) has not only visual but also intermodal components, our data show that haptically and acoustically induced distractor effects show no interaction with parameters of preceding saccadic eye movements.

At the same time, overall results of the present study cannot be easily assimilated by the standard hypothesis of the two modes of visual processing, with its sharp distinction of perception for action and for consciousness (Milner & Goodale, 1995, 2008). In the case of active vision, involvement of saccadic eye movements seems to be rather a matter of balancing between complementary but closely interrelated modes of processing. In view of the contrasting influence of dynamic distractors found in Experiment 2, the difference reminds that of focused and distributed attention (Treisman, 2006). The exact nature of these mechanisms starts to be investigated by a simultaneous analysis of eye movements and neuronal activities (Cornelissen, Marsman, Renken, & Velichkovsky, 2008; Maldonado et al., 2008; Rajkai et al., 2008). Currently available information suggests that large-scale saccades selectively interfere with the magnocellular pathway. The latter is related to forms of global luminance-based processing of transient information, which is under control of dorsal stream structures (Bridgeman, van der Heijden, & Velichkovsky, 1994; Burr et al., 1994; Vallines & Greenlee, 2006).

From this perspective, eye movements have to be considered as a common output of several neurocognitive mechanisms. The neurophysiological data on contrasting functions of frontoparietal system and structures of occipital and temporal cortex (Corbetta et al., 2008; Faillenot, Toni, Decety, Gregoire, & Jeannerod, 1997) suggest two basic mechanisms at work in free exploration of visual images. It remains to be seen, whether the difference of processing in relation to the saccadic amplitude will genera- lise to different tasks, where other brain systems play a role. This may be the case of interpersonal communication where eye-to-eye contacts and the states of joint attention strongly influence the fixation duration (Schrammel, Pannasch, Graupner, Mojzisch, & Velichkovsky, in press; Velichkovsky, 1995). Another example is the comparative visual search: The spatial arrangement of two (nearly) identical parts of search space is well-defined here remaining constant during the task solution (Pomplun, 1998). Reading may be a similar case because in reading too the overall spatial arrangement is known before. Also known is the default saccade target, which normally is the next word. Even for static images, as in the present experiments, the time phase of perception may be of importance as the balance of ambient and focal processing is different at the beginning of scene inspection and after the initial 2–4 s (Pannasch, Helmert, Roth, Herbold, & Walter, 2008; Unema et al., 2005).

The methodological message of this study is therefore that visual processing during fixations has to be investigated in a variety of further conditions and tasks. Both amplitude of preceding saccade and the amount of distractor effect, as a dependent variable, seem to be well suited to testing hypotheses about the modes of visual processing during continuous visual activity in ecologically valid situations. By the beginning of a fixation its status with respect to the parameters of preceding saccade is known, which simplifies decisions on experimental manipulations and on the measures for baseline control. The distractor paradigm is relatively unobtrusive, involving a kind of background stimulation, which only weakly interferes with the task at hand. This makes it a promising instrument for studies of visual cognitive activities, also as a part of neurophysiological experiments with human and subhuman subjects.

REFERENCES

Amlot, R., Walker, R., Driver, J., & Spence, C. (2003). Multimodal visual-somatosensory integration in saccade generation. *Neuropsychologia, 41*(1), 1–15.

Bernstein, N. A. (1947). *O postrojenii dvizhenij [On the construction of movements]*. Moscow: Medgiz.

Billings, R. J. (1989). The origin of the occipital lambda wave in man. *Electroencephalography and Clinical Neurophysiology, 72*(2), 95–113.

Bischof, N., & Kramer, E. (1968). Untersuchungen und Überlegungen zur Richtungswahrneh- mung bei willkürlichen sakkadischen Augenbewegungen [Studies and considerations on the direction perception during saccadic eye movements]. *Psychologische Forschung, 32*, 185–218.

Bridgeman, B., van der Heijden, A. H. C., & Velichkovsky, B. M. (1994). A theory of visual stability across saccadic eye movements. *Behavioral and Brain Sciences, 17*(2), 247–292.

Bruce, V., Green, P. R., & Georgeson, M. A. (1996). *Visual perception: Physiology, psychology and ecology.* Hove, UK: Lawrence Erlbaum Associates Ltd.

Burr, D. C., Morrone, M. C., & Ross, J. (1994). Selective suppression of the magnocellular visual pathway during saccadic eye movements. *Nature, 371*(6497), 511–513.

Buswell, G. T. (1935). *How people look at pictures.* Chicago: University of Chicago Press.

Corbetta, M., Patel, G., & Shulman, G. L. (2008). The reorienting system of the human brain: From environment to theory of mind. *Neuron, 58*(3), 306–324.

Cornelissen, F. W., Marsman, J. B. C., Renken, R., & Velichkovsky, B. M. (2008). Predicting gaze behavior and cognitive task from cortical activity: A fixation based event related (FIBER) fMRI study. In *Proceedings of the third international conference on Cognitive Science* (pp. 535–537). Moscow: Academia Publishing Centre.

Deubel, H., & Schneider, W. X. (1996). Saccade target selection and object recognition: Evidence for a common attentional mechanism. *Vision Research, 36*(12), 1827–1837.

Dodge, R. (1900). Visual perception during eye movement. *Psychological Review, 7*, 454–465.

Faillenot, I., Toni, I., Decety, J., Gregoire, M. C., & Jeannerod, M. (1997). Visual pathways for object-oriented action and object recognition: Functional anatomy with PET. *Cerebral Cortex, 7*, 77–85.

Findlay, J. M., & Walker, R. (1999). A model of saccade generation based on parallel processing and competitive inhibition. *Behavioral and Brain Sciences, 22*(4), 661–721.

Foulsham, T., & Underwood, G. (2008). What can saliency models predict about eye movements? Spatial and sequential aspects of fixations during encoding and recognition. *Journal of Vision, 8*(2), 1–17.

Graupner, S.-T., Velichkovsky, B. M., Pannasch, S., & Marx, J. (2007). Surprise, surprise: Two distinct components in the visually evoked distractor effect. *Psychophysiology, 44*(2), 251–261.

Harris, C. M., Hainline, L., Abramov, I., Lemerise, E., & Camenzuli, C. (1988). The distribution of fixation durations in infants and naive adults. *Vision Research, 28*(3), 419–432.

Hayhoe, M., & Ballard, D. (2005). Eye movements in natural behavior. *Trends in Cognitive Sciences, 9*(4), 188–194.

Henderson, J. M., & Pierce, G. L. (2008). Eye movements during scene viewing: Evidence for mixed control of fixation durations. *Psychonomic Bulletin and Review, 15*(3), 566–573.

Honda, H. (2005). The remote distractor effect of saccade latencies in fixation-offset and overlap conditions. *Vision Research, 45*(21), 2773–2779.

Ingle, D., Schneider, G., Trevarthen, C., & Held, R. (1967). Locating and identifying: Two modes of visual processing. A symposium. *Psychologische Forschung, 31*, 42–43.

Itti, L., & Koch, C. (2001). Computational modeling of visual attention. *Nature Reviews Neuroscience, 2*(3), 194–203.

Kahneman, D. (1973). *Attention and effort.* Englewood Cliffs, NJ: Prentice-Hall.

Lappe, M. (2004). Building blocks for time-to-contact estimation by the brain. In H. Hecht & G. Savelsberg (Eds.), *Theories of time-to-contact* (pp. 39–52). Amsterdam: Elsevier.

Latour, P. L. (1962). Visual threshold during eye movements. *Vision Research, 2*(3), 261–262.

Lee, P. H., Sooksawate, T., Yanagawa, Y., Isa, K., Isa, T., & Hall, W. C. (2007). Identity of a pathway for saccadic suppression. *Proceedings of the National Academy of Sciences of the USA, 104*(16), 6824–6827.

Lévy-Schoen, A. (1969). Determination and latency of oculo-motor response to simultaneous and successive stimuli according to their relative eccentricity. *Anneé Psychologique, 69*(2), 373–392.

Maier, J. X., Neuhoff, J. G., Logothetis, N. K., & Ghazanfar, A. A. (2004). Multisensory integration of looming signals by Rhesus monkeys. *Neuron, 43*(2), 177–181.

Maldonado, P. E., Babul, C. M., Singer, W., Rodriguez, E., Berger, D., & Gruen, S. (2008). Synchronization of neuronal responses in primary visual cortex of monkeys viewing natural images. *Journal of Neurophysiology, 100*, 1523–1532.

McConkie, G. W., & Currie, C. B. (1996). Visual stability across saccades while viewing complex pictures. *Journal of Experimental Psychology: Human Perception and Performance, 22*(3), 563–581.

McConkie, G. W., & Rayner, K. (1975). The span of the effective stimulus during a fixation in reading. *Perception and Psychophysics, 17*(6), 578–586.

Milner, A. D., & Goodale, M. A. (1995). *The visual brain in action.* Oxford, UK: Oxford University Press.

Milner, A. D., & Goodale, M. A. (2008). Two visual systems re-viewed. *Neuropsychologia, 46*(3), 774–785.

Müsseler, J., van der Heijden, A. H. C., Mahmud, S. H., Deubel, H., & Ertsey, S. (1999). Relative mislocalization of briefly presented stimuli in the retinal periphery. *Perception and Psychophysics, 61*(8), 1646–1661.

Norman, J. (2002). Two visual systems and two theories of perception: An attempt to reconcile the constructivist and ecological approaches. *Behavioral and Brain Sciences, 25*(1), 73–144.

Otero-Millan, J., Troncoso, X. G., Macknik, S. L., Serrano-Pedraza, I., & Martinez-Conde, S. (2008). Saccades and microsaccades during visual fixation, exploration and search: Foundations for a common saccadic generator. *Journal of Vision, 8*(14), 1–18.

Pannasch, S., Dornhoefer, S. M., Unema, P. J. A., & Velichkovsky, B. M. (2001). The omnipresent prolongation of visual fixations: Saccades are inhibited by changes in situation and in subject's activity. *Vision Research, 41*(25–26), 3345–3351.

Pannasch, S., Helmert, J. R., Roth, K., Herbold, A.-K., & Walter, H. (2008). Visual fixation durations and saccadic amplitudes: Shifting relationship in a variety of conditions. *Journal of Eye Movement Research, 2*(4), 1–19.

Polyak, S. L. (1941). *The retina.* Chicago: University of Chicago Press.

Pomplun, M. (1998). *Analysis and models of eye movements in comparative visual search.* Göttingen, Germany: Cuvillier.

Rajashekar, U., van der Linde, I., Bovik, A. C., & Cormack, L. K. (2007). Foveated analysis of image features at fixations. *Vision Research, 47*(25), 3160–3172.

Rajkai, C., Lakatos, P., Chen, C. M., Pincze, Z., Karmos, G., & Schroeder, C. E. (2008). Transient cortical excitation at the onset of visual fixation. *Cerebral Cortex, 18*(1), 200–209.

Rayner, K. (1978). Eye movements in reading and information processing. *Psychological Bulletin, 85*(3), 618–660.

Rayner, K. (1998). Eye movements in reading and information processing: 20 years of research. *Psychological Bulletin, 124*(3), 372–422.

Reingold, E. M., & Stampe, D. (2000). Saccadic inhibition and gaze contingent research paradigms. In A. Kennedy, R. Radach, D. Heller, & J. Pynte (Eds.), *Reading as a perceptual process* (pp. 1–26). Amsterdam: Elsevier.

Reingold, E. M., & Stampe, D. (2002). Saccadic inhibition in voluntary and reflexive saccades. *Journal of Cognitive Neuroscience, 14*(3), 371–388.

Reingold, E. M., & Stampe, D. (2004). Saccadic inhibition in reading. *Journal of Experimental Psychology: Human Perception and Performance, 30*(1), 194–211.

Schrammel, F., Pannasch, S., Graupner, S.-T., Mojzisch, A., & Velichkovsky, B. M. (in press). Virtual friend or threat? The effects of facial expression and gaze interaction on psychophysiological responses and emotional experience. *Psychophysiology.*

Stampe, D. M. (1993). Heuristic filtering and reliable calibration methods for video-based pupil-tracking systems. Behavior Research Methods. *Instruments and Computers, 25*(2), 137–142.

Stratton, G. M. (1906). Symmetry, linear illusions, and the movements of the eye. *Psychological Review, 13*(2), 82–96.

Tatler, B. W., Baddeley, R. J., & Vincent, B. T. (2006). The long and the short of it: Spatial statistics at fixation vary with saccade amplitude and task. *Vision Research, 46*(12), 1857–1862.

Tatler, B. W., & Vincent, B. T. (2008). Systematic tendencies in scene viewing. *Journal of Eye Movement Research, 2*(2), 1–18.

Thickbroom, G. W., Knezevic, W., Carroll, W. M., & Mastaglia, F. L. (1991). Saccade onset and offset lambda waves. *Brain Research, 551*(1–2), 150–156.

Torralba, A., Oliva, A., Castelhano, M. S., & Henderson, J. M. (2006). Contextual guidance of eye movements and attention in real-world scenes: The role of global features in object search. *Psychological Review, 113*(4), 766–786.

Treisman, A. (2006). How the deployment of attention determines what we see. *Visual Cognition, 14*(4–8), 411–443.

Unema, P. J. A., Pannasch, S., Joos, M., & Velichkovsky, B. M. (2005). Time course of information processing during scene perception: The relationship between saccade amplitude and fixation duration. *Visual Cognition, 12*(3), 473–494.

Ungerleider, L., & Mishkin, M. (1982). Two cortical visual systems. In D. J. Ingle, M. A. Goodale, & R. J. W. Mansfield (Eds.), *Analysis of visual behavior* (pp. 549–586). Cambridge, MA: MIT Press.

Vallines, I., & Greenlee, M. W. (2006). Saccadic suppression of retinotopically localized blood oxygen level-dependent responses in human primary visual area V1. *Journal of Neuroscience, 26*(22), 5965–5969.

Vaughan, J. (1982). Control of fixation duration in visual search and memory search. *Journal of Experimental Psychology: Human Perception and Performance, 8*(5), 709–723.

Velichkovsky, B. M. (1995). Communicating attention: Gaze position transfer in cooperative problem solving. *Pragmatics and Cognition, 3*(2), 199–222.

Velichkovsky, B. M., Dornhoefer, S. M., Pannasch, S., & Unema, P. J. A. (2000). Visual fixations and level of attentional processing. In A. Duhowski (Ed.), *Proceedings of the symposium on Eye Tracking Research and Applications* (pp. 79–85). Palm Beach Gardens, NY: ACM Press.

Velichkovsky, B. M., Joos, M., Helmert, J. R., & Pannasch, S. (2005). Two visual systems and their eye movements: Evidence from static and dynamic scene perception. In B. G. Bara, L. Barsalou, & M. Bucciarelli (Eds.), *Proceedings of the XXVII conference of the Cognitive Science Society* (pp. 2283–2288). Mahwah, NJ: Lawrence Erlbaum Associates, Inc.

Velichkovsky, B. M., Rothert, A., Kopf, M., Dornhoefer, S. M., & Joos, M. (2002). Towards an express diagnostics for level of processing and hazard perception. *Transportation Research, 5F*(2), 145–156.

Walker, R., Deubel, H., Schneider, W. X., & Findlay, J. M. (1997). Effect of remote distractors on saccade programming: Evidence for an extended fixation zone. *Journal of Neurophysiology, 78*, 1108–1119.

Walker, R., Kentridge, R. W., & Findlay, J. M. (1995). Independent contributions of the orienting of attention, fixation offset and bilateral stimulation on human saccadic latencies. *Experimental Brain Research, 103*, 294–310.

Wyszecki, G., & Stiles, W. S. (1982). Color science: Concepts and methods, quantitative data and formulae (2nd ed.). New York: Wiley.

Yarbus, A. L. (1967). *Eye movements and vision.* New York: Plenum Press.

Zuber, B. L., & Stark, L. (1966). Saccadic suppression: Elevation of visual threshold associated with saccadic eye movements. *Experimental Neurology, 16*(1), 65–79.

VISUAL COGNITION, 2009, 17 (6/7), 1132–1158

Gaze allocation in natural stimuli: Comparing free exploration to head-fixed viewing conditions

Bernard Marius 't Hart[1], Johannes Vockeroth[2],
Frank Schumann[3], Klaus Bartl[2], Erich Schneider[2],
Peter König[3], and Wolfgang Einhäuser[1]

[1]*Department of Neurophysics, Philipps-University Marburg, Germany,* [2]*Chair for Clinical Neurosciences, University of Munich Hospital, Germany,* [3]*Institute of Cognitive Science, University of Osnabrück, Germany*

"Natural" gaze is typically measured by tracking eye positions during scene presentation in laboratory settings. How informative are such investigations for real-world conditions? Using a mobile eyetracking setup ("EyeSeeCam"), we measure gaze during free exploration of various in- and outdoor environments, while simultaneously recording head-centred videos. Here, we replay these videos in a laboratory setup. Half of the laboratory observers view the movies continuously, half as sequences of static 1-second frames. We find a bias of eye position to the stimulus centre, which is strongest in the 1 s frame replay condition. As a consequence, interobserver consistency is highest in this condition, though not fully explained by spatial bias alone. This leaves room for image specific bottom-up models to predict gaze beyond generic biases. Indeed, the "saliency map" predicts eye position in all conditions, and best for continuous replay. Continuous replay predicts real-world gaze better than 1 s frame replay does. In conclusion, experiments and models benefit from preserving the spatial statistics and temporal continuity of natural stimuli to improve their validity for real-world gaze behaviour.

Keywords: Human; Eye movements; Real world; Natural stimuli; Attention.

The question as to which factors guide human eye movements under natural conditions has puzzled researchers for decades. Many have approached this

Please address all correspondence to Wolfgang Einhäuser, Philipps-University Marburg, Physics/Neurophysics, Renthof 7, 35032 Marburg, Germany.

E-mail: wet@physik.uni-marburg.de

The authors gratefully acknowledge the following grants and institutions: BMtH was supported by the Deutsche Forschungsgemeinschaft (DFG) Research Training Group 885-Neuroact; JV received support by the Bayerische Forschungsstiftung (DOK-88-07); PK by the EU project IST-027268-POP "Perception On Purpose". This work was conducted in part within the DFG excellence initiative research cluster Cognition for Technical Systems (CoTeSys).

© 2009 Taylor & Francis
DOI: 10.1080/13506280902812304

issue by showing observers complex natural photographs or pictures, while tracking their eye position (Baddeley & Tatler, 2006; Buswell, 1935; Krieger, Rentschler, Hauske, Schill, & Zetsche, 2000; Mannan, Ruddock, & Wooding, 1996; Parkhurst, Law, & Niebur, 2002; Peters, Iyer, Itti, & Koch, 2005; Privitera & Stark, 2000; Reinagel & Zador, 1999; Tatler, Baddeley, & Gilchrist, 2005; Yarbus, 1967). Such passive-viewing approaches were extended to showing systematically modified photographs (Einhäuser & König, 2003; Kayser, Nielsen, & Logothetis, 2006) or movies (Carmi & Itti, 2006; Itti, 2005; Tosi, Meccacci, & Pasquali, 1997), and combined with computer-game, simulator, or virtual environment settings (Hayhoe et al., 2002; Peters & Itti, 2008). To what extent such laboratory data are informative for unrestrained gaze allocation during natural behaviour has, however, remained largely unaddressed.

Eyetracking in natural scenes has motivated stimulus-driven ("bottom-up") attention models. Most are rooted in the concept of the saliency map (Itti, Koch, & Niebur, 1998; Koch & Ullman, 1985): The stimulus is filtered in different channels (colour, luminance, orientation) to obtain maps of feature contrasts. These are added across spatial scales to a saliency map, the peak of which is predicted to draw most attention. Although not originally designed for fixation prediction or to operate on natural scenes, a location's saliency and its probability to be fixated are (weakly) correlated (Parkhurst et al., 2002; Peters et al., 2005). However, the model's features do not necessarily drive gaze causally (Einhäuser & König, 2003), but rather act through mutual correlations to higher level scene content (Einhäuser, Spain, & Perona, 2008; Elazary & Itti, 2008). Furthermore, if observers search for a template, the correlation vanishes entirely (Henderson, Brockmole, Castelhano, & Mack, 2007) and immediately (Einhäuser, Rutishauser, & Koch, 2008). In a virtual reality setting top-down signals supersede bottom-up saliency for gaze allocation (Rothkopf, Ballard, & Hayhoe, 2007). Consequently, recent extensions of the saliency map include task specific information (Navalpakkam & Itti, 2005). The saliency map's lack of causality and its breakdown for specific tasks has spurred another question: Can *any* purely bottom-up model have predictive power for gaze allocation during real-world behaviour?

Despite the advantages of well-controlled settings and stimuli, eye-movement studies in the laboratory typically suffer from several constraints. First, stimuli must be chosen to be adequate for the natural situation. In particular, biases already present in the stimuli, such as preference for specific features at the centre of gaze (Tatler, 2007), must be matched to the natural setting under investigation. Second, laboratory recordings typically restrain the observer, suppressing head-movement components of gaze allocation, which are particularly relevant for large gaze shifts (Stahl, 1999) and a major source of interindividual differences (Fuller, 1992). Third, vestibular stimuli are typically not matched to the visual input. Finally, the display's limited resolution and extent provide an artificial frame of reference. These constraints necessitate a quantification of differences between laboratory and natural settings.

Several studies measured real-world eye-movement behaviour for specific tasks, including driving (Land & Lee, 1994; Land & Tatler, 2001), food preparation (Land & Hayhoe, 2001; Land, Mennie, & Rusted, 1999), and a variety of sports (Chajka, Hayhoe, Sullivan, Pelz, Mennie, & Droll, 2006; Fairchild, Johnson, Babcock, & Pelz, 2001; Hayhoe, Mannie, Sullivan, & Gorgos, 2005; Land & McLeod, 2000). In contrast, gaze allocation during free exploration of natural settings has rarely been addressed, although its laboratory homologue, "free viewing", provides the typical testbed for bottom-up models.

Virtual reality presents a step towards real-world scenarios that preserves the controllability of laboratory settings. Jovancevic, Sullivan, and Hayhoe (2006) measured eye-movement patterns evoked by surprisingly occurring colliders (other pedestrians) during task performance, and established the scheduling scheme between the bottom-up (collider events) and the top-down (task) signals. Their results were in remarkable agreement with an optimal scheme for such scheduling proposed in earlier theoretical work (Sprague & Ballard, 2004; Sprague, Ballard, & Robinson, 2007): Observers minimize the expected cost of not making a specific eye movement. Unlike static displays, virtual-environment settings readily allow for naturalistic tasks. In contrast to truly real-world experiments, the same trial can be replicated and the environment can be controlled, allowing quantitative manipulations and thus assessment of the interaction between task, stimulus, and context (Rothkopf et al., 2007). Since the statistics of a truly natural environment may influence gaze and in turn gaze shifts affect the selected subset of stimuli to operate upon, the controllability of the environment is, however, virtue *and* challenge. Nonetheless, virtual reality complements truly real-world experiments and will help bridging the gap between laboratory and actual reality.

In earlier work, we used a mobile setup ("EyeSeeCam"; Schneider et al., 2009) to record large amounts of gaze-centred and head-centred movies during free exploration. Eye–head-coordination analysis suggested a profound influence of nonsaccadic eye movements to gaze-centred stimulus statistics (Einhäuser et al., 2007; Einhäuser, Moeller, et al., 2009), and the spatial statistics of features at the centre of gaze transferred the concept of feature saliency from the laboratory to the real world (Einhäuser, Schumann, et al., 2009; Schumann et al., 2008). A direct comparison between free exploration and laboratory data with the same visual input has, however, yet to be performed.

Here we compare gaze-allocation behaviour during free exploration and during replay of videos in a standard head-fixed setup. Laboratory stimuli are taken from head-centred movies recorded simultaneously with the free-exploration data. This ensures that eye-in-head movements operate on the same visual stimuli in all conditions. We dissociate effects on eye movements arising from the visual stimulus alone from effects specific to either free exploration (e.g., resulting from vestibular input) or the laboratory (e.g., resulting from head restraints). To dissociate effects of stimulus continuity, we show static frames from the videos to a second set of laboratory observers. By using data from these three conditions, free exploration, continuous replay, and 1 s frame replay, we address three topics. First, does the spatial distribution of gaze relative to the head differ in active free exploration and head-restrained free viewing? Second, are stimulus locations that are preferentially fixated, consistent within and between the laboratory and real-world conditions? Finally, does the correlation of fixation probability with saliency map values, which here exemplifies a typical bottom-up model of attention, transfer from static images, to movies and to the real world?

METHODS

Free exploration

Gaze-centred and head-centred videos were recorded using the "Eye-SeeCam" setup, which is described in detail elsewhere (Brandt, Glasauer, & Schneider, 2006; Schneider et al., 2005, 2006; Vockeroth, Bardins, Bartl, Dera, & Schneider, 2007), as is the recording procedure and the stimulus material (Schumann et al., 2008). In brief, an eyetracking system attached to swimming goggles controls a gaze-centred camera, while an identical camera (head camera) is fixed to the observer's forehead. Both cameras had a resolution of 752×432 pixels, covered a visual angle of $60° \times 41°$ and recorded digital video at 25 Hz. In the present study, fifteen 90 s excerpts from the head-centred movies recorded in Schumann et al. (2008) were selected as stimuli for the laboratory experiments (Figure 1A). These data were recorded in different environments—German residential areas (four), Munich downtown (three), hospital indoor, forest, open field, scientific conference indoor, park, university building indoor, Californian desert, and beach. Movies were recorded in colour through an IEEE-1394 ("firewire") interface using Bayer encoding with no compression. The total number of observers for recording all used movies was six, but each movie stemmed from a continuous recording in one particular observer. All observers were accustomed to wearing the setup and instructed to "behave naturally". The eye-position data were reconstructed from the motor-control signals of the

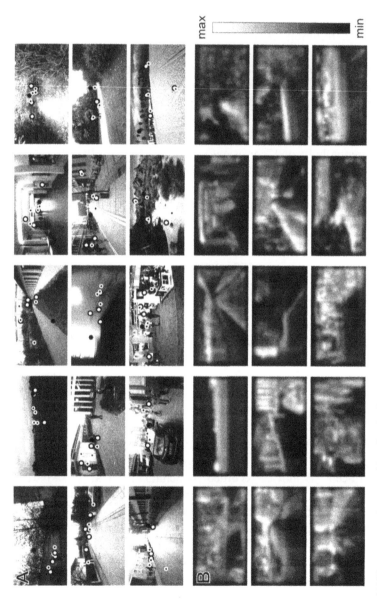

Figure 1. (A) Frames appearing at $t = 20$ s of each of the 90 s movie clips. Markers denote eye positions during presentation of the frame: Black star: Free exploration; black circles: Continuous replay (median eye position during 40 ms of frame presentation); white circles: 1 s frame replay (median eye position 280–320 ms after stimulus onset). Note that the videos were recorded and displayed in colour. All video material is available from the authors. (B) Saliency maps for the frames shown in Panel A.

gaze-centred camera. These data defined the gaze relative to the head-centred stimuli for the free-exploration condition.

The EyeSeeCam records raw eye movements at 192 Hz. By interpolating and subsampling the signal to 25 Hz we obtain one sample per frame. We conservatively defined a saccade as any fast movement (velocity > 35 deg/s, acceleration > 4000 deg/s^2). By this definition $7.2\% \pm 2.1\%$ (mean and *SD* across movies) of samples contained saccades. Excluding all frames for which at least 10% of raw samples in the frame or adjacent frames were saccades, has no qualitative effect on results.

Setup

In the laboratory experiments stimuli were presented in a dark room on a FlexScan F77S (EIZO, Hakusan, Ishikawa, Japan) 19.7-inch CRT monitor at 48 cm distance. Four-pixel wide fringes were cropped from the stimuli at each side, resulting in a resolution of 744×424 pixels. Stimuli were scaled using bilinear interpolation to the central 1280×730 pixels of the 1280×1024 pixels wide screen, thus covering a visual angle of $45° \times 26°$. This is smaller than the cameras' field of view, being the maximum within equipment's constraints at the time of recording. The monitor's frame rate was 100 Hz, an integer multiplier of the 25 Hz at which movies were recorded and presented. Maximum luminance of the monitor was 37 cd/m^2, the minimum below 0.01 cd/m^2. Since the precise characteristics of the cameras were unknown, screen settings were chosen such that the colour movies appeared natural. In particular, the mapping from pixel-values to luminance was nonlinear (gamma of 2.9), and no attempt was made to match the displayed colours physically to the real-world (x/y CIE-coordinates of the screen's guns: 0.610/0.339, 0.282/0.601, 0.151/0.065). Since most measures used in the context of saliency maps are insensitive to monotonic scaling, this restriction should not substantially affect our results.

Throughout the laboratory experiments each observer's eye position was recorded at 2000 Hz using an Eyelink-2000 device (SR Research, Mississauga, Ontario, Canada). Calibration and validation procedures followed manufacturer's recommendation, using a 13-point grid on the effective display area. Eye positions outside the stimulus and blinks were discarded (2.5% of data). To avoid confounds by different dynamics of fixations and eye movements among the conditions, we did not explicitly analyse fixations. Instead, the median eye position during each 40 ms frame or—for the 1 s frame conditions and all temporally resolved analyses—the eye position at each sample point was used. In $4.6\% \pm 1.1\%$ of the frames saccades occurred. Excluding these data has virtually no effect on the results.

All presentation, eye-movement recording and analysis used Matlab (MathWorks, Nattick, MA) with its psychophysics and Eyelink toolbox extensions (Brainard, 1997; Cornelissen, Peters, & Palmer, 2002; Pelli, 1997; http://psychtoolbox.org). All observers had normal or corrected-to-normal vision and normal colour vision, as assessed by a 16-plate Ishihara test and gave written informed consent to participation. All procedures conformed with national and institutional guidelines and the Declaration of Helsinki.

Continuous replay condition. In the continuous replay condition four male observers (aged 21–26) watched a total of fifteen 90 s excerpts of the head-centred free-exploration videos. The observers' heads were stabilized with the chinrest and forehead rest of the Eyelink system. Each observer viewed all movies in random order. Between the movies, observers could rest and the eyetracker was recalibrated. Observers received written instructions prior to the experiment that they were to "watch short video clips", that they should keep their heads "as still as possible", and that they were allowed and encouraged to "move their eyes naturally". The latter was added in distinction to the calibration phases, in which points and crosses had to be fixated.

1 s frame replay condition. Four additional observers (two male, two female; aged 21–27) participated in the 1 s frame replay condition. To create stimuli for this condition, the first frame of each second in each movie was selected, yielding 90 frames per movie and $15 \times 90 = 1350$ frames in total. These were randomly rearranged to 15 new 90 s sequences of 1 s still frames, such that each sequence contained six frames from each original movie. The same sequences were used for all observers, but the presentation order of sequences was randomized. All presentation and setup parameters as well as instructions were otherwise identical to the continuous replay condition.

Taken together, we obtained for each video eye-position data of nine different observers, four from each laboratory condition and one from the free-exploration data. Although the free-exploration videos were recorded by different observers, we will refer to them as a single "free-exploration observer".

Model saliency maps

As a prototypical model of bottom-up guidance of eye movements, we used Itti and Koch's (2000) saliency map (http://ilab.usc.edu). Parameters were unchanged, except that max-norm normalization of the saliency map and randomness were switched off. For analysis the saliency map of each frame was normalized to range from 0 to 1 (Figure 1B).

Eye-position maps.   Average maps of eye positions relative to the image were computed by binning the eye position at each time-point at the image's resolution (744×424) and adding the resulting maps. For display purposes (Figure 2A–C), the maps were smoothed by averaging the 49×49 pixel ($3.1° \times 3.1°$ in the lab, $4.8° \times 4.8°$ in free exploration) neighbourhood of each pixel and truncated with 24 pixels to each side. The binning (kernel size for smoothing) was thus matched in image coordinates (pixels) rather than in world-coordinates (degrees), and was uncritical for the location of the maxima. For each observer and movie, the spatial spread in horizontal direction and vertical direction (σ_x and σ_y, respectively) was computed as the standard deviation of the respective eye-position coordinate, either pooling all 2000 data points per second, or—for time-resolved analysis of the 1 s frame condition—for each of the 2000 time points separately.

Spatial consistency

Spatial consistency between each pair of observers' eye positions was measured by their Euclidian distance at each time-point. As display size differed from the camera field of view for free exploration, we obtain a dimensionless measure by dividing the Euclidian distance by the image diagonal. This value is subtracted from 1 to obtain a consistency measure, which is zero for maximally inconsistent observers, and 1 for identical observers. Since the spatial distribution of eye positions is a priori unknown, there is no analytic expression for the spatial consistency to be expected at random. To estimate the part of the consistency that is stimulus independent and caused by generic spatial biases, we computed a random-reassignment baseline for each observer as follows: The eye positions of each 1 s interval in each movie were randomly attributed to another randomly chosen 1 s interval from the same movie. Shuffling across rather than within movies slightly lowers the baseline, as it is less likely to hit the same or a nearby frame, but qualitatively the observed effects are independent of the baseline choice.

Comparing fixation distributions.   If there are some equally salient or relevant items spread through the scene, which are visited by all observers but in different order, the Euclidian measure would report low degrees of consistency. "Consistency" in an image-related interpretation might therefore be underestimated, especially for static displays. Kullback-Leibler (KL) divergence is an alternative measure of the generic similarity between fixation distributions of different observers and its variation over time. Following Tatler et al. (2005), we binned the display in squares (here: 16×16 pixels) and defined the probability $P(x,y)$ of fixation from this histogram $F(x,y)$ as

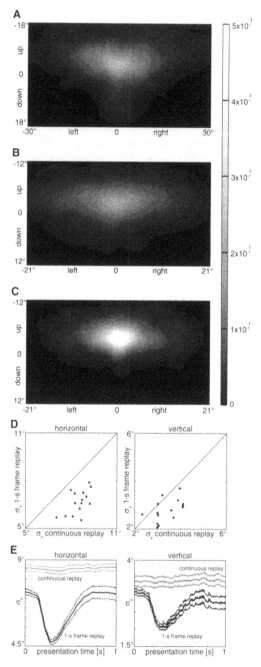

Figure 2 (*See caption opposite*)

$$P(x, y) = \frac{(F(x, y) + \varepsilon)}{\sum_{x',y'}(F(x', y') + \varepsilon)}$$

with $\varepsilon = 10^{-3}$. The KL divergence is then given by

$$KL = -P_a(x, y)\log P_b(x, y) + P_a(x, y)\log P_a(x, y) = P_a(x, y)\log\left(\frac{P_a(x, y)}{P_b(x, y)}\right)$$

where P_a is the eye-position distribution of a given observer, and P_b the eye-position distribution of *all* other observers in the same condition. This measure cannot be used for the instantaneous comparison of fixated locations in any given frame, as the distribution cannot be estimated from a small number of eye positions; here Euclidian distance remains the most straightforward measure complementing the KL analysis.

Signal-detection analysis (ROC).   For the analysis of saliency, we use the same baseline as for spatial consistency. This avoids any confound from shared spatial biases of stimuli and observer (e.g., Tatler, 2007; Tatler et al., 2005) as the baseline and the actual data share condition, setup, and observer biases. Hence any differences between the distribution of saliency at actual gaze and at baseline locations are then guaranteed to result from stimulus specific effects. Using signal-detection analysis, we quantified how well saliency map values discriminate actual eye position from baseline locations. For a given detection threshold, we obtained the rate of hits (true values above threshold divided by number of all true values) and false alarms (baseline values above threshold divided by number of all baseline values). By varying the threshold from the minimum to the maximum of the values, we obtained the receiver operator characteristic (ROC) curve of hit rate versus false alarm rate. The area under this curve (AUC) quantifies how well saliency discriminates eye positions from baseline locations. Note that this usage of the ROC is somewhat different from earlier eyetracking studies (Peters et al., 2005; Tatler et al., 2005), where in an individual image it is asked how well saliency can discriminate fixated from nonfixated locations. Here, with only one or two fixations per subject and frame in free

Figure 2 (opposite). (A)–(C) Density of gaze allocations averaged over all movies and observers, binned at image resolution and smoothed with a mean-filter of 49 pixels width. Maps show the full valid field of view (FoV of the camera of 744×424 pixels cropped by 25 pixels half filter size at each end). Note that the colourmap is brightened compared to the standard Matlab grey colourmap (e.g., Figure 1) for better reproduction of low values. (A) Free exploration. (B) Continuous replay. (C) 1 s frame replay. (D) Standard deviation of eye position in each movie averaged over 1 s frame replay observers (y-axis) and continuous replay observers (x-axis), respectively. Each data point represents one movie clip. Left: Horizontal eye position; right: Vertical eye position. (E) Time course of eye position's standard deviation during 1 s frame replay (black), continuous replay (grey) as reference. Data averaged over observers; lines denote mean $\pm$SEM over movies. Left: Horizontal eye position; right: Vertical eye position.

exploration and continuous replay, the AUC estimate from this frame-based measure would be inaccurate. Instead, we here measured how well saliency discriminates eye positions from baseline locations within observers, movies, and conditions to allow a comparison of the quality of model saliency map predictions between different experimental conditions. As this procedure does not allow tailoring parameters of the decision process to individual images, it returns lower numerical values and is the more conservative measure.

Empirical saliency maps

To test how well laboratory data predicts free-exploration data, we defined empirical saliency maps: For each data sample, we created a map by placing a Gaussian of 2° standard deviation centred at the eye position. These maps were added for all data samples and observers to get two empirical saliency maps for both laboratory conditions in each 40 ms period of each movie (one frame in the continuous replay condition). The empirical maps were then normalized to range from 0 to 1, and the same signal-detection theory analysis as for the model saliency maps was used.

Gaze-centred average saliency maps

To visualize the relationship between gaze allocation and saliency, we computed average saliency maps that were centred at gaze. For each observer, each model saliency map was shifted to align the gaze location with the centre of the to-be-created average saliency map. The saliency values of all pixels in the same new pixel were added. To obtain the mean map for each observer, each coordinate of the map was divided by the number of pixels that went into it after all frames were summed. Finally, we averaged maps over observers. For display, the results were cropped to the central part corresponding to the size of the original map. For this analysis, the median gaze position in a 40 ms time window (corresponding to one frame in the continuous condition) was used. Again, the same analysis was performed for a random-reassignment baseline that paired frames and gaze at random. Depending on the strength of the relationship between gaze and saliency one predicts a peak at the centre of the new average saliency maps. If image specific saliency contributes to gaze allocation, this peak should be more pronounced for the actual than for the baseline data. Unlike other analysis techniques, the average maps do not only use the peak or specific statistics, but consider the entire map's values. This has the advantage that if several points have similar salience but only one attracts attention this is reflected in the map. As all analyses that use the saliency values, rather than the position of peaks, the measure is, however, sensitive to nonlinear scaling of individual maps. Hence, we use it for visualization and to verify the analysis qualitatively, whereas quantification is based on signal-detection theory measures, which are insensitive to any strictly monotonic scaling of the saliency value.

RESULTS

We compare human gaze allocation during three different conditions: Free exploration, continuous replay, and 1 s frame replay of head-centred movies. In laboratory conditions, fixations (periods not containing saccades or blinks) account for 93.2% ± 1.1% of time (1 s frame replay) and 92.4% ± 2.9% (continuous replay), respectively, with no significant difference between the two conditions, $t(6) = 0.53$, $p = .61$. In free exploration, such periods account for 94.8% ± 0.9% of samples, and 72.3% ± 4.7% of frames correspond entirely to a fixation or slow (i.e., nonsaccadic) movement.

Spatial distribution of eye positions

We measured the spatial distribution of eye positions in the head-centred coordinate frame. In all three conditions gaze-allocations show a spatial bias towards the upper centre of the visual field. The peak is above the vertical midline, 3.5° in free exploration (Figure 2A), 2.7° in continuous replay (Figure 2B), and 3.0° in 1 s frame replay (Figure 2C). Horizontally, the peak is displaced slightly to the left in free exploration (0.3°) and continuous replay (1.1°), and virtually at the centre for 1 s frame replay (0.1°). In sum, in all conditions the eyes direct gaze about 3° upwards on average, but show little bias sidewards.

As display sizes were matched in the two laboratory conditions, the height of the peaks can be compared directly to measure how pronounced a spatial bias is. With 5.6×10^{-5} of data in the maximum bin (Figure 2C), the maximum in 1 s frame replay is more than twice as high as in continuous replay (Figure 2B, 2.5×10^{-5}). This is a first indication that the spatial bias is enhanced by the discontinuous presentation in 1 s frame replay. The spatial spread in horizontal and vertical direction in both conditions for each movie quantifies this further. In all 15 movies the standard deviation of horizontal eye position is larger in continuous replay than in 1 s frame replay (Figure 2D, left). A sign-test shows that this fraction of movies is significant ($p = 6.1 \times 10^{-5}$). Similarly, the spread in vertical direction is larger in continuous replay in 12 out of 15 movies (Figure 2D, right), also a significant fraction ($p = .04$, sign-test). Consequently, gaze allocation is spatially more constrained for static than for continuous presentation.

We analyse the time course of spatial spread from the onset of each new stimulus in the 1 s frame condition. We find a dip at 283 ms (horizontal) and 338 ms (vertical) after the onset of a new frame (Figure 2E, black). As baseline, the same spatial spread for the continuous replay, for which the time point relative to the 1 s intervals has no particular meaning, shows little variation, and is above the value for 1 s frame replay (Figure 2E, grey). This shows that the spatial bias in 1 s frame replay is most pronounced about 300 ms after stimulus onset, even though there is no blank or enforced fixation between subsequent frames. These 300 ms may reflect the time needed for processing new visual information and making an according eye movement. We interpret the stronger spatial bias during discontinuous presentation along with its time course as evidence that the central bias often observed in laboratory experiments is to a large degree a consequence of "resetting" eyes to the stimulus centre when new information is onset.

Consistency between observers

Consistency between individuals is a necessary—though not sufficient— prerequisite for bottom-up models to predict gaze allocation from stimulus statistics alone. Hence, we test how consistent different observers are in their eye position, and to what degree this consistency is explained by common spatial biases. Measuring consistency by the average pairwise Euclidian distance between two observers (Figure 3A), we find the highest consistency within the 1 s frame replay observers with $86.7\% \pm 1.0\%$ (mean $\pm SD$ across the six pairs), which is significantly larger than within the continuous-replay observers, who reach $82.6\% \pm 1.4\%$, $t(10) = 5.97$, $p = 1.4 \times 10^{-4}$ (t-test), and across the laboratory conditions of $81.1\% \pm 2.3\%$, $t(20) = 5.63$, $p = 1.7 \times 10^{-5}$. The free-exploration observer is slightly more consistent with the continuous-replay observers ($82.6\% \pm 1.6\%$) than with the 1 s frame replay observers ($81.9\% \pm 1.0\%$), but this difference fails to reach significance, $t(6) = 0.76$, $p = .48$. In summary, observers in 1 s frame replay are more consistent among each other than with observers in other conditions or observers within and across other conditions.

Given the stronger spatial bias in 1 s frame replay, is the larger consistency in this condition an effect of spatial bias alone? We compare the within-condition consistencies to a random-reassignment baseline, which randomly shuffles seconds of presentation within each observer and movie. This baseline reflects the image-independent contribution to consistency, i.e., the contribution of the spatial bias. In both laboratory conditions, the mean baseline consistency remains significantly below the values obtained on the actual data, with $83.4\% \pm 1.2\%$, $t(10) = -5.25$, $p = 3.8 \times 10^{-4}$, for 1 s frame replay and $77.9\% \pm 2.3\%$, $t(10) = -4.38$, $p = .001$, for continuous replay. The

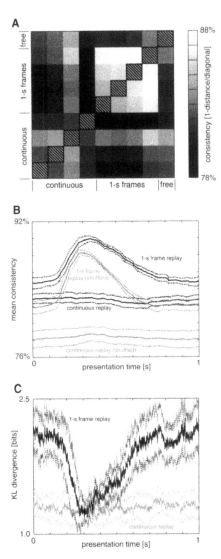

Figure 3. (A) Pairwise consistency measure of eye position for continuous replay (left 4 bins), 1 s frame replay (middle bins), and free exploration. Data averaged over observers and movies; diagonal at 100% by definition. (B) Consistency measure over presentation time for 1 s frame replay condition (upper black trace). Continuous replay (lower black trace) depicted for comparison. Stimulus-independent effects (random-reassignment baseline) presented in grey. All data averaged over subjects, mean ± SEM over movies depicted. (C) KL divergence as alternative measure of consistency of fixation distributions. Black: mean ± SEM KL divergence for the four 1 s frame observers; grey: continuous-replay observers. Note that lower KL implies higher consistency and absolute values are irrelevant in the present context as they depend on discretization.

baseline consistency significantly depends on condition, $t(10) = 5.22$, $p = 3.9 \times 10^{-4}$, suggesting that the difference between consistency in the two conditions is—at least in part—a consequence of the different strength of spatial bias. Furthermore, the baseline values are smaller than the actual values for all pairs of observers in both conditions, a fraction (6/6) that is significant even without taking the absolute values into account ($p = .03$, sign-test). Hence, interobserver consistency by itself is not a consequence of spatial bias alone, but contains a stimulus specific component. There is a stimulus-driven component to gaze allocation that is shared among observers. This effect, however, operates only in addition to consistencies imposed by generic spatial biases, which are consequences of shared preferred heading direction, setup, and presentation mode.

As the spatial bias exhibits a pronounced time course during a 1 s frame presentation, we complemented our analysis of spatial consistency time resolved. We find that consistency peaks at around the same time (at 89.9%, 342 ms after stimulus onset, Figure 3B, black) as the spatial bias. The baseline, which reflects the consistency imposed by spatial biases, peaks slightly earlier (282 ms, Figure 3B, grey) and stays consistently below the actual curve. Analysing the continuous-replay conditions analogously does not show any pronounced peak, neither in baseline nor in actual data.

From the Euclidian consistency measure alone it is unclear to what extent the seemingly increased consistency in 1 s frame replay results from the smaller spatial spread (Figure 2E). To directly compare the spatial distributions of eye positions we measure KL divergence between an observer's distribution and the distribution of all other observers in the same condition. The time course averaged over the four 1 s frame observers is very similar to the results from the Euclidian distance: Consistency increases first during viewing but quickly returns to baseline (Figure 3C, black). Since the time-locking is arbitrary in the continuous-replay condition, we again see a flat line. Remarkably, the consistency in the continuous-replay condition is higher (lower KL) on average and 1 s replay reaches comparable levels only between about 300 and 400 ms after stimulus onset. This implies that the difference in Euclidian distance is fully explained by the larger spatial spread during continuous replay.

Average saliency maps

As prototypical bottom-up model, we use Itti and Koch's (2000) saliency map. To take the entire map's values into account, we average the model saliency maps in a gaze-centred reference frame. The stimuli themselves (in the head-centred reference frame) do not exhibit a pronounced central peak (Figure 4, upper left), rather a stripe of highest saliency 91 pixels (9.0° in free

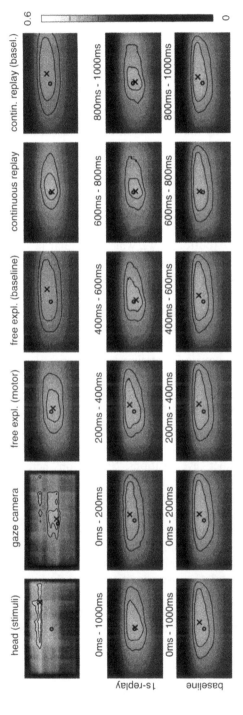

Figure 4. Average saliency maps centred at centre of gaze in various conditions. Circle: Centre of gaze direction (head direction in upper left); cross: Location of maximum; black lines: 95% and 90% contour lines. Top row, from the left: Stimuli (head-centred camera), gaze-centred camera (note that the centre of gaze is slightly offset from the centre of the image), free exploration (reconstructed from camera control signal), random-reassignment baseline for free exploration, continuous replay condition (all observers and movies), random-reassignment baseline for continuous replay. Middle row: 1 s frame replay condition, full presentation time; presentation time in 200 ms intervals after presentation onset. Bottom row: Random-reassignment baseline to middle row. Note that the difference between the gaze-centred camera and the free-exploration data reconstructed from the motor control is partly due to visual impression. The factual difference arises from the unavoidable cropping when reconstructing the gaze-centred map from the head-centred camera during a fixation at high eccentricity. Together with a potential slight misalignment of the cameras, this is the likely cause of the slight (0.5°) difference in estimated peak location.

exploration) above the midline. In gaze-centred coordinates, the peak is centred and found 9 pixels below the centre of gaze by the gaze-camera's image (Figure 4, top row, second panel from left), and 14 pixels below, when using the motor commands and the images of the head-centred camera as in the remainder of the analysis (third panel). These values correspond to 0.9° and 1.4° in free exploration, respectively. Although the peaks are rather broad with the 90th percentile spanning about half the camera's visual field (Figure 4), they are substantially narrower than in the baseline condition (third from right, Figure 4, top row). The continuous-replay result (top right panels) is qualitatively similar to free exploration: A peak centred at the centre of gaze that is wide, but substantially narrower than baseline. Averaged over the full 1 s presentation the peak in 1 s frame replay (middle row, left) is wider than in continuous replay, but narrower than the baseline (bottom row, left). Time-resolved analysis shows little variation for the baseline over presentation time (bottom row), which is similar in shape and peak position for all presentation conditions. In contrast, the peak for the actual data in 1 s frame replay starts narrowing in the 200–400 ms interval and remains at an about constant width for the remainder (Figure 4, middle row). This is a first indication, that saliency becomes more predictive of eye positions in the course of the presentation. In summary, this first qualitative analysis suggests that model saliency is best centred at gaze for continuous replay, and has a distinct time course for static presentations.

Predicting fixations by model saliency

To quantify how saliency relates to eye positions in the different conditions we use model saliency map values to discriminate eye positions from baseline locations, i.e., to "predict" eye positions. "Prediction" here does not imply causality, and it is well conceivable that correlations to other— hidden—scene properties explain away the effects. The area under the curve (AUC) of the receiver operator characteristics (ROC) serves as measure. It reaches 50% if saliency cannot discriminate eye positions from baseline locations and 100% for perfect discrimination. In free exploration, 12/15 movies have AUCs above chance, a significant fraction ($p = .04$, sign-test), with the mean AUC 53.2%±3.4% also significantly exceeding chance, $t(14) = 3.64$, $p = .003$. In the laboratory conditions, there are 60 pairs of observers and movies, of which 56 in each condition exceed chance ($p = 9.1 \times 10^{-13}$, sign-test). When averaging across observers, 13 (1 s replay) and 14 (continuous replay) movies exceed chance, and the means across movies are also significantly larger than chance in both conditions with 53.1%± 2.0%, $t(14) = 6.12$, $p = 2.7 \times 10^{-5}$, and 55.2%±2.7%, $t(14) = 7.58$, $p = 2.6 \times 10^{-6}$, respectively. Comparing the conditions, saliency predicts eye positions better in continuous replay than in 1 s frame replay, $t(14) = 4.00$, $p = .001$, paired t-test (Figure 5A), and slightly better in continuous replay than in free exploration, $t(14) = 2.29$, $p = .04$ (Figure 5B), while there is no difference between the prediction by saliency in 1 s frame replay as compared to free exploration, $t(14) = 0.09$, $p = .93$. In summary, saliency predicts eye positions to some extent in all conditions, and best for continuous replay.

A possible reason why saliency's prediction is worse in 1 s frame presentation than in continuous presentation is the time it takes until saliency gets effective. Subsequent frames are highly correlated in movies (temporal continuity), but independent in 1 s frame presentation. Saliency can thus only be expected to predict eye position after the visual system has processed the new stimulus and initiated an eye movement. To analyse how long it takes for saliency's prediction to become effective, we compute the AUC separately for each time point during the 1 s presentation. As expected, the prediction starts at chance level (50%) because the present frame is unrelated to the preceding one and generic effects are accounted for by baseline. After about 200 ms the prediction by saliency starts to become effective. The mean across movies starts to differ significantly from chance (at an alpha level of .036 corresponding to an expected false discovery rate of .05) for the first time after 256 ms and reaches its maximum after 624 ms (Figure 5C). This characterizes the time it takes until a bottom-up signal related to a novel stimulus affects eye position, and accounts in part for the worse average prediction of 1 s replay by saliency.

Predicting fixations across conditions

To test the mutual prediction between different conditions, we use the empirical saliency maps for the laboratory conditions to predict the other conditions. Within the same condition the prediction of the empirical saliency map, thanks to the small number of observers is always near ceiling, with $97.9\% \pm 1.0\%$ for continuous replay and $79.4\% \pm 3.1\%$ for 1 s replay (maps pooled over the full second). The eye positions on the respective frame in continuous replay condition predicts 1 s frame replay with a similar time course as model saliency and reaches an only slightly higher maximum of 56.2% (Figure 5D) compared to the 55.3% of saliency's prediction (Figure 5C). In turn, we test how well empirical saliency maps generated from 1 s frame replay predict gaze allocation. Prediction is best 280 ms after the stimulus corresponding to the shown frame was encountered in the real world (Figure 5E) or the frame was shown in the continuous-replay condition (Figure 5F). The peak AUC reaches about the same height in the free exploration ($54.8\% \pm 5.4\%$) as in the continuous-replay condition

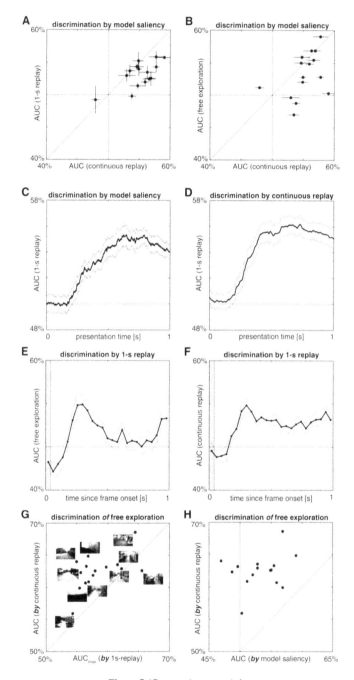

Figure 5 (*See caption opposite*)

(54.2% ± 3.2%), values that are not significantly different, $t(14) = 0.57$, $p = .58$, paired t-test.

As an upper bound for the prediction of free exploration by 1 s frame replay, we compute the best prediction by 1 s frame replay *for each movie*, reaching a mean AUC of 58.4% ± 3.5%. Note that this number is different from the maximum of the mean curve, resulting from the fact that the maximum prediction is reached at different times for different movies. Even in this measure that is beneficial for 1 s frame replay, the eye positions in continuous presentation predict real-world gaze allocation better (AUC 62.5% ± 2.7%) than the individual frame, $t(14) = 5.20$, $p = 1 \times 10^{-4}$, paired t-test. This advantage for predicting the real-world by continuous replay holds for all but one individual movie (14/15, Figure 5G), which constitutes a significant fraction of movies (Figure 5G), $p = 9.8 \times 10^{-4}$, sign-test. Both predictions are, however, correlated, $r = .60$, $p = .03$, and exceed chance for all movies. Qualitatively, both laboratory conditions predict eye positions during free exploration well, when the scene contains artificial structures with plenty of isolated objects (residential areas, indoor environments). In contrast, prediction is worse for natural outdoor sceneries (e.g., desert, open field). The continuous replay condition seems to have particular benefits in situations of highly dynamic character, such as passing uneven terrain or climbing a flight of stairs (Figure 5G).

Empirical saliency maps from continuous replay predict eye positions during free exploration better than the model saliency maps for all movies (15/15, Figure 5H) and significantly better on average, paired t-test, $t(14) = 9.50$, $p = 1.8 \times 10^{-7}$. If the peak prediction in each movie is considered (as in Figure 5G), this also hold for the empirical maps from 1 s replay (better in

---

Figure 5 (opposite). (A) Area under curve (AUC) for saliency map discriminating fixated from baseline locations ("prediction" of fixated locations); each data point corresponds to one movie and depicts mean AUC and SEM over the 4 observers; x-axis continuous replay condition, y-axis 1 s frame replay. (B) As Panel A, with results of free exploration on y-axis. (C) Time course of AUC for saliency predicting fixated locations over the 1 s presentation duration in the 1 s frame replay condition. Mean and SEM over movies. (Note that the curve does *not* need to level off to 0.5 at $t = 1$ s, as there is a sharp transition of stimuli, and the saliency map of the current stimulus can still be predictive in the subsequent frame). (D) Prediction of 1 s replay by continuous replay, using the empirical map recorded in continuous replay at the time the respective frame is shown. (E) Prediction of free exploration by maps generated from 1 s frame replay condition, mean and SEM over movies. The frame corresponding to the 1 s replay frame is shown from 0 to 40 ms (shaded area), but predicts best about 240–280 ms afterwards. (F) Prediction of continuous replay by maps generated from 1 s frame replay condition, analogous to Panel E. (G) Prediction of free exploration data by 1 s frame replay and by continuous replay. Each movie corresponds to one data point. For 1 s frame replay, the maximum AUC over all time points is used for each movie; nevertheless, the continuous replay condition predicts free exploration fixations better in all but one movie. Thumbnails identify selected movies. (H) Comparison of prediction of free exploration eye position between empirical saliency map from continuous replay (y-axis, same data as Panel G's y-axis) and saliency (x-axis, same data as Panel B's y-axis).

13/15 movies), $t(14) = 4.8$, $p = 2.6 \times 10^{-4}$. However, there is no individual time point (0, 40 ms, 80 ms, etc.) for which the mean prediction of this empirical map exceeds the prediction of the model map significantly, and for the first 160 ms the prediction is even significantly worse. Hence only the data from continuous replay is a better predictor of free-exploration eye movements than model saliency. This shows that the eye position in the laboratory has some predictive value for eye positions in the real world, but replicating the dynamic aspect of the scene, especially its temporal continuity, is of importance. In all, our results render the development of models based on laboratory data useful, but also stress the importance of spatially and temporally realistic stimuli, and validation in the real world.

DISCUSSION

We compare laboratory measurements of eye position to free exploration data. Observers' eye positions are more consistent when static frames are presented than for movies, but most of this surplus consistency is explained by spatial biases that are independent of the specific visual stimulus shown. A prototypical bottom-up model of attention, the saliency map, exhibits a weak but significant correlation with eye position inside and outside the laboratory. There is a slight advantage for saliency in continuous input over 1 s frame replay. This may be explained by the time a bottom-up signal needs to be processed and to trigger an eye movement when a novel stimulus is onset. That is, the benefit is a result of temporal continuity in the real world and continuous replay. Finally, we show that gaze recorded in the laboratory possesses some predictive power for gaze allocation in the real world, which is improved if the full dynamics of the stimulus is maintained.

Spatial biases on visual attention and gaze direction have received increasing interest. Mannan et al. (1996) stress that most of their features' effect on eye position vanishes when correcting analysis for shared spatial biases in stimuli and eye position. Similarly, Tatler et al. (2005) demonstrate that a varying spatial bias fully explains the changing effect of low-level features over prolonged viewing (Parkhurst et al., 2002). In turn, spatial biases—or prior knowledge on the likely locations of search targets—complement saliency in guiding eye movements in search (Torralba, Oliva, Castelhano, & Henderson, 2006). A probabilistic model that learns a saliency representation from natural scene statistics—combining bottom-up saliency and generic top-down biases—also outperforms image specific saliency models for free viewing (Zhang, Tong, Marks, Shan, & Cottrell, 2008). A systematic study on spatial biases in free viewing of natural scenes found that—at least under laboratory conditions—central fixation biases prevail irrespective of known biases in stimulus features (Tatler, 2007). This suggested either a role of the artificially limited setup that makes it more effective to look at the centre or a general bias to look straight ahead. Recently, we have used the relation of gaze-centred and head-centred feature statistics to argue against the latter alternative (Schumann et al., 2008). Individual features, as saliency does here, typically show an environment-dependent bias towards the upper half of the head-centred visual field. Gaze centres and refines this bias, which argues against a pure *centring* of eyes in their orbit. By using the camera-control signals relative to the head, we here do find a weak bias in viewing direction for free exploration. This bias is, however, not entirely central in the vertical, although the size of its upward deviation compared to the full oculomotor range still may justify a dubbing as "central". More importantly, however, the bias is strongest in the 1 s frame replay condition, especially compared to continuous replay. It exhibits a time course that suggests that new information arriving triggers this reset to the centre. This suggests that central bias indeed serves to select an optimal starting location for early scene processing on a limited screen when no other prior is available, the first hypothesis proposed by Tatler (2007). Provided the results on spatial priors in search (Torralba et al., 2007), it is likely that task and presentation conditions influence spatial biases. In free exploration, the spatial distribution of gaze suggests a bias towards the open path to be walked on, which is weaker in the laboratory conditions. This might be interpreted as prior for the implicit task of actually navigating the terrain. To what extent such motor planning and action contribute to the difference between "free exploration" and "free viewing" remains an open issue, for which virtual-reality experiments may provide interesting complementary data (cf. Jovancevic et al., 2006).

Interobserver consistency is a necessary condition for a purely bottom-up model to make any predictions (causal or correlative) on gaze allocation. If "bottom-up" is restricted to the presently presented stimulus, a successful prediction needs to exceed that of generic biases. In our small set of laboratory observers, interobserver consistency exceeds the baseline from generic biases alone in all conditions and observer pairs. Remarkably, the stimulus specific consistency in 1 s frame replay persists longer than the generic component. This suggests a prolonged effect of bottom-up signals for static stimuli and shows that bottom-up models can be useful for gaze prediction. Yet, our results stress that—even in the absence of an explicit task—a good part of interobserver consistency is determined by setup, presentation conditions, and—through spatial biases in head-centred videos—the stimuli.

As example for a bottom-up model, we tested Itti and Koch's (2000) saliency map, using its original version rather than its more recent developments (Cerf, Harel, Einhäuser, & Koch, 2008; Itti, 2005; Itti & Baldi, 2006). The correlation between model saliency and fixation probability is weak, but exceeding chance. It is, however, remarkable that even this static model achieves better predictions for the continuous replay condition, at least when compared to a baseline that takes generic biases into account. This stresses the importance to faithfully match not only the spatial but also the temporal statistics of stimuli to the real world. The importance of temporal dynamics is supported by the fact that empirical saliency derived from continuously presented stimuli predicts real-world gaze better than 1 s replay does, even when the latter is used at the optimal latency from stimulus presentation to its prediction. These results highlight that temporal continuity is a key principle not only for object recognition (Einhäuser, Hipp, Eggert, Körner, & König, 2005; Wallis & Rolls, 1997), but also for attention deployment under natural conditions. It thus might be used to learn attention models from natural stimulus statistics (Zhang et al., 2008).

One reason for the worse "prediction" in and by 1 s replay is the time needed to deploy bottom-up attention after stimulus onset. The minimal time needed for a bottom-up effect of a newly onset image that is unrelated to a previous one is the time to process this stimulus by the visual system and to execute one volitional eye movement. Although fast saccades are possible in response to natural scene categorization (Kirchner & Thorpe, 2006), even the fastest express saccades require at least 100 ms (Crouzet, Kirchner, & Thorpe, 2008). Hence, a delay of bottom-up responses till 150–200 ms after stimulus onset is in line with physiological constraints and—by itself—does not argue against the "preattentive" nature of target selection, suggested by the saliency map. Furthermore it is notable that there is no substantial decline of saliency's prediction over the 1 s period. Our data furthermore confirm earlier findings of a decline of interobserver consistency after an initial increase when the starting eye position is random or—in our case—determined by an unrelated stimulus (Tatler et al., 2005).

Provided the task's importance for eye movements (Buswell, 1935; Yarbus, 1967) and saliency map predictions (Henderson et al., 2007), its effect on the comparability of eyetracking in the real world to laboratory settings remains an interesting issue. It is likely that eye movements in highly trained, stereotypic motor tasks that are tied to specific settings (driving, sports, etc.) cannot be reproduced by visual display alone. Hence, eye movements obtained during real-world tasks provide the opportunity to improve and test computational models with data from natural tasks that are difficult to elicit in the laboratory. It is conceivable that such models may then even excel empirical data from the laboratory with respect to gaze prediction in real-world scenarios.

In any case, the comparison between laboratory and real-world data can help in uncovering the role of a specific modality (e.g., vision) in attention allocation during everyday implicit tasks, such as walking on uneven terrain, stair climbing, or navigating. As a first step in this direction, we here followed this approach for the arguably most naïve tasks possible, free viewing and free exploration.

In conclusion, we here quantified for the first time the differences between laboratory and real-world settings. The potential sources of the observed differences are manifold: First, it is unclear whether "free viewing" really represents a laboratory version of "free exploration". Second, there is the limited display in the laboratory; third, the effect of the restriction of head movements; and fourth, the absence of vestibular and other crossmodal information. Future experiments, that systematically modify task, display size, and location, head position, and input from modalities other than vision, and finally a larger number of observers performing multiple conditions, will allow a detailed investigation of all of these issues. Here, we delivered the proof of concept that our novel recording setup allows addressing these topics and provided first quantitative results.

REFERENCES

Baddeley, R. J., & Tatler, B. W. (2006). High frequency edges (but not contrast) predict where we fixate: A Bayesian system identification analysis. *Vision Research, 46*, 2824–2833.

Brainard, D. H. (1997). The Psychophysics Toolbox. *Spatial Vision, 10*, 433–436.

Brandt, T., Glasauer, S., & Schneider, E. (2006). A third eye for the surgeon. *Journal of Neurology, Neurosurgery. and Psychiatry, 77*, 278.

Buswell, G. T. (1935). *How people look at pictures: A study of the psychology of perception in art.* Chicago: University of Chicago Press.

Carmi, R., & Itti, L. (2006). Visual causes versus correlates of attentional selection in dynamic scenes. *Vision Research, 46*(26), 4333–4345.

Cerf, M., Harel, J., Einhäuser, W., & Koch, C. (2008). Predicting human gaze using low-level saliency combined with face detection. *Advances in Neural Information Processing, 20*, 241–248.

Chajka, K., Hayhoe, M., Sullivan, B., Pelz, J., Mennie, N., & Droll, J. (2006). Predictive eye movements in squash [Abstract]. *Journal of Vision, 6*(6), 481, 481a.

Crouzet, S., Kirchner, H., & Thorpe, S.J. (2008). Saccading towards faces in 100 ms. What's the secret? *Perception, 37*(ECVP Abstr. Suppl.), 119.

Cornelissen, F. W., Peters, E. M., & Palmer, J. (2002). The Eyelink Toolbox: Eye tracking with MATLAB and the Psychophysics Toolbox. *Behavior Research Methods, Instruments and Computers, 34*, 613–617.

Einhäuser, W., Hipp, J., Eggert, J., Körner, E., & König, P. (2005). Learning viewpoint invariant object representations using a temporal coherence. principle. *Biological Cybernetics, 93*, 79–90.

Einhäuser, W., & König, P. (2003). Does luminance-contrast contribute to a saliency map for overt visual attention? *European Journal of Neuroscience, 17*, 1089–1097.

Einhäuser, W., Moeller, G. U., Schumann, F., Conradt, J., Vockeroth, J., Bartl, K., et al. (2009). Eye-head coordination during free exploration in human and cat. *Annals of the New York Academy of Sciences, 1164*, 353–366.

Einhäuser, W., Rutishauser, U., & Koch, C. (2008). Task-demands can immediately reverse the effects of sensory-driven saliency in complex visual stimuli. *Journal of Vision, 8*(2), 1–19.

Einhäuser, W., Schumann, F., Bardins, S., Bartl, K., Böning, G., Schneider, E., & König, P. (2007). Human eye-head co-ordination in natural exploration. *Network: Computation in Neural Systems, 18*(3), 267–297.

Einhäuser, W., Schumann, F., Vockeroth, J., Bartl, K., Cerf, M., Harel, J., et al. (2009). Distinct roles for eye and head movements in selecting salient image parts during natural exploration. *Annals of the New York Academy of Sciences, 1164*, 188–193.

Einhäuser, W., Spain, M., & Perona, P. (2008). Objects predict fixations better than early saliency. *Journal of Vision, 8*(14), 1–26.

Elazary, L., & Itti, L. (2008). Interesting objects are visually salient. *Journal of Vision, 8*(3), 1–15.

Fairchild, M. D., Johnson, G. M., Babcock, J., & Pelz, J. B. (2001). *Is your eye on the ball? Eye tracking golfers while putting.* Retrieved from http://www.cis.rit.edu/people/faculty/fairchild/

Fuller, H. J. (1992). Head movement propensity. *Experimental Brain Research, 92*, 152–164.

Hayhoe, M., Ballard, D., Triesch, J., Shinoda, H., Alvar, P., & Sullivan, B. (2002). Vision in natural and virtual environments. *Proceedings of the Symposium on Eye Tracking Research and Applications*, 7–13.

Hayhoe, M., Mannie, N., Sullivan, B., & Gorgos, K. (2005). The role of internal models and prediction in catching balls. *Proceedings of AAAI*, Fall 2005.

Henderson, J. M., Brockmole, J. R., Castelhano, M. S., & Mack, M. (2007). Visual saliency does not account for eye-movements during visual search in real-world scenes. In R. van Gompel, M. Fischer, W. Murray, & R. Hill (Eds.), *Eye movement research: Insights into mind and brain.* (pp. 537–562) Oxford: Elsevier.

Itti, L. (2005). Quantifying the contribution of low-level saliency to human eye movements in dynamic scenes. *Visual Cognition, 12*(6), 1093–1123.

Itti, L., & Baldi, P. (2006). Bayesian surprise attracts human attention. *Advances in Neural Information Processing Systems, 19*, 1–8.

Itti, L., & Koch, C. (2000). A saliency-based search mechanism for overt and covert shifts of visual attention. *Vision Research, 40*(10–12), 1489–1506.

Itti, L., Koch, C., & Niebur, E. (1998). A model of saliency-based visual attention for rapid scene analysis. *IEEE Transactions on Pattern Analysis and Machine Intelligence, 20*(11), 1254–1259.

Jovancevic, J., Sullivan, B., & Hayhoe, M. (2006). Control of attention and gaze in complex environments. *Journal of Vision, 6*, 1431–1450.

Kayser, C., Nielsen, K. K., & Logothetis, N. K. (2006). Fixations in natural scenes: Interaction of image structure and image content. *Vision Research, 46*(16), 2535–2545.

Kirchner, H., & Thorpe, S. J. (2006). Ultra-rapid object detection with saccadic eye movements: Visual processing speed revisited. *Vision Research, 46*(11), 1762–1776.

Koch, C., & Ullman, S. (1985). Shifts in selective visual attention: Towards the underlying neural circuitry. *Human Neurobiology, 4*, 219–227.

Krieger, G., Rentschler, I., Hauske, G., Schill, K., & Zetzsche, C. (2000). Object and scene analysis by saccadic eye-movements: An investigation with higher-order statistics. *Spatial Vision, 13*, 201–214.

Land, M. F., & Hayhoe, M. (2001). In what ways do eye movements contribute to everyday activities? *Vision Research, 41*, 3559–3565.

Land, M. F., & Lee, D. N. (1994). Where we look when we steer. *Nature, 369*, 742–744.

Land, M. F., & McLeod, P. (2000). From eye movements to actions: How batsmen hit the ball. *Nature Neuroscience, 3*, 1340–1345.

Land, M. F., Mennie, N., & Rusted, J. (1999). The roles of vision and eye movements in the control of activities of daily living. *Perception, 28*, 1311–1328.

Land, M. F., & Tatler, B. W. (2001). Steering with the head: The visual strategy of a racing driver. *Current Biology, 11*, 1215–1220.

Mannan, S. K., Ruddock, K. H., & Wooding, D. S. (1996). The relationship between the locations of spatial features and those of fixations made during visual examination of briefly presented images. *Spatial Vision, 10*(3), 165–188.

Navalpakkam, V., & Itti, L. (2005). Modeling the influence of task on attention. *Vision Research, 45*, 205–231.

Parkhurst, D., Law, K., & Niebur, E. (2002). Modeling the role of salience in the allocation of overt visual attention. *Vision Research, 42*, 107–123.

Pelli, D. G. (1997). The VideoToolbox software for visual psychophysics: Transforming numbers into movies. *Spatial Vision, 10*, 437–442.

Peters, R. J., & Itti, L. (2008). Applying computational tools to predict gaze direction in interactive visual environments. *ACM Transactions on Applied Perception, 5*(2), 8.

Peters, R. J., Iyer, A., Itti, L., & Koch, C. (2005). Components of bottom-up gaze allocation in natural images. *Vision Research, 45*(18), 2397–2416.

Privitera, C., & Stark, L. (2000). Algorithms for defining visual regions-of-interest: Comparison with eye fixations. *IEEE Transactions on Pattern Analysis and Machine Intelligence, 22*(9), 970–982.

Reinagel, P., & Zador, A. M. (1999). Natural scene statistics at the centre of gaze. *Network: Computation in Neural Systems, 10*, 341–350.

Rothkopf, C. A., Ballard, D. H., & Hayhoe, M. M. (2007). Task and context determine where you look. *Journal of Vision, 7*(14), 1–20.

Schneider, E., Bartl, K., Bardins, S., Dera, T., Boning, G., & Brandt, T. (2005). Eye movement driven head-mounted camera: It looks where the eyes look. *Proceedings of the IEEE International Conference on Systems, Man and Cybernetics*, 2437–2442.

Schneider, E., Bartl, K., Dera, T., Boning, G., Wagner, P., & Brandt, T. (2006). Documentation and teaching of surgery with an eye movement driven head-mounted camera: See what the surgeon sees and does. *Studies in Health Technology and Informatics, 119*, 486–490.

Schneider, E., Villgrattner, T., Vockeroth, J., Bartl, K., Kohlbecher, S., Bardins, S., et al. (2009). EyeSeeCam: An eye movement-driven head camera for the examination of natural visual exploration. *Annals of the New York Academy of Sciences, 1164*, 461–467.

Schumann, F., Einhäuser, W., Vockeroth, J., Bartl, K., Schneider, E., & König, P. (2008). Salient features in gaze-aligned recordings of human visual input during free exploration of natural environments. *Journal of Vision, 8*(14), 1–17.

Sprague, N., & Ballard, D. (2004). Eye movements for reward maximization. *Advances in Neural Information Processing* (NPIS*2003).

Sprague, N., Ballard, D., & Robinson, A. (2007). Modeling embodied visual behaviors. *ACM Transactions on Applied Perception, 4*(2), 1–23.

Stahl, J. S. (1999). Amplitude of human head movements associated with horizontal saccades. *Experimental Brain Research, 126*, 41–54.

Tatler, B. W. (2007). The central fixation bias in scene viewing: Selecting an optimal viewing position independently of motor biases and image feature distributions. *Journal of Vision, 7*(14), 1–17.

Tatler, B. W., Baddeley, R. J., & Gilchrist, I. D. (2005). Visual correlates of fixation selection: Effects of scale and time. *Vision Research, 45*, 643–659.

Torralba, A., Oliva, A., Castelhano, M. S., & Henderson, J. M. (2006). Contextual guidance of eye movements and attention in real-world scenes: The role of global features in object search. *Psychological Review, 113*, 766786.

Tosi, V., Mecacci, L., & Pasquali, E. (1997). Scanning eye movements made when viewing film: Preliminary observations. *International Journal of Neuroscience, 92*(1–2), 47–52.

Vockeroth, J., Bardins, S., Bartl, K., Dera, T., & Schneider, E. (2007). The combination of a mobile gaze-driven and a head-mounted camera in a hybrid perspective setup. *Proceedings of the IEEE Conference on Systems, Man and Cybernetics*, 2576–2581.

Wallis, G., & Rolls, E. T. (1997). Invariant face and object recognition in the visual system. *Progress in Neurobiology*, *51*(2), 167–194.

Yarbus, A. L. (1967). *Eye movements and vision*. New York: Plenum Press.

Zhang, L., Tong, M. H., Marks, T. K., Shan, H., & Cottrell, G. W. (2008). SUN: A Bayesian framework for saliency using natural statistics. *Journal of Vision*, *8*(7), 1–20.

VISUAL COGNITION, 2009, 17 (6/7), 1159–1184

Gaze control and memory for objects while walking in a real world environment

Jason A. Droll and Miguel P. Eckstein

Department of Psychology, University of California Santa Barbara, CA, USA

Assessments of gaze behaviour and object memory are typically done in the context of experimental paradigms briefly presenting transient static images of synthetic or real scenes. Less is known about observers' gaze behaviour and memory for objects in a real world environment. While wearing a mobile eyetracker, 20 subjects performed a task in which they walked around a building eight times and were either told to walk normally, or to also expect to be asked about what they saw following their walk. During the course of their walk, nine objects along their path were exchanged for similar token objects of the same category (e.g., whisk broom for push broom). Observers told to prepare for a memory test were much more likely to notice object changes than observers simply told to walk normally (32% vs. 5%). Detected object changes were also fixated for longer duration prior to the change, suggesting a role of task demand in gaze control and the selective storage of visual information.

Keywords: Change detection; Eye movements; Walking; Object memory; Real world.

Observers' intrinsic proficiency at coordinating visual tasks is often neglected in laboratory experiments with designs that suppress the ecological context in which vision is most well suited and adapted. Laboratory experiments often employ tasks with a fixed trial structure in which two-dimensional images of sparse synthetic stimuli are briefly presented within the confines of a computer monitor, and observers are instructed how to report their visual judgement with an arbitrary behavioural response. Such controlled methods are necessary for isolating visual and cognitive processes and powerful to test psychological theories, but it is not clear how

Please address all correspondence to Jason A. Droll, Human Factors Practice, Exponent, Inc., 5401 McConnell Avenue, Los Angeles, CA, USA. E-mail: jdroll@exponent.com

This work was supported by National Institutes of Health/Public Health Service Research Grants R01 EY015925 and by IC Postdoctoral Research Fellowship Program Grant 8-444069-23149 (icpostdoc.org). We thank Carter Phelps, Jessica Gaska, Nick Bernstein, Paul Hacker, and Sanjay Athalye for help running subjects and analysis of eyetracking video.

© 2009 Taylor & Francis
DOI: 10.1080/13506280902797125

performance measures acquired in laboratory contexts generalize to an understanding of how vision is used in ordinary, real world behaviour. The purpose of the present paper is to investigate visual processes under more natural circumstances. Specifically, we sought to test the role task demands have in observers' use of eye movements and storage of object information in memory while walking within a real world environment.

TASK DEMANDS AND THE GUIDANCE OF EYE MOVEMENTS

For over 40 years, it has been known that observers direct their gaze towards regions of the scene relevant to their task (Buswell, 1935; Yarbus, 1961, 1967). More recent experiments have reinforced the critical importance of task demand by demonstrating that in real world environments, across a variety of everyday tasks such as driving, walking, sports, playing a piano, visual search, hand-washing, and making tea or sandwiches, fixations are tightly linked to the momentary operations of a task (Chen & Zelinsky, 2006; Hayhoe, Shrivastava, Mruczek, & Pelz, 2003; Land, 2004; Land & Hayhoe, 2001; Land, Mennie, & Rusted, 1999; Mennie, Hayhoe, & Sullivan, 2007; Pelz & Canosa, 2001; Pelz, Hayhoe, & Loeber, 2001; Turano, Geruschat, & Baker, 2003; Turano, Geruschat, Baker, Stahl, & Shapiro, 2001; Zelinsky, Rao, Hayhoe, & Ballard, 1997). Such task-directed behaviour differs from experiments in which subjects simply view images passively, and have no expectation of what information is relevant to their goals or interests. Observers may be engaged in object recognition, remembering object locations and identity, or performing some other visual operation. Although there is some relationship between fixation location and image properties such as contrast or chromatic salience, these factors usually account for only a modest proportion of the variance (Foulsham & Underwood, 2008; Itti & Koch, 2000, 2001; Parkhurst & Niebur, 2003, 2004) and image salience has negligible effect when observers are actively engaged in a task (Einhauser, Rutishauser, & Koch, 2008). In natural behaviour where the task is well defined, the demands of the task also have an overwhelming influence on gaze control. Thus, if the behavioural goals are clearly defined, even such as making a peanut-butter and jelly sandwich, an observer's actions can be reasonably assumed to reflect the internal cognitive representation of the task.

Eye movements can be used to acquire visual information "just-in-time" for the momentary demands of a task (Ballard, Hayhoe, Pook, & Rao, 1997), but there is clearly a need for storing visual information across successive fixations. What is the relationship between eye movements and visual memory? Under what conditions is information expected to be relevant for storage directed by gaze? Is fixated information necessarily stored in memory? Are observers sensitive to a change in visual information that was earlier stored and later refixated?

ESTIMATING MEMORY CAPACITY AND MEMORY USAGE ACROSS TASKS AND CONTEXTS

During an ordinary task such as making a sandwich, observers frequently refixate objects in the scene (Ballard, Hayhoe, & Pelz, 1995; Hayhoe et al., 2003; Land et al., 1999; Pelz & Canosa, 2001; Pelz et al., 2001). Frequent refixations suggest that minimal information is stored internally, as if the world itself is used as a form of "external memory" (Ballard et al., 1997; O'Regan, 1992). Such minimal use of memory is contrasted with performance in memory tasks using traditional experimental paradigms with artificial or synthetic stimuli. Performance in those tasks has suggested the capacity of working memory to be about four objects (Luck & Vogel, 1997; Vogel, Woodman, & Luck, 2001; Wheeler & Treisman, 2002). However, using more realistic stimuli, and after viewing scenes for longer durations or with a greater number of fixations, visual memory may be more robust (Hollingworth, 2006b; Irwin & Zelinsky, 2002; Melcher, 2001, 2006). When viewing images of real world scenes, previously fixated objects are more likely than chance to be identified over novel objects 24 hours after viewing (Hollingworth, 2005). Such robust memory suggests that observers are storing detailed object information, including their position within the scene and their orientation (Hollingworth, 2006a, 2009; Tatler, Gilchrist, & Land, 2005).

Disparate estimates of memory capacity and memory usage across experiments may be due to at least two factors. First, there are significant differences in the task context. Many memory experiments employ artificial tasks in which observers are instructed to store as much information in a scene as possible, or to seek changes between successively presented images. Natural behaviour is unlikely to include such indiscriminate storage of information. Thus, it is not clear how subjects incidentally acquire and store visual information when not instructed to do so. Memory literature has a long history of distinguishing between intentional or incidentally stored information (Craik & Tulving, 1975). For example, observers are more likely to recognize real world objects that they were instructed to remember, with evidence of selective storage for at least 2 days following exposure (Lampinen, Copeland, & Neuschatz, 2001). However, distinctions between intentional or incidental memory are only infrequently addressed in vision studies monitoring the encoding of objects via eye movements and subsequent storage of this information (Castelhano & Henderson, 2005; Williams, Henderson, & Zacks, 2005).

A second reason for disparate estimates of memory capacity is the use of different visual contexts. Although sparse artificial stimuli, such as arrays of coloured rectangles (Luck & Vogel, 1997), are arguably necessary to test vision without contamination from semantic associations, real world environments are tremendously more complex, often including hundreds of objects, with different shapes, sizes, and colours. Stimuli presentation in traditional experiments is also transient and brief, lasting only a few hundred milliseconds. Brief, transient images, are also often static and subtend only the visual angle of the monitor, lacking the larger retinal eccentricities and depth cues of real three-dimensional environments and observers typically exhibit a potentially artificial central-bias in gaze behaviour when viewing images in the laboratory (Schumann et al., 2008; Tatler, 2007). Real environments, on the other hand, are immersive and often perpetually present, allowing observers to scrutinize scene detail with leisure, fixating and attending to objects in a sequence and for durations determined by observers' own internal agenda. This longer viewing time can result in improved retention of visual information (Melcher, 2006). Subjects have also shown improved performance in memory tasks when the scene is representative of a real world environment, suggesting that findings from memory tasks using artificial stimuli may not generalize to ecological behaviour (Tatler et al., 2005; Tatler & Melcher, 2007). It should also be noted that viewing objects in the context of real world scenes influences objects' localization (Eckstein, Dresher, & Shimozaki, 2006) as well as their observers' detection of objects (de Graef, Christiaens, & d'Ydewalle, 1990).

DETECTING CHANGES IN NATURAL SCENES

Perhaps intermediate to the extremes of natural behaviour and traditional laboratory experiments are contexts and scenes that demonstrate the phenomenon of change blindness. Change blindness refers to the occurrence in which observers are unaware of otherwise salient changes to objects in a natural scene when the change is masked by an eye movement (Grimes, 1996), a simulated mud splash (O'Regan, Rensink, & Clark, 1999), a flickering grey screen (Blackmore, Brelstaff, Nelson, & Troscianko, 1995; Rensink, O'Regan, & Clark, 1997), or movie edit (Levin & Simons, 1997). These experimenters have suggested that while we can retain general information about the "gist" of a scene quite easily, memory for scene detail is fleeting and sparse (for reviews, see Simons, 2000).

Failure to notice otherwise salient changes may also be a phenomenon in the real world. For example, only half of observers noticed the change in identity to a person with whom they had been conversing a few seconds earlier (Levin, Simons, Angelone, & Chabris, 2002; Simons & Levin, 1998). It is not clear why observers are so poor at detecting changes. Some instances of change blindness appear to be caused by a failure to compare previously stored information (Angelone, Levin, & Simons, 2003; Hollingworth, 2003; Simons, Chabris, Schnur, & Levin, 2002; Varakin & Levin, 2006). However, when viewing rendered images of natural scenes, observers may also miss changes due to a failure to fixate and attend to the object before or after the change, suggesting a failure to encode the information necessary to make a comparison (Hollingworth & Henderson, 2002). Yet there is also evidence to suggest that observers are capable of encoding peripheral information when detecting object changes (Zelinsky, 2001). The precise role of eye movements and attention in detecting changes in real world environments is not known, as there has not yet been an experiment monitoring gaze while observers encounter object changes.

In an experimental paradigm similar to the present paper, observers infrequently detected changes while navigating through a virtual world, where the changes are separated in time by several seconds (Karacen & Hayhoe, 2008). As observers walked a circular 22 m route, they passed by eight objects. After a variable number of laps, objects disappeared, appeared, were replaced, or underwent a change in their location. Rates of change detection were generally low ($\sim 25\%$). However, observers may have been better at detecting the changes had they been told to either expect changes, or to prepare for some sort of memory test following their walk. Also, although the virtual world was considerably more complex than most experimental displays, it was relatively sparse in comparison to the complexity of real world environments, and it is not clear if observers' rates of change detection would be higher or lower when interacting in a more complex real world environment.

MONITORING GAZE AND MEMORY AS OBSERVERS NAVIGATE THROUGH THE REAL WORLD

The present experimental manipulation was designed to examine the role of task demand on gaze control, and the storage of visual information in a real world environment. If observers are instructed to report what objects they recalled encountering in their environment, they may be more likely to direct gaze towards objects, and to encode and store fixated information. Reflecting this memory, observers may also be more likely to report object changes.

METHODS

Two walking tasks

Subjects were met by the experimenter in the laboratory and escorted to the testing site, approximately a 2 minute walk to the Life Science building. During the escorted walk, subjects were told that the purpose of the experiment was for researchers "to better understand how people moved their eyes while walking". At the testing site, subjects were introduced to two male assistants. The first assistant helped prepare and calibrate the eyetracker. Following calibration, subjects were instructed to walk around the building eight times in a clockwise direction. In both the walking only and the walking and memory condition, subjects were instructed to walk as they would normally, at a comfortable pace. In the walking and memory condition, subjects were given further instruction that after their eight laps, they "would be asked about what they saw". The purpose of the walking and memory condition was to assess how a modest change in task instruction might influence observers' control of gaze and memory for objects. Fifteen subjects participated in the walking only condition and nine subjects participated in the walking and memory condition.[1] During the course of their walk, the second assistant served as an escort and walked alongside, and slightly behind, the subject. The purpose of the escort was to address any possible questions from passing by pedestrians regarding the equipment worn by the subject, and to make the subject more at ease during the walk. Both the subject and the escort were instructed not to converse during the walk to avoid possible interactions between gaze used during walking and gaze during conversation. At the beginning of each lap, the experimenter would hold up a sign indicating the lap number which the subject was beginning (e.g., "3" when starting the third lap). The purpose of the sign was to both keep track of the number of laps navigated during the experiment, and to facilitate video coding. The duration of each lap was approximately 90 seconds.

Object changes

As subjects circumnavigated the building, they passed by nine objects set out by the experimenters. The positions of the nine objects are shown in Figure 1. Each of the nine objects was consistent with the semantic context of the environment. Before each experimental session, all objects were displayed in

---

[1] A different number of subjects were included in each condition because of the variable number of subjects for whom eyetracking data was sufficiently robust to permit analysis. Subjects continued to be run until five subjects in each condition had a sufficient eye track.

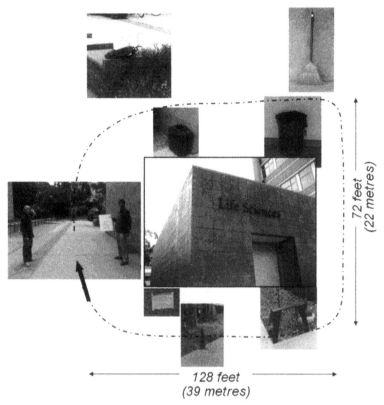

72 feet
(22 metres)

128 feet
(39 metres)

Figure 1.   Observers circumnavigated a building eight times while passing nine objects. Each of the objects was exchanged for an alternate token between the fourth and fifth lap. To view this figure in colour, please see the online issue of the Journal.

either State 1 or State 2, as listed in Table 1. Each of these objects was present during the subjects' first four laps. Between the fourth and the fifth lap, all of the objects were exchanged with another token object of the same category type (e.g., whisk broom to push broom). When not appearing along the course, alternate token objects were hidden either in the building, behind walls, or inside containers. To avoid the possibility of the subject noticing any substitutions being made, object changes were made by the experimenter and assistant as the subject was walking along a different side of the building. The order of object presentation was counterbalanced such that half of the subjects were first exposed to objects in State 1, followed by State 2, and the other half of subjects were presented with the reverse sequence. Before the experiment, subjects were not told about the surrounding objects, or the possibility that any objects might undergo a change between laps.

TABLE 1
Objects and their two possible states

		Object state	
Object		1	2
1.	Sawhorse	green	red
2.	Backpack	purple	grey
3.	Broom	whisk broom	push broom
4.	Luggage (square)	red	purple
5.	Trash can	large grey	small green tin
6.	Traffic cone	tall (28")	short (12")
7.	Assistant's shirt (short sleeve)	red	green
8.	Experimenter's shirt (long sleeve)	green	red
9.	Advertisement	blue	yellow

Between the subjects' fourth and fifth lap, each of the nine objects were exchanged from one state to another. The order of the change was counterbalanced across subjects.

Postexperiment questionnaire

At the completion of the eighth and final lap, subjects were asked to verbally respond to a series of questions. Initial questions were open ended and later questions were more specific. The questionnaire began with, "What did you notice during your walk?" and "What objects do you remember seeing?" The experimenter recorded whether subjects spontaneously mentioned noticing any of the experimental objects, or if they reported noticing their change. Subsequent questions were more detailed, inquiring, "Do you remember seeing a _____?", mentioning one of the seven objects placed around the building (not including the two shirts). Whenever subjects reported seeing a particular object, they were asked to provide more detail, in order to determine if they remembered the object in the initial state, before the change, or the final state, after the change, or if they detected the change. The second to last question asked the subject to report the colour of the assistant's shirt without turning around to face him. The final question was whether the subject remembered the colour of the shirt the experimenter was initially wearing during the beginning of the experiment. Subjects wore a microphone to their collar to record their responses, which were simultaneously transcribed by the experimenter.

Monitoring gaze

Subjects wore an Applied Science Laboratories (ASL) mobile eyetracker which monitored the position of the right eye using corneal IR reflection and pupil. The video-based tracker was mounted on a pair of lightweight goggles and included a scene camera with a field of view coincident with each observer's line of sight. Alternate frames of the 60 Hz video recorded either the scene, or eye, image, resulting in an effective sampling rate of 30 Hz. Spatial accuracy had a lower bound of approximately one degree, although accuracy was sometimes compromised with noise due to outdoor reflections. Video from each camera was recorded by a digital tape recorder placed inside a hip belt worn by the subject.

Before the subject began walking the eight laps, a calibration procedure was performed by asking the subject to stand still and fixate the end of a stick held by the experimenter in twelve different positions, spanning the field of view of the scene camera. The 12 points were on a vertical plane orthogonal to the observers' line of sight, approximately 15 feet from the subject, representing the approximate distance subjects would be when expected to fixate objects in the environment. After walking the eight laps, and after answering the questionnaire, the calibration procedure was repeated on each side of the building in order to accommodate the unique lighting conditions for each path.

After each experiment, ASL software was used to separate alternate video frames to allow for eye calibration. A digital video was then generated, displaying the image from the scene camera, on top of which was projected a cursor indicating the subject's momentary direction of gaze (Figure 2).

Figure 2. Video frame captured from scene camera. Superimposed crosshairs indicate direction of gaze. Scene includes small traffic cone and red sawhorse. To view this figure in colour, please see the online issue of the Journal.

Calibrations for each walkway were used to improve the track. The final video also included a frame count used as a time indicator to document the start and end of fixations.

Data analysis

The timing of each fixation, and the direction of gaze, was determined through frame-by-frame analysis of the output video with fixation cross-hairs. Video coding included documenting the start and end time for each video frame in which gaze was directed to any of the nine objects of interest for each of the eight laps. Due to track noise from outdoor sunlight, the presence of the crosshairs was occasionally intermittent. Thus, rather than classifying fixations by applying an acceleration threshold of eye position, or a minimum number of frames to a particular location, all continuous frames with the crosshairs at a particular location were recorded as a single fixation, regardless of the number of frames in the sequence. Thus, there was an occasional fixation lasting only one frame (33 ms), although this was a minority of fixations (< 10%). Video records were coded blindly with regard to experimental condition. Video-coders were aware of the lap number due to a sign subjects passed by on each lap that indicated their progress. Hand-coded data was then analysed using inhouse software written in Matlab (Mathworks) to calculate each subject's total fixation duration on each of the objects for each of the eight laps, and to sort this data with respect to the subject's responses to the questionnaire.

RESULTS

Memory for objects

Memory for objects was assessed through verbal report during the postexperiment questionnaire. Subjects' questionnaire responses for each object was coded into five possible categories: No memory for the object, incorrect memory (recalled the object, but described an incorrect state), remembered the prechange object state, remembered the postchange object state, or reported a change between the two states, which was described either correctly or incorrectly. Figure 3 plots the frequency of each of these responses for each task condition. There were two main differences in subjects' responses with respect to task condition. First, subjects in the walking only condition were nearly twice as likely to not report seeing one of the experimental objects as subjects in the walking and memory condition (walking vs. memory, chi-square, $df = 1, p < .005$). The second difference was

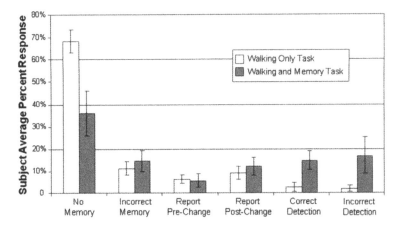

Figure 3. Average percentage of responses across subjects for each possible memory for the object or detection of object change. Possible responses included not remembering an object (no memory), describing the object inaccurately (incorrect memory), reporting the object with features before or after the change (report pre-/postchange), and detecting the change and reporting both object states either correctly or incorrectly (correct/incorrect detection). Subjects instructed to prepare to be asked about what they saw (walking and memory condition) were more likely to detect object changes than subjects asked only to walk. Error bars represent SEMs across subjects.

that subjects in the walking and memory condition were much more likely to report the object change than subjects in the walking only condition (walking vs. memory, chi-square, $df = 1$, $p < .005$). The two groups had similarly low rates of incorrectly describing the recalled object, or reporting the object in the state before, or after, the change. Subjects in neither condition reported seeing objects that had not been present in the environment or changes that did not occur (e.g., false alarms).

The pattern of response to the questionnaire demonstrates how the modest change in task demand, informing subjects that we would ask them "about what they saw" after their walk, strongly influenced what information in the scene subjects chose to store in memory and compare across successive viewings. The higher frequency of change detection for objects in the walking and memory condition suggests that observers in the walking only condition did not use the full capacity of their memory for the objects tested.

Rates of change detection for each object in each task condition are plotted in Figure 4A. A clear result is the different rates of change detection across the nine objects for each experimental condition (chi-square, $df = 8$, both $ps < .001$). Possible influences on the variable rates of detection across the objects will be addressed in the discussion section.

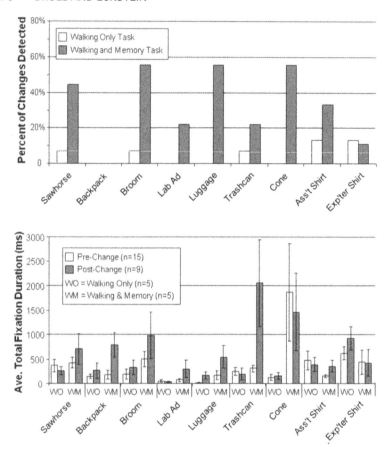

Figure 4. (A) Percentage of subjects who detected changes for each of the nine objects. (B) Average total fixation duration on each object pre- (white) and postchange (grey) for both the walking only (WO) and walking and memory (WM) conditions. Error bars represent SEM between subjects.

Gaze control

While the pattern of subjects' verbal response suggests that the use of working memory is sensitive to the demands of a task, it is not clear from explicit report if observers in the different task conditions had a different strategy for acquiring scene information, which may include a different use of gaze. One possibility is that the two groups had a similar use of gaze, but that observers in the walking and memory condition were more likely to store attended information in memory knowing that that task might probe such information. A second possibility is that the different pattern of explicit report corresponded to a different pattern of eye movements, as subjects attended to the experimental objects before selecting them for storage.

Five subjects in each task condition had sufficiently robust eyetracking data for analysis. Lab assistants aiding as video-coders were provided with digital video of each subject's video but not informed of the subject's task condition. The relatively small fraction of subjects for whom we could recover adequate eye data was due to the wide dynamic range of lighting conditions throughout the walking path, the sensitivity of the eyetracker to sunlight, and the need for the cameras to be stabilized to the head while walking during the entire experimental session, which was upwards of 12 minutes. By visual inspection, video records for each subject were easily categorized into sessions with inconsistent and frequently disappearing eye track, or a consistent and relatively stable eye track, which was used for further analysis.

From casual inspection of the video, there were no clear apparent differences in behaviour between the two experimental groups. Each group took approximately 90 s to circumnavigate the building, and subjects maintained a comfortable walking pace throughout each lap. In other walking tasks, such as being required to step on specific locations, observers' fixations are directed on the path approximately two steps ahead (Palta & Vickers, 2002). However, in the present experiment, and as has been shown in other tasks that encourage participants to walk normally (Pelz & Rothkopf, 2007), our observers typically fixated at much greater distances, including many of the surrounding objects and buildings. The following analysis addresses differences in fixation duration across all experimental objects, and between missed and detected changes in the context of fixations to objects before and after objects underwent a change.

Fixations on objects.   Figure 4B plots the average total fixation duration to each object, for each experimental condition, in the four laps before and after the change. Within each of the four categories (walking only and walking and memory, pre- and postchange), there were differences in fixation duration across the set of experimental objects (chi-square, $df = 8$, all $ps < .001$). Many factors may have contributed to differences in fixation duration across the set of objects. Note that while each of the eight laps took an average of 90 s, there was variation in the exposure duration of each object in the environment. Objects appearing soon after a turn (e.g., luggage) were in observers' field of view for less time than objects appearing at the end of a path, before a turn (e.g., traffic cone). Thus, there was greater opportunity to fixate some objects than others. For the purpose of the present experiment, our analysis concentrates on the relationship between gaze behaviour and change detection. Next, we investigate the relationship between fixation duration on objects whose change was missed and objects whose change was noticed.

Fixation behaviour before object changes. Fixations before object changes are of particular interest because the only difference in the two tasks was that subjects in the walking only condition were simply told to walk around the building as they would normally, and subjects in the walking and memory condition were given the modest additional instruction that they would later be "asked about what they saw". Fixations in the first four laps would thus reflect either a default fixation behaviour, or fixation behaviour specific to the anticipation of reporting what had been in their environment. Fixations that occurred in the context of detecting changes would not yet have occurred, as the changes had not yet been induced.

The most noticeable and relevant result in fixation behaviour before changes occurred is the longer fixation duration on objects in the walking and memory condition (Figure 5). Specifically, fixations before object changes were of longer duration when directed towards objects whose change would later be detected, than on objects whose change would later be missed (789 ms detected, 204 ms missed; before change, red solid vs. red dashed; t-test, $t = -2.10$, $df = 38$, $p < .05$). One interpretation of this result is that the longer fixation duration to objects before the change in the walking and memory condition was a consequence of the unique task instruction. Anticipating that they would later be asked about what they saw

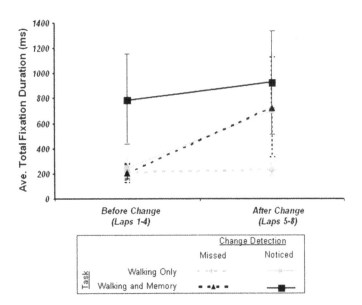

Figure 5. Average fixation behaviour to objects before and after the change for each task and change detection outcome. Error bars represent SEMs across subjects. To view this figure in colour, please see the online issue of the Journal.

during the course of their walk may have inspired subjects to attend to objects in the environment with greater diligence, which was reflected in longer fixations. A second observation of this result is that objects that are fixated for longer durations, and later undergo a change, are more frequently noticed by observers. This finding is consistent with similar observations of fixation behaviour and change detection when viewing images of natural scenes presented on a monitor (Hollingworth & Henderson, 2002).

In the walking only condition, before the change, subjects' average fixation time on objects was the same for those objects whose change was later detected, as on those objects whose change was later missed (247 ms noticed, 216 ms missed; before change, blue solid vs. blue dashed; t-test, $t = 0.192$, $df = 36$, $p = .85$). This suggests that long fixation duration may not be necessary, and that fixations of modest duration may be sufficient, for change detection. However, likely due to the few instances of noticed changes in the walking only condition, the apparent increase in fixation duration for noticed changes before the change in the walking and memory condition did not reach statistical significance (247 ms walking only, 789 ms walking and memory; before change, blue solid vs. red solid; t-test, $t = 0.924$, $df = 17$, $p = .37$). Thus, the relationship between longer fixation duration to objects before a change and observers' detection of object changes is clearer within the walking and memory condition, rather than a comparison between the two conditions.

Fixation behaviour after object changes.   In Laps 5–8, after the object changes, fixation durations to objects generally increased (Figure 5). For example, in the walking only condition, subjects showed a trend towards increased fixation duration on objects whose change was correctly detected, after they underwent the change. (732 ms after noticing, 272 ms before noticing; before vs. after change, blue solid; t-test, $t = -1.83$, $df = 8$, $p = .11$). Similarly, fixations to objects whose change was detected were longer than to those objects whose change was missed (713 ms noticed, 306 ms missed; after change, blue solid vs. blue dashed; t-test, $t = -2.29$, $df = 36$, $p < .05$). These differences in fixation duration after the change may be longer in part due to observers not only encoding the new object, but also in detecting and noticing the change.

Also note that for the walking only condition, objects whose changes were missed were fixated for a shorter duration, both before and after the change (216 ms before, 248 ms after; blue dashed line; t-test, $t = -0.07$, $p = .94$). Because fixation durations were not longer following unnoticed changes, this suggests that changes not reported through explicit report do not necessarily elicit implicit behaviours in response to the change (Fernandez-Duque & Thornton, 2003; Mitroff, Simons, & Franconeri, 2002). It also establishes a baseline for fixation duration on objects possibly considered to be irrelevant by the observers. Also in the walking only condition, the consistent total fixation duration to missed objects after the change suggests that the detection of other changes does not result in a global change in observers' fixation behaviour.

In the walking and memory condition, fixation duration slightly increased, after the change, towards objects whose change was detected, although the increase was not significant (789 ms vs. 931 ms, before vs. after change, red solid; t-test, $t = -0.740$, $df = 26$, $p = .47$). Again, this may include processes involved in the encoding of the object, as well as the change detection itself. It is interesting to note the markedly increased fixation duration after the change for objects whose change was missed (204 ms before; 732 ms after; red dashed line; t-test, $t = -1.97$, $p = .05$). (Note also that this behaviour is nearly identical to behaviour for noticed changes in the walking only condition.) Increased fixation duration for missed changes in later laps may reflect a global change in fixation strategy, and will be addressed in the Discussion.

DISCUSSION

The present experiment investigated the role of task demands on observers' use of gaze and memory for objects within a real world environment. Subjects in the walking only condition, who were simply instructed to walk around the perimeter of a building, were less likely to recall, or notice changes to, objects placed along the pathway, than were subjects in the walking and memory condition, who were given the modest additional instruction that at the end of the experiment they would be "asked about what they saw". Observers instructed in the walking and memory task were not only more likely to recall objects and detect their change, but also had longer fixation durations on objects prior to their change. We now discuss our findings in relation to literature addressing memory for objects in other paradigms, the role of task demands on incidental and intentional visual memory, and consider the nature of object changes in real world environments and future directions of research on vision during natural behaviour.

Probing memory for objects in scenes

Incidental memory vs. intentional representations. A debated question in vision research is how to characterize the nature of visual representations during, and following, scene viewing. There is increasing evidence for robust representations of scene detail (Hollingworth, 2006b; Melcher, 2001, 2006). Previously fixated objects in images of natural scenes are more likely than chance to be identified over novel objects, even 24 hours after viewing (Hollingworth, 2005). Such robust memory suggests that observers are storing detailed object information, including their position within the scene and their orientation (Hollingworth, 2009; Tatler et al., 2005).

However, it is not clear if such robust storage reflects observers' typical usage of memory under normal viewing conditions. For example, evidence for high capacity memory for objects has been found in a task in which observers are instructed to store fixated regions of the scene as they "followed-the-dot" with their gaze, tracking a perpetually repositioned green circle superimposed on each image (Hollingworth, 2004). Observers also typically receive explicit instructions to study the content of images in preparation for a subsequent memory test, including specific descriptions of the information to be tested (Hollingworth & Henderson, 2002). Although comprehensive directions clearly communicate the expectations of behaviour or task to the subjects, such instruction may not be representative of the way in which observers use memory during natural behaviour when the relevance of visual information is not known.

The storage of visual information is undoubtedly selective, and is shaped by the demands of the task. Memory literature has historically distinguished between storage of information through incidental interaction requiring shallow processing, or intentional interaction requiring deeper semantic analysis (Craik & Tulving, 1975). The demands of the task establish the level of processing, including expectations of what information will be tested. For example, in a study similar to the present experiment, but without measures of gaze, Lampinen et al. (2001) found that observers are more likely to recognize real world objects that they were instructed to remember, and this selective storage can endure for at least 2 days following exposure. Also, for stimuli presented on a monitor, fixations on objects are of longer duration during an intentional memory task than a search task (Castelhano & Henderson, 2005).

Indeed, a central function of executive control may be the coordination between intentionally storing select visual information and gaze control. Frequent use of refixations throughout ordinary behaviour, such as making a sandwich or cup of tea (Hayhoe et al., 2003; Land et al., 1999), suggests that items previously fixated are not necessarily stored into memory, but may instead be reacquired with shifts in gaze "just-in-time" for the task. Consistent with this idea of sparse storage, Tatler (2001) has shown that information currently fixated rapidly overwrites previously fixated information. However, if observers can anticipate the use of relevant information, then this information is more likely to be stored in working memory (Droll & Hayhoe, 2007). Incidental storage of visual information may also be reflected in gaze behaviour, even without explicit instructions to store information, if the targeting of visual information is intentional. Objects relevant to a search task are much more likely to be fixated, and consequently stored in memory, than distractor objects incidentally fixated

(Williams et al., 2005). Thus, there appear to be unique cognitive processes recruited during intentional memory storage, including interactions with mechanisms controlling gaze.

The present results serve as reinforcing evidence for selective gaze control and visual storage, and in a context particularly representative of ordinary, ecologically grounded behaviour. Subjects told that they would later be asked what they saw exhibited longer fixation durations to objects. In particular, changes were detected more often in objects that were fixated for longer duration (Figure 5). Two conclusions can be drawn from this finding. First, observers in the walking and memory condition were overtly selecting objects through eye movements, possibly for the purpose of encoding and storage. This is consistent with repeated observations that observers direct gaze towards regions of scenes relevant to their task (Yarbus, 1961, 1967). Second, these longer fixations played a facilitative role in the storage of attended information. Such facilitation is consistent with other studies showing a positive relationship between fixation behaviour and rates of change detection (Droll, Gigone, & Hayhoe, 2007; Droll, Hayhoe, Triesch, & Sullivan, 2005; Hollingworth & Henderson, 2002). However, the role of fixation duration in the task of storage is still not perfectly transparent, as shorter fixations were apparently sufficient for the occasional instances of detection in the walking only condition, and did not differ in duration from fixations to objects whose change was later missed. The rare instances of change detection in the walking only condition may have been a consequence of peripheral encoding, consistent with other observations that real world objects may be encoded without direct fixation (Tatler et al., 2005).

Fixation behaviour following object changes.   In the final four laps, after the changes, objects were generally fixated for longer duration. An increase in fixation duration for noticed changes may include not only encoding the new object, but also processes involved in the detection of the change. However, it is not clear why fixation duration should increase so dramatically for objects whose change was not noticed. One possibility is that this reflects processes engaged in detecting changes, that somehow were not accessible for explicit report (Fernandez-Duque & Thornton, 2003; Mitroff et al., 2002). A second, and more conservative interpretation, is that, upon noticing that several of the objects in the environment had undergone a change, subjects began directing gaze to objects for longer duration, reflecting a global strategy to notice changes elsewhere. This may have particularly been the case in the walking and memory condition, if, upon detecting changes, subjects began to suspect the experimental manipulation since they had been primed to perform a memory task. Due to the limitations of the experimental design, it is not possible to distinguish between these two possibilities.

Differences in change detection between objects.   Objects in the environment had different rates of change detection, from zero to over 50% (Figure 4), and it is beyond the scope of this study to pursue possible reasons for these differences. However, it is worth noting that the backpack and advertisement were the two smallest objects in the environment, and both task conditions had a low (or zero) rate of detection for these objects. Although all nine objects were semantically consistent with the scene, observers may have attended to each object differently due to abstract factors, such as scene gist (Hollingworth & Henderson, 2003), or an expectation that the object would undergo a change (Droll et al., 2007). The role of bottom-up salience (Itti & Koch, 2000, 2001), is likely minimal, as salience has not proved to be a significant predictor of fixations when walking (Rothkopf, Ballard, & Hayhoe, 2007; Turano et al., 2003) or in change detection (Stirk & Underwood, 2007).

In the present experiment, changes occurred between 90 s exposures, a relatively reasonable time frame for real world objects, compared to changes in natural images made during saccadic eye movements lasting less than 100 ms. Thus, the changes in the present experiment are more likely to require long-erm memory than short-term, or working, memory, for changes occurring during saccades.

Change detection in ecologically representative environments

Previous experiments have also found low rates of change detection in real world environments. These experiments often manipulate the identity of a conversation partner with whom the subject had recently been conversing. Because subjects were attending to the changed experimenter(s) immediately before and after the change, and the identity of an individual is presumably meaningful, it is perhaps striking that only half of observers notice this change (Levin et al., 2002; Simons & Levin, 1998). However, the way in which test subjects encoded details of the experimenters who underwent the identity change is not clear. Gaze was not directly monitored, and their interaction was not preceded with instruction as to the relevance of the experimenters' identity. The unexpected disruption of a passing doorway between the observer and conversation partner may have also interfered with observers' attention and memory in unknown ways. Nevertheless, those studies and the present data strongly suggest that observers are frequently insensitive to changes in their environment.

A frequent question in change detection paradigms is whether a failure to notice a change is due to a failure to store the changed information, or a failure to make a comparison between the stored prechange object, and the later encoded (or stored) postchange object (Levin et al., 2002; Simons et al.,

2002; Zelinsky, 2001). In the present experiment, memory for objects was assessed through observers' verbal descriptions, not performance in a recognition task. It is possible that observers still had a visual representation of objects in the scene despite their failure to verbally describe them. Thus, despite having fixated and stored information on the changed objects, observers may have failed to make a comparison of this information. However, revealing the details of the experiment to participants following the questionnaire prompted none of our subjects to make such a comparison, and to then report noticing a change. Thus, it is likely that the failure to notice changes in the present study is due to a failure to attend and store information, rather than a failure to compare. Because we are not able to exhaustively exclude comparison processes, the more modest interpretation of our data simply suggests that prompting observers to store visual information influences gaze behaviour and increases rates of change detection. The present data is unable to resolve whether performance benefits are attributed to recruitment of comparison mechanisms or storage mechanisms and may be an avenue for future research.

What constitutes a "change"?

It is interesting to note that no participant spontaneously mentioned any of the hundreds of naturally occurring changes, such as the shifting position passing pedestrians, movements of tree limbs, scattering of leaves blown by wind, or continuously altering cloud formations. Failure to spontaneously report such incidental changes is curious as such changes would arguably have constituted a change in a task using images of natural scenes depicting real world environments. Failure to mention these naturally occurring changes may suggest the way in which observers apply a priori expectations to memory and change detection tasks.

Because change blindness demonstrations typically occur between two images that differ in a graphic manipulation, scene changes can include arbitrary or impossible events (e.g., disappearance of a jet engine). Also, visual events that might qualify as a change between two images would likely not qualify as a change within a natural environment (e.g., the position of a branch in a tree). Thus, in tasks employing images, observers may consider candidate changes not representative to those considered in real world environments (and vice versa). For example, when viewing images of a scene in which the point of view gradually rotated across successive presentations (Hollingworth & Henderson, 2004), observers did not notice this change until an average of 31 degrees of rotation had occurred. Despite the change of nearly every pixel in the image during each incremental rotation, the real world circumstance of viewing an environment from several viewpoints constitutes an intrinsic change in one's own position, and not an extrinsic change in the world (or image).

With respect to seeking changes between images, Rensink (2002) suggested that changes constitute a transformation or modification of an object that requires memory for detection, such as an object's appearance, disappearance, replacement, or repositioning. Other dynamic events, such as movement or unmasked transients, could not be considered changes because such events can be detected through low-level mechanisms. There may be need for defining criteria for object changes in real world environments.

Computer-based versus naturalistic paradigms

Much work in vision research is grounded on suppositions that performance in repeated trials of simple visual tasks using computer-based stimuli reflect some aspects of natural real world environments and conditions. There are many instances where such suppositions surely hold, but it is not often possible to directly compare performance between computer-based and real world tasks and stimuli. An exception to this is Tatler et al. (2005), who monitored subjects' gaze as they viewed either a real world environment, or a photographic image of the same scene on a monitor. Object memory and fixation behaviour was generally comparable, suggesting that computer-based images may often accurately capture visual processes during real world conditions. Yet the authors also warn against overgeneralizing, particularly in more dynamic environments where observers interact within the scenes, such as when walking.

Many of our results are consistent with the pattern of results obtained from computer-based studies. Subjects were generally poor at detecting visual changes, especially when detecting object changes was not an anticipated task (Simons, 2000). Also consistent with the literature is the finding that longer total fixation durations preceded improved performance in measures of memory (Hollingworth, 2006b; Irwin & Zelinsky, 2002; Melcher, 2001, 2006). Using a natural environment also revealed results not necessarily predicted by literature on computer-based stimuli. Due to the physical constraints of the real world, object changes occurred over several tens of seconds, not within tens of milliseconds, as is the case in many change detection demonstrations. Given the longer time interval between object exposures, it is possible that the detection of changes in real world contexts relies upon different memory and comparison mechanisms as those used in saccade-contingent image manipulations. The presently observed failure to notice multiple real world changes suggests that more stable representations of scene information in long-term memory may not be sufficient to detect the types of changes typically probed in computer-based experiments presenting brief, transient images.

The design of the present experiment drew heavily upon Karacan and Hayhoe (2008), where, in virtual reality, subjects also circumnavigated a building surrounded by objects that underwent changes. The purpose of that study was to investigate the role of observers' familiarity of scenes, and differential sensitivity to changes that introduced, replaced, removed, or displaced surrounding objects. Consistent in both studies is the low rate of change detection for objects undergoing replacement, despite computer-based tasks revealing steady improvement in memory performance with increasing exposure duration of the test scene (Melcher, 2006; Tatler, Gilchrist, & Rusted, 2003). This strengthens the assertion that virtual environments may be sufficiently representative of real world contexts to capture the usage of vision in natural contexts and calls into question any clear linear relationship between duration of scene exposure and observers' accumulation of scene detail.

Although virtual environments allow greater experimental manipulation, such as saccade-contingent object changes (Droll & Hayhoe, 2007), or tracking moving objects such as pedestrians (Jovancevic, Sullivan, & Hayhoe, 2006), their use may be prohibitively expensive for many researchers. Fortunately, as shown in the present experiment, recent technological advances in mobile eyetracking now allow monitoring of eye movements in real world environments with minimal interference on natural behaviour. Despite these technical developments, the application of mobile eyetracking to vision science is still in its infancy (but see Bahill, Adler, & Stark, 1975; Schneider et al., 2005; Schumann et al., 2008). Mobile tracking has been used to study sports performance (Land & McLeod, 2000), walking behaviour (Jovancevic et al., 2006), complex tasks (Hayhoe et al., 2003; Land et al., 1999), and other object memory tasks (Tatler et al., 2005), but has not yet been used in conjunction with probing memory during real world change detection. Thus, although our central aim is to test principles of human vision, a secondary goal is the advancement of more natural paradigms accessible for testing theories of visual cognition and memory that diminish the distinction between laboratory and natural contexts.[2]

---

[2] An area receiving recent interest is the misperceptions during magic tricks, where stage manipulations of objects may arguably be related to laboratory manipulations of images in change detection experiments (Kuhn, Amlani, & Rensink, 2008; Kuhn & Tatler, 2005; Kuhn, Tatler, Findlay, & Cole, 2008)

CONCLUSIONS

First, our results suggest that observers expecting to receive a memory test deploy fixations of longer total duration to experimental objects in the scene, than observers simply instructed to walk as they would normally. This finding contributes to the literature showing how task demands modulate the control of gaze. Second, subjects who fixated experimental objects for longer duration and were told to anticipate discussing what they saw, had higher rates of change detection of those same objects. This suggests that either task demands, or the longer fixations to objects, or both, facilitated the storage of visual information and detection when these objects underwent a change. Last, we have demonstrated a method for testing memory for objects and monitoring gaze in a real world environment and encourage other researchers to expand in a similar direction.

REFERENCES

Angelone, B. L., Levin, D. T., & Simons, D. J. (2003). The relationship between change detection and recognition of centrally attended objects in motion pictures. *Perception, 32*(8), 947–962.

Bahill, A. T., Adler, D., & Stark, L. (1975). Most naturally occurring human saccades have magnitudes of 15 degrees or less. *Investigative Ophthalmology, 14*(6), 468–469.

Ballard, D. H., Hayhoe, M., & Pelz, J. B. (1995). Memory representations in natural tasks. *Journal of Cognitive Neuroscience, 7*(1), 66–80.

Ballard, D. H., Hayhoe, M. M., Pook, P. K., & Rao, R. P. (1997). Deictic codes for the embodiment of cognition. *Behavioral Brain Sciences, 20*(4), 723–742; discussion 743–767.

Blackmore, S. J., Brelstafff, G., Nelson, K., & Troscianko, T. (1995). Is the richness of our visual world an illusion? Transsaccadic memory for complex scenes. *Perception, 24*(9), 1075–1081.

Buswell, G. (1935). *How people look at pictures.* Chicago: University of Chicago Press.

Castelhano, M. S., & Henderson, J. M. (2005). Incidental visual memory for objects in scenes. *Visual Cognition, 12*(6), 1017–1040.

Chen, X., & Zelinsky, G. J. (2006). Real-world visual search is dominated by top-down guidance. *Vision Research, 46*(24), 4118–4133.

Craik, F. I. M., & Tulving, E. (1975). Depth of processing and the retention of words in episodic memory. *Journal of Experimental Psychology: General, 104*(3), 268–294.

De Graef, P., Christiaens, D., & d'Ydewalle, G. (1990). Perceptual effects of scene context on object identification. *Psychological Research, 52*(4), 317–329.

Droll, J. A., Gigone, K., & Hayhoe, M. M. (2007). Learning where to direct gaze during change detection. *Journal of Vision, 7*(14), 1–12.

Droll, J. A., & Hayhoe, M. M. (2007). Trade-offs between gaze and working memory use. *Journal of Experimental Psychology: Human Perception and Performance, 33*(6), 1352–1365.

Droll, J. A., Hayhoe, M. M., Triesch, J., & Sullivan, B. T. (2005). Task demands control acquisition and storage of visual information. *Journal of Experimental Psychology: Human Perception and Performance, 31*(6), 1416–1438.

Eckstein, M. P., Dresher, B. A., & Shimozaki, S. S. (2006). Attentional cues in real scenes, saccadic targeting and Bayesian priors. *Psychological Science, 17*(11), 973–980.

Einhauser, W., Rutishauser, U., & Koch, C. (2008). Task-demands can immediately reverse the effects of sensory-driven saliency in complex visual stimuli. *Journal of Vision, 8*(2), 2 1–19.

Fernandez-Duque, D., & Thornton, I. M. (2003). Explicit mechanisms do not account for implicit localization and identification of change: An empirical reply to Mitroff et al. (2002). *Journal of Experimental Psychology: Human Perception and Performance, 29*(5), 846–858.

Foulsham, T., & Underwood, G. (2008). What can saliency models predict about eye movements? Spatial and sequential aspects of fixations during encoding and recognition. *Journal of Vision, 8*(2), 6 1–17.

Grimes, J. (1996). *On the failure to detect changes in scenes across saccades* (Vol. 2). New York: Oxford University Press.

Hayhoe, M. M., Shrivastava, A., Mruczek, R., & Pelz, J. B. (2003). Visual memory and motor planning in a natural task. *Journal of Vision, 3*(1), 49–63.

Hollingworth, A. (2003). Failures of retrieval and comparison constrain change detection in natural scenes. *Journal of Experimental Psychology: Human Perception and Performance, 29*(2), 388–403.

Hollingworth, A. (2004). Constructing visual representations of natural scenes: The roles of short- and long-term visual memory. *Journal of Experimental Psychology: Human Perception and Performance, 30*(3), 519–537.

Hollingworth, A. (2005). The relationship between online visual representation of a scene and long-term scene memory. *Journal of Experimental Psychology: Learning, Memory, and Cognition, 31*(3), 396–411.

Hollingworth, A. (2006a). Scene and position specificity in visual memory for objects. *Journal of Experimental Psychology: Learning, Memory, and Cognition, 32*(1), 58–69.

Hollingworth, A. (2006b). Visual memory for natural scenes: Evidence from change detection and visual search. *Visual Cognition, 14*(4/5/6/7/8), 781–807.

Hollingworth, A. (2009). Two forms of scene memory guide visual search: Memory for scene context and memory for the binding of target objects to scene location. *Visual Cognition, 17,* 273–291.

Hollingworth, A., & Henderson, J. (2002). Accurate visual memory for previously attended objects in natural scenes. *Journal of Experimental Psychology: Human Perception and Performance, 28,* 113–136.

Hollingworth, A., & Henderson, J. M. (2003). Testing a conceptual locus for the inconsistent object change detection advantage in real-world scenes. *Memory and Cognition, 31*(6), 930–940.

Hollingworth, A., & Henderson, J. M. (2004). Sustained change blindness to incremental scene rotation: A dissociation between explicit change detection and visual memory. *Perception and Psychophysics, 66*(5), 800–807.

Irwin, D. E., & Zelinsky, G. J. (2002). Eye movements and scene perception: Memory for things observed. *Perception and Psychophysics, 64*(6), 882–895.

Itti, L., & Koch, C. (2000). A saliency-based search mechanism for overt and covert shifts of visual attention. *Vision Research, 40*(10–12), 1489–1506.

Itti, L., & Koch, C. (2001). Computational modeling of visual attention. *Nature Reviews Neuroscience, 2*(3), 194–203.

Jovancevic, J., Sullivan, B., & Hayhoe, M. (2006). Control of attention and gaze in complex environments. *Journal of Vision, 6*(12), 1431–1450.

Karacen, H., & Hayhoe, M. M. (2008). Is attention drawn to changes in familiar scenes? *Visual Cognition, 16*(2/3), 356–374.

Kuhn, G., Amlani, A. A., & Rensink, R. A. (2008). Towards a science of magic. *Trends in Cognitive Science, 12*(9), 349–354.

Kuhn, G., & Tatler, B. W. (2005). Magic and fixation: Now you don't see it, now you do. *Perception, 34*(9), 1155–1161.

Kuhn, G., Tatler, B. W., Findlay, J. M., & Cole, G. G. (2008). Misdirection in magic: Implications for the relationship between eye gaze and attention. *Visual Cognition, 16*(2/3), 391–405.

Lampinen, J. M., Copeland, S. M., & Neuschatz, J. S. (2001). Recollections of things schematic: Room schemas revisited. *Journal of Experimental Psychology: Learning, Memory, and Cognition, 27*(5), 1211–1222.

Land, M., Mennie, N., & Rusted, J. (1999). The roles of vision and eye movements in the control of activities of daily living. *Perception, 28*(11), 1311–1328.

Land, M. F. (2004). The coordination of rotations of the eyes, head and trunk in saccadic turns produced in natural situations. *Experimental Brain Research, 159*(2), 151–160.

Land, M. F., & Hayhoe, M. (2001). In what ways do eye movements contribute to everyday activities? *Vision Research, 41*(25–26), 3559–3565.

Land, M. F., & McLeod, P. (2000). From eye movements to actions: How batsmen hit the ball. *Nature Neurosciences, 3*(12), 1340–1345.

Levin, D. T., & Simons, D. J. (1997). Failure to detect changes to attended objects in motion pictures. *Psychonomic Bulletin and Review, 4*, 501–506.

Levin, D. T., Simons, D. J., Angelone, B. L., & Chabris, C. F. (2002). Memory for centrally attended changing objects in an incidental real-world change detection paradigm. *British Journal of Psychology, 93*(3), 289–302.

Luck, S. J., & Vogel, E. K. (1997). The capacity of visual working memory for features and conjunctions. *Nature, 390*(6657), 279–281.

Melcher, D. (2001). Persistence of visual memory for scenes. *Nature, 412*(6845), 401.

Melcher, D. (2006). Accumulation and persistence of memory for natural scenes. *Journal of Vision, 6*(1), 8–17.

Mennie, N., Hayhoe, M., & Sullivan, B. (2007). Look-ahead fixations: Anticipatory eye movements in natural tasks. *Experimental Brain Research, 179*(3), 427–442.

Mitroff, S. R., Simons, D. J., & Franconeri, S. L. (2002). The siren song of implicit change detection. *Journal of Experimental Psychology: Human Perception and Performance, 28*(4), 798–815.

O'Regan, J. K. (1992). Solving the "real" mysteries of visual perception: The world as an outside memory. *Canadian Journal of Psychology, 46*(3), 461–488.

O'Regan, J. K., Rensink, R. A., & Clark, J. J. (1999). Change-blindness as a result of "mudsplashes". *Nature, 398*, 34.

Palta, A. E., & Vickers, J. N. (2002). How far ahead do we look when required to step on specific locations in the travel path during locomotion? *Experimental Brain Research, 148*, 133–138.

Parkhurst, D. J., & Niebur, E. (2003). Scene content selected by active vision. *Spatial Vision, 16*(2), 125–154.

Parkhurst, D. J., & Niebur, E. (2004). Texture contrast attracts overt visual attention in natural scenes. *European Journal of Neuroscience, 19*(3), 783–789.

Pelz, J., Hayhoe, M., & Loeber, R. (2001). The coordination of eye, head, and hand movements in a natural task. *Experimental Brain Research, 139*(3), 266–277.

Pelz, J., & Rothkopf, C. A. (2007). Oculomotor behavior in natural and man-made environments. In R. van Gompel (Ed.), *Eye movements: A window on mind and brain* (pp. 661–676). Oxford, UK: Elsevier.

Pelz, J. B., & Canosa, R. (2001). Oculomotor behavior and perceptual strategies in complex tasks. *Vision Research, 41*(25–26), 3587–3596.

Rensink, R. A. (2002). Change detection. *Annual Reviews Psychology, 53*, 245–277.

Rensink, R. A., O'Regan, J. K., & Clark, J. J. (1997). To see or not to see: The need for attention to perceive changes in scenes. *Psychological Science, 8*, 368–373.

Rothkopf, C. A., Ballard, D. H., & Hayhoe, M. M. (2007). Task and context determine where you look. *Journal of Vision, 7*(14), 11–20.

Schneider, E., Bartl, K., Bardins, S., Dera, T., Boning, G., & Brandt, T. (2005). Eye movement driven head-mounted camera: It looks where the eyes look. *Proceedings of the IEEE International Conference on Systems, Man and Cybernetics*, 2437–2442.

Schumann, F., Einhauser-Treyer, W., Vockeroth, J., Bartl, K., Schneider, E., & Konig, P. (2008). Salient features in gaze-aligned recordings of human visual input during free exploration of natural environments. *Journal of Vision*, *8*(14), 1–17.

Simons, D. J. (2000). Current approaches to change blindness. *Visual Cognition*, *7*(1/2/3), 1–15.

Simons, D. J., Chabris, C. F., Schnur, T., & Levin, D. T. (2002). Evidence for preserved representations in change blindness. *Conscious Cognition*, *11*(1), 78–97.

Simons, D. J., & Levin, D. T. (1998). Failure to detect changes to people during a real-world interaction. *Psychonomic Bulletin and Review*, *5*, 644–649.

Stirk, J. A., & Underwood, G. (2007). Low-level visual saliency does not predict change detection in natural scenes. *Journal of Vision*, *7*(10), 1–10.

Tatler, B. W. (2001). Characterising the visual buffer: Real-world evidence for overwriting early in each fixation. *Perception*, *30*(8), 993–1006.

Tatler, B. W. (2007). The central fixation bias in scene viewing: Selecting an optimal viewing position independently of motor biases and image feature distributions. *Journal of Vision*, *7*(14), 1–17.

Tatler, B. W., Gilchrist, I. D., & Land, M. F. (2005). Visual memory for objects in natural scenes: From fixations to object files. *Quarterly Journal of Experimental Psychology*, *58A*(5), 931–960.

Tatler, B. W., Gilchrist, I. D., & Rusted, J. (2003). The time course of abstract visual representation. *Perception*, *32*, 579–592.

Tatler, B. W., & Melcher, D. (2007). Pictures in mind: Initial encoding of object properties varies with the realism of the scene stimulus. *Perception*, *36*(12), 1715–1729.

Turano, K. A., Geruschat, D. R., & Baker, F. H. (2003). Oculomotor strategies for the direction of gaze tested with a real-world activity. *Vision Research*, *43*(3), 333–346.

Turano, K. A., Geruschat, D. R., Baker, F. H., Stahl, J. W., & Shapiro, M. D. (2001). Direction of gaze while walking a simple route: Persons with normal vision and persons with retinitis pigmentosa. *Optometry and Vision Science*, *78*(9), 667–675.

Varakin, D. A., & Levin, D. T. (2006). Change blindness and visual memory: Visual representations get rich and act poor. *British Journal of Psychology*, *97*(1), 51–77.

Vogel, E. K., Woodman, G. F., & Luck, S. J. (2001). Storage of features, conjunctions and objects in visual working memory. *Journal of Experimental Psychology: Human Perception and Performance*, *27*(1), 92–114.

Wheeler, M. E., & Treisman, A. (2002). Binding in short-term visual memory. *Journal of Experimental Psychology: General*, *131*(1), 48–64.

Williams, C. C., Henderson, J. M., & Zacks, R. T. (2005). Incidental visual memory for targets and distractors in visual search. *Perception and Psychophysics*, *67*(5), 816–827.

Yarbus, A. L. (1961). Eye movements during the examination of complicated objects. *Biofizika*, *6*(2), 52–56.

Yarbus, A. L. (1967). *Eye movements and vision*. New York: Plenum Press.

Zelinsky, G. J. (2001). Eye movements during change detection: Implications for search constraints, memory limitations, and scanning strategies. *Perception and Psychophysics*, *63*(2), 209–225.

Zelinsky, G. J., Rao, R., Hayhoe, M., & Ballard, D. (1997). Eye movements reveal the spatio-temporal dynamics of visual search. *Psychological Science*, *8*, 448–453.

VISUAL COGNITION, 2009, 17 (6/7), 1185–1204

Modelling the role of task in the control of gaze

Dana H. Ballard and Mary M. Hayhoe

Center for Perceptual Systems, University of Texas, Austin, TX, USA

Gaze changes and the resultant fixations that orchestrate the sequential acquisition of information from the visual environment are the central feature of primate vision. How are we to understand their function? For the most part, theories of fixation targets have been image based: The hypothesis being that the eye is drawn to places in the scene that contain discontinuities in image features such as motion, colour, and texture. But are these features the cause of the fixations, or merely the result of fixations that have been planned to serve some visual function? This paper examines the issue and reviews evidence from various image-based and task-based sources. Our conclusion is that the evidence is overwhelmingly in favour of fixation control being essentially task based.

Keywords: Gaze control; Saliency; Task modeling; Saccades.

Yarbus's original work in understanding gaze recordings (Yarbus, 1967) in the 1950s and 1960s revealed the enormous importance of gaze in revealing the underlying structure of human cognition. In his most compelling demonstration, he showed that a subject viewing a painting responded with markedly different eye fixation patterns when asked different questions about the image. Although earlier work by Buswell and Dodge (Buswell, 1935; Erdmann & Dodge, 1898) had implied such cognitive influences on the choice fixations, Yarbus's demonstrations left no doubt about the role of cognition directing gaze.

From this perspective of this pioneering work, it is somewhat surprising that the first significant computational theory of vision (Marr, 1982) avoided the study of gaze as well as any influence of cognition on the extraction of information from the retinal array. In his "principle of least commitment", Marr argued the case for the role of the cortex in building elaborate goal-

---

Please address all correspondence to Dana H. Ballard, Center for Perceptual Systems, SEA 4.328A, 1 University Station, A8000, The University of Texas, Austin, TX 78712-0187, USA. E-mail: dana@cs.rochester.edu

This work was supported by NIH grants RR02983, MH60624, and EY05729. The authors gratefully acknowledge the assistance of the reviewers whose detailed comments and suggestions greatly improved the paper.

© 2009 Taylor & Francis
DOI: 10.1080/13506280902978477

independent descriptions of the physical world. Marr was no doubt influenced by the groundbreaking work of Hubel and Weisel (1962), who showed that striate cortex was organized into a retinotopic map of the visual world, centred on the point of gaze. Subsequent work revealed that all of visual cortex was hierarchically organized into a series of retinotopic maps containing ever more abstract properties of the visual world. At almost the same time work in visual search revealed a stunning difference in search times between displays containing several items with just one feature defining differences between items and displays with conjunctions of two features defining the difference (Treisman & Gelade, 1980), suggesting that groups of features at retinotopic locations was a natural way of organizing the visual stimulus.

As a consequence of the focus on retinotopy, when researchers took on the task of defining computational mechanisms for directing gaze deployment, these turned out to be predominantly image based. Koch and Ullman defined the saliency map: A retinotopic accounting of different retinotopic organizations of specific image features such as colour, texture, and motion (Itti & Koch, 2001; Koch & Ullman, 1985). Retinotopic locations rich in such features were calculated to be salient and potential fixation points. Subsequent additions allowed these locations to be modulated to account to different tasks (Navalpakkam & Itti, 2003; Wolfe, 1994) and the statistics of such features (Itti & Baldi, 2005), and the concept of the saliency map has become a central organizing focus of models of gaze control.

Saliency theories have been compelling, but have many drawbacks. They usually cannot predict the exact fixation points and can leave more than half of the fixations unaccounted for (e.g., Foulsham & Underwood, 2008). It seems likely that the central problem is that they are correlated with fixation behaviours but not their cause. This point has been made by Einhauser, Rutishauser, and Koch (2008), Henderson (2007), and Tatler (2007). Other compelling reasons for this are (1) the dominating role of cognitive goals dictates many image calculations that cannot be expressed in terms of the saliency of conjunctions of features and (2) the situated nature of the human visual system's limited view in a three-dimensional world means that many fixation targets are remembered locations that are not visible when the saccade is initiated.

Recent work has begun to tackle the problem of describing a theory that accounts for the role of the cognitive process and spatial environs that are controlling the subject's behaviours, and there is mounting evidence that such a theory must be central. Experiments using lightweight head-mounted eyetrackers show that fixations are extracting very specific information needed by the human subject's ongoing task (Droll, Hayhoe, Triesch, & Sullivan, 2005; Jovancevic, Sullivan, & Hayhoe, 2006; Triesch, Ballard, Hayhoe, & Sullivan, 2003). The task context introduces enormous economies into this process: If a subject needs to locate a red object near a blue object, the search for that object can be limited to just blue portions of the image followed by a local search for red; vast amounts of extraneous detail can be neglected (Ballard, Hayhoe, Pook, & Rao, 1997; Roelfsema, Khayat, & Spekreijse, 2003; Swain & Ballard, 1991). The visual information-gathering component of almost every task will introduce similar economies.

The purposes of this paper are twofold. We first selectively review research on the deployment of gaze with the view to highlighting difficulties in saliency models. Next we introduce a cognitive model for directing fixations based on learned reward. Rather than offer a *rapprochement* between image-based and task-based approaches, we continue an earlier argument advanced by Ullman (1984) in his classic visual routines paper. That is, that the cognitive processes that operate on image data in order to support cognition have a fundamentally different character than the image structures they use in that process.

EVIDENCE FROM SPORTS

One obvious venue for studying eye movements is sports. Given the time-critical coordination of movements involved, one would suspect that this is a case where eye movements are entirely task based and in fact this turns out to be the case. In classic studies of cricket, Land has shown that batters fixate the area on the pitch where the ball is expected to bounce after first fixating the pitch release to get information on the ball's upcoming trajectory. The best batter's gaze change tends to be about 100 ms before those of average batters (Land & McLeod, 2000). This venue provides an ideal setting to contrast the information gained from saliency methods with information gained by understanding the task. The bowler is of course very salient so it would be easy to produce a high valued saliency measure for the visual area containing him, although perhaps more difficult to highlight the crucially important hand area. On the other hand the area where the ball bounces is virtually featureless, gaining its importance from the surrounding context and the batter's prior knowledge of where pitches typically land. Thus, a saliency model would be able to predict half the fixations but would miss the essence of them. The first fixation's purpose is to measure information that would predict the landing point and spin of the ball; the second fixation is to plan the batter's response.

The use of fixation to plan motor responses in saliency-poor areas is ubiquitous in ball sports. Land and McLeod (2000) have shown that players fixate the predicted bounce point in table tennis, and Hayhoe (McKinney, Chajka, & Hayhoe, 2008) has shown that players fixate the featureless front wall for squash returns. Back wall returns are even more impressive; players fixate a point in empty three-dimensional space that is predicted to be the contact point between the ball and the racquet. In another venue where normal, unskilled subjects have to catch a bounced ball, subjects fixate a three-dimensional point above the bounce point. None of these points could be predicted by a saliency model as the local image features are meaningless for these tasks. Of course the path of the ball, the placement of the player/catcher and their positions in three-dimensional space are all important, but none of this information is part of saliency models.

EVIDENCE FROM COMPLEX TASKS

Sports are interesting in part because the performance of the players is time critical, so they leave open the possibility that in other normal behaviours that are not so demanding, the use of fixations could be less predictable with task information. However, all the emerging evidence implies that this is not the case. It is far more likely that each fixation has a specific purpose even when the observer may not be conscious of it. In studies of car following in a virtual environment, Shinoda, Hayhoe, and Shrivastava (2001) showed that the percentage of fixations on a lead car dropped from 75% to 43% when subjects had to also pay attention to intersection signs. Although it might be possible to adjust a task-based modulation of a saliency map to account for these changes the difficulties are formidable. The visual targets vary hugely in scale as the driver progresses and subjects tend to look at signs at different times.

In a classic experiment, subjects copied patterns of coloured blocks on a display, moving blocks used in the copy from a reservoir of extra blocks with a computer cursor. In this task the modal behaviour was to fixate the pattern to choose a block, remember its colour, find and select the block to be used in the copy, and then use another fixation of the pattern to determine the placement of the selected block in the copy. Even though subjects could obtain both pieces of information (position, colour) with a single fixation, they preferred to use two separate fixations, presumably with the goal of avoiding the carrying cost of remembering the relative position for as long as possible. Thus the first fixation was to determine the colour of the block in turn to compute the subsequent fixation to the reservoir, and the second fixation was to obtain the relative position of the block in the pattern (Hayhoe, Bensinger, & Ballard, 1998).

The focused use of fixations in the block copying task is also a hallmark of subsequent experiments studying natural behaviour in that knowing the task allows the purpose of the fixation to be understood. We will describe these experiments to illustrate this point but before we do let us return to the issue of saliency maps to illustrate their conundrums in this case. One could certainly produce a saliency map for the blocks images and compute points of saliency, but without understanding the task at hand it would be virtually impossible to predict the sequence of eye movements for this task as the static images contain no information as to which salient location is to be preferred over any other.

Another complex task studied by Hayhoe is that of making a peanut butter and jelly sandwich and filling a cup with Coke (Hayhoe, Shrivastrava, Myruczek, & Pelz, 2003). This is a common everyday task but is laden with complexities in eye–hand coordination that challenge the notion of saliency. For example in placing peanut butter on the bread, subjects take advantage of the fact that peanut butter reliably sticks to the knife and make a gaze targeting fixation to the point on the bread where the tip of the knife is to end up to begin spreading. In contrast, jelly is less viscous and more precarious on the knife and thus is guided to the bread with a pursuit eye movement. This kind of knowledge, which is ingrained in any sandwich maker, is way beyond the reach of the capabilities of saliency maps as the knowledge is simply not image based.

At this point it might be germane to discuss one of the ways proposed to extend saliency maps and that is to modulate them with task information. If the information in tasks can be related to image features then, the features themselves can provide a basis for modulating the saliency map. If it is known that jelly is an important component of the task, then one can increase the weight of jelly's dark purple colour in the saliency computation, thus biasing the choice of fixation points. There are lots of difficulties making this work in general but the one that is appropriate for discussion here is that jelly is only important at a few points in the overall task: Finding the jelly jar, extracting the jelly from the jar, and replacing the jelly jar's lid. Thus, any method for routinely increasing saliency would create false targets for all the other moments of sandwich construction and drink pouring. Of course one could introduce knowledge of possible sequences of sandwich making and selectively enhance purple when jelly was important but at this point the idea of task knowledge has been ceded.

Another point that proves problematic for saliency is that of task-based memory. We illustrate this point with another copying example, this time from Aivar, Hayhoe, and Mruczek (2005). Subjects copy a toy model in a virtual environment. The toy is made from German Baufix parts that subjects manipulate with a cursor, as in the previously described block copying task. The important differences here are that (1) subjects copy the same toy repeatedly so that they can learn where the parts are in the reservoir and (2) the distance between the construction site and reservoir is such that when adding parts to the construction, the reservoir is not in view. Nonetheless when subjects have repeated the task they are able to make saccades to the point in virtual three-dimensional space at which the next part is suspended. This is tested by moving the placement of the part when not in view and observing that the initial saccade goes to the vacated spot. Of course this cannot be handled by saliency. In the first place the image is not available at the beginning of the saccade, but even if it were the part is no longer at that position so the resultant saliency of that location is zero. One could try to overcome this difficulty with baroque manipulations of the saliency map, but they would only be shoehorning implicit knowledge of the task into the image-based representation. Furthermore there are other issues not included at this point which are about to be addressed.

Since many aspect of ordinary visually guided behaviour are clearly dominated by the information that is required for the momentary visual operation, what is the potential role of examining the properties of the stimulus as a basis for gaze behaviour? One of implicit rationales might be that tasks are special in some way, and that there is some body of visual processing that does not involve tasks. Consequently, many of the experiments involve what is called "free viewing", with the goal of isolating task-free visual processing. It is possible that the global visual perception of a scene is distinct in some way from the kind of vision involved in tasks. Certainly humans need to extract information about the spatial structure of scenes and the identity of the objects, but is this qualitatively different from specific visual operations such as those involved in visual search, or extracting location information for grasping an object, operations that are performed in the context of a task such as making a sandwich? The suggestion in the next section is that all vision can be conceptualized as a task of some kind. The issue is important and needs to be examined explicitly. What we think of as "seeing" is the consequence of extensive experience in the visual environment during development (Geisler, 2008) and the extraction of information such as gist presumably reflects not only passive visual experience but also the constraint that this information is useful for the organism in some way. Thus it is hard to logically separate the effects of stimulus from the effects of task.

Another important assumption that needs to be examined is that fixation patterns in two-dimensional photographic renderings of a scene will be the same if the observer were actually in that scene. Although this might be the case in some instances, there is no guarantee that it will be true. Real scenes are three-dimensional, and the image changes as a consequence of inevitable body movements. The scale of a rendered image is typically different from the scale of the image if the subject were actually in that scene.

EVIDENCE FOR VISUAL ROUTINES

The discussion up to this point has focused on what might be termed macroscopic issues with respect to eye fixations, that is, specifying their targets broadly and issues as to the overall task context in influencing those choices. But a host of other issues emerge with respect to more microscopic issues, namely the detailed computations that are done during fixation. A variety of experiments have indicated that the visual information acquired during a fixation may be quite specific. In an experiment by Ballard, Hayhoe, and Pelz (1995), observers copied simple coloured block patterns on a computer screen, by picking up blocks with the mouse and moving them to make a copy. In the course of copying a single block, subjects commonly fixated individual blocks in the model patterns twice, once before picking up a matching block, and once before placement. Given the requirements of the task, a reasonable hypothesis is that block colour is acquired during the first fixation, and the next fixation on the block is to acquire its location. A subsequent experiment where changes were made to the block colours at different stages of the task supported the interpretation that the first and second fixations on a model block subserved different visual functions (Hayhoe et al., 1998; Hoffman, Landaub, & Pagani, 2003). Further evidence that fixations are for the purpose of extracting quite specific information is given by Droll et al. (2005), who found that subjects are selectively sensitive to changes made in task relevant features of an object they were manipulating, even though they fixated the object directly for several hundreds of msec. Triesch et al. (2003) also found selective sensitivity to task relevant changes in a manipulated object. This suggests that many simple visual computations involve the ongoing execution of special-purpose "visual routines" that depend on the immediate behavioural context, and extract only the particular information required at the moment. The idea of visual routines was first introduced by Ullman (1984). The essential property of a routine is that it instantiates a procedure for acquiring specific information called for by the current cognitive agenda. Selection of just the task specific information from a scene is an efficient strategy. Task specific strategies not only circumscribe the information that needs to be acquired, but also allow the visual system to take advantage of the known context to simplify the computation (Ballard et al., 1997). This selective acquisition may be reflected in even low-level cortical areas whose neural activity depends not only on stimulus features but on task context (Ito & Gilbert, 1999; Roelfsema, Lamme, & Spekreijse, 1998).

To illustrate the concept of a visual routine, we consider the task of filling a cup with coke. While pouring the coke subjects lock their gaze on the level of coke and track its progress towards the rim. Each subject has a preferred level that he or she can duplicate repeatedly. The obvious conjecture is that subjects are using a template matching approach whereby they are mentally matching a "filled coke cup" template against the current image, stopping when a match criterion is achieved. We have shown with a model in virtual environment that this simple information is adequate for performing the task, and can reproduce the standard deviation of fill levels of a given subject using template matching. Thus, the suggestion is that vision is composed of specialized computations of this kind.

Consider the problem the cup-filling example poses for saliency. Much of the context for the visual routine is provided by the body itself. Since the subject's hands are holding the cup and coke bottle, proprioception can provide the essential geometric information for filling the cup. The weight of the filling cup is another cue. Vision is just needed to detect the final condition of a filled cup. In this venue there are two problems. The first is that the contrast between the liquid and cup colour can be regulated so that their impact on the saliency computation can be reduced to near zero. Thus, without extensive priming the level of the fluid in the cup will be invisible. Second, the subject's gaze tracks the filling level for the duration of the filling process (it is likely that the motion of the fluid relative to the cup is used in doing this, based on a patient studied by Zihl, von Cramon, & Mai, 1983, who had a specific motion deficit and had trouble filling cups). If the knowledge of the task is provided then this behaviour is reasonable, but absent it, there is no reason for using gaze in this way and no way to predict the behaviour purely on the basis of saliency.

A challenging example for saliency models in neuroscience comes from Roelfsema et al.'s (1998) primate studies. In his experimental setup a monkey has to fixate a central point and then on command, make a saccade to one of two radial lines projecting outward from the fixation point. The line that must be chosen is the one that is attached to the fixation point. The experiment takes advantage of the fact that in programming a saccade from a cue onset takes on the order of 250–300 ms so during that time one can record from fixed retinotopic locations in cortical areas such as striate cortex (V1). The experiments show that simple cells on along the line's path increase their firing pattern at a time commensurate with the hypothesis that the monkey solves the task of defining the saccade target by mentally tracing the length of the line to the required end point. The task was made harder by replacing the attachment condition with colouring the fixation point and stubs at the near ends of the lines. The line to be traced is the one that now has the same colour stub as the fixation point. The elevated simple cell response now occurs later in time, consistent with the hypothesis that the monkey now solves two tasks. The main point here for our focus is that line tracing is a technically difficult problem that is outside the domain of static saliency models.

A final example of the use of visual routines posing difficulties for saliency comes from Droll and Hayhoe (2007). In a virtual block task, subjects look a block they are manipulating at different times, but some of those fixations are to obtain its features (e.g., colour), whereas others are to follow task instructions. The point is that the fixation is on the block in both cases but the actual detailed processing that the visual system is doing is very different. The saliency map cannot distinguish these two without having a detailed task model.

HUMAN VISUAL SEARCH

An important aspect of saccadic eye movements that has implications for saliency is their use in visual search. Understanding this venue draws upon the development of reverse correlation in the computation of the search target used by subjects. Given a succession of searches for a target in noise, the experimenter can keep a record of the subject's false positives and true positives and average these in order to produce an image template for the searched target. For example, it has been demonstrated that for searching for targets under low signal-to-noise conditions that the features extracted are often idiosyncratic and not easily related to saliency axes (Rajashekar, Bovik, & Cormack, 2007).

In a related approach, Geisler (2008) asks the question of what is an optimal search pattern for a target embedded in noise given that the retinotopic resolution heavily emphasizes the fovea; a model of the search process predicts subjects' performance accurately. These results have been replicated experimentally by Caspi, Beutter, and Eckstein (2004).

Rao, Zelinsky, Hayhoe, and Ballard (2002) studied a condition where subjects had to search a natural scene such as a tabletop image where one to five objects might appear. Just prior they were shown an image of the target object. There were two conditions, one where at the outset the subjects were given a short view of the tabletop and could memorize the locations of the objects and another where the preview was absent. The instructed response was target present or absent indicated by an appropriate keypress. Although eye movements were not controlled beyond an initial fixation, subjects invariably fixated the target in the course of the response. However, as shown in Figure 1, in the preview condition, subjects usually fixated the target with one saccade, whereas in the no preview condition the modal number of saccades was three.

All these approaches again raise problems for the saliency model. Since the search target is specified by the experimenter, it cannot be a ready product of the priors that saliency computations assume. Of course the actual correlation-based computations that are done can be embraced as saliency, but that would defeat the fundamental stance of saliency as a method of filtering the image ab initio to delimit possible fixation targets. A very nice paper nonetheless blurs this distinction; Navalpakkam and Itti (2007) show that when the search task is cast in terms of artificial distinctions of primitive features, the task can be described in terms of

Figure 1. Separate visual routines. When subjects have had a preview of a scene they can identify a search target's location from memory (A) but without the preview they use a correlation-based technique (B) that takes longer. One could attempt convert the remembered target's location to saliency coordinates, but not without addressing the more complicated question of how the brain manages different dynamic frames of reference.

modulations of such features and, furthermore, human subjects obey the dictates of signal detection theory. Interestingly, the paper does not exhibit eye movements, perhaps because the task is done in a limited part of the visual field.

MODELLING TASK-DIRECTED FIXATIONS

We have made the case that the main source of explanations of fixation locations is not image saliency but rather latent cognitive variables. In this case the task becomes describing the complex human cognitive system in a way that its descriptive components can be related to fixations. This is not an easy task to do without making substantial claims about the workings of cognition interacting with the visual system.

One such system that tackles the cognition–action interface is that of Sprague, Ballard, and Robinson (2007). The central assumption they make is that the system can be composed of modularized sensorimotor behaviours which can cooperate in small sets without interference from each other. For realizing compositions of modular behaviours, following work in psychology and robotics (e.g., Bonasso, Firby, Kortenkamp, Miller, & Slack, 1997), they develop an abstract cognitive architecture composed of three levels: *Central executive, arbitration*, and *behaviour*. The central executive level of the hierarchy maintains an appropriate set of active behaviours from a much larger library of possible behaviours, given the agent's current goals and environmental conditions. The composition of this set was evaluated at every simulation interval, taken to be 300 ms. The arbitration level addresses the issue of managing competing active behaviours. Thus, an intermediate task is that of mapping action recommendations onto the body's resources. Since the active behaviours must share perceptual and motor resources, there must be some mechanism to arbitrate their needs when they make conflicting demands. The behaviour level describes distinct jobs that are necessary, such as interrogating the image array in order to compute the current state.

The models for each of these levels are implemented and tested on a human avatar. The virtual human vision avatar has physical extent and programmable kinematic degrees of freedom that closely mimic those of real humans as well as software for modelling the physics of collisions. This software base has been augmented with our control architecture for managing behaviours. Each behaviour has a very specific goal, and contains all the structure for the extraction of information from visual input that is in

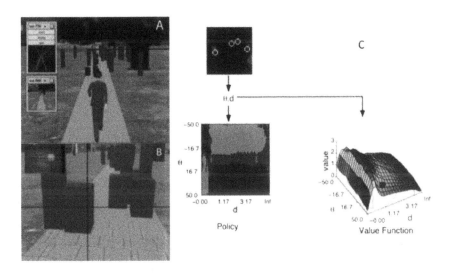

Figure 2. (A) A frame from the human embedded vision system simulation showing the avatar negotiating a pavement strewn with purple litter and blue obstacles, each of which must be dealt with. The insets show the use of vision to guide the avatar through a complex environment. The upper inset shows the particular visual routine that is running at any instant. This instant shows the detection of the edges of the sidewalk that are used in navigation. The lower insert shows the visual field in a head-centred viewing frame. (B) By wearing a Head Mounted Display (HMD), humans can walk in the same environment as the avatar. (C) A basic visually guided behaviour showing steps in the use of the learnt litter cleanup Q-table. The input is a processed colour image with a filled circle on the extreme right-hand side indicating the nearest litter object as a heading angle θ and distance d. This state information, indicated by the circular symbol in the policy table on the lower left, is used to retrieve the appropriate action from the Q-table's policy immediately below. Light regions: Turn $= 45°$; grey regions: Turn $= 0°$; and dark regions: Turn $= -45°$. In this case the selected action is turn $= -45°$. The assumption is that neural circuitry translates this abstract heading into complex walking movements. This is true for the human avatar that has a "walk" command that takes a heading parameter. State information can also be used to retrieve the expected return associated with the optimal action, its learned Q-value, as illustrated on the lower right.

turn mapped onto a library of motor commands. Figure 2A shows the avatar in the act of negotiating a pavement that is strewn with obstacles (blue objects) and litter (purple objects) on the way to crossing a street. Figure 2B shows a human subject in the same environment.

A central problem for task-directed vision concerns the deployment of gaze. The small fovea makes its use to obtain accurate measurements a premium. So in the case of multiple active behaviours, which of them should get the gaze vector at any instant? An elegant solution to this problem is to calculate the amount each behaviour stands to gain by updating its state. Where $Q(s_i,a)$ is the discounted value of behaviour i choosing an action a in state s_i, an agent that chooses an action that is suboptimal for the true state of the environment can expect to lose some reward, estimated as follows:

$$\text{loss} = E\left[\max_a \sum Q_i(s_i, a)\right] - E\left[\sum Q_i(s_i, a_E)\right] \tag{1}$$

The term on the left-hand side of the minus sign expresses the expected return if the agent were able to act with knowledge of the true state of the environment. The term on the right expresses the expected return if forced to choose an action based on the state estimate. The difference between the two can be thought of as the cost of the agent's current uncertainty. The total expected loss does not help to select which of the behaviours should be given access to perception. To make this selection, the loss value can be broken down into the losses associated with the uncertainty for each particular behaviour b:

$$\text{loss}_b = E\left[\max_a \left(Q_b(S_b, a) + \sum_{i \in B, i \neq b} Q_i^E(S_i, a)\right)\right] - \sum_i Q_i^E(S_i, a_E) \tag{2}$$

The expectation on the left is computed only over s_b. This value is the expected return if s_b were known, but the other state variables were not. The value on the right is the expected return if none of the state variables are known. The difference is interpreted as the cost of the uncertainty associated with s_b. This calculation is for all the active behaviours and the one that has the most to lose gets the vector. Figure 3 shows this happening for a walking segment.

As Figure 3C shows, the improvement is small, but nonetheless highly significant. The narrow margin highlights the difficulty of reward-based hypotheses about eye fixations that would attempt to have the results of the fixation directly alter the Q-table. The relative value of any given fixation is small enough so as to be practically undetectable by the learning process. The simulations were unable to detect any systematicity in these variations, and led us to propose the most-to-gain model which uses the state table to calculate the value of an eye fixation, but does not attempt to adjust the Q-table otherwise.

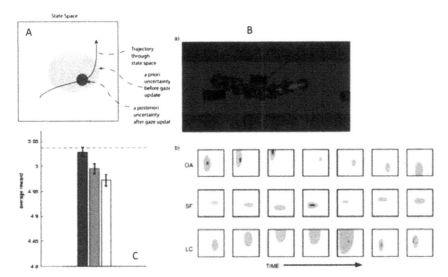

Figure 3. Behaviours compete for gaze in order to update their measurements. (A) A caricature of the basic method. The trajectory through the avatar's state space is estimated using a Kalman filter that allows estimates to propagate in the absence of measurements and build up uncertainty (light grey area). If the behaviour succeeds in obtaining a fixation, uncertainty is reduced (dark grey region). The reinforcement learning model allows the value of reducing uncertainty to be calculated. (B) The top panel shows seven time steps in walking and the associated uncertainties for the state vector grey for obstacle avoidance (OA), sidewalk finding (SF), and litter pickup (LC). The corresponding boxes below show the state spaces where the a priori uncertainty is indicated in light grey and the a posteriori uncertainty is indicated in the darker grey. Uncertainty grows because the internal model has noise that adds to uncertainty in the absence of measurements. Making a measurement with a visual routine that uses gaze reduces the uncertainty. For example, for litter collection (LC), Panel 5 shows a large amount of uncertainty has built up that is greatly reduced by a visual measurement. Overall, obstacle avoidance wins the first three competitions, then sidewalk-finding, and then litter collection wins the last three. (C) Tests of the Sprague algorithm (dark) against the robotics standard round robin algorithm (light) and random gaze allocation (white) show a significant advantage over both.

The simulations can be thought of as tackling the problem of *when* gaze is deployed, but we are also interested in *where* gaze is deployed. Figure 4 shows a case where we obtained Laurent Itti's saliency program and used it to calculate salient points in the walkway setting. Since subjects had walked in this setting their subjects' fixations could be compared directly with those predicted by the program. The program does not return a single point, but a spatial distribution of possible fixation points so some criterion has to be used for selecting a fixation. If the saliency distribution overlapped the object selected by a subject, the result was labelled a "match"' otherwise the label was "no match". The figure shows representative results. Even in this simple setting less than half of the fixations can be accounted for with

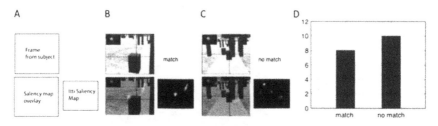

Figure 4. Comparing human gaze locations to those found by the Itti saliency detector. (A) Key. The small inserts show the saliency maps that are overlaid as transparencies on the lower versions of the images. (B) Match example. (C) No match example. (D) In a sample of 18 frames, more than half show fixation locations that are not detected by the maps. The saliency program was provided by Dr. Laurent Itti at the University of Southern California. In this case, for a representative sample, only 8 out of 18 frames were labelled as matches.

saliency. In contrast, the model uses task-directed visual routines based on human performance (Rothkopf, Ballard, & Hayhoe, 2007), so that the landing sites of the routines are qualitatively accurate: Litter fixations are to the centre of the litter; obstacle fixations land on the furthest edge; pavement fixations land on the pavement edge. The reader should compare Figure 3B with Figure 4B and C.

MODELLING TASKS WITH SEQUENTIAL STEPS

In the walking example each behaviour has very a minimal state description. For example, staying on the pavement just requires measuring the pavement edge. The history of the traverse is not needed. However, more complicated behaviours require much more elaborate internal state descriptions. Specifying the details of those descriptions is challenging ongoing research enterprise and is taking many directions. Herein we briefly describe our own work but one could just as easily use other examples such as Nytrøm and Holmqvist (2008) and Oliva and Torralba (2006) as illustrations. The point is that the surface image manipulations are just the tip of an the iceberg of representational structure needed to interpret fixation choices. Furthermore, our example only addresses the recognition issues in interpreting observed fixations. Additional structure is needed to generate the fixations in the process of producing the behaviour.

Consider the process of making a peanut butter sandwich (Hayhoe et al., 2003). If you want to put peanut butter on a slice of bread, you must be holding the knife and you must have taken the lid off the peanut butter jar. Modelling this state is not straightforward owing to a number of factors. Consider the problem of watching someone make a sandwich and describing what has transpired. The basic actions must be measured and recognized.

However, all the steps in the process are noisy and hence the description must necessarily be probabilistic. Now consider describing the order of steps making a sandwich. Since there are over 1000 distinct ways of making it that differ in the order of the steps, any particular sequence of steps is best described probabilistically. A central way of handling probabilistic information goes under the name *graphical models*. These are particularly valuable when the basic dependencies are in the form of conditional probabilities, as in the sandwich-making case. Although some care has to be taken in developing a graphical model, Yi and Ballard (2006) were able to do it. This is a very demanding task, since the model must take head, hand, and eye data from the subjects and, at any given time, recognize what stage in the sandwich making is occurring, as shown in Figure 5.

For this task the graphical model is in the form of a Bayes Net. Such a network is a suitable tool for this class of problems because it uses easily observable evidence to update or infer the probabilistic distribution of the underlying random variables. A Bayesian net represents the causalities with a directed acyclic graph, its nodes denoting variables, and edges denoting causal relations. Since the state of the agent is dynamically changing and the observations are being updated throughout the task execution process, one needs to specify the temporal evolution of the network. Figure 6 illustrates the two slice representation of a Dynamic Bayes Network (DBN). Shaded nodes are observed; the others are hidden. Causalities, represented by straight arrows, are determined by probability distribution matrices.

Each of the states can take on several discrete values as shown by the Tables 1 and 2. Visual and motor routines produce specific values for each of the shaded nodes and the standard Bayes Net propagation rules fill in values

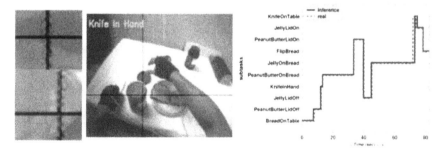

Figure 5. Using the DBN to recognize steps in sandwich making. (A) Two fixations from different points in the task—(top) bread with peanut butter (bottom) peanut butter jar—appear very similar, but do not confuse the Dynamic Bayes Network (DBN), which uses task information. (B) A frame in the video of a human subject in the process of making a sandwich showing that the DBN has correctly identified the subtask as "knife-in-hand". (C) A trace of the entire sandwich-making process showing perfect subtask recognition by the DBN.

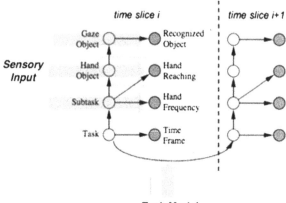

Task Model

Figure 6. The basic structure of the Dynamic Bayes Net (DBN) used to model sandwich making. Two time slices from the sandwich-making DBN. Visual and hand measurements provide input to the shaded nodes, the set of which at any time t comprise the measurement vector O^t. The rest of the nodes comprise the set S^t whose probabilities must be estimated. The sequencing probabilities between subtasks are provided from a task model that in turn is based on human subject data.

for the task nodes. The state of the lowest hidden node is determined by its prior distribution in the first time/slice and thereafter jointly determined by its previous state and the transition matrix, as denoted by the curved arrow shown in Figure 6.

TABLE 1
Number of states for hidden nodes in the task model (Figure 6)

Node name	Number of states
Task	80
Subtask	10
Hand object	4
Gaze object	5

TABLE 2
Number of states for observed data nodes in the task model (Figure 6)

Node name	Number of states
Time frame	20
Hand frequency	2
Hand reaching	2
Recognized object	5

The two-slice representation can be easily unrolled to address behaviours with arbitrary numbers of slices. At each moment, the observed sensory data (grey nodes), along with its history, are used to compute the probability of the hidden nodes being in certain states:

$$p(S^t|O^{[1,t]}) = P(S^1)P(O^1|S^1) \prod_{t=2}^{t} P(S^t|S^{[t-1]})P(O^t|S^{[t]})$$

where S^t is the set of states of hidden nodes at time t, $O^{(1,t)}$ is the observations over time span $(1,t)$. Behaviour recognition computes the states of each hidden node S^t at time t that maximize the probability of observing the given sensory data:

$$S^t = \arg \max_S P(S^t) = S|O^{[1,t]})$$

The point of this elaborate example is simply that all the key variables that direct the progress of interpreting sandwich making are part of an estimate of the sandwich constructor's cognitive program. Image data is important, along with hand measurements, but primarily for conforming hypotheses in the cognitive program. The image structure is not the *cause* of the sandwich being made.

CONCLUSION

The first goal of this paper was to show that it is very unlikely that the saliency map could be the cause of gaze changes. The principal evidence is that almost all behaviour is goal oriented and the object of these goals does readily translate into constellations of image features in a significant number of cases. Thus, these cases are not capable of being modelled as saliency map targets. This is not to say that the saliency map is not without value as in many other cases the features in the saliency map can be used to compute the planned point of fixation. However, the main point still remains that the cause of such a computation comes from the latent variables associated with the subject's internal goals and not directly from the image itself.

In racquet sports where the object is to hit a ball, the position that the racquet must meet the ball is most often a proximal point in three-dimensional space that is determined by distal information. In completing a complex task, often the target of a fixation depends on remembered information obtained on prior fixations and not on the current image. In complex tasks the fixation point can depend on a computation that depends on the image features that cannot be anticipated without knowledge of the task itself.

The conclusion of all these observations is that in order to progress, a substantial effort must be invested in modelling tasks so to have the variables used in computing fixation points made explicit. As an example, we described a way of composing behaviours whose components are learnt using reinforcement. Such behaviours can be used to generate fixations on the basis of rewarding reduction in uncertainty. This idea has at the moment the status of a conjecture, but nonetheless illustrates the motivation for a nonsaliency theory of gaze control.

Finally, to illustrate the possibility of using the information acquired at the point of gaze with that of other body actions to guide behaviour, we showed that the steps in a complex behaviour such as sandwich making could be recognized with just that information as input. Again the status of these variables is provisional, but nonetheless they constitute an existence proof that this sparse information is sufficient to accomplish the task. A huge amount of additional work will need to be done before one could safely establish the role of cognition in gaze control, but the aim of this paper is to argue that this research is necessary and will supplant strictly image-based computational models.

REFERENCES

Aivar, P., Hayhoe, M., & Mruczek, R. (2005). Role of spatial memory in saccadic targeting in natural tasks. *Journal of Vision, 5,* 177–193.

Ballard, D., Hayhoe, M., & Pelz, J (1995). Memory representations in natural tasks. *Journal of Cognitive Neuroscience, 7,* 66–80.

Ballard, D., Hayhoe, M., Pook, P., & Rao, R. (1997). Deictic codes for the embodiment of cognition. *Behavioral and Brain Sciences, 20,* 723–767.

Bonasso, R., Firby, R., Kortenkamp, D., Miller, D., & Slack, M. (1997). Experiences with an architecture for intelligent reactive agents. *Journal of Experimental and Theoretical Artificial Intelligence, 9,* 237–256.

Buswell, G. T. (1935). *How people look at pictures.* Chicago: University of Chicago Press.

Caspi, A., Beutter, B., & Eckstein, M. (2004). The time course of visual information accrual guiding eye movement decisions. *Proceedings of the National Academy of Sciences of the USA, 101,* 13086–13090.

Droll, J., & Hayhoe, M. (2007). Deciding when to remember and when to forget: Trade-offs between working memory and gaze. *Journal of Experimental Psychology: Human Perception and Performance, 33*(6), 1352–1365.

Droll, J., Hayhoe, M., Triesch, J., & Sullivan, B. (2005). Task demands control acquisition and maintenance of visual information. *Journal of Experimental Psychology: Human Perception and Performance, 31*(6), 1416–1438.

Einhauser, W., Rutishauser, U., & Koch, C. (2008). Task-demands can immediately reverse the effects of sensory-driven saliency in complex visual stimuli. *Journal of Vision, 8,* 1–19.

Erdmann, B., & Dodge, R. (1898). *Psychologische Untersuchungen uber das Lesen.* Halle, Germany: N. Niemeyer.

Foulsham, T., & Underwood, G. (2008). What can saliency models predict about eye movements? Spatial and sequential aspects of fixations during encoding and recognition. *Journal of Vision, 8,* 1–17.

Geisler, W. S. (2008). Visual perception and the statistical properties of natural scenes. *Annual Review of Psychology, 59,* 167–192.

Hayhoe, M., Bensinger, D., & Ballard, D. (1998). Task constraints in visual working memory. *Vision Research, 38*, 125–137.

Hayhoe, M., Shrivastrava, A., Myruczek, R., & Pelz, J. (2003). Visual memory and motor planning in a natural task. *Journal of Vision, 3*, 49–63.

Henderson, J. (2007). Regarding scenes. *Current Directions in Psychological Science, 16*, 219–227.

Hoffman, J., Landaub, B., & Pagani, B. (2003). Spatial breakdown in spatial construction: Evidence from eye fixations in children with Williams syndrome. *Cognitive Psychology, 46*, 260–301.

Hubel, D. H., & Wiesel, T. N. (1962). Receptive fields, binocular interaction and functional architecture in the cat's visual cortex. *Journal of Physiology, 160*(1), 106–154.

Ito, M., & Gilbert, G. (1999). Attention modulates contextual influences in the primary visual cortex of alert monkeys. *Neuron, 22*, 593–604.

Itti, L., & Baldi, P. (2005). Bayesian surprise attracts human attention. *Proceedings of Neural Information Processing Systems, 19*, 547–554.

Itti, L., & Koch, C. (2001). Computational modeling of visual attention. *Nature Reviews Neuroscience, 2*, 194–203.

Jovanevic, J., Sullivan, B., & Hayhoe, M. (2006). Control of attention and gaze in complex environments. *Journal of Vision, 6*, 1431–1450.

Koch, C., & Ullman, U. (1985). Shifts in selective visual attention: Towards the underlying neural circuitry. *Human Neurobiology, 4*, 219–227.

Land, M. F., & McLeod, P. (2000). From eye movements to actions: How batsmen hit the ball. *Nature Neuroscience, 3*, 1340–1345.

Marr, D. (1982). *Vision.* New York: Henry Holt & Co.

McKinney, T., Chajka, K., & Hayhoe, M. (2008). Pro-active gaze control in squash [Abstract]. *Journal of Vision, 8*(6), 111a.

Navalpakkam, V., & Itti, L. (2005). Modeling the influence of task on attention. *Vision Research, 45*, 205–231.

Nytrøm, M., & Holmquist, K. (2008). Semantic override of low-level features in image viewing—both initially and overall. *Journal of Eye Movement Research, 2*, 1–11.

Oliva, A., & Torralba, A. (2006). Building the gist of a scene: The role of global image features in recognition. *Progress in Brain Research, 155*, 23–36.

Rajashekar, U., Bovik, A., & Cormack, L. (2007). Visual search in noise: Revealing the influence of structural cues by gaze-contingent classification image analysis. *Journal of Vision, 6*(4), 379–386.

Rao, R., Zelinsky, G., Hayhoe, M., & Ballard, D. (2002). Eye movements in iconic visual search. *Vision Research, 42*, 1447–1463.

Roelfsema, P., Khayat, P. S., & Spekreijse, H. (2003). Subtask sequencing in the primary visual cortex. *Proceedings of the National Academy of Sciences USA, 100*, 5467–5472.

Roelfsema, P., Lamme, V., & Spekreijse, H. (1998). Object-based attention in the primary visual cortex of the macaque monkey. *Nature, 395*, 376–381.

Rothkopf, C., Ballard, D., & Hayhoe, M. (2007). Task and scene context determines where you look. *Journal of Vision, 7*(14), 1–20.

Shinoda, H., Hayhoe, M., & Shrivastava, A. (2001). Attention in natural environments. *Vision Research, 41*, 3535–3546.

Sprague, N., Ballard, D., & Robinson, A. (2007). Modeling embodied visual behaviors. *ACM Transactions in Applied Perception, 4*(2), 11.

Swain, M., & Ballard, D. (1991). Color indexing. *International Journal of Computer Vision, 7*, 11–32.

Tatler, B. (2007). The central fixation bias in scene viewing: Selecting an optimal viewing position independently of motor biases and image feature distributions. *Journal of Vision, 7*, 1–17.

Treisman, A., & Gelade, G. (1980). A feature-integration theory of attention. *Cognitive Psychology, 12*, 136.

Triesch, J., Ballard, D., Hayhoe, M., & Sullivan, B. (2003). What you see is what you need. *Journal of Vision, 3*, 86–94.

Ullman, S. (1984). Visual routines. *Cognition, 18*, 97–157.

Wolfe, J. (1994). Guided Search 2.0: A revised model of visual search. *Psychonomic Bulletin, 1*, 202–238.

Yarbus, A. (1967). *Eye movements and vision*. New York: Plenum Press.

Yi, W., & Ballard, D. (2006). Behavior recognition in human object interactions with a task model. In *IEEE international conference on Advanced Video and Signal Based Surveillance*, Sydney, Australia, IEEE Computer Society.

Zihl, J., von Cramon, D., & Mai, N. (1983). Selective disturbance of movement vision after bilateral brain damage. *Brain, 106*, 313–340.

Subject Index

www.ingramcontent.com/pod-product-compliance
Ingram Content Group UK Ltd.
Pitfield, Milton Keynes, MK11 3LW, UK
UKHW020402010325
455677UK00021B/589